T0364900

Volvo S40 & V50
Owners Workshop Manual

Mark Storey

(6443 - 384)

Models covered
S40 Saloon & V50 Estate
Petrol: 1.8 litre (1798cc), 2.0 litre (1999cc) & 2.4 litre (2435cc) 4- & 5-cylinder
Turbo-diesel: 1.6 litre (1560cc), 2.0 litre (1984cc & 1998cc) & 2.4 litre (2400cc) 4- & 5-cylinder

Does NOT cover 1.6 litre or 2.5 litre 'T5' petrol engines or 2.4 litre 'T9' diesel engine
Does NOT cover 'Classic', AWD (four-wheel-drive) models or 'Powershift' transmission

© Haynes Group Limited 2019

ABCDE
FGHIJ
KLMNO
PQ

A book in the **Haynes Owners Workshop Manual Series**

ISBN **978 1 78521 443 1**

British Library Cataloguing in Publication Data
A catalogue record for this book is available from the British Library.

Printed in India

Haynes Group Limited
Sparkford, Yeovil, Somerset BA22 7JJ, England

Haynes North America, Inc
2801 Townsgate Road, Suite 340, Thousand Oaks, CA 91361

Disclaimer

There are risks associated with automotive repairs. The ability to make repairs depends on the individual's skill, experience and proper tools. Individuals should act with due care and acknowledge and assume the risk of performing automotive repairs.

The purpose of this manual is to provide comprehensive, useful and accessible automotive repair information, to help you get the best value from your vehicle. However, this manual is not a substitute for a professional certified technician or mechanic.

This repair manual is produced by a third party and is not associated with an individual vehicle manufacturer. If there is any doubt or discrepancy between this manual and the owner's manual or the factory service manual, please refer to the factory service manual or seek assistance from a professional certified technician or mechanic.

Even though we have prepared this manual with extreme care and every attempt is made to ensure that the information in this manual is correct, neither the publisher nor the author can accept responsibility for loss, damage or injury caused by any errors in, or omissions from, the information given.

Contents

LIVING WITH YOUR VOLVO S40 & V50

MAINTENANCE

Routine maintenance and servicing

Contents

REPAIRS & OVERHAUL

The original S40/V40 range was introduced to the UK in 1996. In 2004, a completely new range was launched comprising Saloon (S40) and Estate (V50) variants that were based on the 'Focus' platform of the (then) parent company Ford. The range was facelifted in 2007. Although virtually identical in appearance to the models launched in 2004, the revised range saw the introduction of new diesel engines, including an economy-focused 1.6 litre DRIVe unit. Also new for this model were a number of detailed interior changes and a range of new comfort and safety features.

This manual covers the full range of petrol and diesel engines on offer, the only exceptions being the 2.5 litre petrol engines and the 2.4 litre diesel engine that Volvo designates the 'T9' as this unit did not feature in the UK line-up.

Transmissions are either 5 or 6-speed manual, or 5 or 6-speed 'Geartronic' automatics with computer control. The automatic transmission features mode control selection, allowing the driver to alter the transmission characteristics to suit normal or winter driving requirements.

Braking is by discs all round with anti-lock braking (ABS) and power-assisted steering is standard on all models.

A wide range of standard and optional equipment is available within the range to suit virtually all tastes. As with all Volvo models, safety features are of paramount importance, and the comprehensive airbag system and Side Impact Protection System (SIPS) offer an exceptional level of driver and passenger protection throughout the vehicle.

Provided that regular servicing is carried out in accordance with the manufacturer's recommendations, the Volvo S40/V50 should provide many years of reliable service. Despite the engine's complexity, the engine compartment is relatively spacious, and most of the items requiring frequent attention are easily accessible.

Your Volvo manual

The aim of this manual is to help you get the best value from your vehicle. It can do so in several ways. It can help you decide what work must be done (even should you choose to get it done by a garage). It will also provide information on routine maintenance and servicing, and give a logical course of action and diagnosis when random faults occur.

However, it is hoped that you will use the manual by tackling the work yourself. On simpler jobs it may even be quicker than booking the car into a garage and going there twice, to leave and collect it. Perhaps most important, a lot of money can be saved by avoiding the costs a garage must charge to cover its labour and overheads.

The manual has drawings and descriptions to show the function of the various components so that their layout can be understood. Tasks are described and photographed in a clear step-by-step sequence. The illustrations are numbered by the Section number and paragraph number to which they relate – if there is more than one illustration per paragraph, the sequence is denoted alphabetically.

References to the 'left' or 'right' of the vehicle are in the sense of a person in the driver's seat, facing forwards.

Acknowledgements

Certain illustrations are the copyright of Volvo Car Corporation, and are used with their permission. Thanks are due to Draper Tools Limited and AST tools, who provided some of the workshop tools, and to all those people at Sparkford who helped in the production of this manual.

We take great pride in the accuracy of information given in this manual, but vehicle manufacturers make alterations and design changes during the production run of a particular vehicle of which they do not inform us. No liability can be accepted by the authors or publishers for loss, damage or injury caused by any errors in, or omissions from the information given.

Working on your car can be dangerous. This page shows just some of the potential risks and hazards, with the aim of creating a safety-conscious attitude.

General hazards

Scalding

• Don't remove the radiator or expansion tank cap while the engine is hot.
• Engine oil, transmission fluid or power steering fluid may also be dangerously hot if the engine has recently been running.

Burning

• Beware of burns from the exhaust system and from any part of the engine. Brake discs and drums can also be extremely hot immediately after use.

Crushing

• When working under or near a raised vehicle, always supplement the jack with axle stands, or use drive-on ramps.
Never venture under a car which is only supported by a jack.

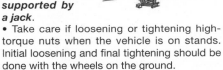

• Take care if loosening or tightening high-torque nuts when the vehicle is on stands. Initial loosening and final tightening should be done with the wheels on the ground.

Fire

• Fuel is highly flammable; fuel vapour is explosive.
• Don't let fuel spill onto a hot engine.
• Do not smoke or allow naked lights (including pilot lights) anywhere near a vehicle being worked on. Also beware of creating sparks (electrically or by use of tools).
• Fuel vapour is heavier than air, so don't work on the fuel system with the vehicle over an inspection pit.
• Another cause of fire is an electrical overload or short-circuit. Take care when repairing or modifying the vehicle wiring.
• Keep a fire extinguisher handy, of a type suitable for use on fuel and electrical fires.

Electric shock

• Ignition HT and Xenon headlight voltages can be dangerous, especially to people with heart problems or a pacemaker. Don't work on or near these systems with the engine running or the ignition switched on.

• Mains voltage is also dangerous. Make sure that any mains-operated equipment is correctly earthed. Mains power points should be protected by a residual current device (RCD) circuit breaker.

Fume or gas intoxication

• Exhaust fumes are poisonous; they can contain carbon monoxide, which is rapidly fatal if inhaled. Never run the engine in a confined space such as a garage with the doors shut.

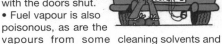

• Fuel vapour is also poisonous, as are the vapours from some cleaning solvents and paint thinners.

Poisonous or irritant substances

• Avoid skin contact with battery acid and with any fuel, fluid or lubricant, especially antifreeze, brake hydraulic fluid and Diesel fuel. Don't syphon them by mouth. If such a substance is swallowed or gets into the eyes, seek medical advice.
• Prolonged contact with used engine oil can cause skin cancer. Wear gloves or use a barrier cream if necessary. Change out of oil-soaked clothes and do not keep oily rags in your pocket.
• Air conditioning refrigerant forms a poisonous gas if exposed to a naked flame (including a cigarette). It can also cause skin burns on contact.

Asbestos

• Asbestos dust can cause cancer if inhaled or swallowed. Asbestos may be found in gaskets and in brake and clutch linings. When dealing with such components it is safest to assume that they contain asbestos.

Special hazards

Hydrofluoric acid

• This extremely corrosive acid is formed when certain types of synthetic rubber, found in some O-rings, oil seals, fuel hoses etc, are exposed to temperatures above 4000C. The rubber changes into a charred or sticky substance containing the acid. *Once formed, the acid remains dangerous for years. If it gets onto the skin, it may be necessary to amputate the limb concerned.*
• When dealing with a vehicle which has suffered a fire, or with components salvaged from such a vehicle, wear protective gloves and discard them after use.

The battery

• Batteries contain sulphuric acid, which attacks clothing, eyes and skin. Take care when topping-up or carrying the battery.
• The hydrogen gas given off by the battery is highly explosive. Never cause a spark or allow a naked light nearby. Be careful when connecting and disconnecting battery chargers or jump leads.

Air bags

• Air bags can cause injury if they go off accidentally. Take care when removing the steering wheel and trim panels. Special storage instructions may apply.

Diesel injection equipment

• Diesel injection pumps supply fuel at very high pressure. Take care when working on the fuel injectors and fuel pipes.

⚠ *Warning: Never expose the hands, face or any other part of the body to injector spray; the fuel can penetrate the skin with potentially fatal results.*

Remember...

DO

• Do use eye protection when using power tools, and when working under the vehicle.

• Do wear gloves or use barrier cream to protect your hands when necessary.

• Do get someone to check periodically that all is well when working alone on the vehicle.

• Do keep loose clothing and long hair well out of the way of moving mechanical parts.

• Do remove rings, wristwatch etc, before working on the vehicle – especially the electrical system.

• Do ensure that any lifting or jacking equipment has a safe working load rating adequate for the job.

DON'T

• Don't attempt to lift a heavy component which may be beyond your capability – get assistance.

• Don't rush to finish a job, or take unverified short cuts.

• Don't use ill-fitting tools which may slip and cause injury.

• Don't leave tools or parts lying around where someone can trip over them. Mop up oil and fuel spills at once.

• Don't allow children or pets to play in or near a vehicle being worked on.

The following pages are intended to help in dealing with common roadside emergencies and breakdowns. You will find more detailed fault finding information at the back of the manual, and repair information in the main chapters.

If your car won't start and the starter motor doesn't turn

☐ If it's a model with automatic transmission, make sure the selector is in 'P' or 'N'.
☐ Open the bonnet and make sure that the battery terminals are clean and tight.
☐ Switch on the headlights and try to start the engine. If the headlights go very dim when you're trying to start, the battery is probably flat. Get out of trouble by jump starting using a friend's car.

If your car won't start even though the starter motor turns as normal

☐ Is there fuel in the tank?
☐ Is there moisture on electrical components under the bonnet? Switch off the ignition, then wipe off any obvious dampness with a dry cloth. Spray a water-repellent aerosol product (WD-40 or equivalent) on fuel system electrical connectors like those shown in the photos.

A Check the security and condition of the battery connections – unclip and lift the battery cover for access

B Check the mass airflow sensor wiring plug

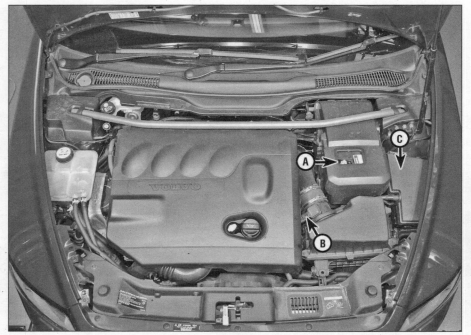

Check that all electrical connections are secure (with the ignition switched off). Spray the connector plugs with a water-dispersant spray like WD-40 if you suspect a problem due to damp. Diesel models do not usually suffer from damp starting problems, but check all visible connector plugs just in case

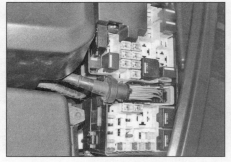

C Check that none of the engine compartment fuses have blown

Jump starting

Jump starting will get you out of trouble, but you must correct whatever made the battery go flat in the first place. There are three possibilities:

1 The battery has been drained by repeated attempts to start, or by leaving the lights on.

2 The charging system is not working properly (alternator drivebelt slack or broken, alternator wiring fault or alternator itself faulty).

3 The battery itself is at fault (electrolyte low, or battery worn out).

When jump-starting a car, observe the following precautions:

✓ Before connecting the booster battery, make sure that the ignition is switched off.

Caution: Remove the key in case the central locking engages when the jump leads are connected

✓ Ensure that all electrical equipment (lights, heater, wipers, etc) is switched off.
✓ Take note of any special precautions printed on the battery case.
✓ Make sure that the booster battery is the same voltage as the discharged one in the vehicle.

✓ If the battery is being jump-started from the battery in another vehicle, the two vehicles MUST NOT TOUCH each other.

✓ Make sure that the transmission is in neutral (or PARK, in the case of automatic transmission).

Budget jump leads can be a false economy, as they often do not pass enough current to start large capacity or diesel engines. They can also get hot.

1 Connect the red jump lead to the battery positive (+) terminal through the hole in the cover of the flat battery

2 Connect the other end of the red lead to the positive (+) terminal of the booster battery

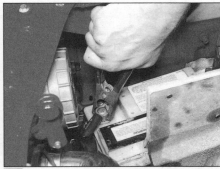

3 Connect one end of the black jump lead to the negative (-) terminal of the booster battery

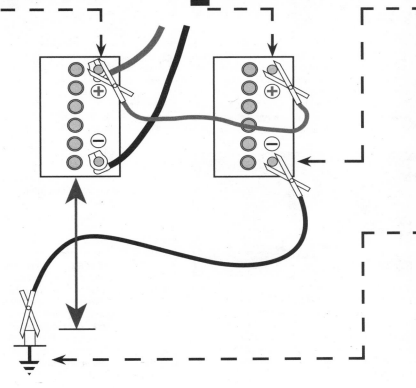

4 Connect the other end of the black jump lead to the earth terminal on the left-hand front suspension turret in the engine compartment

5 Make sure that the jump leads will not come into contact with the cooling fan. Drive belts or other moving parts on the engine

6 Start the engine, then with the engine running at fast idle speed, disconnect the jump leads in the reverse order of connection

Wheel changing

⚠️ *Warning: Do not change a wheel in a situation where you risk being hit by other traffic. On busy roads, try to stop in a lay-by or a gateway. Be wary of passing traffic while changing the wheel – it is easy to become distracted by the job in hand.*

Preparation

☐ When a puncture occurs, stop as soon as it is safe to do so.

☐ Park on firm level ground, if possible, and well out of the way of other traffic.

☐ Use hazard warning lights if necessary.

☐ If you have one, use a warning triangle to alert other drivers of your presence.

☐ Apply the handbrake and engage first or reverse gear (or Park on models with automatic transmission).

☐ Chock the wheel diagonally opposite the one being removed – a couple of large stones will do for this.

☐ If the ground is soft, use a flat piece of wood to spread the load under the jack.

Changing the wheel

1 The spare wheel and tools are stored under the floor in the luggage compartment. Lift up the cover panel.

2 Unscrew the retaining bolt, and lift the spare wheel out. The jack and wheel brace are located beneath the spare wheel. The screw-in towing eye is located alongside the spare wheel

3 Using the flat end of the wheel brace, prise off the wheel trim (if applicable) for access to the wheel nuts. Models with alloy wheels have locking nuts – these are removed with a special tool, which should be with the wheel brace (or in the glovebox)

4 Slacken each wheel nut by half a turn, using the wheel brace. If the nuts are too tight, DON'T stand on the wheel brace to undo them – call for assistance from one of the motoring organisations

5 Two jacking points are provided on each side – use the one nearest the punctured tyre. Locate the jack head in the groove at the jacking point in the lower sill flange (don't jack the vehicle at any other point of the sill, nor on a plastic panel). Turn the jack handle clockwise until the wheel is raised clear of the ground.

6 Unscrew the wheel nuts, noting which way round they fit (tapered side inwards), and remove the wheel

Finally...

☐ Remove the wheel chocks.

☐ Stow the jack and tools in the correct locations in the car.

☐ Check the tyre pressure on the wheel just fitted. If it is low, or if you don't have a pressure gauge with you, drive slowly to the nearest garage and inflate the tyre to the right pressure.

☐ Have the damaged tyre or wheel repaired as soon as possible.

7 Fit the spare wheel, and screw on the nuts. Lightly tighten the nuts with the wheel brace, then lower the vehicle to the ground. Securely tighten the nuts, then refit the wheel trim where applicable. Note that the wheel nuts should be slackened and retightened to the specified torque at the earliest opportunity

Instead of a spare wheel, some models may be provided with a kit that includes an electrically-operated pump and a container of sealant, to be used in the event of a puncture. The kit is located in the space otherwise occupied by a spare wheel. Should a puncture occur, follow the operating instructions that are included with the kit.

Note: *If a temporary 'space-saver' spare wheel has been fitted, special conditions apply to its use. This type of spare wheel is only intended for use in an emergency, and should not remain fitted any longer than it takes to get the punctured wheel repaired. While the temporary wheel is in use, do not exceed 50 mph, and avoid harsh acceleration, braking or cornering. Note that the temporary wheel is of smaller diameter and since ground clearance will be slightly reduced with the temporary spare in use, take care when travelling over rough ground.*

Identifying leaks

Puddles on the garage floor or drive, or obvious wetness under the bonnet or underneath the car, suggest a leak that needs investigating. It can sometimes be difficult to decide where the leak is coming from, especially if an engine undershield is fitted. Leaking oil or fluid can also be blown rearwards by the passage of air under the car, giving a false impression of where the problem lies.

 Warning: Most automotive oils and fluids are poisonous. Wash them off skin, and change out of contaminated clothing, without delay.

 The smell of a fluid leaking from the car may provide a clue to what's leaking. Some fluids are distinctively coloured. It may help to remove the engine undershield, clean the car carefully and to park it over some clean paper overnight as an aid to locating the source of the leak. Remember that some leaks may only occur while the engine is running.

Sump oil

Engine oil may leak from the drain plug...

Oil from filter

...or from the base of the oil filter.

Gearbox oil
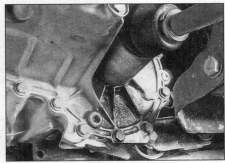
Gearbox oil can leak from the seals at the inboard ends of the driveshafts.

Antifreeze

Leaking antifreeze often leaves a crystalline deposit like this.

Brake fluid

A leak occurring at a wheel is almost certainly brake fluid.

Power steering fluid

Power steering fluid may leak from the pipe connectors on the steering rack.

Towing

When all else fails, you may find yourself having to get a tow home – or of course you may be helping somebody else. Long-distance recovery should only be done by a garage or breakdown service. For shorter distances, DIY towing using another car is easy enough, but observe the following points:

☐ Use a proper tow-rope or solid towing bar – they are not expensive. The vehicle being towed must display an ON TOW sign in its rear window.

☐ Always insert the remote unit when the vehicle is being towed, so that the steering lock is released, and that the direction indicator and brake lights will work.

☐ A rear towing eye is provided below the right-hand side of the bumper. The front towing eye is provided behind the cover on the right-hand side of the front bumper – pull the cover from the bumper and screw in the towing hook supplied with the vehicle.

☐ Before being towed, release the handbrake and select neutral on the transmission. On models with automatic transmission, do not exceed 30 mph or tow for more than 30 miles. If in doubt, do not tow, or transmission damage may result.

☐ Note that greater-than-usual pedal pressure will be required to operate the brakes, since the vacuum servo unit is only operational with the engine running.

☐ Greater-than-usual steering effort will also be required.

☐ The driver of the car being towed must keep the tow-rope taut at all times to avoid snatching.

☐ Make sure that both drivers know the route before setting off.

☐ Only drive at moderate speeds and keep the distance towed to a minimum. Drive smoothly and allow plenty of time for slowing down at junctions.

Introduction

There are some very simple checks which need only take a few minutes to carry out, but which could save you a lot of inconvenience and expense.

These checks require no great skill or special tools, and the small amount of time they take to perform could prove to be very well spent, for example:

☐ Keeping an eye on tyre condition and pressures, will not only help to stop them wearing out prematurely, but could also save your life.

☐ Many breakdowns are caused by electrical problems. Battery-related faults are particularly common, and a quick check on a regular basis will often prevent the majority of these.

☐ If your car develops a brake fluid leak, the first time you might know about it is when your brakes don't work properly. Checking the level regularly will give advance warning of this kind of problem.

☐ If the oil or coolant levels run low, the cost of repairing any engine damage will be far greater than fixing the leak, for example.

Underbonnet check points

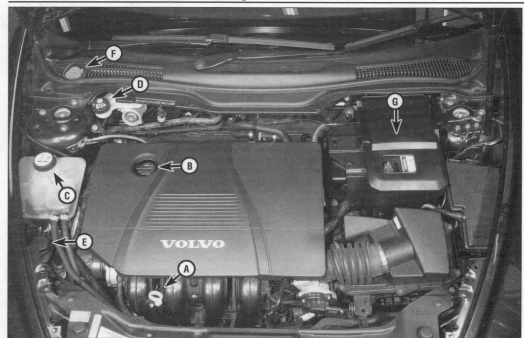

◄ Petrol engine (1.8 litre shown)

A *Engine oil level dipstick*

B *Engine oil filler cap*

C *Coolant expansion tank*

D *Brake and clutch fluid reservoir*

E *Power steering reservoir*

F *Screen washer fluid reservoir*

G *Battery*

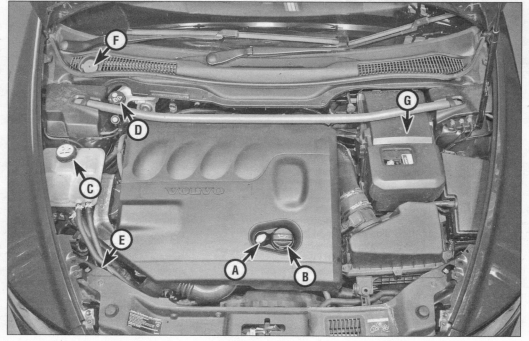

◄ Diesel engine (2.0 litre shown)

A *Engine oil level dipstick*

B *Engine oil filler cap*

C *Coolant expansion tank*

D *Brake and clutch fluid reservoir*

E *Power steering reservoir*

F *Screen washer fluid reservoir*

G *Battery*

Engine oil level

Before you start
✔ Make sure that the car is on level ground.
✔ Check the oil level before the car is driven, or at least 5 minutes after the engine has been switched off.

HAYNES HiNT *If the oil is checked immediately after driving the vehicle, some of the oil will remain in the upper engine components, resulting in an inaccurate reading on the dipstick.*

The correct oil
Modern engines place great demands on their oil. It is very important that the correct oil for your car is used (see *Lubricants and fluids*).

Car care
● If you have to add oil frequently, you should check whether you have any oil leaks. Place some clean paper under the car overnight, and check for stains in the morning. If there are no leaks, then the engine may be burning oil.
● Always maintain the level between the upper and lower dipstick marks. If the level is too low, severe engine damage may occur. Oil seal failure may result if the engine is overfilled by adding too much oil.

1 The dipstick top is yellow for easy identification (see *Underbonnet check points* for exact location). Withdraw the dipstick. Using a clean rag or paper towel, remove all oil from the dipstick

3 Oil is added through the filler cap. Unscrew the filler cap...

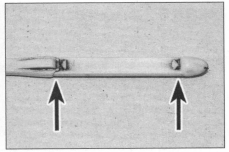
2 Insert the clean dipstick into the tube as far as it will go, the withdraw it again. Note the oil level on the end of the dipstick, which should be between the MAX and MIN marks. If the oil level is only just above, or below, the MIN mark, topping up is required

4 ...and top-up the level. Add the oil slowly, checking the level on the dipstick often, and allowing time for the oil to fall to the sump. Add oil until the level is just up to the MAX mark on the dipstick – don't overfill (see *Car care*)

Coolant level

 Warning: Do not attempt to remove the expansion tank pressure cap when the engine is hot, as there is a very great risk of scalding. Do not leave open containers of coolant about, as it is poisonous.

Car care
● With a sealed-type cooling system, adding coolant should not be necessary on a regular basis. If frequent topping-up is required, it is likely there is a leak. Check the radiator, all hoses and joint faces for signs of staining or wetness, and rectify as necessary.

● It is important that antifreeze is used in the cooling system all year round, not just during the winter months. Don't top up with water alone, as the antifreeze will become diluted.

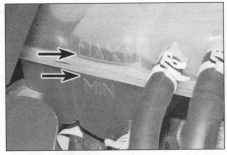
1 The coolant level varies with the temperature of the engine, and is visible through the expansion tank. When the engine is cold, the coolant level should be between the MAX and MIN marks on the front of the reservoir. When the engine is hot, the level may rise slightly above the MAX mark.

2 If topping up is necessary, wait until the engine is cold. Slowly unscrew the expansion tank cap to release any pressure present in the cooling system, and remove it.

3 Add a mixture of water and antifreeze to the expansion tank until the coolant level is halfway between the level marks. Use only the specified antifreeze – if using Volvo antifreeze, make sure it is the same type and colour as that already in the system. Refit the cap and tighten it securely.

Brake (and clutch) fluid level

Warning:
• *Brake fluid can harm your eyes and damage painted surfaces, so use extreme caution when handling and pouring it.*
• *Do not use fluid that has been standing open for some time, as it absorbs moisture from the air, which can cause a dangerous loss of braking effectiveness.*
• *The fluid level in the reservoir will drop slightly as the brake pads wear down, but the fluid level must never be allowed to drop below the MIN mark.*

Before you start

✔ Make sure that your car is on level ground.

Safety first!

● If the reservoir requires repeated topping-up this is an indication of a fluid leak somewhere in the system, which should be investigated immediately.
● If a leak is suspected, the car should not be driven until the braking system has been checked. Never take any risks where brakes are concerned.

1 The brake fluid reservoir is located on the right-hand side of the engine compartment

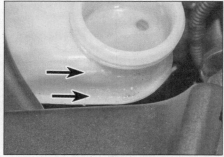

2 The MAX and MIN marks are indicated on the front of the reservoir. The fluid level must be kept between the marks at all times

3 If topping up is necessary, first wipe clean the area around the filler cap to prevent dirt entering the hydraulic system. Unscrew the reservoir cap and carefully lift it out of position, holding the wiring connector plug and taking care not to damage the level sender float. Inspect the reservoir; if the fluid is dirty, the hydraulic system should be drained and refilled (see relevant part of Chapter 1)

4 Carefully add fluid, taking care not to spill it onto the surrounding components. Use only the specified fluid; mixing different types can cause damage to the system. After topping up to the correct level, securely refit the cap and wipe off any spilt fluid

Washer fluid level

● Screenwash additives not only keep the windscreen clean during bad weather, they also prevent the washer system freezing in cold weather – which is when you are likely to need it most. Don't top-up using plain water, as the screenwash will become diluted, and will freeze in cold weather.

Caution: On no account use coolant antifreeze in the washer system – this could discolour or damage paintwork.

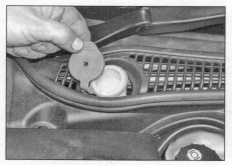

1 The washer fluid reservoir filler neck is located in the right-hand rear corner of the engine compartment. The washer level cannot easily be seen. Remove the filler cap, and look down the filler neck – if fluid is not visible, topping-up may be required

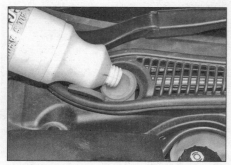

2 When topping-up the reservoir, add a screenwash additive in the quantities recommended on the bottle

Battery

Caution: Before carrying out any work on the vehicle battery, read the precautions given in 'Safety first!' at the start of this manual.

✔ Make sure that the battery tray is in good condition, and that the clamp is tight. Corrosion on the tray, retaining clamp and the battery itself can be removed with a solution of water and baking soda. Thoroughly rinse all cleaned areas with water. Any metal parts damaged by corrosion should be covered with a zinc-based primer, then painted.

✔ Periodically (approximately every three months), check the charge condition of the battery, as described in Chapter 5A, Section 2.

✔ If the battery is flat, and you need to jump start your vehicle, see *Roadside repairs*.

HAYNES HiNT *Battery corrosion can be kept to a minimum by applying a layer of petroleum jelly to the clamps and terminals after they are reconnected.*

1 The battery is located in the left-hand rear corner of the engine compartment – remove the engine compartment crossmember (where fitted)

2 Unclip and remove the battery cover to gain access. The exterior of the battery should be inspected periodically for damage such as a cracked case or cover

3 Check the tightness of the battery clamps to ensure good electrical connections. You should not be able to move them. Also check each cable for cracks and frayed conductors

4 If corrosion (white, fluffy deposits) is evident, remove the cables from the battery terminals, clean them with a small wire brush, then refit them. Automotive stores sell a tool for cleaning the battery post…

5 =…as well as the battery cable clamps

Tyre condition and pressure

It is very important that tyres are in good condition, and at the correct pressure - having a tyre failure at any speed is highly dangerous. Tyre wear is influenced by driving style - harsh braking and acceleration, or fast cornering, will all produce more rapid tyre wear. As a general rule, the front tyres wear out faster than the rears. Interchanging the tyres from front to rear ("rotating" the tyres) may result in more even wear. However, if this is completely effective, you may have the expense of replacing all four tyres at once!

Remove any nails or stones embedded in the tread before they penetrate the tyre to cause deflation. If removal of a nail does reveal that the tyre has been punctured, refit the nail so that its point of penetration is marked. Then immediately change the wheel, and have the tyre repaired by a tyre dealer.

Regularly check the tyres for damage in the form of cuts or bulges, especially in the sidewalls. Periodically remove the wheels, and clean any dirt or mud from the inside and outside surfaces. Examine the wheel rims for signs of rusting, corrosion or other damage. Light alloy wheels are easily damaged by "kerbing" whilst parking; steel wheels may also become dented or buckled. A new wheel is very often the only way to overcome severe damage.

New tyres should be balanced when they are fitted, but it may become necessary to re-balance them as they wear, or if the balance weights fitted to the wheel rim should fall off. Unbalanced tyres will wear more quickly, as will the steering and suspension components. Wheel imbalance is normally signified by vibration, particularly at a certain speed (typically around 50 mph). If this vibration is felt only through the steering, then it is likely that just the front wheels need balancing. If, however, the vibration is felt through the whole car, the rear wheels could be out of balance. Wheel balancing should be carried out by a tyre dealer or garage.

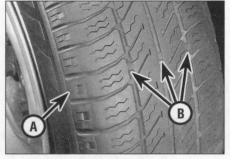

1 Tread Depth - visual check
The original tyres have tread wear safety bands (B), which will appear when the tread depth reaches approximately 1.6 mm. The band positions are indicated by a triangular mark on the tyre sidewall (A).

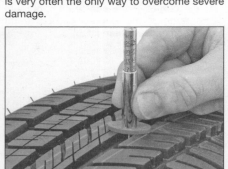

2 Tread Depth - manual check
Alternatively, tread wear can be monitored with a simple, inexpensive device known as a tread depth indicator gauge.

3 Tyre Pressure Check
Check the tyre pressures regularly with the tyres cold. Do not adjust the tyre pressures immediately after the vehicle has been used, or an inaccurate setting will result.

Tyre tread wear patterns

Shoulder Wear

Underinflation (wear on both sides)
Under-inflation will cause overheating of the tyre, because the tyre will flex too much, and the tread will not sit correctly on the road surface. This will cause a loss of grip and excessive wear, not to mention the danger of sudden tyre failure due to heat build-up.
Check and adjust pressures
Incorrect wheel camber (wear on one side)
Repair or renew suspension parts
Hard cornering
Reduce speed!

Centre Wear

Overinflation
Over-inflation will cause rapid wear of the centre part of the tyre tread, coupled with reduced grip, harsher ride, and the danger of shock damage occurring in the tyre casing.
Check and adjust pressures

If you sometimes have to inflate your car's tyres to the higher pressures specified for maximum load or sustained high speed, don't forget to reduce the pressures to normal afterwards.

Uneven Wear

Front tyres may wear unevenly as a result of wheel misalignment. Most tyre dealers and garages can check and adjust the wheel alignment (or "tracking") for a modest charge.
Incorrect camber or castor
Repair or renew suspension parts
Malfunctioning suspension
Repair or renew suspension parts
Unbalanced wheel
Balance tyres
Incorrect toe setting
Adjust front wheel alignment
Note: *The feathered edge of the tread which typifies toe wear is best checked by feel.*

Electrical systems

✔ Check all external lights and the horn. Refer to Chapter 12 Section 2 for details if any of the circuits are found to be inoperative.

✔ Visually check all accessible wiring connectors, harnesses and retaining clips for security, and for signs of chafing or damage.

HAYNES HiNT *If you need to check your brake lights and indicators unaided, back up to a wall or garage door and operate the lights. The reflected light should show if they are working properly.*

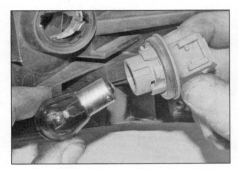

1 If a single indicator light, stop light, or headlight has failed, it is likely that a bulb has blown and will need to be renewed. Refer to Chapter 12 for details. If both stop lights have failed, it is possible that the switch has failed (Chapter 9)

2 If more than one indicator or tail light has failed, it is likely that either a fuse has blown or that there is a fault in the circuit. The main fusebox is located below the glovebox on the passenger's side. Refer to Chapter 12 for instructions on accessing the main fusebox.

3 To renew a blown fuse, simply pull it out and a fit a new fuse of the correct rating. Spares fuses and a fuse removal tool are provided on the inside of the auxiliary fusebox lid. If the fuse blows again, it is important that you find out why – a complete checking procedure is given in Chapter 12.

Wiper blades

Only fit good-quality replacement blades. When removing an old wiper blade, note how it is fitted. Fitting new blades can be a tricky exercise, and noting how the old blade came off can save time.
While the wiper blade is removed, take care

not to knock the wiper arm from its locked position or it could damage the glass.
Offer the new blade into position the same way round as the old one. Ensure that it clicks home securely, otherwise it may come off in use, damaging the glass.

Note: *Fitting details for wiper blades vary according to model, and according to whether genuine Volvo wiper blades have been fited. Use the procedures and illustrations as a guide for your car.*

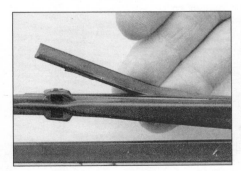

1 Check the condition of the wiper blades; if they are cracked or show any signs of deterioration, or if the glass area swept is smeared, renew them. Wiper blades should be renewed annually, regardless of their apparent condition

2 To remove a windscreen wiper blade, pull the arm fully away from the glass until it locks. Depress the clip on the front of the arm and slide the blade from place

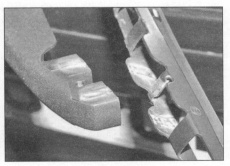

3 The tailgate blade simply pulls from place

Lubricants and fluids

Note: *Using lubricants and fluids which do not meet the Volvo standard may invalidate the warranty.*

Petrol engines:
1.8, 2.0 and 2.4 litre engines . . . . SAE 5W-30 ACEA A5/B5
2.4 litre engines (from 2007) . . . . SAE 0W-30 ACEA A5/B5

Diesel engines:
1.6 and 2.0 litre 4-cylinder engines . . . . SAE 5W-30 ACEA A5/B5
2.0 and 2.4 litre 5-cylinder engines . . . . SAE 0W/30 ACEA A5/B5

Cooling system . . . . Refer to dealer

Gearbox:
Manual transmission:
IB5 . . . . BOT 130 M3
B6, MTX75 and M66 . . . . BOT 350 M3
Automatic transmission:
AW55-51 . . . . JWS 3309
TF-80SC AW1

Braking system . . . . Hydraulic fluid to DOT 4+

Power steering system . . . . M2C204-A or equivalent

Air conditioning system R134a

Tyre pressures

Note: *The recommended tyre pressures for each vehicle are given on a sticker attached to the driver's door pillar. The pressures given are for the original equipment tyres – the recommended pressures may vary if any other make or type of tyre is fitted; check with the tyre manufacturer or supplier for latest recommendations.*

Chapter 1 Part A:
Routine maintenance and servicing – petrol models

Contents

Degrees of difficulty

Easy, suitable for novice with little experience

Fairly easy, suitable for beginner with some experience

Fairly difficult, suitable for competent DIY mechanic

Difficult, suitable for experienced DIY mechanic

Very difficult, suitable for expert DIY or professional

Lubricants and fluids.. See *Lubricants, fluids and tyre pressures* on page 0•16

Capacities

Engine oil (including filter)
1.8 and 2.0 litre engines.. 4.3 litres
2.4 litre engines .... 5.8 litres

Cooling system (approximate)
1.8 litre engines .... 7.5 litres
2.0 litre engines .... 6.5 litres
2.4 litre engines:
  Manual transmission.. 8.0 litres
  Automatic transmission .... 8.5 litres

Transmission
Manual transmission:
  IB5 .... 2.1 litres
  B6 .... 1.6 litres
  MTX75 .... 1.8 litres
  M66 .... 1.9 litres
  MMT6 .... 1.65 litres
Automatic transmission (total capacity):
  AW55-50/51 .... 7.7 litres
  TF-80SC... 7.0

Washer fluid reservoir
4-cylinder engines .... 4.0 litres
5-cylinder engines .... 6.5 litres

Fuel tank
1.8 and 2.0 litre models .... 55.0 litres
2.4 litre models .... 62.0 litres

Cooling system

Antifreeze mixture:
  50% antifreeze .... Protection down to –37°C
  55% antifreeze .... Protection down to –45°C
Note: *Refer to antifreeze manufacturer for latest recommendations.*

Ignition system

Spark plugs:	Type	Gap
1.8 and 2.0 litre engines	Volvo 30777349 Denso IT20 NGK TR6AP-13	1.25 mm to 1.35 mm (Gap is preset. Do not adjust)
2.4 litre engines	Volvo 30650843 NGK LFR6D	0.5 mm to 0.7 mm (3 electrode type. Do not adjust)

Brakes

Friction material minimum thickness:
  Front or rear brake pads.................................... 2.0 mm

Remote control battery

Type CR2032, 3V

Torque wrench settings

	Nm	lbf ft
Automatic transmission fluid filler/drain plug (AW55-51)	35	26
Automatic transmission filler plug (TF-80SC)	35	8
Automatic transmission drain plug (TF-80SC)	8	6
Compressor mounting bolts	20	15
Engine oil drain plug:		
1.8 and 2.0 litre engines	28	21
2.4 litre engines	38	28
Ignition coil retaining bolts	10	7
Oil filter cap (2.4 litre engines only)	25	18
Roadwheel nuts:		
Stage 1 (All nuts)	20	15
Stage 2:		
Standard, locking and nuts with fixed conical seating	110	81
Nuts with rotating conical seating	130	96
Spark plugs:		
1.8 and 2.0 litre models	12	9
2.4 litre models	25	18

1 Maintenance schedule

The maintenance intervals in this manual are provided with the assumption that you, not the dealer, will be carrying out the work. These are the minimum maintenance intervals recommended by us for vehicles driven daily. If you wish to keep your vehicle in peak condition at all times, you may wish to perform some of these procedures more often. We encourage frequent maintenance, because it enhances the efficiency, performance and resale value of your vehicle.

If the vehicle is driven in dusty areas, used to tow a trailer, or driven frequently at slow speeds (idling in traffic) or on short journeys, more frequent maintenance intervals are recommended.

When the vehicle is new, it should be serviced by a dealer service department (or other workshop recognised by the vehicle manufacturer as providing the same standard of service) in order to preserve the warranty. The vehicle manufacturer may reject warranty claims if you are unable to prove that servicing has been carried out as and when specified, using only original equipment parts or parts certified to be of equivalent quality.

Every 250 miles or weekly
- [ ] Refer to Weekly checks

Every 6000 miles or 6 months, whichever comes first
- [ ] Renew the engine oil and filter (Section 4)

Note: *Volvo recommend that the engine oil and filter are changed every 12 500 miles or 12 months. However, oil and filter changes are good for the engine and we recommend that the oil and filter are renewed more frequently, especially if the vehicle is used on a lot of short journeys.*
- [ ] Check the power steering fluid level (Section 5)

Every 12 500 miles or 12 months, whichever comes first
In addition to the items listed above, carry out the following:
- [ ] Check the automatic transmission park/neutral position switch (Section 6)
- [ ] Check the condition of the auxiliary drivebelt (Section 7)
- [ ] Check the operation of the lights and the horn (Section 8)
- [ ] Check under the bonnet for fluid leaks and hose condition (Section 9)
- [ ] Check the condition of the engine compartment wiring (Section 10)
- [ ] Check the automatic transmission fluid level (Section 11)
- [ ] Check the condition of the brake pads and discs (Section 12)
- [ ] Check the exhaust system (Section 13)
- [ ] Check the steering and suspension components for condition and security (Section 14)
- [ ] Check the condition of the driveshaft joints and gaiters (Section 15)

Every 12 500 miles or 12 months, whichever comes first (continued)
- [ ] Check the underbody and all fuel/brake lines (Section 16)
- [ ] Lubricate all hinges and locks (Section 17)
- [ ] Roadwheel check (Section 18)
- [ ] Carry out a road test (Section 19)
- [ ] Renew the pollen filter (Section 20)

Note: *If the vehicle is used in dusty conditions, the pollen filter should be renewed more frequently.*
- [ ] Renew the fuel filter (Section 21)
- [ ] Check and if necessary adjust the handbrake (Section 22)
- [ ] Check the condition of the seat belts (Section 23)
- [ ] Check the antifreeze/inhibitor strength (Section 24)
- [ ] Reset the service reminder indicator (Section 25)

Every 36 000 miles
In addition to the items listed above, carry out the following:
- [ ] Renew the air filter (Section 26)

Note: *If the vehicle is used in dusty conditions, the air filter should be renewed more frequently.*
- [ ] Renew the spark plugs (Section 27)

Note: *Volvo recommend that the spark plugs are replaced at 72, 000 miles or every 4 years.*
- [ ] Renew the automatic transmission fluid (Section 11)

Note: *The automatic transmission fluid does not normally require changing. It's only necessary on vehicles that are used predominantly for towing or as taxis.*

Every 60 000 miles
In addition to the items listed above, carry out the following:
- [ ] Renew the timing belt and tensioner (Section 28)

Note: *The Volvo interval for belt renewal is actually at a much higher mileage than this (100 000 miles or 10 years). It is strongly recommended, however, that the interval is reduced to 60 000 miles, particularly on vehicles which are subjected to intensive use, ie, mainly short journeys or a lot of stop-start driving. The actual belt renewal interval is therefore very much up to the individual owner, but bear in mind that severe engine damage will result if the belt breaks.*

Every 2 years, regardless of mileage
- [ ] Renew the brake fluid (Section 29)
- [ ] Renew the coolant (Section 30)

Note: *This work is not included in the Volvo schedule, and should not be required if the recommended Volvo antifreeze/inhibitor is used.*
- [ ] Renew remote control battery (Section 31)

Every 100 000 miles or 9 years, whichever comes first
- [ ] Renew the auxiliary drivebelt (Section 32)

2 Maintenance – component location

Underbonnet view of a 1.8 litre model

1 Oil level dipstick
2 Oil filler cap
3 Coolant expansion tank cap
4 Power steering fluid reservoir
5 Air filter element cover
6 Battery
7 Brake and clutch fluid reservoir
8 Washer fluid reservoir
9 ECM cover
10 Fuse/relay box

Underbonnet view of a 2.4 litre model

1 Oil level dipstick
2 Oil filler cap
3 Air filter element cover
4 Brake and clutch fluid reservoir
5 Washer fluid reservoir
6 Power steering fluid reservoir
7 Coolant expansion tank
8 Battery
9 Fuse/relay box
10 ECM cover

Front underbody view – 1.8 litre model

1 Oil filter cartridge
2 Engine oil drain plug
3 Transmission drain plug
4 Catalytic converter
5 Track rod end
6 Right-hand driveshaft
7 Air conditioning compressor
8 Suspension control arm
9 Brake caliper

Rear underbody view – 1.8 litre model

1 Anti-roll bar
2 Carbon canister
3 Fuel tank
4 Silencer
5 Shock absorber
6 Lateral link
7 Lower control arm
8 Tie rod

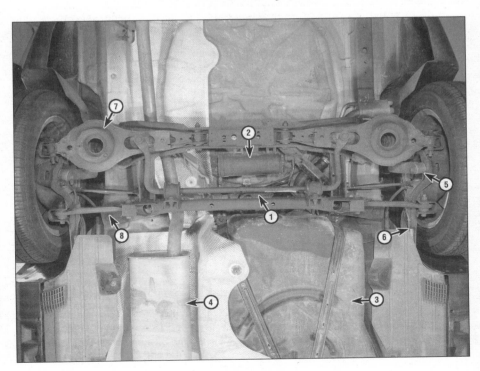

3 General information and regular maintenance

General information

1 This Chapter is designed to help the home mechanic maintain his/her vehicle for safety, economy, long life and peak performance.

2 The Chapter contains a master maintenance schedule, followed by Sections dealing specifically with each task in the schedule. Visual checks, adjustments, component renewal and other helpful items are included. Refer to the accompanying illustrations of the engine compartment and the underside of the vehicle for the locations of the various components.

3 Servicing your vehicle in accordance with the mileage/time maintenance schedule and the following Sections will provide a planned maintenance programme, which should result in a long and reliable service life. This is a comprehensive plan, so maintaining some items but not others at the specified service intervals will not produce the same results.

4 As you service your vehicle, you will discover that many of the procedures can – and should – be grouped together, because of the particular procedure being performed, or because of the proximity of two otherwise-unrelated components to one another. For example, if the vehicle is raised for any reason,

the exhaust can be inspected at the same time as the suspension and steering components.

5 The first step in this maintenance programme is to prepare yourself before the actual work begins. Read through all the Sections relevant to the work to be carried out, then make a list and gather all the parts and tools required. If a problem is encountered, seek advice from a parts specialist, or a dealer service department.

Regular maintenance

6 If, from the time the vehicle is new, the routine maintenance schedule is followed closely, and frequent checks are made of fluid levels and high-wear items, as suggested throughout this manual, the engine will be kept in relatively good running condition, and the need for additional work will be minimised.

7 It is possible that there will be times when the engine is running poorly due to the lack of regular maintenance. This is even more likely if a used vehicle, which has not received regular and frequent maintenance checks, is purchased. In such cases, additional work may need to be carried out, outside of the regular maintenance intervals.

8 If engine wear is suspected, a compression test (refer to Chapter 2A or 2B, as applicable) will provide valuable information regarding the overall performance of the main internal components. Such a test can be used as a basis to decide on the extent of the work to be carried out. If, for example, a compression test indicates serious internal engine wear,

conventional maintenance as described in this Chapter will not greatly improve the performance of the engine, and may prove a waste of time and money, unless extensive overhaul work is carried out first.

9 The following series of operations are those most often required to improve the performance of a generally poor-running engine:

Primary operations

a) Clean, inspect and test the battery (refer to 'Weekly checks').
b) Check all the engine-related fluids (refer to 'Weekly checks').
c) Check the condition and tension of the auxiliary drivebelt (Section 7).
d) Renew the spark plugs (Section 27).
e) Check the condition of the air filter, and renew if necessary (Section 26).
f) Renew the fuel filter (Section 21).
g) Check the condition of all hoses, and check for fluid leaks (Section 9).

10 If the above operations do not prove fully effective, carry out the following secondary operations:

Secondary operations

All items listed under Primary operations, plus the following:

a) Check the charging system (refer to Chapter 5A, Section 4).
b) Check the ignition system (refer to Chapter 5B).
c) Check the fuel system (refer to Chapter 4A).

Every 6000 miles or 6 months

4 Engine oil and filter renewal

1 Frequent oil and filter changes are the most important preventative maintenance procedures which can be undertaken by the DIY owner. As engine oil ages, it becomes diluted and contaminated, which leads to premature engine wear.

2 Before starting this procedure, gather

together all the necessary tools and materials. Also make sure that you have plenty of clean rags and newspapers handy, to mop-up any spills. Ideally, the engine oil should be warm, as it will drain more easily, and more built-up sludge will be removed with it.

3 Take care not to touch the exhaust (especially the catalytic converter) or any other hot parts of the engine when working under the vehicle. To avoid any possibility of scalding, and to protect yourself from possible skin irritants and other harmful contaminants

in used engine oils, it is advisable to wear gloves when carrying out this work.

4 Firmly apply the handbrake, then jack up the front of the vehicle and support it on axle stands (see Jacking and vehicle support). Where fitted, release the 7 Torx screws and remove the engine undershield (see illustration).

5 Remove the oil filler cap.

6 Using a spanner, or preferably a socket and bar, slacken the sump drain plug about half a turn (see illustrations). Position the draining container under the drain plug, then remove the plug completely.

4.4 Undo the 7 Torx screws (arrowed) and remove the engine undershield

4.6a Engine oil sump drain plug (arrowed) – 1.8 and 2.0 litre models

4.6b Engine oil sump drain plug (arrowed) – 2.4 litre models

4.9 On 1.8 and 2.0 litre models, the oil filter is located at the front of the engine

4.10 Slacken the filter cartridge using a tool which grips the casing

4.15 Use a 36 mm socket to unscrew the filter cap

HAYNES HiNT *As the plug releases from the threads, move it away sharply, so that the stream of oil from the sump runs into the container, not up your sleeve.*

7 Allow some time for the oil to drain, noting that it may be necessary to reposition the container as the oil flow slows to a trickle.

8 After all the oil has drained, wipe the drain plug with a clean rag. Examine the condition of the drain plug sealing ring, and renew it if it shows signs of flattening or other damage which may prevent an oil-tight seal (it is generally considered good practice to fit a new seal every time, but on the 1.8 and 2.0 litre models, the seal is not available separately from the drain plug). Clean the area around the drain plug opening, and refit the plug complete with the seal and tighten it to the specified torque.

1.8 and 2.0 litre models

9 Move the container into position under the oil filter, which is located on the front of the cylinder block **(see illustration)**.

10 Use an oil filter removal tool if necessary to slacken the filter initially, then unscrew it by hand the rest of the way **(see illustration)**. Empty the oil from the old filter into the container, then puncture the top of the filter, and allow the remaining oil to drain from the filter into the container.

11 Use a clean rag to remove all oil, dirt and sludge from the filter sealing area on the engine.

12 Apply a light coating of clean engine oil to the sealing ring on the new filter, then screw the filter into position on the engine. Tighten the filter firmly by hand only – do not use any tools.

13 Remove the old oil and all tools from under the car, refit the engine undershield (where applicable), then lower the car to the ground.

2.4 litre models

14 Remove the old oil and all tools from under the car, refit the engine undershield (where applicable), then lower the car to the ground.

15 Using a 36 mm socket on an extension unscrew and remove the oil filter housing cap **(see illustration)**. Discard the O-ring seal, a new one must be fitted.

16 Lift the filter insert from the housing and dispose of it. Be prepared for oil spillage **(see illustration)**.

17 Clean the filter housing and cap using rags, then install the new O-ring seal on the cap, and lubricate it with a little clean engine oil **(see illustration)**.

18 Position the new filter insert into the filter housing, then refit the cap and tighten it to the specified torque **(see illustration)**.

19 Refit the air cleaner resonator, and intake ducting.

All models

20 Fill the engine, using the correct grade and type of oil (refer to *Weekly checks* for details of topping-up). An oil can spout or funnel may help to reduce spillage. Pour in half the specified quantity of oil first, then wait a few minutes for the oil to run to the sump.

21 Continue adding oil a small quantity at a time until the level is up to the MIN mark on the dipstick. Adding around 0.5 litre of oil will now bring the level up to the MAX on the dipstick – do not worry if a little too much goes in, as some of the excess will be taken up in filling the oil filter. Refit the dipstick and the filler cap.

22 Start the engine and run it for a few minutes; check for leaks around the oil filter and the sump drain plug. Note that there may be a few seconds' delay before the oil pressure warning light goes out when the engine is started, as the oil circulates through the engine oil galleries and the new oil filter before the pressure builds up.

23 Switch off the engine, and wait a few minutes for the oil to settle in the sump once more. With the new oil circulated and the filter completely full, recheck the level on the dipstick, and add more oil as necessary.

24 Dispose of the used engine oil and the old oil filter safely, with reference to *General repair procedures* in the *Reference* section of this manual. Many local recycling points have containers for waste oil, with oil filter disposal receptacles alongside.

5 Power steering fluid level check

Caution: The need for frequent topping-up indicates a leak, which should be investigated immediately.

4.16 Lift the oil filter element from the housing

4.17 Fit a new O-ring seal to the filter cap

4.18 The new filter element can be fitted either way up

1 Park the vehicle on level ground, set the steering wheel straight-ahead. The engine should be turned off and cold.

 HAYNES HiNT *For the check to be accurate, the steering must not be turned once the engine has been stopped.*

2 The reservoir is mounted at the right-hand side of the engine compartment, behind the headlight. Remove the headlight as described in Chapter 12. The fluid level can be viewed through the reservoir body, and should be between the MIN and MAX marks when the engine is cold **(see illustration)**. If the level is checked when the engine is running or hot, the level may rise slightly above the MAX mark.

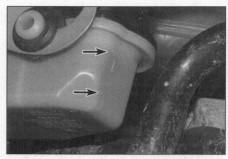

5.2 The power steering fluid level should be between the MIN and MAX marks

3 If topping-up is necessary, use the specified type of fluid – do not overfill the reservoir. Undo the reservoir cap **(see illustration)**.

5.3 Power steering reservoir cap

Take care not to introduce dirt into the system when topping-up. When the level is correct, securely refit the cap.

Every 12 500 miles or 12 months

6 Automatic transmission park/neutral switch check

1 The transmission selection system is designed so that the engine can only be started with the selector lever in position P or N.
2 Park the car on level ground, and apply the handbrake very firmly. Move the selector lever to position P and check that the engine can be started. Repeat this check with the lever in position N.
3 Move the lever to the other positions, and check that the engine cannot be started.
4 If it is possible to start the engine in a position other than P or N adjust the selector cable as described in Chapter 7B.

7 Auxiliary drivebelt check and renewal

Drivebelt check

1 On 1.8 and 2.0 litre models, two auxiliary drivebelts are fitted – one from the crankshaft pulley to the alternator and coolant pump,

and one from the crankshaft pulley to the air conditioning compressor. On 2.4 litre models, two auxiliary drivebelts are fitted at the right-hand side of the engine. On all engines, an automatic adjuster is fitted to the main auxiliary drivebelt, so checking the drivebelt tension is unnecessary. On 1.8 and 2.0 litre models, no provision is made to adjust the air conditioning drivebelt tension.
2 Due to their function and material make-up, drivebelts are prone to failure after a long period of time, and should therefore be inspected regularly.
3 Since the drivebelt is located very close to the right-hand side of the engine compartment, it is possible to gain better access by raising the front of the vehicle and removing the right-hand wheel, then undoing the 7 Torx screws and removing the engine undershield (where fitted) **(see illustration 4.4)**.
4 With the engine stopped, inspect the full length of the drivebelt for cracks and separation of the belt plies. It will be necessary to turn the engine (using a spanner or socket and bar on the crankshaft pulley bolt) in order to move the belt from the pulleys so that the belt can be inspected thoroughly. Twist the belt between the pulleys so that both sides can be viewed. Also check for fraying,

and glazing which gives the belt a shiny appearance. Check the pulleys for nicks, cracks, distortion and corrosion.
5 Note that it is not unusual for a ribbed belt to exhibit small cracks in the edges of the belt ribs, and unless these are extensive or very deep, belt renewal is not essential.

Drivebelt renewal

1.8 and 2.0 litre engines

6 Slacken the right-hand front roadwheel nuts, raise the front of the vehicle and support on axle stands (see *Jacking and vehicle support*). Where fitted - undo the 7 fasteners and remove the engine undershield **(see illustration 4.4)**. Remove the roadwheel.
7 Undo the Torx screws and the plastic nut, then remove the wheel arch liner.
8 Disconnect the air conditioning wiring plug, then slacken and remove bolts securing the compressor, protection plate and pipe bracket to the sump. Allow the compressor to pivot and remove the belt from the pulleys **(see illustrations)**.
9 Using a spanner on the tensioner centre bolt, turn the tensioner anti-clockwise to release the drivebelt tension. Note how the drivebelt is routed, then remove the belt from the pulleys **(see illustration)**.

7.8a Undo the protection plate/ compressor mounting bolts (arrowed)

7.8b With the compressor released, slip the belt from the pulleys

7.9 Rotate the tensioner anti-clockwise

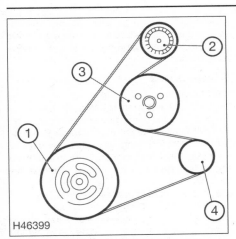

7.10 **Auxiliary drivebelt routing – 1.8 and 2.0 litre models**

1 Crankshaft pulley
2 Tensioner pulley
3 Coolant pump pulley
4 Alternator pulley

10 Fit the new drivebelt onto the crankshaft, alternator, and coolant pump, then turn the tensioner anti-clockwise and locate the drivebelt on the pulley. Make sure that the drivebelt is correctly seated in all of the pulley grooves, then release the tensioner **(see illustration)**.
11 Fit the new belt to the compressor and crankshaft pulleys, then refit the protection plate and tighten the bolts to the specified torque. Take care not to cross-thread the mounting bolts. Reconnect the wiring plug and refit the pipe bracket.
12 Refit the wheel arch liner, and engine undershield (where applicable). The fit the roadwheel and lower the car to the ground.

2.4 litre engines

13 Slacken the right-hand front roadwheel nuts, raise the front of the vehicle and support on axle stands (see *Jacking and vehicle support*). Undo the 7 fasteners and remove the engine undershield **(see illustration 4.4)**. Remove the roadwheel.
14 Undo the Torx screws and the plastic nuts, then remove the wheel arch liner.
15 To remove the outer belt, insert a Torx bit into the tensioner arm, then rotate the tensioner clockwise as far as possible, and remove the belt **(see illustration)**.
16 Insert a Torx bit into the centre of the inner belt tensioner pulley, then rotate the tensioner anti-clockwise as far as it will go. Remove the belt.
17 Ensure the pulley grooves are clean, rotate the tensioner anti-clockwise and fit the new belt to the pulleys. Check the belt is correctly located in the pulley grooves, then gently release the tensioner.
18 Rotate the outer belt tensioner clockwise, and fit the new belt to the pulleys. Check the belt is correctly located in the pulley grooves, then gently release the tensioner.

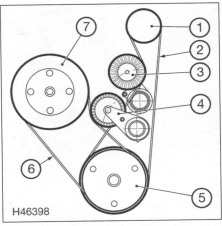

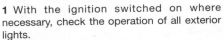

7.15 **Auxiliary drivebelt details – 2.4 litre models**

1 Alternator pulley
2 Inner drivebelt
3 Inner drivebelt tensioner
4 Outer drivebelt tensioner
5 Air conditioning compressor
6 Outer drivebelt
7 Crankshaft pulley

19 Refit the undershield, the wheel arch liner and the roadwheel, then lower the vehicle to the ground.

8 Lights and horn operation check

1 With the ignition switched on where necessary, check the operation of all exterior lights.
2 Check the brake lights with the help of an assistant, or by reversing up close to a reflective door. Make sure that all the rear lights are capable of operating independently, without affecting any of the other lights – for example, switch on as many rear lights as possible, then try the brake lights. If any unusual results are found, this is usually due to an earth fault or other poor connection at that rear light unit.
3 Again with the help of an assistant or using a reflective surface, check as far as possible that the headlights work on both main and dipped beam.
4 Renew any defective bulbs with reference to Chapter 12 **(see Haynes Hint)**.

> **HAYNES HINT** *Particularly on older vehicles, bulbs can stop working as a result of corrosion build-up on the bulb or its holder – fitting a new bulb may not cure the problem in this instance. When renewing any bulb, if you find any green or white-coloured powdery deposits, these should be cleaned off using emery cloth.*

5 Check the operation of all interior lights, including the glovebox and luggage area illumination lights. Switch on the ignition, and check that all relevant warning lights come on as expected – the vehicle handbook should give details of these. Now start the engine, and check that the appropriate lights go out. When you are next driving at night, check that all the instrument panel and facia lighting works correctly. If any problems are found, refer to Chapter 12.
6 Finally, choose an appropriate time of day to test the operation of the horn.

9 Underbonnet check for fluid leaks and hose condition

> ⚠ *Warning: Renewal of air conditioning hoses must be left to a dealer service department or air conditioning specialist who has the equipment to depressurise the system safely. Never remove air conditioning components or hoses until the system has been depressurised.*

General

1 Visually inspect the engine joint faces, gaskets and seals for any signs of water or oil leaks. Pay particular attention to the areas around the cylinder head cover, cylinder head, oil filter and sump joint faces. Bear in mind that, over a period of time, some very slight seepage from these areas is to be expected – what you are really looking for is any indication of a serious leak. Should a leak be found, renew the offending gasket or oil seal by referring to the appropriate Chapters in this manual.
2 High temperatures in the engine compartment can cause the deterioration of the rubber and plastic hoses used for engine, accessory and emission systems operation. Periodic inspection should be made for cracks, loose clamps, material hardening and leaks.
3 When checking the hoses, ensure that all the cable-ties or clips used to retain the hoses are in place, and in good condition. Clips which are broken or missing can lead to chafing of the hoses, pipes or wiring, which could cause more serious problems in the future.
4 Carefully check the large top and bottom radiator hoses, along with the other smaller-diameter cooling system hoses and metal pipes; do not forget the heater hoses/pipes which run from the engine to the bulkhead. Inspect each hose along its entire length, renewing any that is cracked, swollen or shows signs of deterioration. Cracks may become more apparent if the hose is squeezed, and may often be apparent at the hose ends.
5 Make sure that all hose connections are tight. If the large-diameter air hoses from the air cleaner are loose, they will leak air, and

9.5 Check the security of the air intake hoses

9.16 Check the fuel hose where it joins the fuel rail

upset the engine idle quality **(see illustration)**. If the spring clamps that are used to secure some of the hoses appear to be slackening, they should be updated with worm-drive clips to prevent the possibility of leaks.

6 Some other hoses are secured to their fittings with clamps. Where clamps are used, check to be sure they haven't lost their tension, allowing the hose to leak. If clamps aren't used, make sure the hose has not expanded and/or hardened where it slips over the fitting, allowing it to leak.

7 Check all fluid reservoirs, filler caps, drain plugs and fittings, etc, looking for any signs of leakage of oil, transmission and/or brake hydraulic fluid, coolant and power steering fluid. Also check the clutch hydraulic fluid lines which lead from the fluid reservoir and slave cylinder (on the transmission).

8 If the vehicle is regularly parked in the same place, close inspection of the ground underneath it will soon show any leaks; ignore the puddle of water which will be left if the air conditioning system is in use. Place a clean piece of cardboard below the engine, and examine it for signs of contamination after the vehicle has been parked over it overnight – be aware, however, of the fire risk inherent in placing combustible material below the catalytic converter.

9 Remember that some leaks will only occur with the engine running, or when the engine is hot or cold. With the handbrake firmly applied, start the engine from cold, and let the engine idle while you examine the underside of the engine compartment for signs of leakage.

10 If an unusual smell is noticed inside or around the car, especially when the engine is thoroughly hot, this may point to the presence of a leak.

11 As soon as a leak is detected, its source must be traced and rectified. Where oil has been leaking for some time, it is usually necessary to use a steam cleaner, pressure washer or similar, to clean away the accumulated dirt, so that the exact source of the leak can be identified.

Vacuum hoses

12 It's quite common for vacuum hoses, especially those in the emissions system, to be colour-coded, or to be identified by coloured

stripes moulded into them. Various systems require hoses with different wall thicknesses, collapse resistance and temperature resistance. When renewing hoses, be sure the new ones are made of the same material.

13 Often the only effective way to check a hose is to remove it completely from the vehicle. If more than one hose is removed, be sure to label the hoses and fittings to ensure correct installation.

14 When checking vacuum hoses, be sure to include any plastic T-fittings in the check. Inspect the fittings for cracks, and check the hose where it fits over the fitting for distortion, which could cause leakage.

15 A small piece of vacuum hose (quarter-inch inside diameter) can be used as a stethoscope to detect vacuum leaks. Hold one end of the hose near your ear, and probe around vacuum hoses and fittings, listening for the 'hissing' sound characteristic of a vacuum leak.

⚠️ *Warning: When probing with the vacuum hose stethoscope, be very careful not to come into contact with moving engine components such as the auxiliary drivebelt, radiator electric cooling fan, etc.*

Fuel hoses

⚠️ *Warning: There are certain precautions which must be taken when inspecting or servicing fuel system components. Work in a well-ventilated area, and do not allow open flames (cigarettes, appliance pilot lights, etc) or bare light bulbs near the work area. Mop-up any spills immediately, and do not store fuel-soaked rags where they could ignite.*

16 Check all fuel hoses for deterioration and chafing. Check especially for cracks in areas where the hose bends, and also just before fittings, such as where a hose attaches to the fuel rail **(see illustration)**.

17 High-quality fuel line, usually identified by the word 'Fluoroelastomer' printed on the hose, should be used for fuel line renewal. Never, under any circumstances, use non-reinforced vacuum line, clear plastic tubing or water hose as a substitute for fuel lines.

18 Spring-type clamps may be used on fuel lines. These clamps often lose their tension

over a period of time, and can be 'sprung' during removal. Update all spring-type clamps with proper petrol pipe clips whenever a hose is renewed.

Metal pipes

19 Sections of metal piping are often used for fuel line between the fuel filter and the engine, and for some power steering and air conditioning applications. Check carefully to be sure the piping has not been bent or crimped, and that cracks have not started in the line; also check for signs of excessive corrosion.

20 If a section of metal fuel line must be renewed, only seamless steel piping should be used, since copper and aluminium piping don't have the strength necessary to withstand normal engine vibration.

21 Check the metal lines where they enter the brake master cylinder, ABS hydraulic unit or clutch master/slave cylinders (as applicable) for cracks in the lines or loose fittings. Any sign of brake fluid leakage calls for an immediate and thorough inspection.

10 Engine compartment wiring check

1 With the vehicle parked on level ground, apply the handbrake firmly and open the bonnet. Using an inspection light or a small electric torch, check all visible wiring within and beneath the engine compartment.

2 What you are looking for is wiring that is obviously damaged by chafing against sharp edges, or against moving suspension/transmission components and/or the auxiliary drivebelt, by being trapped or crushed between carelessly-refitted components, or melted by being forced into contact with the hot engine castings, coolant pipes, etc. In almost all cases, damage of this sort is caused in the first instance by incorrect routing on reassembly after previous work has been carried out.

3 Depending on the extent of the problem, damaged wiring may be repaired by rejoining the break or splicing-in a new length of wire, using solder to ensure a good connection, and remaking the insulation with adhesive insulating tape or heat-shrink tubing, as appropriate. If the damage is extensive, given the implications for the vehicle's future reliability, the best long-term answer may well be to renew that entire section of the loom, however expensive this may appear.

4 When the damage has been repaired, ensure that the wiring loom is re-routed correctly, so that it is clear of other components, and not stretched or kinked, and is secured out of harm's way using the plastic clips, guides and ties provided.

5 Check all electrical connectors, ensuring that they are clean, securely fastened, and that each is locked by its plastic tabs or wire

10.5 Ensure all electrical connectors are securely clipped together

clip, as appropriate **(see illustration)**. If any connector shows external signs of corrosion (accumulations of white or green deposits, or streaks of 'rust'), or if any is thought to be dirty, it must be unplugged and cleaned using electrical contact cleaner. If the connector pins are severely corroded, the connector must be renewed; note that this may mean the renewal of that entire section of the loom – see your local Volvo dealer for details.

6 If the cleaner completely removes the corrosion to leave the connector in a satisfactory condition, it would be wise to pack the connector with a suitable material which will exclude dirt and moisture, preventing the corrosion from occurring again; a Volvo dealer may be able to recommend a suitable product.

7 Check the condition of the battery connections – remake the connections or renew the leads if a fault is found (see Chapter 5A). Use the same techniques to ensure that all earth points in the engine compartment provide good electrical contact through clean, metal-to-metal joints, and that all are securely fastened.

11 Automatic transmission fluid level checking and renewal

Level check

1 The level of the automatic transmission fluid should be carefully maintained. Low fluid level can lead to slipping or loss of drive, while overfilling can cause foaming, loss of fluid and transmission damage.

2 Ideally, the transmission fluid level should be checked when the transmission is hot (at its normal operating temperature). If the vehicle has just been driven for about 30 minutes, the fluid temperature will be around 80°C, and the transmission is hot.

3 Raise the vehicle and support it securely on axle stands (see *Jacking and vehicle support*). Undo the 7 Torx screws and remove the engine undershield **(see illustration 4.4)**.

4 Firmly apply the handbrake, and start the engine. While the engine is idling, depress the brake pedal and move the selector lever through all gear positions (pausing in each position for at least 3 seconds), returning finally to the P position.

5 Wait two minutes then, with the engine still idling, remove the dipstick (yellow handle) from its tube which is located at the front of the transmission **(see illustration)**. Note the condition and colour of the fluid on the dipstick.

6 Wipe the fluid from the dipstick with a clean rag, and re-insert it into the filler tube until the cap seats.

7 Pull the dipstick out again, and note the fluid level. The level should be towards the top of the HOT range of the dipstick. If the level is below the HOT range, stop the engine.

8 To add fluid to the transmission, disconnect the oil cooler hose from the return port on the transmission cover. The hose is secured by a quick-release connector. Connect a length of rubber hose to the return port with a funnel in the other end of the hose. Add the specified automatic transmission fluid. It is essential not to introduce dirt into the transmission when topping-up.

9 Add the fluid a little at a time, and keep checking the level as previously described until it is correct. The difference between the top and bottom of the HOT or COLD ranges is approximately 0.3 litres.

10 If the vehicle has not been driven and the engine and transmission are cold, carry out the procedures in paragraphs 3 to 6, but use the marks of the dipstick marked COLD. It is, however, preferable to check the level when the transmission is hot, as a more accurate reading will be obtained.

11 The need for regular topping-up of the transmission fluid indicates a leak, which should be found and rectified without delay.

12 The condition of the fluid should also be checked along with the level. If the fluid at the end of the dipstick is black or a dark reddish-brown colour, or if it has a burned smell, the fluid should be changed. If you are in doubt about the condition of the fluid, purchase some new fluid, and compare the two for colour and smell.

13 If the car is used regularly for short trips, taxi work, or does a lot of towing, the transmission fluid should be renewed on a regular basis. Likewise, if a high mileage has been completed, or the history of the car is unknown, it might be worth renewing the fluid for peace of mind. Normally, however, renewal of the fluid is not a service requirement.

Fluid renewal

14 Raise the vehicle and support it securely on axle stands (see *Jacking and vehicle support*). Undo the 7 Torx screws and remove the engine undershield **(see illustration 4.4)**.

15 Position a container under the transmission drain plug, then remove the plug and allow the fluid to drain into the container **(see illustration)**. Discard the sealing washer, a new one must be fitted.

16 Once all the fluid has drained, refit the drain plug with a new washer, and tighten it to the specified torque.

17 To add fluid to the transmission, disconnect the oil cooler hose from the return port on the transmission cover **(see illustration)**. The hose is secured by a quick-release connector. Connect a length of clear plastic hose to the return port with a funnel in the other end of the hose.

18 Ensure the selector lever is in position P, then add approximately 2.0 litres of the specified automatic transmission fluid through the hose into the transmission. It is essential not to introduce dirt into the transmission when topping-up.

19 Start the engine, and allow it to idle so the transmission pumps out the fluid. Turn the engine off as soon as air bubbles appear in the plastic tube.

20 Repeat the operation described in paragraph 19 above.

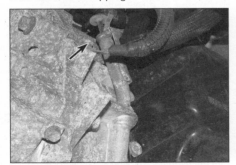

11.5 Automatic transmission oil level dipstick (arrowed) – viewed from underneath

11.15 Automatic transmission oil drain plug (arrowed)

11.17 Disconnect the oil return hose from the front/top of the transmission (arrowed)

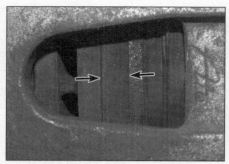

12.4 Measure the thickness of the brake pad friction material (arrowed)

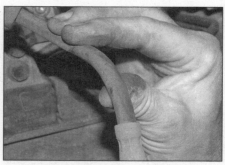

12.12 Check the condition of the rubber brake hoses by bending them slightly and looking for cracks

13.2 Check the condition of the exhaust mounting rubbers

21 Add a further 2 litres of fluid, then check the oil level as previously described in this Section.
22 Refit the engine undershield upon completion.

12 Brake pads and discs check

1 The work described in this Section should be carried out at the specified intervals, or whenever a defect is suspected in the braking system. Any of the following symptoms could indicate a potential brake system defect:
a) *The vehicle pulls to one side when the brake pedal is depressed.*
b) *The brakes make squealing, scraping or dragging noises when applied.*
c) *Brake pedal travel is excessive, or pedal feel is poor.*
d) *The brake fluid requires repeated topping-up. Note that, because the hydraulic clutch shares the same fluid as the braking system (see Chapter 6), this problem could be due to a leak in the clutch system.*

Front disc brakes

2 Apply the handbrake, then loosen the front wheel nuts. Jack up the front of the vehicle, and support it on axle stands (see *Jacking and vehicle support*).
3 For better access to the brake calipers, remove the wheels.
4 Look through the inspection window in the caliper, and check that the thickness of the friction lining material on each of the pads is not less than the recommended minimum thickness given in the Specifications **(see illustration)**.

HAYNES HINT *Bear in mind that the lining material is normally bonded to a metal backing plate. To differentiate between the metal and the lining material, it is helpful to turn the disc slowly at first – the edge of the disc can then be identified, with the lining material on each pad either side of it, and the backing plates behind.*

5 If it is difficult to determine the exact thickness of the pad linings, or if you are at all concerned about the condition of the pads, then remove them from the calipers for further inspection (refer to Chapter 9, Section 4).
6 Check the other caliper in the same way.
7 If any one of the brake pads has worn down to, or below, the specified limit, *all four* pads at that end of the car must be renewed as a set. If the pads on one side are significantly more worn than the other, this may indicate that the caliper pistons have partially seized – refer to the brake pad renewal procedure in Chapter 9, and push the pistons back into the caliper to free them.
8 Measure the thickness of the discs with a micrometer, if available, to make sure that they still have service life remaining. Do not be fooled by the lip of rust which often forms on the outer edge of the disc, which may make the disc appear thicker than it really is – scrape off the loose rust if necessary, without scoring the disc friction (shiny) surface.
9 If any disc is thinner than the specified minimum thickness, renew both (refer to Chapter 9).
10 Check the general condition of the discs. Look for excessive scoring and discolouration caused by overheating. If these conditions exist, remove the relevant disc and have it resurfaced or renewed (refer to Chapter 9).
11 Make sure that the handbrake is firmly applied, then check that the transmission is in neutral. Spin the wheel, and check that the brake is not binding. Some drag is normal with a disc brake, but it should not require any great effort to turn the wheel – also, do not confuse brake drag with resistance from the transmission.
12 Before refitting the wheels, check all brake lines and hoses (refer to Chapter 9). In particular, check the flexible hoses in the vicinity of the calipers, where they are subjected to most movement **(see illustration)**. Bend them between the fingers (but do not actually bend them double, or the casing may be damaged) and check that this does not reveal previously-hidden cracks, cuts or splits.
13 On completion, refit the wheels and lower the car to the ground. Tighten the wheel nuts to the specified torque.

Rear disc brakes

14 Loosen the rear wheel nuts, then chock the front wheels. Jack up the rear of the car, and support it on axle stands. Release the handbrake and remove the rear wheels.
15 The procedure for checking the rear brakes is much the same as described in paragraphs 2 to 13 above. Check that the rear brakes are not binding, noting that transmission resistance is not a factor on the rear wheels. Abnormal effort may indicate that the handbrake needs adjusting – see Chapter 9.

13 Exhaust system check

1 With the engine cold (at least three hours after the vehicle has been driven), check the complete exhaust system, from its starting point at the engine to the end of the tailpipe. Ideally, this should be done on a hoist, where unrestricted access is available; if a hoist is not available, raise and support the vehicle on axle stands (see *Jacking and vehicle support*).
2 Make sure that all brackets and rubber mountings are in good condition, and tight; if any of the mountings are to be renewed, ensure that the new ones are of the correct type – in the case of the rubber mountings, their colour is a good guide. Those nearest to the catalytic converter are more heat-resistant than the others **(see illustration)**.
3 Check the pipes and connections for evidence of leaks, severe corrosion, or damage. One of the most common points for a leak to develop is around the welded joints between the pipes and silencers. Leakage at any of the joints or in other parts of the system will usually show up as a black sooty stain in the vicinity of the leak. **Note:** *Exhaust sealants should not be used on any part of the exhaust system upstream of the catalytic converter (between the converter and engine) – even if the sealant does not contain additives harmful to the converter, pieces of it may break off and foul the element, causing local overheating.*
4 At the same time, inspect the underside of the body for holes, corrosion, open seams,

14.2 Check the condition of the steering rack gaiters

14.4 Check for wear in the wheel bearing by grasping the wheel and trying to rock it

15.2 Squeeze the driveshaft gaiters and check for cracks

etc, which may allow exhaust gases to enter the passenger compartment. Seal all body openings with silicone or body putty.

5 Rattles and other noises can often be traced to the exhaust system, especially the rubber mountings. Try to move the system, silencer(s), heat shields and catalytic converter. If any components can touch the body or suspension parts, secure the exhaust system with new mountings.

6 Check the running condition of the engine by inspecting inside the end of the tailpipe; the exhaust deposits here are an indication of the engine's state of tune. The inside of the tailpipe should be dry, and should vary in colour from dark grey to light grey/brown; if it is black and sooty, or coated with white deposits, this may indicate the need for a full fuel system inspection.

14 Steering and suspension check

Front suspension and steering

1 Apply the handbrake, then raise the front of the vehicle and support it on axle stands (see *Jacking and vehicle support*).

2 Visually inspect the balljoint dust covers and the steering rack gaiters for splits, chafing or deterioration **(see illustration)**. Any wear of these components will cause loss of lubricant, together with dirt and water entry, resulting in rapid deterioration of the balljoints or steering gear.

3 Check the power-assisted steering fluid hoses for chafing or deterioration, and the pipe and hose unions for fluid leaks. Also check for signs of fluid leakage under pressure from the steering gear rubber gaiters, which would indicate failed fluid seals within the steering gear.

4 Grasp the roadwheel at the 12 o'clock and 6 o'clock positions, and try to rock it **(see illustration)**. Very slight free play may be felt, but if the movement is appreciable, further investigation is necessary to determine the source. Continue rocking the wheel while an assistant depresses the footbrake. If the

movement is now eliminated or significantly reduced, it is likely that the hub bearings are at fault. If the free play is still evident with the footbrake depressed, then there is wear in the suspension joints or mountings.

5 Now grasp the wheel at the 9 o'clock and 3 o'clock positions, and try to rock it as before. Any movement felt now may again be caused by wear in the hub bearings or the steering track rod balljoints. If the outer track rod balljoint is worn, the visual movement will be obvious. If the inner joint is suspect, it can be felt by placing a hand over the rack-and-pinion rubber gaiter, and gripping the track rod. If the wheel is now rocked, movement will be felt at the inner joint if wear has taken place.

6 Using a large screwdriver or flat bar, check for wear in the suspension mounting and subframe bushes by levering between the relevant suspension component and its attachment point. Some movement is to be expected as the mountings are made of rubber, but excessive wear should be obvious. Also check the condition of any visible rubber bushes, looking for splits, cracks or contamination of the rubber.

7 With the vehicle standing on its wheels, have an assistant turn the steering wheel back-and-forth, about an eighth of a turn each way. There should be very little, if any, lost movement between the steering wheel and roadwheels. If this is not the case, closely observe the joints and mountings previously described, but in addition, check the steering column joints for wear, and also check the rack-and-pinion steering gear itself.

Rear suspension

8 Chock the front wheels, then raise the rear of the vehicle and support it on axle stands (see *Jacking and vehicle support*).

9 Check the rear hub bearings for wear, using the method described for the front hub bearings (paragraph 4).

10 Using a large screwdriver or flat bar, check for wear in the suspension mounting bushes by levering between the relevant suspension component and its attachment point. Some movement is to be expected as the mountings are made of rubber, but excessive wear should be obvious.

15 Driveshaft rubber gaiter and joint check

1 The driveshaft rubber gaiters are very important, because they prevent dirt, water and foreign material from entering and damaging the joints. External contamination can cause the gaiter material to deteriorate prematurely, so it's a good idea to wash the gaiters with soap and water occasionally.

2 With the vehicle raised and securely supported on axle stands, turn the steering onto full-lock, then slowly rotate each front wheel. Inspect the condition of the outer constant velocity (CV) joint rubber gaiters, squeezing the gaiters to open out the folds. Check for signs of cracking, splits, or deterioration of the rubber, which may allow the escape of grease, and lead to the ingress of water and grit into the joint. Also check the security and condition of the retaining clips. Repeat these checks on the inner tripod joints **(see illustration)**. If any damage or deterioration is found, the gaiters should be renewed as described in Chapter 8.

3 At the same time, check the general condition of the outer CV joints themselves, by first holding the driveshaft and attempting to rotate the wheels. Repeat this check on the inner joints, by holding the inner joint yoke and attempting to rotate the driveshaft.

4 Any appreciable movement in the joint indicates wear in the joint, wear in the driveshaft splines, or a loose driveshaft retaining nut.

16 Underbody and fuel/brake line check

1 With the vehicle raised and supported on axle stands or over an inspection pit, thoroughly inspect the underbody and wheelarches for signs of damage and corrosion. In particular, examine the bottom of the side sills, and any concealed areas where mud can collect.

2 Where corrosion and rust is evident, press and tap firmly on the panel with a screwdriver,

16.5 Check the fuel and brake pipes under the vehicle body

and check for any serious corrosion which would necessitate repairs.

3 If the panel is not seriously corroded, clean away the rust, and apply a new coating of underseal. Refer to Chapter 11 for more details of body repairs.

4 At the same time, inspect the lower body panels for stone damage and general condition.

5 Inspect all of the fuel and brake lines on the underbody for damage, rust, corrosion and leakage. Also make sure that they are correctly supported in their clips **(see illustration)**. Where applicable, check the PVC coating on the lines for damage.

17 Hinge and lock lubrication

1 Work around the vehicle and lubricate the hinges of the bonnet, doors and tailgate with a light machine oil.

2 Check carefully the security and operation of all hinges, latches and locks, adjusting them where required. Check the operation of the central locking system (if fitted).

3 Where applicable, check the condition and operation of the tailgate struts, renewing them if either is leaking or no longer able to support the tailgate securely when raised.

18 Roadwheel check

Roadwheel nut tightness check

1 Checking the tightness of the wheel nuts is more relevant than you might think. Apart from the obvious safety aspect of ensuring they are sufficiently tight, this check will reveal whether they have been overtightened, as may have happened the last time new tyres were fitted, for example. If the car suffers a puncture, you may find that the wheel nuts cannot be loosened with the wheel brace.

2 Apply the handbrake, chock the wheels, and engage 1st gear (or P).

3 Remove the wheel cover (or wheel centre cover), using the flat end of the wheel brace supplied in the tool kit.

4 Loosen the first wheel nut, using the wheel brace if possible. If the nut proves stubborn, use a close-fitting socket and a long extension bar.

⚠️ **Warning: Do not use makeshift means to loosen the wheel nuts if the proper tools are not available. If extra force is required, make sure that the tools fit properly, and are of good quality. Even so, consider the consequences of the tool slipping or breaking, and take precautions – wearing stout gloves is advisable to protect your hands. Do not be tempted to stand on the tools used – they are not designed for this, and there is a high risk of personal injury if the tool slips or breaks. If the wheel nuts are simply too tight, take the car to a garage equipped with suitable power tools.**

5 Once the nut has been loosened, remove it and check that the wheel stud threads are clean. Use a small wire brush to clean any rust or dirt from the threads, if necessary.

6 Refit the nut, with the tapered side facing inwards. Tighten it fully, using the wheel brace alone – no other tools. This will ensure that the wheel nuts can be loosened using the wheel brace if a puncture occurs. However, if a torque wrench is available, tighten the nut to the specified torque wrench setting.

7 Repeat the procedure for the remaining three nuts, then refit the wheel cover or centre cover, as applicable.

8 Work around the car, checking and retightening the nuts for all four wheels.

Roadwheel check and balancing

9 Periodically remove the roadwheels, and clean any dirt or mud from the inside and outside surfaces. Examine the wheel rims for signs of rusting, corrosion or other damage. Light alloy wheels are easily damaged by 'kerbing' whilst parking, and similarly, steel wheels may become dented or buckled. Renewal of the wheel is very often the only course of remedial action possible.

10 The balance of each wheel and tyre assembly should be maintained, not only to avoid excessive tyre wear, but also to avoid wear in the steering and suspension components. Wheel imbalance is normally signified by vibration through the vehicle's bodyshell, although in many cases it is particularly noticeable through the steering wheel. Conversely, it should be noted that wear or damage in suspension or steering components may cause excessive tyre wear. Out-of-round or out-of-true tyres, damaged wheels and wheel bearing wear/maladjustment also fall into this category. Balancing will not usually cure vibration caused by such wear.

11 Wheel balancing may be carried out with the wheel either on or off the vehicle.

If balanced on the vehicle, ensure that the wheel-to-hub relationship is marked in some way prior to subsequent wheel removal, so that it may be refitted in its original position.

19 Road test

Braking system

1 Make sure that the vehicle does not pull to one side when braking, and that the wheels do not lock when braking hard.

2 Check that there is no vibration through the steering when braking. As all models are equipped with ABS brakes, if vibration is felt through the pedal under heavy braking, this is a normal characteristic of the system operation, and is not a cause for concern.

3 Check that the handbrake operates correctly, without excessive movement of the lever, and that it holds the vehicle stationary on a slope, in both directions (facing up and down a slope).

4 With the engine switched off, test the operation of the brake servo unit as follows. Depress the footbrake four or five times to exhaust the vacuum, then start the engine. As the engine starts, there should be a noticeable 'give' in the brake pedal as vacuum builds-up. Allow the engine to run for at least two minutes, and then switch it off. If the brake pedal is now depressed again, it should be possible to detect a hiss from the servo as the pedal is depressed. After about four or five applications, no further hissing should be heard, and the pedal should feel considerably harder.

Steering and suspension

5 Check for any abnormalities in the steering, suspension, handling or road 'feel'.

6 Drive the vehicle, and check that there are no unusual vibrations or noises.

7 Check that the steering feels positive, with no excessive sloppiness or roughness, and check for any suspension noises when cornering and driving over bumps.

Drivetrain

8 Check the performance of the engine, transmission and driveshafts.

9 Check that the engine starts correctly, both when cold and when hot.

10 Listen for any unusual noises from the engine and transmission.

11 Make sure that the engine runs smoothly when idling, and that there is no hesitation when accelerating.

12 On manual transmission models, check that all gears can be engaged smoothly without noise, and that the gear lever action is smooth and not abnormally vague or 'notchy'.

13 On automatic transmission models, make sure that all gearchanges occur smoothly

20.1 Push in the centre pins, prise out the plastic rivets and lower the insulation

20.2a Undo the 2 fasteners . . .

20.2b . . . and lower the fusebox/central electrical module

without snatching, and without an increase in engine speed between changes. Check that all the gear positions can be selected with the vehicle at rest. If any problems are found, they should be referred to a Volvo dealer.

14 Listen for a metallic clicking sound from the front of the vehicle as the vehicle is driven slowly in a circle with the steering on full-lock. Carry out this check in both directions. If a clicking noise is heard, this indicates wear in a driveshaft joint, in which case renew the joint if necessary.

Clutch

15 Check that the clutch pedal moves smoothly and easily through its full travel, and that the clutch itself functions correctly, with no trace of slip or drag.

16 If the clutch is slow to release, it is possible that the system requires bleeding (see Chapter 6). Also check the fluid pipes under the bonnet for signs of leakage.

17 Check the clutch as described in Chapter 6.

Instruments and electrical equipment

18 Check the operation of all instruments and electrical equipment.

19 Make sure that all instruments read correctly, and switch on all electrical equipment in turn, to check that it functions properly.

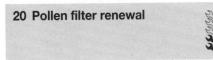

20 Pollen filter renewal

Pollen filter

1 Push in the centre pins and prise out the plastic expanding rivets holding the sound insulation in place under the passenger's side of the facia (see illustration). Pull the insulation downwards, then rearwards to remove it.

2 Undo the 2 fasteners securing the fusebox/central electrical module to its mounting bracket by rotating them anti-clockwise, then

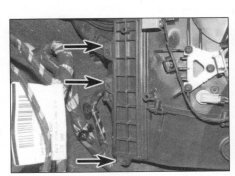

20.3a Undo the 3 bolts and remove the cover . . .

move the fusebox/module downwards and rearwards and detach it from the bracket (see illustrations). Move the fusebox/module to one side, there is no need to disconnect the wiring plugs.

3 Undo the bolts, remove the cover and pull the filter from the housing (see illustrations).

4 Fit the new filter using a reversal of the removal procedure, ensuring that the filter is fitted with the airflow arrows pointing straight back into the cabin.

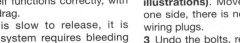

21 Fuel filter renewal

⚠ *Warning: Petrol is extremely flammable, so extra precautions must be taken when working on any part of the fuel system. Do not smoke, or allow open flames or bare light bulbs, near the work area. Also, do not work in a garage if a natural gas-type appliance with a pilot light is present. While performing any work on the fuel system, wear safety glasses, and have a suitable (Class B) fire extinguisher on hand. If you spill any fuel on your skin, rinse it off immediately with soap and water.*

Note: *Volvo do not suggest a replacement interval for the fuel filter. Renewal of the external fuel filter will only be necessary on a vehicle that have covered a high mileage or where contaminated fuel has been used. The filter should always be replaced if the vehicle is accidentally filled with diesel.*

20.3b . . . then pull the pollen filter from the housing

1 The fuel filter is located adjacent to the fuel tank. The filter performs a vital role in keeping dirt and other foreign matter out of the fuel system, and so must be renewed at regular intervals (see note above), or whenever you have reason to suspect that it may be clogged.

2 Before disturbing any fuel pipes which may contain fuel under pressure, any residual pressure in the system must be relieved as follows.

3 With the ignition switched off, open the passenger's compartment fusebox and remove the fuel pump fuse (No 74).

4 If the engine starts, allow it to idle until it dies. Turn the engine over once or twice on the starter, to ensure that all pressure is released, then switch off the ignition.

⚠ *Warning: This procedure will merely relieve the increased pressure necessary for the engine to run – remember that fuel will still be present in the system components, and take precautions accordingly before disconnecting any of them.*

5 Jack up the rear right-hand side of the vehicle, and support it securely on an axle stand (see *Jacking and vehicle support*).

6 Slacken the fuel filter clamp screw.

7 Depress the release buttons, then separate the fuel pipe fittings at either end of the filter by pulling apart – be prepared for fuel spillage. Note the positions of the pipes for refitting.

8 Lower the filter out from under the car – note that the filter will still contain fuel; care should be taken to avoid spillage and to minimise the risk of fire.

9 Slide the new filter fully into its clamp so that the arrow marked on it faces the same direction as when removing the old filter. Do not tighten the clamp screw yet.

10 Slide each pipe union onto its (correct) respective filter stub, until the fittings click into their groove.

11 Tighten the filter clamp screw securely.

12 Refit the fuel pump fuse. Check for any sign of fuel leakage around the filter unions before lowering the vehicle to the ground and starting the engine.

22 Handbrake check and adjustment

In service, the handbrake should be fully applied within 3 to 5 clicks of the handbrake lever ratchet. Should adjustment be necessary, refer to Chapter 9 for the full procedure.

23 Seat belt check

1 Check the seat belts for satisfactory operation and condition. Inspect the webbing for fraying and cuts. Check that they retract smoothly and without binding into their reels.

2 Check the seat belt mountings, ensuring that all the bolts are securely tightened.

24 Antifreeze/inhibitor strength check

See Section 30.

25 Service reminder indicator reset

1 Turn the ignition switch to position I.

2 Press and hold the trip odometer reset button, then turn the ignition switch to position II within 2 seconds.

3 Hold the button in until the warning light extinguishes and then release the button within 4 seconds. The instrument panel gives an audible signal when the resetting has been successful. **Note:** *If the odometer is already reset, the button must be held in for a minimum of 10 seconds and a maximum of 14 seconds.*

4 Turn off the ignition switch.

Every 36 000 miles

26 Air filter element renewal

Caution: Never drive the vehicle with the air cleaner filter element removed. Excessive engine wear could result, and backfiring could even cause a fire under the bonnet.

1.8 and 2.0 litre models

1 The air filter element is located in the air cleaner assembly on the left-hand side of the engine compartment.

2 Remove the 6 Torx screws securing the cover to the air cleaner housing **(see illustration)**.

3 The left-hand end of the cover can now be lifted, and the filter element removed **(see illustration)**. If preferred, the cover can be removed completely – this will allow a more thorough cleaning of the filter housing.

4 Loosen the clip and disconnect the air inlet duct from the air cleaner.

5 Withdraw the cover and remove the filter element, noting its direction of fitting.

2.4 litre models

6 The air filter is located at the front of the

26.2 Undo the 6 Torx screws (arrowed) and lift the air filter cover

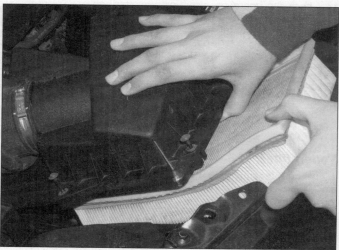

26.3 Slide out the filter element

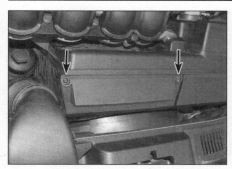

26.6a Undo the two screws (arrowed) . . .

26.6b . . . and pull the filter element holder from the housing

26.7 Pull the filter element from the holder

engine compartment. Undo the 2 screws and pull the filter element holder from the air filter housing **(see illustrations)**.

7 Pull the filter element from the holder. Note which way round it's fitted **(see illustration)**.

All models

8 If carrying out a routine service, the element must be renewed regardless of its apparent condition.

9 If you are checking the element for any other reason, inspect its lower surface; if it is oily or very dirty, renew the element. If it is only moderately dusty, it can be re-used by blowing it clean from the upper to the lower surface with compressed air. Because it is a pleated-paper type filter, it cannot be washed or re-oiled. If it cannot be cleaned satisfactorily with compressed air, renew it.

 Warning: Wear eye protection when using compressed air.

10 Where the air cleaner cover was removed, wipe out the inside of the housing. Check that no foreign matter is visible, either in the air intake or in the air mass meter.

11 Refitting is the reverse of the removal procedure, noting the following points:

a) *Make sure that the filter is fitted the correct way up (observe any direction-of-fitting markings).*

b) *Ensure that the element and cover are securely seated, so that unfiltered air cannot enter the engine.*

c) *Where removed, secure the cover with the screws, and ensure that the air inlet duct securing clip is fully tightened.*

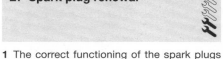

27 Spark plug renewal

1 The correct functioning of the spark plugs is vital for the correct running and efficiency of the engine. It is essential that the plugs fitted are appropriate for the engine; suitable types are specified at the beginning of this Chapter.

2 If the correct type is used and the engine is in good condition, the spark plugs should not need attention between scheduled renewal intervals. Spark plug cleaning is rarely necessary, and should not be attempted unless specialised equipment is available, as damage can easily be caused to the firing ends.

3 Spark plug removal and refitting requires a spark plug socket, with an extension which can be turned by a ratchet handle or similar. This socket is lined with a rubber sleeve, to protect the porcelain insulator of the spark plug, and to hold the plug while you insert it into the spark plug hole. You may also need feeler blades, to

check and adjust the spark plug electrode gap, and (ideally) a torque wrench to tighten the new plugs to the specified torque.

1.8 and 2.0 litre models

4 To remove the spark plugs, first open the bonnet; the plugs are easily reached at the top of the engine. Pull the plastic cover on the top of the engine straight up to release its mountings **(see illustration)**.

5 The ignition coils are fitted one-per-plug, on the top of each spark plug. To aid refitment, use paint (or similar) to identify the ignition coils so they are refitted to their original positions. Undo the retaining bolts and lift each coil from place **(see illustrations)**.

27.4 Pull the plastic cover upwards to release the mountings

27.5a Undo the coil retaining bolt . . .

27.5b . . . and lift it from place

27.7a The intake manifold is secured by 6 bolts at the front . . .

27.7b . . . and 2 at the rear (arrowed)

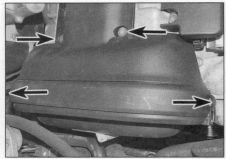

27.8 Undo the 2 screws, release the clips, and remove the timing belt upper cover (arrowed)

2.4 litre models

6 Slacken the clamp and disconnect the air intake hose from the throttle body.

7 Undo the 8 retaining bolts and lift the upper intake manifold from place, and lay it over the battery box **(see illustrations)**.

8 Unclip and remove the timing belt upper cover, and disconnect the variable valve timing solenoid wiring plug **(see illustration)**.

9 The ignition coils are fitted one-per-plug, on the top of each spark plug. To aid refitment, use paint (or similar) to identify the ignition coils so they are refitted to their original positions. Undo the coil retaining bolt and pull each one from the top of the spark plugs **(see illustrations)**.

All models

10 It is advisable to soak up any water in the spark plug recesses with a rag, and to remove any dirt from them using a clean brush, vacuum cleaner or compressed air before removing the plugs to prevent any dirt or water from dropping into the cylinders.

 Warning: Wear eye protection when using compressed air.

11 Unscrew the spark plugs, ensuring that the socket is kept in alignment with each plug – if the socket is forcibly moved to either side, the porcelain top of the plug may be broken off. Remove the plug from the engine.

12 If any undue difficulty is encountered when unscrewing any of the spark plugs, carefully check the cylinder head threads and

sealing surfaces for signs of wear, excessive corrosion or damage; if any of these conditions is found, seek the advice of a Volvo dealer or engine overhaul specialist as to the best method of repair.

13 As each plug is removed, examine it as follows – this will give a good indication of the condition of the engine:

a) *If the insulator nose of the spark plug is clean and white, with no deposits, this is indicative of a weak mixture.*

b) *If the tip and insulator nose are covered with hard black-looking deposits, then this is indicative that the mixture is too rich.*

c) *Should the plug be black and oily, then it is likely that the engine is fairly worn, as well as the mixture being too rich.*

d) *If the insulator nose is covered with light tan to greyish-brown deposits, then the mixture is correct, and it is likely that the engine is in good condition.*

14 If you are renewing the spark plugs, purchase the new plugs, then check each of them first for faults such as cracked insulators or damaged threads.

15 The spark plug electrode gap is of considerable importance as, if it is too large or too small, the size of the spark and its efficiency will be seriously impaired. Note that several models covered by this manual use spark plugs with multiple earth electrodes.

16 The electrode gap on plugs with one earth electrode can be measured with a feeler gauge. It is difficult (but not impossible) to check the gap on multiple earth spark plugs. If the gap is outside the specification it should

be replaced – no attempt should be made to adjust the gap. Replacement spark plugs are supplied preset to the correct gap, but it is always worth checking that the gap is correct before fitting the new spark plugs.

17 Before fitting the spark plugs, check that the threaded connector sleeves at the top of the plugs are tight, and that the plug exterior surfaces and threads are clean. Brown staining on the porcelain, immediately above the metal body, is quite normal, and does not necessarily indicate a leak between the body and insulator.

18 On installing the spark plugs, first check that the cylinder head thread and sealing surface are as clean as possible; use a clean rag wrapped around a paintbrush to wipe clean the sealing surface. Apply a smear of copper-based grease or anti-seize compound to the threads of each plug, and screw them in by hand where possible. Take extra care to enter the plug threads correctly, as the cylinder head is made of aluminium alloy – it's often difficult to insert spark plugs into their holes without cross-threading them **(see Haynes Hint)**.

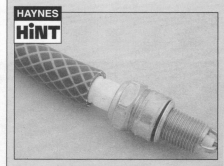

HAYNES HINT

It is often difficult to insert spark plugs into their holes without cross-threading them. To avoid this possibility, fit a short length of 8 mm diameter rubber/plastic hose over the end of the spark plug. The flexible hose acts as a universal joint to help align the plug with the hole. Should the plug begin to cross-thread, then the hose will slip on the spark plug, preventing thread damage to the cylinder head.

27.9a Undo the coil retaining bolt (arrowed) . . .

27.9b . . . and lift the coil from position

19 When each spark plug is started correctly on its threads, screw it down until it just seats lightly, then tighten it to the specified torque wrench setting. If a torque wrench is not available – and this is one case where the use of a torque wrench is strongly recommended – tighten each spark plug through *no more than* 1/16th of a turn. *Do not* exceed the specified torque setting, and *NEVER* overtighten spark plugs.

20 Align the coil with the mounting bolt hole, then push it down firmly onto the spark plug. Tighten the retaining bolt to the specified torque.

21 The remainder of refitting is a reversal of removal.

Every 60 000 miles

28 Timing belt renewal

The procedure (applicable only to the 2.4 litre engine) is described in Chapter 2B, Section 3.

Every 2 years

29 Brake fluid renewal

 Warning: Brake hydraulic fluid can harm your eyes and damage painted surfaces, so use extreme caution when handling and pouring it. Do not use fluid that has been standing open for some time, as it absorbs moisture from the air. Excess moisture can cause a dangerous loss of braking effectiveness. Brake fluid is also highly flammable – treat it with the same respect as petrol.

1 The procedure is similar to that for the bleeding of the hydraulic system as described in Chapter 9, Section 2.

2 Reduce the fluid level in the reservoir (by syphoning or using a poultry baster), but do not allow the fluid level to drop far enough to allow air into the system – if air enters the ABS hydraulic unit, the unit may need be bled using special Volvo test equipment (see Chapter 9).

 Warning: Do not syphon the fluid by mouth; it is poisonous.

3 Working as described in Chapter 9, open the first bleed screw in the sequence, and pump the brake pedal gently until nearly all the old fluid has been emptied from the master cylinder reservoir. Top-up to the MAX level with new fluid, and continue pumping until only the new fluid remains in the reservoir, and new fluid can be seen emerging from the bleed screw. Tighten the screw, and top the reservoir level up to the MAX level line. Old hydraulic fluid is invariably much darker in colour than the new, making it easy to distinguish the two.

4 Work through all the remaining bleed screws in the sequence until new fluid can be seen at all of them. Be careful to keep the master cylinder reservoir topped-up to above the MIN level at all times, or air may enter the system and greatly increase the length of the task.

5 When the operation is complete, check that all bleed screws are securely tightened, and that their dust caps are refitted. Wash off all traces of spilt fluid, and recheck the master cylinder reservoir fluid level.

6 Check the operation of the brakes before taking the car on the road.

7 Finally, check the operation of the clutch. Since the clutch shares the same fluid reservoir as the braking system, it may also be necessary to bleed the clutch as described in Chapter 6, Section 5.

30 Coolant renewal

 Warning: Do not allow antifreeze to come in contact with your skin or painted surfaces of the vehicle. Flush contaminated areas immediately with plenty of water. Don't store new coolant, or leave old coolant lying around, where it's accessible to children or pets – they're attracted by its sweet smell. Ingestion of even a small amount of coolant can be fatal. Wipe up garage-floor and drip-pan spills immediately. Keep antifreeze containers covered, and repair cooling system leaks as soon as they're noticed.

 Warning: Never remove the expansion tank filler cap when the engine is running, or has just been switched off, as the cooling system will be hot, and the consequent escaping steam and scalding coolant could cause serious injury.

 Warning: Wait until the engine is cold before starting these procedures.

Strength check

1 Use a hydrometer to check the strength of the antifreeze. Follow the instructions provided with your hydrometer. The antifreeze strength should be approximately 50%. If it is significantly less than this, drain a little coolant from the radiator (see this Section), add antifreeze to the coolant expansion tank, then recheck the strength.

Coolant draining

2 To drain the system, first remove the expansion tank filler cap.

3 If the additional working clearance is required, raise the front of the vehicle and

30.4a The radiator drain plug is located on the left-hand side of the radiator – 1.8 and 2.0 litre models . . .

30.4b . . . and on the right-hand side (arrowed) for 2.4 litre models

support it securely on axle stands (see *Jacking and vehicle support*). Where fitted, undo the 7 fasteners and remove the engine undershield (see illustration 4.4).

4 Place a large drain tray underneath, and unscrew the radiator drain plug (see illustrations); direct as much of the escaping coolant as possible into the tray.

5 Once the coolant has stopped draining from the radiator, close the drain plug.

System flushing

6 With time, the cooling system may gradually lose its efficiency, as the radiator core becomes choked with rust, scale deposits from the water, and other sediment. To minimise this, as well as using only good-quality antifreeze and clean soft water, the system should be flushed as follows whenever any part of it is disturbed, and/or when the coolant is renewed.

7 With the coolant drained, refit the drain plug and refill the system with fresh water. Refit the expansion tank filler cap, start the engine and warm it up to normal operating temperature, then stop it and (after allowing it to cool down completely) drain the system again. Repeat as necessary until only clean water can be seen to emerge, then refill finally with the specified coolant mixture.

8 If only clean, soft water and good-quality antifreeze (even if not to Volvo's specification) has been used, and the coolant has been renewed at the suggested intervals, the above procedure will be sufficient to keep clean the system for a considerable length of time. If, however, the system has been neglected, a more thorough operation will be required, as follows.

9 First drain the coolant, then disconnect the radiator top and bottom hoses. Insert a garden hose into the radiator top hose connection, and allow water to circulate through the radiator until it runs clean from the bottom outlet.

10 To flush the engine, insert the garden hose into the radiator bottom hose, wrap a piece of rag around the garden hose to seal the connection, and allow water to circulate until it runs clear.

11 Try the effect of repeating this procedure

in the top hose, although this may not be effective, since the thermostat will probably close and prevent the flow of water.

12 In severe cases of contamination, reverse-flushing of the radiator may be necessary. This may be achieved by inserting the garden hose into the bottom outlet, wrapping a piece of rag around the hose to seal the connection, then flushing the radiator until clear water emerges from the top hose outlet.

13 If the radiator is suspected of being severely choked, remove the radiator (Chapter 3, Section 5), turn it upside-down, and repeat the procedure described in paragraph 12.

14 Flushing the heater matrix can be achieved using a similar procedure to that described in paragraph 12, once the heater inlet and outlet hoses have been identified. These two hoses will be of the same diameter, and pass through the engine compartment bulkhead (refer to the heater matrix removal procedure in Chapter 3 for more details).

15 The use of chemical cleaners is not recommended, and should be necessary only as a last resort; the scouring action of some chemical cleaners may lead to other cooling system problems. Normally, regular renewal of the coolant will prevent excessive contamination of the system.

Coolant filling

16 With the cooling system drained and flushed, ensure that all disturbed hose unions are correctly secured, and that the radiator/engine drain plug(s) is securely tightened. Refit the engine undershield (where applicable). If it was raised, lower the vehicle to the ground.

17 Prepare a sufficient quantity of the specified coolant mixture (see below); allow for a surplus, so as to have a reserve supply for topping-up.

18 Slowly fill the system through the expansion tank. Since the tank is the highest point in the system, all the air in the system should be displaced into the tank by the rising liquid. Slow pouring reduces the possibility of air being trapped and forming airlocks.

19 Continue filling until the coolant level reaches the expansion tank MAX level line (see *Weekly checks*), then cover the filler opening to prevent coolant splashing out.

20 Start the engine and run it at idle speed, until it has warmed-up to normal operating temperature and the radiator electric cooling fan has cut in; watch the temperature gauge to check for signs of overheating. If the level in the expansion tank drops significantly, top-up to the MAX level line, to minimise the amount of air circulating in the system.

21 Stop the engine, wash off any spilt coolant from the engine compartment and bodywork, then leave the car to cool down *completely* (overnight, if possible).

22 With the system cool, uncover the expansion tank filler opening, and top-up the tank to the MAX level line. Refit the filler cap, tightening it securely, and clean up any further spillage.

23 After refilling, always check carefully all components of the system (but especially any unions disturbed during draining and flushing) for signs of coolant leaks. Fresh antifreeze has a searching action, which will rapidly expose any weak points in the system.

Antifreeze type and mixture

Note: *Do not use engine antifreeze in the windscreen/tailgate washer system, as it will damage the vehicle's paintwork. A screenwash additive should be added to the washer system in its maker's recommended quantities.*

24 If the vehicle's history (and therefore the quality of the antifreeze in it) is unknown, owners are advised to drain and thoroughly reverse-flush the system, before refilling with fresh coolant mixture. If the Volvo antifreeze is used, the coolant can then be left indefinitely, providing the strength of the mixture is checked every year (see this Section).

25 If any antifreeze other than Volvo's is to be used, the coolant must be renewed at regular intervals to provide an equivalent degree of protection; the conventional recommendation is to renew the coolant every two years.

26 If the antifreeze used is to Volvo's specification, the levels of protection it affords are indicated in the coolant packaging. To give the recommended *standard* mixture ratio for antifreeze, 50% (by volume) of antifreeze must be mixed with 50% of clean, soft water; if you are using any other type of antifreeze, follow its manufacturer's instructions to achieve the correct protection.

27 You are unlikely to fully drain the system at any one time (unless the engine is being completely stripped), and the capacities quoted in Specifications are therefore slightly academic for routine coolant renewal. As a guide, only two-thirds of the system's total capacity is likely to be needed for coolant renewal.

28 As the drained system will be partially filled with flushing water, in order to establish the recommended mixture ratio, measure out 50% of the system capacity in antifreeze and pour it into the hose/expansion tank as described above, then top-up with water. Any topping-up while refilling the system should be done with water.

29 Before adding antifreeze, the cooling system should be drained, preferably flushed, and all hoses checked for condition and security. As noted earlier, fresh antifreeze will rapidly find any weaknesses in the system.

30 After filling with antifreeze, a label should be attached to the expansion tank, stating the type and concentration of antifreeze used, and the date installed. Any subsequent topping-up should be made with the same type and concentration of antifreeze.

General cooling system checks

31 The engine should be cold for the cooling system checks, so perform the following procedure before driving the vehicle, or after it has been shut off for at least three hours.

32 Remove the expansion tank filler cap, and clean it thoroughly inside and out with a rag. Also clean the filler neck on the expansion tank. The presence of rust or corrosion in the filler neck indicates that the coolant should be changed. The coolant inside the expansion tank should be relatively clean and transparent. If it is rust-coloured, drain and flush the system, and refill with a fresh coolant mixture.

33 Carefully check the radiator hoses and heater hoses along their entire length; renew any hose which is cracked, swollen or deteriorated (see Section 9).

34 Inspect all other cooling system components (joint faces, etc) for leaks. A leak in the cooling system will usually show up as white- or antifreeze-coloured deposits on the area adjoining the leak **(see illustration)**. Where any problems of this nature are found on system components, renew the component or gasket with reference to Chapter 3.

35 Clean the front of the radiator with a soft brush to remove all insects, leaves, etc, embedded in the radiator fins. Be careful not to damage the radiator fins, or cut your fingers on them. To do a more thorough job, remove the radiator grille as described in Chapter 11.

Airlocks

36 If, after draining and refilling the system, symptoms of overheating are found which did not occur previously, then the fault is almost certainly due to trapped air at some point in the system, causing an airlock and restricting the flow of coolant; usually, the air is trapped because the system was refilled too quickly.

30.34 A leak in the cooling system will usually show up as white- or antifreeze-coloured deposits on the areas adjoining the leak

37 If an airlock is suspected, first try gently squeezing all visible coolant hoses. A coolant hose which is full of air feels quite different to one full of coolant when squeezed. After refilling the system, most airlocks will clear once the system has cooled, and been topped-up.

38 While the engine is running at operating temperature, switch on the heater and heater fan, and check for heat output. Provided there is sufficient coolant in the system, lack of heat output could be due to an airlock in the system.

39 Airlocks can have more serious effects than simply reducing heater output – a severe airlock could reduce coolant flow around the engine. Check that the radiator top hose is hot when the engine is at operating temperature – a top hose which stays cold could be the result of an airlock (or a non-opening thermostat).

40 If the problem persists, stop the engine and allow it to cool down **completely**, before unscrewing the expansion tank filler cap or loosening the hose clips and squeezing the hoses to bleed out the trapped air. In the worst case, the system will have to be at least partially drained (this time, the coolant can be saved for re-use) and flushed to clear the problem. If all else fails, have the system evacuated and vacuum filled by a suitably-equipped garage.

Expansion tank cap check

41 Wait until the engine is completely cold

– perform this check before the engine is started for the first time in the day.

42 Place a wad of cloth over the expansion tank cap, then unscrew it slowly and remove it.

43 Examine the condition of the rubber seal on the underside of the cap. If the rubber appears to have hardened, or cracks are visible in the seal edges, a new cap should be fitted.

44 If the car is several years old, or has covered a large mileage, consider renewing the cap regardless of its apparent condition – they are not expensive. If the pressure relief valve built into the cap fails, excess pressure in the system will lead to puzzling failures of hoses and other cooling system components.

31 Remote control battery renewal
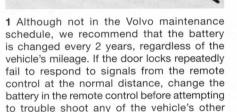

1 Although not in the Volvo maintenance schedule, we recommend that the battery is changed every 2 years, regardless of the vehicle's mileage. If the door locks repeatedly fail to respond to signals from the remote control at the normal distance, change the battery in the remote control before attempting to trouble shoot any of the vehicle's other systems.

2 Pull out the key blade from the remote control **(see illustration)**.

3 Undo the small screw, and remove the control cover **(see illustration)**.

4 Note the fitted position of the battery, then prise the battery from place, and insert the new one **(see illustration)**. Avoid touching the battery or the terminals with bare fingers.

5 Refit the cover and tighten the screw securely.

6 Refit the key blade, and check for correct operation.

Every 100 000 miles or 9 years

32 Auxiliary drivebelt renewal

See Section 7.

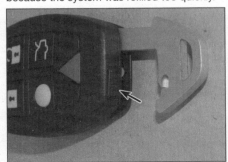

31.2 Slide across the button (arrowed) and pull out the key blade

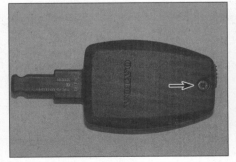

31.3 Turn the controller over and undo the small screw (arrowed)

31.4 Insert the battery with the negative side facing upwards

Chapter 1 Part B:
Routine maintenance and servicing – diesel models

Contents

Degrees of difficulty

Easy, suitable for novice with little experience | **Fairly easy,** suitable for beginner with some experience | **Fairly difficult,** suitable for competent DIY mechanic | **Difficult,** suitable for experienced DIY mechanic | **Very difficult,** suitable for expert DIY or professional

Lubricants and fluids.. See *Lubricants, fluids and tyre pressures* on page 0•16

Capacities

Engine oil

1.6 litre (80kW):

    2005-2009 models .... 3.7 litres

    2010 onwards... 3.9 litres

1.6 litre (85kW) .... 3.9 litres

2.0 litre 4-cylinder... 4.8 litres

2.0 litre 5-cylinder... 5.9 litres

2.4 litre .... 5.5 litres

Cooling system (approx.)

1.6 litre engines .... 5.8 litres

1.6 litre engines (D2 and DRIVe)................................ 6.2 litres

2.0 litre engines (D3 and D4) .... 8.5 litres

2.4 litre engines .... 11.0 litres

Fuel tank

Approximate and depending on model .... 52 - 60 litres

Cooling system

Specified antifreeze mixture................................... 50% antifreeze/50% water

Note: *Refer to Chapter* **3** *for further details.*

Brakes

Brake pad minimum lining thickness 2.0mm

Remote control battery

Type .... CR 2032 3V

Tyres

Tyre pressures .... See sticker on the driver's door aperture pillar

Torque wrench settings	Nm	lbf ft
Automatic transmission fluid filler/drain plug (AW55-51)	35	26
Automatic transmission filler plug (TF-80SC)	35	26
Automatic transmission drain plug (TF-80SC)	8	6
Engine oil drain plug:		
1.6 litre engines	34	25
All other engines..	38	28
Oil filter cover	25	18
Roadwheel nuts:		
Stage 1 (All nuts)..	20	15
Stage 2:		
Standard, locking and nuts with fixed conical seating	110	81
Nuts with rotating conical seating	130	96

1 Maintenance schedule

The maintenance intervals in this manual are provided with the assumption that you, not the dealer, will be carrying out the work. These are the minimum maintenance intervals recommended by us for vehicles driven daily. If you wish to keep your vehicle in peak condition at all times, you may wish to perform some of these procedures more often. We encourage frequent maintenance, because it enhances the efficiency, performance and resale value of your vehicle.

If the vehicle is driven in dusty areas, used to tow a trailer, or driven frequently at slow speeds (idling in traffic) or on short journeys, more frequent maintenance intervals are recommended.

When the vehicle is new, it should be serviced by a dealer service department (or other workshop recognised by the vehicle manufacturer as providing the same standard of service) in order to preserve the warranty. The vehicle manufacturer may reject warranty claims if you are unable to prove that servicing has been carried out as and when specified, using only original equipment parts or parts certified to be of equivalent quality.

Every 250 miles or weekly
☐ Refer to *Weekly checks*

Every 6000 miles or 6 months, whichever comes first
☐ Renew the engine oil and filter (Section 4)
Note: *Volvo recommend that the engine oil and filter are changed every 12 500 miles or 12 months. However, oil and filter changes are good for the engine and we recommend that the oil and filter are renewed more frequently, especially if the vehicle is used on a lot of short journeys.*
☐ Check the power steering fluid level (Section 5)

Every 12 500 miles or 12 months, whichever comes first
In addition to the items listed above, carry out the following:
☐ Check the condition of the auxiliary drivebelt (Section 6)
☐ Check the operation of the lights and the horn (Section 7)
☐ Check under the bonnet for fluid leaks and hose condition (Section 8)
☐ Check the condition of the engine compartment wiring (Section 9)
☐ Check the condition of the seat belts (Section 10)
☐ Check the condition of the brake pads and discs (Section 11)
☐ Check the exhaust system (Section 12)
☐ Check the steering and suspension components for condition and security (Section 13)
☐ Check the condition of the driveshaft joints and gaiters (Section14)
☐ Check the underbody and all fuel/brake lines (Section 15)
☐ Lubricate all hinges and locks (Section 16)
☐ Roadwheel check (Section 17)

Every 12 500 miles or 12 months, whichever comes first (continued)
☐ Carry out a road test (Section 18)
☐ Renew the pollen filter (Section 19)
Note: *If the vehicle is used in dusty conditions, the pollen filter should be renewed more frequently.*
☐ Drain the water from the fuel filter (Section 20)
☐ Check and, if necessary, adjust the handbrake (Section 21)
☐ Check the antifreeze/inhibitor strength (Section 22)
☐ Reset the service reminder indicator (Section 23)

Every 37 000 miles
In addition to the items listed above, carry out the following:
☐ Renew the fuel filter (Section 20)
Note: *In countries where the fuel is contaminated, renew every 12 500 miles or 12 months*
☐ Renew the air filter (Section 24)
Note: *If the vehicle is used in dusty conditions, the air filter should be renewed more frequently.*
☐ Top-up the additive tank for the particulate filter (Section 25)
☐ Check and renew the automatic transmission fluid (Section 26)
Note: *Dependent on vehicle usage*

Every 62 000 miles
In addition to the items listed above, carry out the following:
☐ Renew the timing belt and tensioner (Section 27)
Note: *The Volvo interval for belt renewal is actually at a much higher mileage than this (125 000 miles or 10 years). It is strongly recommended, however, that the interval is reduced to 62 500 miles, particularly on vehicles which are subjected to intensive use, ie, mainly short journeys or a lot of stop-start driving. The actual belt renewal interval is therefore very much up to the individual owner, but bear in mind that severe engine damage will result if the belt breaks.*

Every 2 years, regardless of mileage
☐ Renew the brake fluid (Section 28)
☐ Renew the coolant (Section 29)
Note: *This work is not included in the Volvo schedule, and should not be required if the recommended Volvo antifreeze/inhibitor is used.*
☐ Renew remote control battery (Section 30)

Every 75 000 miles or 6 years, whichever comes first
☐ Renew the exhaust particulate filter (Section 31)

Every 100 000 miles or 9 years, whichever comes first
☐ Renew the auxiliary drivebelt (Section 32)

2 Maintenance – component location

Underbonnet view of a 1.6 litre model

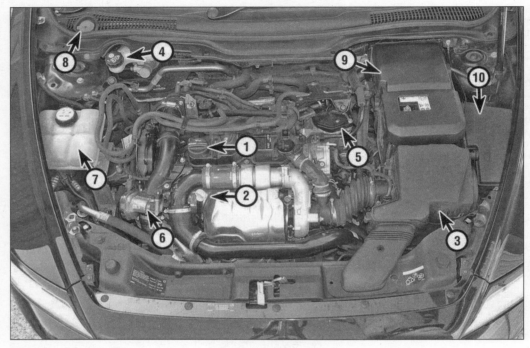

1 Engine oil filler cap
2 Engine oil level dipstick
3 Air filter
4 Brake and clutch fluid reservoir
5 Fuel filter
6 Throttle body
7 Coolant expansion tank
8 Washer fluid reservoir
9 Battery
10 Engine compartment fuse and relay box

Front underbody view of a 1.6 litre model

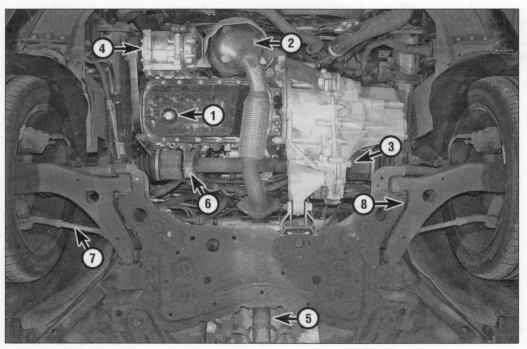

1 Engine oil (sump) drain plug
2 Catalytic convertor/diesel particulate filter
3 Manual transmission drain plug
4 Air-conditioning compressor
5 Exhaust pipe
6 Driveshaft intermediate bearing
7 Steering track rod
8 Suspension control arm

Rear underbody view

1 Fuel tank
2 Anti-roll bar
3 Shock absorber
4 Fuel filler and breather pipes
5 Handbrake cable
6 Hub carrier/lateral link
7 Lower control arm
8 Tie rod

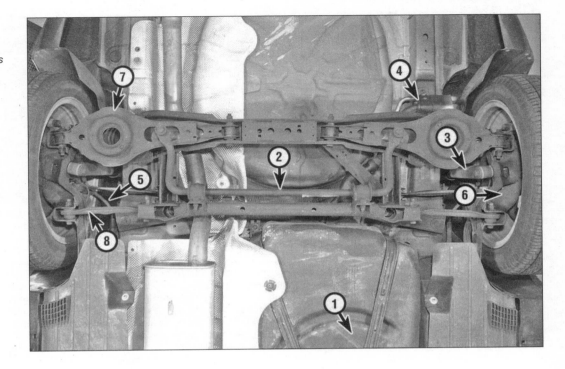

3 General information and regular maintenance

General information

1 This Chapter is designed to help the home mechanic maintain his/her vehicle for safety, economy, long life and peak performance.

2 The Chapter contains a master maintenance schedule, followed by Sections dealing specifically with each task in the schedule. Visual checks, adjustments, component renewal and other helpful items are included. Refer to the accompanying illustrations of the engine compartment and the underside of the vehicle for the locations of the various components.

3 Servicing your vehicle in accordance with the mileage/time maintenance schedule and the following Sections will provide a planned maintenance programme, which should result in a long and reliable service life. This is a comprehensive plan, so maintaining some items but not others at the specified service intervals will not produce the same results.

4 As you service your vehicle, you will discover that many of the procedures can – and should – be grouped together, because of the particular procedure being performed, or because of the proximity of two otherwise-unrelated components to one another. For example, if the vehicle is raised for any reason, the exhaust can be inspected at the same time as the suspension and steering components.

5 The first step in this maintenance programme is to prepare yourself before the actual work begins. Read through all the Sections relevant to the work to be carried out, then make a list and gather all the parts and tools required. If a problem is encountered, seek advice from a parts specialist, or a dealer service department.

Regular maintenance

6 If, from the time the vehicle is new, the routine maintenance schedule is followed closely, and frequent checks are made of fluid levels and high-wear items, as suggested throughout this manual, the engine will be kept in relatively good running condition, and the need for additional work will be minimised.

7 It is possible that there will be times when the engine is running poorly due to the lack of regular maintenance. This is even more likely if a used vehicle, which has not received regular and frequent maintenance checks, is purchased. In such cases, additional work may need to be carried out, outside of the regular maintenance intervals.

8 If engine wear is suspected, a compression test or leakdown test (refer to Section 2 of Chapter 2C, 2D, or 2E) will provide valuable information regarding the overall performance of the main internal components. Such a test can be used as a basis to decide on the extent of the work to be carried out. If, for example, a compression or leakdown test indicates serious internal engine wear, conventional maintenance as described in this Chapter will not greatly improve the performance of the engine, and may prove a waste of time and money, unless extensive overhaul work is carried out first.

9 The following series of operations are those most often required to improve the performance of a generally poor-running engine:

Primary operations

a) Clean, inspect and test the battery (refer to 'Weekly checks').
b) Check all the engine-related fluids (refer to 'Weekly checks').
c) Check the condition and tension of the auxiliary drivebelt (Section 6).
d) Check the condition of the air filter, and renew if necessary (Section 24).
e) Renew the fuel filter (Section 20).
f) Check the condition of all hoses, and check for fluid leaks (Section 8).

10 If the above operations do not prove fully effective, carry out the following secondary operations:

Secondary operations

All items listed under *Primary operations*, plus the following:

a) Check the charging system (refer to Chapter 5A).
b) Check the preheating system (refer to Chapter 5C).
c) Check the fuel system (refer to Chapter 4B).

4.2 Undo the Torx screws (arrowed) and remove the engine undershield

4.3a Undo the engine oil drain plug (arrowed) – 2.0 litre 4-cylinder model shown

Every 6000 miles or 6 months

4 Engine oil and filter renewal

1 Make sure that you have all the necessary tools before you begin this procedure. You should also have plenty of rags or newspapers handy, for mopping-up any spills. The oil should preferably be changed when the engine is still fully warmed-up to normal operating temperature, just after a run warm oil and sludge will flow out more easily. Take care, however, not to touch the exhaust or any other hot parts of the engine when working under the vehicle. To avoid any possibility of scalding, and to protect yourself from possible skin irritants and other harmful contaminants in used engine oils, it is advisable to wear gloves when carrying out this work.
2 Access to the underside of the vehicle is greatly improved if the vehicle can be lifted on a hoist, driven onto ramps, or supported by axle stands (see *Jacking and vehicle support*). Whichever method is chosen, make sure that the vehicle remains level, or if it is at an angle, that the drain point is at the lowest point. Release the screws and remove the engine

undershield (see illustration) for access to the sump and drain plug.
3 Position the draining container under the drain plug, and unscrew the plug (see illustrations). If possible, try to keep the plug pressed into the sump while unscrewing it by hand the last couple of turns.
4 Allow the oil to drain into the container, and discard the drain plug sealing washer. A new one must be fitted.
5 Allow some time for the old oil to drain, noting that it may be necessary to reposition the container as the oil flow slows to a trickle; when the oil has completely drained, wipe clean the drain plug and its threads in the sump and refit the plug with a new sealing washer, tightening it to the specified torque (see illustration).
6 Remove the old oil and all tools from under the vehicle, then lower the vehicle to the ground.
7 Renew the oil filter as described below.
8 Remove the dipstick and the oil filler cap from the engine.
9 On models fitted with the 1.6 litre engine, fill the engine with oil, using the correct grade and type of oil (see *Lubricants and fluids* and Specifications). Pour in half the specified quantity of oil first, then wait a few minutes for the oil to run to the sump. Continue adding

oil a small quantity at a time, until the level is up to the lower mark on the dipstick. Adding approximately 1.0 litre will raise the level to the upper mark on the dipstick.
10 Start the engine. The oil pressure warning light will take a few seconds to go out while the new filter fills with oil; do not race the engine while the light is on. Run the engine for a few minutes, while checking for leaks around the oil filter seal and the drain plug. Refit the engine undershield.
11 Switch off the engine, and wait a few minutes for the oil to settle in the sump once more. With the new oil circulated and the filter now completely full, recheck the level on the dipstick, and add more oil as necessary.
12 On models fitted with the 2.0 litre (4-cylinder) or 5-cylinder engines, fresh engine oil should only be added until the level is two thirds of the way between the minimum and maximum marks on the dipstick.
13 Dispose of the used engine oil safely and in accordance with environmental regulations (see *General repair procedures*).

Oil filter renewal

14 Remove the plastic cover on top of the engine by pulling it straight up from its mountings (see illustration).

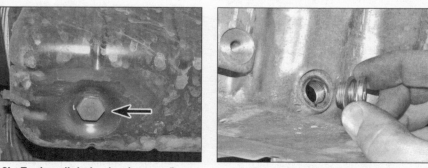

4.3b Engine oil drain plug (arrowed) on 1.6 litre (85kW) engine

4.5 Fit a new sealing washer to the oil drain plug

4.14 Pull up the front and right-hand rear corner, then pull the cover upwards

4.15 Oil filter cap (arrowed) on 1.6 litre engines

4.16 Undo the oil filter cap (arrowed) . . .

4.17a . . . then lift up the cap with the filter element . . .

4.17b . . . pull the element from the cap . . .

4.17c . . . and discard the O-ring seal

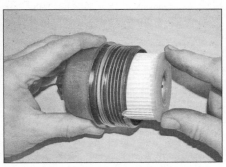

4.19 Insert the new filter element into the cap

15 On 1.6 litre engines the oil filter is located on the front, left-hand end of the engine, accessible from above **(see illustration)**. On models fitted with the 80kW engine, remove the air cleaner housing as described in Chapter 4B, Section 3. Undo the bolts for the air inlet pipe support brackets. One is located behind the oil filter housing, the other below the filter on the left hand side. Move the pipe to one side. On models fitted with the 85kW engine, slacken the clamps and remove the air inlet pipe between the mass air flow meter and the turbocharger.

16 On all other engines the oil filter is located at the front of the engine, accessible from above **(see illustration)**. If other components need to be removed to improve access to the filter, refer to the relevant Chapter of this manual.

17 Using a socket on an extension bar, undo the oil filter housing cap. Lift the cap up, with the filter element inside it. Discard the filter and the O-ring seal around the circumference of the cap **(see illustrations)**.

18 Using a clean, lint-free rag, wipe clean the inside of the filter housing and cover.

19 Apply a light coating of clean engine oil to the new O-ring seal and fit it to the filter cover. Insert the filter element into the cover **(see illustration)**, then screw the filter cover into position on the engine until it seats, then tighten it to the specified torque.

5 Power steering fluid level check

Caution: The need for frequent topping-up indicates a leak, which should be investigated immediately.

1 Park the vehicle on level ground, set the steering wheel straight-ahead. The engine should be turned off and cold.

2 The reservoir is mounted at the right-hand side of the engine compartment, behind the headlight. Remove the headlight as described in Chapter 12. The fluid level can be viewed through the reservoir body, and should be

5.3 Power steering reservoir cap

between the MIN and MAX marks when the engine is cold. If the level is checked when the engine is running or hot, the level may rise slightly above the MAX mark.

3 If topping-up is necessary, use the specified type of fluid – do not overfill the reservoir. Undo the reservoir cap **(see illustration)**. Take care not to introduce dirt into the system when topping-up. When the level is correct, securely refit the cap.

Every 12 500 miles or 12 months

6 Auxiliary drivebelt check

Drivebelt check

1 On 1.6 litre and 2.0 litre (4-cylinder) engines, a single auxiliary drivebelt is fitted at the right-hand side of the engine. On 5-cylinder engines, two belts are fitted - one from the crankshaft pulley to the air-conditioning compressor and one from the air-conditioning compressor to components such as the alternator **(see illustration)**. An automatic adjuster is

fitted, so checking the drivebelt tension is unnecessary.

2 Due to their function and material make-up, drivebelts are prone to failure after a long period of time, and should therefore be inspected regularly.

3 Since the drivebelt is located very close to the right-hand side of the engine

6.1 Inner auxiliary drivebelt on 5-cylinder engines (arrowed) between the air-conditioning compressor and the alternator

6.7 Use a 15mm open-ended spanner to rotate the tensioner clockwise

compartment, it is possible to gain better access by raising the front of the vehicle, undoing the 7 Torx screws and removing the engine undershield (see illustration 4.2).

4 With the engine stopped, inspect the full length of the drivebelt for cracks and separation of the belt plies. It will be necessary to turn the engine (using a spanner or socket and bar on the crankshaft pulley bolt) in order to move the belt from the pulleys so that the belt can be inspected thoroughly. Twist the belt between the pulleys so that both sides can be viewed. Also check for fraying, and glazing which gives the belt a shiny appearance. Check the pulleys for nicks, cracks, distortion and corrosion.

5 Note that it is not unusual for a ribbed belt to exhibit small cracks in the edges of the belt ribs, and unless these are extensive or very deep, belt renewal is not essential.

Drivebelt renewal

1.6 litre engines

6 Raise the front of the vehicle and support on axle stands (see *Jacking and vehicle support*). Undo the 7 fasteners and remove the engine undershield, followed by the wheelarch liner (see illustration 4.2)

7 Use a 15mm spanner to rotate the tensioner, while an assistant lifts the belt from the pulleys (see illustration).

8 Fit the tool or spanner to the tensioner arm and rotate the tensioner clockwise until the tensioner arm passes the hole in the housing, and a 5.0mm drill bit can be inserted, locking the tensioner in position (see illustration).

9 Note how the belt is routed, then remove the belt from the pulleys (see illustration).

10 Fit the new drivebelt onto the crankshaft, air conditioning compressor, alternator and tensioner/idler pulleys. Hold the tensioner stationary with the spanner and remove the locking drill bit. Slowly allow the tensioner arm

6.8 Insert a 5mm drill bit/rod into the hole (arrowed) in the tensioner housing

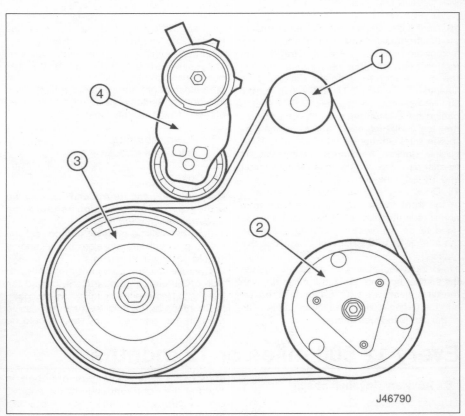

6.9. Auxiliary belt routing –
1.6 litre (80kw) engine

1 Alternator pulley
2 Air-conditioning compressor pulley
3 Crankshaft pulley
4 Tensioner

6.12 Rotate the tensioner pulley bolt anti-clockwise, then insert a 5mm drill or rod through the locking holes once they align (arrowed)

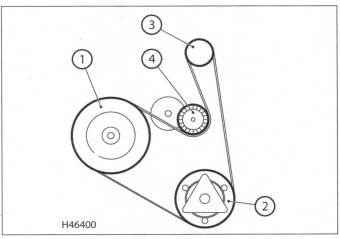

6.13 Auxiliary drivebelt routing – 2.0 litre 4 cylinder engine

1 Crankshaft pulley
2 Air-conditioning compressor pulley
3 Alternator pulley
4 Tensioner

to rotate and tension the belt. Remove the spanner.

2.0 litre 4-cylinder engine

11 Raise the front of the vehicle and support on axle stands (see *Jacking and vehicle support*). Undo the 7 fasteners and remove the engine undershield, followed by the wheelarch liner **(see illustration 4.2)**.

12 Using a spanner on the tensioner centre bolt, turn the tensioner clockwise to release the drivebelt tension, then insert a 5mm drill bit or rod through the holes in the arm/body when they align to lock the tensioner in this position **(see illustration)**.

13 Note how the drivebelt is routed, then remove the belt from the pulleys **(see illustration)**.

14 Fit the new drivebelt onto the crankshaft, air conditioning compressor, alternator, and tensioner pulleys. Use a spanner to hold the tensioner centre bolt, then remove the locking drill bit/rod, and allow the tensioner to rotate anti-clockwise and gently tension the belt.

5-cylinder engines

15 Slacken the right-hand front roadwheel nuts, raise the front of the vehicle and support on axle stands (see *Jacking and vehicle support*). Undo the 7 fasteners and remove the engine undershield **(see illustration 4.2)**. Remove the roadwheel.

16 Undo the Torx screws and the plastic nuts, then remove the wheel arch liner.

17 To remove the outer belt between the crankshaft pulley and the air-conditioning compressor, insert a Torx bit into the tensioner arm, then rotate the tensioner clockwise as far as possible, and remove the belt.

18 To remove the inner belt between the air-conditioning compressor and the alternator, insert a Torx bit into the tensioner arm, then rotate the tensioner anti-clockwise as far as it will go **(see illustration)**. Remove the belt.

19 Ensure the pulley grooves are clean, rotate the tensioner, and fit the new belt to the pulleys. Check the belt is correctly located in the pulley grooves, then allow the tensioner arm to rotate and tension the belt.

20 Refit the undershield, the wheel arch liner and the roadwheel, then lower the vehicle to the ground.

7 Lights and horn operation check

1 With the ignition switched on where necessary, check the operation of all exterior lights.

2 Check the brake lights with the help of an assistant, or by reversing up close to a reflective door. Make sure that all the rear lights are capable of operating independently, without affecting any of the other lights – for example, switch on as many rear lights as possible, then try the brake lights. If any unusual results are found, this is usually due to an earth fault or other poor connection at that rear light unit.

3 Again with the help of an assistant or using a reflective surface, check as far as possible

6.18 Insert a Torx bit into the inner belt tensioner

that the headlights work on both main and dipped beam.

4 Renew any defective bulbs with reference to Chapter 12.

5 Check the operation of all interior lights, including the glovebox and luggage area illumination lights. Switch on the ignition, and check that all relevant warning lights come on as expected – the vehicle handbook should give details of these. Now start the engine, and check that the appropriate lights go out. When you are next driving at night, check that all the instrument panel and facia lighting works correctly. If any problems are found, refer to Chapter 12.

6 Finally, choose an appropriate time of day to test the operation of the horn.

8 Underbonnet check for fluid leaks and hose condition

 Warning: Renewal of air conditioning hoses must be left to a dealer service department or air conditioning specialist who has the equipment to depressurise the system safely. Never remove air conditioning components or hoses until the system has been depressurised.

1 Visually inspect the engine joint faces, gaskets and seals for any signs of water or oil leaks. Pay particular attention to the areas around the cylinder head cover, cylinder head, oil filter and sump joint faces. Bear in mind that, over a period of time, some very slight seepage from these areas is to be expected – what you are really looking for is any indication of a serious leak. Should a leak be found, renew the offending gasket or oil seal by referring to the appropriate Chapters in this manual.

2 High temperatures in the engine

compartment can cause the deterioration of the rubber and plastic hoses used for engine, accessory and emission systems operation. Periodic inspection should be made for cracks, loose clamps, material hardening and leaks.

3 When checking the hoses, ensure that all the cable-ties or clips used to retain the hoses are in place, and in good condition. Clips which are broken or missing can lead to chafing of the hoses, pipes or wiring, which could cause more serious problems in the future.

4 Carefully check the large top and bottom radiator hoses, along with the other smaller-diameter cooling system hoses and metal pipes; do not forget the heater hoses/pipes which run from the engine to the bulkhead. Inspect each hose along its entire length, renewing any that is cracked, swollen or shows signs of deterioration. Cracks may become more apparent if the hose is squeezed, and may often be apparent at the hose ends.

5 Make sure that all hose connections are tight. If the large-diameter air hoses from the air cleaner are loose, they will leak air, and upset the engine idle quality. If the spring clamps that are used to secure many of the hoses appear to be slackening, they should be updated with worm-drive clips to prevent the possibility of leaks.

6 Some other hoses are secured to their fittings with clamps. Where clamps are used, check to be sure they haven't lost their tension, allowing the hose to leak. If clamps aren't used, make sure the hose has not expanded and/or hardened where it slips over the fitting, allowing it to leak.

7 Check all fluid reservoirs, filler caps, drain plugs and fittings, etc, looking for any signs of leakage of oil, transmission and/or brake hydraulic fluid, coolant and power steering fluid. Also check the clutch hydraulic fluid lines which lead from the fluid reservoir and slave cylinder (on the transmission).

8 If the vehicle is regularly parked in the same place, close inspection of the ground underneath it will soon show any leaks; ignore the puddle of water which will be left if the air conditioning system is in use. Place a clean piece of cardboard below the engine, and examine it for signs of contamination after the vehicle has been parked over it overnight.

9 Remember that some leaks will only occur with the engine running, or when the engine is hot or cold. With the handbrake firmly applied, start the engine from cold, and let the engine idle while you examine the underside of the engine compartment for signs of leakage.

10 If an unusual smell is noticed inside or around the car, especially when the engine is thoroughly hot, this may point to the presence of a leak.

11 As soon as a leak is detected, its source must be traced and rectified. Where oil has been leaking for some time, it is usually necessary to use a steam cleaner, pressure washer or similar, to clean away the accumulated dirt, so that the exact source of the leak can be identified.

Vacuum hoses

12 It's quite common for vacuum hoses, especially those in the emissions system, to be colour-coded, or to be identified by coloured stripes moulded into them. Various systems require hoses with different wall thicknesses, collapse resistance and temperature resistance. When renewing hoses, be sure the new ones are made of the same material.

13 Often the only effective way to check a hose is to remove it completely from the vehicle. If more than one hose is removed, be sure to label the hoses and fittings to ensure correct installation.

14 When checking vacuum hoses, be sure to include any plastic T-fittings in the check. Inspect the fittings for cracks, and check the hose where it fits over the fitting for distortion, which could cause leakage.

15 A small piece of vacuum hose (quarter-inch inside diameter) can be used as a stethoscope to detect vacuum leaks. Hold one end of the hose near your ear, and probe around vacuum hoses and fittings, listening for the 'hissing' sound characteristic of a vacuum leak.

⚠ *Warning: When probing with the vacuum hose stethoscope, be very careful not to come into contact with moving engine components such as the auxiliary drivebelt, radiator electric cooling fan, etc.*

Fuel hoses

⚠ *Warning: There are certain precautions which must be taken when inspecting or servicing fuel system components. Work in a well-ventilated area, and do not allow open flames (cigarettes, appliance pilot lights, etc) or bare light bulbs near the work area. Mop-up any spills immediately, and do not store fuel-soaked rags where they could ignite.*

16 Check all fuel hoses for deterioration and chafing. Check especially for cracks in areas where the hose bends, and also just before fittings, such as where a hose attaches to the fuel filter.

17 It is not unusual for a high-mileage diesel engine to exhibit a 'film' of diesel fuel around the injectors, resulting in an oily appearance. Unless there is clear evidence of a significant fuel leak, this is not normally a matter for concern. The best course of action would be to first clean the engine thoroughly; then, after several more miles have been covered, the source of the leak can be identified and its severity assessed.

18 High-quality fuel line, usually identified by the word 'Fluoroelastomer' printed on the hose, should be used for fuel line renewal. Never, under any circumstances, use non-reinforced vacuum line, clear plastic tubing or water hose as a substitute for fuel lines.

19 Spring-type clamps are commonly used on fuel lines. These clamps often lose their tension over a period of time, and can be 'sprung' during removal. Update all spring-type clamps with proper fuel pipe clips whenever a hose is renewed.

Metal lines

20 Sections of metal piping are often used for fuel line between the fuel filter and the engine. Check carefully to be sure the piping has not been bent or crimped, and that cracks have not started in the line.

21 If a section of metal fuel line must be renewed, only seamless steel piping should be used, since copper and aluminium piping don't have the strength necessary to withstand normal engine vibration.

22 Check the metal lines where they enter the brake master cylinder, ABS hydraulic unit or clutch master/slave cylinders (as applicable) for cracks in the lines or loose fittings. Any sign of brake fluid leakage calls for an immediate and thorough inspection.

9 Engine compartment wiring check

1 With the vehicle parked on level ground, apply the handbrake firmly and open the bonnet. Using an inspection light or a small electric torch, check all visible wiring within and beneath the engine compartment. Make sure that the ignition is switched off – take out the key.

2 What you are looking for is wiring that is obviously damaged by chafing against sharp edges, or against moving suspension/transmission components and/or the auxiliary drivebelt, by being trapped or crushed between carelessly-refitted components, or melted by being forced into contact with the hot engine castings, coolant pipes, etc. In almost all cases, damage of this sort is caused in the first instance by incorrect routing on reassembly after previous work has been carried out.

3 Depending on the extent of the problem, damaged wiring may be repaired by rejoining the break or splicing-in a new length of wire, using solder to ensure a good connection, and remaking the insulation with adhesive insulating tape or heat-shrink tubing, as appropriate. If the damage is extensive, given the implications for the vehicle's future reliability, the best long-term answer may well be to renew that entire section of the loom, however expensive this may appear.

4 When the actual damage has been repaired, ensure that the wiring loom is re-routed correctly, so that it is clear of other components, and not stretched or kinked, and is secured out of harm's way using the plastic clips, guides and ties provided.

5 Check all electrical connectors, ensuring that they are clean, securely fastened, and that each is locked by its plastic tabs or wire clip, as appropriate. If any connector shows external signs of corrosion (accumulations of white or green deposits, or streaks of 'rust'), or if any is thought to be dirty, it must be unplugged and cleaned using electrical contact cleaner. If the connector pins are

severely corroded, the connector must be renewed; note that this may mean the renewal of that entire section of the loom – see your local Volvo dealer for details.

6 If the cleaner completely removes the corrosion to leave the connector in a satisfactory condition, it would be wise to pack the connector with a suitable material which will exclude dirt and moisture, preventing the corrosion from occurring again; a Volvo dealer may be able to recommend a suitable product.

7 Check the condition of the battery connections – remake the connections or renew the leads if a fault is found (see Chapter 5A). Use the same techniques to ensure that all earth points in the engine compartment provide good electrical contact through clean, metal-to-metal joints, and that all are securely fastened.

8 Check the wiring to the glow plugs.

10 Seat belt check

1 Check the seat belts for satisfactory operation and condition. Inspect the webbing for fraying and cuts. Check that they retract smoothly and without binding into their reels.
2 Check the seat belt mountings, ensuring that all the bolts are securely tightened.

11 Brake pads and discs check

1 The work described in this Section should be carried out at the specified intervals, or whenever a defect is suspected in the braking system. Any of the following symptoms could indicate a potential brake system defect:
 a) *The vehicle pulls to one side when the brake pedal is depressed.*
 b) *The brakes make squealing, scraping or dragging noises when applied.*
 c) *Brake pedal travel is excessive, or pedal feel is poor.*
 d) *The brake fluid requires repeated topping-up. Note that, because the hydraulic clutch shares the same fluid as the braking system (see Chapter 6), this problem could be due to a leak in the clutch system.*

Front disc brakes

2 Apply the handbrake, then loosen the front wheel nuts. Jack up the front of the vehicle, and support it on axle stands (see *Jacking and vehicle support*).
3 For better access to the brake calipers, remove the wheels.
4 Look through the inspection window in the caliper, and check that the thickness of the friction lining material on each of the pads is not less than the recommended minimum thickness given in the Specifications **(see illustration)**.
5 If it is difficult to determine the exact

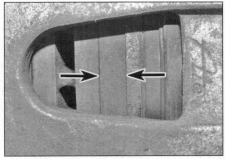
11.4 Check the brake pad friction material thickness (arrowed)

thickness of the pad linings, or if you are at all concerned about the condition of the pads, then remove them from the calipers for further inspection (refer to Chapter 9).
6 Check the other caliper in the same way.
7 If any one of the brake pads has worn down to, or below, the specified limit, *all four* pads at that end of the car must be renewed as a set. If the pads on one side are significantly more worn than the other, this may indicate that the caliper pistons have partially seized – refer to the brake pad renewal procedure in Chapter 9, and push the pistons back into the caliper to free them.
8 Measure the thickness of the discs with a micrometer, if available, to make sure that they still have service life remaining. Do not be fooled by the lip of rust which often forms on the outer edge of the disc, which may make the disc appear thicker than it really is – scrape off the loose rust if necessary, without scoring the disc friction (shiny) surface.
9 If any disc is thinner than the specified minimum thickness, renew both (refer to Chapter 9).
10 Check the general condition of the discs. Look for excessive scoring and discolouration caused by overheating. If these conditions exist, remove the relevant disc and replace both front discs (refer to Chapter 9). Never replace a single disc. They must be replaced in pairs.
11 Make sure that the handbrake is firmly applied, then check that the transmission is in neutral. Spin the wheel, and check that the brake is not binding. Some drag is normal with a disc brake, but it should not require any great effort to turn the wheel – also, do not confuse brake drag with resistance from the transmission.

12.5a Check the condition of the exhaust system rubber mountings (arrowed)

12 Before refitting the wheels, check all brake lines and hoses (refer to Chapter 9). In particular, check the flexible hoses in the vicinity of the calipers, where they are subjected to most movement. Bend them between the fingers (but do not actually bend them double, or the casing may be damaged) and check that this does not reveal previously-hidden cracks, cuts or splits.
13 On completion, refit the wheels and lower the car to the ground. Tighten the wheel nuts to the specified torque.

Rear disc brakes

14 Loosen the rear wheel nuts, then chock the front wheels. Jack up the rear of the car, and support it on axle stands. Release the handbrake and remove the rear wheels.
15 The procedure for checking the rear brakes is much the same as described in paragraphs 2 to 13 above. Check that the rear brakes are not binding, noting that transmission resistance is not a factor on the rear wheels. Abnormal effort may indicate that the handbrake needs adjusting – see Section 21.

12 Exhaust system check

1 With the engine cold (at least three hours after the vehicle has been driven), check the complete exhaust system from its starting point at the engine to the end of the tailpipe. Ideally, this should be done on a hoist, where unrestricted access is available; if a hoist is not available, raise and support the vehicle on axle stands (see *Jacking and vehicle support*).
2 Make sure that all brackets and rubber mountings are in good condition, and tight; if any of the mountings are to be renewed, ensure that the new ones are of the correct type – in the case of the rubber mountings, their colour is a good guide. Those nearest to the catalytic converter are more heat-resistant than the others.
3 Check the pipes and connections for evidence of leaks, severe corrosion, or damage. Leakage at any of the joints or in other parts of the system will usually show up as a black sooty stain in the vicinity of the leak. **Note:** *Exhaust sealants should not be used on any part of the exhaust system upstream of the catalytic converter (between the engine and the converter) – even if the sealant does not contain additives harmful to the converter, pieces of it may break off and foul the element, causing local overheating.*
4 At the same time, inspect the underside of the body for holes, corrosion, open seams, etc, which may allow exhaust gases to enter the passenger compartment. Seal all body openings with silicone or body putty.
5 Rattles and other noises can often be traced to the exhaust system, especially the rubber mountings **(see illustrations)**. Try to

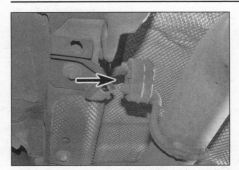

12.5b Tailpipe rubber mounting (arrowed)

move the system, silencer(s) and catalytic converter. If any components can touch the body or suspension parts, secure the exhaust system with new mountings.

13 Steering and suspension check

Front suspension and steering

1 Apply the handbrake, then raise the front of the vehicle and support it on axle stands (see *Jacking and vehicle support*).
2 Visually inspect the balljoint dust covers and the steering gear gaiters for splits, chafing or deterioration **(see illustration)**. Any wear of these components will cause loss of lubricant, together with dirt and water entry, resulting in rapid deterioration of the balljoints or steering gear.
3 Check the power-assisted steering fluid hoses for chafing or deterioration, and the pipe and hose unions for fluid leaks. Also check for signs of fluid leakage under pressure from the steering gear rubber gaiters, which would indicate failed fluid seals within the steering gear.
4 Grasp the roadwheel at the 12 o'clock and 6 o'clock positions, and try to rock it **(see illustration)**. Very slight free play may be felt, but if the movement is appreciable, further investigation is necessary to determine the source. Continue rocking the wheel while an assistant depresses the footbrake. If the movement is now eliminated or significantly

reduced, it is likely that the hub bearings are at fault. If the free play is still evident with the footbrake depressed, then there is wear in the suspension joints or mountings.
5 Now grasp the wheel at the 9 o'clock and 3 o'clock positions, and try to rock it as before. Any movement felt now may again be caused by wear in the hub bearings or the steering track rod balljoints. If the outer track rod balljoint is worn, the visual movement will be obvious. If the inner joint is suspect, it can be felt by placing a hand over the rack-and-pinion rubber gaiter, and gripping the track rod. If the wheel is now rocked, movement will be felt at the inner joint if wear has taken place.
6 Using a large screwdriver or flat bar, check for wear in the suspension mounting and subframe bushes by levering between the relevant suspension component and its attachment point. Some movement is to be expected as the mountings are made of rubber, but excessive wear should be obvious. Also check the condition of any visible rubber bushes, looking for splits, cracks or contamination of the rubber.
7 With the vehicle standing on its wheels, have an assistant turn the steering wheel back-and-forth, about an eighth of a turn each way. There should be very little, if any, lost movement between the steering wheel and roadwheels. If this is not the case, closely observe the joints and mountings previously described, but in addition, check the steering column joints for wear, and also check the rack-and-pinion steering gear itself.

Rear suspension check

8 Chock the front wheels, then raise the rear of the vehicle and support it on axle stands (see *Jacking and vehicle support*).
9 Check the rear hub bearings for wear, using the method described for the front hub bearings (paragraph 4).
10 Using a large screwdriver or flat bar, check for wear in the suspension mounting bushes by levering between the relevant suspension component and its attachment point. Some movement is to be expected as the mountings are made of rubber, but excessive wear should be obvious.

14 Driveshaft rubber gaiter and joint check

1 The driveshaft rubber gaiters are very important, because they prevent dirt, water and foreign material from entering and damaging the joints. External contamination can cause the gaiter material to deteriorate prematurely, so it's a good idea to wash the gaiters with soap and water occasionally.
2 With the vehicle raised and securely supported on axle stands (see *Jacking and vehicle support*), turn the steering onto full-lock, then slowly rotate each front wheel in turn. Inspect the condition of the outer constant velocity (CV) joint rubber gaiters, squeezing the gaiters to open out the folds. Check for signs of cracking, splits, or deterioration of the rubber, which may allow the escape of grease, and lead to the ingress of water and grit into the joint. Also check the security and condition of the retaining clips. Repeat these checks on the inner joints **(see illustration)**. If any damage or deterioration is found, the gaiters should be renewed as described in Chapter 8, Section 3.
3 At the same time, check the general condition of the outer CV joints themselves, by first holding the driveshaft and attempting to rotate the wheels. Repeat this check on the inner joints, by holding the inner joint yoke and attempting to rotate the driveshaft.
4 Any appreciable movement in the joint indicates wear in the joint, wear in the driveshaft splines, or a loose driveshaft retaining nut.

15 Underbody and fuel/brake line check

1 With the vehicle raised and supported on axle stands or over an inspection pit, thoroughly inspect the underbody and wheel arches for signs of damage and corrosion. In particular, examine the bottom of the side sills, and any concealed areas where mud can collect.

13.2 Check the condition of the steering rack rubber gaiters

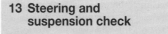

13.4 Grasp the roadwheel at the 12 o'clock and 6 o'clock positions, and try to rock it

14.2 Check the condition of the driveshaft joint rubber gaiters

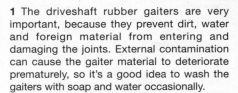

2 Where corrosion and rust is evident, press and tap firmly on the panel with a screwdriver, and check for any serious corrosion which would necessitate repairs.

3 If the panel is not seriously corroded, clean away the rust, and apply a new coating of underseal. Refer to Chapter 11 for more details of body repairs.

4 At the same time, inspect the lower body panels for stone damage and general condition.

5 Inspect all of the fuel and brake lines on the underbody for damage, rust, corrosion and leakage. Also make sure that they are correctly supported in their clips **(see illustration).** Where applicable, check the PVC coating on the lines for damage.

16 Hinge and lock lubrication

1 Work around the vehicle and lubricate the hinges of the bonnet, doors and tailgate with a light machine oil.

2 Check carefully the security and operation of all hinges, latches and locks, adjusting them where required. Check the operation of the central locking system.

3 Where applicable, check the condition and operation of the tailgate struts, renewing them if either is leaking or no longer able to support the tailgate securely when raised.

17 Roadwheel check

Roadwheel nut tightness check

1 Checking the tightness of the wheel nuts is more relevant than you might think. Apart from the obvious safety aspect of ensuring they are sufficiently tight, this check will reveal whether they have been overtightened, as may have happened the last time new tyres were fitted, for example. If the car suffers a puncture, you may find that the wheel nuts cannot be loosened with the wheel brace.

2 Apply the handbrake, chock the wheels, and engage 1st gear.

3 Remove the wheel cover (or wheel centre cover), using the flat end of the wheel brace supplied in the tool kit.

4 Loosen the first wheel nut, using the wheel brace if possible. If the nut proves stubborn, use a close-fitting socket and a long extension bar.

⚠️ *Warning: Do not use makeshift means to loosen the wheel nuts if the proper tools are not available. If extra force is required, make sure that the tools fit properly, and are of good quality. Even so, consider the consequences of the tool slipping or breaking, and take precautions – wearing stout gloves is*

advisable to protect your hands. Do not be tempted to stand on the tools used – they are not designed for this, and there is a high risk of personal injury if the tool slips or breaks. If the wheel nuts are simply too tight, take the car to a garage equipped with suitable power tools.

5 Once the nut has been loosened, remove it and check that the wheel stud threads are clean. Use a small wire brush to clean any rust or dirt from the threads, if necessary.

6 Refit the nut, with the tapered side facing inwards. Tighten it fully, using the wheel brace alone – no other tools. This will ensure that the wheel nuts can be loosened using the wheel brace if a puncture occurs. However, if a torque wrench is available, tighten the nut to the specified torque wrench setting.

7 Repeat the procedure for the remaining three nuts, then refit the wheel cover or centre cover, as applicable.

8 Work around the car, checking and retightening the nuts for all four wheels.

Roadwheel check and balancing

9 Periodically remove the roadwheels, and clean any dirt or mud from the inside and outside surfaces. Examine the wheel rims for signs of rusting, corrosion or other damage. Light alloy wheels are easily damaged by 'kerbing' whilst parking, and similarly, steel wheels may become dented or buckled. Renewal of the wheel is very often the only course of remedial action possible.

10 The balance of each wheel and tyre assembly should be maintained, not only to avoid excessive tyre wear, but also to avoid wear in the steering and suspension components. Wheel imbalance is normally signified by vibration through the vehicle's bodyshell, although in many cases it is particularly noticeable through the steering wheel. Conversely, it should be noted that wear or damage in suspension or steering components may cause excessive tyre wear. Out-of-round or out-of-true tyres, damaged wheels and wheel bearing wear/maladjustment also fall into this category. Balancing will not usually cure vibration caused by such wear.

11 Wheel balancing may be carried out with the wheel either on or off the vehicle. If balanced off the vehicle, ensure that the wheel-to-hub relationship is marked in some way prior to subsequent wheel removal, so that it may be refitted in its original position.

18 Road test

Braking system

1 Make sure that the vehicle does not pull to one side when braking, and that the wheels do not lock when braking hard.

2 Check that there is no vibration through the steering when braking. On cars equipped

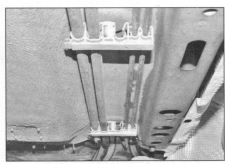

15.5 Check the security and condition of the fuel and brake lines under the body

with ABS brakes, if vibration is felt through the pedal under heavy braking, this is a normal characteristic of the system operation, and is not a cause for concern.

3 Check that the handbrake operates correctly, without excessive movement of the lever, and that it holds the vehicle stationary on a slope, in both directions (facing up and down a slope).

4 With the engine switched off, test the operation of the brake servo unit as follows. Depress the footbrake four or five times to exhaust the vacuum, then start the engine. As the engine starts, there should be a noticeable 'give' in the brake pedal as vacuum builds-up. Allow the engine to run for at least two minutes, and then switch it off. If the brake pedal is now depressed again, it should be possible to detect a hiss from the servo as the pedal is depressed. After about four or five applications, no further hissing should be heard, and the pedal should feel considerably harder.

Steering and suspension

5 Check for any abnormalities in the steering, suspension, handling or road 'feel'.

6 Drive the vehicle, and check that there are no unusual vibrations or noises.

7 Check that the steering feels positive, with no excessive sloppiness or roughness, and check for any suspension noises when cornering and driving over bumps.

Drivetrain

8 Check the performance of the engine, transmission and driveshafts.

9 Check that the engine starts correctly, both when cold and when hot. Observe the glow plug warning light, and check that it comes on and goes off correctly.

10 Listen for any unusual noises from the engine and transmission.

11 Make sure that the engine runs smoothly when idling, and that there is no hesitation when accelerating.

12 Check that all gears can be engaged smoothly without noise, and that the gear lever action is smooth and not abnormally vague or 'notchy'.

13 Listen for a metallic clicking sound from the front of the vehicle as the vehicle is driven slowly in a circle with the steering on full-lock.

19.1 Push in the centre pins, prise out the plastic rivets and lower the insulation

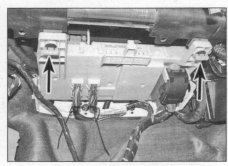

19.2a Undo the 2 fasteners (arrowed) . . .

19.2b . . . and lower the fusebox/module

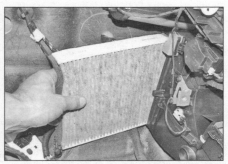

19.3a Undo the 3 bolts (arrowed), remove the cover . . .

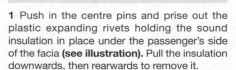

19.3b . . . and pull the pollen filter from the housing

Carry out this check in both directions. If a clicking noise is heard, this indicates wear in a driveshaft joint, in which case renew the joint if necessary.

Clutch

14 Check that the clutch pedal moves smoothly and easily through its full travel, and that the clutch itself functions correctly, with no trace of slip or drag.

15 If the clutch is slow to release, it is possible that the system requires bleeding (see Chapter 6). Also check the fluid pipes under the bonnet for signs of leakage.

Instruments and electrical equipment

16 Check the operation of all instruments and electrical equipment.

17 Make sure that all instruments read correctly, and switch on all electrical equipment in turn, to check that it functions properly.

19 Pollen filter renewal

1 Push in the centre pins and prise out the plastic expanding rivets holding the sound insulation in place under the passenger's side of the facia (see illustration). Pull the insulation downwards, then rearwards to remove it.

2 Undo the 2 fasteners securing the fusebox/ central electrical module to its mounting bracket by rotating them anti-clockwise, then move the fusebox/module downwards and rearwards and detach it from the bracket (see illustrations). Move the fusebox/module to one side, there is no need to disconnect the wiring plugs.

3 Undo the bolts, remove the cover and pull the filter from the housing (see illustrations).

4 Fit the new filter using a reversal of the removal procedure, ensuring that the filter is

fitted with the airflow arrows pointing straight back into the cabin.

20 Fuel filter water draining and renewal

Caution: Use barrier cream or (preferably) wear disposable gloves before doing work which involves coming into contact with diesel fuel.

Water draining

Note: The process described below is for the 2.0 litre 4-cylinder engine but it is similar for 1.6 litre engines

1 The fuel filter is located at the front of the engine compartment. Remove the plastic cover on the top of the engine. Pull up the right-hand rear corner and the front edges, then pull the cover forwards to release it.

2 Cover the alternator with a cloth, then attach a length of plastic/rubber hose to the drain screw, with the other end of the hose in a container (see illustration).

3 Slacken the drain screw and the top bleed screw a few turns, and allow the fuel to drain, until it appears clean and free from water droplets. Tighten the bleed screw and drain screw (see illustration).

4 Remove the hose, and bleed the fuel system as described in Chapter 4B.

5-cylinder engines

5 The fuel filter is located near the right-hand side rear roadwheel, within the rear suspension subframe. Connect a length of

20.2 Attach a length of hose to the drain screw (arrowed)

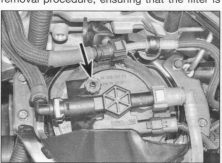

20.3 Slacken the top bleed screw (arrowed)

20.5 Attach a length of hose and slacken the drain screw of the fuel filter

20.9 Undo the 3 screws (arrowed) for the engine cover mounting bracket

20.10a Disconnect the wiring plug from the fuel filter…

20.10b …and release the locking tabs and disconnect the fuel hoses from the filter head

20.11 Filter securing bolts (arrowed) on the 1.6 litre (85kW) engine

20.14 Depress the locking tabs and disconnect the fuel hoses from the filter head

20.16 Unscrew the filter head

hose to the drain screw and place the open end in a container. Slacken the drain screw on the underside of the filter by no more than 4 turns (see illustration).
6 Drain off approximately 100cc of fluid and tighten the drain screw.
7 Start the engine and check for leaks.

Filter renewal

1.6 litre engines

8 Remove the plastic cover on top of the engine.
9 Undo the 3 screws and remove the bracket above the filter that supports the plastic engine cover (see illustration).
10 Release the locking tabs and disconnect the fuel hoses from the filter head. Be prepared for fuel spillage. Disconnect the wiring plug (see illustrations).
11 On models fitted with the 80kW engine, undo the 3 bolts for the securing bracket and lift the filter from its mounting. On models fitted with the 85kW engine, undo the 2 bolts on top of the filter and withdraw the filter from its housing (see illustration).
12 Refitting is a reversal of removal. Bleed the fuel system as described in Chapter 4B.

2.0 litre 4-cylinder engine

13 Release the wiring harnesses from the cable ties on the fuel filter bracket, then disconnect the filter wiring plug, release the fuel pipe from the clip, undo the 4 bolts, then remove the bracket.
14 Depress the locking tabs and disconnect

the fuel hoses from the filter head (see illustration). Be prepared for fuel spillage.
15 Disconnect the wiring plug from the filter head.
16 Unscrew the filter head, and lift it from place (see illustration).
17 Remove the filter element, and discard the O-ring seal (see illustration).
18 Fit the new filter element and O-ring seal, then position the filter head and tighten it by rotating it clockwise.
19 The remainder of refitting is a reversal of removal. Bleed the fuel system as described in Chapter 4B.

5-cylinder engines

Note: *Ensure the fuel tank level is less than 3/4 full before renewing the filter.*
20 The fuel filter is located near the

20.17 Renew the filter element and the O-ring seal

right-hand side rear roadwheel, within the rear suspension subframe (see illustration).
21 Place a container under the filter, then slacken the drain screw on the filter underside and allow the fuel to drain.
22 Use a strap wrench or filter removal tool to unscrew the filter from the housing. Be prepared for fuel spillage.
23 Ensure the small O-ring seal is fitted to the top of the element, then fit the large O-ring seal to the filter housing. Fit the new element into the filter holder, then fit the assembly to the housing, ensuring the top of the element locates in the housing. Tighten the filter by hand until the seal contacts the holder, then tighten it a further 1/2 to 3/4 of a turn.
24 Start the engine and check for leaks.

20.20 The fuel filter is located under the right-hand side of the vehicle within the rear suspension subframe

23.2 Press and hold the trip odometer reset button

21 Handbrake check and adjustment

In service, the handbrake should be fully applied within 3 to 5 clicks of the handbrake lever ratchet. Should adjustment be necessary, refer to Chapter 9, Section 13 for the full procedure description.

22 Antifreeze/inhibitor strength check

See Section 29.

23 Service reminder indicator reset

1 Turn the ignition switch to position I.
2 Press and hold the trip odometer reset button **(see illustration),** then turn the ignition switch to position II within 2 seconds.
3 Hold the button in until the warning light extinguishes and then release the button within 4 seconds. The instrument panel gives an audible signal when the resetting has been successful. **Note:** *If the odometer is already reset, the button must be held in for a minimum of 10 seconds and a maximum of 14 seconds.*
4 Turn off the ignition switch.

Every 37 000 miles

24 Air filter element renewal

Caution: Never drive the vehicle with the air cleaner filter element removed. Excessive engine wear could result, and backfiring could even cause a fire under the bonnet.

1 The air filter element is located in the air cleaner assembly on the left-hand side of the engine compartment.
2 Undo the Torx screws, and remove the air cleaner top cover **(see illustrations).**
3 Unclip the mass airflow sensor wiring

harness clip from the cover where required **(see illustration).**
4 The cover can now be removed, and the filter element removed noting its direction of fitting **(see illustrations).**
5 If carrying out a routine service, the element must be renewed regardless of its apparent condition.
6 If you are checking the element for any other reason, inspect its lower surface; if it is oily or very dirty, renew the element. If it is only moderately dusty, it can be re-used by blowing it clean from the upper to the lower surface with compressed air. Because it is a pleated-paper type filter, it cannot be washed or oiled. If it cannot be

cleaned satisfactorily with compressed air, renew it.

 Warning: Wear eye protection when using compressed air.

7 With the filter removed, wipe out the inside of the housing. Check that no foreign matter is visible, either in the air intake or in the air mass meter.
8 Refitting is the reverse of the removal procedure, noting the following points:
a) *Make sure that the filter is fitted the correct way up (observe any direction-of-fitting markings). On 1.6 litre engines, a small lug at the rear of the filter locates in a slot in the filter housing (see illustration).*

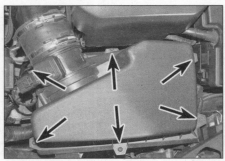

24.2a The air filter cover is retained by 6 Torx screws (arrowed)...

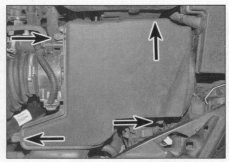

24.2b ...or 4 Torx screws depending on the engine fitted

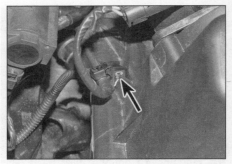

24.3 Unclip the wiring harness from the cover (arrowed)

24.4a Air filter on the 2.0 4-cylinder engine...

24.4b ...and on 1.6 litre engines

24.8 On 1.6 litre engines, a lug (arrowed) at the rear of the filter locates in the filter housing

b) *Ensure that the element and cover are securely seated, so that unfiltered air cannot enter the engine.*

c) *Where removed, secure the cover with the screws, and ensure that the air inlet duct securing clip is fully tightened.*

25 Particulate filter additive tank refilling

Note: *Although refilling the additive tank is straightforward, after topping it up the tank level counter in the control module must be reset in order for the system to function correctly. This can only be done with Volvo test equipment. If you do not have access to this equipment, entrust this task to a Volvo dealer or suitably-equipped specialist.*

1 Chock the front wheels, raise the rear of the vehicle and support it securely on axle stands (see *Jacking and vehicle support*).

2 Place a container under the additive tank, then depress the release button and disconnect the level control pipe from the tank. Be prepared for additive spillage.

Caution: Do not allow the additive to come into contact with skin, eyes or vehicle paintwork.

3 Depress the release button and remove the plug from the additive filler pipe. Attach the new additive container to the filler pipe, raise the container up, and fill the tank.

4 As soon as additive starts to flow through the level control pipe port, lower the additive container and cease filling. Reconnect the pipes to the tank, and mop-up any additive spills.

5 The level counter in the control module must now be reset using Volvo's dedicated test equipment. Note that this function may also be available on professional diagnostic equipment. If the counter is not reset, the ECM will assume the additive tank is empty, and cease to inject the additive into the fuel tank. Particles will no longer be burnt off, and will eventually block the exhaust particulate filter.

26 Automatic transmission fluid level check

Note: *If the 'Gearbox oil change' indicator illuminates, this can only be reset using dedicated Volvo test equipment. Entrust this task to a Volvo dealer or suitably-equipped specialist.*

General

1 The need for regular topping-up of the transmission fluid indicates a leak, which should be found and rectified without delay.

2 The condition of the fluid should also be checked along with the level. If the fluid at the end of the dipstick is black or a dark

reddish-brown colour, or if it has a burned smell, the fluid should be changed. If you are in doubt about the condition of the fluid, purchase some new fluid, and compare the two for colour and smell.

3 If the car is used regularly for short trips, taxi work, or does a lot of towing, the transmission fluid should be renewed on a regular basis. Likewise, if a high mileage has been completed, or the history of the car is unknown, it might be worth renewing the fluid for peace of mind. Normally, however, renewal of the fluid is not a service requirement.

Fluid level check

AW55-51SN Transmission

4 The level of the automatic transmission fluid should be carefully maintained. Low fluid level can lead to slipping or loss of drive, while overfilling can cause foaming, loss of fluid and transmission damage.

5 Ideally, the transmission fluid level should be checked when the transmission is hot (at its normal operating temperature). If the vehicle has just been driven for about 30 minutes, the fluid temperature will be around 80°C, and the transmission is hot.

6 Raise the vehicle and support it securely on axle stands (see *Jacking and vehicle support*). Undo the 7 Torx screws and remove the engine undershield **(see illustration 4.2)**.

7 Firmly apply the handbrake, and start the engine. While the engine is idling, depress the brake pedal and move the selector lever through all gear positions (pausing in each position for at least **3** seconds), returning finally to the P position.

8 Wait two minutes then, with the engine still idling, remove the dipstick (yellow handle) from its tube which is located at the front of the transmission **(see illustration)**. Note the condition and colour of the fluid on the dipstick.

9 Wipe the fluid from the dipstick with a clean rag, and re-insert it into the filler tube until the cap seats.

10 Pull the dipstick out again, and note the fluid level. The level should be towards the top of the HOT range of the dipstick. If the level is below the HOT range, stop the engine.

11 To add fluid to the transmission, disconnect the oil cooler hose from the return port on the transmission cover. The hose is secured by a quick-release connector. Connect a length of rubber hose to the return port with a funnel in the other end of the hose. Add the specified automatic transmission fluid. It is essential not to introduce dirt into the transmission when topping-up.

12 Add the fluid a little at a time, and keep checking the level as previously described until it is correct. The difference between the top and bottom of the HOT or COLD ranges is approximately 0.3 litres.

13 If the vehicle has not been driven and the engine and transmission are cold, carry out

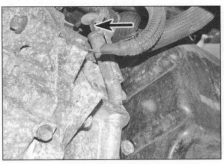

26.8 Automatic transmission oil level dipstick (arrowed) – viewed from underneath

the procedures in paragraphs 3 to 6, but use the marks of the dipstick marked COLD. It is, however, preferable to check the level when the transmission is hot, as a more accurate reading will be obtained.

TF-80SC Transmission

14 The level of the automatic transmission fluid should be carefully maintained. Low fluid level can lead to slipping or loss of drive, while overfilling can cause foaming, loss of fluid and transmission damage.

15 Ideally, the transmission fluid level should be checked when the transmission is hot – 50°C to 60°C.

16 Park the vehicle on level ground, firmly apply the handbrake, and remove the engine undershield **(see illustration 4.2)**.

17 Remove the air cleaner housing as described in Chapter 4B, Section 3.

18 Clean the area on the top of the transmission around the filler plug, then using a T55 Torx bit, unscrew the filler plug **(see illustration)**.

19 Position the end of a hose in the filler aperture, and attach a funnel to the other end. Temporarily refit the air cleaner housing.

20 Start the engine. While the engine is idling, depress the brake pedal and move the selector lever through all gear positions (pausing in each position for 2 seconds), returning finally to the P position.

21 With the engine still running, unscrew the level plug from the centre of the transmission drain plug using a T40 Torx bit

26.18 Oil filler plug on the TF-80SC transmission

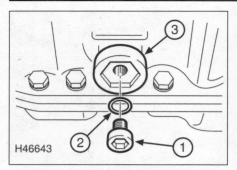

26.21 Transmission level plug (1), drain plug (3) and sealing washer (2)

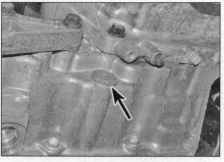

26.25 Automatic transmission oil drain plug (arrowed)

(see illustration). If no fluid emerges from the level aperture, add specified fluid through the funnel and hose until it does emerge. Refit the level plug and tighten it to the specified torque, using a new sealing washer.

22 Stop the engine, remove the air cleaner housing, and tighten the fluid filler plug to the specified torque, using a new sealing washer.

23 Refit the air cleaner housing as described in Chapter 4B, then refit the engine undershield.

Fluid renewal

AW55-51SN Transmission

24 Raise the vehicle and support it securely on axle stands (see *Jacking and vehicle support*). Undo the 7 Torx screws and remove the engine undershield (see illustration 4.2).

25 Position a container under the transmission drain plug, then remove the plug and allow the fluid to drain into the container (see illustration). Discard the sealing washer, a new one must be fitted.

26 Once all the fluid has drained, refit the drain plug with a new washer, and tighten it to the specified torque.

27 To add fluid to the transmission, disconnect the oil cooler hose from the return port on the transmission cover. The hose is secured by a quick-release connector. Connect a length of clear plastic hose to the return port with a funnel in the other end of the hose.

28 Ensure the selector lever is in position P, then add approximately 2.0 litres of the specified automatic transmission fluid through the hose into the transmission. It is essential not to introduce dirt into the transmission when topping-up.

29 Start the engine, and allow it to idle so the transmission pumps out the fluid. Turn the engine off as soon as air bubbles appear in the plastic tube.

30 Repeat the operation described in paragraph 29 above.

31 Add a further 2 litres of fluid, then check the oil level as previously described in this Section.

32 Refit the engine undershield upon completion.

TF-80SC Transmission

Note: *The automatic transmission fluid does not normally require changing. It's only necessary on vehicles which are used predominantly for towing or as taxis.*

33 Ideally, the transmission fluid should be drained when the transmission is hot (at its normal operating temperature). Take care however not to be scalded by the hot fluid – wear protective gloves.

34 Jack up the front and rear of the vehicle and support it securely on axle stands (see *Jacking and vehicle support*). The vehicle should be level.

35 Release the screws and remove the engine undershield (see illustration 4.2).

36 Position a container beneath the transmission and unscrew the level plug from the centre of the drain plug using a T40 Torx bit (see illustration 26.21).

37 Unscrew the drain plug from the transmission and allow the fluid to drain. Refit the drain plug with a new seal and tighten it to the specified torque.

38 Refit the level plug, but only finger-tighten it at this stage.

39 Remove the air cleaner housing as described in Chapter 4B, Section 3.

40 Clean the area on the top of the transmission around the filler plug, then using a T55 Torx bit, unscrew the filler plug (see illustration 26.18).

41 Disconnect the fluid return hose from the cooler adjacent to the radiator, and attach a length of clear hose to the cooler outlet. Volvo special tool No 999 7363 may be available for this purpose. Place the end of the hose into a container.

42 Using a funnel, add 4.0 litres of the specified fluid into the transmission casing through the filler hole.

43 Fully apply the handbrake, and check the selector lever is in position P.

44 Start the engine, and allow it to idle. Shift through all the selector positions, pausing for 2 seconds at each position. Switch the engine off when air bubbles are visible in the clear hose attached to the cooler.

45 Add 2.0 litres of the specified fluid, then start the engine again and allow it to idle. Switch the engine off when air bubbles are visible in the clear hose.

46 Disconnect the clear hose from the cooler, and reconnect the fluid return hose.

47 Unscrew the level plug from the centre of the drain plug, and add fluid through the filler hole until It begins to run out of the level plug hole. Refit the level and filler plugs and tighten them to their specified torques.

48 Refit the air cleaner housing as described in Chapter 4B.

Every 62 000 miles

<table>
<tr><td>**27 Timing belt renewal**</td><td>The procedure is described in Chapter 2C, Section 7 (1.6 litre engine), Chapter 2D, Section 6 (2.0 litre 4-cylinder engine) or Chapter 2E, Section 4 (2.0 and 2.4 litre 5-cylinder engines).</td></tr>
</table>

Every 2 years

28 Brake fluid renewal

⚠ *Warning: Brake hydraulic fluid can harm your eyes and damage painted surfaces, so use extreme caution when handling and pouring it. Do*

not use fluid that has been standing open for some time, as it absorbs moisture from the air. Excess moisture can cause a dangerous loss of braking effectiveness. Brake fluid is also highly flammable – treat it with the same respect as petrol.

1 The procedure is similar to that for the bleeding of the hydraulic system as described in Chapter 9, Section 2.

2 Reduce the fluid level in the reservoir (by syphoning or using a poultry baster), but do not allow the fluid level to drop far enough to allow air into the system – if air enters the ABS hydraulic unit, the unit may need be bled using special Volvo test equipment (see Chapter 9).

⚠ *Warning: Do not syphon the fluid by mouth; it is poisonous.*

3 Working as described in Chapter 9, open the first bleed screw in the sequence, and pump the brake pedal gently until nearly all the old fluid has been emptied from the master cylinder reservoir. Top-up to the MAX level with new fluid, and continue pumping until only the new fluid remains in the reservoir, and new fluid can be seen emerging from the bleed screw. Tighten the screw, and top the reservoir level up to the MAX level line. Old hydraulic fluid is invariably much darker in colour than the new, making it easy to distinguish the two.

4 Work through all the remaining bleed screws in the sequence until new fluid can be seen at all of them. Be careful to keep the master cylinder reservoir topped-up to above the MIN level at all times, or air may enter the system and greatly increase the length of the task.

5 When the operation is complete, check that all bleed screws are securely tightened, and that their dust caps are refitted. Wash off all traces of spilt fluid, and recheck the master cylinder reservoir fluid level.

6 Check the operation of the brakes before taking the car on the road.

7 Finally, check the operation of the clutch. Since the clutch shares the same fluid reservoir as the braking system, it may also be necessary to bleed the clutch as described in Chapter 6, Section 5.

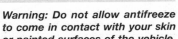

29 Coolant renewal

⚠ **Warning: Do not allow antifreeze to come in contact with your skin or painted surfaces of the vehicle. Flush contaminated areas immediately with plenty of water. Don't store new coolant, or leave old coolant lying around, where it's accessible to children or pets – they're attracted by its sweet smell. Ingestion of even a small amount of coolant can be fatal. Wipe up garage-floor and drip-pan spills immediately. Keep antifreeze containers covered, and repair cooling system leaks as soon as they're noticed.**

⚠ **Warning: Never remove the expansion tank filler cap when the engine is running, or has just been switched off, as the cooling system will be hot, and the consequent escaping steam and scalding coolant could cause serious injury.**

⚠ **Warning: Wait until the engine is cold before starting these procedures.**

Note: *Volvo do not include coolant renewal in the service schedule. Providing the strength of the coolant mixture is maintained with the correct Volvo specification antifreeze, the coolant should not normally require renewal.*

Strength check

1 Use a hydrometer to check the strength of the antifreeze. Follow the instructions provided with your hydrometer. The antifreeze strength should be approximately 50%. If it is significantly less than this, drain a little coolant from the radiator (see this Section), add antifreeze to the coolant expansion tank, then recheck the strength.

Coolant draining

2 To drain the system, first remove the expansion tank filler cap.

3 If the additional working clearance is required, raise the front of the vehicle and support it securely on axle stands (see *Jacking and vehicle support*). Undo the 7 Torx screws **(see illustration 4.2)** and remove the engine undershield.

4 Place a large drain tray underneath, and unscrew the drain plug located at the bottom left-hand side of the radiator **(see illustration)**; direct as much of the escaping coolant as possible into the tray.

5 On models fitted with an oil cooler, once the coolant has stopped draining from the radiator, close the drain plug, and position the container under the engine. Slacken the clamp and disconnect the coolant hose from the oil cooler, and allow the coolant to drain into the container.

System flushing

6 With time, the cooling system may gradually lose its efficiency, as the radiator core becomes choked with rust, scale deposits from the water, and other sediment. To minimise this, as well as using only good-quality antifreeze and clean soft water, the system should be flushed as follows whenever any part of it is disturbed, and/or when the coolant is renewed.

7 With the coolant drained, refit the drain plug and refill the system with fresh water. Refit the expansion tank filler cap, start the engine and warm it up to normal operating temperature, then stop it and (after allowing it to cool down completely) drain the system again. Repeat as necessary until only clean water can be seen to emerge, then refill finally with the specified coolant mixture.

8 If only clean, soft water and good-quality antifreeze (even if not to Volvo's specification) has been used, and the coolant has been renewed at the suggested intervals, the above procedure will be sufficient to keep clean the system for a considerable length of time. If, however, the system has been neglected, a more thorough operation will be required, as follows.

9 First drain the coolant, then disconnect the radiator top and bottom hoses. Insert a garden hose into the radiator top hose connection, and allow water to circulate through the radiator until it runs clean from the bottom outlet.

10 To flush the engine, insert the garden hose into the radiator bottom hose, wrap a piece of rag around the garden hose to seal the connection, and allow water to circulate until it runs clear.

11 Try the effect of repeating this procedure

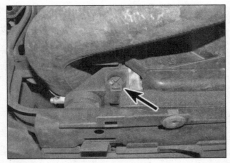

29.4 Drain plug is located on the left-hand side of the radiator

in the top hose, although this may not be effective, since the thermostat will probably close and prevent the flow of water.

12 In severe cases of contamination, reverse-flushing of the radiator may be necessary. This may be achieved by inserting the garden hose into the bottom outlet, wrapping a piece of rag around the hose to seal the connection, then flushing the radiator until clear water emerges from the top hose outlet.

13 If the radiator is suspected of being severely choked, remove the radiator (Chapter 3), turn it upside-down, and repeat the procedure described in paragraph 12.

14 Flushing the heater matrix can be achieved using a similar procedure to that described in paragraph 12, once the heater inlet and outlet hoses have been identified. These two hoses will be of the same diameter, and pass through the engine compartment bulkhead (refer to the heater matrix removal procedure in Chapter 3 for more details).

15 The use of chemical cleaners is not recommended, and should be necessary only as a last resort; the scouring action of some chemical cleaners may lead to other cooling system problems. Normally, regular renewal of the coolant will prevent excessive contamination of the system.

Coolant filling

16 With the cooling system drained and flushed, ensure that all disturbed hose unions are correctly secured, and that the radiator/engine drain plug(s) is securely tightened. Refit the engine undershield. If it was raised, lower the vehicle to the ground.

17 Prepare a sufficient quantity of the specified coolant mixture (see below); allow for a surplus, so as to have a reserve supply for topping-up.

18 Where fitted, slacken the bleed screw located on the EGR cooler hose at the rear of the engine.

19 Slowly fill the system through the expansion tank. Since the tank is the highest point in the system, all the air in the system should be displaced into the tank by the rising liquid. Slow pouring reduces the possibility of air being trapped and forming airlocks.

20 As soon as a steady stream of bubble-free coolant emerges from the bleed screw on the EGR hose, tighten the screw.

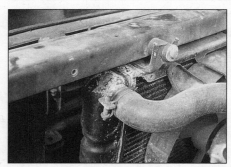

29.36 A leak in the cooling system will usually show up as white- or antifreeze-coloured deposits on the areas adjoining the leak

21 Continue filling until the coolant level reaches the expansion tank MAX level line (see *Weekly checks*), then cover the filler opening to prevent coolant splashing out.

22 Start the engine and run it at idle speed, until it has warmed-up to normal operating temperature and the radiator electric cooling fan has cut in; watch the temperature gauge to check for signs of overheating. If the level in the expansion tank drops significantly, top-up to the MAX level line to minimise the amount of air circulating in the system.

23 Stop the engine, wash off any spilt coolant from the engine compartment and bodywork, then leave the car to cool down *completely* (overnight, if possible).

24 With the system cool, uncover the expansion tank filler opening, and top-up the tank to the MAX level line. Refit the filler cap, tightening it securely, and clean up any further spillage.

25 After refilling, always check carefully all components of the system (but especially any unions disturbed during draining and flushing) for signs of coolant leaks. Fresh antifreeze has a searching action, which will rapidly expose any weak points in the system.

Antifreeze type and mixture

Note: *Do not use engine antifreeze in the windscreen/tailgate washer system, as it will damage the vehicle's paintwork. A screenwash additive should be added to the washer system in its maker's recommended quantities.*

26 If the vehicle's history (and therefore the quality of the antifreeze in it) is unknown, owners are advised to drain and thoroughly reverse-flush the system, before refilling with fresh coolant mixture. If the Volvo antifreeze is used, the coolant can then be left indefinitely, providing the strength of the mixture is checked every year (see this Section).

27 If any antifreeze other than Volvo's is to be used, the coolant must be renewed at regular intervals to provide an equivalent degree of protection; the conventional recommendation is to renew the coolant every two years.

28 If the antifreeze used is to Volvo's specification, the levels of protection it affords are indicated in the coolant packaging. To give the recommended standard mixture ratio for antifreeze, 50% (by volume) of antifreeze must be mixed with 50% of clean, soft water; if you are using any other type of antifreeze, follow its manufacturer's instructions to achieve the correct protection.

29 You are unlikely to fully drain the system at any one time (unless the engine is being completely stripped), and the capacities quoted in Specifications are therefore slightly academic for routine coolant renewal. As a guide, only two-thirds of the system's total capacity is likely to be needed for coolant renewal.

30 As the drained system will be partially filled with flushing water, in order to establish the recommended mixture ratio, measure out 50% of the system capacity in antifreeze and pour it into the hose/expansion tank as described above, then top-up with water. Any topping-up while refilling the system should be done with water – for Weekly checks use a suitable mixture.

31 Before adding antifreeze, the cooling system should be drained, preferably flushed, and all hoses checked for condition and security. As noted earlier, fresh antifreeze will rapidly find any weaknesses in the system.

32 After filling with antifreeze, a label should be attached to the expansion tank, stating the type and concentration of antifreeze used, and the date installed. Any subsequent topping-up should be made with the same type and concentration of antifreeze.

General cooling system checks

33 The engine should be cold for the cooling system checks, so perform the following procedure before driving the vehicle, or after it has been shut off for at least three hours.

34 Remove the expansion tank filler cap, and clean it thoroughly inside and out with a rag. Also clean the filler neck on the expansion tank. The presence of rust or corrosion in the filler neck indicates that the coolant should be changed. The coolant inside the expansion tank should be relatively clean and transparent. If it is rust-coloured, drain and flush the system, and refill with a fresh coolant mixture.

35 Carefully check the radiator hoses and heater hoses along their entire length; renew any hose which is cracked, swollen or deteriorated (see Section 8).

36 Inspect all other cooling system components (joint faces, etc) for leaks. A leak in the cooling system will usually show up as white- or antifreeze-coloured deposits on the area adjoining the leak **(see illustration)**. Where any problems of this nature are found on system components, renew the component or gasket with reference to Chapter 3.

37 Clean the front of the radiator with a soft brush to remove all insects, leaves, etc, embedded in the radiator fins. Be careful not to damage the radiator fins, or cut your fingers on them. To do a more thorough job, remove the radiator grille as described in Chapter 11.

Airlocks

38 If, after draining and refilling the system, symptoms of overheating are found which did not occur previously, then the fault is almost certainly due to trapped air at some point in the system, causing an airlock and restricting the flow of coolant; usually, the air is trapped because the system was refilled too quickly.

39 If an airlock is suspected, first try gently squeezing all visible coolant hoses. A coolant hose which is full of air feels quite different to one full of coolant when squeezed. After refilling the system, most airlocks will clear once the system has cooled, and been topped-up.

40 While the engine is running at operating temperature, switch on the heater and heater fan, and check for heat output. Provided there is sufficient coolant in the system, lack of heat output could be due to an airlock in the system.

41 Airlocks can have more serious effects than simply reducing heater output – a severe airlock could reduce coolant flow around the engine. Check that the radiator top hose is hot when the engine is at operating temperature – a top hose which stays cold could be the result of an airlock (or a non-opening thermostat).

42 If the problem persists, stop the engine and allow it to cool down **completely**, before unscrewing the expansion tank filler cap or loosening the hose clips and squeezing the hoses to bleed out the trapped air. In the worst case, the system will have to be at least partially drained (this time, the coolant can be saved for re-use) and flushed to clear the problem. If all else fails, have the system evacuated and vacuum filled by a suitably-equipped garage.

Expansion tank cap check

43 Wait until the engine is completely cold – perform this check before the engine is started for the first time in the day.

44 Place a wad of cloth over the expansion tank cap, then unscrew it slowly and remove it.

45 Examine the condition of the rubber seal on the underside of the cap. If the rubber appears to have hardened, or cracks are visible in the seal edges, a new cap should be fitted.

46 If the car is several years old, or has covered a large mileage, consider renewing the cap regardless of its apparent condition – they are not expensive. If the pressure relief valve built into the cap fails, excess pressure in the system will lead to puzzling failures of hoses and other cooling system components.

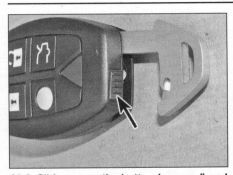

30.2 Slide across the button (arrowed) and pull out the key blade

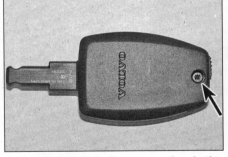

30.3 Turn the controller over and undo the small screw (arrowed)

30.4 Insert the battery with the negative side facing upwards

30 Remote control battery renewal

1 Although not in the Volvo maintenance schedule, we recommend that the battery be changed every 2 years, regardless of the vehicle's mileage. If the door locks repeatedly fail to respond to signals from the remote control at the normal distance, change the battery in the remote control before attempting to troubleshoot any of the vehicle's other systems.

2 Slide the button across and pull out the key blade from the remote control **(see illustration).**

3 Undo the small screw, and remove the control cover **(see illustration).**

4 Note the fitted position of the battery (positive side against the cover), then prise the battery from place, and insert the new one **(see illustration).** Avoid touching the battery or the terminals with bare fingers.

5 Refit the cover and tighten the screw securely.

6 Refit the key blade, and check for correct operation.

Every 75 000 miles or 6 years

31 Particulate filter renewal

This procedure is described in Chapter 4B, Section 18.

Every 100 000 miles or 9 years

32 Auxiliary drivebelt renewal

See Section 6.

Chapter 2 Part A:
1.8 and 2.0 litre petrol engine in-car repair procedures

Contents

Degrees of difficulty

Easy, suitable for novice with little experience	**Fairly easy,** suitable for beginner with some experience	**Fairly difficult,** suitable for competent DIY mechanic	**Difficult,** suitable for experienced DIY mechanic	**Very difficult,** suitable for expert DIY or professional

Specifications

General

Engine type	Four-cylinder, in-line, chain-driven double overhead camshafts, aluminium alloy cylinder head and engine block
Engine code:	
1.8 litre	B4184S11 (CSDA or CSDB)
2.0 litre	B4204S3
Capacity:	
1.8 litre	1798 cc
2.0 litre	1999 cc
Bore:	
1.8 litre	83.0 mm
2.0 litre	87.0 mm
Stroke:	
1.8 litre	83.1 mm
2.0 litre	83.1 mm
Compression ratio:	
1.8 litre	10.8:1
2.0 litre	10.8:1
Output:	
Power:	
1.8 litre	88 kW @ 6000 rpm (120 bhp)
2.0 litre	107 kW @ 6000 rpm (145 bhp)
Torque:	
1.8 litre	165 Nm @ 4000 rpm
2.0 litre	185 Nm @ 4500 rpm
Firing order	1-3-4-2 (No 1 cylinder at timing chain end)
Direction of crankshaft rotation	Clockwise (seen from right-hand side of vehicle)

Camshafts

Camshaft endfloat . . . . 0.09 to 0.24 mm
Camshaft bearing journal diameter . . . . 24.96 to 24.98 mm

Valves

	Intake	Exhaust
Valve clearances:		
Cold	0.22 to 0.28 mm	0.27 to 0.33 mm

Lubrication

Engine oil type/specification . . . . See *Lubricants, fluids and tyre pressures* on page 0•16
Engine oil capacity . . . . See Chapter 1A Specifications
Oil pressure (engine at operating temperature):
   At 1500 rpm . . . . 1.3 to 2.7 bar
   At 3000 rpm . . . . 2.3 to 5.2 bar
Oil pressure relief valve opens at . . . . 5.0 bar

Torque wrench settings

	Nm	lbf ft
Air conditioning compressor	25	18
Auxiliary belt tensioner	24	18
Camshaft bearing cap bolts:		
Stage 1	7	5
Stage 2	16	12
Camshaft position sensor	6	4
Camshaft sprocket	72	53
Crankshaft oil seal carrier bolts	10	7
Crankshaft pulley bolt: *		
Stage 1	100	74
Stage 2	Angle-tighten a further 90°	
Cylinder head bolts: *		
Stage 1	5	4
Stage 2	15	11
Stage 3	45	33
Stage 4	Angle-tighten a further 90°	
Stage 5	Angle-tighten a further 90°	
Cylinder head cover bolts	10	7
Engine mountings:		
Left-hand mounting (transmission):		
M12 bolt	80	59
M14 bolt:		
Stage 1	60	44
Stage 2	Angle-tighten a further 60°	
M10 nuts:		
Stage 1	35	26
Stage 2	Angle-tighten a further 60°	
Rear mounting bolts	80	59
Right-hand mounting nuts	60	44
Right-hand mounting (to body) bolts	90	66
Flywheel bolts: *		
Stage 1	30	22
Stage 2	Angle-tighten a further 90°	
Oil pick-up pipe bolts	10	7
Oil pressure switch	15	11
Oil pump chain guide	10	7
Oil pump chain tensioner	10	7
Oil pump sprocket bolt	25	18
Oil pump to engine block bolts:		
Stage 1	20	15
Stage 2	23	17
Sump drain plug	28	21
Sump to block bolts	25	18
Sump to transmission	50	37
Timing chain covers:		
M6 bolts	10	7
M8	48	35
Timing chain guide bolts	10	7
Timing chain tensioner	10	7

* *Do not re-use*

1 General information

How to use this Chapter

This Part of Chapter 2 is devoted to repair procedures possible while the engine is still installed in the vehicle. Since these procedures are based on the assumption that the engine is installed in the vehicle, if the engine has been removed from the vehicle and mounted on a stand, some of the preliminary dismantling steps outlined will not apply.

Information concerning engine/transmission removal and refitting and engine overhaul, can be found in Part F of this Chapter.

Engine description

The engine is of sixteen-valve, double overhead camshaft (DOHC), four-cylinder, in-line type, mounted transversely at the front of the vehicle, with the transmission on its left-hand end. It is available in 1.8 and 2.0 litre versions.

All major engine castings are of aluminium alloy, with cast-iron cylinder liners, and a crankshaft made from forged nodular iron.

The crankshaft runs in five main bearings, the centre main bearing's upper half incorporating thrustwashers to control crankshaft endfloat. The connecting rods rotate on horizontally-split bearing shells at their big-ends. The pistons are attached to the connecting rods by gudgeon pins which are an interference fit in the connecting rod small-end eyes. The aluminium alloy pistons are fitted with three piston rings: two compression rings and an oil control ring. After manufacture, the cylinder bores and piston skirts are measured and classified into three grades, which must be carefully matched together to ensure the correct piston/cylinder clearance; no oversizes are available to permit reboring. New cylinder blocks are supplied complete with crankshafts, pistons and connecting rods assembled. These components are not available separately.

The intake and exhaust valves are each closed by coil springs; they operate in guides which are shrink-fitted into the cylinder head, as are the valve seat inserts.

The two camshafts are driven by the same timing chain, each operating eight valves via solid cam followers (bucket tappets). The followers are graded for thickness, and are changed in order to adjust the valve clearances. Each camshaft rotates in five bearings that are line-bored directly in the cylinder head and the (bolted-on) bearing caps; this means that the bearing caps are not available separately from the cylinder head, and must not be interchanged with caps from another engine.

The coolant pump is bolted to the right-hand end of the cylinder block, and is driven with the alternator by a multi-ribbed auxiliary drivebelt from the crankshaft pulley.

When working on this engine, note that Torx-type (both male and female heads) and hexagon socket (Allen head) fasteners are widely used; a good selection of bits, with the necessary adapters, will be required, so that these can be unscrewed without damage and, on reassembly, tightened to the torque wrench settings specified.

Lubrication system

Lubrication is by means of an eccentric-rotor pump, which is mounted at right-hand end of the cylinder block, and is driven by a chain from a sprocket on the crankshaft, and draws oil through a strainer located in the sump. The pump forces oil through an externally-mounted full-flow cartridge-type filter. From the filter, the oil is pumped into a main gallery in the cylinder block/crankcase, from where it is distributed to the crankshaft (main bearings) and cylinder head.

The big-end bearings are supplied with oil via internal drillings in the crankshaft. Each piston crown is cooled by a spray of oil directed at its underside by a jet. These jets are fed by passages off the crankshaft oil supply galleries, with spring-loaded valves to ensure that the jets open only when there is sufficient pressure to guarantee a good oil supply to the rest of the engine components.

The cylinder head is provided with two oil galleries, one on the intake side and one on the exhaust, to ensure constant oil supply to the camshaft bearings and cam followers. A retaining valve (inserted into the cylinder head's top surface, in the middle, on the intake side) prevents these galleries from being drained when the engine is switched off. The valve incorporates a ventilation hole in its upper end, to allow air bubbles to escape from the system when the engine is restarted.

While the crankshaft and camshaft bearings receive a pressurised supply, the camshaft lobes and valves are lubricated by splash, as are all other engine components.

Operations with engine in car

The following major repair operations can be accomplished without removing the engine from the vehicle. However, owners should note that any operation involving the removal of the sump requires careful forethought, depending on the level of skill and the tools and facilities available; refer to the relevant text for details.

a) Compression pressure – testing.
b) Cylinder head cover – removal and refitting.
c) Timing chain covers – removal and refitting.
d) Timing chain – renewal.
e) Timing chain tensioner and sprockets – removal and refitting.
f) Camshaft oil seals – renewal.
g) Camshafts and cam followers – removal and refitting.
h) Cylinder head – removal, overhaul and refitting.

i) Cylinder head and pistons – decarbonising.
j) Sump – removal and refitting.
k) Crankshaft oil seals – renewal.
l) Oil pump – removal and refitting.
m) Flywheel – removal and refitting.
n) Engine/transmission mountings – removal and refitting.

Clean the engine compartment and the exterior of the engine with some type of degreaser before any work is done (and/or clean the engine using a steam cleaner). It will make the job easier and will help to keep dirt out of the internal areas of the engine.

Depending on the components involved, it may be helpful to remove the bonnet, to improve access to the engine as repairs are performed (refer to Chapter 11 if necessary). Cover the wings to prevent damage to the paint; special covers are available, but an old bedspread or blanket will also work.

2 Compression test – description and interpretation

1 When engine performance is down, or if misfiring occurs which cannot be attributed to the ignition or fuel systems, a compression test can provide diagnostic clues as to the engine's condition. If the test is performed regularly, it can give warning of trouble before any other symptoms become apparent.

2 The engine must be fully warmed-up to normal operating temperature, the oil level must be correct, the battery must be fully-charged. The aid of an assistant will also be required.

3 Referring to Chapter 12, identify and remove the fuel pump fuse from the fusebox. Now start the engine and allow it to run until it stalls. If the engine will not start, at least keep it cranking for about 10 seconds. The fuel system should now be depressurised, preventing unburnt fuel from soaking the catalytic converter as the engine is turned over during the test.

4 Disable the ignition system by unplugging the crankshaft speed/position sensor (see Chapter 4A). Remove the spark plugs as described in Chapter 1A.

5 Fit a compression tester to the No 1 cylinder spark plug hole – the type of tester which screws into the plug thread is to be preferred.

6 Have the assistant hold the throttle wide open and crank the engine on the starter motor; after one or two revolutions, the compression pressure should build-up to a maximum figure and then stabilise. Record the highest reading obtained.

7 The compression will build-up fairly quickly in a healthy engine. Low compression on the first stroke, followed by gradually-increasing pressure on successive strokes, indicates worn piston rings. A low compression on the first stroke which does not rise on successive strokes, indicates leaking valves or a blown

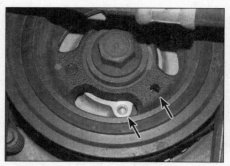

3.8a These 2 holes (arrowed) will align at TDC

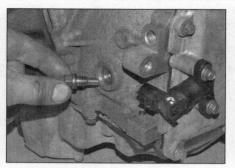

3.8b Remove the timing hole plug . . .

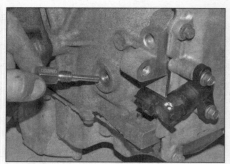

3.8c . . . and insert the timing pin

head gasket (a cracked cylinder head could also be the cause). Deposits on the underside of the valve heads can also cause low compression. Record the highest gauge reading obtained, then repeat the procedure for the remaining cylinders.

8 Due to the variety of testers available, and the fluctuation in starter motor speed when cranking the engine, different readings are often obtained when carrying out the compression test. For this reason, specific compression pressure figures are not quoted by Volvo. However, the most important factor is that the compression pressures are uniform in all cylinders, and that is what this test is mainly concerned with.

9 If the pressure in any cylinder is considerably lower than the others, introduce a teaspoonful of clean oil into that cylinder through its spark plug hole and repeat the test.

10 If the addition of oil temporarily improves the compression pressure, this indicates that bore or piston wear is responsible for the pressure loss. No improvement suggests that leaking or burnt valves, or a blown head gasket, may be to blame.

11 A low reading from two adjacent cylinders is almost certainly due to the head gasket having blown between them; the presence of coolant in the engine oil will confirm this.

12 If one cylinder is about 20 percent lower than the others and the engine has a slightly rough idle, a worn camshaft lobe or faulty cam follower could be the cause.

13 If the compression is unusually high, the combustion chambers are probably coated

with carbon deposits. If this is the case, the cylinder head should be removed and decarbonised.

14 On completion of the test, refit the spark plugs, then reconnect the crankshaft speed/position sensor, and refit the fuel pump fuse. Note that carrying out this test as described, may result in one or more fault codes being stored by the engine management ECM. Have these codes erased by a Volvo dealer or suitably-equipped specialist.

3 Top Dead Centre (TDC) for No 1 piston – locating

Note: *Only turn the engine in the normal direction of rotation – clockwise from the right-hand side of the vehicle.*

General

1 Top Dead Centre (TDC) is the highest point in its travel up-and-down its cylinder bore that each piston reaches as the crankshaft rotates. While each piston reaches TDC both at the top of the compression stroke and again at the top of the exhaust stroke, for the purpose of timing the engine, TDC refers to the No 1 piston position at the top of its compression stroke.

2 It is useful for several servicing procedures to be able to position the engine at TDC.

3 No 1 piston and cylinder are at the right-hand (timing chain) end of the engine (right- and left-hand are always quoted as seen from the driver's seat).

Locating TDC

4 Remove all the spark plugs, this will make it easier to turn the engine (Chapter 1A).

5 Disconnect the battery negative (earth) lead (refer to Chapter 5A).

6 Apply the handbrake, then jack up the front of the vehicle and support it on axle stands (see *Jacking and vehicle support*). Remove the right-hand front roadwheel.

7 Undo the 2 plastic nuts, and Torx screws, then remove the right-hand front wheel arch liner.

8 There is a timing hole provided on the rear of the cylinder block (behind the TDC sensor) to position the crankshaft at TDC. Using a spanner or socket on the crankshaft pulley bolt, rotate the crankshaft clockwise until it is positioned approximately 45° before TDC **(see illustrations)**. Unscrew the timing hole plug and insert a timing peg (obtainable from Volvo dealers (999 7152) – or a tool supplier).

9 Rotate the crankshaft clockwise until it stops against the timing peg.

10 There is a bolt hole in the crankshaft pulley which should align with the thread in the timing chain cover, insert a bolt (M6 x 18 mm) to locate the pulley at TDC **(see illustration)**.

11 Number 1 and 4 pistons are now at TDC, one of them on the compression stroke. To determine which cylinder is on the compression stroke the cylinder head cover will need to be removed (as described in Section 4).

12 Obtain Volvo service tool 999 7151 or an aftermarket alternative – AST tools part number AST 4404C for example. Alternatively fabricate a substitute from a strip of metal 5 mm thick (while the strip's thickness is critical, its length and width are not, but should be approximately 180 to 230 mm by 20 to 30 mm). If number 1 cylinder is on the compression stroke – rest the tool on the cylinder head mating surface, and slide it into the slot in the left-hand end of both camshafts **(see illustration)**. The tool should slip snugly into both slots while resting on the cylinder head mating surface; if one camshaft is only slightly out of alignment, it is permissible to use an open-ended spanner to rotate the camshaft gently and carefully until the tool will fit.

13 If both camshaft slots (they are machined significantly off-centre) are below the level of the cylinder head mating surface, rotate the

3.10 Insert an M6 bolt though the pulley into the hole in the casing – TDC position

3.12 Slide the tool/metal bar into the slots in the end of the camshafts

4.2 Pull the plastic cover straight upwards to release its mountings

4.3 Disconnect the camshaft position sensor wiring plug

4.7 Undo the retaining screw and lift out the ignition coils (arrowed)

crankshaft through one full turn clockwise and fit the tool again; it should now fit as described in the previous paragraph. **Note:** *The timing peg and crankshaft pulley locking bolt will have to be removed before turning the engine.*

14 Do not use the locked camshafts to prevent the crankshaft from rotating – use only the locking methods described in Section 8 for removing the crankshaft pulley.

15 Once No 1 cylinder has been positioned at TDC on the compression stroke, TDC for any of the other cylinders can then be located by rotating the crankshaft clockwise 180° at a time and following the firing order (see Specifications).

16 Before turning the engine again, make sure that the timing peg and crankshaft pulley locating bolt have been removed.

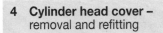

4 Cylinder head cover – removal and refitting

Removal

1 Disconnect the battery negative (earth) lead (refer to Chapter 5A).

2 Remove the plastic cover on the top of the engine by pulling it straight up from its mountings **(see illustration)**.

3 Disconnect the electrical connector from the camshaft position sensor **(see illustration)**.

4 Detach the wiring harness from the cylinder head cover.

5 Disconnect the positive crankcase ventilation (PCV) hose from the left-hand rear corner of the cylinder head cover.

6 Unscrew the three engine upper plastic cover retaining pegs from the cylinder head cover retaining studs, note the position of the retaining studs.

7 Carefully undo the retaining screws and lift out the ignition coils above the spark plugs **(see illustration)**.

8 Working progressively, unscrew the cylinder head cover retaining bolts and withdraw the cover.

9 Discard the cover gasket; this must be renewed whenever it is disturbed. Check that the sealing faces are undamaged, and

4.9 Check the rubber seal on the cylinder head cover retaining bolts for damage

that the rubber seal at each retaining bolt is serviceable **(see illustration)**; renew any worn or damaged seals.

Refitting

10 On refitting, clean the cover and cylinder head gasket faces carefully, then fit a new gaskets to the cover, ensuring that they locate correctly in the cover grooves.

11 Insert the retaining bolts, complete with rubber seals and spacer at each bolt location then refit the cover to the cylinder head **(see illustration)**. Start all bolts finger-tight, ensuring that the gasket remains seated in its groove.

12 Working in the sequence shown **(see illustration)**, tighten the cover bolts to the

4.11 Insert the retaining bolts into the cylinder head cover gasket, ensuring the gasket is correctly located in the groove

specified torque wrench setting. Refit the three engine upper plastic cover retaining pegs to the cover retaining studs noted on removal.

13 The remainder of reassembly is the reverse of the removal procedure. Make sure the HT leads are clipped into place and are correctly routed; each is numbered, and can also be identified by the numbering on its respective coil terminal.

5 Valve clearances – checking and adjustment

Note: *Only turn the engine in the normal direction of rotation – clockwise viewed from the right-hand side of the vehicle.*

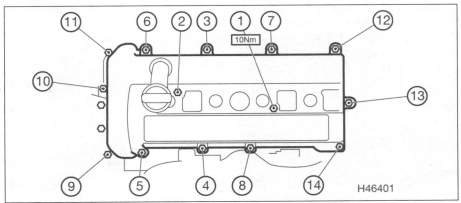

4.12 Cylinder head cover bolt tightening sequence

5.3 Measure the clearance between the base of the cam lobe and the bucket using feeler gauges

5.6 The tappet bucket has a number engraved on the inside

Checking

1 Remove the cylinder head cover as described in Section 4.

2 Set the engine to TDC on cylinder No 1 as described in Section 3. The inlet and exhaust cam lobes of No 1 cylinder will be pointing upwards (though not vertical) and the valve clearances can be checked.

3 Working on each valve, measure the clearance between the base of the cam lobe and the bucket tappet using feeler blades **(see illustration)**. Record the thickness of the blade required to give a firm sliding fit on all the valves of No 1 cylinder. The desired clearances are given in the Specifications. Note that the clearances for inlet and exhaust valves are different. The intake camshaft is at the front of the engine and the exhaust camshaft at the rear. Record all four clearances.

4 Now turn the crankshaft clockwise through 180° so that the valves of cylinder No 3 are pointing upwards. Check and record the four valve clearances for cylinder No 3. The clearances for cylinders 4 and 2 can be checked after turning the crankshaft through 180° each time.

Adjustment

5 If adjustment is required, the bucket tappets must be changed by removing the camshafts as described in Section 9.

6 If the valve clearance was too small, a thinner bucket tappet must be fitted. If the clearance was too large, a thicker bucket tappet must be fitted. The bucket tappet

has a number engraved on the inside **(see illustration)**, if the marking is missing or illegible, a micrometer will be needed to establish bucket tappet thickness.

7 When the bucket tappet thickness and the valve clearance are known, the required thickness of the new bucket tappet can be calculated as follows:

Sample calculation – clearance too small

Desired clearance (A)	= 0.25 mm
Measured clearance (B)	= 0.20 mm
Tappet thickness found (C)	= 2.55 mm
Thickness required (D)	= C + B – A
	= 2.50 mm

Sample calculation – clearance too large

Desired clearance (A)	= 0.30 mm
Measured clearance (B)	= 0.36 mm
Tappet thickness found (C)	= 2.19 mm
Thickness required (D)	= C + B – A
	= 2.25 mm

8 With the correct thickness bucket tappets fitted in the cylinder head, refit the camshafts as described in Section 9.

9 Check the valve clearances are now correct, as described in paragraphs 2 to 4. If any clearances are still not within specification then carry out the adjustment procedure again.

10 It will be helpful for future adjustment if a record is kept of the thickness of bucket fitted at each position. The buckets required can be purchased in advance once the clearances and the existing bucket thicknesses are known.

11 When all the clearances are correct, refit the cylinder head cover as described in Section 4.

6.3 Using a flywheel locking tool to prevent the flywheel from rotating

6.6 A new retaining bolt must be fitted

6 Crankshaft pulley – removal and refitting

Note: *Only turn the engine in the normal direction of rotation – clockwise from the right-hand side of the vehicle.*
Caution: The pulley and crankshaft timing gear are not on a keyway, they are held in place by the crankshaft retaining bolt. Make sure the engine is set at TDC (see Section 3) before the pulley is removed.
Note: *The crankshaft pulley retaining bolt is very tight and Volvo use a special tool (999 7128 or aftermarket equivalent) to lock the pulley to prevent it from turning. A new pulley retaining bolt will be required on refitting.*

Removal

1 Remove the auxiliary drivebelts – either remove the drivebelts completely, or just secure them clear of the crankshaft pulley, depending on the work to be carried out (see Chapter 1A).

2 Set the engine to TDC (see Section 3).

3 The crankshaft must now be locked to prevent its rotation while the pulley bolt is unscrewed. If the Volvo Special tool is not available proceed as follows:

a) Remove the rubber plug from the transmission bellhousing and use a large screwdriver or similar to lock the flywheel ring gear teeth while an assistant slackens the pulley bolt; take care not to damage the teeth or the surrounding castings when using this method.

b) If the engine/transmission has been removed and separated, lock the flywheel using a locking tool **(see illustration)**.

4 Unscrew the pulley bolt and remove the pulley.

Refitting

5 Refitting is the reverse of the removal procedure; making sure the engine has not moved from its setting at TDC (see Section 3).

6 Ensure that a new retaining bolt is used **(see illustration)**, and tightened to the torque specified at the beginning of this Chapter.

7 Timing chain cover – removal and refitting

Note: *Only turn the engine in the normal direction of rotation – clockwise from the right-hand side of the vehicle.*

Removal

1 Remove the cylinder head cover as described in Section 4.

2 Apply the handbrake, then jack up the front of the vehicle and support it on axle stands

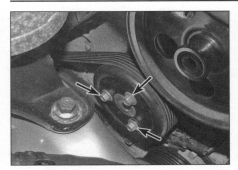

7.3 Slacken the 3 retaining bolts (arrowed)

7.5 Compressor protective cover retaining bolts (arrowed)

7.7 Disconnect the crankshaft position sensor wiring plug

(see *Jacking and vehicle support*). Remove the right-hand front roadwheel and remove the cover from under the right-hand front wheel arch.

3 Slacken the water pump pulley retaining bolts by approximately three turns **(see illustration)**.

4 Remove the auxiliary drivebelts (Chapter 1A).

5 Undo the screws securing the protective cover over the air conditioning compressor, and remove the cover. Disconnect the wiring plug, then undo the compressor mounting bolts, and the refrigerant pipe bracket bolt, and move the compressor to one side **(see illustration)**. Suspend the compressor using wire or a strap, from the vehicle bodywork/suspension. Note there is no need to disconnect any refrigerant pipes.

6 Remove the crankshaft pulley (Section 6).

7 Disconnect the crankshaft position (CKP) sensor wiring connector **(see illustration)**.

8 Unscrew the retaining bolts and remove the water pump pulley.

9 Detach the wiring harness from the studs on the lower edge of the timing chain cover.

10 Lift the coolant expansion tank from its mountings and move it to one side. If better access is required, drain sufficient coolant (see Chapter 1A), then disconnect the lower coolant hose from the expansion tank.

11 Support the engine using a trolley jack and block of wood beneath the sump, then unscrew the nuts/bolts securing the engine/transmission right-hand mounting bracket and

remove the mounting from the engine **(see illustration)**. Unclip the air conditioning pipe as the mounting is removed.

12 Remove the auxiliary drivebelt tensioner lower screw.

13 Unscrew the timing chain cover retaining bolts (noting their positions for refitting) and withdraw the cover from the engine.

Refitting

14 Refitting is the reverse of the removal procedure (using the relevant Sections); note the following points:

a) Clean the sealant from the timing cover, cylinder block and cylinder head mating surfaces. When using a scraper and solvent to remove all traces of old gasket/sealant from the mating surfaces, be careful to ensure that you do not scratch or damage the material of either component – any solvents used must be suitable for this application. If the gasket was leaking, have the mating surfaces checked for warpage at an automotive engineering workshop.

b) Renew the crankshaft front oil seal fitted into the timing chain cover as described in Section 10.

c) Ensure the drive shim is still fitted to the end of the crankshaft before the timing chain cover oil seal is fitted is refitted **(see illustration)**.

d) Provided the relevant mating surfaces are clean and flat, apply a (3.0mm) bead of silicone sealant around the timing

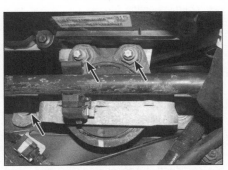

7.11 Undo the right-hand mounting bolts/nuts (arrowed)

chain cover and the inner bolt holes **(see illustration)**. **Note:** The cover must be fitted within 10 minutes of applying the sealant.

e) Tighten the timing chain cover bolts to the specified torque settings at the beginning of this Chapter, following the sequence shown **(see illustration)**.

7.14a Ensure the crankshaft pulley drive shim (arrowed) is fitted before fitting the new oil seal

7.14b Apply a 3.0 mm bead of sealant around the timing chain cover, including the inner bolt holes

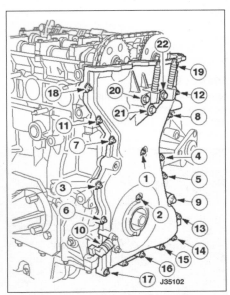

7.14c Timing chain cover bolt tightening sequence

8 Timing chain, tensioner and guides – removal, inspection and refitting

Note: *Only turn the engine in the normal direction of rotation – clockwise from the right-hand side of the vehicle.*

Removal

1 Remove the cylinder head cover as described in Section 4.

2 Set the engine to TDC as described in Section 3.

3 Remove the timing chain cover as described in Section 7.

4 Slacken the timing chain tensioner by inserting a small screwdriver into the access hole in the tensioner and releasing the pawl mechanism. Press against the timing chain guide to depress the piston into the tensioner housing, when fully depressed, insert a locking pin (approximately 1.5 mm) to lock the piston in its compressed position **(see illustration)**.

5 Hold the camshafts by the hexagon sections on the shafts to prevent them from turning, using an open-ended spanner.

6 With the camshafts held in position, undo the camshaft sprocket retaining bolts and remove the camshaft sprockets and timing chain. Do not rotate the crankshaft until the timing chain is refitted **(see illustration)**.

7 If required, unbolt the fixed timing chain guide and withdraw the tensioner timing chain guide from its pivot pin on the cylinder head **(see illustrations)**.

8 To remove the tensioner, undo the two retaining bolts and remove the timing chain tensioner from the cylinder block, taking care not to remove the locking pin **(see illustration)**.

9 To remove the timing chain sprocket from the crankshaft, the oil pump drive chain will need to be removed as described in Section 13 of this Chapter. Note which way round it is fitted and mark the sprocket to ensure it is refitted the same way round.

Inspection

Note: *Keep all components identified for position to ensure correct refitting.*

10 Clean all components thoroughly and wipe dry.

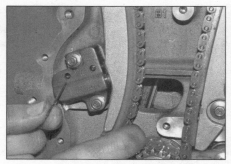

8.4 Press against the timing chain guide and insert a locking pin (approximately 1.5 mm)

8.7a Withdraw the tensioner guide from the pivot pin . . .

11 Examine the chain tensioner and tensioner guide for excessive wear or other damage. Check the guides for deep grooves made by the timing chain. Renew them both if there is any doubt concerning their condition.

12 Examine the timing chain for excessive wear. Hold it horizontally and check how much movement exists in the chain links. If there is any doubt, compare it to a new chain. Renew as necessary.

13 Examine the teeth of the camshaft and crankshaft sprockets for excessive wear and damage.

14 Before refitting the timing chain tensioner, the piston must be compressed and locked until refitted (if not already done on removal). To do this, insert a small screwdriver into the access hole in the tensioner and release the pawl mechanism. Now lightly clamp the tensioner in a soft-jawed vice and slowly compress the piston. Do not apply excessive

8.6 Use a spanner to hold the camshafts whilst undoing the retaining bolts

8.7b . . . then undo the retaining bolts (arrowed) and remove the fixed guide

force and make sure that the piston remains aligned with its cylinder. When completely compressed, insert a locking pin/1.5 mm diameter wire rod into the special hole to lock the piston in its compressed position.

Refitting

15 If not already fitted, slide the crankshaft drive sprocket (and drive shim) onto the crankshaft. Ensure it is refitted the same way round as noted on removal (see Section 13 for further information on refitting the oil pump drive chain).

16 Refit the tensioner to the cylinder block and tighten the retaining bolts to the specified torque setting. Take care not to remove the locking pin **(see illustration)**.

17 Refit the fixed timing chain guide and tighten the two retaining bolts, then slide the tensioner timing chain guide back into place on the upper pivot pin **(see illustration)**.

8.8 Timing chain tensioner bolts (arrowed)

8.16 Refit the timing chain tensioner (still in the locked position)

8.17 Refit the tensioner guides to the engine

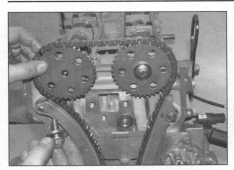

8.19 Refit the camshaft sprockets into position, complete with timing chain

8.20 Press against the tensioner guide and withdraw the locking pin (arrowed)

8.22 Use a spanner on the camshaft hexagon section to prevent them from rotating

18 Refit the intake camshaft sprocket onto the camshaft, DO NOT tighten the retaining bolt at this stage.

19 With the timing chain around the exhaust camshaft sprocket refit the timing chain and sprocket, feeding the timing chain around the crankshaft drive sprocket and intake camshaft sprocket **(see illustration)**.

20 With the timing chain in place, press against the tensioner guide and withdraw the tensioner locking pin. This will then tension the timing chain **(see illustration)**.

21 Check that the engine is still set to TDC (as described in Section 3).

22 Tighten the both camshaft retaining bolts to the torque setting specified in the Specifications at the beginning of this Chapter. **Note:** Use an open-ended spanner on the hexagon on the camshafts to stop them from turning **(see illustration)**.

23 Refit the timing chain cover as described in Section 7.

24 Remove the camshaft locking plate and crankshaft timing peg, and turn the engine (in the direction of engine rotation) two full turns. Refit the camshaft locking plate and crankshaft timing peg to make sure the engine is still set at TDC (see Section 3 for further information).

25 Refit the cylinder head cover as described in Section 4.

9 Camshafts and tappets – removal, inspection and refitting

Note: *Only turn the engine in the normal direction of rotation – clockwise from the right-hand side of the vehicle.*

Removal

1 Remove the cylinder head cover as described in Section 4.

2 Set the engine to TDC on No 1 cylinder as described in Section 3.

3 Remove the timing chain cover lower and upper blanking plugs, to gain access to the timing chain tensioner and guide **(see illustrations)**.

4 Slacken the timing chain tensioner by

inserting a small screwdriver into the lower access hole in the timing chain cover and releasing the pawl mechanism in the tensioner **(see illustration)**.

5 Carefully turn the exhaust camshaft (by using an open-ended spanner on the hexagon on the shaft) in the normal direction of rotation (clockwise), to compress the timing chain tensioner **(see illustration)**.

6 Holding the exhaust camshaft in position, insert a bolt (M6 x 25 mm) into the upper access hole in the timing chain cover to lock the tensioner guide rail in position **(see illustration)**.

7 With the camshafts held in position (by using an open-ended spanner on the hexagon section on the shaft), slacken the camshaft sprocket retaining bolts.

8 Using a cable tie or similar, fasten the timing chain to the camshaft sprockets.

9.3a Remove the timing chain cover lower . . .

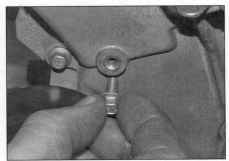

9.3b . . . and upper blanking plugs

9.4 Insert a small screwdriver into the lower access hole to release the timing chain tensioner

9.5 Carefully turn the exhaust camshaft in the direction of the arrow to slacken the timing chain tensioner

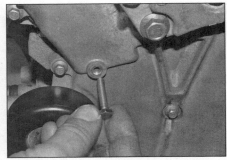

9.6 Whilst holding the exhaust camshaft in position, insert a bolt (M6 x 18 mm) to lock the tensioner guide rail

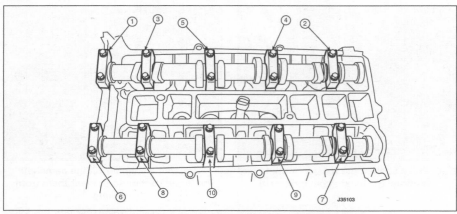

9.10 Sequence for slackening the camshaft bearing cap bolts

9.11a Note the identification markings (arrowed) on the camshaft bearing caps . . .

9.11b . . . and the reference lobe (arrowed) on the intake camshaft for the position sensor

9.12a Remove the tappet bucket with a rubber sucker

9.12b Note the thickness number on the underside of the tappet bucket

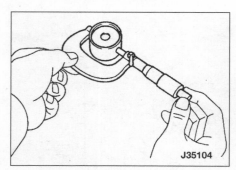

9.14 Use a micrometer to measure the diameter of the tappets

9.15 Check the cam lobes for pitting, wear and score marks – if necessary, renew the camshaft

9 Remove the camshaft sprocket retaining bolts and remove the sprockets, complete with timing chain, away from the camshafts. Using a suitable piece of wire secure the sprockets and timing chain to prevent them dropping into the timing cover.

10 Working in the sequence shown (see illustration), slacken the camshaft bearing cap bolts progressively by half a turn at a time. Work only as described, gradually and evenly release the pressure of the valve springs on the caps.

11 Withdraw the camshaft bearing caps, noting their markings, then remove the camshafts. The intake camshaft can be identified by the reference lobe for the camshaft position sensor; therefore, there is no need to mark the camshafts (see illustrations).

12 Obtain sixteen small, clean containers, and number them 1 to 16. Using a rubber sucker, withdraw each bucket tappet in turn and place them in the containers. Do not interchange the bucket tappets as they are of different sizes; the shim is part of the bucket tappet (see illustrations). Different sizes of bucket tappets are available in the event of wear on the valves or repair on the cylinder head assembly.

Inspection

13 With the camshafts and tappets removed, check each for signs of obvious wear (scoring, pitting, etc) and for ovality, and renew if necessary.

14 Measure the outside diameter of each tappet (see illustration) – take measurements at the top and bottom of each tappet, then a second set at right-angles to the first; if any measurement is significantly different from the others, the tappet is tapered or oval (as applicable) and must be renewed. If the necessary equipment is available, measure the inside diameter of the corresponding cylinder head bore. If the tappets or the cylinder head bores are excessively worn, new tappets and/or a new cylinder head will be required.

15 Visually examine the camshaft lobes for score marks, pitting, galling (wear due to rubbing) and evidence of overheating (blue, discoloured areas). Look for flaking away of the hardened surface layer of each lobe (see illustration). If any such signs are evident, renew the component concerned.

16 Examine the camshaft bearing journals and the cylinder head bearing surfaces for signs of obvious wear or pitting. If any such signs are evident, renew the component concerned.

17 Using a micrometer, measure the diameter of each journal at several points (see illustration). If any measurement is significantly different from the others, renew the camshaft.

18 To check camshaft endfloat, remove the tappets, clean the bearing surfaces carefully, and refit the camshafts and bearing caps. Tighten the bearing cap bolts to the specified

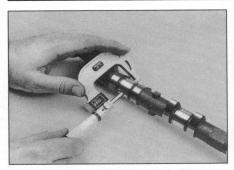

9.17 Measure each journal with a micrometer

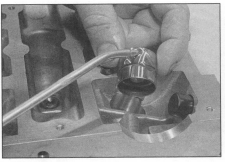

9.20 Liberally oil the tappets when refitting

9.22 Apply clean engine oil to the cam lobes and journals

torque wrench setting, then measure the endfloat using a DTI (Dial Test Indicator, or dial gauge) mounted on the cylinder head so that its tip bears on the camshaft right-hand end.

19 Tap the camshaft fully towards the gauge, zero the gauge, then tap the camshaft fully away from the gauge, and note the gauge reading. If the endfloat measured is found to be at or beyond the specified service limit, fit a new camshaft and repeat the check; if the clearance is still excessive, the cylinder head must be renewed.

Refitting

20 On reassembly, liberally oil the cylinder head tappet bores and the tappets **(see illustration)**. Carefully refit the tappets to the cylinder head, ensuring that each tappet is refitted to its original bore. Some care will be required to enter the tappets squarely into their bores.

21 Turn the engine back approximately 45° so that there are no pistons at the top of the cylinders.

22 Liberally oil the camshaft bearings and lobes **(see illustration)**. Ensuring that each camshaft is in its original location, refit the camshafts, locating each so that the slot in its left-hand end is approximately parallel to, and just above, the cylinder head mating surface.

23 All camshaft bearing caps have an identifying number and letter etched on

them. The exhaust camshaft's bearing caps are numbered in sequence E1 to E5 and the inlet camshaft's bearing caps I1 to I5 **(see illustration 9.11a)**.

24 Ensuring that each cap is kept square to the cylinder head as it is tightened down, and working in sequence **(see illustration)**, tighten the camshaft bearing cap bolts slowly and by one turn at a time, until each cap touches the cylinder head. Next, go round again in the same sequence, tightening the bolts to the first stage torque wrench setting specified, then once more, tightening them to the second stage setting. Work only as described, to gradually and evenly impose the pressure of the valve springs on the caps.

25 Fit the camshaft aligning tool; it should slip into place as described in Section 3 **(see illustration)**.

26 Refit the camshaft sprockets, complete with timing chain to the ends of the camshafts. DO NOT tighten the camshaft sprocket retaining bolts at this stage. Remove the cable ties from the timing chain and camshaft sprockets.

27 Remove the tensioner guide rail locking bolt from the upper access hole in the timing chain cover. It may be necessary to hold some pressure against the tensioner guide rail to remove the locking bolt.

28 Turn the engine (in the direction of rotation) approximately 45° to TDC. For further

information on setting the engine to TDC, see Section 3.

29 With the camshafts held in position (by using an open-ended spanner on the hexagon on the shaft), tighten the camshaft sprocket retaining bolts to the specified torque.

30 Remove the camshaft locking plate and crankshaft timing peg and turn the engine (in the direction of engine rotation) two full turns. Refit the camshaft locking plate and crankshaft timing peg to make sure the engine is still set at TDC (see Section 3 for further information).

31 Refit the timing chain cover upper and lower blanking plugs, coat the blanking plug threads with a suitable sealant to prevent leaks.

32 Refit the cylinder head cover as described in Section 4.

10 Crankshaft oil seals – renewal

Timing chain end oil seal

1 Remove the crankshaft pulley as described in Section 6 of this Chapter.

2 Using a screwdriver, prise the old oil seal from the timing cover. Take care not to damage the surface of the timing cover and

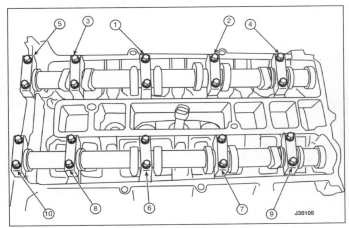

9.24 Camshaft bearing cap bolts tightening sequence

9.25 Fit the camshaft aligning tool to set TDC position

10.4a Ensure the oil seal remains square as it is being fitted

10.4b A socket of the correct size can be used for fitting the new seal

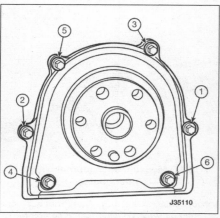

10.13 Oil seal carrier retaining bolts tightening sequence

crankshaft. If the oil seal is tight, carefully drill two holes diagonally opposite each other in the oil seal, then insert self-tapping screws and use a pair of pliers to pull out the oil seal.

3 Wipe clean the seating in the timing cover and the nose of the crankshaft.

4 Smear clean engine oil on the outer periphery and sealing lips of the new oil seal, then start it into the timing cover by pressing it in squarely. Using a large socket or metal tubing, drive in the oil seal until flush with the outer surface of the timing cover. Make sure the oil seal remains square as it is being inserted. Wipe off any excess oil **(see illustrations)**.

5 Refit the crankshaft pulley as described in Section 6 of this Chapter.

Transmission end oil seal

Note: *The oil seal can only be renewed as a complete unit with the carrier.*

6 Remove the transmission (see Chapter 7A or 7B).

7 Remove the clutch assembly (see Chapter 6).

8 Unbolt the flywheel (Section 15).

9 Remove the sump (see Section 12).

10 Undo the six retaining bolts and remove the oil seal carrier from the cylinder block. Where applicable, remove and discard its gasket.

11 Clean the seal housing and crankshaft, polishing off any burrs or raised edges which may have caused the seal to fail in the first place. Where applicable, clean also the mating surfaces of the cylinder block/crankcase, using a scraper to remove all traces of the

old gasket/sealant – be careful not to scratch or damage the material of either – then use a suitable solvent to degrease them.

12 Use a special sleeve to slide the seal over the crankshaft, if this is not available, make up a guide from a thin sheet of plastic or similar, lubricate the lips of the new seal and the crankshaft shoulder with oil, then offer up the oil seal carrier, with the guide feeding the seal's lips over the crankshaft shoulder.

13 Being careful not to damage the oil seal, move the carrier into the correct position, aligning the guide pins, and tighten its bolts in the correct sequence to the specified torque wrench setting **(see illustration)**.

14 Wipe off any surplus oil or grease; the remainder of the reassembly procedure is the reverse of dismantling, referring to the relevant text for details where required. Check for signs of oil leakage when the engine is restarted.

11 Cylinder head – removal and refitting

Note: *Only turn the engine in the normal direction of rotation – clockwise from the right-hand side of the vehicle.*

Removal

1 Remove the battery as described in Chapter 5A, then remove the lower section of the battery box.

2 Whenever you disconnect any vacuum lines, coolant and emissions hoses, wiring

loom connectors, earth straps and fuel lines as part of the following procedure, always label them clearly, so that they can be correctly reassembled.

3 Drain the cooling system as described in Chapter 1A.

4 Remove the air cleaner assembly as described in Chapter 4A.

5 Remove the exhaust manifold and heat shields as described in Chapter 4A.

6 Place rags around the pipes, then depress the locking tab and disconnect the fuel feed pipe from the fuel rail.

7 Undo the two screws and remove the fuel rail. Plug the openings to prevent dirt ingress. Refer to Chapter 4A for more information.

8 Remove the intake manifold as described in Chapter 4A.

9 Note their fitted locations, then disconnect the various wiring plugs from the components on the cylinder head, and release any relevant wiring loom from any retaining clips.

10 Undo the four bolts and detach the coolant housing from the left-hand end of the cylinder head **(see illustration)**.

11 Undo the two bolts securing the EGR valve. Discard the gasket **(see illustration)**.

12 Remove the cylinder head cover as described in Section 4.

13 Remove the timing chain as described in Section 8.

14 Remove the camshafts and tappets as described in Section 9.

15 Make a final check to ensure that all relevant coolant/vacuum hoses and wiring connectors have been disconnected.

16 Working in sequence **(see illustration)**, slacken the ten cylinder head bolts progressively and by one turn at a time. Remove each bolt in turn, and ensure that new ones are obtained for reassembly; these bolts are subjected to severe stresses and so must be renewed, regardless of their apparent condition, whenever they are disturbed.

17 Lift the cylinder head away; use assistance if possible, as it is a heavy assembly. Remove the gasket and discard it, note the position of the dowels.

11.10 Remove the coolant outlet housing from the left-hand end of the cylinder head

11.11 Remove the EGR valve from the left-hand end of the cylinder head

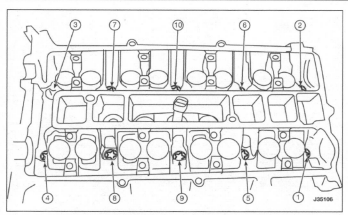

11.16 Cylinder head bolt slackening sequence

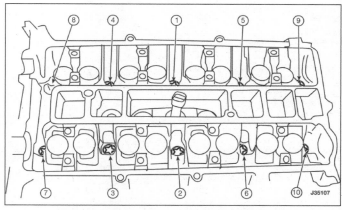

11.25a Cylinder head bolt tightening sequence

Refitting

18 The mating faces of the cylinder head and cylinder block must be perfectly clean before refitting the head. Use a hard plastic or wood scraper to remove all traces of gasket and carbon; also clean the piston crowns. Take particular care, as the soft aluminium alloy is easily damaged. Also, make sure that the carbon is not allowed to enter the oil and water passages – this is particularly important for the lubrication system, as carbon could block the oil supply to any of the engine's components. Using adhesive tape and paper, seal the water, oil and bolt holes in the cylinder block. Clean all the pistons in the same way.

19 Check the mating surfaces of the cylinder block and the cylinder head for nicks, deep scratches and other damage. If excessive, machining may be the only alternative to renewal.

20 If warpage of the cylinder head gasket surface is suspected, use a straight-edge to check it for distortion. Refer to Chapter 2, Part F, Section 5, if necessary.

21 Wipe clean the mating surfaces of the cylinder head and cylinder block. Check that the locating dowels are in position in the cylinder block, and that all cylinder head bolt holes are free from oil.

22 Position a new gasket over the dowels on the cylinder block surface, making sure it is fitted the correct way around.

23 Rotate the crankshaft anti-clockwise so that No 1 cylinder's piston is lowered to approximately 20 mm before TDC, thus avoiding any risk of valve/piston contact and damage during reassembly.

24 Refit the cylinder head, locating it on the dowels. Lubricate the threads, then fit the new cylinder head bolts; carefully enter each into its hole and screw it in, by hand only, until finger-tight.

25 Working progressively and in sequence, use first a torque wrench, then an ordinary socket extension bar and an angle gauge to tighten the cylinder head bolts **(see illustrations)**. This is completed in stages given in the Specifications Section at the beginning of this Chapter. **Note:** *Once tightened correctly, following this procedure, the cylinder head bolts do not require check-tightening, and must not be re-torqued.*

26 Refit the tappets, the camshafts, and the timing chain as described in Sections 8 and 9.

27 The remainder of reassembly is the reverse of the removal procedure, noting the following points:

a) *See the refitting procedures in the relevant Sections and tighten all nuts and bolts to the torque wrench settings specified.*

b) *Refill the cooling system, and top-up the engine oil.*

c) *Check all disturbed joints for signs of oil or coolant leakage, once the engine has been restarted and warmed-up to normal operating temperature.*

12 Sump – removal and refitting

Note: *To carry out this task with the engine/ transmission installed in the vehicle it requires the assistance of at least one person, plus the equipment necessary to raise and support the front of the vehicle (high enough that the sump can be withdrawn from underneath). It will also need a support bar across the top of the engine bay to hold the complete engine/ transmission unit in place while the vehicle is raised. Precise details of the procedure will depend on the equipment available – the following is typical.*

Removal

1 Apply the handbrake, then jack up the front of the vehicle and support it on axle stands (see *Jacking and vehicle support*).

2 Drain the engine oil, then clean and refit the engine oil drain plug, tightening it to the specified torque wrench setting. **Note:** *If the drain plug seal is damaged, a new drain plug will be required.* Although not strictly necessary as part of the dismantling procedure, owners are advised to remove and discard the oil filter, so that it can be renewed with the oil (see Chapter 1A).

3 Support the engine with a cross-beam or hoist.

4 Remove the timing chain cover as described in Section 7.

5 Unscrew and remove the sump-to-transmission bolts **(see illustration)**.

6 Progressively unscrew the sump retaining bolts. Use a scraper to break the sealant around the sump, taking care not to damage the mating surfaces of the sump and cylinder block. Lower the sump and withdraw it with the engine/transmission.

Refitting

7 On reassembly, thoroughly clean and degrease the mating surfaces of the cylinder block/crankcase and sump, then use a clean rag to wipe out the sump.

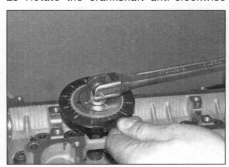

11.25b Use an angle-gauge for the final stages

12.5 Remove the bolts

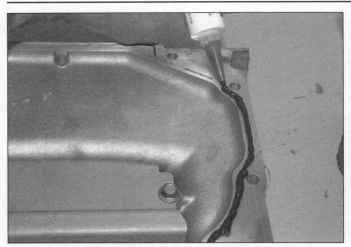

12.8 Apply a 3.0 mm bead of sealant to the sump flange

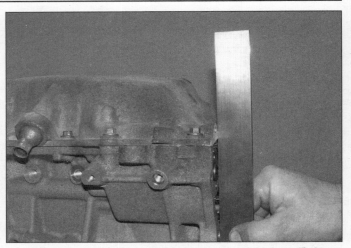

12.10a Use a straight-edge to align the sump to the cylinder block

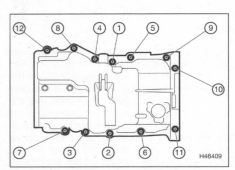

12.10b Sump bolt tightening sequence

8 Apply a 3.0 mm bead of sealant to the sump flange so that the bead is around the inside edge of the bolt holes **(see illustration)**. **Note:** *The sump must be refitted within 10 minutes of applying the sealant.*
9 Offer up the sump and insert the retaining bolts, do not tighten them at this stage.
10 Using a straight-edge, align the sump to the cylinder block on the timing chain end. With the sump held in position, progressively tighten the retaining bolts to the specified torque in sequence **(see illustrations)**.
11 Refit the sump bolts and tighten them to the specified torque.
12 Refit the timing chain cover as described in Section 7.
13 Lower the car to the ground and refill the engine with oil (and fit new oil filter) and the cooling system with coolant (see Chapter 1A).
14 Check for signs of oil or coolant leaks once the engine has been restarted and warmed-up to normal operating temperature.

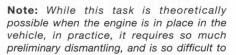

13 Oil pump –
removal, inspection and refitting

Note: *While this task is theoretically possible when the engine is in place in the vehicle, in practice, it requires so much preliminary dismantling, and is so difficult to* carry out due to the restricted access, that owners are advised to remove the engine from the vehicle first. All the illustrations used in this Section are with the engine out of the vehicle and the engine upside down on a work bench.
Note: *In addition to the new pump gasket and other parts required, read through this Section, and ensure that the necessary tools and facilities are available.*

Removal

1 Remove the timing chain as described in Section 8.
2 Remove the sump as described in Section 12.
3 Undo the two bolts securing the oil pump pick-up pipe to the pump **(see illustration)**. Discard the O-ring/gasket.
4 Undo the two retaining bolts and remove the oil pump chain guide, then undo the retaining bolt and remove the oil pump chain tensioner **(see illustration)**.

13.3 Remove the oil pump pick-up pipe retaining bolts

13.4 Oil pump check guide and tensioner retaining bolts (arrowed)

13.5 Hold the oil pump sprocket whilst undoing the sprocket bolt

13.7 Undo the 4 retaining bolts (arrowed) and remove the oil pump

5 Hold the oil pump drive sprocket to prevent it from turning and slacken the sprocket retaining bolt (see illustration).

6 Undo the bolt and remove the oil pump sprocket complete with the oil pump drive chain.

7 Unbolt the pump from the cylinder block/crankcase (see illustration). Withdraw and discard the gasket.

Inspection

8 At the time of writing there were no parts for the pump, if there is any doubt in the operation of the oil pump, then the complete pump assembly should be renewed.

Refitting

9 Thoroughly clean and degrease all components, particularly the mating surfaces of the pump, the sump, and the cylinder block/

crankcase. When using a scraper and solvent to remove all traces of old gasket/sealant from the mating surfaces, be careful to ensure that you do not scratch or damage the material of either component – any solvents used must be suitable for this application.

10 The oil pump must be primed on installation, by pouring clean engine oil into it and rotating its inner rotor a few turns.

11 Fit the new gasket in place on the oil pump using one of the retaining bolts to locate it, refit the pump to the cylinder block/crankcase and insert the retaining bolts, tightening them to the specified torque wrench setting (see illustration).

12 Fit the new O-ring/gasket in place and refit the pump pick-up pipe to the pump, tightening its retaining bolts securely (see illustration).

13 Refit the oil pump drive chain complete with oil pump sprocket (see illustration) and tighten the retaining bolt to the specified torque setting. Hold the oil pump drive

13.11 Use one of the retaining bolts to locate the new gasket in place on the oil pump

sprocket (using the same method as removal) to prevent it from turning when tightening the sprocket retaining bolt.

14 Refit the oil pump chain tensioner to the cylinder block, making sure the spring is

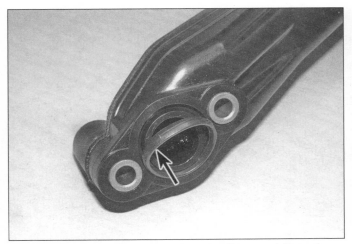

13.12 Fit a new O-ring (arrowed) to the oil pump pick-up pipe

13.13 Align the flats (arrowed) on the oil pump driveshaft and oil pump sprocket when refitting

13.14 Ensure the spring on the tensioner is hooked behind the bolt (arrowed) to tension the chain

14.1 Oil pressure warning light switch (arrowed)

located correctly **(see illustration)**. Tighten the retaining bolt to its specified torque setting.

15 Refit the oil pump chain guide to the cylinder block, tightening the two retaining bolts to their specified torque setting.

16 Refit the timing chain as described in Section 8.

17 Refit the sump as described in Section 12.

14 Oil pressure warning light switch – removal and refitting

Removal

1 The switch is screwed into the oil filter housing on the front of the cylinder block **(see illustration)**.

2 With the vehicle parked on firm level ground, open the bonnet and disconnect the battery negative (earth) lead as described in Chapter 5A.

3 If required, raise the front of the vehicle, and support it securely on axle stands, this will give better access to the switch. Where fitted, undo the 7 Torx screws and remove the engine undershield **(see illustration)**.

4 Disconnect the wiring connector from the switch, and unscrew it; be prepared for some oil loss.

Refitting

5 Refitting is the reverse of the removal procedure; apply a thin smear of suitable sealant to the switch threads, and tighten it to the specified torque wrench setting.

6 Check the engine oil level, and top-up as necessary (see *Weekly checks*). Check for signs of oil leaks once the engine has been restarted and warmed-up to normal operating temperature.

15 Flywheel – removal, inspection and refitting

Removal

1 Remove the transmission (see Chapter 7A). Now is a good time to check components such as oil seals and renew them if necessary.

2 Remove the clutch (Chapter 6). Now is a good time to check or renew the clutch components.

3 Use a centre-punch or paint to make alignment marks on the flywheel and crankshaft to ensure correct alignment during refitting.

4 Prevent the flywheel from turning by locking the ring gear teeth, or by bolting a strap between the flywheel and the cylinder block/crankcase **(see illustration)**. Slacken the bolts evenly until all are free.

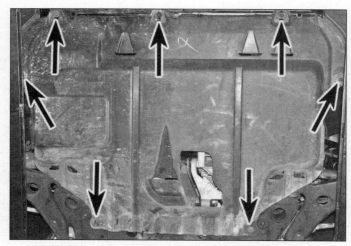

14.3 Undo the 7 Torx screws (arrowed) and remove the engine undershield – where fitted

15.4 Lock the flywheel whilst the bolts (arrowed) are removed

15.10 Apply suitable locking fluid to the threads of the new bolts on fitting

15.11 Tighten the new bolts, using method used on dismantling for locking the flywheel

5 Remove each bolt in turn, and ensure that new ones are obtained for reassembly; these bolts are subjected to severe stresses, and so must be renewed, regardless of their apparent condition, whenever they are disturbed.

6 Withdraw the flywheel from the end of the crankshaft. **Note:** *Take care when removing the flywheel as it is a very heavy component.*

Inspection

7 Clean the flywheel to remove grease and oil. Inspect the surface for cracks, rivet grooves, burned areas and score marks. Light scoring can be removed with emery cloth. Check for cracked and broken ring gear teeth. Lay the flywheel on a flat surface, and use a straight-edge to check for warpage.

8 Clean and inspect the mating surfaces of the flywheel and the crankshaft. If the crankshaft left-hand oil seal is leaking, renew it (see Section 10) before refitting the flywheel.

9 While the flywheel is removed, clean carefully its inboard (right-hand) face. Thoroughly clean the threaded bolt holes in the crankshaft – this is important, since if old sealer remains in the threads, the bolts will settle over a period and will not retain their correct torque wrench settings.

Refitting

10 On refitting, fit the flywheel to the crankshaft so that all bolt holes align – it will fit only one way – check this using the marks made on removal. Apply suitable sealer to the threads of the new bolts then insert them **(see illustration)**.

11 Lock the flywheel by the method used on dismantling. Working in a diagonal sequence to tighten them evenly, and increasing to the final amount in three stages, tighten the new bolts to the specified torque wrench setting **(see illustration)**.

12 The remainder of reassembly is the reverse of the removal procedure, referring to the relevant text for details where required.

16 Engine/transmission mountings – inspection and renewal

General

1 The engine/transmission mountings seldom require attention, but broken or deteriorated mountings should be renewed immediately, or the added strain placed on the driveline components may cause damage or wear.

2 While separate mountings may be removed and refitted individually, if more than one is disturbed at a time – such as if the engine/transmission unit is removed from its mountings – they must be reassembled and their fasteners tightened in the position marked on removal.

3 On reassembly, the complete weight of the engine/transmission unit must not be taken by the mountings until all are correctly aligned with the marks made on removal. Tighten the engine/transmission mounting fasteners to their specified torque wrench settings.

Inspection

4 During the check, the engine/transmission unit must be raised slightly, to remove its weight from the mountings.

5 Raise the front of the vehicle, and support it securely on axle stands. Position a jack under the sump, with a large block of wood between the jack head and the sump, then carefully raise the engine/transmission just enough to take the weight off the mountings.

 Warning: DO NOT place any part of your body under the engine when it is supported only by a jack.

6 Check the mountings to see if the rubber is cracked, hardened or separated from the metal components. Sometimes the rubber will split right down the centre.

7 Check for relative movement between

each mounting's brackets and the engine/transmission or body (use a large screwdriver or lever to attempt to move the mountings). If movement is noted, lower the engine and check-tighten the mounting fasteners.

Renewal

Note: *The following paragraphs assume the engine is supported beneath the sump as described earlier.*

Right-hand mounting

8 Pull the plastic cover on the top of the engine upwards from its mountings.

9 Lift up the coolant expansion tank and position it to one side. Note there is no need to disconnect the coolant pipes.

10 Mark the position of the mounting on the vehicle, right-hand inner wing panel, then unclip the refrigerant pipe from the clip on the mounting.

11 With the engine/transmission supported, unscrew the two locking nuts from the engine casing, then undo the two retaining bolts to the vehicle inner wing panel and withdraw the mounting from the vehicle **(see illustration 7.11)**.

12 On refitting, tighten all fasteners to the torque wrench settings specified. Tighten the two locking nuts to the engine casing first, then release the hoist or jack to allow the mounting bracket to rest on the vehicle inner wing panel. Re-align the marks made on removal, then tighten the two mounting bracket-to-inner wing retaining bolts.

Left-hand mounting

13 Remove the air cleaner assembly as described in Chapter 4A.

14 Remove the battery as described in Chapter 5A, then undo the 3 screws and remove the battery tray. Disconnect any wiring as the tray is withdrawn.

15 With the transmission supported, note the position of the mounting then unscrew the

centre retaining screw to release the mounting from the transmission **(see illustration)**.

16 Unscrew the four outer retaining nuts, and 2 screws to dismantle the mounting from the mounting bracket.

17 On refitting, renew the self-locking nuts. Re-align the mounting in the position noted on removal, then tighten all fasteners to the specified torque wrench settings.

Rear mounting (roll restrictor)

18 Unbolt the mounting from the subframe and the transmission by unscrewing the mounting's centre bolts **(see illustration)**.

19 On refitting, ensure that the bolts are securely tightened to the specified torque wrench setting.

16.15 Undo the centre bolt (arrowed) to release the mounting from the transmission

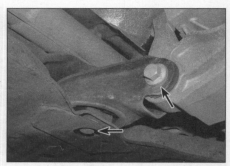

16.18 Undo the 2 bolts (arrowed) and remove the rear mounting

Chapter 2 Part B:
2.4 litre petrol engine in-car repair procedures

Degrees of difficulty

| **Easy,** suitable for novice with little experience | 🔧 | **Fairly easy,** suitable for beginner with some experience | 🔧 | **Fairly difficult,** suitable for competent DIY mechanic | 🔧 | **Difficult,** suitable for experienced DIY mechanic | 🔧 | **Very difficult,** suitable for expert DIY or professional | 🔧 |

Specifications

General

Engine code:
B5244 S4	2.4 litre (2435 cc) 20-valve
B5244 S5	2.4 litre (2435 cc) 20-valve
B5244 S7	2.4 litre (2435 cc) 20-valve
Bore	83.0 mm
Stroke	93.0 mm
Compression ratio	10.3 : 1
Compression pressure	13 to 15 bar
Maximum difference between cylinders.	2 bar

Output:
  Power
B5244 S4	125 kW @ 6000 rpm
B5244 S5	103 kW @ 6000 rpm
B5244 S7	123 kW @ 6000 rpm
B5254 T3/T7	162 kW @ 5000 rpm

  Torque:
B5244 S4	230 Nm @ 1500-4800 rpm
B5244 S5	220 Nm @ 4000 rpm
B5244 S7	230 Nm @ 4000 rpm
B5244 T3/T7	320 Nm @ 1500 – 4800 rpm
Firing order	1-2-4-5-3 (No 1 at timing belt of engine)
Direction of rotation	Clockwise (viewed from timing belt end of engine)

Camshaft

	Intake	Exhaust
Identification letter	PGI	PGE
Maximum lift.	8.65 mm	8.65mm
Camshaft endfloat	0.05 to 0.20 mm	0.05 to 0.20 mm
Valve clearances (engine cold):		
Checking dimension.	0.15 to 0.45 mm	0.35 to 0.60 mm
Setting dimension.	0.20 ± 0.03 mm	0.40 ± 0.03 mm

Lubrication

Engine oil type/specification	See *Lubricants, fluids and tyre pressures* on page 0•16
Engine oil capacity	See Chapter 1A Specifications
Oil pressure (warm engine):	
At idle speed.	1.0 bar
At 4000 rpm	3.5 bars
Oil pump type.	Gear – driven from crankshaft
Maximum pump gear to housing clearance.	0.35 mm
Pressure relief valve spring free height.	82.13 mm

Torque wrench settings

	Nm	lbf ft
Camshaft sprocket bolts (non-VVT)	20	15
Connecting rod cap bolt: *		
Stage 1	15	11
Stage 2	25	18
Stage 3	Angle-tighten a further 100°	
Crankshaft pulley-to-sprocket bolts: *		
Stage 1	25	18
Stage 2	Angle-tighten a further 60°	
Crankshaft sprocket centre nut	180	133
Crankshaft stop tool hole plug in cylinder block	40	30
Cylinder head lower section to block: *		
Stage 1	20	15
Stage 2	60	44
Stage 3	Angle-tighten a further 130°	
Cylinder head upper section to lower section	14	10
Driveplate: *		
Stage 1	45	33
Stage 2	Angle-tighten a further 50°	
Engine mountings:		
Right-hand mounting to inner wing	90	66
Right-hand mounting-to-engine nuts:		
M12		
Stage 1	65	48
Stage 2	Angle-tighten a further 90°	
M14	133	98
Left-hand mounting M10 nuts:		
Stage 1	35	26
Stage 2	Angle-tighten a further 90°	
Left-hand mounting bolts:		
M12	80	59
M14:		
Stage 1	60	44
Stage 2	Angle-tighten a further 50°	
Lower torque rod bolts: *		
M10	60	44
M12	80	59
M12 (to upper chassis member)	130	96
Engine oil drain plug	38	28
Flywheel: *		
Stage 1	45	33
Stage 2	Angle-tighten a further 65°	
Inlet manifold:		
Upper section	10	7
Lower section	20	15
Intermediate section to cylinder block:		
Tighten in the following sequence:		
M10*	20	5
M10	45	33
M8	24	18
M7	17	13
M10	Angle-tighten a further 90°	
Oil filter	25	18
Oil pump to cylinder block	6	4
Oil pressure switch	25	18
Piston cooling jet	17	13
Piston cooling oil valve	32	24
Spark plugs	28	21
Subframe front and rear mounting bolts:		
Front bolts	120	89
Rear bolts	280	207
Subframe rear mounting brackets to body	50	37
Sump:		
Sump to engine	17	13
Sump to transmission:		
Stage 1	25	18
Stage 2	48	35

Torque wrench settings (continued)

	Nm	lbf ft
Timing belt cover screws:		
Rear:		
M7	12	9
M8	25	18
Upper	10	7
Front	8	6
Timing belt idler pulley	25	18
Timing belt tensioner bolt (see text):		
Models up to 2005 model year	20	15
Models from 2006 model year	24	18
Variable valve timing (VVT) unit central screw	120	89
Variable valve timing (VVT) unit central plug.	35	26

* Do not re-use

1 General information

How to use this Chapter

This Part of Chapter 2 describes those repair procedures that can reasonably be carried out on the engine while it remains in the car. If the engine has been removed from the car and is being dismantled as described in Part F, any preliminary dismantling procedures can be ignored.

Note that, while it may be possible physically to overhaul items such as the piston/connecting rod assemblies while the engine is in the car, such tasks are not normally carried out as separate operations. Usually, several additional procedures (not to mention the cleaning of components and oilways) have to be carried out. For this reason, all such tasks are classed as major overhaul procedures, and are described in Part F of this Chapter.

Part F describes the removal of the engine/transmission from the vehicle, and the full overhaul procedures that can then be carried out.

Engine description

The five-cylinder engine is of the double overhead camshaft type, incorporating four valves per cylinder. The cylinders are in line and the engine is mounted transversely on a subframe in the engine bay. The engine codes (which appear only where necessary) are quite logical to follow – the first digit is the number of cylinders, the second and third together give the engine capacity in litres, and the final digit is the number of valves per cylinder. An S designation after the digits denotes a non-turbocharged engine. Thus, the B5244 S is a five-cylinder, 2.4 litre engine, with 4 valves per cylinder (total: 20 valves) and is not turbocharged.

The entire engine is constructed of aluminium alloy, and consists of five sections. The cylinder head comprises an upper and lower section, with the cylinder block, intermediate section and sump forming the other three. The upper and lower sections of the cylinder head are mated along the centre-line of the camshafts, while the cylinder block and intermediate section are mated along the crankshaft centre-line. A conventional cylinder head gasket is used between the cylinder head and block, with liquid gaskets being used in the joints between the other main sections.

The cylinder block incorporates five cast-iron dry cylinder liners which are cast into the block and cannot be renewed. Cast-iron reinforcements are also used in the intermediate section as strengthening agents in the main bearing areas.

Drive to the camshaft is by a toothed timing belt and sprockets, incorporating an automatic tensioning mechanism. The timing belt also drives the coolant pump. All accessories are driven from the crankshaft pulley by a single multi-ribbed auxiliary drivebelt.

The cylinder head is of the crossflow type, the intake ports being at the front of the engine and the exhaust ports at the rear. The upper section of the cylinder head functions as a combined valve cover and camshaft cover, and the camshafts run in six plain bearings integral to the two cylinder head sections. Valve actuation is by solid tappets, acted upon directly by the camshaft lobes. Correct valve clearance is maintained by substituting tappets of the correct size.

A variable valve timing system is fitted to the intake camshaft, whilst the position of the exhaust camshaft pulley is fixed.

The crankshaft runs in six shell type main bearings; the connecting rod big-end bearings are also of the shell type. Crankshaft endfloat is taken by thrustwashers which are an integral part of the No 5 main bearing shells.

The lubrication system is of the full-flow, pressure-feed type. Oil is drawn from the sump by a gear type pump, driven from the front of the crankshaft. Oil under pressure passes through a filter before being fed to the various shaft bearings and to the valve gear. All models have an external oil cooler mounted on the rear of the sump.

Operations with engine in car

The following work can be carried out with the engine in the car:

a) *Compression pressure – testing.*
b) *Timing belt – removal and refitting.*
c) *Camshaft oil seals – renewal.*
d) *Camshafts and tappets – removal and refitting.*
e) *Cylinder head – removal and refitting.*
f) *Cylinder head and pistons – decarbonising.*
g) *Crankshaft oil seals – renewal.*
h) *Oil pump – removal and refitting.*
i) *Flywheel/driveplate – removal and refitting.*
j) *Engine mountings – removal and refitting.*

Clean the engine compartment and the exterior of the engine with some type of degreaser before any work is done (and/or clean the engine using a steam cleaner). It will make the job easier and will help to keep dirt out of the internal areas of the engine.

Depending on the components involved, it may be helpful to remove the bonnet, to improve access to the engine as repairs are performed (refer to Chapter 11 if necessary). Cover the wings to prevent damage to the paint; special covers are available, but an old bedspread or blanket will also work.

2 Compression test – description and interpretation

1 When engine performance is down, or if misfiring occurs which cannot be attributed to the ignition or fuel systems, a compression test can provide diagnostic clues as to the engine's condition. If the test is performed regularly, it can give warning of trouble before any other symptoms become apparent.

2 The engine must be fully warmed-up to normal operating temperature, the battery must be fully-charged, and all the spark plugs must be removed (Chapter 1A). The aid of an assistant will also be required.

3 Disable the ignition system by disconnecting the crankshaft speed/position sensor (see Chapter 4A).

4 Fit a compression tester to the No 1 cylinder spark plug hole – the type of tester which screws into the plug thread is to be preferred.

5 Have the assistant hold the throttle wide open, and crank the engine on the starter motor; after one or two revolutions, the compression pressure should build-up to a maximum figure, and then stabilise. Record the highest reading obtained.

6 Repeat the test on the remaining cylinders, recording the pressure in each.

7 All cylinders should produce very similar pressures; a difference of more than 2 bars between the highest and lowest reading indicates a fault.

8 Note that the compression should build-up quickly in a healthy engine; low compression on the first stroke, followed by gradually-increasing pressure on successive strokes, indicates worn piston rings.

9 A low compression reading on the first stroke, which does not build-up during successive strokes, indicates leaking valves or a blown head gasket (a cracked head could also be the cause). Deposits on the undersides of the valve heads can also cause low compression.

10 If the pressure in any cylinder is low, carry out the following test to isolate the cause. Introduce a teaspoonful of clean oil into that cylinder through its spark plug hole, and repeat the test.

11 If the addition of oil temporarily improves the compression pressure, this indicates that bore or piston wear is responsible for the pressure loss. No improvement suggests that leaking or burnt valves, or a blown head gasket, may be to blame.

12 A low reading from two adjacent cylinders is almost certainly due to the head gasket having blown between them; the presence of coolant in the engine oil will confirm this.

13 If one cylinder is about 20 percent lower than the others and the engine has a slightly rough idle, a worn camshaft lobe could be the cause.

14 If the compression reading is unusually high, the combustion chambers are probably coated with carbon deposits. If this is the case, the cylinder head should be removed and decarbonised.

15 On completion of the test, refit the spark plugs and reconnect the crankshaft speed/position sensor. Note that carrying out this test as described may result in one or more fault codes being stored by the engine management ECM. Have these codes erased by a Volvo dealer or suitably-equipped specialist.

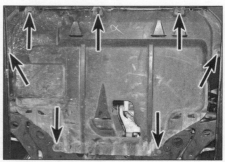

3.2 Undo the 7 Torx screws (arrowed) and remove the engine undershield

3 Timing belt –
  removal and refitting

Removal

1 Disconnect the battery negative lead as described in Chapter 5A.

2 Loosen the right-hand front wheel bolts, then jack up the front of the car and support it on axle stands (see *Jacking and vehicle support*). Remove the right-hand front roadwheel. Undo the 7 Torx screws and remove the engine undershield **(see illustration)**.

3 Release the two nuts securing the inner wheel arch liner, then undo the Torx screws and remove the liner.

4 Position a trolley jack under the engine, with

3.6a Undo the 2 screws securing the top-inner cover (arrowed) . . .

3.5 Undo the bolts (arrowed) and remove the right-hand engine mounting

a block of wood between the jack head and the sump to prevent damage, and to spread the load. Lift out the coolant expansion tank – no need to disconnect the hoses.

5 Mark the position of the right-hand engine mounting in relation to the inner wing, then undo the bolts and remove the mounting assembly **(see illustration)**.

6 Undo the Torx screws, release the clips and remove the timing belt covers **(see illustrations)**.

7 Remove the main auxiliary drivebelt as described in Chapter 1A.

8 Temporarily refit the timing belt inner, upper cover.

9 Using a socket on the crankshaft pulley centre nut, rotate the crankshaft clockwise (viewed from the right-hand side of the car) until the timing marks on the camshaft

3.6b . . . and the Torx screw (arrowed) securing the lower cover . . .

3.6c . . . then lift off the top-inner cover . . .

3.6d . . . followed by the outer cover . . .

3.6e . . . and the lower cover

3.9 Align the camshaft sprocket marks (A) with the notches (B) on the timing belt rear cover

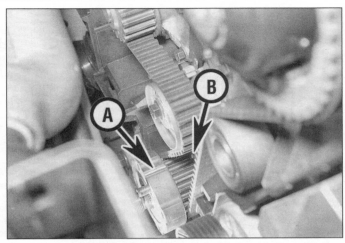

3.10 The crankshaft sprocket flange rib (A) should align with the oil pump housing mark (B)

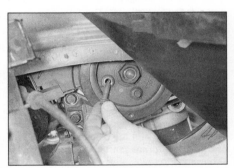

3.13a Slacken and remove 2 of the outer bolts . . .

3.13b . . . then fit a home-made pulley holding tool . . .

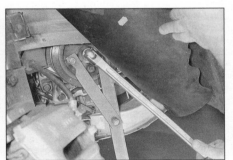

3.13c . . . and slacken the central nut

sprocket rims align with the notches on the timing belt upper cover **(see illustration)**.

10 In this position, the timing mark on the edge of the crankshaft sprocket flange should also be aligned with the cast projection on the oil pump housing **(see illustration)**.

11 The timing marks are not at all easy to see – the camshaft sprocket marks can be hardly more than faint scratches on the edges of the sprockets. Similarly, the mark on the crankshaft sprocket flange can only just be seen from above. It will probably take two or three attempts until you are sure that the marks are correctly aligned.

12 The crankshaft (auxiliary drivebelt) pulley must now be removed – this is secured to the crankshaft (timing belt) sprocket by four bolts, and to the crankshaft itself by a large central nut.

13 Loosen the four outer bolts, and remove two of them. Using a home-made sprocket holding tool bolted to the pulley using the two vacated bolt holes, hold the pulley as the central nut is loosened – this is tightened to a very high torque **(see illustrations)**.

14 Once the central nut is loose, check the alignment of the timing belt sprockets as described in paragraphs 9 and 10 before removing the pulley and the upper timing belt cover.

15 The crankshaft pulley locates on a roll-pin,

and a puller may be required to work the pulley off **(see illustration)**. Levering the pulley off is not advisable – the rim of the pulley itself is easily broken if care is not taken.

Models up to 2006 model year up to Chassis No 206721 (V50) or 202464 (S40)

16 Insert a 6 mm Allen key into the hole in the tensioner arm, then loosen the timing belt tensioner retaining bolt, and rotate the tensioner assembly clockwise to approximately the 10 o'clock position to relieve the tension on the belt **(see illustration)**. If a new belt is being fitted, remove the tensioner completely,

noting how the protruding lug on the tensioner engages with the engine. Volvo recommend that a new tensioner is fitted whenever a new timing belt is fitted.

Models from 2006 model year from Chassis No 206722 (V50) or 202465 (S40)

17 Undo the tensioner retaining bolt to relieve the tension on the belt. Discard the tensioner – Volvo recommend a new one is fitted.

All models

18 Mark the running direction of the belt if it is to be re-used, then slip it off the sprockets

3.15 The crankshaft pulley locates on a roll-pin (arrowed)

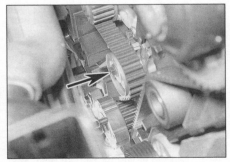

3.16 Slacken the tensioner retaining bolt (arrowed)

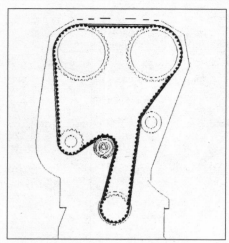

3.28 Timing belt routing

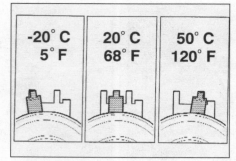

3.30a Timing belt tensioner settings at various ambient temperatures

3.30b Timing belt tensioner aligned with the central notch

and idler pulleys and remove it. Clearance is very limited at the crankshaft sprocket, and a certain amount of manipulation is necessary. **Do not** rotate the crankshaft or camshafts with the belt removed.

19 Volvo recommend that the idler pulley is also renewed whenever a new belt is fitted.

20 Check the timing belt carefully for any signs of uneven wear or splitting. Pay particular attention to the roots of the teeth. Renew the belt if there is the slightest doubt about its condition.

21 If the engine is undergoing an overhaul, and has covered more than 36 000 miles with the existing belt fitted, renew the belt as a matter of course, regardless of its apparent condition. The cost of a new belt is nothing when compared to the cost of repairs should the belt break in service.

22 If signs of oil or coolant contamination are found on the old belt, trace the source of the leak, and rectify it. Wash down the engine timing belt area and all related components to remove all traces of oil.

23 Even if the old timing belt does not show signs of coolant contamination, examine the coolant pump carefully for any indication that it may be leaking. When a coolant pump fails, it often starts leaking from the 'weep hole' in the top of the unit, just behind the pump's timing

belt sprocket (see Chapter 3). A coolant leak normally shows up as a white, crusty stain. If the engine has covered a high mileage, and is known to be using the original pump, it would be worth considering renewing the coolant pump at the same time as the timing belt. If this is not done, and the pump subsequently starts leaking, the belt will have to be taken off again to fit a new pump.

Refitting and tensioning

24 Before refitting the timing belt, make sure that the sprockets are in the correct positions (paragraphs 9 and 10). It will be necessary to temporarily refit the timing belt upper cover to do this.

25 Fit the new belt tensioner in the same position as noted on removal, ensuring the tensioner 'fork' locates over the cylinder block rib.

Models up to 2006 model year up to Chassis No 206721 (V50) or 202464 (S40)

26 With the tensioner arm at the 10 o'clock position, lightly tighten the retaining bolt.

27 Fit the new idler pulley, and tighten the retaining bolts to the specified torque.

28 Slip the belt over the crankshaft sprocket. Keeping it taut, and taking care not to rotate the camshaft sprockets in particular, feed the belt over the idler pulley, front camshaft sprocket, rear camshaft sprocket, coolant pump sprocket and finally over the tensioner pulley **(see illustration)**. Observe the correct running direction if the old belt is being re-used.

29 Recheck the alignment of the sprocket marks.

30 Using a 6 mm Allen key, turn the belt tensioner anti-clockwise until its pointer reaches the stop to the right of the central notch, then turn it back to align with the central notch **(see illustrations)**. The tensioner must always be set in this way, so that it is being set from the right of the central position.

31 With the tensioner aligned with the central notch, hold the tensioner using the Allen key, and tighten the retaining bolt to the specified torque **(see illustration)**.

32 Press on the belt at a point midway between the sprockets, and check that the tensioner pointer moves freely.

33 Temporarily refit the crankshaft pulley nut, and turn the crankshaft clockwise through two complete revolutions, then check that all the timing marks can be realigned.

34 Also check that the tensioner pointer is aligned with the central notch. If not, loosen the tensioner retaining bolt and reset the belt tension as described in paragraphs 30 to 34.

Models from 2006 model year from Chassis No 206722 (V50) or 202465 (S40)

35 Fit the new tensioner, ensuring it engages correctly with the cylinder block, and tighten the retaining bolt to the specified torque.

36 Rotate the tensioner arm anti-clockwise until a locking pin can be inserted through the holes in the arm and backplate once they are aligned **(see illustration)**.

37 Fit the new idler pulley and tighten the bolts to the specified torque.

38 Slip the belt over the crankshaft sprocket. Keeping it taut, and taking care not to rotate the camshaft sprockets in particular, feed the belt over the idler pulley, front camshaft sprocket, rear camshaft sprocket, coolant pump sprocket and finally over the tensioner pulley **(see illustration 3.28)**. Observe the correct running direction if the old belt is being re-used.

39 Recheck the alignment of the sprocket marks.

40 Pull out the tensioner locking pin. This should allow the pulley to spring back and tension the belt.

41 Temporarily refit the crankshaft pulley

3.31 Hold the tensioner with an Allen key and tighten the nut

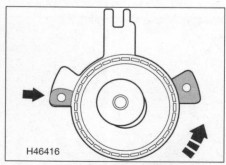

3.36 Rotate the tensioner anti-clockwise and insert a locking pin into the hole (arrowed)

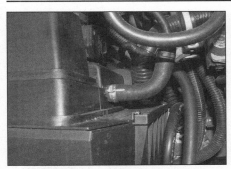

4.3a Disconnect the EVAP pipe . . .

4.3b . . . then press-in the collar and disconnect the servo hose

4.5 Oxygen sensor wiring plug and EVAP valve

nut, and turn the crankshaft clockwise through two complete revolutions, then check that all the timing marks can be realigned.

All models

42 Refit the crankshaft pulley over the roll-pin, then fit and tighten the central nut and the four new outer bolts to the specified torques.
43 Fold back the wheel arch liner, and secure with the two nuts.
44 Refit the roadwheel and lower the car to the ground. Tighten the wheel bolts in a diagonal sequence to the specified torque.
45 Refit all the remaining components removed for access, using a reversal of the removal procedure.

4 Camshaft sprockets, VVT units and right-hand oil seals – removal and refitting

Note: *For this procedure, the Volvo camshaft locking tool 999 5452 will be required to prevent the camshafts from rotating while the sprockets are removed. Details for fabricating a home-made alternative are given in the text. Do not attempt to carry out the work without locking the camshafts, or the valve timing will be lost.*

Removal

1 Remove the timing belt as described in Section 3.
2 Referring to Chapter 4A, remove the air cleaner assembly and intake ducts as

4.6 Prise out the blanking plugs at the end of the camshafts

necessary for clear access to the left-hand end of both camshafts.
3 Press-in the collar and disconnect the brake servo vacuum pipe and EVAP pipe from the intake manifold **(see illustrations)**. Refer to Chapter 4A if necessary.
4 Undo the 8 screws (6 at the front, 2 at the rear), disconnect the MAP sensor and throttle body wiring plugs, and remove the manifold. Plug the lower manifold openings to prevent contamination.
5 Unhook the EVAP canister valve from the lifting eye on the cylinder head, then undo the fuel pipe bracket bolt, and the 2 bolts securing the eye to the cylinder head. Disconnect the oxygen sensor wiring plug as the eye is withdrawn **(see illustration)**.
6 Using a screwdriver, prise out the plastic

blanking plug at the end of the camshafts, then undo the screws and remove the rotors **(see illustration)**. Be prepared for oil spillage.
7 Observe the position of the slots in the ends of the camshafts. Before the sprockets are removed, the camshafts must be positioned so that these slots are parallel to the join between the upper and lower cylinder head sections, and then locked in that position. Note also that the slots are very slightly offset from the centre-line; one slightly above and one slightly below.
8 To lock the camshafts in the correct position for refitting, obtain Volvo tool 999 5452 or fabricate a home-made alternative **(see Tool Tip)**.
9 Check that the crankshaft sprocket timing marks are still aligned, then attach the Volvo

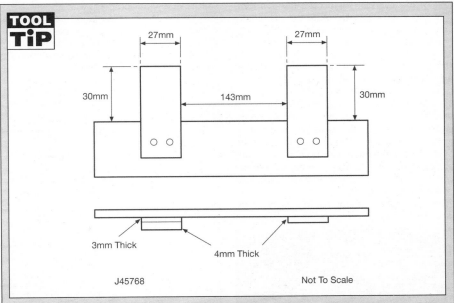

TOOL TiP

27mm | 27mm
30mm | 143mm | 30mm
3mm Thick | 4mm Thick
J45768 | Not To Scale

To make a camshaft locking tool, obtain a length of strip steel or angle-iron, and cut it so that it will fit across the left-hand end of the cylinder head. Obtain another length of strip steel of suitable thickness to fit snugly in the slots in the camshafts. Cut the strip into two lengths and drill accordingly so that both strips can be bolted to the angle-iron/strip. Using spacer washers, nuts and bolts, position and secure the strips to the angle-iron/strip so that the camshafts can be locked with their slots horizontal. Pack out the strips with spacers to cater for the offset of the slots. Bear in mind that the tool must be strong enough to hold the camshaft whilst the sprocket bolts are tightened.

4.9 Engage the locking tool with the slots in the end of the camshafts, to prevent the camshafts from rotating. The tool and the camshafts must be secure

4.11 Undo the plug, then undo the retaining screw

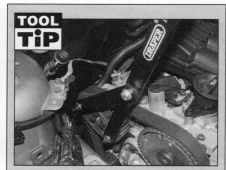

Restrain the sprockets through the holes in the sprocket faces.

4.15 Fit the oil seal over the end of the shaft, lips inwards

4.19a With the starter motor removed, undo the blanking plug (arrowed) . . .

Refitting

14 Clean the seal seat. Examine the shaft sealing face for wear or damage which could cause premature failure of the new seal.

15 Lubricate the new oil seal with clean engine oil. Fit the seal over the shaft, lips inwards, and tap it home with a large socket or piece of tube until its outer face is flush with the housing **(see illustration)**.

16 Temporarily refit the timing belt upper/inner cover.

Variable valve timing (VVT) sprocket

17 Check the crankshaft is still positioned as described in Section 3, then rotate it clockwise a few degrees.

18 Remove the starter motor as described in Chapter 5A.

19 Unscrew the blanking plug from the engine block, and insert Volvo tool 999 5451 **(see illustrations)**.

20 Rotate the crankshaft anti-clockwise until

tool or the home-made alternative to the end of the cylinder head **(see illustration)**. It may be necessary to rotate the camshafts very slightly to bring their slots exactly to the horizontal position to allow the tool to fit.

10 If both camshaft sprockets are to be removed, mark them intake and exhaust for identification when refitting. The intake sprocket is nearest the front of the car.

11 If a sprocket with a variable valve timing unit is to be removed, use a Torx 55 key to undo and remove the plug at the front of the unit, then use the same key to undo the central retaining screw. Pull the camshaft sprocket from the camshaft complete with the variable valve timing unit **(see illustration)**. Be prepared for oil spillage.

12 If a sprocket without variable valve timing is to be removed, undo the three bolts and

remove the sprocket for access to the failed seal. Restrain the sprockets with a suitable tool through the holes in their faces **(see Tool Tip)**. Withdraw the sprocket from the camshaft.

13 Carefully extract the seal by prising it out with a small screwdriver or hooked tool. Do not damage the shaft sealing face.

4.19b . . . and insert the crankshaft stop tool

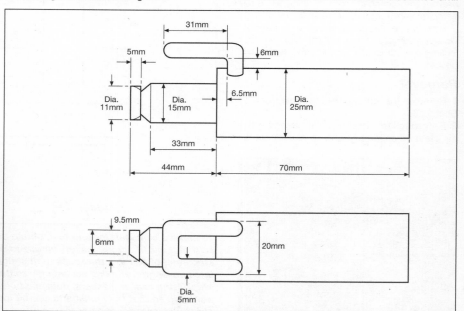

4.19c If you have access to a lathe, you may be able to produce a replica of the Volvo crankshaft stop tool

5.7 Fit the new oil seal with the lips facing inwards until its outer face is flush with the housing

the crankweb stops against the Volvo tool. Check that the marking on the crankshaft sprocket aligns with the mark on the oil pump housing.

21 Press the VVT unit/camshaft sprocket onto the camshaft, and refit the central retaining Torx screw. Do not tighten the screw.

Non-VVT sprocket

22 Refit the camshaft sprocket with the timing marks aligned, refit the retaining bolts but only tighten the bolts so that they just touch the sprockets, but allow the sprockets to turn within the limits of their elongated bolt holes. Check that the crankshaft pulley marks still align as described in Section 3, paragraph 10.

Both sprockets

23 Remove the upper timing belt cover, then fit a new timing belt as described in Section 3.

24 Tighten the VVT unit central retaining screw to the specified torque.

25 Tighten the non-VVT sprocket bolts to their specified torque.

26 Refit the centre plug to the VVT unit and tighten it to the specified torque.

27 Check the position of the timing belt tensioner arm, and adjust if necessary (models up to 2006 model year – see Section 3).

28 Remove the camshaft locking tools and the crankshaft stop tool.

29 Turn the crankshaft clockwise through two complete revolutions, then check that all the timing marks can be realigned.

30 Also check that the tensioner pointer is aligned with the central notch – models up to 2006 models year. If not, loosen the tensioner retaining bolt, and reset the belt tension as described in Section 3.

31 The remainder of refitting is a reversal of removal.

5 Camshaft left-hand oil seals – renewal

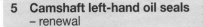

1 Refer to Chapter 4A and remove the air cleaner assembly and intake ducts as necessary for clear access to the rear end of both camshafts.

2 Note their fitted positions, then disconnect the EVAP canister hose and brake servo vacuum pipe from the intake manifold **(see illustration 4.3a and 4.3b)**. Refer to Chapter 4A if necessary.

3 Unhook the EVAP canister valve from the lifting eye on the cylinder head, then undo the fuel pipe bracket bolt, and the 2 bolts securing the eye to the cylinder head. Disconnect the oxygen sensor wiring plug as the eye is withdrawn **(see illustration 4.5)**.

4 Using a screwdriver, prise out the plastic blanking plug at the end of the camshafts, then undo the screws and remove the rotors **(see illustration 4.6)**. Be prepared for oil spillage.

5 Carefully extract the seal by prising it out

with a small screwdriver or hooked tool. Do not damage the shaft sealing face.

6 Clean the seal seat. Examine the shaft sealing face for wear or damage which could cause premature failure of the new seal.

7 Lubricate the new oil seal with clean engine oil. Fit the seal over the shaft, lips inwards, and tap it home with a large socket or piece of tube until its outer face is flush with the housing **(see illustration)**. Note: *If the camshaft journal shows signs of wear, the seal can be pressed in up to 2.0 mm further so it bears upon an unworn part of the camshaft surface.*

8 Refit the components removed for access, using a reversal of removal.

9 Refit the air cleaner and ducts.

6 Camshafts and tappets – removal, inspection and refitting

Note: *For this procedure, Volvo tools 999 5452, 999 5754, 999 5453 and 999 5454 will be required to lock the camshafts in position in the cylinder head upper section during refitting, and to pull the upper section into place. These tools are available in the aftermarket (e.g AST 5087). Details for fabricating home-made alternatives are given in the text. Do not attempt to carry out the work without these tools. A tube of liquid gasket and a short-haired application roller (available from Volvo dealers) will also be required.*

Removal

1 Remove the camshaft sprockets and right-hand oil seals as described in Section 4.

2 Remove the cylinder head earth strap **(see illustration)**.

3 Disconnect the crankcase breather hose from the camshaft cover **(see illustration)**.

4 Remove the spark plugs as described in Chapter 1A.

6.2 Disconnect the cylinder head earth strap

6.3 Disconnect the breather hose (arrowed)

6.5 VVT solenoid bolt (arrowed)

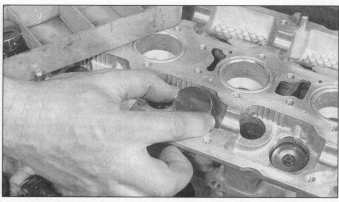

6.14 Remove the tappets and place them in a segmented container

5 Undo the retaining bolt and remove the VVT solenoid **(see illustration)**.

6 In a diagonal sequence, working inwards, gently, progressively slacken then remove all the bolts securing the cylinder head upper section.

7 Using a soft-faced mallet, gently tap, or alternatively prise, the cylinder head upper section upwards off the lower section. Note that parting lugs are provided to allow the upper section to be struck or prised against without damage. Do not insert a screwdriver or similar tool into the joint between the two sections as a means of separation. In practice, the upper section will be quite tight as it is located on numerous dowels; patience is necessary.

8 Once the upper section is free, carefully lift it off. The camshafts will rise up under the pressure of the valve springs – be careful they don't tip and jam in the upper section.

9 Withdraw the sealing O-rings from the top of the spark plug recesses in the lower section. Obtain new O-rings for reassembly

10 Suitably mark the camshafts, intake and exhaust, and lift them out complete with rear oil seals. Be careful of the lobes, which may have sharp edges.

11 Remove the oil seals from the camshafts, noting their fitted positions. Obtain new seals for reassembly.

12 Have ready a suitable box divided into twenty segments, or some containers and other means of storing and identifying the tappets after removal.

13 Mark the segments in the box or the containers with the cylinder number for each tappet, together with identification for intake and exhaust, and front and rear of the particular cylinder.

14 Lift out the tappets, using a suction cup or magnet if necessary. Keep them identified for position, and place them upright in their respective positions in the box or containers **(see illustration)**.

Inspection

15 Inspect the cam lobes and the camshaft bearing journals for scoring or other visible evidence of wear. Once the surface hardening

of the lobes has been penetrated, wear will progress rapidly.

16 No specific bearing journal diameters or running clearances are specified by Volvo for the camshafts or journals. However, if there is a visual deterioration, then component renewal will be necessary.

17 Inspect the tappets for scuffing, cracking or other damage. Note that where either the camshafts, valves or cylinder head have been renewed, the valve clearances must be checked and, if necessary, the correct size tappet fitted as described below.

Preparation for refitting

18 Thoroughly clean the sealer from the mating surfaces of the upper and lower cylinder head sections. Use a suitable liquid gasket dissolving agent together with a soft putty knife; do not use a metal scraper, or the faces will be damaged. As there is no conventional gasket used, the condition of the faces is of the utmost importance.

19 Clean off any oil, dirt or grease from both components and dry with a clean lint-free cloth. Ensure that all the oilways are completely clean.

Valve clearances checking and adjustment

20 If the camshaft(s), cylinder head or valves have been renewed, or the valve seats/faces ground, the valve clearances must be checked and if necessary adjusted.

21 Install two tappets (both intake or both exhaust) for the first cylinder to be checked.

22 Lay the camshaft in position over the tappets with the relevant lobes pointing away from their tappets.

23 Use hand pressure to clamp the camshaft onto the cylinder head, and measure the clearance between the underside of the camshaft and the tappet surface. If the measurement is different from that given in Specifications, make a note of the clearance, remove the camshaft and tappet. The tappet size is marked on its underside.

24 Once the size of the tappet is established, it must be changed for a thicker or thinner one to bring the previously recorded clearance

within specification. For example, if the measured valve clearance was 0.20 mm too great, a tappet *thicker* by this amount will be required. Conversely, if the clearance was 0.20 mm too small, a tappet thicker by this amount will be required. Note the different clearance specifications for *Checking* (with the camshaft cover, timing belt, etc, installed) and *Setting* (with the camshaft cover, etc, removed).

25 For reassembly, the camshafts are installed in the upper section, and retained in place in the correct position using special tools. This assembly is then fitted to the lower section, clamped in place against the pressure of the valve springs with more special tools, and finally bolted down. If possible, obtain the Volvo special tools mentioned in the note at the beginning of this section and use them in accordance with the instructions provided. Alternatively, fabricate a set of home-made tools as follows.

26 To position and secure the camshafts at the left-hand end, make up the camshaft locking tool described in the Tool Tip in Section 4.

27 To secure the camshafts at the right-hand end, make up a strap as shown **(see Tool Tip)**.

TOOL TiP

To retain the camshafts in the cylinder head upper section at the right-hand end when refitting, make a retaining strap out of welding rod, bent to shape, which will locate under the camshaft projections and can be secured to the upper section with two bolts.

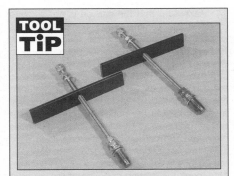

TOOL TiP

To pull the cylinder head upper section down against the valve spring pressure, obtain two old spark plugs and carefully break away all the porcelain so that only the lower threaded portion remains. Drill out the centre of the spark plugs as necessary, then fit a long bolt or threaded rod to each, and secure tightly with nuts. The bolts or rods must be long enough to project up from the spark plug wells to above the level of the assembled cylinder head. Drill a hole in the centre of two 6 mm thick strips of steel which are long enough to fit across the cylinder head upper section. Fit the strips then fit a nut and locknut to each bolt or rod.

28 Finally, it will be necessary to make up a tool which will allow the upper section to be clamped down against the pressure of the valve springs **(see Tool Tip)**.

Refitting

29 Commence refitting by liberally oiling the tappet bores and the camshaft bearings in the cylinder head lower section with clean engine oil.

30 Insert the tappets into their original bores (unless new tappets are being fitted).

31 Ensure that the mating faces of both cylinder head sections are clean and free of any oil or grease.

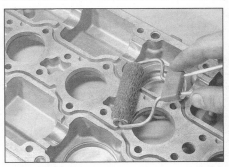

6.33 Apply the liquid sealant using a short-haired roller

32 Check that the crankshaft timing marks are still aligned.

33 Using the short-haired roller, apply an even coating of Volvo liquid gasket solution (1161 059) to the mating face of the cylinder head upper section only **(see illustration)**. Ensure that the whole surface is covered, but take care to keep the solution out of the oilways; a thin coating is sufficient for a good seal.

34 Lubricate the camshaft journals in the upper section sparingly with oil, taking care not to allow the oil to spill over onto the liquid gasket.

35 Lay the camshafts in their correct locations in the upper section, remembering that the intake camshaft must be at the front of the engine.

36 Turn the camshafts so that their slots are parallel to the upper section join, noting that the slots in each camshaft are offset with regards to the centre-line **(see illustration)**. When viewing the upper section the right way up, ie, as it would be when fitted, the slot on the intake camshaft is offset above the centre-line, and the exhaust camshaft slot is offset below the centre-line. Verify this by looking at the other end of the camshafts. Again, with the upper section the right way up, there should be two sprocket bolt holes above the centre-

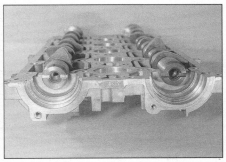

6.36 Position the camshafts so that their slots are parallel to the upper section joint (see text)

line on the intake camshaft, and two bolt holes below the centre-line on the exhaust camshaft.

37 With the camshafts correctly positioned, lock them at the rear by fitting the left-hand locking and holding tool. It should not be possible to rotate the camshafts at all with the tool in place. Now secure the camshafts at the right using the holding tool or the home-made alternative.

38 Place new sealing O-rings into the recesses around each spark plug well in the lower section **(see illustration)**.

39 Lift up the assembled upper section, with camshafts, and lay it in place on the lower section.

40 Insert the pull-down tools into Nos 1 and 5 spark plug holes and tighten securely. If using the home-made tool, make sure that the bolt or threaded rod is a secure fit in the spark plug, or you will not be able to remove the tool later.

41 Lay the pull-down tool top plates, or the home-made steel strips, over the bolts or threaded rods, and secure with the nuts **(see illustration)**. Slowly and carefully tighten the nuts, a little at a time, so that the tools pull the upper section down onto the lower section. Remember there will be considerable resistance from the valve springs. Make sure

6.38 Place new sealing O-rings around each spark plug well

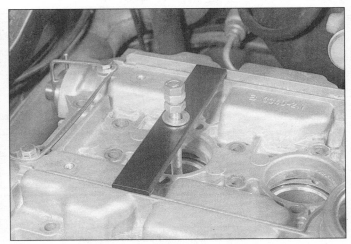

6.41 Home-made pull-down tool in position

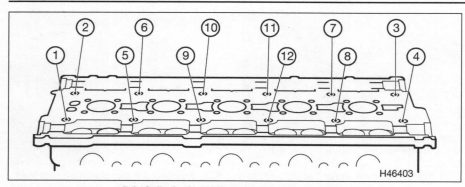

7.9 Cylinder head bolt slackening sequence

that the upper section stays level, or the locating dowels will jam.

42 Refit the upper section retaining bolts and tighten them in a progressive diagonal sequence, working outwards, to the specified torque. Don't forget the earth lead on the rear bolt.

43 With the upper section secure, remove the pull-down tool and the camshaft right-hand end holding tool. Leave the left-hand locking tool in place.

44 Lubricate the lips of four new camshaft oil seals. Fit each seal the correct way round over the camshaft, and tap it home with a large socket or piece of tube until its outer face is flush with the housing (see Sections 4 and 5).

45 Refit the camshaft sprockets, timing belt, etc, as described in Section 4.

46 The remainder of refitting is a reversal of removal.

47 Check the coolant level as described in Chapter 1A on completion.

7 Cylinder head – removal and refitting

Removal

1 Disconnect the battery negative lead (Chapter 5A).

2 Drain the engine coolant as described in Chapter 1A.

3 Remove the intake and exhaust manifolds as described in Chapter 4A.

4 Remove the camshafts and tappets as described in Section 6.

5 Undo the bolts securing the engine mounting bracket to the right-hand end of the cylinder head/block, then where applicable, undo the bolt securing the timing belt rear cover to the cylinder head (see illustration 3.5).

6 If not already done, undo the bolt and remove the earth lead(s) at the rear of the cylinder head.

7 Slacken the clips and remove the radiator top hose from the thermostat housing and radiator. Remove the expansion tank hose from the thermostat housing.

8 Disconnect the coolant hose from the left-hand end of the cylinder head.

9 Slacken the cylinder head bolts, half a turn at a time to begin with, in the order shown (see illustration). Remove the bolts. Note that new bolts will be required for refitting.

10 Lift off the cylinder head and set it down on wooden blocks to avoid damage to protruding valves. Recover the old head gasket.

11 If the cylinder head is to be dismantled for overhaul, refer to Part F of this Chapter.

Preparation for refitting

12 The mating faces of the cylinder head and cylinder block must be perfectly clean before refitting the head.

13 Use a plastic scraper to remove all traces of gasket and carbon; also clean the piston crowns. Take particular care during the cleaning operations, as aluminium alloy is easily damaged.

14 Make sure that the carbon is not allowed to enter the oil and water passages – this is particularly important for the lubrication system, as carbon could block the oil supply to the engine's components. Using adhesive tape and paper, seal the water, oil and bolt holes in the cylinder block. To prevent carbon entering the gap between the pistons and bores, smear a little grease in the gap. After cleaning each piston, use a small brush to remove all traces of grease and carbon from the gap, then wipe away the remainder with a clean rag. Clean all the pistons in the same way.

15 Check the mating surfaces of the cylinder block and the cylinder head for nicks, deep scratches and other damage. If slight, they may be removed carefully with a file, but if excessive, machining may be the only alternative to renewal.

16 If warpage of the cylinder head gasket surface is suspected, use a straight-edge to check it for distortion. Refer to Part F of this Chapter if necessary.

17 Check that the cylinder head bolt holes in the block are clean and dry. If available, run a correct-size tap down each threaded hole – failing this, an old head bolt with two slots cut along the length of the threads can be used. It is most important that no oil or coolant is present in the bolt holes, otherwise the block may be cracked by the hydraulic action as the head bolts are inserted and tightened.

Refitting

18 Commence refitting by placing a new head gasket on the cylinder block. Make sure it is the right way up; it should be marked TOP.

19 Lower the head into position, then lightly oil the threads of the new cylinder head bolts. Fit the bolts and tighten them to the specified Stage 1 torque in the sequence shown (see illustration).

20 In the same sequence, tighten the bolts to the Stage 2 torque, then, again in the same sequence, tighten the bolts through the angle specified for Stage 3 using an angle-tightening gauge (see illustration).

21 Using a new gasket, refit the coolant pipe flange to the rear of the cylinder head and secure with the two bolts.

22 Refit the radiator top hose to the thermostat housing and radiator.

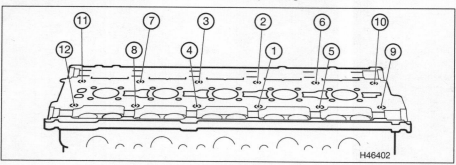

7.19 Cylinder head bolt tightening sequence

7.20 Tighten the bolts through the specified angle using an angle-tightening gauge

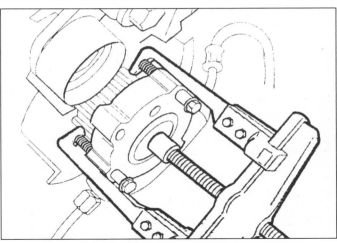

8.2 Use a puller to draw off the crankshaft pulley flange

9.3 Parting lugs (arrowed) for oil pump removal

23 Refit the timing belt cover retaining bolt and the bolt securing the rear earth lead.
24 Refit the right-hand engine mounting to the cylinder head/block, and tighten the bolts securely.
25 Refit the camshaft and tappets as described in Section 6, but do not reconnect the battery at this stage.
26 Refit the intake and exhaust manifolds as described in Chapter 4A.
27 Refill the engine cooling system as described in Chapter 1A.

8 Crankshaft oil seals – renewal

Right-hand end seal

1 Remove the timing belt as described in Section 3.
2 With the crankshaft pulley removed, insert two of the retaining bolts and draw the sprocket/flange off the crankshaft using a two-legged puller. Engage the puller legs with the protruding bolts at the rear (see illustration).
3 With the sprocket removed, carefully prise out the old oil seal. Do not damage the oil pump housing or the surface of the crankshaft. Alternatively, punch or drill two small holes opposite each other in the oil seal. Screw a self-tapping screw into each, and pull on the screws with pliers to extract the seal.
4 Clean the oil seal location and the crankshaft. Inspect the crankshaft for a wear groove or ridge left by the old seal.
5 Lubricate the housing, the crankshaft and the new seal with clean engine oil – not grease. Fit the seal, lips inwards, and use a piece of tube (or the old seal, inverted) to tap it into place until flush.
6 Refit the crankshaft sprocket using the reverse of the removal procedure, aligning the master spline.
7 Refit the timing belt as described in Section 3.

Left-hand end seal

8 Remove the flywheel or driveplate as described in Section 10.
9 Remove the old seal and fit the new one as described previously in paragraphs 3 to 5.
10 Refit the flywheel or driveplate as described in Section 10.

9 Oil pump – removal, inspection and refitting

Removal

1 Carry out the operations described in Section 8, paragraphs 1 to 4.
2 Undo the four bolts securing the oil pump to the cylinder block.
3 Carefully withdraw the pump assembly by levering behind the upper and lower parting lugs using a screwdriver (see illustration). Remove the pump and recover the gasket.
4 Thoroughly clean the pump and cylinder block mating faces and remove all traces of old gasket.

Inspection

5 Remove the two screws which hold the two halves of the pump together.
6 Remove the gear cover from the pump body. Be prepared for the ejection of the pressure relief valve spring.
7 Remove the relief valve spring and plunger and the pump gears.
8 Remove the crankshaft oil seal by carefully levering it out of the cover. Obtain a new seal for refitting.
9 Clean all components thoroughly, then inspect the gears, body and gear cover for signs of wear or damage.
10 If any parts appear worn, or damaged, renew them. At the time of writing no information concerning valve spring length or rotor/gear clearance was available.

11 Refit the gears to the pump body, with the markings on the large gear uppermost.
12 Liberally lubricate the gears. Lubricate and fit the relief valve plunger and spring.
13 Fit a new O-ring seal to the pump body, then fit the cover and secure with the two screws.

Refitting

14 Using a new gasket, fit the pump to the block. Use the pump retaining bolts as guides, and draw the pump into place with the crankshaft pulley nut and spacers. With the pump seated, tighten the retaining bolts diagonally to the specified torque.
15 Lubricate the cover, crankshaft and the new oil seal. Fit the seal, lips inwards, and use a piece of tube (or the old seal, inverted) to tap it into place until flush.
16 Refit the crankshaft sprocket and pulley using a reverse of the removal procedure.
17 Refit the timing belt as described in Section 3.

10 Flywheel/driveplate – removal, inspection and refitting

Note: New flywheel/driveplate retaining bolts will be required for refitting.

Removal

Flywheel

1 Remove the transmission as described in Chapter 7A.
2 Remove the clutch assembly as described in Chapter 6.
3 Make alignment marks so that the flywheel can be refitted in the same position relative to the crankshaft.
4 Loosen the flywheel bolts. Prevent crankshaft rotation by inserting a large screwdriver in the ring gear teeth and in contact with an adjacent dowel in the engine/transmission mating face.

5 With the flywheel supported, remove the bolts and lower it to the floor. Take care not to drop it, as it is heavy, and not easy to hold on to.

Driveplate

6 Remove the automatic transmission as described in Chapter 7B.
7 Make alignment marks so that the driveplate can be refitted in the same position relative to the crankshaft.
8 Unbolt the driveplate and remove it as described in paragraphs 4 and 5.

Inspection

9 On manual transmission models, if the flywheel's clutch mating surface is deeply scored, cracked or otherwise damaged, the flywheel must be renewed. However, it may be possible to have it surface-ground; seek the advice of a Volvo dealer or engine reconditioning specialist. If the ring gear is badly worn or has missing teeth, flywheel renewal will also be necessary.
10 On models with automatic transmission, check the torque converter driveplate carefully for signs of distortion. Look for any hairline cracks around the bolt holes or radiating outwards from the centre, and inspect the ring gear teeth for signs of wear or chipping. If any signs of wear or damage are found, the driveplate must be renewed.

Refitting

Flywheel

11 Clean the mating surfaces of the flywheel and crankshaft. Remove any remaining locking compound from the threads of the crankshaft holes, using the correct-size tap, if available **(see Haynes Hint)**.

> **HAYNES HINT** *If a suitable tap is not available, cut two slots into the threads of one of the old flywheel bolts and use the bolt to remove the locking compound from the threads.*

12 Continue refitting by reversing the removal operations. Apply thread-locking compound to the new flywheel retaining bolts (if not already precoated) and tighten them to the specified torque. **Note:** *Ensure the flywheel is located against the crankshaft mating surface before the bolts are inserted, to avoid the possibility of thread-locking compound getting between the flywheel and crankshaft surfaces.*
13 Refit the clutch as described in Chapter 6, and the transmission as described in Chapter 7A.

Driveplate

14 Proceed as described above for manual transmission models, ignoring any references to the clutch. Refit the transmission as described in Chapter 7B.

---

11 Engine mountings – removal and refitting

Removal

Right-hand mounting

1 Support the engine with an engine compartment cross-beam, or remove the engine undershield and place a trolley jack under the engine with a block of wood between the engine and jack head to spread the load and prevent damage. Take the weight of the engine.
2 Lift the coolant expansion tank upwards from its mountings, and place it over the engine. There is no need to disconnect the coolant hoses.
3 Mark the position of the mounting bracket on the inner wing to aid reassembly, then undo the screws securing the mounting to the inner wing and the engine **(see illustration)**.

Left-hand mounting

4 Undo the 7 Torx screws and remove the engine/transmission undershield, and support the transmission with a trolley jack. Use a block of wood between the jack head and the transmission casing to spread the load and prevent damage. Take the weight of the transmission.
5 Remove the battery as described in Chapter 5A, then undo the screws and remove the battery tray. Release the connector under the tray as it's withdrawn.
6 Remove the air cleaner assembly as described in Chapter 4A.
7 Undo the 4 nuts and 2 bolts and remove the mounting plate **(see illustration)**.
8 Undo the centre bolt and remove the mounting pad.

Lower torque rod

9 Release the 7 Torx screws and remove the engine undershield **(see illustration 3.2)**.
10 Undo the 2 bolts and remove the torque rod **(see illustration)**.

Refitting

11 Refit by reversing the removal operations, tightening all fastenings to the specified torque.

11.3 Mark the position of the mounting bracket in relation to the inner wing

11.7 Undo the 4 nuts and 2 bolts (arrowed) and remove the mounting plate

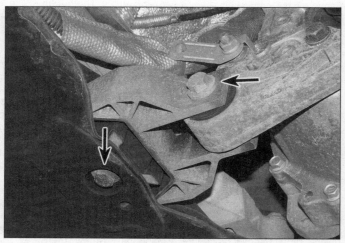

11.10 Undo the 2 bolts and remove the torque rod (arrowed)

12.6 Oil cooler mounting bolts (arrowed)

12.8 Disconnect the power steering fluid supply and return hose (arrowed)

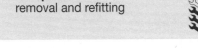

12 Sump –
removal and refitting

Removal

1 Slacken the right-hand front roadwheel nuts, then jack up the front of the vehicle and support it securely on axle stands (see *Jacking and vehicle support*). Remove the roadwheel.

2 Undo the 7 Torx screws and remove the engine undershield, and right-hand front wheel arch liner **(see illustration 3.2)**.

3 Drain the engine oil as described in Chapter 1A.

4 Remove the intake manifold as described in Chapter 4A.

5 Undo the bolt/nut and pull the oil level dipstick guide tube from the sump.

6 The oil cooler (where fitted) is secured to the sump by four bolts. Undo the bolts and pull the cooler to the rear **(see illustration)**. Be prepared for oil spillage.

7 Disconnect the oil level sensor wiring plug.

8 Position a container under the power steering pump, then disconnect the fluid delivery and return hose from the pump **(see illustration)**. Plug/seal the openings to prevent fluid loss and contamination.

9 Undo the bolts securing the power steering pipe bracket to the sump.

10 Remove the air conditioning compressor drivebelt as described in Chapter 1A.

11 Undo the air conditioning compressor retaining bolts, and detach it from the sump. Suspend the compressor from the radiator crossmember using wire or straps.

12 Remove all the screws securing the sump to the engine, with the exception of one

screw in each corner, which should just be slackened a few turns.

13 Gently tap the sides and ends of the sump until the joint between the engine and sump releases. Undo the remaining screws and remove the sump. Discard the O-rings at the right-hand end of the sump, new ones must be fitted.

Refitting

14 Ensure the mating faces of the sump and engine are clean and free from any remaining gasket residue.

15 Using a short-haired roller, apply a thin layer of Volvo liquid sealant (1161 059-9) to the sump mating face.

16 Position the new O-rings, and refit the sump, securing it with a screw in each corner, finger-tightened only.

17 Insert the sump-to-transmission screws, and tighten them to the specified torque.

18 Refit the remaining sump-to-engine screws and tighten them to the specified torque starting from the transmission end.

13.1 The oil pressure warning light switch (arrowed) is located on the front of the cylinder block

19 The remainder of refitting is a reversal of removal, noting the following points:
   a) *Refit the oil cooler to the sump using new O-ring seals.*
   b) *Reconnect the power steering pipes using new seals where applicable.*
   c) *Refit the oil level dipstick tube using a new O-ring seal.*
   d) *Renew the oil filter and fill the engine with new oil as described in Chapter 1A.*

13 Oil pressure warning light switch –
removal and refitting

Removal

1 The switch is screwed into the front of the cylinder block **(see illustration)**.

2 With the vehicle parked on firm level ground, open the bonnet and disconnect the battery negative (earth) lead.

3 If required, raise the front of the vehicle, and support it securely on axle stands, this will give better access to the switch. Undo the 7 Torx screws and remove the engine undershield **(see illustration 3.2)**.

4 Disconnect the wiring connector from the switch, and unscrew it; be prepared for some oil loss.

Refitting

5 Refitting is the reverse of the removal procedure; apply a thin smear of suitable sealant to the switch threads, and tighten it to the specified torque wrench setting. Check the engine oil level, and top-up as necessary (see *Weekly checks*). Check for signs of oil leaks once the engine has been restarted and warmed-up to normal operating temperature.

Notes

Chapter 2 Part C:
1.6 litre diesel engine in-car repair procedures

Contents

Degrees of difficulty

Easy, suitable for novice with little experience	Fairly easy, suitable for beginner with some experience	Fairly difficult, suitable for competent DIY mechanic	Difficult, suitable for experienced DIY mechanic	Very difficult, suitable for expert DIY or professional

Specifications

General

Engine code	D4162T, D4164T
Capacity	1560 cc
Bore	75.0mm
Stroke	88.3mm
Direction of crankshaft rotation	Clockwise (viewed from the right-hand side of vehicle)
No 1 cylinder location.	At the transmission end of block
Maximum power output (D4162T)	85 kW @ 3600 rpm
Maximum power output (D4164T)	80 kW @ 4000 rpm
Maximum torque output (D4162T)	270 Nm @ 1750 rpm
Maximum torque output (D4164T)	240 Nm @ 1750 rpm
Compression ratio (D4162T).	16.0:1
Compression ratio (D4164T).	18.3:1

The engine code is stamped on a plate attached to the front of the cylinder block, next to the oil filter

Cylinder head gasket identification (D4164T)

	Piston protrusion	Gasket thickness
1 notch	0.53 to 0.63mm	1.35mm
2 notches	0.63 to 0.68mm	1.25mm
3 notches	0.68 to 0.73mm	1.30mm
4 notches	0.73 to 0.78mm	1.40mm
5 notches	0.78 to 0.89mm	1.45mm

Camshaft

Drive	Toothed belt

Lubrication

Engine oil type/specification	See *Lubricants, fluids and tyre pressures* on page 0•16
Engine oil capacity	See Chapter 1B Specifications
Oil pump type.	Gear-type, driven directly by the right-hand end of the crankshaft, by two flats machined along the crankshaft journal.

Oil pressure - minimum (engine at operating temperature):

At idle	1.0 to 2.0 bar
At 2000 rpm	2.3 to 3.7 bar

Valves

Valve clearances.	Hydraulic compensators – no adjustment necessary

Torque wrench settings

	Nm	lbf ft
Ancillary drivebelt tensioner roller	24	18
Big-end bolts: *		
Stage 1	10	7
Stage 2	Slacken	180°
Stage 3	10	7
Stage 4	Angle-tighten a further	130°
Camshaft bearing caps	10	7
Camshaft cover/bearing ladder:		
Stage 1	5	4
Stage 2	10	7
Camshaft carrier bolts (D4162T)	10	7
Camshaft position sensor bolt:		
D4162T	7	5
D4164T	5	4
Camshaft sprocket	43	32
Coolant outlet housing bolts	8	6
Crankshaft position/speed sensor bolt	10	7
Crankshaft pulley/sprocket bolt: *		
Stage 1	30	22
Stage 2	Angle-tighten a further	180°
Cylinder head bolts: *		
Stage 1	20	15
Stage 2	40	30
Stage 3 (D4164T)	Angle-tighten a further	220°
Stage 3 (D4162T)	Angle-tighten a further	260°
Cylinder head cover/manifold	10	7
EGR valve	10	7
Engine-to-transmission fixing bolts	50	37
Engine-to-transmission lower M8 bolts (D4162T)	24	18
Flywheel bolts: *		
Stage 1	30	22
Stage 2	Angle-tighten a further	90°
Fuel pump sprocket	50	37
Left-hand engine/transmission mounting:		
Mounting-to-bracket centre nut	130	96
M12 nuts	24	18
M12 to engine block	90	66
Lower torque rod		
Rod to engine	50	37
Centre link bolt	80	59
Rod to subframe	80	59
Main bearing ladder outer seam bolts:		
Stage 1	6	4
Stage 2	8	6
Main bearing ladder to cylinder block:		
Stage 1	10	7
Stage 2	Slacken	180°
Stage 3	30	22
Stage 4	Angle-tighten a further	140°
Piston oil jet spray tube bolt	20	15
Oil cooler retaining bolts	10	7
Oil filter cover	25	18
Oil pick-up pipe	10	7
Oil pressure switch	30	22
Oil pump to cylinder block	10	7
Right-hand engine mounting:		
M6	10	7
M10	50	37
Centre retaining bolt	130	96
Mounting-to-engine	80	59
Mounting-to-subframe	80	59
Sump drain plug	34	25
Sump bolts/nuts	10	7
Timing belt idler pulley	45	33
Timing belt tensioner pulley	30	22
Timing belt cover bolts	5	4
Timing chain tensioner	10	7
Vacuum pump	20	15

* Do not re-use

1 General information

How to use this Chapter

This Part of Chapter 2 describes the repair procedures that can reasonably be carried out on the engine while it remains in the vehicle. If the engine has been removed from the vehicle and is being dismantled as described in Part F, any preliminary dismantling procedures can be ignored.

Note that, while it may be possible physically to overhaul items such as the piston/connecting rod assemblies while the engine is in the car, such tasks are not usually carried out as separate operations. Usually, several additional procedures are required (not to mention the cleaning of components and oilways); for this reason, all such tasks are classed as major overhaul procedures, and are described in Part F of this Chapter.

Part F describes the removal of the engine/transmission from the car, and the full overhaul procedures that can then be carried out.

Introduction

The 1.6 litre engines are available in two states of tune, 80kw or 85kw. The former is of double overhead camshaft (DOHC) 16-valve design, the latter a single overhead camshaft (SOHC) 8-valve design. The direct injection, turbocharged, four-cylinder engines are mounted transversely, with the transmission mounted on the left-hand side.

A toothed timing belt drives the camshaft(s), high-pressure fuel pump and coolant pump. On models fitted with the 80kw engine, the inlet camshaft drives the exhaust camshaft via a chain. The camshaft(s) operates the inlet and exhaust valves via rocker arms which are supported at their pivot ends by hydraulic self-adjusting tappets. The camshafts are supported by bearings machined directly in the cylinder head or camshaft carrier and camshaft bearing housing.

The high-pressure fuel pump supplies fuel to the fuel rail, and subsequently to the electronically-controlled injectors which inject the fuel direct into the combustion chambers.

The crankshaft runs in five main bearings of the usual shell type. Endfloat is controlled by thrustwashers either side of No 2 main bearing.

The pistons are selected to be of matching weight, and incorporate fully-floating gudgeon pins retained by circlips.

Repair operations precaution

The engine is a complex unit with numerous accessories and ancillary components. The design of the engine compartment is such that every conceivable space has been utilised, and access to many of the engine components is limited. In many cases, ancillary components will have to be removed, or moved to one side, and wiring, pipes and hoses will have to be disconnected or removed from various cable clips and support brackets.

When working on this engine, read through the entire procedure first, look at the car and engine at the same time, and establish whether you have the necessary tools, equipment, skill and patience to proceed. Allow considerable time for any operation, and be prepared for the unexpected.

Because of the limited access, many of the engine photographs appearing in this Chapter were, by necessity, taken with the engine removed from the vehicle.

⚠ **Warning: It is essential to observe strict precautions when working on the fuel system components of the engine, particularly the high-pressure side of the system. Before carrying out any engine operations that entail working on, or near, any part of the fuel system, refer to the special information given in Chapter 4B.**

Operations with engine in vehicle

a) Compression pressure – testing.
b) Cylinder head cover – removal and refitting.
c) Crankshaft pulley – removal and refitting.
d) Timing belt covers – removal and refitting.
e) Timing belt – removal, refitting and adjustment.
f) Timing belt tensioner and sprockets – removal and refitting.
g) Camshaft oil seal – renewal.
h) Camshaft, rocker arms and hydraulic tappets – removal, inspection and refitting.
i) Sump – removal and refitting.
j) Oil pump – removal and refitting.
k) Crankshaft oil seals – renewal.
l) Engine/transmission mountings – inspection and renewal.
m) Flywheel – removal, inspection and refitting.

2 Compression and leakdown tests – description and interpretation

Compression test

Note: A compression tester specifically designed for diesel engines must be used for this test.

1 When engine performance is down, or if misfiring occurs which cannot be attributed to the fuel system, a compression test can provide diagnostic clues as to the engine's condition. If the test is performed regularly, it can give warning of trouble before any other symptoms become apparent.

2 A compression tester specifically intended for diesel engines must be used, because of the higher pressures involved. The tester is connected to an adapter which screws into the glow plug or injector hole. On this engine, an adapter suitable for use in the glow plug holes will be required, so as not to disturb the fuel system components. It is unlikely to be worthwhile buying such a tester for occasional use, but it may be possible to borrow or hire one – if not, have the test performed by a garage.

3 Unless specific instructions to the contrary are supplied with the tester, observe the following points:
a) The battery must be in a good state of charge, the air filter must be clean, and the engine should be at normal operating temperature.
b) All the glow plugs should be removed as described in Chapter 5C before starting the test.
c) Disconnect the fuel injector wiring plugs.

4 The compression pressures measured are not so important as the balance between cylinders. You should refer to a Volvo dealer for compression pressures.

5 The cause of poor compression is less easy to establish on a diesel engine than on a petrol one. The effect of introducing oil into the cylinders ('wet' testing) is not conclusive, because there is a risk that the oil will sit in the swirl chamber or in the recess on the piston crown instead of passing to the rings. However, the following can be used as a rough guide to diagnosis.

6 All cylinders should produce very similar pressures; any difference greater than that specified indicates the existence of a fault. Note that the compression should build-up quickly in a healthy engine; low compression on the first stroke, followed by gradually-increasing pressure on successive strokes, indicates worn piston rings. A low compression reading on the first stroke, which does not build-up during successive strokes, indicates leaking valves or a blown head gasket (a cracked head could also be the cause). Deposits on the undersides of the valve heads can also cause low compression.

7 A low reading from two adjacent cylinders is almost certainly due to the head gasket having blown between them; the presence of coolant in the engine oil will confirm this.

8 If the compression reading is unusually high, the cylinder head surfaces, valves and pistons are probably coated with carbon deposits. If this is the case, the cylinder head should be removed and decarbonised (see Part F).

Note: After performing this test, a fault code may be generated and stored in the ECM memory. Have the ECM self-diagnosis facility interrogated by a Volvo dealer or suitably-equipped specialist, and the fault code erased.

Leakdown test

9 A leakdown test measures the rate at which compressed air fed into the cylinder is lost. It is an alternative to a compression test, and in many ways it is better, since the escaping air provides easy identification of where pressure loss is occurring (piston rings, valves or head gasket).

3.8 Insert a 5mm drill bit/rod through the round hole in the sprocket flange into the hole in the oil pump housing (lower timing belt cover removed for clarity)

10 The equipment needed for leakdown testing is unlikely to be available to the home mechanic. If poor compression is suspected, have the test performed by a suitably-equipped garage.

3 Engine assembly/ valve timing holes – general information and usage

Note: *Do not attempt to rotate the engine whilst the crankshaft and camshaft are locked in position. If the engine is to be left in this state for a long period of time, it is a good idea to place suitable warning notices inside the vehicle, and in the engine compartment. This will reduce the possibility of the engine being accidentally cranked on the starter motor, which is likely to cause damage with the locking pins in place.*

1 Timing holes or slots are located only in the crankshaft sprocket flange and camshaft sprocket hub. The holes/slots are used to position the pistons halfway up the cylinder bores. This will ensure that the valve timing is maintained during operations that require removal and refitting of the timing belt.

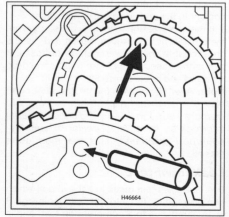

3.10 Insert the Volvo tool or a 5mm drill bit/rod through the hole in the fuel pump sprocket into the fuel pump mounting bracket

3.9 Insert an 8mm drill bit/rod through the hole in the camshaft sprocket into the corresponding hole in the cylinder head

When the holes/slots are aligned with their corresponding holes in the cylinder block and cylinder head, suitable diameter bolts/pins can be inserted to lock the crankshaft and camshaft in position, preventing rotation.

2 Note that the fuel system used on these engines does not have a conventional diesel injection pump, but instead uses a high-pressure fuel pump. However, the fuel pump sprocket must be pegged in position in a similar fashion to the camshaft sprocket.

3 To align the engine assembly/valve timing holes, proceed as follows.

4 Apply the handbrake, then jack up the front of the vehicle and support it on axle stands (see *Jacking and vehicle support*). Remove the right-hand front roadwheel.

5 To gain access to the crankshaft pulley, to enable the engine to be turned, the wheel arch plastic liner must be removed. The crankshaft can then be turned using a suitable socket and extension bar fitted to the pulley bolt.

6 Remove the crankshaft pulley as described in Section 5 and the timing belt covers as described in Section 6.

7 Temporarily refit the crankshaft pulley bolt, remove the crankshaft locking tool, then turn the crankshaft until the timing hole in the camshaft sprocket hub is aligned with the corresponding hole in the cylinder head. Note that the crankshaft must always be turned in a clockwise direction (viewed from the right-hand side of vehicle). Use a small mirror so that the position of the sprocket hub timing slot can be observed. When the

4.5 Depress the release buttons (arrowed) and disconnect the fuel hoses

slot is aligned with the corresponding hole in the cylinder head the camshaft is positioned correctly.

8 Insert a 5mm diameter bolt, rod or drill through the hole in crankshaft sprocket flange and into the corresponding hole in the oil pump **(see illustration)**, if necessary, carefully turn the crankshaft either way until the rod enters the timing hole in the block.

9 Insert an 8mm bolt, rod or drill through the hole in the camshaft sprocket hub and into engagement with the cylinder head **(see illustration)**.

10 When refitting the timing belt, insert the Volvo tool through the hole in the fuel pump sprocket and into the corresponding hole in the fuel pump mounting bracket **(see illustration)**. In the absence of this tool use a 5mm bolt or drill bit.

11 The crankshaft and camshaft are now locked in position, preventing unnecessary rotation.

4 Cylinder head cover/manifold – removal and refitting

Removal

80 kW engine

1 Disconnect the battery negative lead as described in Chapter 5A.

2 Pull the plastic cover upwards from the top of the engine.

3 Remove the fuel injectors as described in Chapter 4B.

4 Undo the 3 bolts and remove the engine cover mounting bracket from the left-hand end of the cylinder head, located above the fuel filter.

5 Unclip the fuel feed and return hoses from their mountings above the timing belt cover **(see illustration)**.

6 Undo the 3 bolts and disconnect the air inlet pipe from the head cover/manifold flange at the right-hand end of the cylinder head, then undo the 2 Torx screws securing the EGR pipe.

7 Undo the 7 retaining bolts and remove the oil separator from the top of the cylinder head **(see illustration)**. Recover the rubber seal.

8 Undo the remaining bolt securing the

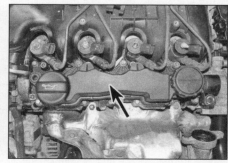

4.7 Undo the bolts and remove the oil separator (arrowed)

4.8 Undo the remaining bolt (arrowed) and pull the cover/manifold upwards

4.10 Undo the 3 screws (arrowed) and remove the engine cover mounting bracket

4.12a Disconnect the inlet hose from the throttle body...

4.12b ...and loosen the mounting bolt below the throttle body

4.13a Disconnect the pipe from the flange (arrowed) at the rear of the cylinder head

4.13b Undo the nut and bolt that secures the throttle body pipe

cylinder head cover/inlet manifold. Lift the assembly away **(see illustration)**. Recover the manifold rubber seals.

85kW engine

9 Pull the plastic cover upwards from the top of the engine.

10 Undo the 3 screws and remove the engine cover mounting bracket above the fuel filter **(see illustration)**. Disconnect the fuel hoses and the wiring plug from the top of the fuel filter with reference to Chapter 1B, Section 20. Unclip the fuel pipes from their fixings on top of the engine.

11 Undo the clip and disconnect the coolant hose below the fuel filter. Unclip the wiring loom from the fuel filter housing. undo the 3 bolts, and remove the fuel filter housing.

12 Slacken the clamp and disconnect the inlet hose from the throttle body **(see illustration)**. Loosen the throttle body mounting bolt below the unit - this is difficult to reach and access can be improved by removing the flexible section of the outlet pipe from the turbocharger **(see illustration)**.

13 Slacken the clamp and disconnect the throttle body pipe from the flange at the rear of the cylinder head **(see illustration)**. Undo the nut and bolt for the pipe support bracket **(see illustration)**.

14 Working at the rear of the engine, disconnect the wiring plug for the EGR valve, undo the EGR bracket bolt, and the two bolts connecting the EGR pipe to the intake pipe.

15 Undo the bolt for the EGR valve lower support bracket, and the 2 bolts for the pipe

connecting the EGR valve to the EGR cooler. Ensuring that all relevant pipework has been disconnected, the EGR valve assembly can now be withdrawn.

16 Undo the 2 bolts connecting the intake pipe to the flange at the rear of the cylinder head, and undo the 3 bolts securing the intake pipe to the engine. The pipe can now be removed.

Refitting

17 Refitting is a reversal of removal, bearing in mind the following points:

a) *Examine any seals or gaskets for signs of damage and deterioration, and renew if necessary.*

b) *On the 80kW engine, renew the fuel injector high-pressure pipes – see Chapter 4B.*

5.2 The locking pin/rod (arrowed) must be located in the hole in the flywheel (arrowed) to prevent rotation

5 Crankshaft pulley – removal and refitting

Removal

1 Remove the auxiliary drivebelt as described in Chapter 1.

2 To lock the crankshaft, working underneath the engine, insert Volvo tool No 999 7169 into the hole in the right-hand face of the engine block casting over the lower section of the flywheel. Rotate the crankshaft until the tool engages in the corresponding hole in the flywheel. In the absence of the Volvo tool, insert a 12mm rod or drill into the hole **(see illustration). Note:** *The hole in the casting and the hole in the flywheel are provided purely to lock the crankshaft whilst the pulley bolt is undone, it does not position the crankshaft at TDC.*

3 Using a suitable socket and extension bar, unscrew the retaining bolt, remove the washer, then slide the pulley off the end of the crankshaft **(see illustration)**. If the pulley is tight fit, it can be drawn off the crankshaft using a suitable puller. If a puller is being used, refit the pulley retaining bolt without the washer, to avoid damaging the crankshaft as the puller is tightened.

Refitting

4 Refit the pulley to the end of the crankshaft.

5 Thoroughly clean the threads of the pulley

5.3 Undo the crankshaft pulley retaining bolt (arrowed)

retaining bolt, then apply a coat of locking compound to the bolt threads.

6 Refit the crankshaft pulley retaining bolt and washer. Tighten the bolt to the specified torque, then through the specified angle, preventing the crankshaft from turning using the method employed on removal.

7 Refit and tension the auxiliary drivebelt as described in Chapter 1B, Section 32.

6 Timing belt covers – removal and refitting

> **Warning: Refer to the precautionary information contained in Section 1 before proceeding.**

Removal

1 Remove the plastic cover from the top of the engine.

6.5a Upper timing cover bolts (arrowed)

7.7 Undo the bolt (arrowed) and remove the crankshaft position sensor

2 Remove the engine undershield.
3 Unclip the fuel hoses from the bracket on the top of the upper cover.
4 Remove the crankshaft pulley as described in Section 5.
5 Undo the 5 bolts and remove the upper cover. Undo the 5 bolts and remove the lower cover **(see illustrations)**.

Refitting

6 Refitting of all the covers is a reversal of the relevant removal procedure, ensuring that each cover section is correctly located, and that the cover retaining bolts are securely tightened. Ensure that all disturbed hoses are reconnected and retained by their relevant clips.

7 Timing belt – removal, inspection, refitting and tensioning

General

1 The timing belt drives the camshaft, high-pressure fuel pump, and coolant pump from a toothed sprocket on the end of the crankshaft. If the belt breaks or slips in service, the pistons are likely to hit the valve heads, resulting in expensive damage.
2 The timing belt should be renewed at the specified intervals, or earlier if it is contaminated with oil, or at all noisy in operation (a 'scraping' noise due to uneven wear).
3 If the timing belt is being removed, it is a

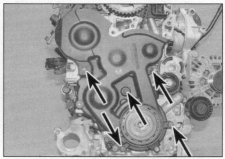

6.5b Lower timing cover bolts (arrowed)

7.9 Remove the timing belt protection bracket

wise precaution to check the condition of the coolant pump at the same time (check for signs of coolant leakage). This may avoid the need to remove the timing belt again at a later stage, should the coolant pump fail.

Removal

4 Apply the handbrake, then jack up the front of the vehicle and support it on axle stands (see *Jacking and vehicle support*). Remove the front right-hand roadwheel, wheel arch liner (to expose the crankshaft pulley), and the engine undershield. The wheel arch liner is secured by screws. The engine undershield is retained by 7 Torx screws.
5 Remove the upper and lower timing belt covers, as described in Section 6.
6 Position a trolley/workshop jack under the engine. Place a block of wood on the jack head, then take the weight of the engine. Unclip the coolant expansion tank from its mountings and move it to one side. Undo the nuts/bolts and remove the right-hand engine mounting as described in Chapter 2E, Section 11
7 Undo the bolt and remove the crankshaft position sensor adjacent to the crankshaft sprocket flange, and move it to one side **(see illustration)**.
8 Undo the 4 bolts and remove the plate below the camshaft sprocket.
9 Undo the retaining bolt and remove the timing belt protection bracket, again, adjacent to the crankshaft sprocket flange **(see illustration)**.
10 Lock the crankshaft and camshaft in the correct position as described in Section 3. If necessary, temporarily refit the crankshaft pulley bolt to enable the crankshaft to be rotated.
11 Insert a hexagon key into the belt tensioner pulley centre, slacken the pulley bolt by no more than 2 turns, and allow the tensioner to rotate, relieving the belt tension **(see illustration)**. With belt slack, temporarily tighten the pulley bolt. Undo the bolt for the idler pulley.
12 Note its routing, then remove the timing belt from the sprockets.

Inspection

13 Renew the belt as a matter of course, regardless of its apparent condition. The

7.11 Slacken the bolt and allow the tensioner to rotate, relieving the tension on the belt

7.15 Timing belt routing

7.17 The index arm must align with the lug (arrowed)

cost of a new belt is nothing compared with the cost of repairs should the belt break in service. If signs of oil contamination are found, trace the source of the oil leak and rectify it. Wash down the engine timing belt area and all related components, to remove all traces of oil. Check that the tensioner and idler pulleys rotate freely without any sign of roughness, and also check that the coolant pump pulley rotates freely. If necessary, renew these items.

Refitting and tensioning

14 Commence refitting by ensuring that the crankshaft, camshaft and fuel pump sprocket timing pins are in position as described in Section 8.

15 Locate the timing belt on the crankshaft sprocket, then keeping it taut, locate it around the idler pulley, camshaft sprocket, high-pressure pump sprocket, coolant pump sprocket, and the tensioner roller **(see illustration)**.

16 Refit the timing belt protection bracket and tighten the retaining bolt securely.

17 Slacken the tensioner pulley bolt, and using a hexagonal key, rotate the tensioner anti-clockwise, which moves the index arm clockwise, until the index arm is aligned as shown **(see illustration)**.

18 Remove the camshaft, crankshaft and fuel pump sprocket (where applicable) timing pins and, using a socket on the crankshaft

pulley bolt, rotate the crankshaft clockwise 10 complete revolutions. Refit the crankshaft and camshaft locking pins.

19 Check that the tensioner index arm is still aligned between the edges of the area shown. If it is not, remove and belt and begin the refitting process again, starting at Paragraph 14.

20 The remainder of refitting is a reversal of removal. Tighten all fasteners to the specified torque where given.

8 Timing belt sprockets and tensioner – removal and refitting

Camshaft sprocket

Removal

1 Remove the timing belt as described in Section 7.

2 Remove the locking tool from the camshaft sprocket/hub. Slacken the sprocket hub retaining bolt. To prevent the camshaft rotating as the bolt is slackened, a sprocket holding tool will be required. In the absence of the special Volvo tool, an acceptable substitute can be fabricated at home **(see Tool Tip 1)**. *Do not* attempt to use the engine assembly/valve timing locking tool to prevent the sprocket from rotating whilst the bolt is slackened.

3 Remove the sprocket hub retaining bolt, and slide the sprocket and hub off the end of the camshaft.

4 Clean the camshaft sprocket thoroughly, and renew it if there are any signs of wear, damage or cracks.

Refitting

5 Refit the camshaft sprocket to the camshaft **(see illustration)**.

6 Refit the sprocket hub retaining bolt. Tighten the bolt to the specified torque, preventing the camshaft from turning as during removal.

7 Align the engine assembly/valve timing slot in the camshaft sprocket hub with the hole in the cylinder head and refit the timing pin to lock the camshaft in position.

8 Fit the timing belt around the pump sprocket and camshaft sprocket, and tension the timing belt as described in Section 7.

Crankshaft sprocket

Removal

9 Remove the timing belt as described in Section 7.

10 Check that the engine assembly/valve timing holes are still aligned as described in Section 3, and the camshaft sprocket and flywheel are locked in position.

11 Slide the sprocket off the end of the crankshaft and collect the Woodruff key **(see illustrations)**.

8.5 Ensure the lug on the sprocket hub engages with the slot on the end of the camshaft (arrowed)

8.11a Slide the sprocket from the crankshaft...

8.11b ...and recover the woodruff key

8.17 Insert a suitable drill bit through the sprocket into the hole in the backplate

12 Examine the crankshaft oil seal for signs of oil leakage and, if necessary, renew it as described in Section 14.

13 Clean the crankshaft sprocket thoroughly, and renew it if there are any signs of wear, damage or cracks. Recover the crankshaft locating key.

Refitting

14 Refit the key to the end of the crankshaft, then refit the crankshaft sprocket (with the flange facing the crankshaft pulley).

15 Fit the timing belt around the crankshaft sprocket, and tension the timing belt as described in Section 7.

Fuel pump sprocket

Removal

16 Remove the timing belt as described in Section 7.

17 Using a suitable socket, undo the pump sprocket retaining nut. The sprocket can be held stationary by inserting a suitably-sized locking pin, drill or rod through the hole in the sprocket, and into the corresponding hole in the backplate **(see illustration)**, or by using a suitable forked tool engaged with the holes in the sprocket **(see Tool Tip 1)**.

18 The pump sprocket is a taper fit on the pump shaft and it will be necessary to make up another tool to release it from the taper **(see Tool Tip 2)**.

19 Partially unscrew the sprocket retaining nut, fit the home-made tool, and secure it to the sprocket with two suitable bolts. Prevent the sprocket from rotating as before, and unscrew the sprocket retaining nut. The nut will bear

8.31 Timing belt idler pulley retaining nut (arrowed)

Tool Tip 1 A sprocket holding tool can be made from two lengths of steel strip bolted together to form a forked end. Drill holes and insert bolts in the ends of the fork to engage with the sprocket spokes

against the tool as it is undone, forcing the sprocket off the shaft taper. Once the taper is released, remove the tool, unscrew the nut fully, and remove the sprocket from the pump shaft.

20 Clean the sprocket thoroughly, and renew it if there are any signs of wear, damage or cracks.

Refitting

21 Refit the pump sprocket and retaining nut, and tighten the nut to the specified torque. Prevent the sprocket rotating as the nut is tightened using the sprocket holding tool.

22 Refit the timing belt as described in Section 7.

Coolant pump sprocket

23 The coolant pump sprocket is integral with the pump, and cannot be removed. Coolant pump removal is described in Chapter 3.

Tensioner pulley

Removal

24 Remove the timing belt as described in Section 7.

25 Remove the tensioner pulley retaining bolt, and slide the pulley off its mounting stud.

26 Clean the tensioner pulley, but do not use any strong solvent which may enter the pulley bearings. Check that the pulley rotates freely, with no sign of stiffness or free play. Renew the pulley if there is any doubt about its condition, or if there are any obvious signs of wear or damage.

27 Examine the pulley mounting stud for signs of damage and if necessary, renew it.

Refitting

28 Refit the tensioner pulley to its mounting stud, and fit the retaining bolt.

29 Refit the timing belt as described in Section 7.

Idler pulley

Removal

30 Remove the timing belt as described in Section 7.

Tool Tip 2 Make a sprocket releasing tool from a short strip of steel. Drill two holes in the strip to correspond with the two holes in the sprocket. Drill a third hole just large enough to accept the flats of the sprocket retaining nut

31 Undo the retaining bolt/nut and withdraw the idler pulley from the engine **(see illustration)**.

32 Clean the idler pulley, but do not use any strong solvent which may enter the bearings. Check that the pulley rotates freely, with no sign of stiffness or free play. Renew the idler pulley if there is any doubt about its condition, or if there are any obvious signs of wear or damage.

Refitting

33 Locate the idler pulley on the engine, and fit the retaining bolt/nut. Tighten the bolt/nut to the specified torque.

34 Refit the timing belt as described in Section 7.

9 Camshafts, rocker arms and hydraulic tappets – removal, inspection and refitting

Removal

80kw engine

1 Remove the cylinder head cover/manifold as described in Section 4.

2 Remove the camshaft position sensor as described in Chapter 4B, and the camshaft oil seal as described in Section 14.

3 Undo the bolts and remove the vacuum pump (see Chapter 9). Recover the pump O-ring seals **(see illustration)**.

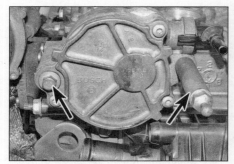

9.3 Vacuum pump bolts (arrowed)

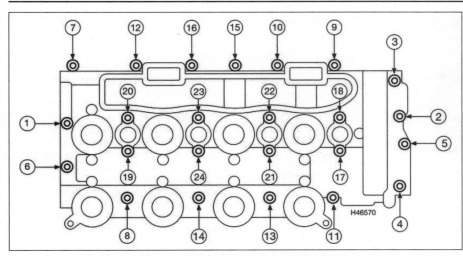

9.7 Camshaft cover/bearing ladder bolt slackening sequence

9.8 The camshaft bearing caps are numbered 1 to 4 from the flywheel end A for inlet, and E for exhaust (arrowed)

4 Remove the fuel filter (see Chapter 1B), then undo the bolts and remove the fuel filter mounting bracket.

5 Remove the short section of pipe between the turbocharger and the intercooler pipe. Slacken the clamp at the intercooler pipe, slacken the clamp and disconnect the pipe to the throttle body assembly. Loosen the 2 bolts (but don't remove them completely) securing the pipe to the turbocharger.

6 Remove the mounting bolt at the cylinder head that secures the throttle body, and move the assembly to one side.

7 Working gradually and evenly, slacken and remove the bolts securing the camshaft cover/bearing ladder to the cylinder head in sequence **(see illustration)**. Lift the cover/ladder from position complete with the camshafts.

8 Undo the retaining bolts and remove the bearing caps. Note their fitted positions, as they must be refitted into their original positions **(see illustration)**. Note that the bearing caps are marked A for inlet, and E for exhaust, and 1 to 4 from the flywheel end of the cylinder head.

9 Undo the bolts securing the chain tensioner assembly to the camshaft cover/bearing ladder, then lift the camshafts, chain and tensioner from place **(see illustrations)**. Discard the camshaft oil seal.

10 Obtain 16 small, clean plastic containers,

and number them 1 to 8 inlet and 1 to 8 exhaust; alternatively, divide a larger container into 16 compartments.

11 Lift out each rocker arm. Put the rocker arms in their respective positions in the containers.

12 A compartmentalised container filled with engine oil is now required to retain the hydraulic tappets while they are removed from the cylinder head. Withdraw each hydraulic tappet and place it in the container, keeping them each identified for correct refitting. The tappets must be totally submerged in the oil to prevent air entering them.

85kw engine

13 To remove the camshaft, start by removing the brake vacuum pump as described in Chapter 9. Recover the pump O-ring seals.

14 Follow the steps in the relevant Section of this Chapter and remove the timing belt and camshaft oil seal.

15 Remove the fuel filter as described in Chapter 1B, undo the 3 bolts, and remove the filter housing.

16 Remove the foam padding at the rear of the camshaft cover. Slacken the inlet pipe clamp at the flange at the rear of the cylinder head, undo the nut and bolt for the support bracket **(see illustration)**, and move the inlet air pipe to one side.

17 Ensure that all pipes/hoses are disconnected then undo the 11 bolts and remove the camshaft cover.

18 Undo the 12 bolts and remove the camshaft bearing ladder. The camshaft can now be lifted from position.

19 To remove the rockers and hydraulic tappets, refer to Section 10.

Inspection

All engines

20 Inspect the cam lobes and the camshaft bearing journals for scoring or other visible evidence of wear. Once the surface hardening of the cam lobes has been eroded, wear will occur at an accelerated rate. **Note:** *If these symptoms are visible on the tips of the camshaft lobes, check the corresponding rocker arm, as it will probably be worn as well.*

21 Examine the condition of the bearing surfaces in the cylinder head and camshaft bearing housing. If wear is evident, the cylinder head and bearing housing will both have to be renewed, as they are a matched assembly.

22 Inspect the rocker arms and tappets for scuffing, cracking or other damage and renew any components as necessary. Also check the condition of the tappet bores in the cylinder head. As with the camshafts, any wear in this area will necessitate cylinder head renewal.

Refitting

80kw engine

23 Thoroughly clean the sealant from the

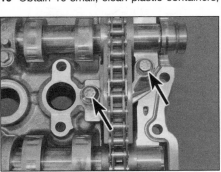

9.9a Undo the tensioner bolts (arrowed)...

9.9b ...then lift the camshafts, chain and tensioner from place

9.16 Undo the nut and bolt that secures the throttle body pipe

9.26 Refit the hydraulic tappets...

9.27 ...and rocker arms to their original locations

mating surfaces of the cylinder head and camshaft bearing housing. Use a suitable liquid gasket dissolving agent (available from Volvo dealers) together with a soft putty knife; do not use a metal scraper or the faces will be damaged. As there is no conventional gasket used, the cleanliness of the mating faces is of the utmost importance.

24 Clean off any oil, dirt or grease from both components and dry with a clean lint-free cloth. Ensure that all the oilways are completely clean.

25 Liberally lubricate the hydraulic tappet bores in the cylinder head with clean engine oil.

26 Insert the hydraulic tappets into their original bores in the cylinder head unless they have been renewed **(see illustration)**.

27 Lubricate the rocker arms and place them over their respective tappets and valve stems **(see illustration)**.

28 Engage the timing chain around the camshaft sprockets, aligning the black-coloured links with the marked teeth on the camshaft sprockets **(see illustration)**. If the black colouring has been lost, there must be 12 chain link pins between the marks on the sprockets.

29 Fit the chain tensioner between the upper and lower runs of the chain, then lubricate the bearing surfaces with clean engine oil, and fit the camshafts into position on the underside of the camshaft cover/bearing ladder. Refit the bearing caps to their original positions and tighten the retaining bolts to the specified torque **(see illustrations)**. Tighten the tensioner retaining bolts to the specified torque.

30 Apply a thin bead of silicone sealant to the mating surface of the camshaft cover/bearing ladder as shown **(see illustration)**. Do not allow the sealant to obstruct the oil channels for the hydraulic chain tensioner.

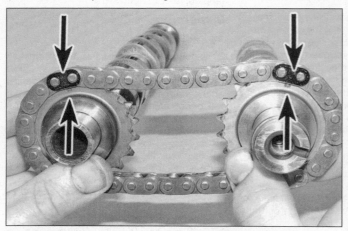

9.28 Align the marks on the sprockets with the centre of the black-coloured chain links (arrowed). There must be 12 link pins between the sprocket marks

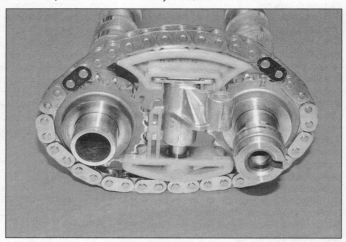

9.29a Assemble the chain tensioner between the upper and lower runs of the chain...

9.29b ...and lower the camshaft, chain and tensioner into position

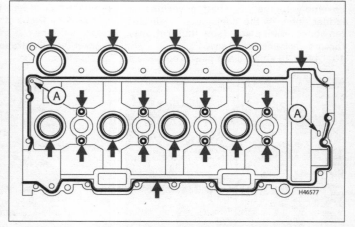

9.30 Apply sealant to the camshaft cover/bearing ladder as indicated by the heavy black lines. Ensure sealant doesn't enter the tensioner oil holes marked A

31 Check that the black-coloured links on the chain are still aligned with the marks on the camshaft sprockets, then refit the camshaft cover/bearing ladder, and gradually and evenly tighten the retaining bolts until the cover/ladder is in contact with the cylinder head. Tighten the bolts to the specified torque in sequence **(see illustration)**. **Note:** *Ensure the cover/ladder is correctly located by checking the bores of the vacuum pump and camshaft oil seal at each end of the cover/ladder.*

32 Fit a new camshaft oil seal as described in Section 14.

33 Refit the camshaft sprocket, and tighten the retaining bolt finger-tight.

34 Using a spanner on the camshaft sprocket bolt, rotate the camshafts approximately 40 complete revolutions clockwise. Check the black-coloured links on the chain still align with the marks on the camshaft sprockets.

35 If the marks still align, refit the camshaft sprocket as described in Section 8.

36 Refit and adjust the camshaft position sensor as described in Chapter 4B.

37 Press the new oil seals into the bearing housing, using a tube/socket of approximately 20mm outside diameter, ensuring the inner lip of the seal fits around the injector guide tube **(see illustrations)**. Refit the injectors as described in Chapter 4B.

38 Refit the cylinder head cover/manifold as described in Section 4.

85kw engine

39 To refit the camshaft, first note the points above regarding the cleaning of mating surfaces. Apply a thin bead of sealant (Volvo 31330209) to the mating surface of the camshaft carrier. Note that the camshaft bearing ladder must be installed within 5 minutes of applying the sealant.

40 Refit the camshaft, lubricating the bearings with engine oil.

41 Refit the camshaft bearing ladder, tightening the bolts to the specified torque.

42 The remainder of refitting is a reversal of removal.

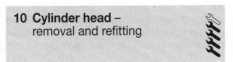

10 Cylinder head –
removal and refitting

Removal

80kw engine

1 Disconnect the battery negative lead as described in Chapter 5A.

2 Remove the air cleaner housing as described in Chapter 4B.

3 Remove the intake manifold and the exhaust manifold as described in Chapter 4B Section 17.

4 Remove the brake vacuum pump as described in Chapter 9.

5 Remove the thermostat (see Chapter 3) and the fuel pump (see Chapter 4B).

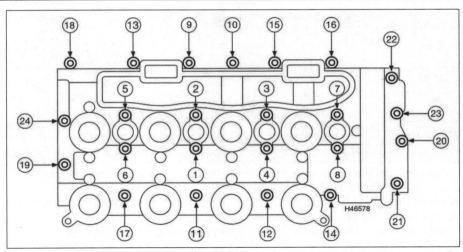

9.31 Camshaft cover/bearing ladder bolt tightening sequence

9.37a Fit the new seal around a 20mm outside diameter socket…

9.37b …and push it into place

6 Remove the camshafts, rocker arms and hydraulic tappets as described in Section 9.

7 Working in the sequence shown **(see illustration)** undo the cylinder head bolts. Discard the bolts – new ones must be fitted.

8 Release the cylinder head from the cylinder block and location dowels by rocking it. Do not prise between the mating faces of the cylinder head and block, as this may damage the gasket faces.

9 Lift the cylinder head from the block, and recover the gasket.

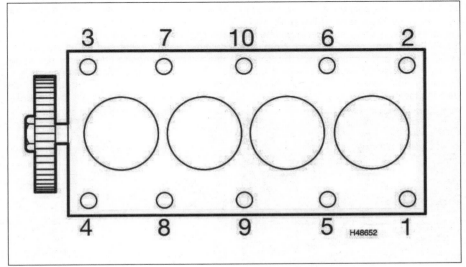

10.7 Cylinder head bolt slackening sequence

10.23a Pull the non-return valve from the cylinder head...

85kw engine

10 Remove the fuel injectors as described in Chapter 4B, and the glow plugs as described in Chapter 5C.

11 Remove the brake vacuum pump as described in Chapter 9.

12 Remove the camshaft oil seal as described in Section 14.

13 Remove the thermostat as described in Chapter 3, and the exhaust manifold as described in Chapter 4B.

14 Ensure that all pipes/hoses are disconnected then undo the 11 bolts and remove the camshaft cover.

15 Undo the 13 bolts and remove the camshaft carrier. Undo the support bracket bold located behind the high pressure fuel pump.

16 Lift out each rocker arm. Place the rocker arms in their respective positions in suitable boxes or containers.

17 A compartmentalised container filled with engine oil is now required to retain the hydraulic tappets while they are removed from the cylinder head. Withdraw each hydraulic follower and place it in the container, keeping them each identified for correct refitting. The tappets must be totally submerged in the oil to prevent air entering them.

18 Working in the sequence shown, undo the cylinder head bolts **(see illustration 10.7)**. Discard the bolts - new ones must be fitted.

19 Release the cylinder head from the cylinder block and location dowels by rocking it. Do not prise between the mating faces of the cylinder head and block, as this may damage the gasket faces.

10.28 Measure the piston protrusion using a DTi gauge

10.23b ...and push a new one into place

20 Lift the cylinder head from the block, and recover the gasket.

Preparation for refitting

21 The mating faces of the cylinder head and cylinder block must be perfectly clean before refitting the head. Use a hard plastic or wood scraper to remove all traces of gasket and carbon. The same method can be used to clean the piston crowns. Take particular care to avoid scoring or gouging the cylinder head/cylinder block mating surfaces during the cleaning operations, as aluminium alloy is easily damaged. Make sure that the carbon is not allowed to enter the oil and water passages – this is particularly important for the lubrication system, as carbon could block the oil supply to the engine's components. Using adhesive tape and paper, seal the water, oil and bolt holes in the cylinder block. To prevent carbon entering the gap between the pistons and bores, smear a little grease in the gap. After cleaning each piston, use a small brush to remove all traces of grease and carbon from the gap, then wipe away the remainder with a clean rag.

22 Check the mating surfaces of the cylinder block and the cylinder head for nicks, deep scratches and other damage. If slight, they may be removed carefully with a file, but if excessive, machining may be the only alternative to renewal. If warpage of the cylinder head gasket surface is suspected, use a straight-edge to check it for distortion. Refer to Part F of this Chapter if necessary.

23 Thoroughly clean the threads of the cylinder head bolt holes in the cylinder

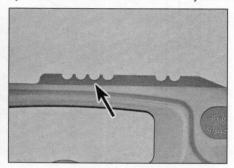

10.30 Cylinder head gasket thickness identification notches

block. Ensure that the bolts run freely in their threads, and that all traces of oil and water are removed from each bolt hole. If required, pull the oil feed non-return valve from the cylinder head, and check the ball moves freely. Push a new valve into place if necessary **(see illustrations)**.

Gasket selection

24 The gasket thickness is indicated by notches/holes on the front edge of the gasket. If the crankshaft or pistons/connecting rods have not been disturbed, fit a new gasket with the same number of notches/holes as the previous one. If the crankshaft/piston or connecting rods have been disturbed, it's necessary to work out the piston protrusion as follows:

25 Remove the crankshaft timing pin, then turn the crankshaft until pistons 1 and 4 are at TDC (Top Dead Centre). Position a dial test indicator (dial gauge) on the cylinder block adjacent to the rear of No 1 piston, and zero it on the block face. Transfer the probe to the crown of No 1 piston (10.0 mm in from the rear edge), then slowly turn the crankshaft back-and-forth past TDC, noting the highest reading on the indicator. Record this reading as protrusion A.

26 Repeat the check described in paragraph 25, this time 10.0 mm in from the front edge of the No 1 piston crown. Record this reading as protrusion B.

27 Add protrusion A to protrusion B, then divide the result by 2 to obtain an average reading for piston No 1.

28 Repeat the procedure described in paragraph 25 on piston 4, then turn the crankshaft through 180° and carry out the procedure on the piston Nos 2 and 3 **(see illustration)**. Check that there is a maximum difference of 0.07 mm protrusion between any two pistons.

29 If a dial test indicator is not available, piston protrusion may be measured using a straight-edge and feeler blades or Vernier calipers. However, this is much less accurate, and cannot therefore be recommended.

30 Note the greatest piston protrusion measurement, and use this to determine the correct cylinder head gasket from the table below. The series of notches/holes on the side of the gasket are used for thickness identification **(see illustration)**.

Refitting

31 Turn the crankshaft and position Nos 1 and 4 pistons at TDC, then turn the crankshaft a quarter turn (90°) anti-clockwise.

32 Thoroughly clean the surfaces of the cylinder head and block.

33 Make sure that the locating dowels are in place, then fit the correct gasket the right way round on the cylinder block **(see illustration)**.

34 Carefully lower the cylinder head onto the gasket and block, making sure that it locates correctly onto the dowels.

35 Apply a smear of grease to the threads,

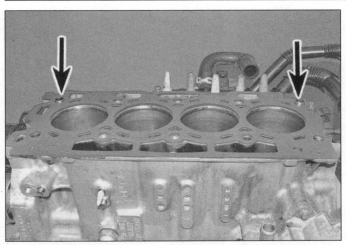

10.33 Ensure the gasket locates over the dowels (arrowed)

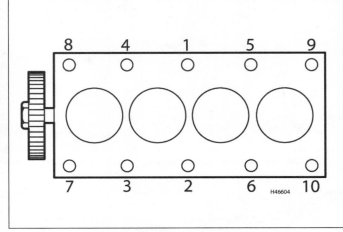

10.37 Cylinder head bolt tightening sequence

and to the underside of the heads of the new cylinder head bolts.

36 Carefully insert the cylinder head bolts into their holes (*do not drop them in*) and initially finger-tighten them.

37 Working progressively and in sequence, tighten the cylinder head bolts to their Stage 1 torque setting, using a torque wrench and suitable socket **(see illustration)**.

38 Once all the bolts have been tightened to their Stage 1 torque setting, working again in the specified sequence, tighten each bolt to the specified Stage 2 setting. Finally, angle-tighten the bolts through the specified Stage 3 angle. It is recommended that an angle-measuring gauge is used during this stage of tightening, to ensure accuracy. **Note:** *Retightening of the cylinder head bolts after running the engine is not required.*

39 Refit the hydraulic tappets, rocker arms, and camshaft housing (complete with camshafts) as described in the relevant section. Note that on models fitted with the 85kw engine, a thin bead of sealant (Volvo 116 1771) should be applied to the mating surface of the cylinder head before the camshaft carrier is refitted.

40 The remainder of refitting is a reversal of removal, noting the following points.

a) *When refitting a cylinder head, it is good practice to renew the thermostat.*

b) *Tighten all fasteners to the specified torque where given.*

c) *Top-up or replenish the coolant and engine oil as required, with reference to Chapter 1B.*

d) *The engine may run erratically for the first few miles, until the engine management ECM relearns its stored values.*

11 Sump – removal and refitting

Removal

1 Drain the engine oil, then clean and refit the engine oil drain plug, tightening it securely. If the engine is nearing its service interval when the oil and filter are due for renewal, it is recommended that the filter is also removed, and a new one fitted. After reassembly, the engine can then be refilled with fresh oil. Refer to Chapter 1B for further information.

2 Apply the handbrake, then jack up the front of the vehicle and support it on axle stands (see *Jacking and vehicle support*). Undo the Torx screws and remove the engine undershield.

3 Progressively slacken and remove all the sump retaining bolts/nuts. Since the sump bolts may vary in length, remove each bolt in turn, and store it in its correct fitted order by pushing it through a clearly-marked cardboard template. This will avoid the possibility of installing the bolts in the wrong locations on refitting.

4 Try to break the joint by striking the sump with the palm of your hand, then lower and withdraw the sump from under the car. If the sump is stuck (which is quite likely) use a putty knife or similar, carefully inserted between the sump and block. Ease the knife along the joint until the sump is released. While the sump is removed, take the opportunity to check the oil pump pick-up/

strainer for signs of clogging or splitting. If necessary, remove the pump as described in this chapter, and clean or renew the strainer.

Refitting

5 Clean all traces of sealant from the mating surfaces of the cylinder block/crankcase and sump, then use a clean rag to wipe out the sump and the engine's interior.

6 On engines where the sump was fitted without a gasket, ensure that the sump mating surfaces are clean and dry, then apply a thin coating of silicone sealant to the sump or crankcase mating surface **(see illustration)**. Ensure the sealant is applied to the inside of the retaining bolt holes Note that the sump must be installed within 5 minutes of applying the sealant.

7 Offer up the sump to the cylinder block/crankcase. Refit its retaining bolts/nuts, ensuring that each bolt is screwed into its original location. Tighten the bolts evenly and progressively to the specified torque setting **(see illustration)**

8 Lower the vehicle to the ground, then refill the engine with oil as described in Chapter 1B.

9 After applying sealant Volvo recommend waiting a minimum of 2 hours before starting the engine.

11.6 Apply a bead of sealant to the sump or crankcase mating surface

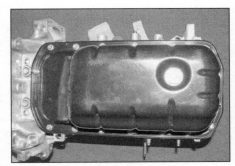

11.7 Refit the sump and tighten the bolts

12.3 Oil pick-up tube bolts (arrowed)

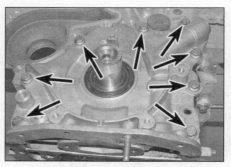

12.4 Oil pump retaining bolts (arrowed)

12.6 Apply a bead of sealant to the cylinder block mating surfaces

12.7a Fit a new seal…

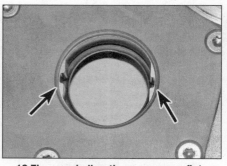

12.7b …and align the pump gear flats (arrowed)…

12.7c …with those of the crankshaft

12 Oil pump – removal and refitting

Removal

1 Remove the sump as described in Section 11.
2 Remove the timing belt as described in Section 7.
3 Undo the three bolts and remove the oil pump pick-up tube from the pump/block (see illustration). Discard the oil seal, a new one must be fitted.
4 Undo the 8 bolts, and remove the oil pump (see illustration).

Refitting

5 Remove all traces of sealant, and thoroughly clean the mating surfaces of the oil pump and cylinder block.
6 Apply a 4mm wide bead of silicone sealant (Volvo 116 1771) to the mating face of the cylinder block (see illustration). Ensure that no sealant enters any of the holes in the block.
7 With a new oil seal fitted, refit the oil pump over the end of the crankshaft, aligning the flats in the pump drive gear with the flats machined in the crankshaft (see illustrations). Note that new oil pumps are supplied with the oil seal already fitted, and a seal protector sleeve. The sleeve fits over the end of the crankshaft to protect the seal as the pump is fitted.
8 Install the oil pump bolts and tighten them to the specified torque.
9 Refit the oil pick-up tube to the pump/cylinder block using a new O-ring seal.

Ensure the oil dipstick guide tube is correctly refitted.
10 Refit the woodruff key to the crankshaft, and slide the crankshaft sprocket into place.
11 The remainder of refitting is a reversal of removal.

13 Oil cooler – removal and refitting

Removal

1 Drain the coolant as described in Chapter 1B. Drain the engine oil as described in Chapter 1B, or be prepared for fluid spillage.
2 On models fitted with the 85 kW engine, remove the diesel particulate filter as described in Chapter 4D.
3 Undo the bolts/stud and remove the oil cooler located on the front of the oil filter housing. Recover the O-ring seals (see illustrations).

Refitting

4 Fit new O-ring seals into the recesses in the oil filter housing, and refit the cooler. Tighten the bolts securely.
5 Refit the diesel particulate filter if removed with reference to Chapter 4D.
6 Refill or top-up the cooling system and engine oil level as described in Chapter 1B or Weekly Checks (as applicable). Start the engine, and check the oil cooler for signs of leakage.

13.3a Undo the oil cooler bolts/stud (arrowed)

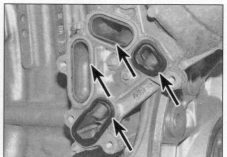

13.3b Renew the O-ring seals

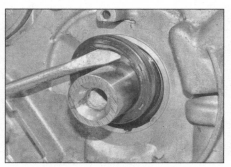

14.3 Take great care not to mark the crankshaft while levering out the seal

14.5a Slide the seal and protective sleeve over the end of the crankshaft...

14.5b ...and press the seal into place

14.12 Slide the seal and protective sleeve over the left-hand end of the crankshaft

14.16 Drill a hole, insert a self-tapping screw and pull the seal from place using pliers

14.18 Fit the protective sleeve and seal over the end of the camshaft

14 Oil seals – renewal

Crankshaft

Right-hand oil seal

1 Remove the crankshaft sprocket and Woodruff key as described in Section 8.
2 Measure and note the fitted depth of the oil seal.
3 Pull the oil seal from the housing using a screwdriver. Alternatively, drill a small hole in the oil seal, and use a self-tapping screw and a pair of pliers to remove it **(see illustration)**.
4 Clean the oil seal housing and the crankshaft sealing surface.
5 The seal has a Teflon lip and must not be oiled or marked. The new seal should be supplied with a protective sleeve, which fits over the end of the crankshaft to prevent any damage to the seal lip. With the sleeve in place, press the seal (open end first) into the pump to the previously-noted depth, using a suitable tube or socket **(see illustrations)**.
6 Where applicable, remove the plastic sleeve from the end of the crankshaft.
7 Refit the crankshaft sprocket as described in Section 8.

Left-hand oil seal

8 Remove the flywheel, as described in Section 16.
9 Measure and note the fitted depth of the oil seal.

10 Pull the oil seal from the housing using a screwdriver. Alternatively, drill a small hole in the oil seal, and use a self-tapping screw and a pair of pliers to remove it.
11 Clean the oil seal housing and the crankshaft sealing surface.
12 The seal should be lubricated with engine oil before refitting. The new seal should be supplied with a protective sleeve, which fits over the end of the crankshaft to prevent any damage to the seal lip **(see illustration)**. With the sleeve in place, press the seal (open end first) into the housing to the previously-noted depth using a suitable tube or socket.
13 Where applicable, remove the plastic sleeve from the end of the crankshaft.
14 Refit the flywheel, as described in Section 16.

Camshaft

15 Remove the camshaft sprocket as described in Section 8. In principle there is no need to remove the timing belt completely, but remember that if the belt has been contaminated with oil, it must be renewed. Undo the 3 bolts and remove the inner timing belt cover where fitted.
16 Pull the oil seal from the housing using a hooked instrument. Alternatively, drill a small hole in the oil seal and use a self-tapping screw and a pair of pliers to remove it **(see illustration)**.
17 Clean the oil seal housing and the camshaft sealing surface.
18 The seal has a Teflon lip and must not

be oiled or marked. The new seal should be supplied with a protective sleeve. which fits over the end of the camshaft to prevent any damage to the seal lip **(see illustration)**. With the sleeve in place, press the seal (open end first) into the housing to the previously-noted depth, using a suitable tube or socket which bears only of the outer edge of the seal.
19 Refit the camshaft sprocket as described in Section 8.
20 Where necessary, fit a new timing belt with reference to Section 7.

15 Oil pressure switch – removal and refitting

Removal

1 The oil pressure switch is located at the front of the cylinder block, adjacent to the oil dipstick guide tube. Note that on some models, access to the switch may be improved if the vehicle is jacked up and supported on axle stands, then undo the 7 Torx screws and remove the engine undershield so that the switch can be reached from underneath (see *Jacking and vehicle support*).
2 Remove the protective sleeve from the wiring plug (where applicable), then disconnect the wiring from the switch.
3 Unscrew the switch from the cylinder block, and recover the sealing washer **(see**

15.3 The oil pressure switch is located on the front face of the cylinder block (arrowed)

illustration). Be prepared for oil spillage, and if the switch is to be left removed from the engine for any length of time, plug the hole in the cylinder block.

Refitting

4 Examine the sealing washer for any signs of damage or deterioration, and if necessary renew.

5 Refit the switch, complete with washer, and tighten it to the specified torque where given.

6 Refit the engine undershield, and lower the vehicle to the ground.

16 Flywheel –
removal, inspection and refitting

Removal

1 Remove the transmission as described in Chapter 7A, then remove the clutch assembly as described in Chapter 6.

16.8 Flywheel retaining torx bolts

2 Make alignment marks between the flywheel and crankshaft to aid refitment.

3 Prevent the flywheel from turning. Volvo recommend the use of a locking tool (part number 999 7120) that is bolted to the engine/transmission mounting face but a large screwdriver can be inserted in the ring gear teeth. Slacken and remove the flywheel retaining bolts, and remove the flywheel from the end of the crankshaft. Be careful not to drop it; it is heavy. If the flywheel locating dowel (where fitted) is a loose fit in the crankshaft end, remove it and store it with the flywheel for safe-keeping. Discard the flywheel bolts; new ones must be used on refitting.

Inspection

4 Examine the flywheel for scoring of the clutch face, and for wear or chipping of the ring gear teeth. If the clutch face is scored, the flywheel may be surface-ground, but renewal is preferable. Seek the advice of a Volvo

dealer or engine reconditioning specialist to see if machining is possible. If the ring gear is worn or damaged, the flywheel must be renewed, as it is not possible to renew the ring gear separately.

Refitting

5 Clean the mating surfaces of the flywheel and crankshaft. Remove any remaining locking compound from the threads of the crankshaft holes, using the correct size of tap, if available.

6 If the new flywheel retaining bolts are not supplied with their threads already pre-coated, apply a suitable thread-locking compound to the threads of each bolt.

7 Ensure that the locating dowel is in position. Offer up the flywheel, locating it on the dowel (where fitted), and fit the new retaining bolts. Where no locating dowel is fitted, align the previously-made marks to ensure the flywheel is refitted in its original position. Ensure the flywheel is in full contact with the crankshaft flange before installing the bolts.

8 Lock the flywheel using the method employed on dismantling, and tighten the retaining bolts to the specified torque **(see illustration)**.

9 Refit the clutch as described in Chapter 6. Remove the flywheel locking tool if used, and refit the transmission as described in Chapter 7A.

17 Engine/transmission mountings –
inspection and renewal

Refer to Chapter 2E, Section 11.

Chapter 2 Part D:
2.0 litre 4-cylinder diesel engine in-car repair procedures

Contents

Degrees of difficulty

Easy, suitable for novice with little experience	**Fairly easy,** suitable for beginner with some experience	**Fairly difficult,** suitable for competent DIY mechanic	**Difficult,** suitable for experienced DIY mechanic	**Very difficult,** suitable for expert DIY or professional

Specifications

General

Engine type.	Four-cylinder, in-line, double overhead camshaft, aluminium cylinder head and cast iron engine block with turbocharger
Engine code	D4204T
Power output	100 kW @ 4000 rpm
Torque output	320 Nm @ 1750 rpm
Capacity	1998 cc
Bore	85.0mm
Stroke.	88.0mm
Compression ratio	18.1:1
Firing order	1-3-4-2 (No 1 cylinder at transmission)
Direction of crankshaft rotation	Clockwise (seen from right-hand side of vehicle)

Cylinder head gasket identification

	Piston protrusion	Gasket thickness
1 notch	0.55 to 0.60mm	1.21 to 1.29mm
2 notches	0.61 to 0.65mm	1.26 to 1.34mm
3 notches	0.66 to 0.70mm	1.31 to 1.39mm
4 notches	0.71 to 0.75mm	1.36 to 1.40mm

Camshaft

Drive	Toothed belt for exhaust camshaft and roller chain to inlet camshaft

Lubrication

Engine oil type/specification	See *Lubricants, fluids and tyre pressures* on page 0•16
Engine oil capacity	See Chapter 1B Specifications
Oil pressure – minimum (engine at operating temperature):	
At 2000 rpm	2.0 bar
At 4000 rpm	4.0 bar

Valves

Valve clearances.	Hydraulic compensators – no adjustment necessary

Torque wrench settings

	Nm	lbf ft
Big-end bearing cap bolts: *		
Stage 1	20	15
Stage 2	Angle-tighten a further 70°	
Camshaft bearing housing:		
Stage 1	5	4
Stage 2	10	7
Camshaft sprocket bolt:		
Stage 1	20	15
Stage 2	Angle-tighten a further 60°	
Camshaft position sensor	2	1.5
Crankshaft oil seal carrier..	17	12
Crankshaft pulley bolt: *		
Stage 1	70	52
Stage 2	Angle-tighten a further 60°	
Cylinder head lower section-to-block bolts:		
Stage 1	60	44
Stage 2	Angle-tighten a further 220°	
Cylinder head upper section-to-lower section bolts:		
Stage 1	5	4
Stage 2	10	7
Cylinder head cover/intake manifold:		
Stage 1	5	4
Stage 2	10	7
Engine mountings:		
Right-hand mounting nuts (M12)	90	66
Right-hand mounting bolts-to-cylinder head	90	66
Left-hand mounting bolts:		
M8	24	18
Bracket nuts:		
Stage 1	35	26
Stage 2	Angle-tighten a further 60°	
Centre mounting bolt	150	111
Lower torque rod bolts..	80	59
Engine oil drain plug..	38	28
Flywheel bolts*...	48	35
Fuel high-pressure pump mounting bolts	20	15
Fuel high-pressure pipe unions:		
Stage 1	19	14
Stage 2	30	22
Fuel injector mounting studs	13	11
Main bearing bolts:		
Stage 1	25	18
Stage 2	Angle-tighten a further 60°	
Oil cooler retaining bolts...	10	7
Oil pressure switch...	15	11
Oil pump bolts	17	13
Piston cooling jet	10	7
Sump bolts:		
M7	17	13
M10	50	37
Thermostat housing to cylinder head............................	17	13
Timing belt cover bolts...	10	7
Timing belt tensioner	24	18
Timing chain tensioner	6	4
Vacuum pump	10	7

* Do not re-use

---

1 General information

How to use this Chapter

This Part of Chapter 2 describes the repair procedures that can reasonably be carried out on the engine while it remains in the vehicle. If the engine has been removed from the vehicle and is being dismantled as described in Part F, any preliminary dismantling procedures can be ignored.

Note that, while it may be possible physically to overhaul items such as the piston/connecting rod assemblies while the engine is in the car, such tasks are not usually carried out as separate operations. Usually, several additional procedures are required (not to mention the cleaning of components and oilways); for this reason, all such tasks are classed as major overhaul procedures, and are described in Part F of this Chapter.

Part F describes the removal of the engine/transmission from the car, and the full overhaul procedures that can then be carried out.

Engine description

This DOHC (double overhead camshaft) 16-valve engine features common rail direct injection, and a VNT (Variable Nozzle Turbine) turbocharger.

All major components are made from aluminium, apart from the cast-iron cylinder block – no liners are fitted, the cylinders are bored directly into the block. An aluminium main bearing ladder is fitted. This arrangement offers greater rigidity than the normal sump arrangement, and helps to reduce engine vibration.

The crankshaft runs in five main bearings, thrustwashers are fitting either side of the No 1 cylinder main bearings to control crankshaft endfloat. The connecting rods rotate on horizontally-split bearing shells at their big-ends. The pistons are attached to the connecting rods by gudgeon pins which are a floating fit in the connecting rod small-end eyes, secured by circlips. The aluminium alloy pistons are fitted with three piston rings: two compression rings and an oil control ring. After manufacture, the cylinder bores and piston skirts are measured and classified into four weight grades, which must be carefully matched together to ensure the correct piston/cylinder clearance; no oversizes are available to permit reboring.

The intake and exhaust valves are each closed by coil springs; they operate in guides which are shrink-fitted into the cylinder head, as are the valve seat inserts.

A rubber toothed-belt driven by the crankshaft sprocket rotates the coolant pump, injection high-pressure pump, and the exhaust camshaft sprocket. The intake camshaft is driven by a short timing chain from the exhaust sprocket.

The camshafts operate the 16 valves via roller-rocker arms with hydraulic clearance compensators. The camshafts rotate in five bearings that are line-bored directly into the two sections of the cylinder head.

The vacuum pump (used for the brake servo and other vacuum actuators) is driven from the end of the intake camshaft, whilst the fuel pump is driven from the end of the exhaust camshaft.

The coolant pump is bolted to the right-hand end of the cylinder block, and driven by the timing belt.

When working on this engine, note that Torx-type (both male and female heads) and hexagon socket (Allen head) fasteners are widely used; a good selection of bits, with the necessary adapters, will be required so that these can be unscrewed without damage and, on reassembly, tightened to the torque wrench settings specified.

Lubrication system

The oil pump is mounted under the cylinder block, and is chain driven from a crankshaft sprocket. The pump forces oil through an externally-mounted full-flow cartridge-type filter. From the filter, the oil is pumped into a main gallery in the cylinder block/crankcase, from where it is distributed to the crankshaft (main bearings) and cylinder head. An oil cooler is fitted next to the oil filter, at the rear of the block. The cooler is supplied with coolant from the engine cooling system.

While the crankshaft and camshaft bearings receive a pressurised supply, the camshaft lobes and valves are lubricated by splash, as are all other engine components. The undersides of the pistons are cooled by oil, sprayed from nozzles fitted above the upper main bearing shells. The turbocharger receives its own pressurised oil supply.

Operations with engine in car

The following major repair operations can be accomplished without removing the engine from the vehicle. However, owners should note that any operation involving the removal of the sump requires careful forethought, depending on the level of skill and the tools and facilities available; refer to the relevant text for details.

a) Compression pressure – testing.
b) Cylinder head cover – removal and refitting.
c) Timing belt cover – removal and refitting.
d) Timing belt/chain – renewal.
e) Timing belt tensioner and sprockets – removal and refitting.
f) Camshaft oil seal – renewal.
g) Camshaft and cam followers – removal and refitting.
h) Cylinder head – removal, overhaul and refitting.
i) Cylinder head and pistons – decarbonising.
j) Sump – removal and refitting.
k) Crankshaft oil seals – renewal.
l) Oil pump – removal and refitting.
m) Piston/connecting rod assemblies – removal and refitting (but see note below).
n) Flywheel – removal and refitting.
o) Engine/transmission mountings – removal and refitting.

Note: *It is possible to remove the pistons and connecting rods (after removing the cylinder head and sump) without removing the engine, however, this is not recommended. Work of this nature is more easily and thoroughly completed with the engine on the bench, as described in Chapter 2F.*

Clean the engine compartment and the exterior of the engine with some type of degreaser before any work is done (and/or clean the engine using a steam cleaner). It will make the job easier and will help to keep dirt out of the internal areas of the engine.

Depending on the components involved, it may be helpful to remove the bonnet, to improve access to the engine as repairs are performed (refer to Chapter 11 if necessary). Cover the wings to prevent damage to the paint; special covers are available, but an old bedspread or blanket will also work.

2 Compression and leakdown tests – description and interpretation

Compression test

Note: *A compression tester suitable for use with diesel engines will be required for this test.*

1 When engine performance is down, or if misfiring occurs which cannot be attributed to the fuel or emissions systems, a compression test can provide diagnostic clues as to the engine's condition. If the test is performed regularly, it can give warning of trouble before any other symptoms become apparent.

2 The engine must be fully warmed-up to normal operating temperature, the battery must be fully-charged and the glow plugs must be removed. The aid of an assistant will be required.

3 Make sure that the ignition is switched off (take out the remote unit). Remove the fuel pump fuse from the engine compartment fusebox (see diagram on the fusebox lid), and disconnect the crankshaft speed/position sensor as described in Chapter 4A.

4 Remove the glow plugs as described in Chapter 5C.

5 Fit a compression tester to the No 1 cylinder glow plug hole. The type of tester which screws into the plug thread is preferred.

6 Crank the engine for several seconds on the starter motor. After one or two revolutions, the compression pressure should build-up to a maximum figure and then stabilise. Record the highest reading obtained.

7 Repeat the test on the remaining cylinders, recording the pressure in each.

8 The cause of poor compression is less easy to establish on a diesel engine than on a petrol engine. The effect of introducing oil into the cylinders (wet testing) is not conclusive, because there is a risk that the oil will sit in the recess on the piston crown, instead of passing to the rings. However, the following can be used as a rough guide to diagnosis.

9 All cylinders should produce very similar pressures. Any difference greater than that specified indicates the existence of a fault. Note that the compression should build-up quickly in a healthy engine. Low compression on the first stroke, followed by gradually increasing pressure on successive strokes, indicates worn piston rings. A low compression reading on the first stroke, which does not build-up during successive strokes, indicates leaking valves or a blown head gasket (a cracked head could also be the cause).

10 A low reading from two adjacent cylinders is almost certainly due to the head gasket having blown between them and the presence of coolant in the engine oil will confirm this.

11 On completion, remove the compression tester, and refit the glow plugs.

12 Take out the remote unit, then refit the fuel

3.4 Undo the bolt and remove the camshaft position sensor from the right-hand end of the cylinder head cover

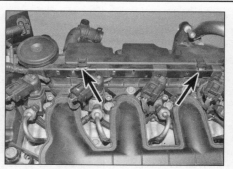

3.6 Release the clips (arrowed) and detach the injector wiring harness duct

3.7a Release the clamps and disconnect the breather hose (arrowed) from the cylinder head cover…

3.7b …and the EGR pipe from the intake manifold…

3.7c …then slide out the clip and disconnect the breather hose from the rear of the cylinder head cover

pump fuse and reconnect the crankshaft speed/position sensor. Note that carrying out this test as described may result in one or more fault codes being stored by the engine management ECU. Have these codes erased by a Volvo dealer or suitably-equipped specialist.

Leakdown test

13 A leakdown test measures the rate at which compressed air fed into the cylinder

is lost. It is an alternative to a compression test, and in many ways it is better, since the escaping air provides easy identification of where pressure loss is occurring (piston rings, valves or head gasket).

14 The equipment required for leakdown testing is unlikely to be available to the home mechanic. If poor compression is suspected, have the test performed by a suitably-equipped garage.

3 Cylinder head cover – removal and refitting

Removal

1 The cylinder head cover is integral with the intake manifold. Begin by removing the plastic cover from the top of the engine.
2 Release the clips and detach the wiring harness and fuel pipes from the timing belt upper cover.
3 Undo the bolt and remove the wiring bracket from the right-hand rear corner of the cylinder head. Undo the bolt and remove the pipe support bracket located in front of the brake vacuum pump.
4 Disconnect the wiring plug, undo the retaining bolt and remove the camshaft position sensor **(see illustration)**.
5 Undo the bolts, slacken the nut, then remove the timing belt upper cover.
6 Disconnect the injectors' wiring plugs, then detach the harness duct from the intake manifold/cover and position it to one side **(see illustration)**.
7 Disconnect the crankcase ventilation hoses from the intake manifold/cover, then release the clamp and disconnect the EGR pipe from the intake manifold **(see illustrations)**.
8 Release the glow plugs' wiring harness from the 2 clips on the manifold.
9 Undo the screws and disconnect the intake hose from the intake manifold.
10 Unclip the fuel temperature sensor (located on underside the intake manifold).
11 Undo the manifold/cover retaining bolts in the **reverse** of the sequence shown **(see illustration 3.13)**. Discards the gaskets, new ones must be fitted.

Refitting

12 Clean the sealing surfaces of the manifold/cover and the head.
13 Fit the new seals to the intake manifold/cover, then fit it to the cylinder head. Use a little petroleum jelly on the manifold O-rings to ease assembly. Tighten the bolts to the specified torque in sequence **(see illustration)**.

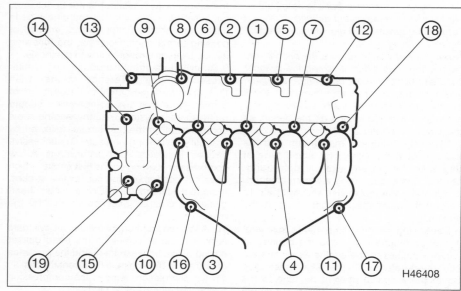

3.13 Intake manifold/cylinder head cover bolt tightening sequence

H46408

14 The remainder of refitting is a reversal of removal, noting the following points:
a) *Tighten all fasteners to their specified torque where given.*
b) *The camshaft position sensor must be refitted in accordance with the instructions given in Chapter 4B, otherwise it will not function correctly.*

4 Crankshaft pulley – removal and refitting

Removal

1 Loosen the right-hand front roadwheel nuts, then raise the front of the vehicle, and support securely on axle stands (see *Jacking and vehicle support*). Remove the roadwheel. Access is greatly improved once the wheel arch liner has been removed.
2 Release the 7 Torx screws and withdraw the engine undershield from under the car.
3 Remove the auxiliary drivebelt as described in Chapter 1B.
4 The centre bolt which secures the crankshaft pulley must now be slackened. This bolt is tightened to a very high torque, and it is first of all essential to ensure that the car is adequately supported, as considerable effort will be needed.
5 Volvo technicians use a special holding tool (999 7119/999 7120) which bolts to the transmission housing and engages with the starter ring gear teeth once the starter motor has been removed. If this is not available, select a gear, and have an assistant apply the handbrake and footbrake as the bolt is loosened.
6 Unscrew the bolt securing the pulley to the crankshaft, and remove the pulley. It is essential to obtain a new bolt for reassembly **(see illustrations)**. If required, remove the sensor ring/spacer.
7 With the pulley removed, it is advisable to check the crankshaft oil seal for signs of oil leakage. If necessary, fit a new seal as described in Section 15.

Refitting

8 Refit the pulley to the crankshaft sprocket, then fit the new pulley securing bolt and tighten it as far as possible before the crankshaft starts to rotate.
9 Holding the pulley against rotation as for removal, first tighten the bolt to the specified Stage 1 torque.
10 Stage 2 involves tightening the bolt though an angle, rather than to a torque. The bolt must be rotated through the specified angle – special angle gauges are available from tool outlets. As a guide, a 180° angle is equivalent to a half-turn, and this is easily judged by assessing the start and end positions of the socket handle or torque wrench.
11 The remainder of refitting is a reversal of removal.

4.6a Undo the bolt and remove the crankshaft pulley...

5 Timing belt covers – removal and refitting

⚠ *Warning: Refer to the precautionary information contained in Section 1 before proceeding.*

Removal

1 Jack up the front of the vehicle and support it on axle stands (see *Jacking and vehicle support*).
2 Remove the right-hand side front wheel, and the wheelarch liner.
3 Remove the crankshaft pulley as described in Section 4.
4 Undo the 3 bolts and remove the lower cover **(see illustration)**. Undo the 3 bolts and remove the upper cover.

Refitting

5 Refitting of all the covers is a reversal of the relevant removal procedure, ensuring that each cover section is correctly located, and that the cover retaining bolts are securely tightened. Ensure that all disturbed hoses are reconnected and retained by their relevant clips.

6 Timing belt and tensioner – removal and refitting

Removal

1 Disconnect the battery negative lead as described in Chapter 5A and remove the plastic cover on top of the engine.
2 Lift the coolant expansion tank up from its position, and move the tank to one side without disconnecting the hoses.
3 Slacken the front right-hand roadwheel bolts, then jack up the front of the vehicle and support it securely on axle stands (see *Jacking and vehicle support*). Remove the roadwheel.
4 Release the 7 Torx screws and remove the engine undershield.
5 Remove the auxiliary drivebelt as described in Chapter 1B.
6 The engine must now be supported before the right-hand mounting is removed. Volvo technicians use an engine support bar, which locates in the channels at the top of each

4.6b ...followed by the TDC sensor ring/ spacer

inner wing, and a further beam attached to this, which rests on the front crossmember. If such an arrangement is not available, use an engine crane; either way, use a suitable length of chain and hooks to attach the lifting gear to the engine lifting eye. If the engine must be supported from below (and this is not recommended), use a large piece of wood on a trolley jack to spread the load and reduce the chance of damage to the sump.
7 With the weight of the engine supported remove the right-hand engine mounting as described in Chapter 2E, Section 11.
8 Release the cable clip from the timing belt cover.
9 Undo the 2 bolts, slacken the nut, and remove the upper timing belt cover.
10 Slacken the crankshaft pulley bolt as described in Section 4. Do not discard the old bolt yet – it is used during reassembly.
11 Two special tools are now required to set the engine at TDC (Top Dead Centre) for No 1 cylinder (at the transmission end). Volvo tool No 999 7121 locates through a hole in the rear flange of the cylinder block into a corresponding hole in the rear of the flywheel, whilst tool No 999 7122 locates through a hole in the exhaust camshaft sprocket into a hole in the cylinder head casting. In the absence of these tools, use an 8mm drill bit to lock the camshaft sprocket, and an 8mm rod to lock the flywheel. **Note:** *The flywheel locking rod must be flat (not tapered at all) at the end.*
12 Undo the starter motor bolts and position the motor to one side, to expose the crankshaft setting tool hole in the cylinder block flange. Refer to Chapter 5A if necessary.

5.4 Timing belt lower cover bolts (arrowed)

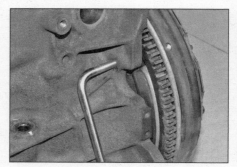

6.14a The tool fits through the hole in the cylinder block flange…

6.14b …and into a hole in the rear of the flywheel

6.15 The tool fits through a hole in the exhaust camshaft sprocket, into the timing hole in the cylinder head

13 Using a spanner or socket on the crankshaft pulley bolt, rotate the engine in a clockwise direction (viewed from the timing belt end of the engine) until the hole in the camshaft sprocket begins to align with the corresponding hole in the cylinder head.

14 Insert the crankshaft setting tool though the hole in the cylinder block flange and press it against the back of the flywheel. Have an assistant very slowly rotate the crankshaft clockwise, and the tool should slide into the back of the flywheel as the holes align **(see illustrations)**.

15 It should now be possible to insert the camshaft locking tool (999 7122) or equivalent through the hole in the camshaft sprocket into the hole in the cylinder head **(see illustration)**. Note that it may be necessary to rotate the camshaft sprocket backwards or forwards very slightly to be able to insert the tool.

16 At this point, Volvo technicians use the tool

described in paragraph 5 of Section 4 to lock the crankshaft in this position. The use of this tool, or an equivalent, is strongly recommended.

17 Disconnect the crankshaft position sensor wiring plug, then undo the bolt and remove the sensor **(see illustration)**.

18 Remove the crankshaft pulley, followed by the sensor ring/spacer.

19 Undo the bolts and remove the lower timing belt cover **(see illustration)**.

20 Raise the engine slightly, then relieve the timing belt tension by slackening the bolt in the centre of the tensioning pulley **(see illustration)**.

21 Remove the timing belt from the sprockets. Note that the belt must not be re-used.

22 Slacken the 4 bolts a few turns, remove the engine mounting bracket and the idler pulley, then undo the tensioner bolt **(see illustration)**. Discard both the tensioner and idler pulleys – new ones must be fitted.

23 If a new timing belt is not being fitted straight away (or if the belt is being removed as part of another procedure, such as cylinder head removal), temporarily refit the engine right-hand mounting and tighten the bolts securely.

Refitting

24 Ensure that the crankshaft and camshaft are still set to TDC on No 1 cylinder.

25 Position the new idler pulley and insert the retaining bolt **(see illustration)**.

26 Refit the engine mounting bracket, then tighten the retaining bolts (including the idler pulley bolt) to the specified torque.

27 Fit the new timing belt tensioner into position, but tighten the retaining finger-tight only at this stage.

28 Fit the new timing belt over the various sprockets in the following order: crankshaft, idler pulley, camshaft, tensioner and coolant pump **(see illustrations)**. Pay attention to

6.17 Crankshaft position sensor bolt (arrowed)

6.19 Timing belt lower cover bolts (arrowed)

6.20 Slacken the tensioner pulley bolt (arrowed)

6.22 Slacken the engine mounting bracket bolts and remove the idler pulley

6.25 Fit the new idler pulley

6.28a Timing belt routing

6.28b The arrows on the belt must point in the direction of rotation

6.29a Use an allen key in the tensioner arm hole (arrowed)

6.29b Rotate the arm anti-clockwise until the pointer is between the sides of the adjustment 'window' (arrowed)

any arrows on the belt indicating direction of rotation.

29 Using an Allen key in the tensioner arm, rotate the arm anti-clockwise until the pointer is positioned between the sides of the adjustment 'window' (see illustrations). Fully tighten the tensioner retaining bolt.

30 Refit the timing belt lower cover and tighten the bolts securely.

31 Refit the sensor ring/spacer and the crankshaft pulley, then tighten the old pulley bolt to 50 Nm (37 lbf ft).

32 Remove the crankshaft and camshaft setting/locking tools, then rotate the crankshaft 2 complete revolutions clockwise, until the crankshaft setting tool can be re-inserted. Check that the camshaft locking tool can be inserted.

33 Check position of the tensioner pointer, and if necessary slacken the retaining bolt and use the Allen key to align the pointer in the centre of the adjustment 'window'. Tighten the retaining bolt securely.

34 Remove the old crankshaft pulley bolt, and fit the new one. Tighten the bolt to the specified torque, using the method employed during removal to prevent the crankshaft from rotating.

35 Remove the crankshaft and camshaft locking tools.

36 The remainder of refitting is a reversal of removal, remembering to tighten all fasteners to their specified torque where given.

7 Timing chain and tensioner – removal and refitting

Timing chain

1 Removal of the timing chain is included in the camshaft removal and refitment procedure, as described in Section 8.

Tensioner

2 Remove the cylinder head cover as described in Section 3.

3 Press the tensioner upper guide rail upwards into the housing, then insert a 2.0mm locking pin/drill bit to secure the rail in position (see illustration).

4 Undo the 2 retaining bolts and withdrawn the tensioner (see illustration).

5 Begin refitting by ensuring the tensioner

7.3 Lift up the chain upper guide rail and insert a 2mm drill bit/rod into the hole in the tensioner housing

and cylinder head mating faces are clean and free of debris.

6 Install the tensioner and tighten the retaining bolts to the specified torque.

7 Press the tensioner upper guide rail into the housing, pull out the locking pin/drill bit, then slowly release the guide rail.

8 Refit the cylinder head cover as described in Section 3.

8 Camshaft, rocker arms and hydraulic adjusters – removal, inspection and refitting

Note: A new camshaft oil seal will be required on refitting.

Removal

1 Remove the timing belt as described in Section 6.

8.4a Depress the release tab (arrowed) and disconnect the servo hose from the pump

7.4 Undo the tensioner retaining bolts (arrowed)

2 Remove the timing chain tensioner as described in Section 7.

3 Remove the air cleaner assembly as described in Chapter 4B.

4 Working at the left-hand end of the cylinder head, depress the release tab and disconnect the hose from the vacuum pump, undo the nut securing the EGR pipe and fuel supply hose, then undo the 3 Allen bolts and remove the pump from the cylinder head (see illustrations). Check the condition of the pump O-ring seals and renew if necessary.

5 Undo the unions and remove the high-pressure fuel pipe between the fuel rail and the high-pressure pump located at the left-hand end of the cylinder head (see illustration). Discard the pipe, a new one must be fitted. Plug or seal the openings to prevent contamination.

6 Slide off the retaining clip/depress the

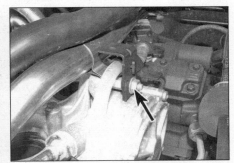

8.4b Undo the nut securing the EGR pipe and fuel hose

8.4c Vacuum pump securing bolts (arrowed)

8.5 Undo the unions and remove the high-pressure fuel pipe between the fuel rail and pump

8.6a Disconnect the fuel return hose...

8.6b ...then slide out the clip and disconnect the fuel supply hose

8.8 High-pressure fuel pump retaining bolts (arrowed)

release tab and disconnect the fuel supply and return hoses from the high-pressure pump **(see illustrations)**. Plug or seal the openings to prevent contamination.

7 Note their fitted positions, and disconnect the wiring plug(s) from the high-pressure fuel pump.

8 Undo the 3 retaining bolts and pull the high-pressure fuel pump out from the cylinder head **(see illustration)**. Be prepared for fuel spillage.

9 Remove the injectors as described in Chapter 4B.

10 Undo the retaining bolt and pull the sprocket from the exhaust camshaft. Use

a tool to prevent the camshaft and sprocket from rotating whilst the nut is released **(see Haynes Hint)**.

11 Undo the bolts and remove the engine mounting bracket from the right-hand end of the cylinder head/block.

12 Undo the bolts securing the timing belt inner cover to the cylinder head **(see illustration)**.

13 Undo the 2 bolts and remove the EGR pipe from over the left-hand end of the cylinder head.

14 Unscrew the injector mounting studs using a Torx socket, in sequence **(see illustration)**.

15 Working in the **reverse** of the sequence

HAYNES HiNT

To make a camshaft sprocket holding tool, obtain two lengths of steel strip about 6mm thick by 30mm wide or similar, one 600mm long, the other 200mm long (all dimensions are approximate). Bolt the two strips together to form a forked end, leaving the bolt slack so that the shorter strip can pivot freely. At the end of each 'prong' of the fork, use nuts and bolts or bend the strips through 90° about 50mm from their ends to act as fulcrums; these will engage with the holes in the sprockets. It may be necessary to grind or cut off the side slightly to allow them to fit in the sprocket holes

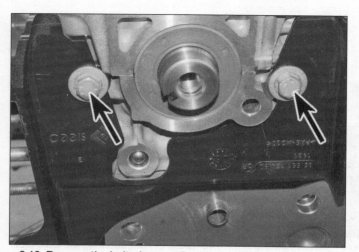

8.12 Remove the bolts (arrowed) securing the inner belt cover

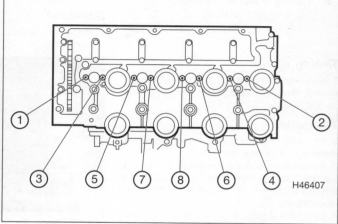

8.14 Injector mounting stud removal sequence

given in paragraph 28 **(see illustration 8.28)**, gradually and evenly remove the bolts securing the upper section of the cylinder head.

16 Carefully tap around the edge of the cylinder head upper section and lift it from position. Note that the cover will probably be reluctant to lift due to the sealant used, and possible corrosion around the two locating dowels at the front edge.

17 Lift the camshafts from position, disengage the timing chain from the sprockets, and remove the exhaust camshaft seal.

18 Have ready a box divided into 16 segments, or some containers or other means of storing and identifying the rockers arms and hydraulic adjusters after removal. It's essential that if they are to be refitted, they return to their original positions. Mark the segments in the box or the containers with the cylinder number for each rocker arm/adjuster, and left or right, for the particular cylinder.

19 Lift out the rockers arms and hydraulic adjusters, Keep them identified for position, and place them in their respective positions in the box or container **(see illustration)**.

Inspection

20 With the camshaft removed, examine the bearing surfaces in the upper and lower sections of the cylinder head for signs of obvious wear or pitting. If evident, a new cylinder head will probably be required. Also check that the oil supply holes in the cylinder head are free from obstructions.

21 Visually inspect the camshaft for evidence of wear on the surfaces of the lobes and journals. Normally their surfaces should be smooth and have a dull shine; look for scoring, erosion or pitting and areas that appear highly polished, indicating excessive wear. Accelerated wear will occur once the hardened exterior of the camshaft has been damaged, so always renew worn items. **Note:** *If these symptoms are visible on the tips of the camshaft lobes, check the rocker arm, as it will probably be worn as well.*

22 If any doubt exists as to the condition of the camshafts or cylinder head, have them examined at a Volvo dealer workshop or suitably-equipped automotive repair facility.

23 Inspect the rocker arms and hydraulic adjusters for obvious signs of wear or damage, and renew if necessary.

Refitting

24 Make sure that the top surfaces of the cylinder head, and in particular the camshaft bearings and the mating surfaces are completely clean. Ensure the secondary timing chain lower guide rail is in place **(see illustration)**.

25 Smear some clean engine oil onto the sides of the hydraulic adjusters, and offer each one into position in their original bores in the cylinder head, together with its rocker arm **(see illustrations)**.

26 Locate the timing chain on the camshaft sprockets, aligning the two coloured chain

8.19 Lift out the rocker arms and hydraulic adjusters

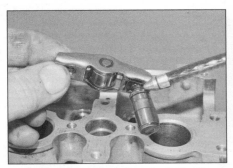

8.25a Apply clean oil to the hydraulic adjusters...

links with the marks on the camshaft sprockets, then lubricate the camshaft and cylinder head bearing journals with clean engine oil, and lower the camshafts into position **(see illustrations)**. The mark on the

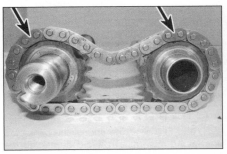

8.26a Align the coloured links on the chain with the marks on the camshaft sprockets...

8.26c ...then fit the camshafts with the mark on the intake camshaft (arrowed) in the 12 o'clock position

8.24 Fit the secondary timing chain lower guide rail

8.25b ...and refit them to their original positions

intake camshaft must be in the 12 o'clock position.

27 Apply a thin bead of Volvo sealant (No 116 1771) to the mating surface of the cylinder head **(see illustration)**. Take great care to

8.26b ...the mark on the sprockets is a dot and a line...

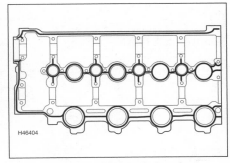

8.27a Apply a thin bead of sealant as indicated by the heavy black line

8.27b We inserted a tapered rod into the tensioner oil supply hole to prevent any sealant from entering

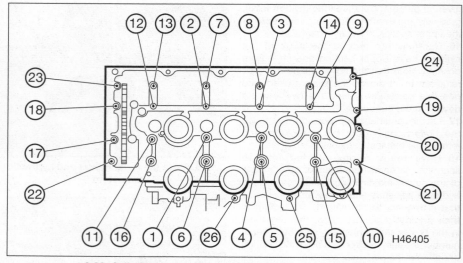

8.28 Cylinder head upper section bolt tightening sequence

ensure the chain tensioner oil supply hole is free from sealant **(see illustration)**.

28 Lower the upper section of the cylinder head into place, and tighten the retaining bolts to the specified torque in sequence **(see illustration)**.

29 Refit the injector mounting studs and tighten them to the specified torque.

30 Refit the camshaft timing chain tensioner assembly, and tighten the retaining bolts to the specified torque. Press the tensioner guide rail up into the housing and pull out the locking pin/drill bit. Slowly release the guide rail to tension the chain.

31 Fit a new exhaust camshaft oil seal as described in Section 9.

32 Refit the 2 bolts securing the timing belt inner cover to the cylinder head, and the single bolt to the cylinder block, then tighten the bolts securely.

33 Slide the exhaust camshaft sprocket into place, aligning the integral key with the camshaft and fit the camshaft sprocket locking tool.

34 Fit the sprocket retaining bolt and tighten it to the specified torque, preventing the sprocket from turning using the tool used during removal.

35 Refit the engine mounting bracket to the right-hand end of the cylinder head/block, and tighten the bolts to the specified torque.

36 The remainder of refitting is a reversal of removal, noting the following points:

a) Refit the injectors as described in Chapter 4B.

b) Fit the new timing belt, tensioner and idler pulley as described in Section 6.
c) Tighten all fasteners to their specified torque, where given.
d) Check the engine oil and coolant levels as described in Weekly checks.

9 Camshaft oil seal – renewal

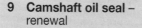

1 Remove the timing belt as described in Section 6, and the camshaft sprocket as described in paragraph 10 of the previous Section. Recover the sprocket locating key from the end of the camshaft.

2 Carefully prise or pull the seal from position.

3 Clean out the seal housing and the sealing surface of the camshaft by wiping it with a lint-free cloth. Remove any swarf or burrs that may cause the seal to leak.

4 Apply a little oil to the new camshaft oil seal, and fit it over the end of the camshaft, lips facing inwards. To avoid damaging the seal lips, wrap a little tape over the end of the camshaft. Volvo dealers have a special tool (No 999 7123) for fitting the seal, but if this is

not available, a deep socket of suitable size can be used. **Note:** *Select a socket that bears only on the hard outer surface of the seal, not the inner lip which can easily be damaged. It is important that the seal is fitted square to the shaft, and is fully-seated* **(see illustrations)**.

5 Refit the camshaft sprocket (and key – Section 8) and timing belt as described in Section 6.

10 Cylinder head – removal, inspection and refitting

Removal

1 Remove the battery as described in Chapter 5A, then unscrew the 4 bolts securing the battery tray, and remove the tray from the engine compartment.

2 Drain the coolant as described in Chapter 1B.

3 Remove the camshafts, rocker arms and hydraulic adjusters as described in Section 8.

4 Undo the 4 bolts, and remove the bracket over the fuel filter.

5 Undo the Torx screw, lift out the filter housing, then undo the bolts and remove the fuel filter bracket. Refit the bolt securing

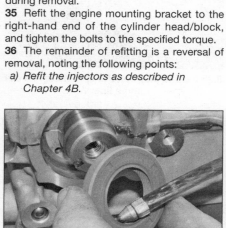

9.4a Apply a little clean oil to the oil seal inner lip...

9.4b ...then using a socket (or similar) to drive the seal into place...

9.4c ...until the seal is flush with the casing surface

10.5 Undo the bolts (arrowed) and remove the filter bracket

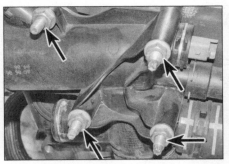

10.7 Thermostat housing studs (arrowed)

10.20 Zero the DTi gauge on the gasket face

the lifting bracket to the cylinder head **(see illustration)**.

6 Remove the turbocharger/exhaust manifold as described in Chapter 4B.

7 Disconnect the wiring plugs, then undo the 4 nuts, unscrew the 4 mounting studs and detach the thermostat housing from the left-hand of the cylinder head. Be prepared for coolant spillage **(see illustration)**.

8 Disconnect the wiring plug from the pressure sensor on the underside of the common fuel rail at the front of the cylinder head, and remove the fuel rail as described in Chapter 4B.

9 Undo the retaining bolt, and remove the oil filler pipe support bracket.

10 Working in the **reverse** of the sequence shown in paragraph 34, gradually and evenly slacken and remove the cylinder head bolts. Discard the bolts, new ones must be fitted.

11 Lift the cylinder head away; use assistance if possible, as it is a very heavy assembly. Do not place the cylinder head flat on its sealing surface, as the ends of the glow plugs may be damaged – support the ends of the cylinder head on wooden blocks.

12 If the head is stuck (as is possible), be careful how you choose to free it. Striking the head with tools carries the risk of damage, and the head is located on two dowels, so its movement will be limited. Do not, under any circumstances, lever the head between the mating surfaces, as this will certainly damage the sealing surfaces for the gasket, leading to leaks.

13 Once the head has been removed, recover the gasket from the two dowels.

14 Do not discard the gasket at this stage – it will be needed for correct identification of the new gasket.

Inspection

15 If required, dismantling and inspection of the cylinder head is covered in Part F of this Chapter.

Cylinder head gasket selection

16 Examine the old cylinder head gasket for manufacturer's identification markings. These will be in the form of holes on the front edge of the gasket, which indicate the gasket's thickness.

17 Unless new components have been fitted,

or the cylinder head has been machined (skimmed), the new cylinder head gasket must be of the same type as the old one. Purchase the required gasket, and proceed to paragraph 24.

18 If the head has been machined, or if new pistons have been fitted, it is likely that a head gasket of different thickness to the original will be needed.

19 Gasket selection is made on the basis of the measured piston protrusion above the cylinder head gasket surface (the protrusion must fall within the range specified at the start of this Chapter).

20 To measure the piston protrusion, anchor a dial test indicator (DTI) to the top face (cylinder head gasket mating face) of the cylinder block, and zero the gauge on the gasket mating face **(see illustration)**.

21 Rest the gauge probe above No 1 piston crown, and turn the crankshaft slowly by hand until the piston reaches TDC (its maximum height). Measure and record the maximum piston projection at TDC.

22 Repeat the measurement for the remaining pistons, and record the results.

23 If the measurements differ from piston to piston, take the highest figure, and use this to determine the thickness of the head gasket required.

Preparation for refitting

24 The mating faces of the cylinder head and cylinder block must be perfectly clean before refitting the head. Use a hard plastic or wooden scraper to remove all traces of gasket

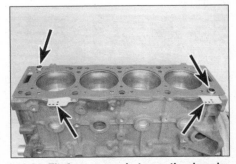

10.31 Fit the new gasket over the dowels with the thickness identification holes at the front (arrowed)

and carbon; also clean the piston crowns. **Note:** *The new head gasket has rubber-coated surfaces, which could be damaged from sharp edges or debris left by a metal scraper.* Take particular care when cleaning the piston crowns, as the soft aluminium alloy is easily damaged.

25 Make sure that the carbon is not allowed to enter the oil and water passages – this is particularly important for the lubrication system, as carbon could block the oil supply to the engine's components. Using adhesive tape and paper, seal the water, oil and bolt holes in the cylinder block.

26 To prevent carbon entering the gap between the pistons and bores, smear a little grease in the gap.

27 After cleaning each piston, use a small brush to remove all traces of grease and carbon from the gap, then wipe away the remainder with a clean rag. Clean all the pistons in the same way.

28 Check the mating surfaces of the cylinder block and the cylinder head for nicks, deep scratches and other damage (refer to the Note in paragraph 24). If slight, they may be removed carefully with a file, but if excessive, machining may be the only alternative to renewal.

29 If warpage of the cylinder head gasket surface is suspected, use a straight-edge to check it for distortion. Refer to Part F of this Chapter if necessary.

30 Ensure that the cylinder head bolt holes in the crankcase are clean and free of oil. Syringe or soak up any oil left in the bolt holes. This is most important in order that the correct bolt tightening torque can be applied, and to prevent the possibility of the block being cracked by hydraulic pressure when the bolts are tightened.

Refitting

31 Ensure that the cylinder head locating dowels are in place at the corners of the cylinder block, then fit the new cylinder head gasket over the dowels, ensuring that the identification holes are at the front **(see illustration)**. Take care to avoid damaging the gasket's rubber coating.

32 Lower the cylinder head into position on the gasket, ensuring that it engages correctly over the dowels.

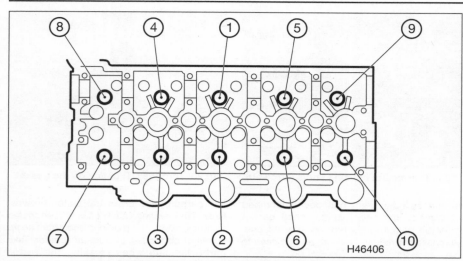

10.34 Cylinder head lower section bolt tightening sequence

10.35 Use an angle gauge for the Stage 2 torque setting

33 Fit the new cylinder head bolts and screw them in as far as possible by hand.

34 Working in the sequence shown (see illustration), tighten all the cylinder head bolts to the specified Stage 1 torque using an E14 Torx socket.

35 Stage 2 involves tightening the bolts though an angle, rather than to a torque (see illustration). Each bolt in sequence must be rotated through the specified angle – special angle gauges are available from tool outlets. As a guide, a 180° angle is equivalent to a half-turn, and this is easily judged by assessing the start and end positions of the socket handle or torque wrench.

36 The remainder of the refitting procedure is a reversal of the removal procedure, bearing in mind the following points:

a) *Refit the camshafts, rocker arms and hydraulic adjusters as described in Section 8.*

b) *Reconnect the exhaust front section to the exhaust manifold with reference to Chapter 4B.*

c) *Fit new high-pressure fuel delivery pipes as described in Chapter 4B.*

d) *Refit the intake manifold/cylinder head cover with reference to Section 3.*

e) *Refit the air cleaner as described in Chapter 4B.*

f) *Refill the cooling system as described in Chapter 1B.*

g) *Check and if necessary top-up the engine oil level and power steering fluid level as described in 'Weekly checks'.*

h) *Before starting the engine, read through the section on engine restarting after overhaul, at the end of Chapter 2F.*

11 Sump –
removal and refitting

Note: *The full procedure outlined below must be followed so that the mating surfaces can be cleaned and prepared to achieve an oil-tight joint on reassembly.*

Removal

1 Apply the handbrake, then jack up the front of the vehicle and support it on axle stands (see *Jacking and vehicle support*). Undo the 7 Torx screws and remove the engine undershield.

2 Referring to Chapter 1B if necessary, drain the engine oil, then clean and refit the engine oil drain plug, tightening it to the specified torque wrench setting. We strongly advise renewing the oil filter element, also described in Chapter 1B.

3 Pull the plastic cover on the top of the engine upwards from its mountings.

4 Slacken the hose clamps, undo the bracket bolt and remove the charge air pipe from the underside of the engine (see illustration).

5 Remove the air conditioning compressor drivebelt as described in Chapter 1B, then undo the mounting bolts and move the compressor to one side without disconnecting the refrigerant pipes. Suspend the compressor from the radiator crossmember using wires or straps.

6 Progressively unscrew the sump retaining Allen bolts, including the 2 bolts securing the sump to the transmission housing (see illustration). Don't forget the 4 bolts at the left-hand end accessed through the holes. Break the joint by carefully inserting a putty knife (or similar) between the sump and cylinder block (see illustration). Take care not to damage the sealing surfaces.

Refitting

7 On reassembly, thoroughly clean and degrease the mating surfaces of the cylinder block/crankcase and sump, removing all traces of sealant, then use a clean rag to wipe out the sump and the engine's interior.

8 Apply a 3mm thick bead of sealant (Volvo part No 116 1771) to the sump flange, making sure the bead is around the inside edge of the bolt holes. Do not allow the sealant to enter the bolt holes (see illustration). **Note:** *The sump must be refitted within 5 minutes of applying the sealant.*

9 Refit the sump and fit the retaining bolts, tightening them by hand only at this stage.

11.4 Undo the charge air pipe bracket bolt (arrowed)

11.6a Undo the 2 bolts securing the sump to the transmission (arrowed)...

11.6b ...access to the sump end bolts is through the holes (arrowed)

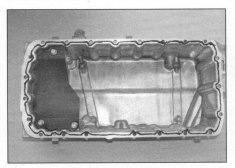

11.8 Apply sealant around the inside of the bolt holes

10 Tighten the 2 bolts securing the sump to the transmission casing to the specified torque, then tighten the remaining bolts, gradually and evenly to the specified torque.
11 Lower the car to the ground. Refill the engine with oil, and if removed fit a new oil filter with reference to Chapter 1B.
12 Volvo recommend waiting a minimum of 2 hours before starting the car to allow the sealant to cure fully.

---

12 Oil pump –
removal, inspection
and refitting

Removal

1 Remove the timing belt as described in Section 6, then slide off the crankshaft sprocket **(see illustrations)**.
2 Remove the sump as described in Section 11.

12.4 Oil level pipe bracket bolt (arrowed)

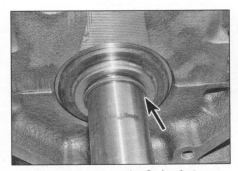

12.5c ...and recover the O-ring between the sprocket and the crankshaft

12.1a Slide off the crankshaft sprocket...

3 Undo the retaining bolts and remove the front cover and crankshaft seal. Note the original locations of the cover screws – they are of different lengths.
4 Undo the bolt securing the oil level pipe **(see illustration)**.
5 Pull out the key from the crankshaft sprocket, then undo the pump mounting bolts, slide the pump, chain, and crankshaft sprocket from the end of the engine **(see illustrations)**. Recover the O-ring between the sprocket and crankshaft.

Inspection

6 Undo the retaining screws and remove the cover from the oil pump **(see illustration)**. Note the location of any identification marks on the inner and outer rotors for refitting.
7 Unscrew the plug and remove the pressure relief valve, spring and plunger, clean out and check the condition of the components **(see illustration)**.

12.5a Remove the sprocket key...

12.6 Oil pump cover bolts

12.1b ...and recover the crankshaft key

8 No specifications for the pump internal components are given by Volvo.
9 Check the general condition of the oil pump, and in particular, its mating face to the cylinder block. If the mating face is damaged significantly, this may lead to oil loss (and a resulting drop in available oil pressure).
10 Inspect the rotors for obvious signs of wear or damage; at the time of writing, no parts are available. If the pump is faulty, it must be renewed as a complete unit. Lubricate the rotors with fresh engine oil and refit them into the body, making sure that the identification marks are positioned as noted on removal.
11 If the oil pump has been removed as part of a major engine overhaul, it is assumed that the engine will have completed a substantial mileage. In this case, it is often considered good practice to fit a new (or reconditioned) pump as a matter of course. In other words, if the rest of the engine is being rebuilt, the

12.5b ...undo the oil pump mounting bolts (arrowed) and slide the assembly from the crankshaft...

12.7 Oil pressure relief valve plug

12.13 Fit the O-ring to the end of the crankshaft

engine has completed a large mileage, or there is any question as to the old pump's condition, it is preferable to fit a new oil pump.

Refitting

12 Before fitting the oil pump, ensure that the mating faces on the pump and the engine block are completely clean.

13 Fit the O-ring to the end of the crankshaft **(see illustration)**.

14 Engage the drive chain with the oil pump and crankshaft sprockets, then slide the crankshaft sprocket into place (aligning the slot in the sprocket with the keyway in the crankshaft) as the pump is refitted. Refit the crankshaft key.

15 Refit the mounting bolts and tighten them to the specified torque. Note that the front, left-hand bolt is slightly longer than the others.

16 Apply a 3mm wide bead of sealant (part No 116 1771) to the oil seal carrier flange.

13.1 Oil pressure warning light switch

15.4a Drill a small hole in the seal...

Refit the cover and tighten the bolts to the specified torque. Note that the bolts must be tightened within 4 minutes of the sealant being applied.

17 Fit a new oil seal to the cover as described in Section 15.

18 Refit the bolt securing the oil level pipe.

19 The remainder of refitting is a reversal of removal, remembering to fit a new oil filter element, and replenish the engine oil.

13 Oil pressure warning light switch – removal and refitting

Removal

1 The switch is screwed into the oil filter housing **(see illustration)**. Access is from under the vehicle. Undo the 7 Torx screws and remove the engine undershield. To further improve access, undo the mounting bolts and move the air conditioning compressor to one side. Suspend the compressor from the radiator crossmember using wire or straps. There is no need to disconnect the refrigerant pipes.

2 Disconnect the switch wiring plug.

3 Unscrew the switch from the housing; be prepared for some oil loss.

Refitting

4 Refitting is the reverse of the removal procedure; fit a new pressure switch sealing washer, and tighten the switch to the specified torque wrench setting.

14.2 Oil cooler retaining bolts (arrowed)

15.4b ...insert a self-tapping screw and pull out the seal

5 Reconnect the switch wiring plug.

6 Refit all components removed for access to the switch.

7 Check the engine oil level and top-up as necessary (see *Weekly checks*).

8 Check for correct warning light operation, and for signs of oil leaks, once the engine has been restarted and warmed-up to normal operating temperature.

14 Oil cooler – removal and refitting

Note: *New sealing rings will be required on refitting – check for availability prior to commencing work.*

Removal

1 The cooler is fitted to the oil filter housing on the front of the cylinder block. Access is from under the vehicle. Undo the 7 Torx screws and remove the engine undershield. To further improve access, remove the auxiliary drivebelt (refer to Chapter 1B), undo the mounting bolts and move the air conditioning compressor to one side. Suspend the compressor from the radiator crossmember using wire or straps. There is no need to disconnect the refrigerant pipes.

2 Undo the 4 retaining bolts and detach the cooler from the housing **(see illustration)**. Recover the sealing rings and be prepared for oil/coolant spillage.

Refitting

3 Refitting is a reversal of removal, bearing in mind the following points:
 a) Use new sealing rings.
 b) Tighten the cooler mounting bolts securely.
 c) On completion, lower the car to the ground. Check and if necessary top-up the oil and coolant levels, then start the engine and check for signs of oil or coolant leakage.

15 Crankshaft oil seals – renewal

Timing belt end seal

1 Remove the timing belt as described in Section 6.

2 Slide the belt sprocket from the crankshaft, and recover the locating key from the groove on the crankshaft.

3 Note the fitted depth of the oil seal as a guide for fitting the new one.

4 Using a screwdriver or similar tool, carefully prise the oil seal from its location. Take care not to damage the oil seal contact surfaces or crankshaft. Alternatively, drill a small hole in the seal (taking care not to drill any deeper than necessary), then insert a self-tapping screw and use pliers to pull out the seal **(see illustrations)**.

15.7a Locate the new seal and guide over the end of the crankshaft...

15.7b ...then drive the seal home until it's flush with the cover

15.11a Drill a hole in the seal...

15.11b ...then insert a self-tapping screw and pull out the seal

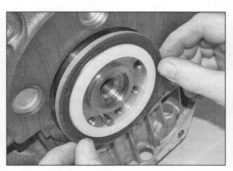

15.14 Locate the seal and locating sleeve over the end of the crankshaft

15.15 Press the seal in until it's flush with the surface

5 Wipe clean the oil seal contact surfaces and seating, and clean up any sharp edges or burrs which might damage the new seal as it is fitted, or which might cause the seal to leak once in place.

6 No oil should be applied to the oil seal, which is made of PTFE. Volvo technicians use a special seal-fitting tool (999-7124), but an adequate substitute can be achieved using a large socket or piece of tubing of sufficient size to bear on the outer edge of the new seal. Note that the new seal is supplied with a guide which fits over the end of the crankshaft.

7 Locate the new seal (with guide still fitted) over the end of the crankshaft, using the tool **(see illustrations)**, socket, or tubing to press the seal squarely and fully into position, to the previously-noted depth. Remove the guide from the end of the crankshaft.

8 The remainder of reassembly is the reverse of the removal procedure, referring to the relevant text for details where required. Check for signs of oil leakage when the engine is restarted.

Flywheel end seal

9 Remove the transmission as described in Chapter 7A, and the clutch assembly as described in Chapter 6.

10 Unbolt the flywheel (see Section 16).

11 Using a screwdriver or similar, carefully prise the oil seal from place. Take great care not to damage the seal seating area or the crankshaft sealing surface. Alternatively, punch or drill two small holes opposite each other in the oil seal, then screw a self-tapping

screw into each hole, and pull the screws with pliers to extract the seal **(see illustrations)**.

12 Clean the end of the crankshaft, polishing off any burrs or raised edges, which may have caused the seal to fail in the first place. Clean also the seal mating face on the engine block, using a suitable solvent for degreasing if necessary.

13 The new oil seal is supplied fitted with a locating sleeve, which must **not** be removed prior to fitting (it will drop out on its own when the seal is fitted). Do not lubricate the seal.

14 Offer the new seal into position, feeding the locating sleeve over the end of the crankshaft **(see illustration)**.

15 Volvo technicians use a special tool (999 7126) to pull the seal into position. In the absence of the tool, use a large socket/piece of tubing which bears only on the hard outer edge of the seal, and carefully tap the seal into position **(see illustration)**.

16.5 Flywheel retaining bolts

16 If the seal locating sleeve is still in position, remove it now.

17 The remainder of the reassembly procedure is the reverse of dismantling, referring to the relevant text for details where required. Check for signs of oil leakage when the engine is restarted.

16 Flywheel – removal, inspection and refitting

Removal

1 Remove the transmission as described in Chapter 7A. Now is a good time to check components such as the oil seals and renew them if necessary.

2 Remove the clutch as described in Chapter 6. Now is a good time to check or renew the clutch components and release bearing.

3 Use a centre-punch or paint to make alignment marks on the flywheel and crankshaft, to ensure correct alignment during refitting.

4 Prevent the flywheel from turning by locking the ring gear teeth, or by bolting a strap between the flywheel and the cylinder block/crankcase. Slacken the Torx bolts evenly until all are free.

5 Remove each bolt in turn and ensure that new ones are obtained for reassembly; these bolts are subjected to severe stresses and so must be renewed, regardless of their apparent condition, whenever they are disturbed **(see illustration)**.

16.10 Note the locating dowel and corresponding hole (arrowed)

16.11 A simple home-made tool to lock the flywheel

6 Withdraw the flywheel, remembering that it is very heavy – do not drop it.

Inspection

7 Clean the flywheel to remove grease and oil. Inspect the surface for cracks, rivet grooves, burned areas and score marks. Light scoring can be removed with emery cloth.

Check for cracked and broken ring gear teeth. Lay the flywheel on a flat surface and use a straight-edge to check for warpage.
8 Clean and inspect the mating surfaces of the flywheel and the crankshaft. If the crankshaft seal is leaking, renew it before refitting the flywheel. If the engine has covered a high mileage, it may be worth fitting a new

seal as a matter if course, given the amount of work needed to access it.
9 Thoroughly clean the threaded bolt holes in the crankshaft, removing all traces of locking compound.

Refitting

10 Fit the flywheel to the crankshaft ensuring the dowel aligns with the hole in the crankshaft – it will fit only one way **(see illustration)**. Insert the new bolts.
11 Lock the flywheel by the method used on dismantling **(see illustration)**. Working in a diagonal sequence, tighten the bolts to the specified torque wrench setting.
12 Refit the clutch (Chapter 6) and the transmission (Chapter 7A).

17 Engine/transmission mountings – inspection and renewal

Refer to Chapter 2E, Section 11.

Chapter 2 Part E:
2.0 & 2.4 litre 5-cylinder diesel engine in-car repair procedures

Contents

Degrees of difficulty

Easy, suitable for novice with little experience	**Fairly easy,** suitable for beginner with some experience	**Fairly difficult,** suitable for competent DIY mechanic	**Difficult,** suitable for experienced DIY mechanic	**Very difficult,** suitable for expert DIY or professional

Specifications

General

Capacity:
- D5204T/T5 — 1984 cc
- D5244 T8 and T13 — 2400 cc

Bore:
- D5204T/T5 — 81.0mm
- D5244 T8 and T13 — 81.0mm

Stroke:
- D5204T/T5 — 77.0mm
- D5244 T8 and T13 — 93.15mm

Engine code:	Power output	Torque
D5204T5	100kW at 4000 rpm	350 Nm at 1500 to 2750 rpm
D5204T	125 kW at 4000 rpm	400 Nm at 1750 to 2750 rpm
D5244 T8	132 kW at 4000 rpm	350 Nm at 1750 to 3250 rpm
D5244 T13	132 kW at 4000 rpm	400 Nm at 1750 to 3250 rpm

Firing order — 1-2-4-5-3
Cylinder No 1 location — Timing belt end

Camshaft

Drive — Toothed belt

Lubrication

Engine oil type/specification — See *Lubricants, fluids and tyre pressures* on page 0•16
Engine oil capacity — See Chapter 1B Specifications
Oil pump type — Mounted on front of cylinder block and driven directly from crankshaft
Oil pressure - minimum (engine at operating temperature):
- At idle (figure at 800 rpm on 2.0 litre 5-cylinder engine) — 1.0 bar
- At 4000 rpm — 3.5 bar

Valves

Valve clearances — Hydraulic compensators – no adjustment necessary

Torque wrench settings

	Nm	lbf ft
Camshaft bearing cap	10	7
Camshaft cover	10	7
Camshaft end sealing/bearing caps (M7)	17	13
Camshaft position sensor	10	7
Camshaft pulley bolts	17	13
Connecting rod cap*:		
Stage 1	30	22
Stage 2	Angle-tighten a further 90°	
Coolant temperature sensor	22	16
Crankcase intermediate section:		
Tighten in the following sequence:		
M10*	20	15
M10	40	30
M8	24	18
M7	17	13
M10	Angle-tighten a further 110°	
Crankshaft pulley/sprocket:		
Nut	300	221
Screws:		
Stage 1	35	26
Stage 2	Angle-tighten a further 50°	
Cylinder head bolts*:		
Stage 1	20	15
Stage 2	50	37
Stage 3	50	37
Stage 4	Angle-tighten a further 90°	
Stage 5	Angle-tighten a further 90°	
Driveplate*:		
Stage 1	45	33
Stage 2	Angle-tighten a further 50°	
Engine mounting bolts	Refer to Volvo dealer	
Flywheel*:		
Stage 1	45	33
Stage 2	Angle-tighten a further 65°	
Fuel injection pump	18	13
Fuel rail/injector pipe unions:		
Stage 1	10	7
Stage 2	Angle-tighten a further 60°	
Fuel rail mounting bolts	24	18
Injector screws*	13	10
Lower torque rod bolts	Refer to Volvo dealer	
Upper torque rod bolts	Refer to Volvo dealer	
Oil cooler retaining bolts	17	13
Oil filter	25	18
Oil pick-up pipe	17	13
Oil pressure switch	27	20
Oil pump bolts	10	7
Piston cooling jets	17	13
Piston cooling valve	51	38
Sump:		
Sump to transmission	50	37
Sump to engine	17	13
Sump drain plug (engine oil)	38	28
Timing belt idler pulley	24	18
Timing belt tensioner	24	18
Torque converter bolts*	60	44
Vacuum pump	17	13

* Do not re-use

1 General information

Using this Chapter

This Part of Chapter 2 describes the repair procedures that can reasonably be carried out on the engine while it remains in the vehicle. If the engine has been removed from the vehicle and is being dismantled as described in Part F, any preliminary dismantling procedures can be ignored.

Note that, while it may be possible physically to overhaul items such as the piston/connecting rod assemblies while the engine is in the car, such tasks are not usually carried out as separate operations. Usually, several additional procedures are required (not to mention the cleaning of components and oilways); for this reason, all such tasks are classed as major overhaul procedures, and are described in Part F of this Chapter.

Part F describes the removal of the engine/transmission from the car, and the full overhaul procedures that can then be carried out.

Engine description

The engines are water-cooled, double overhead camshaft, 20 valve, in-line five cylinder units of 2.0 and 2.4 litre capacities, with both the cylinder block and cylinder head made from aluminium-alloy, with cast-iron cylinder sleeves. The engine is mounted transversely at the front of the vehicle, with the transmission bolted to the left-hand end of the engine.

The cylinder head carries the camshafts, which are driven by a toothed timing belt from the crankshaft to the intake camshaft. A toothed gear on the intake shaft drives a corresponding gear on the exhaust camshaft. An Oldham coupling on the left-hand end of the intake camshaft drives the low/high pressure fuel pump, whilst the vacuum pump is driven from the left-hand end of the exhaust camshaft. The cylinder head also incorporates the 20 inlet and exhaust valves (4 per cylinder), which are closed by single coil springs, and which run in guides pressed into the cylinder head. The camshafts actuate the valves via roller type rocker arms acting upon hydraulic tappets, mounted in the cylinder head. The cylinder head contains internal oilways which supply and lubricate the hydraulic tappets.

All engines are of direct injection design where the swirl chambers are incorporated in the tops of the pistons. The cylinder head incorporates two separate intake ports per cylinder. These ports are of different length and geometry to ensure more efficient combustion and reduced emissions.

The forged steel crankshaft is of six-bearing type, and the No 5 (from timing belt end) main bearing shells incorporate separate thrustwashers to control crankshaft endfloat. The intake camshaft is driven by a toothed belt from the crankshaft sprocket, and the belt also drives the water pump mounted on the rear of the block.

The pistons are manufactured from aluminium-silicon alloy, with graphite coated skirts to reduce friction. The pistons incorporate cooling channels, through which oil flows, supplied by fixed jets mounted at the base of the cylinders. As each piston reaches the lower end of its stroke, the oil jet aligns with a hole in the base of the piston, and oil is forced through the cooling channel.

The engine has a full-flow lubrication system. A duocentric internal gear type oil pump is mounted on the front of the crankshaft. The oil filter is of the paper element type, mounted on the front side of the cylinder block.

The two specified power outputs are achieved using different turbochargers and ECM software.

Operations with engine in car

The following operations can be performed without removing the engine:

a) *Auxiliary drivebelt – removal and refitting.*
b) *Camshafts – removal and refitting.*
c) *Camshaft oil seals – renewal.*
d) *Coolant pump – removal and refitting (refer to Chapter 3)*
e) *Crankshaft oil seals – renewal.*
f) *Cylinder head – removal and refitting.*
g) *Engine mountings – inspection and renewal.*
h) *Oil pump and pickup assembly – removal and refitting.*
i) *Sump – removal and refitting.*
j) *Timing belt and cover – removal, inspection and refitting.*

Note: *It is possible to remove the pistons and connecting rods (after removing the cylinder head and sump) without removing the engine from the vehicle. However, this procedure is not recommended. Work of this nature is more easily and thoroughly completed with the engine on the bench – refer to Chapter 2F.*

2 Compression and leakdown tests – description and interpretation

Compression test

Note: *A compression tester specifically designed for diesel engines must be used for this test.*

1 When engine performance is down, or if misfiring occurs, a compression test can provide diagnostic clues as to the engine's condition. If the test is performed regularly, it can give warning of trouble before any other symptoms become apparent.

2 A compression tester specifically intended for diesel engines must be used, because of the higher pressures involved. The tester is connected to an adapter which screws into the glow plug hole. It is unlikely to be worthwhile buying such a tester for occasional use, but it may be possible to borrow or hire one – if not, have the test performed by a garage.

3 Unless specific instructions to the contrary are supplied with the tester, observe the following points:

a) *The battery must be in a good state of charge, the air filter clean, and the engine should be at normal operating temperature.*
b) *All the glow plugs should be removed before starting the test.*
c) *The engine management ECM relay must be removed from the fuse/relay box.*

4 There is no need to hold the accelerator pedal down during the test, because the diesel engine air inlet is not throttled.

5 The manufacturers specify a wear limit for compression pressure. Seek the advice of a Volvo dealer or other diesel specialist if in doubt as to whether a particular pressure reading is acceptable.

6 The cause of poor compression is less easy to establish on a diesel engine than on a petrol one. The effect of introducing oil into the cylinders (wet testing) is not conclusive, because there is a risk that the oil will sit in the recess on the piston crown, instead of passing to the rings. However, the following can be used as a rough guide to diagnosis.

7 All cylinders should produce very similar pressures; a difference of more than 5.0 bars between any two cylinders indicates the existence of a fault. Note that the compression should build-up quickly in a healthy engine; low compression on the first stroke, followed by gradually-increasing pressure on successive strokes, indicates worn piston rings. A low compression reading on the first stroke, which does not build-up during successive strokes, indicates leaking valves or a blown head gasket (a cracked head could also be the cause).

8 A low reading from two adjacent cylinders is almost certainly due to the head gasket having blown between them.

Leakdown test

9 A leakdown test measures the rate at which compressed air fed into the cylinder is lost. It is an alternative to a compression test, and in many ways it is better, since the escaping air provides easy identification of where pressure loss is occurring (piston rings, valves or head gasket).

10 The equipment needed for leakdown testing is unlikely to be available to the home mechanic. If poor compression is suspected, have the test performed by a suitably-equipped garage.

3 Timing belt covers – removal and refitting

 Warning: Refer to the precautionary information contained in Section 1 before proceeding.

Removal

1 Jack up and support the front of the vehicle (see *Jacking and vehicle support*). Remove the under shield.

2 Using a block of wood on the head of a trolley jack (to spread the load) place a trolley jack under the sump. Raise the engine and remove the right-hand engine mount as described in Section 11.

3 Remove the auxiliary drive belt as described in Chapter 1B Section 6.

4 Remove the crankshaft pulley as described in Section 4.

5 Undo the bolt and remove the pipe bracket on the front face of the timing belt cover **(see illustration)**.

6 Release the 5 securing clips and remove the cover This is a single piece on 2.4 litre

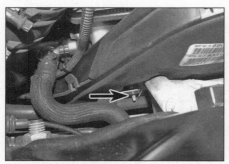

3.5 Unbolt the bracket (arrowed) on the front of the timing belt cover

engines **(see illustration)** and in two sections on 2.0 litre engines. Note that on 2.0 litre engines, bolts are used and not spring clips.
7 Remove the lower timing belt cover (2.0 litre engines) or the lower belt guard (2.4 litre engines).

Refitting

8 Refitting of the cover is a reversal of the relevant removal procedure. Ensure that all disturbed hoses are reconnected and retained by their relevant clips.

4	Timing belt – removal, inspection and refitting

Note: *Whenever the timing belt is renewed, the tensioner and idler pulley should also be renewed.*

4.6 Remove the wheelarch liner for access to the crankshaft pulley

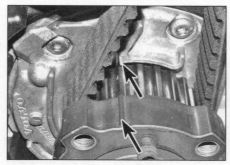

4.13 The mark on the crankshaft pulley flange should align with the mark on the oil pump housing (arrowed)

3.6 Release the clips (arrowed) securing the timing belt cover

Removal

1 The camshaft and coolant pump sprockets are driven by the timing belt from the crankshaft sprocket. The crankshaft and camshaft sprockets move in phase with each other to ensure correct valve timing. Should the timing belt slip or break in service, the valve timing will be disturbed and piston-to-valve contact will occur, resulting in serious engine damage.
2 The design of the engines covered in this Chapter is such that piston-to-valve contact will occur if the crankshaft is turned with the timing belt removed. For this reason, it is important that the correct phasing between the camshaft and crankshaft is preserved whilst the timing belt is off the engine. This is achieved by setting the engine in a reference condition (known as Top Dead Centre or TDC) before the timing belt is removed, and then not rotating the shafts until the belt is refitted.

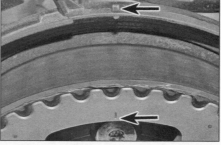

4.11 Align the mark on the camshaft sprocket with the mark on the timing belt cover (arrowed)

4.14 Use a 6mm Allen key to position the tensioner arm (arrowed) at approximately the 10 o'clock position

Similarly, if the engine has been dismantled for overhaul, the engine must be set to TDC during reassembly to ensure that the correct shaft phasing is restored.
3 TDC is the highest position a piston reaches within its respective cylinder – in a four-stroke engine, each piston reaches TDC twice per cycle, once on the compression stroke and once on the exhaust stroke. In general, TDC normally refers to No 1 cylinder on the compression stroke. The cylinders are numbered one to five, starting from the timing belt end of the engine. Note that on this particular engine, when the timing marks are aligned, the No 1 piston is positioned very slightly before TDC.
4 Before starting work, disconnect the battery (see Chapter 5A).
5 Slacken the right-hand front road wheel bolts, then jack up the front of the vehicle and support it securely on axle stands (see *Jacking and vehicle support*). Remove the roadwheel.
6 Remove the engine under shield and the right-hand wheel arch liner **(see illustration)**.
7 Remove the auxiliary drivebelt as described in Chapter 1B, Section 32.
8 The engine must now be supported before the right-hand mounting is removed. Use a large piece of wood on a trolley jack to spread the load and reduce the chance of damage to the sump.
9 With the weight of the engine supported, remove the right-hand engine mounting as described in Section 11.
10 Remove the timing belt outer cover(s) as described in Section 3. Note that the crankshaft pulley must be removed first (as described below) on 2.0 litre engines with a two part timing belt cover.
11 Using a socket on the crankshaft pulley nut, rotate the crankshaft clockwise until the markings on the camshaft sprocket and timing belt rear cover align **(see illustration)**.
12 Undo the four bolts and one nut securing the crankshaft pulley to the crankshaft sprocket and remove the crankshaft pulley, leaving the sprocket in place. Note that the centre nut is very tight. In order to prevent the crankshaft from rotating remove the starter motor as described in Chapter 5A, Section 8, and use a large flat-bladed screwdriver wedged between the flywheel (or driveplate) ring gear teeth and the transmission housing. Note that Volvo list a crank pulley tool (999-5433) that fits the crankshaft pulley outer bolt holes and holds the crankshaft stationary whilst the centre bolt is slackened. Versions of this tool are available in the aftermarket (AST 5039A for example)..
13 Check that the marks on the camshaft sprocket and timing belt rear cover are still aligned, and the lug on the oil pump housing aligns with the mark cast into crankshaft pulley mounting boss. If the marks do not align, temporarily refit two of the crankshaft pulley retaining bolts and the centre nut loosely and, using a large screwdriver/lever, rotate the crankshaft anti-clockwise until the marks are in alignment **(see illustration)**. In actual fact, in this position the No1 piston is slightly before TDC.

14 Slacken the timing belt tensioner centre bolt slightly, and use a 6mm Allen key to rotate the tensioner arm clockwise to the 10 o'clock position, then lightly tighten the centre bolt **(see illustration)**. Slacken the bolt for the idler pulley.
15 Remove the timing belt from the sprockets, without turning the crankshaft or camshaft.

Inspection

16 Examine the belt for evidence of contamination by coolant or lubricant. If this is the case, find the source of the contamination before progressing any further. Check the belt for signs of wear or damage, particularly around the leading edges of the belt teeth. Renew the belt if its condition is in doubt; the cost of belt renewal is negligible compared with potential cost of the engine repairs, should the belt fail in service. The belt must be renewed if it has covered the mileage stated by the manufacturer (see Chapter 1B), however if it has covered less it is prudent to renew it regardless of condition, as a precautionary measure. **Note:** *If the timing belt is not going to be refitted for some time, it is a wise precaution to hang a warning label on the steering wheel, to remind yourself (and others) not to attempt to start the engine.*
17 Spin the belt tensioner and idler pulleys and listen for noise which may indicate wear in the pulley bearings. If in any doubt, renew the pulleys.
Note: *It is considered best practise to always replace the idler pulley and belt tensioner when the belt is replaced. Consideration should also be given to replacing the coolant pump at the same time. Note that most timing belt manufacturers will not usually warrant a belt failure if the tensioner and idler have not been replaced.*

Refitting

18 Ensure that the crankshaft and camshaft are still aligned as described in paragraphs 13 and 15.
19 Fit the new belt around the crankshaft sprocket, idler pulley, camshaft sprocket, coolant pump sprocket, and finally, the tensioner pulley. Ensure the belt teeth seat correctly on the sprockets.
20 Ensure that the front run of the belt is taut – ie, all the slack should be in the section of the belt that passes over the tensioner roller.
21 Slacken the tensioner roller centre bolt slightly, then using a 6mm Allen key, rotate the tensioner arm anti-clockwise until it passes the position shown, then rotate it clockwise until the indicator reaches the correct position as shown **(see illustration)**. Tighten the centre bolt to the specified torque.
22 Gently press the belt between the camshaft sprocket and coolant pump sprocket, and check the tensioner arm moves freely as the belt is pressed.
23 Turn the crankshaft through two complete turns, then check that the timing marks on the crankshaft pulley boss and camshaft sprocket align correctly as described in paragraphs 13 and 15.

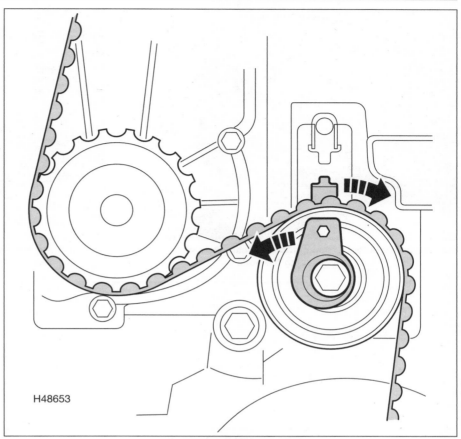

4.21 Timing belt tensioner position

24 Check that the timing belt tensioner indicator is still position as described in paragraph 21.
25 The remainder of refitting is a reversal of removal, remembering to tighten all fasteners to their specified torque where given.

5 Cylinder head cover/inlet manifold – removal and refitting

Removal

1 Remove the plastic cover on top of the engine.
2 Remove the high pressure fuel pipes and the fuel injectors as described in Chapter 4B, Section 11. Discard the fuel pipes as new ones must be fitted on refitting.
3 Remove the air inlet pipe at the front of the engine. Slacken the clamp at the left-hand end of the pipe, the clamp at the rear of the cylinder head on the right-hand side, the clamp for the breather hose, and undo the bolt for the support bracket.
4 Slacken the clamps and remove the air inlet hose from the bottom of the inlet manifold and from the EGR assembly. Undo the clamp and disconnect the breather hose from the cylinder head cover.
5 Undo the 3 bolts and remove the oil filler

neck from the cover, and disconnect the wiring plug for the camshaft position sensor.
6 Undo the 18 securing bolts and carefully lift the cover from place.

Refitting

7 Refit the camshaft cover by following the removal procedure in reverse, noting the following points:
a) *A rubber sealing gasket is fitted to the underside of the camshaft cover* **(see illustration)**. *Ensure the gasket remains in place whilst the cover is refitted.*
b) *Tighten the camshaft cover retaining nuts to the specified torque, starting from the centre and working outwards.*

5.7 An intricate rubber gasket is fitted to the camshaft cover

6.3 Use a simple tool to counterhold the camshaft sprocket whilst slackening the bolts

6.6a Insert the camshaft aligning tool through the hole in the cylinder head and into the exhaust camshaft sprocket

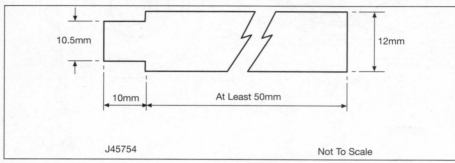

J45754   Not To Scale

6.6b Camshaft aligning tool

6.7a Unscrew the blanking plug...

6.7b ...and insert the crankshaft stop tool

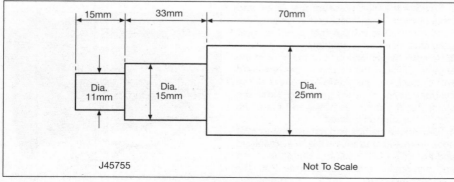

J45755   Not To Scale

6.7c Crankshaft stop tool

6 Camshaft oil seal – renewal

Removal

1 Remove the timing belt as described in Section 4.

2 Remove the brake vacuum pump as described in Chapter 9, and the starter motor as described in Chapter 5A.

3 Unscrew the camshaft pulley bolts, while holding the sprocket stationary using a tool which engages the holes in the sprocket **(see illustration)**. Do not allow the camshaft to rotate. Remove the pulley from the camshaft.

4 Remove the pulley from the camshaft.

5 Using a screwdriver or lever, carefully prise out the oil seal taking care not to damage the camshaft surface.

Refitting

6 Insert a camshaft locking pin (Volvo No 999 7007) into the hole in the cylinder head, exposed by removal of the brake vacuum pump. If necessary, rotate the camshaft slightly to enable the pin to be inserted. If the Volvo pin is not available, a home-made equivalent can be fabricated **(see illustrations)**.

7 Unscrew the blanking plug from the front left-hand face of the cylinder block, and insert Volvo Tool No 999 7005, then rotate the crankshaft anti-clockwise (viewed from the timing belt of the engine) until the crankshaft web of No 5 cylinder comes to a stop against the tool. Check the marks on the crankshaft pulley flange and oil pump housing align. If the tool is not available, a home-made equivalent may be fabricated using the dimensions shown **(see illustrations)**.

8 Clean the seating in the bearing cap, then smear a little oil on the lips of the new oil seal. Fit the new oil seal and tap it into position carefully, using a tubular spacer, socket, or block of wood that bears only on the hard outer surface of the seal (see illustrations).

9 Refit the pulley to the camshaft, but only insert 3 of the retaining bolts finger tight. Ensure the hole in the sprocket for the remaining bolt (at roughly the 1 o'clock position) is exactly in the centre of the hole in the pulley itself. Refit the remaining pulley bolt.

10 Refit the timing belt as described in Section 4, and tighten the camshaft pulley bolts to the specified torque.

11 The remainder of refitting is a reversal of removal.

---

7 Crankshaft oil seals – renewal

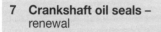

Right-hand oil seal

1 Remove the timing belt as described in Section 4.

2 Remove the crankshaft sprocket. The sprocket locates on a master spline on the crankshaft, and a puller may be required to work the sprocket off. Levering the sprocket is not advisable - the rim at the sprocket itself is easily broken if care if not taken.

3 The seal may be renewed without removing the oil pump by drilling a small hole, inserting a self-tapping screw, and pulling on the head of the screw with pliers (see illustrations). Take great care not to mark the crankshaft surface with the drill bit.

6.8a Fit the new seal using a tubular spacer which bears only on the hard, outer surface of the seal

4 Wrap some adhesive tape around the end of the crankshaft to prevent damage to the new oil seal. Dip the new seal in engine oil and drive it into the oil pump housing with a block of wood or a socket until flush. Make sure that the closed end of the seal is facing outwards (see illustrations).

5 Remove the adhesive tape.

6 Refit the timing belt and crankshaft sprocket.

Left-hand oil seal

7 Remove the flywheel/driveplate with reference to Section 10.

8 Clean the surfaces of the block and crankshaft.

9 Remove the old oil seal and fit the new one as described in paragraphs 3 to 5 above (see illustration).

10 Refit the flywheel/driveplate (Section 10).

6.8b The outside edge of the seal should be flush with the outer edge of the sealing cap/cylinder head casting

---

8 Cylinder head – removal, inspection and refitting

Removal

1 Disconnect the battery negative lead (see Chapter 5A).

2 Jack up the front of the vehicle and support it securely on axle stands (see *Jacking and vehicle support*).

3 Drain the engine oil with reference to Chapter 1B, Section 4.

4 Drain the cooling system with reference to Chapter 1B, Section 29.

5 Remove the timing belt as described in Section 4.

6 Remove the intake manifold as described in Section 5.

7.3a Drill a small hole into the hard, outer edge of the seal...

7.3b ...then insert a self-tapping screw and pull the seal from place

7.4a Wrap tape around the shoulder on the crankshaft to protect the seal lips...

7.4b ...then use a tubular spacer or socket...

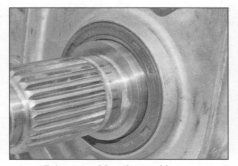

7.4c ...to drive the seal home

7.9 Drill a hole, insert a self-tapping screw and pull the crankshaft left-hand oil seal from place

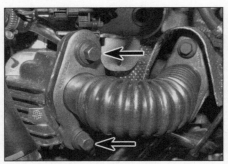

8.11 Undo the 2 bolts (arrowed) and disconnect the pipe at the left-hand end of the cylinder head

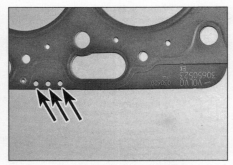

8.22 The holes (arrowed) along the edge of the cylinder head gasket indicate the thickness

8.25 Ensure the cylinder head gasket locates over the dowels in the block surface

7 Remove the fuel injectors and fuel rail as described in Chapter 4B. Remove the glow plugs as described in Chapter 5C.

8 Remove the high pressure fuel pump as described in Chapter 4B, and the brake vacuum pump as described in Chapter 9.

9 At the EGR cooler, slacken the clamp for the pipe connecting the cooler to the exhaust manifold, then undo the bolts securing the EGR valve/cooler assembly to the cylinder head and move it to one side. If necessary, the EGR assembly can be removed completely with reference to the relevant part of Chapter 4D.

10 Undo the securing bolts/nuts and remove the exhaust manifold heat shield.

11 Undo the bolts securing the exhaust manifold to the cylinder head as described in Chapter 4B. Undo the 2 bolts securing the pipe at the left-hand end of the exhaust manifold to the cylinder head (see illustration).

12 Remove the camshafts and rockers as described in Section 9.

13 Make a final check to ensure all wiring plugs and hoses have been disconnected from the cylinder head.

14 Following the reverse of the tightening sequence (see illustration 8.29), progressively slacken the cylinder head bolts, by half a turn at a time, until all bolts can be unscrewed by hand and removed. Discard the bolts – new ones must be fitted on reassembly.

15 Check that nothing remains connected to the cylinder head, then lift the head away from the cylinder block; seek assistance if possible, as it is heavy. Do not lay the cylinder head on

the worktop face down – this may damage the sealing face.

16 Remove the gasket from the top of the block, noting the identification holes on its front edge. If the dowels are a loose fit, remove them and store them with the head for safe-keeping. Do not discard the gasket yet – it will be needed for identification purposes.

17 If the cylinder head is to be dismantled for overhaul, refer to Chapter 2F.

Inspection

18 The mating faces of the cylinder head and cylinder block/crankcase must be perfectly clean before refitting the head. Use a hard plastic or wood scraper to remove all traces of gasket and carbon; also clean the piston crowns. Take particular care during the cleaning operations, as aluminium alloy is easily damaged. Also, make sure that the carbon is not allowed to enter the oil and water passages – this is particularly important for the lubrication system, as carbon could block the oil supply to the engine's components. Using adhesive tape and paper, seal the water, oil and bolt holes in the cylinder block/crankcase.

19 Check the mating surfaces of the cylinder block/crankcase and the cylinder head for nicks, deep scratches and other damage. If slight, they may be removed carefully with abrasive paper, but note that head machining will not be possible – refer to Chapter 2F.

20 If warpage of the cylinder head gasket surface is suspected, use a straight-edge to check it for distortion.

21 Clean out the cylinder head bolt drillings

using a suitable tap. If a tap is not available, use an old head bolt with two slots cut along the length of the threads. It is most important that no oil or coolant is present in the bolts holes, otherwise the block may be cracked by the hydraulic action as the head bolts are inserted and tightened.

Refitting

22 Examine the old cylinder head gasket for manufacturer's identification markings. These are in the form of holes along the front edge of the gasket (see illustration). Unless new pistons have been fitted, the new cylinder head gasket must be the same type as the old one.

23 If new piston assemblies have been fitted as part of an engine overhaul, before purchasing the new cylinder head gasket, refer to Chapter 2F and measure the piston projection. Purchase a new gasket according to the results of the measurement.

24 Check the marks on the crankshaft pulley flange and oil pump housing align.

25 Lay the new head gasket on the cylinder block, engaging it with the locating dowels (see illustration). Ensure that the manufacturer's part number markings are facing upwards.

26 With the help of an assistant, place the cylinder head centrally on the cylinder block, ensuring that the locating dowels engage with the recesses in the cylinder head. Check that the head gasket is correctly seated before allowing the full weight of the cylinder head to rest on it.

27 Apply a smear of grease to the threads, and to the underside of the heads, of the new cylinder head bolts.

28 Carefully enter each bolt into its relevant hole (do not drop them in) and screw in, by hand only, until finger-tight.

29 Working progressively and in the sequence shown, tighten the cylinder head bolts to the settings specified, using a torque wrench and socket (see illustration).

30 Once all the bolts have been tightened to their Stage 3 settings, working again in the given sequence, angle-tighten the bolts through the specified Stage 4 angle, using a socket and extension bar (see illustration). It is recommended that an angle-measuring gauge is used during this stage of the tightening, to ensure accuracy. If a gauge is not

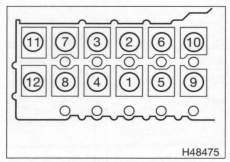

8.29 Cylinder head bolt tightening sequence

H48475

8.30 Use an angle-measuring gauge to accurately tighten the bolts

9.4 Inner timing cover screw

9.5a Undo the screws and remove the left-hand…

9.5b ..and right-hand bearing caps

9.6 The bearing caps should be numbered, starting from the timing belt end

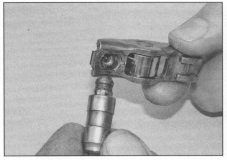

9.10 Unclip the tappets from the rocker arms

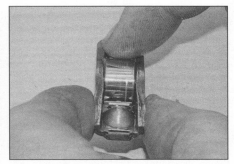

9.11 Spin the roller and listen for any noise

available, use paint to make alignment marks between the bolt head and cylinder head prior to tightening; the marks can then be used to check the bolt has been rotated through the correct angle during tightening. Repeat the procedure, tightening the bolts to the Stage 5 angle.

31 Refit the camshafts and rockers as described in Section 9. Fit a new camshaft oil seal as described in Section 6.

32 The remainder of refitting is a reversal of removal, noting the following points:

a) *No retightening of the cylinder head bolts is required.*

b) *Tighten all fasteners to their specified torque where given.*

c) *Refill the cooling system and replenish the engine oil as described in Chapter 1B.*

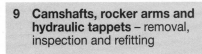

9 Camshafts, rocker arms and hydraulic tappets – removal, inspection and refitting

Removal

1 Remove the camshaft oil seal as described in Section 6.

2 Remove the high pressure fuel pump as described in Chapter 4B.

3 Remove the inlet manifold as described in Section 5.

4 Undo the bolt securing the timing inner cover to the right-hand camshaft bearing cap **(see illustration)**.

5 Undo the 3 bolts securing the camshaft bearing cap at the left-hand end of the engine,

adjacent to the camshaft gears. Undo the 2 bolts and remove the inlet camshaft bearing cap at the right-hand end of the engine. **(see illustrations)**.

6 The camshaft bearing caps should be marked to indicate their position. If they are not, number them starting from the timing belt end **(see illustration)**. It is essential they are refitted to their original positions.

7 Starting on the intake camshaft, slacken each of the bearing cap bolts one turn at a time until the camshaft is no longer under tension, then remove the bolts and caps. The bolts must be released gradually and evenly to prevent excess stress and possible damage to the camshaft. Repeat this procedure on the exhaust camshaft.

8 Lift out the camshafts, and discard the oil seal on the intake camshaft.

9 Carefully lift the rocker arms and hydraulic tappets from the cylinder head. Lay them out

9.15 Ensure the end of the rocker arms are correctly located over the end of the valve stems

on a clean, dry surface and, using paint, mark their positions in the cylinder head, eg, E1, E2 (exhaust 1, exhaust 2, etc).

Inspection

10 Unclip the hydraulic tappets from the rocker arms, and check for any signs of damage **(see illustration)**. Renew as necessary.

11 Spin the roller on each of the rocker arms and listen for any noise from the bearing **(see illustration)**. Renew as necessary.

12 Inspect the cam lobes and the camshaft bearing journals for scoring or other visible evidence of wear. Once the surface hardening of the lobes has been penetrated, wear will progress rapidly.

13 No specific bearing journal diameters or running clearances are given by Volvo for the camshafts. However, if there is a visual deterioration, then component renewal will be necessary.

Refitting

14 Clip each tappet onto the underside of their respective rocker arms.

15 Ensure the bores for the tappets in the cylinder head are clean and free of debris, then lubricate the tappets with clean engine oil, and lower them into their original positions. Check the ends of the rocker arms are correctly located over the valve stems **(see illustration)**.

16 Check to make sure the camshaft bearing positions in the cylinder head are clean, then lubricate them, and the rocker arm rollers, with clean engine oil.

17 Position the camshafts together, so the marks on the drive gears align, then lower the

9.17 Position the camshafts together so the marks (arrowed) on the drive gears align

camshafts into position on the cylinder head (see illustration). Lubricate the camshaft journals with clean engine oil.

18 Refit the camshaft bearing caps and screws into their original positions, and hand-tighten the screws evenly until the caps lie flat against the camshaft journals. Do not install the right- and left-hand bearing/sealing caps yet.

19 Tighten the bearing cap screws one turn at a time on both camshafts, until the bearing caps contact the cylinder head. It's essential the bearing caps are tightened down gradually and evenly, or damage to the camshaft may result. Finally, tighten the bearing cap screws to the specified torque.

20 Insert a camshaft locking pin (Volvo No 999 7007) though the hole in the cylinder head, exposed by removal of the brake vacuum pump. If necessary, rotate the camshaft slightly to enable the pin to be inserted using a large screwdriver in the camshaft end slots – do not turn the camshafts more than is absolutely necessary. If the Volvo pin is not available, a home-made equivalent can be fabricated.

21 Ensure the mating surfaces of the right-hand and left-hand camshaft bearing/sealing caps are clean and dry, then apply a light, even film of Volvo liquid sealant (Volvo No 11 61 059) to the mating surfaces (see illustration). Ideally, use a short haired roller.

22 Refit the right- and left-hand bearing/sealing caps, and tighten the retaining screws to their specified torque.

23 Refit the camshaft oil seal as described in Section 6.

9.21 Apply sealant to the cylinder head/bearing cap sealing surfaces

24 The remainder of refitting is a reversal of removal, noting the following points:
a) Tighten all fasteners to the specified torque where given.
b) Wait a minimum of 30 minutes (or preferably, leave overnight) after fitting the hydraulic tappets before turning the engine over, to allow the tappets time to settle, otherwise the valve heads will strike the pistons.

10 Flywheel/driveplate – removal, inspection and refitting

Removal

1 On manual transmission models, remove the gearbox (see Chapter 7A) and clutch (see Chapter 6).

2 On automatic transmission models, remove the automatic transmission as described in Chapter 7B.

3 Undo the bolts and move the engine speed sensor complete with bracket, to one side (see illustration).

4 Temporarily insert a bolt in the cylinder block, and use a wide-bladed screwdriver to hold the flywheel/driveplate, or make up a holding tool (see illustration).

5 Slacken and remove the multi-spline bolts securing the flywheel/driveplate to the crankshaft, and lift the flywheel/driveplate from place – the flywheel's heavy! Discard the bolts, new ones must be fitted.

Inspection

6 Check the flywheel/driveplate for wear and damage. Examine the starter ring gear for excessive wear to the teeth. If the driveplate or ring gear are damaged, the complete driveplate must be renewed. The flywheel ring gear, however, may be renewed separately from the flywheel, but the work should be entrusted to a Volvo dealer. If the clutch friction face is discoloured or scored excessively, it may be possible to regrind it, but this work should also be entrusted to a Volvo dealer. Always renew the flywheel/driveplate bolts.

7 On models with a dual mass flywheel, check the radial play by turning the flywheel secondary mass one way until the spring begins to tension, then allow the flywheel to spring back – make an alignment mark between the primary and secondary masses. Now turn the flywheel in the opposite direction until the spring begins to tension – make another alignment mark between the two masses. The distance between the 2 marks must be less than 35mm.

Refitting

8 Position the flywheel/driveplate against the crankshaft, aligning the locating dowel with the corresponding hole in the flywheel/driveplate (see illustration).

9 Insert the new bolts, and tighten them gradually and evenly, in a diagonal pattern to the Stage 1 torque setting, followed by the Stage 2 angle setting. Prevent the flywheel from rotating using the same method as during removal.

10 The remainder of refitting is a reversal of removal.

11 Engine mountings – inspection and renewal

Inspection

1 If improved access is required, raise the front of the car and support it securely on axle stands (see *Jacking and vehicle support*) then remove the undershield.

2 Check the mounting rubbers to see if they are cracked, hardened or separated from the

10.3 Undo the bolts and remove the engine speed sensor complete with bracket

10.4 Ideally, make up a tool to lock the flywheel in place

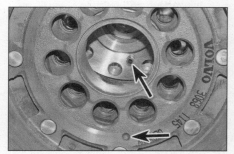

10.8 Align the locating dowel in the crankshaft with the hole in the flywheel marled by the dimple (arrowed)

metal at any point; renew the mounting if any such damage or deterioration is evident.

3 Check that all the mounting's fasteners are securely tightened; use a torque wrench to check if possible.

4 Using a large screwdriver or a crowbar, check for wear in the mounting by carefully levering against it to check for free play. Where this is not possible, enlist the aid of an assistant to move the engine/transmission back-and-forth, or from side-to-side, while you watch the mounting. While some free play is to be expected even from new components, excessive wear should be obvious. If excessive free play is found, check first that the fasteners are correctly secured, then renew any worn components as described below.

Renewal

Right-hand mounting

5 Pull the plastic cover on the engine straight upwards and remove it from the engine compartment.

6 Release the coolant expansion from its mountings and move it to one side **(see illustration)**.

7 Remove the upper torque rod (where fitted) as described below.

8 Place a trolley jack under the right-hand end of the engine sump and take the weight. Position a block of wood between the jack head and sump to prevent damage to the casing.

9 Unscrew the 2 locking nuts from the engine casing, then undo the 2 retaining bolts to the vehicle inner wing panel, and withdraw the mounting **(see illustration)**.

10 Refitting is a reversal of removal, tightening the mounting bolts to the correct torque.

Left-hand mounting

11 Pull the plastic cover on the engine straight upwards and remove it from the engine compartment.

12 Remove the air cleaner housing as described in Chapter 4B.

13 Remove the battery and battery tray as described in Chapter 5A.

14 Place a trolley jack under the left-hand end of the engine sump and take the weight. Position a block of wood between the jack head and sump to prevent damage to the casing.

15 Undo the 4 large nuts and the 2 small bolts on top of the mounting, then undo the main mounting bolt **(see illustration)**. The mounting can now be removed.

16 Refitting is a reversal of removal, tightening the mounting bolts to the correct torque.

Upper torque rod (where fitted)

17 Pull the plastic cover on the engine straight upwards and remove it from the engine compartment.

18 Undo the torque rod bolt at the suspension strut turret, and the 3 mounting

11.6 With the coolant tank released from its mountings, it can be moved to one side

bolts, and manoeuvre the torque rod from place.

19 Position the torque rod and tighten the new fasteners to the specified torque.

Lower torque rod

20 Jack up the front of the vehicle and support it securely on axle stands (see *Jacking and vehicle support*).

21 On models fitted with 1.6 litre and 2.0 litre (4-cylinder) engines, release the 7 Torx screws and remove the engine undershield. Undo the 2 bolts and remove the torque rod **(see illustration)**.

22 On models fitted with 5-cylinder engines, undo the 4 torque rod mounting bolts, and the lower torque rod bolt and manoeuvre the torque rod from place.

23 Position the torque rod and tighten the new fasteners to the specified torque.

24 Refit the roadwheel (and engine undershield where removed) and lower the vehicle to the ground.

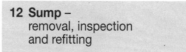

12 Sump –
removal, inspection and refitting

Removal

1 Jack up the front of the vehicle and support it securely on axle stands (see *Jacking and vehicle support*).

2 Undo the screws and remove the engine undershield.

11.15 Undo the centre bolt (arrowed) to release the mounting from the transmission

11.9 Undo the right-hand mounting bolts/ nuts (arrowed)

3 Drain the engine oil as described in Chapter 1B, Section 4.

4 Remove the auxiliary drive belt as described in Chapter 1B, Section 32.

5 Undo the 3 bolts and move the air-conditioning compressor to one side. Use wire to secure the compressor to a suitable part of the bodywork or chassis.

6 Undo the bolt/nut and pull the oil level dipstick guide tube from the sump.

7 Disconnect the wiring plug, undo the 3 bolts, and remove the oil level sensor from the sump.

8 The oil cooler (where fitted) is secured to the sump by four bolts. Undo the bolts and pull the cooler to the rear. Be prepared for oil spillage.

9 Remove the charge air pipe below the sump. Undo the clips at each end and undo the bolt securing the mounting bracket.

10 Slacken the bolts securing the sump, and remove them all apart from one bolt in each corner.

11 Gently tap the sides and ends of the sump until the joint between the engine and sump releases. Undo the remaining bolts and remove the sump. Discard the O-rings at the right-hand end/front edge of the sump, new ones must be fitted.

Refitting

12 Clean the contact faces of the sump and block.

13 Apply a thin and even layer of Volvo sealant (No 116 1771) to the sump mating face, and position the new O-ring seals on the engine

11.21 Undo the 2 bolts (arrowed) and remove the torque rod

12.13a Apply a thin and even layer of Volvo sealant...

12.13b ...and renew the O-rings (arrowed)

12.14 The four slightly shorter bolts are fitted at the transmission end

block face (see illustrations). The sump must be refitted within 5 minutes of applying the sealant.

14 Refit the sump casing and refit the retaining bolts, finger-finger tight only at this stage. Note that the three longest bolts are fitted to the oil pump end, and the four slightly shorter bolts are fitted at the transmission end (see illustration).

15 Refit the sump-to-transmission bolts and tighten them to the specified torque setting.

16 Starting from the transmission end, tighten the sump-to-engine bolts in pairs to the specified torque.

17 The remainder of refitting is a reversal of refitting, noting the following points:
 a) Renew the oil cooler-to-sump O-ring seals.
 b) Tighten all fasteners to their specified torque where given.
 c) Fit a new engine oil filter, and refill the engine with oil as described in Chapter 1B.

 d) Volvo recommend waiting a minimum of 2 hours before starting the engine to allow the sealant to cure fully.

13 Oil pump – removal, inspection and refitting

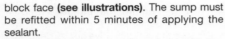

Removal

1 Remove the crankshaft right-hand oil seal as described in Section 7.

2 Undo the four bolts securing the oil pump to the front of the cylinder block (see illustration).

3 Carefully withdraw the pump assembly by levering behind the upper and lower parting lugs using a screwdriver. Remove the pump and recover the gasket.

4 Thoroughly clean the pump and cylinder

block mating faces and remove all traces of old gasket. Discard the O-ring seal, a new one must be fitted.

Inspection

5 Undo the two pump cover retaining Allen screws whilst holding the two halves of the pump together, then remove the cover. Be prepared for the ejection of the pressure relief valve spring (see illustration).

6 Note their fitted positions, then remove the pressure relief valve spring, plunger and pump rotors (see illustrations).

7 If not already done, lever out the crankshaft oil seal.

8 Clean all the components thoroughly, then inspect the rotors, body and cover for damage or signs of wear.

9 At the time of writing, no specifications concerning the overhaul or inspection of the pump were available, and it would appear that no pump internal parts are available separately.

10 Refit the inner rotor with the marks facing the pump body (see illustration).

11 Refit the outer rotor to the body, ensuring the mark on the rotor faces the cylinder block (see illustration).

12 Refit the pressure relief valve spring and plunger, and fit the cover, tightening the retaining screws securely.

Refitting

13 Using a new gasket and O-ring, fit the pump to the block. Use the pump retaining bolts as guides, and draw the pump into place with the crankshaft pulley nut and spacers.

13.2 Undo the four oil pump bolts (arrowed)

13.5 Undo the two oil pump cover screws (arrowed)

13.6a Remove the plunger...

13.6b ...spring...

13.6c ...and rotors

With the pump seated, tighten the retaining bolts diagonally to the specified torque.
14 Fit a new crankshaft right-hand oil seal as described in Section 7.

14 Oil cooler –
removal and refitting

Removal

1 Drain the engine oil and coolant as described in Chapter 1B, Sections 4 and 29.
2 Release the hose clamp and disconnect the coolant hoses from the cooler, located on the rear face of the sump.
3 Undo the bolts securing the cooler to the sump, and recover the O-ring seals as the cooler is withdrawn. Be prepared for fluid spillage **(see illustration)**.

Refitting

4 Check the mating faces of the sump and oil cooler are clean, then refit the cooler using new O-ring seals. Tighten the retaining bolts securely **(see illustration)**.
5 Reconnect the coolant hoses and secure them with new clips where necessary.
6 Refill the engine oil and cooling systems as described in Chapter 1B.

13.10 Fit the inner rotor with the marks (arrowed) facing the pump body...

13.11 ...and the outer rotor with the mark (arrowed) facing the cylinder block

14.3 Undo the oil cooler bolts (arrowed)

14.4 Oil cooler O-rings

Chapter 2 Part F:
Engine removal and overhaul procedures

Contents

Degrees of difficulty

| Easy, suitable for novice with little experience | | Fairly easy, suitable for beginner with some experience | | Fairly difficult, suitable for competent DIY mechanic | | Difficult, suitable for experienced DIY mechanic | | Very difficult, suitable for expert DIY or professional | |

Specifications

Cylinder head

Warp limit – maximum acceptable for use:
  Petrol engines:
    1.8 litre engines. . . . . 0.10 mm
    2.0 litre engines. . . . . 0.10 mm
    2.4 litre engines:
      Lengthways. . . . . 0.50 mm
      Across. . . . . 0.20 mm
  Diesel engines:
    1.6 litre engines. . . . . 0.025 mm
    2.0 litre engines (4 cylinder) . . . . 0.030 mm
    2.0 litre engines (5-cylinder) . . . . 0.05 mm
    2.4 litre engines (5-cylinder) . . . . 0.05 mm

Inlet valves

Stem diameter:
  Petrol engines:
    1.8 litre engines. . . . . 5.470 to 5.485 mm
    2.0 litre engines. . . . . 5.470 to 5.485 mm
    2.4 litre engines. . . . . Not available
  Diesel engines:
    1.6 litre engines. . . . . Not available
    2.0 litre engines (4 cylinder) . . . . 5.969 to 5.987mm
    2.0 litre engines (5-cylinder) . . . . 5.975 ± 0.015mm
    2.4 litre engines (5-cylinder) . . . . 5.975 ± 0.015mm

Exhaust valves

Stem diameter:
  Petrol engines:
    1.8 litre engines. . . . . 5.465 to 5.480 mm
    2.0 litre engines. . . . . Not available
    2.4 litre petrol engines . . . . Not available
  Diesel engines:
    1.6 litre engines. . . . . Not available
    2.0 litre engines (4-cylinder) . . . . 5.969 to 5.987 mm
    2.0 litre engines (5-cylinder) . . . . 5.975 ± 0.015 mm
    2.4 litre engines (5-cylinder) . . . . 5.975 ± 0.015 mm

Pistons

Piston-to-bore clearance:	
Petrol engines (all engines)...........................	0.01 to 0.03 mm
Diesel engines:	
1.6 litre engines..................................	0.164 to 0.196mm
2.0 litre 4-cylinder engine........................	0.056 to 0.103mm
5-cylinder engines	0.010 to 0.030mm

Piston rings

Clearance in groove:	
Petrol engines:	
1.8 and 2.0 litre engines...........................	Not available
2.4 litre engines	
Top compression	0.030 to 0.070 mm
Second compression	0.030 to 0.070 mm
Oil control	0.038 to 0.142 mm
Diesel engines	
1.6 litre diesel engine:	
Top compression	0.200 to 0.350 mm
Second compression	0.200 to 0.400 mm
Oil control	0.800 to 1.000 mm
2.0 litre diesel engine (4-cylinder):	
Top compression	0.200 to 0.350 mm
Second compression	0.800 to 1.000 mm
Oil control	0.250 to 0.500 mm
2.0 and 2.5 litre diesel engines (5-cylinder):	
Top compression	0.120 to 0.160 mm
Second compression	0.070 to 0.110 mm
Oil control	0.25 to 0.0500 mm
End gap (measured in cylinder):	
Petrol engines:	
1.8 and 2.0 litre engines:	
Compression rings	0.30 to 0.50 mm
Oil control ring.............................	0.20 to 1.40 mm
2.4 litre engine:	
Compression rings	0.20 to 0.40 mm
Oil control ring.............................	0.25 to 0.50 mm
Diesel engines:	
1.6 litre engines:	
Compression rings	Not available
Oil control	Not available
2.4 litre engines (4-cylinder):	
Compression rings	Not available
Oil control ring.............................	Not available
2.0 and 2.5 litre engines (5-cylinder):	
Compression rings	0.20 to 0.40 mm
Oil control ring.............................	0.25 to 0.50 mm

Crankshaft

Endfloat:	
Petrol engines:	
1.8 and 2.0 litre engines..............................	0.09 to 0.26 mm
2.4 litre engines.....................................	0.19 mm max
Diesel engines:	
1.6 litre engines.....................................	0.10 to 0.30mm
2.0 litre 4-cylinder engine............................	0.07 to 0.32mm
5-cylinder engines	0.08 to 0.19mm

Torque wrench settings

Refer to Chapter 2A, 2B, 2C, 2D or 2E depending on engine.

---

1 General Information

1 Included in this part of Chapter 2 are details of removing the engine/transmission from the car and general overhaul procedures for the cylinder head, cylinder block and all other engine internal components.

2 The information ranges from advice concerning preparation for an overhaul and the purchase of parts, to detailed step-by-step procedures covering removal, inspection, renovation and refitting of engine internal components.

3 After Section 6, all instructions are based on the assumption that the engine has been removed from the car. For information concerning engine in-car repair, as well as removal and installation of those external components necessary for full overhaul, refer to Part A, B, C, D or E of this Chapter as applicable, and to Section 2. Ignore any

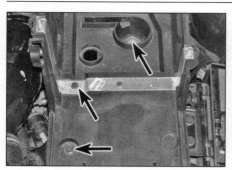

3.3 Undo the bolts and remove the battery tray

3.6a Depress the clip and remove the ECM cover – 1.8 and 2.0 litre models

3.6b Slide up and remove the ECM cover – 2.4 litre models

preliminary dismantling operations described in Part A, B, C, D or E that are no longer relevant once the engine has been removed from the car.

2 Engine/transmission removal – preparation and precautions

1 If you have decided that an engine must be removed for overhaul or major repair work, several preliminary steps should be taken.
2 Locating a suitable place to work is extremely important. Adequate work space, along with storage space for the car, will be needed. If a workshop or garage is not available, at the very least, a flat, level, clean work surface is required.
3 If possible, clear some shelving close to the work area, and use it to store the engine components and ancillaries as they are removed and dismantled. In this manner, the components stand a better chance of staying clean and undamaged during the overhaul. Laying out components in groups together with their fixing bolts, screws, etc, will save time and avoid confusion when the engine is refitted.
4 Clean the engine compartment and engine/transmission before beginning the removal procedure; this will help visibility and help to keep tools clean.
5 The help of an assistant should be available; there are certain instances when one person cannot safely perform all of the operations required to remove the engine from the vehicle. Safety is of primary importance, considering the potential hazards involved in this kind of operation. A second person should always be in attendance to offer help in an emergency. If this is the first time you have removed an engine, advice and aid from someone more experienced would also be beneficial.
6 Plan the operation ahead of time. Before starting work, obtain (or arrange for the hire of) all of the tools and equipment you will need. Access to the following items will allow the task of removing and refitting the engine/transmission to be completed safely and with relative ease: an engine hoist – rated in

excess of the combined weight of the engine/transmission, a heavy-duty trolley jack, complete sets of spanners and sockets as described at the rear this manual, wooden blocks, and plenty of rags and cleaning solvent for mopping-up spilled oil, coolant and fuel. A selection of different sized plastic storage bins will also prove useful for keeping dismantled components grouped together. If any of the equipment must be hired, make sure that you arrange for it in advance, and perform all of the operations possible without it beforehand; this may save you time and money.
7 Plan on the vehicle being out of use for quite a while, especially if you intend to carry out an engine overhaul. Read through the whole of this Section and work out a strategy based on your own experience and the tools, time and workspace available to you. Some of the overhaul processes may have to be carried out by a Volvo dealer or an engineering works – these establishments often have busy schedules, so it would be prudent to consult them before removing or dismantling the engine, to get an idea of the amount of time required to carry out the work.
8 When removing the engine from the vehicle, be methodical about the disconnection of external components. Labelling cables and hoses as they removed will greatly assist the refitting process.
9 Always be extremely careful when lifting the engine/transmission assembly from the engine bay. Serious injury can result from

3.8a Oxygen sensor wiring plugs located at the left-hand end of the cylinder head – 1.8 and 2.0 litre models

careless actions. If help is required, it is better to wait until it is available rather than risk personal injury and/or damage to components by continuing alone. By planning ahead and taking your time, a job of this nature, although major, can be accomplished successfully and without incident.

3 Engine and transmission – removal, separation and refitting

Note: *This procedure describes removing the engine and transmission a complete assembly downwards out the of the engine compartment. When raising the vehicle bear in mind that the front underside of the vehicle must be at least 700 mm above the ground to provide sufficient clearance.*

Removal

1 On petrol models, remove the fuel pump fuse from the engine compartment fusebox, then start the engine (if possible) and allow it to run until it stops (having relieved the fuel pressure).
2 Open the bonnet. If there is any possibility of the engine hoist being obstructed, remove the bonnet as described in Chapter 11, Section 6.
3 Remove the battery as described and then undo the 3 bolts and remove the battery tray as described in Chapter 5A, Section 3. Disconnect the sensor connector from the lower section (see illustration).
4 Drain the coolant as described in Chapter 1A (petrol) or Chapter 1B (diesel).
5 Pull the plastic cover on top of the engine (where fitted) straight-up, then undo the 7 Torx screws and remove the engine undershield (where fitted).

Petrol models

6 Remove the cover over the engine control module (ECM), then disconnect the wiring connectors and pull out the wiring harness (see illustrations).
7 Disconnect the fuel supply pipe, brake servo vacuum hose, and the hose for the EVAP canister.
8 Disconnect the oxygen sensors' wiring plugs (see illustrations).

3.8b Front oxygen sensor wiring plug located at the left-hand end of the cylinder head – 2.4 litre models

3.9a Disconnect the coolant hoses at the left-hand end of the engine – 1.8 litre model shown

3.9b Rotate the grey catches to disconnect the heater pipes

3.10a The ECU wiring plugs

3.10b Fold back the catches…

3.10c …and pull the plugs from the ECU

9 Disconnect the coolant hoses at the coolant outlet terminal at the left-hand end of the cylinder head, then disconnect the heater hoses at the engine compartment bulkhead (see illustrations). On some models the hoses are disconnected by depressing the release tabs, on others the grey catches must be rotated.

Diesel models

10 Detach the front edge of the left-hand front wheel arch liner, then undo the 4 Torx screws and remove the engine control unit (ECU) cover. Disconnect the 3 wiring plugs from the ECU (see illustrations).

11 Release the clamps, undo the support bracket bolt, and remove the charge air pipe under the engine.

12 Slide up the retaining clip and disconnect the coolant bleed hose, then slacken the clamp and disconnect the upper coolant hose

from the thermostat housing (see illustration).

13 Disconnect the vacuum hose from the vacuum pump at the quick-release connector.

14 Depress the release tabs and disconnect the fuel hoses from the filter assembly. Plug or cover the openings to prevent contamination.

All models

15 Remove the air cleaner assembly, and all air ducting, including turbocharger inlet (where applicable) with reference to Chapter 4A (petrol) or Chapter 4B (diesel).

16 Remove the cover from the central electrical unit, then disconnect the engine harness connector, undo the earth connections, and the positive lead connection from the battery clamp (see illustration). Note that the number of connections will vary depending on the engine version fitted.

17 Remove both driveshafts as described in Chapter 8 Section 2.

18 If the engine is to be dismantled, refer to Chapter 1A (petrol) or Chapter 1B (diesel) and drain the engine oil.

19 Remove the auxiliary drivebelts as described in Chapter 1A (petrol) or Chapter. 1B (diesel).

20 Disconnect the selector cables from the transmission as described in Chapter 7A (petrol) or Chapter 7B (diesel).

21 On 2.4 litre models, remove the right-hand wheel arch liner, and disconnect the power steering pump fluid delivery and return hoses. Plug or cover the openings to prevent contamination.

22 On manual transmission models, prise out the retaining clip and separate the clutch slave cylinder fluid pipe at the connection on the bulkhead. Plug to cover the openings to prevent contamination.

23 On automatic transmission models, disconnect the oil hoses and coolant hoses

3.12 Slide up the clip and disconnect the coolant bleed hose

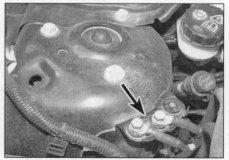

3.16a Disconnect the engine loom earth connections from the right-hand front strut tower…

3.16b …and from the left-hand strut tower

for the transmission (see Chapter 7B). Plug or cover the openings to prevent contamination.
24 Move the coolant expansion tank to one side for access to the engine mounting.
25 Remove the exhaust manifold, turbocharger (where applicable) and catalytic converter as described in Chapter 4A or Chapter 4B.
26 Undo the bolts, then remove the lower torque rod and mounting bracket from the lower, rear of the engine/transmission.
27 Undo the air conditioning compressor mounting bolts and refrigerant pipe bracket bolt, then suspend the compressor from the radiator crossmember using wire or straps. There is no need to disconnect the refrigerant pipes.
28 On 1.8 and 2.0 litre petrol and diesel models, undo the steering rack mounting bolts and suspend the rack with wire or straps from a suitable point above it. Note that the left-hand bolt is accessed from above.
29 On 2.4 litre petrol models, undo the steering column lower universal joint pinch-bolt. Then make alignment marks between the joint and the steering rack pinion, and push the joint upwards and off the pinion.
30 Position a trolley jack and block of wood to support the front subframe. Undo the subframe retaining bolts and lower the subframe a little to access the anti-roll bar clamp bolts. Undo the bolts and lower the subframe to the ground. The help of an assistant will be required.
31 Slacken the clamp and disconnect the radiator bottom hose from the engine. Make a final check to ensure all relevant coolant hoses and electrical wiring has been disconnected from the engine/transmission.
32 Attach lifting chains/straps to the engine/transmission lifting eyes, and position an engine hoist to take the weight of the engine/transmission assembly.
33 Undo the nuts and bolts, then remove the right-hand engine mounting assembly.
34 Remove the central bolt from the left-hand transmission mounting. The engine and transmission should now be suspended from the hoist. Check to ensure nothing will obstruct the engine/transmission assembly as it is lowered.
35 Enlist the help of an assistant, and lower the engine/transmission downwards onto a trolley jack or similar. Once the assembly is fully lowered, disconnect the engine hoist and pull the assembly from under the vehicle.

Separation

36 Remove the starter motor as described in Chapter 5A Section 8.

Manual transmission models

37 Remove the bolts securing the transmission to the engine.
38 With the aid of an assistant, draw the transmission off the engine. Once it is clear of the dowels, do not allow it to hang on the input shaft.

Automatic transmission models

39 Rotate the crankshaft, using a socket on the pulley nut, until one of the torque converter-to-driveplate retaining bolts becomes accessible through the opening on the rear facing side of the engine. Working through the opening, undo the bolt using a TX50 socket. Rotate the crankshaft as necessary and remove the remaining bolts in the same way. Note that new bolts will be required for refitting.
40 Remove the bolts securing the transmission to the engine.
41 With the aid of an assistant, draw the transmission squarely off the engine dowels making sure that the torque converter remains in position on the transmission. Use the access hole in the transmission housing to hold the converter in place.

Refitting

Manual transmission models

42 Make sure that the clutch is correctly centred and that the clutch release components are fitted to the bellhousing. Do not apply any grease to the transmission input shaft, the guide sleeve, or the release bearing itself, as these components have a friction-reducing coating which does not require lubrication.
43 Manoeuvre the transmission squarely into position, and engage it with the engine dowels. Refit the bolts securing the transmission to the engine, and tighten them to the specified torque. Refit the starter motor as described in Chapter 5A Section 8.

Automatic transmission models

44 Before refitting the transmission, flush out the fluid cooler with fresh transmission fluid. To do this, attach a hose to the upper union, pour ATF through the hose and collect it in a container positioned beneath the return hose.
45 Clean the contact surfaces on the torque converter and driveplate, and the transmission and engine mating faces. Lightly lubricate the torque converter guide projection and the engine/transmission locating dowels with grease.
46 Manoeuvre the transmission squarely into position, and engage it with the engine dowels. Refit the bolts securing the transmission to the engine and tighten lightly first in a diagonal sequence, then again to the specified torque.
47 Attach the torque converter to the driveplate using new bolts. Rotate the crankshaft for access to the bolts as was done for removal, then rotate the torque converter by means of the access hole in the transmission housing. Fit and tighten all the bolts hand-tight first, then tighten again to the specified torque.

All models

48 The remainder of refitting is essentially a reversal of removal, noting the following points:

a) Tighten all fastenings to the specified torque and, where applicable, torque angle. Refer to the relevant Chapters of this manual for torque wrench settings not directly related to the engine.
b) Refit the front subframe as described in Chapter 10, Section 15.
c) Reconnect and if necessary, adjust the manual transmission selector cables as described in Chapter 7A Section 3.
d) On automatic transmission models, reconnect and adjust the selector cable as described in Chapter 7B Section 2.
e) Refit the air cleaner assembly as described in Chapter 4A Section 3 or Chapter 4B Section 3.
f) Refit the auxiliary drivebelts, then refill the engine with coolant and oil as described in Chapter 1A or Chapter 1B.
g) Refill the transmission with lubricant if necessary as described in Chapter 1A Section 11 (automatic transmissions) or Chapter 7A Section 6 (manual transmissions).
h) Refer to Section 16 before starting the engine.

4 Engine overhaul – preliminary information

1 It is much easier to dismantle and work on the engine if it is mounted on a portable engine stand. These stands can often be hired from a tool hire shop. Before the engine is mounted on a stand, the flywheel/driveplate should be removed so that the stand bolts can be tightened into the end of the cylinder block/crankcase.
2 If a stand is not available, it is possible to dismantle the engine with it suitably supported on a sturdy, workbench or on the floor. Be careful not to tip or drop the engine when working without a stand.
3 If you intend to obtain a reconditioned engine, all ancillaries must be removed first, to be transferred to the new engine (just as they will if you are doing a complete engine overhaul yourself). These components include the following:
a) Engine mountings and brackets (Chapter 2E Section 11).
b) Alternator including accessories mounting bracket (Chapter 5A Section 5).
c) Starter motor (Chapter 5A Section 8).
d) The fuel pump and common rail – diesel models (Chapter 4B Section 10).
e) The ignition system and HT components including all sensors, ignition coils and spark plugs, as applicable (Chapters 1A Section 27 and Chapter 5B Section 4).
f) Exhaust manifold, with turbocharger if fitted (Chapter 4A Section 12 or Chapter 4B Section 14).
g) Inlet manifold with fuel injection components (Chapter 4A Section 11 or Chapter 4B Section 17).

5.4a Compress the valve spring with a suitable valve spring compressor

5.4b Extract the collets and release the spring compressor

Note: *New and reconditioned cylinder heads are available from the manufacturer and from engine overhaul specialists. Specialist tools are required for the dismantling and inspection procedures, and new components may not be readily available. It may, therefore, be more practical and economical for the home mechanic to purchase a reconditioned head rather than dismantle, inspect and recondition the original head.*

h) All electrical switches, actuators and sensors, and the engine wiring harness.
i) Coolant pump, thermostat, hoses, and distribution pipe (Chapter 3).
j) Clutch components – manual transmission models (Chapter 6 Section 6).
k) Flywheel/driveplate (Chapter 2A Section 15, Chapter 2B Section 10, Chapter 2B Section 10, Chapter 2C Section 16 or Chapter 2E Section 10.
l) Oil filter (Chapter 1A Section 4 or Chapter 1B Section 4).
m) Dipstick, tube and bracket.
Note: *When removing the external components from the engine, pay close attention to details that may be helpful or important during refitting. Note the fitting positions of gaskets, seals, washers, bolts and other small items.*
4 If you are obtaining a 'short' engine (cylinder

block/crankcase, crankshaft, pistons and connecting rods all assembled), then the cylinder head, timing belt (together with tensioner, tensioner and idler pulleys and covers) and auxiliary drivebelt tensioner will have to be removed also.
5 If a complete overhaul is planned, the engine can be dismantled in the order given below:
a) Inlet and exhaust manifolds and turbocharger (where applicable).
b) Timing belt, sprockets, tensioner, pulleys and covers.
c) Cylinder head.
d) Oil pump.
e) Flywheel/driveplate.
f) Sump.
g) Oil pick-up pipe.
h) Intermediate section.
i) Pistons/connecting rods.
j) Crankshaft.

Dismantling

1 Remove the cylinder head as described in the relevant part of Chapter 2, depending on engine.
2 According to components still fitted, remove the thermostat housing (Chapter 3 Section 8), the glow plugs (Chapter 5C Section 3) and any other unions, pipes, sensors or brackets as necessary. On 5-cylinder diesel engines, lift the swirl valve assembly from the top of the cylinder head.
3 Tap each valve stem smartly, using a light hammer and a block of wood to free the spring and associated items.
4 Fit a deep-reach type valve spring compressor to each valve in turn, and compress each spring until the collets are exposed. Lift out the collets; a small screwdriver, a magnet or a pair of tweezers may be useful **(see illustrations)**. Carefully release the spring compressor and remove it.
5 Remove the valve spring upper seat and the valve spring. Pull the valve out of its guide **(see illustrations)**.
6 Pull off the valve stem oil seal with a pair of long-nosed pliers. It may be necessary to use a tool such as a pair of electrician's wire strippers, the 'legs' of which will engage under the seal, if the seal is tight **(see illustration)**. Note that specialised valve stem oil seal pliers are also available.
7 Recover the valve spring lower seat. If there is much carbon build-up round the outside of the valve guide, this will have to be scraped off before the seat can be removed **(see illustration)**. Note that on diesel models, the spring seat is integral with the stem seal.

All engines

8 It is essential that each valve is stored together with its collets, spring and seats. The valves should also be kept in their correct sequence, unless they are so badly worn or burnt that they are to be renewed. If they are going to be kept and used again, place each valve assembly in a labelled polythene bag or similar container **(see illustration)**.
9 Continue removing all the remaining valves in the same way.

Cleaning

10 Thoroughly clean all traces of old gasket

5.5a Remove the spring retainer...

5.5b ...followed by the valve spring

5.6 Pull out the valve stem oil seal with a pair of long-nosed pliers

5.7 Remove the spring seat

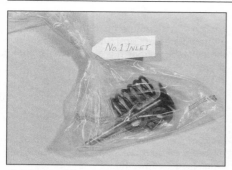

5.8 Keep groups of components together in labelled bags or boxes

5.15 Check the cylinder head gasket surface for distortion

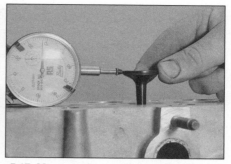

5.17 Measure the maximum deflection of the valve in its guide using a dial gauge

material and sealing compound from the cylinder head upper and lower mating surfaces. Use a suitable liquid gasket dissolving agent together with a soft putty knife; do not use a metal scraper, or the faces will be damaged. Note that on diesel engines, the gasket surface cannot be refaced.

11 Remove the carbon from the combustion chambers and ports, then clean all traces of oil and other deposits from the cylinder head, paying particular attention to the bearing journals, tappet bores, valve guides and oilways.

12 Wash the head thoroughly with paraffin or a suitable solvent. Take plenty of time and do a thorough job. Be sure to clean all oil holes and galleries very thoroughly, dry the head completely and coat all machined surfaces with light oil.

13 Scrape off any heavy carbon deposits that may have formed on the valves, then use a power-operated wire brush to remove deposits from the valve heads and stems.

Inspection

Note: Be sure to perform all the following inspection procedures before concluding that the services of an engineering works are required. Make a list of all items that require attention.

Cylinder head

14 Inspect the head very carefully for cracks, evidence of coolant leakage, and other damage. If cracks are found, a new cylinder head should be obtained.

15 Use a straight-edge and feeler blade to check that the cylinder head gasket surface is not distorted **(see illustration)**.

16 Examine the valve seats in each of the combustion chambers. If they are severely pitted, cracked or burned, then they will need to be renewed or recut by an engine overhaul specialist. If they are only slightly pitted, this can be removed by grinding-in the valve heads and seats with fine valve-grinding compound, as described below.

17 If the valve guides appear worn, indicated by a side-to-side motion of the valve, new guides must be fitted. Verify this by mounting a dial gauge on the cylinder head, and check the side-to-side rock with the valve lifted 2.0 to 3.0mm clear of its seat **(see illustration)**.

Measure the diameter of the existing valve stems (see below) and the bore of the guides, renew the valves or guides as necessary. The renewal of valve guides should be carried out by an engine overhaul specialist.

18 If the valve seats are to be recut, this must be done *only after* the guides have been renewed.

19 The threaded holes in the cylinder head must be clean to ensure accurate torque readings when tightening fixings during reassembly. Carefully run the correct size tap (which can be determined from the size of the relevant bolt which fits in the hole) into each of the holes to remove rust, corrosion, thread sealant or other contamination, and to restore damaged threads. If possible, use compressed air to clear the holes of debris produced by this operation. Do not forget to clean the threads of all bolts and nuts as well.

20 Any threads which cannot be restored in this way can often be reclaimed by the use of thread inserts. If any threaded holes are damaged, consult your dealer or engine overhaul specialist and have them install any thread inserts where necessary.

Valves

21 Examine the head of each valve for pitting, burning, cracks and general wear, and check the valve stem for scoring and wear ridges. Rotate the valve, and check for any obvious indication that it is bent. Look for pits and excessive wear on the tip of each valve stem. Renew any valve that shows any such signs of wear or damage.

22 If the valve appears satisfactory at this

stage, measure the valve stem diameter at several points, using a micrometer **(see illustration)**. Any significant difference in the readings obtained indicates wear of the valve stem. Should any of these conditions be apparent, the valve(s) must be renewed.

23 If the valves are in satisfactory condition, they should be ground (lapped) into their respective seats, to ensure a smooth gas-tight seal. If the seat is only lightly pitted, or if it has been recut, fine grinding compound *only* should be used to produce the required finish. Coarse valve-grinding compound should *not* be used unless a seat is badly burned or deeply pitted; if this is the case, the cylinder head and valves should be inspected by an expert, to decide whether seat recutting, or even the renewal of the valve or seat insert, is required.

24 Valve grinding is carried out as follows. Place the cylinder head upside-down on a bench, with a block of wood at each end to give clearance for the valve stems.

25 Smear a trace of (the appropriate grade) valve-grinding compound on the seat face, and press a suction grinding tool onto the valve head. With a semi-rotary action, grind the valve head to its seat, lifting the valve occasionally to redistribute the grinding compound. A light spring placed under the valve head will greatly ease this operation **(see illustration)**.

26 If coarse grinding compound is being used, work only until a dull, matt even surface is produced on both the valve seat and the valve, then wipe off the used compound, and repeat the process with fine compound. When a smooth unbroken ring of light grey matt

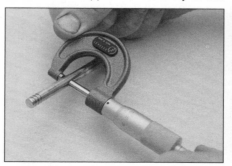

5.22 Measure the valve stem diameter with a micrometer

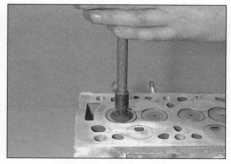

5.25 Grinding-in a valve

5.31 Lubricate the stem of the valve and insert it into the guide

finish is produced on both the valve and seat, the grinding operation is complete. *Do not grind in the valves any further than absolutely necessary, or the seat will be prematurely sunk into the cylinder head.*

27 When all the valves have been ground-in, carefully wash off *all* traces of grinding compound, using paraffin or a suitable solvent, before reassembly of the cylinder head.

Valve components

28 Examine the valve springs for signs of damage and discoloration, and also measure their free length by comparing each of the existing springs with a new component.

29 Stand each spring on a flat surface, and check it for squareness. If any of the springs are damaged, distorted, or have lost their tension, obtain a complete set of new springs. It is normal to fit new springs as a matter of course if a major overhaul is being carried out.

30 Renew the valve stem oil seals regardless of their apparent condition.

Reassembly

31 Oil the stem of one valve and insert it into its guide then fit the spring lower seat **(see illustration)**.

32 The new valve stem oil seals should be supplied with a plastic fitting sleeve to protect the seal when it is fitted over the valve. If not, wrap a thin piece of polythene around the valve stem allowing it to extend about 10mm above the end of the valve stem.

33 With the fitting sleeve, or polythene in place around the valve, fit the valve stem oil seal, pushing it onto the valve guide as far

as it will go with a suitable socket or piece of tube. Once the seal is seated, remove the protective sleeve or polythene.

34 Fit the valve spring and upper seat. Compress the spring and fit the two collets in the recesses in the valve stem. Carefully release the compressor.

35 Cover the valve stem with a cloth and tap it smartly with a light hammer to verify that the collets are properly seated.

36 Repeat these procedures on all the other valves.

37 Refit the remainder of the disturbed components then refit the cylinder head as described in the relevant part of Chapter 2, depending on engine.

6 Intermediate section/ main bearing caps – removal

Note: *On 1.6 diesel, 1.8 and 2.0 litre petrol engines, it is not possible to remove the intermediate/main bearing section or to remove the crankshaft or pistons. No separate parts appear to be available, and new/exchange units are supplied with crankshaft, pistons, connecting rods, etc, already fitted.*

1 If not already done, drain the engine oil then remove the oil filter, referring to Chapter 1A (petrol) or Chapter 1B (diesel) if necessary.

2 Remove the oil pump as described in Chapter 2B Section 9, Chapter 2D Section 12 or Chapter 2E Section 13.

2.4 litre petrol engines

3 Undo the mounting bracket bolt and remove the oil pick-up pipe **(see illustration)**. Recover the O-ring seal on the end of the pipe.

4 Remove the pistons and connecting rods as described in Section 7.

5 Undo all the M7 bolts securing the intermediate section to the cylinder block working from the outside in. With all the M7 bolts removed, undo the M8, then the M10 bolts in the same order.

6 Carefully tap the intermediate section free using a rubber or hide mallet. Lift off the intermediate section complete with crankshaft lower main bearing shells. If any of the shells have stayed on the crankshaft, transfer them

to their correct locations in the intermediate section. Do not rotate the crankshaft with the intermediate section removed. Recover the thrustwashers from the No 1 main bearing position.

7 Remove the crankshaft oil seal.

5-cylinder diesel engines

8 On models with an oil cooler mounted on the rear face of the sump, remove the four retaining bolts and take off the cooler, if possible without disconnecting the coolant pipes **(see illustration)**.

9 Undo the bolts securing the sump to the intermediate section, noting the different bolt lengths and their locations.

10 Carefully tap the sump free using a rubber or hide mallet. Recover the O-ring seals.

11 Undo the mounting bracket bolt and remove the oil pick-up pipe **(see illustration 6.3)**. Recover the O-ring seal on the end of the pipe.

12 Remove the pistons and connecting rods as described in Section 7.

13 Undo all the M7 bolts securing the intermediate section to the cylinder block working from the outside in. With all the M7 bolts removed, undo the M8, then the M10 bolts in the same order.

14 Carefully tap the intermediate section free using a rubber or hide mallet. Lift off the intermediate section complete with crankshaft lower main bearing shells. If any of the shells have stayed on the crankshaft, transfer them to their correct locations in the intermediate section. Do not rotate the crankshaft with the intermediate section removed.

15 Remove the crankshaft left-hand oil seal.

2.0 litre 4-cylinder engine

16 Remove the pistons and connecting rods as described in Section 7.

17 Undo the rear main bearing cap bolts, then remove the cap. Screw 2 sump bolts into the cap, and pull on them to remove the cap **(see illustration)**.

18 Make identification/alignment marks on the remaining bearing caps, then unscrew the retaining bolts and remove the caps. Note the fitted locations of the thrustwashers at the bearing position for No.1 cylinder.

19 Prise out the oil seal.

6.3 Undo the oil pick-up pipe bracket bolt

6.8 Oil cooler mounting bolts

6.17 Screw two sump bolts into the main bearing cap, then lever it upwards

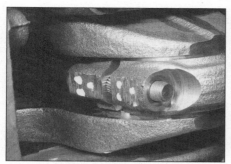

7.3 Connecting rod and big-end bearing cap identification marks

7.10 Remove the big-end bearing cap and shell

7.11 To protect the crankshaft journals, tape over the connecting rod stud threads

7 Pistons and connecting rods – removal and inspection

Note: *On 1.8 and 2.0 litre petrol engines, it is not possible to remove the intermediate/main bearing section or to remove the crankshaft or pistons. No separate parts appear to be available, and new/exchange units are supplied with crankshaft, pistons, connecting rods, etc, already fitted.*

Removal

1 Remove the cylinder head, oil pump and flywheel/driveplate as described in Chapter 2B, Chapter 2C or Chapter 2D. On 5-cylinder models, remove the intermediate section as described in Section 6.

2 Feel inside the tops of the bores for a pronounced wear ridge. Some experts recommend that such a ridge be removed (with a scraper or ridge reamer) before attempting to remove the pistons. However, a ridge big enough to damage the pistons and/ or piston rings will almost certainly mean that a rebore and new pistons/rings are needed anyway.

2.0 and 2.4 litre engines (petrol and diesel)

3 Check that there are identification numbers or marks on each connecting rod and cap; paint or punch suitable marks if necessary, so that each rod can be refitted in the same position and the same way round **(see illustration)**. Note their positions, eg, markings on the exhaust side, etc.

4 Remove the two connecting rod bolts. Tap the cap with a soft-faced hammer to free it. Remove the cap and lower bearing shell. Note that new bolts will be needed for reassembly. New shells should always be fitted.

5 Push the connecting rod and piston up and out of the bore. Recover the other half bearing shell if it is loose.

6 Refit the cap to the connecting rod, the correct way round, so that they do not get mixed up. Note that on some engines, the surface between the cap and rod is not machined, but fractured. Take great care not to damage or mark the fractured surfaces otherwise the cap will not fit properly with

the shell, and new connecting rods will be required.

7 Check to see if there is an arrow on the top of the piston which should be pointing toward the timing belt end of the engine. If no arrow can be seen, make a suitable direction mark yourself.

8 Repeat the operations on the remaining connecting rods and pistons.

1.6 litre engines

9 Turn the crankshaft to bring pistons 1 and 4 to BDC (bottom dead centre).

10 Unscrew the nuts or bolts, as applicable from No 1 piston big-end bearing cap. Take off the cap, and recover the bottom half bearing shell **(see illustration)**. If the bearing shells are to be re-used, tape the cap and the shell together.

11 Where applicable, to prevent the possibility of damage to the crankshaft bearing journals, tape over the connecting rod stud threads **(see illustration)**.

12 Using a hammer handle, push the piston up through the bore, and remove it from the top of the cylinder block. Recover the bearing shell, and tape it to the connecting rod for safe-keeping.

13 Loosely refit the big-end cap to the connecting rod, and secure with the nuts/ bolts – this will help to keep the components in their correct order.

14 Remove No 4 piston assembly in the same way.

15 Turn the crankshaft through 180° to bring pistons 2 and 3 to BDC (bottom dead centre), and remove them in the same way.

Inspection

16 Before the inspection process can be carried out, the piston/connecting rod assemblies must be cleaned, and the original piston rings removed from the pistons.

17 Carefully expand the old rings and remove them from the top of the pistons. The use of two or three old feeler blades will be helpful in preventing the rings dropping into empty grooves **(see illustration)**. Be careful not to scratch the pistons with the ends of the ring. The rings are brittle and will snap if they are spread too far. They are also very sharp – protect your hands and fingers.

18 Scrape all traces of carbon from the top of

the piston. A hand-held wire brush (or a piece of fine emery cloth) can be used, once the majority of the deposits have been scraped away.

19 Remove the carbon from the ring grooves in the piston, using an old ring. Break the ring in half to do this (be careful not to cut your fingers – piston rings are sharp). Be careful to remove only the carbon deposits – do not remove any metal, and do not nick or scratch the sides of the ring grooves.

20 Once the deposits have been removed, clean the piston/rod assemblies with paraffin or a suitable solvent, and dry thoroughly. Make sure the oil return holes in the ring grooves, are clear.

21 If the pistons and cylinder bores are not damaged or worn excessively, and if the cylinder block does not need to be rebored (where applicable), the original pistons can be refitted. Normal piston wear appears as even vertical wear on the piston thrust surfaces, and slight looseness of the top ring in its groove. New piston rings should always be used when the engine is reassembled.

22 Carefully inspect each piston for cracks around the skirt, around the gudgeon pin holes, and at the ring 'lands' (between the ring grooves).

23 Look for scoring and scuffing on the piston skirt, holes in the piston crown, and burned areas at the edge of the crown.

24 If the skirt is scored or scuffed, the engine may have been suffering from overheating and/or abnormal combustion, which caused excessively-high operating temperatures. The cooling and lubrication systems should

7.17 Remove the piston rings with the aid of feeler gauges

7.30a Prise out the circlip...

7.30b ...and withdraw the gudgeon pin

7.33 Measure the ring-to-groove clearance using feeler gauges

be checked thoroughly. Scorch marks on the sides of the piston show that blow-by has occurred.

25 A hole in the piston crown or burned areas at the edge of the piston crown, indicates that abnormal combustion (pre-ignition, knocking, or detonation) has been occurring.

26 If any of the above piston problems exist, the causes must be investigated and corrected, or the damage will occur again. The causes may include inlet air leaks, incorrect fuel/air mixture or an emission control system fault.

27 Corrosion of the piston, in the form of pitting, indicates that coolant has been leaking into the combustion chamber and/or the crankcase. Again, the cause must be corrected, or the problem may persist in the rebuilt engine.

28 Examine each connecting rod carefully for signs of damage, such as cracks around the big-end and small-end bearings. Check that the rod is not bent or distorted. Damage is highly unlikely, unless the engine has been seized or badly overheated. Detailed checking of the connecting rod assembly can only be carried out by an engine overhaul specialist with the necessary equipment.

29 The gudgeon pins are of the floating type, secured in position by two circlips. Where necessary, the pistons and connecting rods can be separated as follows.

30 Remove one of the circlips which secure the gudgeon pin. Push the gudgeon pin out of the piston and connecting rod **(see illustrations)**.

31 If any doubt exists concerning the condition of the pistons, have them measured by an automotive engine reconditioning specialist. If new pistons are required, the specialist will be able to supply new pistons and rebore the cylinder block to the appropriate size (where applicable).

32 If any one of the pistons is worn, then all the pistons must be renewed. Note that if the cylinder block was rebored during a previous overhaul, oversize pistons may have been fitted.

33 Hold a new piston ring in the appropriate groove, and measure the ring-to-groove clearance using a feeler blade **(see illustration)**. Note that the rings are of different sizes, so use the correct ring for the groove.

Compare the measurements with those listed in the Specifications; if the clearances are outside the tolerance range, then the pistons must be renewed.

34 Check the fit of the gudgeon pin in the connecting rod bush and in the piston. If there is perceptible play, a new bush or an oversize gudgeon pin must be fitted. Consult a Volvo dealer or engine reconditioning specialist.

35 Examine all components and obtain any new parts required. If new pistons are purchased, they will be supplied complete with gudgeon pins and circlips. Circlips can also be purchased separately.

36 Oil the gudgeon pin. Reassemble the connecting rod and piston, making sure the rod is the right way round as noted during removal, and secure the gudgeon pin with the circlip. Position the circlip so that its opening is facing downward.

37 Repeat these operations for the remaining pistons.

8 Crankshaft – removal and inspection

Note: *On 1.8 and 2.0 litre petrol engines, it is not possible to remove the intermediate/main bearing section or to remove the crankshaft or pistons. No separate parts appear to be available, and new/exchange units are supplied with crankshaft, pistons, connecting rods, etc, already fitted. Consequently, the following only applies to 2.4 litre petrol and diesel models.*

8.2 Check the crankshaft end float using a dial gauge

Note: *If no work is to be done on the pistons and connecting rods, then removal of the cylinder head and pistons will not be necessary. Instead, the pistons need only be pushed far enough up the bores so that they are positioned clear of the crankpins.*

Removal

1 With reference to Chapter 2B, Chapter 2C, Chapter 2D, Chapter 2E and earlier Sections of this part as applicable, carry out the following:
a) *Remove the oil pump.*
b) *Remove the sump.*
c) *Remove the clutch components and flywheel/driveplate.*
d) *Remove the pistons and connecting rods (refer to the Note above).*

2 Before the crankshaft is removed, it is advisable to check the endfloat. To do this, temporarily refit the intermediate section then mount a dial gauge with the stem in line with the crankshaft and just touching the crankshaft **(see illustration)**.

3 Push the crankshaft fully away from the gauge, and zero it. Next, lever the crankshaft towards the gauge as far as possible, and check the reading obtained. The distance that the crankshaft moved is its endfloat; if it is greater than specified, check the crankshaft thrust surfaces for wear. If no wear is evident, new thrustwashers (which are integral with the main bearing shells on 2.4 litre models) should correct the endfloat.

2.0 and 2.4 litre engines (petrol and diesel)

4 Remove the intermediate section again (see Section 6), then lift out the crankshaft. Do not drop it, it is heavy.

5 Remove the upper half main bearing shells from their seats in the crankcase by pressing the end of the shell furthest from the locating tab. Keep all the shells in order.

1.6 litre engines

6 Working around the inner periphery of the crankcase, unscrew the small bolts securing the crankshaft bearing cap housing to the base of the cylinder block. Note the correct fitted depth of the left-hand crankshaft oil seal in the cylinder block/bearing cap housing.

7 Working in the **reverse** of the tightening sequence, evenly and progressively slacken the ten large bearing cap housing retaining bolts by a turn at a time. Once all the bolts are loose, remove them from the housing. **Note:** *Prise up the two caps at the flywheel end of the housing to expose the two end main bearing bolts* **(see illustration).**

8 With all the retaining bolts removed, tap around the outer periphery of the bearing cap housing using a soft-faced mallet to break the seal between the housing and cylinder block. Once the seal is released and the housing is clear of the locating dowels, lift it up and off the crankshaft and cylinder block **(see illustration).** Recover the lower main bearing shells, and tape them to their respective locations in the housing. If the two locating dowels are a loose fit, remove them and store them with the housing for safe-keeping.

9 Lift out the crankshaft, and collect the left-hand oil seal.

10 Recover the upper main bearing shells, and store them along with the relevant lower bearing shell. Also recover the two thrustwashers (one fitted either side of No 2 main bearing) from the cylinder block.

Inspection

11 Clean the crankshaft using paraffin or a suitable solvent, and dry it, preferably with compressed air if available. Be sure to clean the oil holes with a pipe cleaner or similar probe to ensure that they are not obstructed.

 Warning: Wear eye protection when using compressed air.

12 Check the main and big-end bearing journals for uneven wear, scoring, pitting and cracking.

13 Big-end bearing wear is accompanied by distinct metallic knocking when the engine is running (particularly noticeable when the engine is pulling from low speed) and some loss of oil pressure.

14 Main bearing wear is accompanied by severe engine vibration and rumble – getting progressively worse as engine speed increases – and again by loss of oil pressure.

15 Check the bearing journal for roughness by running a finger lightly over the bearing surface. Any roughness (which will be accompanied by obvious bearing wear) indicates that the crankshaft requires regrinding (where possible) or renewal.

16 Have the crankshaft measured and inspected by an engine reconditioning specialist. They will be able to advise concerning the availability of undersize bearings, and crankshaft reconditioning.

9 Cylinder block/crankcase – cleaning and inspection

Cleaning

1 Prior to cleaning, remove all external components and senders, and any gallery plugs or caps that may be fitted. Remove

8.7 Prise up the two caps to expose the main bearing bolts at the flywheel end

the piston cooling valve, and the cooling jets (where applicable) **(see illustration).**

2 If any of the castings are extremely dirty, all should be steam-cleaned.

3 After the castings are returned from steam-cleaning, clean all oil holes and oil galleries one more time. Flush all internal passages with warm water until the water runs clear. If you have access to compressed air, use it to speed the drying process, and to blow out all the oil holes and galleries.

 Warning: Wear eye protection when using compressed air.

4 If the castings are not very dirty, you can do an adequate cleaning job with hot soapy water (as hot as you can stand!) and a stiff brush. Take plenty of time, and do a thorough job. Regardless of the cleaning method used, be sure to clean all oil holes and galleries very thoroughly, and to dry all components completely. Apply clean engine oil to the cylinder bores to prevent rusting.

5 The threaded holes in the cylinder block must be clean to ensure accurate torque readings when tightening fixings during reassembly. Carefully run the correct size tap (which can be determined from the size of the relevant bolt which fits in the hole) into each of the holes to remove rust, corrosion, thread sealant or other contamination, and to restore damaged threads. If possible, use compressed air to clear the holes of debris produced by this operation. Do not forget to clean the threads of all bolts and nuts as well.

6 Any threads which cannot be restored in this way can often be reclaimed by the use

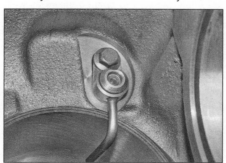
9.1 Piston cooling jets may be fitted to the base of each cylinder bore

8.8 Remove the crankshaft bearing cap housing

of thread inserts. If any threaded holes are damaged, consult your dealer or engine overhaul specialist and have them install any thread inserts where necessary.

7 If the engine is not going to be reassembled right away, cover it with a large plastic bag to keep it clean; protect the machined surfaces as described above, to prevent rusting.

Inspection

8 Visually check the castings for cracks and corrosion. Look for stripped threads in the threaded holes. If there has been any history of internal coolant leakage, it may be worthwhile having an engine overhaul specialist check the cylinder block/crankcase for cracks with special equipment. If defects are found, have them repaired, if possible, or renew the assembly.

9 Check the condition of the cylinder head mating face and the intermediate section mating surfaces. Check the surfaces for any possible distortion using the straight-edge and feeler blade method described earlier for cylinder head inspection. If distortion is slight, consult an engine overhaul specialist as to the best course of action.

10 Check each cylinder bore for scuffing and scoring. Check for signs of a wear ridge at the top of the cylinder, indicating that the bore is excessively worn.

11 Have the bores inspected and measured by an automotive engine reconditioning specialist. They will be able to advise on possible cylinder reboring and supply appropriate pistons to match.

12 If the bores are in reasonably good condition and not excessively-worn, then it may only be necessary to renew the piston rings.

13 If this is the case, the bores should be honed, to allow the new rings to bed in correctly and provide the best possible seal. Honing is an operation that will be carried out for you by an engine reconditioning specialist.

14 After all machining operations are completed, the entire block/crankcase must be washed very thoroughly with warm soapy water to remove all traces of abrasive grit produced during the machining operations. When the cylinder block/crankcase is completely clean, rinse it thoroughly and dry it, then lightly oil all exposed machined surfaces, to prevent rusting.

15 Refit the piston cooling jets to the base of the cylinder bores, and tighten the retaining bolts to the specified torque.

16 Fit a new sealing washer to the piston cooling oil valve, or apply thread sealing compound to valve threads (as applicable), then refit the valve and tighten it to the specified torque.

10 Main and big-end bearings – inspection and selection

Inspection

1 Even though the main and big-end bearing shells should be renewed during the engine overhaul, the old shells should be retained for close examination, as they may reveal valuable information about the condition of the engine.

2 Bearing failure occurs because of lack of lubrication, the presence of dirt or other foreign particles, overloading the engine, and corrosion **(see illustration)**. Regardless of the cause of bearing failure, the cause must be corrected (where applicable) before the engine is reassembled, to prevent it from happening again.

3 When examining the bearing shells, remove them from the cylinder block/crankcase and main bearing caps, and from the connecting rods and the big-end bearing caps, then lay them out on a clean surface in the same general position as their location in the engine. This will enable you to match any bearing problems with the corresponding crankshaft journal. *Do not* touch any of the shell's bearing surface with your fingers while checking it, or the delicate surface may be scratched.

4 Dirt or other foreign matter gets into the engine in a variety of ways. It may be left in the engine during assembly, or it may pass

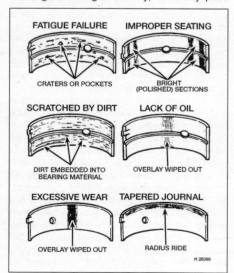

10.2 Typical bearing failures

FATIGUE FAILURE

CRATERS OR POCKETS

IMPROPER SEATING

BRIGHT (POLISHED) SECTIONS

SCRATCHED BY DIRT

DIRT EMBEDDED INTO BEARING MATERIAL

LACK OF OIL

OVERLAY WIPED OUT

EXCESSIVE WEAR

OVERLAY WIPED OUT

TAPERED JOURNAL

RADIUS RIDE

H 28395

through filters or the crankcase ventilation system. It may get into the oil, and from there into the bearings. Metal chips from machining operations and normal engine wear are often present. Abrasives are sometimes left in engine components after reconditioning, especially when parts are not thoroughly cleaned using the proper cleaning methods.

5 Whatever the source, any foreign objects often end up embedded in the soft bearing material, and are easily recognised. Large particles will not embed in the material, and will score or gouge the shell and journal. The best prevention for this cause of bearing failure is to clean all parts thoroughly, and to keep everything spotlessly-clean during engine assembly. Frequent and regular engine oil and filter changes are also recommended.

6 Lack of lubrication (or lubrication breakdown) has a number of inter-related causes. Excessive heat (which thins the oil), overloading (which squeezes the oil from the bearing face) and oil leakage (from excessive bearing clearances, worn oil pump or high engine speeds) all contribute to lubrication breakdown. Blocked oil passages, which usually are the result of misaligned oil holes in a bearing shell, will also starve a bearing of oil, and destroy it.

7 When lack of lubrication is the cause of bearing failure, the bearing material is wiped or extruded from the shell's steel backing. Temperatures may increase to the point where the steel backing turns blue from overheating.

8 Driving habits can have a definite effect on bearing life. Full-throttle, low-speed operation (labouring the engine) puts very high loads on bearings, which tends to squeeze out the oil film. These loads cause the shells to flex, which produces fine cracks in the bearing face (fatigue failure). Eventually, the bearing material will loosen in pieces, and tear away from the steel backing.

9 Short-distance driving leads to corrosion of bearings, because insufficient engine heat is produced to drive off condensed water and corrosive gases. These products collect in the engine oil, forming acid and sludge. As the oil is carried to the engine bearings, the acid attacks and corrodes the bearing material.

10 Incorrect shell refitting during engine assembly will lead to bearing failure as well. Tight-fitting shells leave insufficient bearing running clearance, and will result in oil starvation. Dirt or foreign particles trapped behind a bearing shell result in high spots on the bearing, which lead to failure.

11 *Do not* touch any shell's bearing surface with your fingers during reassembly; there is a risk of scratching the delicate surface, or of depositing particles of dirt on it.

Bearing selection

12 Have the crankshaft measured and examined by an automotive engine reconditioning specialist, who will be able to supply the appropriate bearing shells.

11 Engine overhaul – reassembly sequence

1 Before reassembly begins, ensure that all new parts have been obtained and that all necessary tools are available. Read through the entire procedure to familiarise yourself with the work involved, and to ensure that all items necessary for reassembly of the engine are at hand. In addition to all normal tools and materials, thread-locking compound will be needed in most areas during engine reassembly. A tube of Volvo liquid gasket solution together with a short-haired application roller will also be needed to assemble the main engine sections.

2 In order to save time and avoid problems, engine reassembly can be carried out in the following order:
a) *Crankshaft.*
b) *Intermediate section.*
c) *Pistons/connecting rods.*
d) *Sump.*
e) *Oil pump.*
f) *Flywheel/driveplate.*
g) *Cylinder head.*
h) *Camshaft and tappets.*
i) *Timing belt, tensioner, sprockets and idler pulleys.*
j) *Engine external components.*

3 At this stage, all engine components should be absolutely clean and dry, with all faults repaired. The components should be laid out (or in individual containers) on a completely clean work surface.

12 Crankshaft – refitting

1 Crankshaft refitting is the first stage of engine reassembly following overhaul. It is assumed at this point that the cylinder block/crankcase and crankshaft have been cleaned, inspected and repaired or reconditioned as necessary, and the piston cooling jets and valve have been refitted. Position the cylinder block on a clean level work surface, with the crankcase facing upwards.

Petrol engines

2 Using the short-haired application roller, apply an even coating of Volvo liquid gasket solution (No 11 61 059) to the cylinder block mating face of the intermediate section. Ensure that the whole surface is covered, but note that a thin coating is sufficient for a good seal.

3 Wipe clean the main bearing shell seats in the intermediate section and clean the backs of the bearing shells. Insert the previously selected lower shells into their correct position in the intermediate section. Press the shells home so that the tangs engage in the recesses provided.

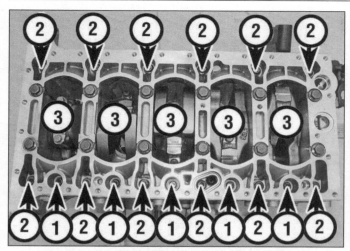

12.5 Intermediate section bolts – 2.4 litre models

1 M7   2 M8   3 M10

12.8 Place the thrustwashers each side of the No 2 bearing upper location

4 Lightly lubricate the bearing shells in the intermediate section, but take care to keep the oil away from the liquid gasket solution.

5 Lay the intermediate section on the crankshaft and cylinder block, and insert the (new M10) retaining bolts. Tighten the bolts in the five stages listed in the Specifications, to the specified torque and torque angle, starting from the outside in **(see illustration)**.

1.6 litre engines

6 Place the bearing shells in their locations. If new shells are being fitted, ensure that all traces of protective grease are cleaned off using paraffin. Wipe dry the shells with a lint-free cloth. The upper bearing shells all have a grooved surface, whereas the lower shells have a plain surface. It's essential that the lower bearing shells are centrally located in the bearing cap housing/ladder.

7 Liberally lubricate each bearing shell in the cylinder block with clean engine oil then lower the crankshaft into position.

8 Insert the thrustwashers to either side of No 2 main bearing upper location and push them around the bearing journal until their edges are horizontal **(see illustration)**. Ensure that the oilway grooves on each thrustwasher face outwards (away from the bearing journal).

9 Thoroughly degrease the mating surfaces of the cylinder block and the crankshaft bearing cap housing. Apply a thin bead of silicone sealant to the bearing cap housing mating surface **(see illustration)**.

10 Lubricate the lower bearing shells with clean engine oil, then refit the bearing cap housing, ensuring that the shells are not displaced, and that the locating dowels engage correctly.

11 Install the ten large diameter, and sixteen smaller diameter crankshaft bearing cap housing retaining bolts, and screw them in until they are just making contact with the housing.

12 Working in sequence, tighten the bolts to the torque settings given in the Specifications **(see illustration)**.

13 With the bearing cap housing in place, check that the crankshaft rotates freely.

14 Refit the piston/connecting rod assemblies to the crankshaft as described in Section 7.

15 Refit the oil pump and sump.

16 Fit a new crankshaft left-hand oil seal, then refit the flywheel.

17 Where removed, refit the cylinder head, crankshaft sprocket and timing belt.

2.0 litre 4-cylinder engine

18 Wipe clean the bearing shell seats in the

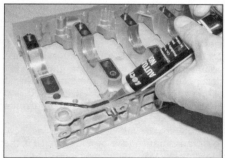

12.9 Apply a thin bead of sealant to the bearing cap housing mating surface

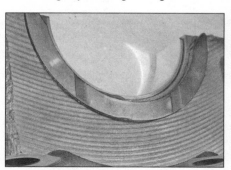

12.19a Ensure the thrustwashers are fitted with the oil grooves facing outwards

main bearing caps, and clean the back of the shells. Insert the previously-selected lower shells into their correct locations in the bearing caps. Press the shells home so that the tangs engage in the recesses provided.

19 Lightly lubricate the bearing shells in the main bearing caps, then refit the caps to their original positions, aligning the previously-made marks. Ensure the thrustwashers are fitted with the oil grooves against the bearing surfaces. Note that new rubber seals must be fitted to each side of the main bearing cap fitted at the transmission end **(see illustrations)**. The cap is then fitted

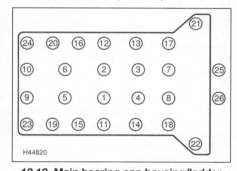

12.12 Main bearing cap housing/ladder retaining bolt tightening sequence

12.19b Fit new rubber seals to the main bearing cap at the transmission end

12.19c Apply a bead of sealant to the corners of the recess...

12.19d ...then fit the cap using strips of shim steel to ease the seals into position

using a Volvo special tool No 999 7223 (or strips of shim steel) to ease the cap and seals into position (see illustrations). Apply a bead of silicone sealant to the corners of the main bearing cap recess in the block. Note that even with the Volvo tool it is impossible to fit the seals completely flush with the sump mating surface – a protrusion of approximately 1.0mm is acceptable.

20 Tighten the main bearing cap bolts to the specified Stage 1 torque setting, working gradually from the centre outwards. Repeat the sequence tightening the bolts to the Stage 2 angle-tightening setting.

5-cylinder engines

21 If they're still in place, remove the old bearing shells from the block and the intermediate section.

22 Wipe clean the main bearing shell seats in the crankcase and clean the backs of the new bearing shells. Insert the previously selected upper shells into their correct position in the crankcase. Note the shells incorporating the thrustwashers must be fitted to the No 5 bearing position. Press the shells home so that the tangs engage in the recesses provided. Note the thicker of the two shells must be fitted to the intermediate section.

23 Liberally lubricate the bearing shells in the crankcase with clean engine oil.

24 Wipe clean the crankshaft journals, then lower the crankshaft into position. Make sure that the shells are not displaced.

25 Inject oil into the crankshaft oilways, then wipe any traces of excess oil from the crankshaft and intermediate section mating faces.

26 Using the short-haired application roller, apply an even coating of Volvo liquid gasket solution (No 116 1771) to the cylinder block mating face of the intermediate section. Ensure that the whole surface is covered, but note that a thin coating is sufficient for a good seal.

27 Wipe clean the main bearing shell seats in the intermediate section and clean the backs of the bearing shells. Insert the previously selected lower shells into their correct position in the intermediate section. Press the shells home so that the tangs engage in the recesses provided.

28 Lightly lubricate the bearing shells in the intermediate section, but take care to keep the oil away from the liquid gasket solution.

29 Lay the intermediate section on the crankshaft and cylinder block, and insert the retaining bolts. Tighten the bolts in the five stages listed in the Specifications, to the specified torque and torque angle, starting from the outside in (see illustration 12.5).

30 Rotate the crankshaft. Slight resistance is to be expected with new components, but there must be no tight spots or binding.

31 It is a good idea at this stage to once again check the crankshaft endfloat as described in Section 8. If the thrust surfaces of the crankshaft have been checked and new bearing shells have been fitted, then the endfloat should be within specification.

32 Lubricate the left-hand oil seal location, the crankshaft, and a new oil seal. Fit the seal, lips inwards, and use a piece of tube (or the old seal, inverted) to tap it into place until flush.

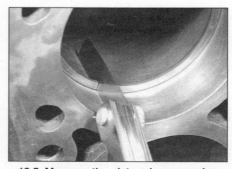

13.5 Measure the piston ring gap using feeler gauges

13 Pistons and piston rings – assembly

1 At this stage, it is assumed that the pistons have been correctly assembled to their respective connecting rods, and that the piston ring-to-groove clearances have been checked. If not, refer to the end of Section 7.

2 Before the rings can be fitted to the pistons, the end gaps must be checked with the rings inserted into the cylinder bores.

3 Lay out the piston assemblies and the new ring sets so the components are kept together in their groups, during and after end gap checking. Position the cylinder block on the work surface, on its side, allowing access to the top and bottom of the bores.

4 Take the No 1 piston top ring and insert it into the top of the first cylinder. Push it down the bore using the top of the piston; this will ensure that the ring remains square with the cylinder walls. Position the ring near the bottom of the cylinder bore, at the lower limit of ring travel. Note that the top and second compression rings are different. The second ring is easily identified by the step on its lower surface.

5 Measure the ring gap using feeler blades (see illustration).

6 Repeat the procedure with the ring at the top of the cylinder bore, at the upper limit of its travel, and compare the measurements with the figures given in the Specifications.

7 If new rings are being fitted, it is unlikely that the end gaps will be too small. If a measurement is found to be undersize, it must be corrected, or there is the risk that the ring ends may contact each other during engine operation, possibly resulting in engine damage. Ideally, new piston rings providing the correct end gap should be fitted; however, as a last resort the end gaps can be increased by filing the ring ends very carefully with a fine file. Mount the file in a vice equipped with soft

jaws, slip the ring over the file with the ends contacting the file face, and slowly move the ring to remove material from the ends. Take care, as piston rings are sharp and are easily broken.

8 It is equally unlikely that the end gap will be too large. If the gaps are too large, check that you have the correct rings for your engine and for the cylinder bore size.

9 Repeat the checking procedure for each ring in the first cylinder, and then for the rings in the remaining cylinders. Remember to keep rings, pistons and cylinders matched up.

10 Once the ring end gaps have been checked and if necessary corrected, the rings can be fitted to the pistons.

11 Fit the piston rings using the same technique as for removal. Fit the bottom scraper ring first, and work up. Observe the text markings on one side of the top and bottom rings; this must face upwards when the rings are fitted. The middle ring is bevelled (or stepped), and the bevel (or step) must face downwards when installed **(see illustration)**. Do not expand the compression rings too far, or they will break. **Note:** *Always follow any instructions supplied with the new piston ring sets – different manufacturers may specify different procedures. Do not mix up the top and second compression rings, as they have different cross-sections.*

12 When all the rings are in position, arrange the ring gaps 120° apart, with the exception of the 3-part oil scraper ring where the two plain rings should be 90° apart from each other.

14 Pistons and connecting rod assemblies – refitting

1 Before refitting the piston/connecting rod assemblies, the cylinder bores must be perfectly clean, and the crankshaft and intermediate section must be in place.

2 Remove the big-end bearing cap from No 1 cylinder connecting rod (refer to the marks noted or made on removal). Remove the original bearing shells, and wipe the bearing recesses of the connecting rod and cap with a clean, lint-free cloth. They must be kept spotlessly-clean. Ensure that new big-end bearing cap retaining bolts are available.

3 Clean the back of the new upper bearing shell, fit it to No 1 connecting rod, then fit the other shell of the bearing to the big-end bearing cap. Note that shell with the black-coloured size marker on its edge must be fitted to the connecting rod. On 'fractured' type rods and caps, no locating notch for the bearing shell tab is provided. On these rods/caps, simply position the shells as centrally as possible. Where tabs and notches are provided, make sure the tab on each shell fits into the notch in the rod or cap recess.

4 Position the piston ring gaps in their correct positions around the piston, lubricate the piston and rings with clean engine oil, and

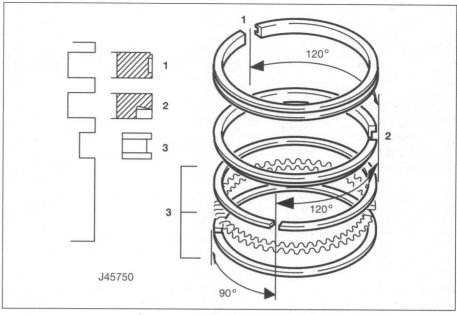

13.11 Piston ring details

1 Top compression ring   *2 2nd compression ring*   *3 Oil scraper ring assembly*

attach a piston ring compressor to the piston. Leave the skirt protruding slightly, to guide the piston into the cylinder bore. The rings must be compressed until they're flush with the piston.

5 Rotate the crankshaft until No 1 big-end journal is at BDC (Bottom Dead Centre), and apply a coat of engine oil to the cylinder walls.

6 Arrange the No 1 piston/connecting rod assembly so that the arrow on the piston crown points to the timing belt end of the engine (petrol engines), or the channel in the base of the piston aligns with the piston cooling jet at the base of the cylinder bore. Gently insert the assembly into the No 1 cylinder bore, and rest the bottom edge of the ring compressor on the engine block.

7 Tap the top edge of the ring compressor to make sure it's contacting the block around its entire circumference.

8 Gently tap on the top of the piston with the end of a wooden hammer handle while guiding the connecting rod big-end onto the crankpin. The piston rings may try to pop out of the ring compressor just before entering the cylinder bore, so keep some pressure on the ring compressor. Work slowly, and if any resistance is felt as the piston enters the cylinder, stop immediately. Find out what is binding, and fix it before proceeding. *Do not,* for any reason, force the piston into the cylinder – you might break a ring and/or the piston. Take great care not to damage the piston cooling jets **(see illustration)**.

9 Make sure the bearing surfaces are perfectly clean, then apply a uniform layer of clean engine oil to both of them. You may have to push the piston back up the cylinder bore slightly to expose the bearing surface of the shell in the connecting rod.

10 Slide the connecting rod back into place on the big-end journal, refit the big-end bearing cap. Lubricate the bolt threads, fit the bolts and tighten them in two stages to the specified torque.

11 Repeat the entire procedure for the remaining piston/connecting rod assemblies.

12 The important points to remember are:

a) *Keep the backs of the bearing shells and the recesses of the connecting rods and caps perfectly clean when assembling them.*

b) *Make sure you have the correct piston/rod assembly for each cylinder.*

c) *The channel in the base of the piston must align with the piston cooling jet.*

d) *Lubricate the cylinder bores with clean engine oil.*

e) *Lubricate the bearing surfaces before fitting the big-end bearing caps.*

13 After all the piston/connecting rod assemblies have been properly installed, rotate the crankshaft a number of times by hand, to check for any obvious binding.

14.8 Tap the piston into the bore using a hammer handle

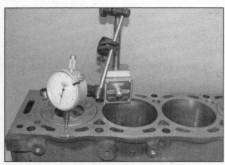

14.16 Measure the piston protrusion using a dial gauge

14 If new pistons, connecting rods, or crankshaft are fitted, or if a new short engine is installed, the projection of the piston crowns above the cylinder head surface at TDC must be measured, to determine the correct head gasket required.

15 Fit the sump as described in Section 15.

Diesel engines

16 Anchor a DTI gauge to the cylinder block, and zero it on the head gasket mating surface. Rest the gauge probe on No 1 piston crown and turn the crankshaft slowly by hand so that the piston reaches TDC (Top Dead Centre). Measure and record the maximum projection at TDC **(see illustration)**.

17 Repeat the measurement for the remaining pistons and record.

18 If the measurements differ from piston-to-piston, take the highest figure and use this to determine the head gasket type required – refer to the Specifications for details.

15 Sump – refitting

1 Refer to the relevant part of Chapter 2 depending on engine.

16 Engine – initial start-up after overhaul and reassembly

1 Refit the remainder of the engine components in the order listed in Section 11, with reference to the relevant Sections of Chapter 2 depending on engine. Refit the engine and transmission to the vehicle as described in Section 3 of this Part. Double-check the engine oil and coolant levels and make a final check that everything has been reconnected. Make sure that there are no tools or rags left in the engine compartment.

2 Remove the spark plugs (Chapter 1A) or glow plugs (Chapter 5C).

3 On petrol engines disable the ignition system by disconnecting the camshaft position sensor wiring at the connector. Disconnect the fuel injector wiring connectors to prevent fuel being injected into the cylinders

4 On diesel engines disconnect the wiring plugs from the fuel injectors.

5 Turn the engine over on the starter motor until the oil pressure warning light goes out. If the light fails to extinguish after several seconds of cranking, check the engine oil level and that the oil filter is fitted securely. Assuming these are correct, check the security of the oil pressure sensor wiring – do not progress any further until you are sure that oil is being pumped around the engine at sufficient pressure.

6 Refit the glow plugs and spark plugs and reconnect the disconnected wiring plugs.

7 Start the engine, noting that this also may take a little longer than usual, due to the fuel system components being empty.

8 While the engine is idling, check for fuel, coolant and oil leaks. Don't be alarmed if there are some odd smells and smoke from parts getting hot and burning off oil deposits. Note also that it may initially be a little noisy until the hydraulic tappets fill with oil.

9 Keep the engine idling until hot water is felt circulating through the top hose, check that it idles reasonably smoothly and at the usual speed, then switch it off.

10 After a few minutes, recheck the oil and coolant levels, and top-up as necessary (see *Weekly checks*).

11 If new components such as pistons, rings or crankshaft bearings have been fitted, the engine must be run-in for the first 500 miles (800 km). Do not operate the engine at full-throttle, or allow it to labour in any gear during this period. It is recommended that the oil and filter be changed at the end of this period.

Chapter 3
Cooling, heating and air conditioning systems

Contents

Degrees of difficulty

Easy, suitable for novice with little experience	Fairly easy, suitable for beginner with some experience	Fairly difficult, suitable for competent DIY mechanic	Difficult, suitable for experienced DIY mechanic	Very difficult, suitable for expert DIY or professional

Specifications

General
System type . . . . Water-based coolant, pump-assisted circulation, thermostatically controlled

System pressure
Pressure test . . . . 1.2 bars approximately – see cap for actual value (should hold this pressure for 2 minutes)
Expansion tank filler cap pressure . . . . 1.2 bars approximately – see cap for actual value

Thermostat
Starts to open:
  Petrol engines. . . . . 90° C
  Diesel engines . . . . 82° C

Coolant temperature sensor
Resistance:
  1.8 litre petrol models. . . . . 280 k ohms at -20°C and 32 k ohms at 20°C
  2.4 litre petrol models. . . . . 2.4 k ohms at 0°C and 318 ohms at 80°C
  2.0 litre petrol and all diesel models . . . . Not available

Air conditioning system
Refrigerant:
  Type R134a
  Capacity. . . . . 535 g

Torque wrench settings	Nm	lbf ft
Compressor mounting bolts (all engines).	20	15
Coolant pump bolts:		
2.0 litre 4-cylinder engine (diesel).	17	13
All other engines.	10	7
Coolant pump pulley bolts (1.8 and 2.0 litre petrol)	10	7
Coolant temperature sensor:		
1.8 and 2.0 litre petrol engines.	12	9
1.6 litre diesel engine	10	7
2.4 litre diesel engine	22	16
Expansion valve screws.	4.5	3
Radiator-to-condenser bolts	5	4
Radiator mounting screws	24	18
Thermostat housing:		
1.8 and 2.0 litre petrol engines.	10	7
2.4 litre petrol engines	Not available	
1.6 litre diesel engines	10	7
2.0 litre diesel engines (4-cylinder)	17	13
2.0 litre diesel engines (5-cylinder)	10	7
2.4 litre diesel engine (5-cylinder)	17	13

1 General information and precautions

General information

1 The cooling system is of pressurised semi-sealed type with the inclusion of an expansion tank to accept coolant displaced from the system when hot and to return it when the system cools.

2 Water-based coolant is circulated around the cylinder block and head by the coolant pump which is driven by the engine timing belt. As the coolant circulates around the engine it absorbs heat as it flows then, when hot, it travels out into the radiator to pass across the matrix. As the coolant flows across the radiator matrix, airflow created by the forward motion of the vehicle cools it, and it returns to the cylinder block. Airflow through the radiator matrix is assisted by a two-speed electric fan, which is controlled by the engine management system ECU.

3 A thermostat is fitted to control coolant flow through the radiator. When the engine is cold, the thermostat valve remains closed so that the coolant flow which occurs at normal operating temperatures through the radiator matrix is interrupted.

4 As the coolant warms up, the thermostat valve starts to open and allows the coolant flow through the radiator to resume.

5 The engine temperature will always be maintained at a constant level (according to the thermostat rating) whatever the ambient air temperature.

6 Most models have an oil cooler mounted on the sump – this is basically a heat exchanger with a coolant supply, to take heat away from the oil in the sump.

7 The vehicle interior heater operates by means of coolant from the engine cooling system. Coolant flow through the heater matrix is constant; temperature control being achieved by blending cool air from outside the vehicle with the warm air from the heater matrix, in the desired ratio.

8 Air entering the passenger compartment is filtered by a pleated paper filter element, known as a pollen filter whilst a pollution sensor monitors the quality of the incoming air, and opens and closes the recirculation flaps accordingly.

9 The standard climate control (air conditioning) system is described in detail in Section 9.

10 Available as options are additional electric and fuel-fired cabin and engine block heaters. These can be remotely operated, or programmed to operate for a suitable period before the vehicle is required.

Precautions

⚠️ *Warning: Do not attempt to remove the expansion tank filler cap, or to disturb any part of the cooling system, while it or the engine is hot, as there is a very great risk of scalding. If the expansion tank filler cap must be removed before the engine and radiator have fully cooled down (even though this is not recommended) the pressure in the cooling system must first be released. Cover the cap with a thick layer of cloth, to avoid scalding, and slowly unscrew the filler cap until a hissing sound can be heard. When the hissing has stopped, showing that pressure is released, slowly unscrew the filler cap further until it can be removed; if more hissing sounds are heard, wait until they have stopped before unscrewing the cap completely. At all times, keep well away from the filler opening.*

⚠️ *Warning: Do not allow antifreeze to come in contact with your skin, or with the painted surfaces of the vehicle. Rinse off spills immediately with plenty of water. Never leave antifreeze lying around in an open container, or in a puddle in the driveway or on the garage floor. Children and pets are attracted by its sweet smell, but antifreeze is fatal if ingested.*

⚠️ *Warning: Refer to Section for precautions to be observed when working on vehicles equipped with air conditioning.*

2 Cooling system hoses – disconnection and renewal

Note: *Refer to the warnings given in Section 1 of this Chapter before proceeding. Hoses should only be disconnected once the engine has cooled sufficiently to avoid scalding.*

1 If the checks described in Chapter 1A Section 9 or Chapter 1B Section 8 reveal a faulty hose, it must be renewed as follows.

2 First drain the cooling system as described in Chapter 1A (petrol) or Chapter 1B (diesel); if the antifreeze is not due for renewal, the drained coolant may be re-used, if it is collected in a clean container.

3 To disconnect any hose, use a pair of pliers to release the spring clamps (or a screwdriver to slacken screw-type clamps), then move them along the hose clear of the union **(see illustrations)**. Carefully work the hose off its stubs. The hoses can be removed with relative ease when new – on an older vehicle, they may have stuck.

4 If a hose proves to be difficult to remove, try to release it by rotating it on its unions before attempting to work it off. Gently prise the end of the hose with a blunt instrument (such as a flat-bladed screwdriver), but do not apply too much force, and take care not to damage the pipe stubs or hoses. Note in particular that the radiator hose unions are fragile; do not use excessive force when attempting to remove the hoses.

5 When refitting a hose, first slide the clamps onto the hose, then engage the hose with its unions. Work the hose into position, then check that the hose is settled correctly and is properly routed. Slide each clamp along the hose until it is behind the union flared end, before tightening it securely.

6 Refill the system with coolant as described in Chapter 1A Section 30 (petrol engines) or Chapter 1B Section 29 (diesel engines).

7 Check carefully for leaks as soon as possible after disturbing any part of the cooling system.

3 Antifreeze – general information

Note: *Refer to the warnings given in Section 1 of this Chapter before proceeding.*

1 The cooling system should be filled with Volvo (antifreeze) in a ratio of 50/50 with pure water. At this strength, the coolant will protect against freezing down to -35°C. Antifreeze also provides protection against corrosion, and increases the coolant boiling point. Also as the engine uses aluminium in its construction, the corrosion protection properties of the antifreeze are critical. Only Volvo antifreeze should be used in the system, and should never be mixed with different antifreeze types.

2 The cooling system should be maintained

2.3a Screw-type hose clamp

2.3b Special tools are available to release the spring type hose clips

4.3 Undo the 2 screws securing the air intake hose

4.5 The cooling fan wiring plug is located on the top, left-hand corner of the shroud

4.8 Depress the clip each side to release the cooling fan shroud

according to the schedule described in Chapter 1A, Section 30 or Chapter 1B, Section 29. If antifreeze is used that is not to Volvo's specification, old or contaminated coolant mixtures are likely to cause damage, and encourage the formation of corrosion and scale in the system.

3 Before adding antifreeze, check all hoses and hose connections, because antifreeze tends to leak through very small openings. Engines don't normally consume coolant, so if the level goes down, find the cause and correct it.

4 The specified mixture is 50% antifreeze and 50% clean soft water (by volume). Mix the required quantity in a clean container and then fill the system as described in Chapter 1A or Chapter 1B and *Weekly checks* . Save any surplus mixture for topping-up.

4 Radiator cooling fan – removal and refitting

Removal

1.8 and 2.0 litre petrol models

1 Remove the air cleaner housing as described in Chapter 4A.

2 Undo the 3 retaining screws and remove the panel from above the radiator.

3 Undo the 2 screws and remove the air cleaner housing bracket from the bonnet slam panel (see illustration).

4 Release the hoses from the retaining clips at the top of the fan shrouding.

5 Disconnect the cooling fan wiring plug (see illustration).

6 Jack up the front of the vehicle, and support it securely on axle stands (see *Jacking and vehicle support*).

7 Where fitted, release the 7 Torx screws and remove the engine undershield (see illustration 4.25).

8 Press-in the clips and release the catches at the bottom of the fan shroud on each side (see illustration).

9 Lift the fan shroud upwards to disengage the upper and lower locking hooks each side. Lower the fan shroud downwards and withdraw it from under the vehicle.

10 Note that the fan is only supplied complete with the shroud.

2.4 litre petrol models

11 Remove the front bumper as described in Chapter 11 Section 21.

12 Drain the cooling system as described in Chapter 1A Section 30.

13 Remove the cover from the engine control module (see illustration).

14 Disconnect the cooling fan wiring plug (see illustration 4.5).

15 Release the hoses at the top of the cooling fan shroud from the retaining clips.

16 Jack up the front of the vehicle and support it securely on axle stands (see *Jacking and vehicle support*).

17 Undo the 7 Torx screws and remove the engine undershield (see illustration 4.25).

18 Place a trolley jack under the radiator and take its weight.

4.13 Slide up the ECM cover at the front of the air cleaner housing

4.19b ...and the right-hand side

19 Undo the 4 bolts and remove the radiator/ fan shroud lower mounting bracket (see illustrations).

20 Release the clips and disconnect the coolant hoses from each side of the radiator.

21 On automatic transmission models, undo the Torx screw and detach the oil cooler from the left-hand side of the radiator. There is no need to disconnect the hoses.

22 Depress the retaining clips at the upper section of the fan shroud each side, lift the shroud up from its lower catches, then lower the fan and shroud downwards from place (see illustration).

23 Note that the fan is only supplied complete with the shroud.

1.6 litre diesel engines

24 Raise the vehicle and support it securely on axle stands (see *Jacking and vehicle support*).

4.19a Remove the radiator bracket bolts on the left-hand side...

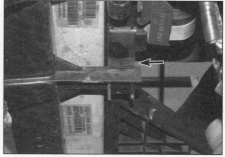

4.22 Depress the clip each side and lift the cooling fan upwards a little to disengage the lower catches

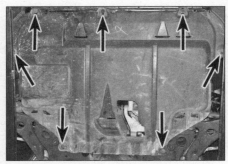

4.25 Undo the 7 Torx screws and remove the engine undershield

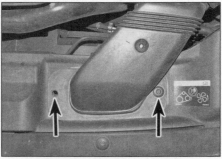

4.28 Release the plastic rivets and remove the inlet trunking

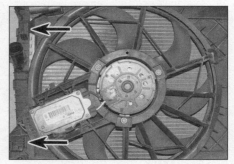

4.31 1.6 litre engine cooling fan shroud retaining clips – left-hand clips shown

4.33 Depress the clip each side and lift the fan shroud

25 Undo the 7 Torx screws and remove the engine undershield **(see illustration)**. Drain the cooling system as described in Chapter 1A or Chapter 1B.
26 Remove the air cleaner housing as

described in Chapter 4A (petrol) or Chapter 4B (diesel).
27 Undo the 5 screws along the top edge of the bumper, the 3 remaining screws, and remove the panel above the radiator.

5.5 Unclip the plastic cover

5.8a Undo the retaining screw each side...

5.8b ...and remove the lower air baffle

5.9 Suspend the condenser from the vehicle bodywork

28 Release the plastic rivets and remove the air inlet from the left-hand side of the lock panel **(see illustration)**. Working at the rear of the lock panel, undo the 2 screws and remove the air cleaner housing mounting bracket.
29 Release the clips, and move the hoses across the rear of the lock panel to one side.
30 Disconnect the wiring plug for the cooling fan **(see illustration 4.5)**. Release the clamps and disconnect the coolant hoses from the radiator.
31 Release the retaining clips, undo any screws at the bottom of the fan shroud, and lift the cooling fan from position **(see illustration)**.

2.0 and 2.4 litre diesel engines

32 Remove the radiator as described in Section 5.
33 Release the retaining clips each side **(see illustration)**, and lift the fan shroud upwards from the radiator.

Refitting

34 Refitting is the reversal of removal. Replenish the cooling system as described in Chapter 1A Section 30 (petrol) or Chapter 1B Section 29 (diesel).

5 Radiator – removal and refitting

Removal

1 Drain the cooling system (as described in Chapter 1A (petrol) or Chapter 1B (Diesel).

1.8 and 2.0 litre petrol engines

2 Remove the front bumper as described in Chapter 11 Section 21.
3 Remove the cooling fan assembly as described in Section 4.
4 Undo the 2 screws and remove the plastic panel under the radiator.
5 Unclip the plastic cover from the bumper mounting bar **(see illustration)**.
6 Undo the mounting bolts, disconnect the wiring plugs and remove the horns.
7 Remove the upper air baffle from the mounting studs.
8 Undo the 2 Torx screws and remove the lower air baffle **(see illustrations)**.
9 Use cable ties/straps to suspend the condenser from the vehicle bodywork **(see illustration)**.
10 Release the clips and disconnect the coolant hoses from each side of the radiator.
11 Disconnect the expansion hose from the radiator **(see illustration)**.
12 Undo the 4 bolts and remove the radiator lower mounting bracket **(see illustrations 4.19a and 4.19b)**.
13 Press-in the condenser retaining clips, and lower the radiator from place **(see illustrations)**.

5.11 Disconnect the expansion hose

5.13a Depress the clip each side...

5.13b ...and lower the radiator from place

5.15 Undo the 2 screws and remove the air intake duct

2.4 litre petrol models

14 Remove the radiator cooling fan as described in Section 4.
15 Undo the screws and detach the intake duct from the bonnet slam panel **(see illustration)**.
16 Undo the 2 screws and remove the bonnet slam panel at the top of the radiator **(see illustration)**.
17 Undo the screw each side and remove the upper radiator mounting **(see illustration)**.
18 Lift up the air conditioning condenser and suspend it from the bodywork using wire or straps.
19 Support the radiator, then undo the screws each side at the top, and lower the radiator from position **(see illustration)**.

Diesel engines

20 Remove the front bumper as described in Chapter 11 Section 21, then release the clips and remove the plastic bumper bar cover.
21 Undo the mounting bolt and remove the horn each side. Disconnect the wiring plugs as the horn is removed.
22 Jack up the front of the vehicle and support it securely on axle stands (see *Jacking and vehicle support)*. Release the 7 Torx screws and remove the engine undershield **(see illustration 4.25)**.
23 Release the expansion hoses from the clips at the top of the radiator.
24 Disconnect the cooling fan wiring plug.
25 On models fitted with the 2.0 4-cylinder engine release the clamp and disconnect the charge air pipe from the intake manifold **(see illustration)**.
26 Remove the upper air baffle by pulling

5.16 Undo the screw at each end securing the panel cover

the fixing in each top corner from place **(see illustration)**.
27 Remove the 2 lower air baffle Torx screws. Note that these are located behind the bumper bar and access is awkward – a degree of patience is required **(see illustration)**.

5.19 Undo the screw each side at the top of the radiator

5.26 Pull the fixing from place and remove the upper air baffle

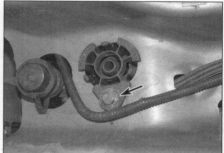

5.17 Undo the screw and pull up the radiator mounting each side

28 Undo the clamps and disconnect the air hoses from the intercooler.
29 Undo the 2 mounting bolts, lift the intercooler up from the lugs, then lower the intercooler and lower air baffle from position **(see illustration)**.

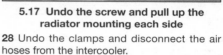

5.25 Slacken the clamp and disconnect the intake pipe

5.27 One of the lower air baffle screws

5.29 Lift up the intercooler to disengage the lugs, then lower it complete with air baffle

5.30a Undo the screw at the air-conditioning pipe block

5.30b Release the catch each side...

5.30c ...then lift the condenser up and suspend it

5.31a Radiator bottom hose...

5.31b ...and upper hose

30 Release the catch either side, undo the screw securing the air-conditioning pipe union block to the radiator, and lift the air conditioning condenser upwards a little from position, then suspend it from the bodywork using wire or straps **(see illustrations)**.

31 Release the clamps and disconnect the coolant hoses from the radiator **(see illustrations)**. Release the hoses from any retaining clips on the radiator.

32 With the help of an assistant, support the radiator, then undo the lower mounting bracket retaining bolts (2 each side), and lower the radiator a little to gain access to the expansion hose at its upper edge. Disconnect the hose, and lower the radiator completely **(see illustrations)**.

33 If required, remove the cooling fan and shroud as described in Section 4, then pull the lower mounting bracket from the rubber fittings, and the fittings from the base of the radiator **(see illustration)**.

Refitting

34 Refit by reversing the removal operations, ensuring that all hoses are re-connected and tightened securely. With reference to Chapter 1A (petrol) or Chapter 1B (diesel) refill the cooling system on completion.

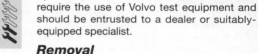

6 Coolant temperature sensor
– testing, removal and refitting

Testing

1 The coolant temperature sensor is located in the thermostat housing, and is used by both the engine management system and the instrument panel temperature gauge to supply an engine temperature source signal.

2 In the event of a fault in the sensor, or a loss of signal due to poor electrical connections, a fault

code will be logged in the engine management system ECU, which can be read out via the diagnostic connector beneath the facia on the driver's side (using a suitable fault code reader).

3 Should a fault code be logged, a careful check should be made of the sensor wiring and the wiring connector. Apart from testing by substitution with a new unit, further checks require the use of Volvo test equipment and should be entrusted to a dealer or suitably-equipped specialist.

Removal

All engines

4 Drain the cooling system as described in Chapter 1A (petrol) or Chapter 1B (diesel). Note that if a replacement sensor is to hand, in many cases it is possible to swap the sensors with little loss of coolant and without draining the system.

5 Pull the plastic cover on the top of the

5.32a Undo the radiator lower bracket bolts each side

5.32b As the radiator is lowered, disconnect the expansion hose

5.33 Pull the rubber fitting from the base of the radiator

engine straight up and remove it from the engine compartment.

1.8 and 2.0 litre petrol models

6 Pull the plastic cover on the top of the engine straight upwards from its mountings.
7 Disconnect the wiring plug, then unscrew the sensor from its location in the coolant outlet housing using a deep socket **(see illustration)**.

2.4 litre petrol models

8 Remove the air cleaner assembly as described in Chapter 4A Section 3.
9 Disconnect the sensor wiring plug, then pull out the retaining clip and remove the sensor from the thermostat housing at the left-hand end of the cylinder head **(see illustration)**. Where fitted, discard the sensor seal – a new one must be fitted.

1.6 litre engines

10 The sensor is fitted to the thermostat housing at the left-hand end of the cylinder head. Disconnect the wiring plug, pull out the retaining clip, and remove the sensor.

2.0 litre 4-cylinder engine

11 Remove the air cleaner housing as described in Chapter 4A Section 3.
12 Disconnect the wiring plug, then prise out the retaining clip and pull the sensor from the thermostat housing **(see illustration)**.

5-cylinder engines

13 On 2.0 litre models only, slacken the clamps at the air cleaner housing and at the rear of the engine on the right-hand side, disconnect the pipe at the cylinder head, and remove the air intake pipe at the front of the engine. Disconnect and remove the pipe between the EGR valve and the intake manifold.
14 Disconnect the wiring plug, release the retaining clamp, and pull the sensor from the thermostat housing **(see illustration)**.
15 On 2.4 litre models, disconnect the wiring plug and use a deep 19mm socket to unscrew the sensor.

Refitting

16 Screw or push in the new sensor unit, using a smear of sealant on the threads or new seal as applicable. Reconnect the wiring plug, and refit components as applicable.
17 Replenish or top-up the cooling system as described in Chapter 1A or Chapter 1B.

7 Coolant pump – removal and refitting

Note: *Refer to the warnings given in Section 1 of this Chapter before proceeding.*

Removal

1 Drain the cooling system as described in Chapter 1A (petrol) or Chapter 1B (diesel).

1.8 and 2.0 litre petrol models

2 Pull the plastic cover on the top of the engine straight up from its mountings.

6.7 The engine coolant temperature sensor is located at the left-hand end of the cylinder head – viewed from the rear of the engine

6.12 The coolant temperature sensor is located at the left-hand end of the cylinder head, and retained by a clip

3 Remove the auxiliary drivebelt as described in Chapter 1A and then slacken the coolant pump pulley bolts **(see illustration)**. Note that it is also possible to slacken the pulley bolts before removing the auxiliary drivebelt.

7.3 Use a strap wrench hold the coolant pump pulley whilst slackening the bolts

7.5b ...remove the coolant pump...

6.9 Engine coolant temperature sensor – 2.4 litre models

6.14 Coolant sensor wiring plug

4 Remove the bolts and then pull the pulley from the coolant pump.
5 Undo the 3 bolts, and remove the coolant pump **(see illustrations)**. Remove the O-ring seal and discard it.

7.5a Unscrew the mounting bolts...

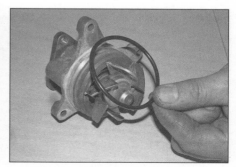

7.5c ...and remove the O-ring seal

7.10a Undo the mounting bolts...

2.4 litre petrol models

6 Remove the timing belt as described in Chapter 2B Section 3.

7 Undo the retaining bolts and remove the coolant pump (see illustrations 7.17 and 7.19). Note that access is limited, and it may be necessary to raise or lower the engine slightly to access the bolts.

8 Thoroughly clean all traces of old gasket from the pump and cylinder block mating faces.

1.6 and 2.0 litre 4-cylinder diesel engines

9 Remove the remove the timing belt as described in Chapter 2C Section 7 or Chapter 2D Section 6.

10 Undo the bolts (7 bolts on the 1.6 litre engine, 5 bolts on the 2.0 litre engine), and remove the coolant pump from its locating dowels (see illustrations). Recover the gasket, and the O-ring seal where applicable, after removing the pump.

11 Thoroughly clean all traces of old gasket from the pump and cylinder block mating faces.

5-cylinder diesel engines

12 Drain the cooling system as described in Chapter 1B Section 29.

13 Remove the timing belt as described in Chapter 2E Section 4.

14 Remove the brake vacuum pump as described in Chapter 9 Section 21, and the lower torque rod as described in Chapter 2E Section 11.

15 Insert a camshaft locking tool (Volvo part no. 999 7007) into the aperture exposed by removal of the vacuum pump.

7.17 Undo the mounting bolts

7.10b ...remove the coolant pump and recover the gasket

16 Undo the 4 bolts and remove the upper timing belt sprocket. Undo the 3 securing bolts for the rear timing belt cover.

17 Undo the 7 bolts for the coolant pump, and move the rear timing belt cover forward a little (see illustration).

18 Using an engine hoist, support the engine from above and move it slightly towards the right-hand side of the engine compartment. Move the water pump forwards a little.

19 Move the engine back towards the left-hand side of the engine compartment, and withdraw the coolant pump (see illustration).

Refitting

20 Using a new gasket, and O-ring seal where applicable, locate the pump in position.

21 Apply a little thread-locking compound, then tighten the bolts progressively and in a diagonal sequence to the specified torque.

22 Refit all components as described in the relevant Chapter, and replenish the cooling system as described in Chapter 1A or Chapter 1B.

8	Thermostat – removal, testing and refitting

1 As the thermostat ages, it will become slower to react to changes in water temperature. Ultimately, the unit may stick in the open or closed position, and this causes problems. A thermostat which is stuck open will result in a very slow warm-up; a thermostat which is stuck shut will lead to rapid overheating.

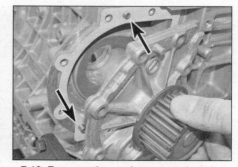

7.19 Remove the coolant pump from its locating dowels

2 Before assuming the thermostat is to blame for a cooling system problem, check the coolant level. If the system is draining due to a leak, or has not been properly filled, there may be an air-lock in the system (see Chapter 1A or Chapter 1B).

3 If the engine seems to be taking a long time to warm up (based on heater output or temperature gauge operation), the thermostat is probably stuck open.

4 Equally, a lengthy warm-up period might suggest that the thermostat is missing – it may have been removed or inadvertently omitted by a previous owner or mechanic. Don't drive the vehicle without a thermostat – the engine management system's ECU will stay in warm-up mode for longer than necessary, causing emissions and fuel economy to suffer.

5 If the engine runs hot, use your hand to check the temperature of the radiator top hose. If the hose isn't hot, but the engine is, the thermostat is probably stuck closed, preventing the coolant inside the engine from escaping to the radiator – renew the thermostat. Again, this problem may also be due to an air-lock (see Chapter 1A Section 30 or Chapter 1B Section 29).

6 If the radiator top hose is hot, it means that the coolant is flowing and the thermostat is open. Consult the *Fault diagnosis* section at the end of this manual to assist in tracing possible cooling system faults.

7 To gain a rough idea of whether the thermostat is working properly when the engine is warming up, without dismantling the system, proceed as follows.

8 With the engine completely cold, start the engine and let it idle, while checking the temperature of the radiator top hose. Periodically check the temperature indicated on the coolant temperature gauge – if overheating is indicated, switch the engine off immediately.

9 The top hose should feel cold for some time as the engine warms up, and should then get warm quite quickly as the thermostat opens.

10 The above is not a precise or definitive test of thermostat operation, but if the system does not perform as described, remove and test the thermostat as described below.

Removal

Note: *Refer to the warnings given in Section 1 of this Chapter before proceeding.*

11 The engine must be completely cold before starting this procedure – the engine should have been switched off for several hours, and ideally, left to cool overnight.

12 Drain the cooling system as described in Chapter 1A (petrol) or Chapter 1B (diesel).

13 where fitted, pull the plastic engine cover straight-up and remove it from the engine compartment.

1.8 and 2.0 litre petrol models

14 Remove the inlet manifold as described in Chapter 4A.

15 Note their fitted locations, then release the

8.15 Disconnect the coolant hoses from the thermostat housing – 1.8 and 2.0 litre models

8.18 Thermostat housing – 2.4 litre models

8.25 Thermostat mounting bolts on 1.6 litre engines

clamps and disconnect the hoses from the thermostat housing **(see illustration)**.
16 Undo the 3 bolts and remove the thermostat housing. Remove all traces of the old gasket from the housing and cylinder block mating faces. Note that the thermostat is not available separately from the housing.

2.4 litre petrol models

2.4 litre petrol models

17 Remove the air cleaner assembly as described in Chapter 4A Section 3.
18 Release the clips and disconnect the hoses from the thermostat housing **(see illustration)**.
19 Disconnect the temperature sensor wiring plug.
20 Undo the retaining bolts and remove the thermostat housing. Discard the housing seal, a new one must be fitted. Although it is possible to separate the thermostat from the housing, it would appear that it is not available as a separate part. Check with a Volvo dealer or parts specialist. The temperature sensor should be transferred to the new housing as described in Section 6.

1.6 litre diesel engines

21 Remove the air cleaner housing as described in Chapter 4B Section 3. On models fitted with the 85kw engine, remove the fuel filter as described in Chapter 1B Section 20.
22 The thermostat housing is located at the left-hand end of the cylinder head. Release the clips and disconnect the coolant hoses from the thermostat housing.
23 Disconnect the wiring plug from the engine coolant temperature sensor.

24 Undo the coolant bypass pipe retaining bolt.
25 Undo the 4 retaining bolts and remove the thermostat housing **(see illustration)**. Note that the thermostat is integral with the housing. If the thermostat is faulty, the housing must be renewed

2.0 litre 4-cylinder engine

26 Release the clips and disconnect the hoses from the thermostat housing. Disconnect the wiring plug for the engine coolant temperature sensor.
27 Undo the 4 nuts and remove the thermostat housing from the left-hand end of the cylinder head **(see illustrations)**. Disconnect the coolant hose from the rear of the thermostat housing as its withdrawn. Although it may be possible to separate the thermostat from the cover, it would appear that it is not available as a separate part. Check with a Volvo dealer or parts specialist.

5-cylinder engines

28 Disconnect the wiring plug for the engine coolant temperature sensor.
29 Undo the clips and disconnect the hoses from the thermostat housing. Undo the retaining bolts (there are 3 bolts on 2.0 litre engines, 2 bolts on 2.4 litre engines) and remove the housing from the engine **(see illustration)**.

Testing

30 Check the temperature marking stamped on the thermostat, which will typically be 82°C.
31 Using a thermometer and container of

water, heat the water until the temperature corresponds with the temperature marking stamped on the thermostat.
32 Suspend the (closed) thermostat on a length of string in the water, and check that maximum opening occurs within two minutes.
33 Remove the thermostat and allow it to cool down; check that it closes fully.
34 If the thermostat does not open and close as described, or if it sticks in either position, it must be renewed.

Refitting

35 Refitting is a reversal of removal using new gaskets and seals where applicable. Top-up the cooling system as described in *Weekly checks*.

9 Heating, ventilation and air conditioning systems – general information

Automatic climate control

1 With automatic climate control, the temperature inside the car can be automatically maintained at the level selected by the operator, irrespective of outside temperature. The computer-controlled system operates the heater, air conditioner and fan functions as necessary to achieve this. The refrigeration side of the air conditioning system functions in a similar way to a domestic refrigerator. A compressor, belt-driven from the crankshaft pulley, draws refrigerant in its gaseous phase from an evaporator. The compound refrigerant

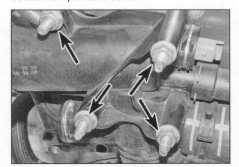

8.27a On 2.0 litre 4-cylinder engines, undo the thermostat securing nuts

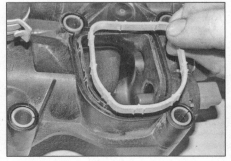

8.27b Renew the thermostat housing sealing ring

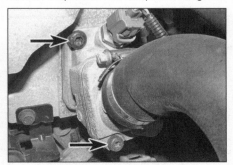

8.29 Thermostat housing bolts on 2.4 litre engine

9.8 The air conditioning service ports

passes through a condenser where it loses heat and enters its liquid phase. After dehydration the refrigerant returns to the evaporator where it absorbs heat from air passing over the evaporator fins. The refrigerant becomes a gas again and the cycle is repeated. The fully automatic electronic control operates as follows.

2 An electronic control unit (ECU) receives signal inputs from sensors that detect the air duct temperatures on the driver's and passenger's side, and interior temperature on the driver's and passenger's side. A solar sensor is used to detect the presence of sunlight. Signals are also received from the dampers (air flaps) on their position at any given time. Information on engine temperature, outside temperature, whether or not the engine is running, and if so, the vehicle roadspeed, are also sent to the ECU from the engine management system.

3 When the automatic function is engaged, the ECU can establish the optimum settings needed, based on the sensor signals, for the selected temperature and air distribution. These settings can then be maintained irrespective of driving conditions and weather.

4 Distribution of air to the various vents, and the blending of hot or cold air to achieve the selected temperature, are controlled by dampers (flaps). These are operated by electric motors, which are in turn controlled by the ECU. A variable speed fan which can be manually or automatically controlled is used to boost airflow through the system.

5 Should a fault occur, the ECU stores a series of fault codes for subsequent read-out via the diagnostic connector located in the lower facia panel above the driver's pedals.

Precautions

6 When an air conditioning system is fitted, it is necessary to observe special precautions whenever dealing with any part of the system, or its associated components. If for any reason the system must be discharged, entrust this task to your Volvo dealer, local garage or a mobile AC specialist.

⚠ **Warning: The refrigeration circuit contains R134a liquid refrigerant, and it is therefore dangerous to disconnect any part of the system without specialised knowledge and equipment.**

7 The refrigerant is potentially dangerous, and should only be handled by qualified persons. If it is splashed onto the skin, it can cause frostbite. It is not itself poisonous, but in the presence of a naked flame (including a cigarette) it forms a poisonous gas. Uncontrolled discharging of the refrigerant is dangerous, and potentially damaging to the environment.

8 The refrigerant circuit service ports are located on the right-hand side of the engine compartment, and under the plastic panel attached to the bonnet slam panel (see illustration).

10 Climate control system components – removal and refitting

Climate control module (CCM) control panel

Removal

Note: *Variations to the procedure may occur, depending on the vehicle trim level and/or year of manufacture, however the procedure for removal is essentially the same for all variants.*

1 Ensure the ignition switch is in the 'Off' position.

2 Remove the centre console as described in Chapter 11 Section 27.

3 Carefully pull the panel behind the CCM, releasing its 4 retaining clips (see illustration).

4 Using a small screwdriver, push the retaining clip each side away from the centre and remove the audio panel (see illustrations).

5 Pull the infotainment control module from the centre console (see illustration). Disconnect the wiring plugs as the module is withdrawn.

6 Starting at the sides, prise the cigarette lighter/electrical socket panel from behind the heater lever/selector lever position (see illustration). Disconnect the wiring plugs as the panel is withdrawn.

7 Undo the retaining screws (see illustrations).

8 Where required unclip the gearchange lever gaiter and remove the console. Disconnect the wiring plug(s) as the console is withdrawn.

10.3 Pull the panel rearwards to release the clips

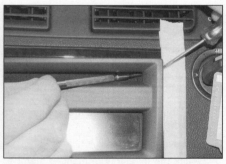

10.4a Insert a screwdriver through the loading slot and press the clip each side outwards – use tape to protect the trim

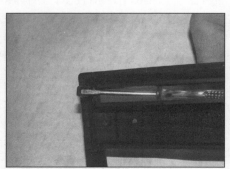

10.4b Viewed from the inside of the panel to show how the clips are released

10.5 Reach behind and push the module from place

10.6 Unclip the cigarette lighter/power outlet panel

10.7a Undo the screws at the top...

10.7b ...and at the bottom

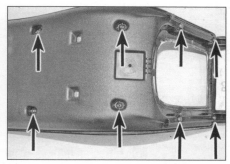

10.9 Undo the screws and remove the rear panel

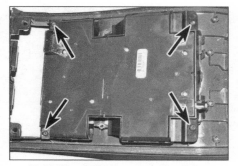

10.10 The CCM is secured by 4 Torx screws

10.14 Twist the air quality sensor anti-clockwise and remove it

10.16 Undo the damper cover screws

9 Undo the 8 screws on the reverse of the console, and remove the panel **(see illustration)**.
10 Remove the 4 retaining screws and remove the CCM **(see illustration)**.

Refitting

11 Refit by reversing the removal operations. Take care not to overtighten the panel retaining screws as it is easily cracked.
12 If the CCM assembly has been renewed, it may need to be programmed prior to use. This can only be carried out by a Volvo dealer or suitably-equipped specialist.

Heater blower motor

Removal

13 Remove the facia as described in Chapter 11 Section 28.
14 Remove the air quality sensor as described in this Section **(see illustration)**.

15 Disconnect the wiring plug, then undo the 3 retaining screws and remove the recirculation damper motor module (DMM) **(see illustration 10.30)**.
16 Undo the 3 retaining screws and remove the air distribution damper cover **(see illustration)**.
17 Disconnect the blower motor wiring plug, then depress the lock button, rotate the fan motor body anti-clockwise to the stop position, then pull the motor from the housing **(see illustrations)**.

Refitting

18 Refit by reversing the removal operations.

Heater matrix

Note: *Refer to the warnings given in Section 1 of this Chapter before proceeding.*

Removal

19 Remove the centre console as described in Chapter 11 Section 27.
20 Undo the bolts and remove the driver's side facia support bracket (where fitted). Release any wiring harness clips as necessary **(see illustration)**.
21 From the factory, the matrix is installed with integral coolant pipes that extend from the engine compartment side of the bulkhead down to the matrix (one-piece pipes). However, repair matrices are supplied with short pipe stubs – 2 extra pipes are available (included in the matrix service kit) to supply/return the coolant to the hoses on other side of the bulkhead (split pipes).
22 Undo the cover retaining Torx screws, the remove the cover from the matrix **(see illustration)**.

10.17a Rotate the fan motor body anti-clockwise...

10.17b ...and pull the motor from the housing

10.20 Remove the driver's side facia support bracket

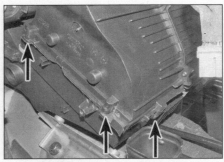

10.22 Undo the matrix cover screws (left-hand side shown)

10.23 Cut through the matrix pipes

10.24 Lift the matrix from the housing

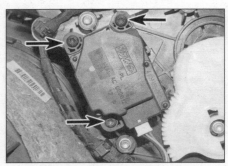

10.31 Air distribution damper motor module Torx screws

10.32 When refitting, ensure the large gap on the white gear is occupied by the large tooth of the black gear

10.36 Air recirculation damper motor module Torx screws

23 Cut the matrix pipes, and push the pipes slightly into the engine compartment **(see illustration)**. If necessary, undo the 2 Torx screws securing the right-hand half of the bulkhead grommet seal.
24 Pull the matrix from the housing **(see illustration)**. Note how the seal is located.

Refitting

25 Fit the new pipes into the bulkhead grommet.
26 Fit a new seal to the matrix, and insert the matrix into the heater housing.
27 Lubricate the new O-ring seals with a little clean oil, and fit them on the pipes.
28 Secure the pipe connections using the clips. The clips are fully installed when they are heard to 'click' as they are pressed together.
29 The remainder of refitting is a reversal of removal. Replenish the cooling system as described in Chapter 1A Section 30 or Chapter 1B Section 29.

Air distribution damper motor module (DMM)

Removal

30 Remove the glovebox compartment as described in Chapter 11 Section 25.
31 Disconnect the wiring plug, then undo the 3 screws and remove the DMM **(see illustration)**.

Refitting

32 Adjust the position of the motor/flap gears as shown **(see illustration)**, then refit the motor and tighten the screws securely.
33 The remainder of refitting is a reversal of removal.

Air recirculation damper motor module (DMM)

Removal

34 Remove the glovebox compartment as described in Chapter 11 Section 25.

35 Working through the glovebox aperture, disconnect the damper motor wiring connector.
36 Undo the 3 screws and remove the DMM from the side of the heater blower motor housing **(see illustration)**.

Refitting

37 Refit by reversing the removal operations.

Defroster damper motor module (DMM)

Removal

38 Remove the facia as described in Chapter 11 Section 28.
39 Disconnect the wiring plug, then undo the 3 retaining screws and pull the DMM from position **(see illustration)**.

Refitting

40 Refit by reversing the removal operations.

Temperature damper motor module (DMM)

Note: *There are two temperature DMMs – one on the right-hand side, and one on the left.*

Removal

41 Remove the facia as described in Chapter 11 Section 28.
42 Disconnect the wiring plug, then undo the 3 retaining screws and pull the DMM from position **(see illustration)**.

Refitting

43 Refit by reversing the removal operations.

10.39 Defroster damper motor module

10.42 Temperature damper motor module

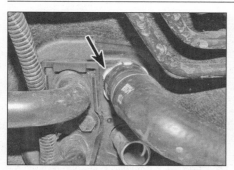

10.49 Rotate the clamp anti-clockwise and disconnect the heater hoses

10.50 Undo the bolt and disconnect the air conditioning pipes

10.53a Release the wiring harness...

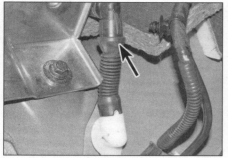

10.53b ...and disconnect the drain tube

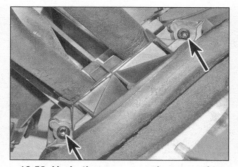

10.56 Undo the screws and remove the bulkhead seal cover

10.58 Undo the evaporator cover

Facia panel centre and side vents

Removal

44 Carefully lever the vents out of the facia panel, using a screwdriver with a piece of card beneath it to protect the trim. Disconnect the wiring plugs from the vents as they are withdrawn (where applicable).

Refitting

45 Refitting is a reversal of removal.

Heater housing

Removal

46 Have the air conditioning refrigerant discharged by a suitably-equipped specialist.
47 Drain the cooling system as described in Chapter 1A (petrol) or Chapter 1B (diesel).
48 Remove the complete facia assembly as described in Chapter 11 Section 28.
49 Rotate the clamps anti-clockwise and disconnect the heater hoses from the engine compartment bulkhead **(see illustration)**.
50 Undo the retaining bolt and detach the air conditioning pipes from the evaporator connection at the engine compartment bulkhead **(see illustration)**. Recover the O-ring seals, and seal the openings.
51 With reference to the relevant part of this section, separate the pipes for the heater matrix and the evaporator.
52 Undo the bolts and remove the right-hand support bracket from the floor **(see illustration 10.20)**.
53 Disconnect the drain tube, and release the wiring harness on the right-hand lower edge of the housing, then remove the complete

housing from the passenger cabin **(see illustrations)**.

Refitting

54 Refitting is a reversal of removal, bearing in mind the following points:
a) *Ensure the rubber grommet between the coolant/refrigerant pipes and the bulkhead is correctly positioned.*
b) *Renew the matrix coolant pipe O-rings.*
c) *Volvo insist that the receiver/drier is renewed if the heater housing is renewed.*
d) *Have the refrigerant circuit recharged by a suitably-equipped specialist.*

Evaporator

Note: *Whenever disconnecting air conditioning pipes or components, always plug the openings to prevent dirt ingress, and to prevent the receiver/drier from becoming saturated.*

10.59 Pull the evaporator from the housing

Removal

55 Remove the heater housing as described in this Section.
56 Undo the 2 retaining screws, remove the right-hand half of the bulkhead seal cover **(see illustration)**.
57 Remove the heater matrix pipes.
58 Undo the 3 screws and remove the evaporator cover **(see illustration)**.
59 Pull the evaporator from the housing. It may be difficult to remove – pull alternatively on the top and bottom edges. Note how the seal is located on the evaporator **(see illustration)**.

Refitting

60 Fit a new seal to the evaporator, then insert the evaporator into position in the heater housing **(see illustration)**. Insert the evaporator far enough into the housing so the cover can be fitted (approximately 3 to 4mm).

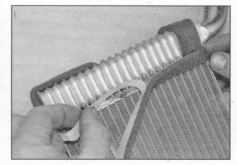

10.60 Fit the new seals to the evaporator

10.64 Undo the 2 nuts and disconnect the refrigerant pipes

Position the front edge of the cover between the evaporator and the heater unit and tighten the cover retaining screws securely.

61 When the vehicles leave the factory, they are fitted with evaporators that have integral refrigerant pipes. However, repair evaporators are supplied with separate pipes. Install the pipes into the seal in the bulkhead, then fit them to the evaporator using new O-ring seals.

62 The remainder of refitting is a reversal of removal, noting the following points:

a) *Fit new O-ring seals to the refrigerant pipe connections at the engine compartment bulkhead, lubricated with refrigerant oil.*

b) *Upon completion have the air conditioning system recharged, and checked for leaks*

Condenser

Note: *Whenever disconnecting air conditioning pipes or components, always plug the openings to prevent dirt ingress, and to prevent the receiver/drier from becoming saturated.*

63 Have the air conditioning refrigerant discharged by a suitably-equipped specialist.

Removal

64 Remove the radiator as described in Section 5, but instead of suspending the condenser, undo the refrigerant pipe unions and remove it along with the radiator **(see illustration)**.

65 Depress the clip then slide the condenser from the mounting frame **(see illustration 5.13a)**.

Refitting

66 Refitting is a reversal of removal, noting the following points:

a) *Fit new O-ring seals to the air conditioning pipe connections, lubricated with refrigerant oil.*

b) *Replenish the cooling system as described in Chapter 1A Section 30 (petrol engines) or Chapter 1B Section 32 (diesel engines).*

c) *Upon completion, have the air conditioning system recharged, and checked for leaks.*

Expansion valve

Note: *Whenever disconnecting air conditioning pipes or components, always plug the openings to prevent dirt ingress, and to prevent the receiver/drier from becoming saturated.*

Removal

67 Have the air conditioning refrigerant discharged by a suitably-equipped specialist.

68 The expansion valve is located in the lower air conditioning pipe at the engine compartment bulkhead. Undo the union nut and pull the pipe evaporator inlet pipe from the connection at the engine compartment bulkhead.

69 Note its fitted position, then pull the expansion valve from the pipe using pliers. Recover the valve O-ring seal. Note that the valve incorporates a filter. Should a component such as a compressor fail, it's possible that the filter may become clogged with debris.

Refitting

70 Refitting is a reversal of removal, noting the following points:

a) *Tighten the expansion valve union nut to the specified torque.*

b) *Renew all O-ring seals where disturbed, lubricated with refrigerant oil.*

c) *Upon completion, have the air conditioning system recharged and checked for leaks.*

Receiver/drier

Note: *Whenever disconnecting air conditioning pipes or components, always plug the openings to prevent dirt ingress, and to prevent the receiver/drier from becoming* saturated.

Note: *Volvo insist that the receiver/drier must be renewed if the refrigerant circuit has been opened/unplugged for more than 10 minutes, or the compressor has been renewed.*

Removal

71 Remove the right-hand headlight as described in Chapter 12 Section 11.

72 Remove the front bumper as described in Chapter 11 Section 21.

73 Undo the fasteners and pull back the front edge of the wheel arch liner.

74 Undo the nut behind the wheel arch liner **(see illustration)**.

75 Undo the bolts and disconnect the receiver/drier refrigerant pipes. Recover the O-ring seals.

76 Undo the 3 retaining bolts and remove the receiver/drier **(see illustration)**.

Refitting

77 Refitting is a reversal of removal, noting the following points:

a) *Tighten the receiver/drier bolts to the specified torque.*

b) *Renew all O-ring seals where disturbed, lubricated with refrigerant oil.*

c) *Upon completion, have the air conditioning system recharged and checked for leaks.*

Compressor

Note: *Whenever disconnecting air conditioning pipes or components, always plug the openings to prevent dirt ingress, and to prevent the receiver/drier from becoming saturated.*

Note: *Volvo insist that the receiver/drier must be renewed if the compressor has been renewed.*

Removal

78 Have the air conditioning refrigerant discharged by a suitably-equipped specialist.

79 Remove the auxiliary drivebelt as described in Chapter 1A (petrol) or Chapter 1B (diesel).

80 Jack up the front of the vehicle and support it securely on axle stands (see *Jacking and vehicle support*). Release the 7 Torx screws and remove the engine undershield **(see illustration 4.25)**.

81 Undo the screws and detach the air conditioning pipes from the compressor. Discard the O-ring seals, new ones must be fitted.

82 Disconnect the wiring plug, then undo the bolts securing the compressor to the engine, and manoeuvre it downwards and out from the vehicle **(see illustration)**.

Note: *The compressor is secured by either 3 or 4 bolts depending on the engine fitted.*

10.74 Undo the nut behind the wheel arch liner

10.76 Receiver/drier retaining bolts

10.82 Compressor lower mounting bolts on the 1.6 litre engine

10.85 Carefully prise the solar sensor up from the facia

11.4a Undo the 2 Torx screws...

11.4b ...and pull the heater from the housing

On models fitted with the 2.0 litre 4-cylinder engine, the lower mounting has a spacer that must be removed and which must be tightened last on refitting. On 5-cylinder engines, the bolts are of differing lengths. The longer bolt should be installed and tightened first on refitting.

Refitting

83 Refitting is a reversal of removal, noting the following points:

a) *Renew all O-ring seals where disturbed, lubricated with refrigerant oil.*

b) *Upon completion, have the air conditioning system recharged and checked for leaks.*

c) *The amount of refrigerant oil to be added after compressor refitting depends on the amount drained during refrigerant evacuation. If more than 70 cm 3 was drained, add the amount that was drained. If less than this amount, add 70 cm 3.*

Solar sensor

Removal

84 The solar sensor is located on top of the facia cover.

85 Carefully prise up the sensor using a screwdriver inserted under its base at the side **(see illustration)**.

86 Disconnect the wiring connector and remove the sensor.

Refitting

87 Refitting is a reversal of removal.

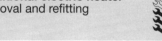

11 Additional electric heater – removal and refitting

Note: *The additional electric heater is only available on models supplied to some markets.*

Removal

1 Remove the centre console as described in Chapter 11, Section 27.

2 Release the wiring harness from the mounting bracket, then undo the 4 bolts and remove the right-hand mounting bracket **(see illustration 10.14)**.

3 Disconnect the heater wiring plugs.

4 Undo the 2 retaining bolts and pull the heater from the housing **(see illustrations)**.

Refitting

5 Refit the heater to the housing, ensuring the guide pins on the end of the heater engage correctly with the heater housing.

6 The remainder of refitting is a reversal of removal.

Chapter 4 Part A:
Fuel and exhaust systems – petrol models

Contents

Degrees of difficulty

Easy, suitable for novice with little experience	Fairly easy, suitable for beginner with some experience	Fairly difficult, suitable for competent DIY mechanic	Difficult, suitable for experienced DIY mechanic	Very difficult, suitable for expert DIY or professional

Specifications

General

System type . . . . Integrated engine management system with sequential electronic fuel injection and ignition. Both the idle speed and mixture are under the control of the ECM (Electronic Control Module), and cannot be adjusted

Fuel system data

Note: *The resistance values quoted below are typical, but may be used for guidance. Generally, a faulty component will be indicated by a zero or infinity reading, rather than a slight deviation from the values given. Always have your findings verified before buying a new component (if possible, perform the same test on a new component, and compare the results).*

Fuel injectors

Resistance . . . . 12.5 ohms at 20°C

Crankshaft position sensor

Resistance:
  1.8 and 2.0 litre models . . . . 450 ohms at 20°C
  2.4 litre models . . . . 125 ohms at 20°C

Camshaft position sensor

Resistance:
  1.8 and 2.0 litre models . . . . 450 ohms at 20°C

Inlet camshaft reset valve

Resistance:
  2.4 litre models . . . . 3 to 5 ohms

Intake air temperature sensor

Resistance:
  1.8 and 2.0 litre models . . . . 15 k ohms at -20°C
                        2.5 k ohms at 20°C
  2.4 litre models . . . . 2.3 k ohms at 20°C

Fuel temperature sensor

Resistance:
  2.4 litre models . . . . 2.5 k ohms at 20°C

EGR valve

Resistance:
  1.8 and 2.0 litre models . . . . 12 to 22 ohms on each stepper motor coil

Fuel system data (continued)

Manifold absolute pressure sensor

Resistance:
1.8 and 2.0 litre models .... 3 to 5 k ohms at 20°C
2.4 litre models .... 10 ohms

Variable intake vacuum valve

Resistance:
1.8 and 2.0 litre models .... 31 ohms at 20°C

Swirl throttle vacuum valve

Resistance:
1.8 and 2.0 litre models .... 31 ohms at 20°C

Torque wrench settings	Nm	lbf ft
Camshaft position sensor		
1.8 and 2.0 litre models	6	4
2.4 and 2.5 litre models	Not available	
Crankshaft position sensor:		
1.8 and 2.0 litre models	6	4
2.4 and 2.5 litre models*.....................	25	18
Electronic throttle module	10	7
Exhaust manifold:		
1.8 and 2.0 litre models*.....................	48	35
2.4 and 2.5 litre models*.....................	25	18
Front subframe bolts		
Front bolts	120	89
Rear bolts	280	207
Fuel gauge sender unit/pump plastic retaining nut	70	52
Fuel rail to inlet manifold:		
1.8 and 2.0 litre models	25	18
2.4 and 2.5 litre models	10	7
Inlet manifold bolts:		
2.4 litre models:		
Upper section	10	7
Lower section	20	15
Lower torque rod:		
M10	60	44
M12	80	59

* Do not re-use

1 General information and precautions

General information

The fuel system consists of a centrally-mounted fuel tank, an electric fuel pump, a fuel filter and a fully-electronic fuel injection system. Further details of the fuel injection systems will be found in Sections 5 and 7.

Depending on engine type, models for some market territories are also equipped with an exhaust gas recirculation (EGR) system, as part of an emissions control package. Further details of these systems will be found in Part C of this Chapter.

Depressurising the fuel system

Before working on any part of the fuel system, it is recommended that the residual fuel pressure is relieved. Even if the engine has been switched off for some time, there is a risk that, when fuel lines are disconnected, the residual fuel pressure will cause fuel to spray out uncontrollably. This is at best unpleasant

(if it sprays in your face, for instance), and at worst, presents a fire risk.

Whenever a fuel line is to be disconnected, particularly if the system pressure has not been relieved, wrap plenty of absorbent rag around the connection to be disturbed. Loosen the fittings or clips slowly, and remove any pipes carefully, so that the pressure is relieved in a controlled fashion, and/or so that any fuel spillage can be contained.

Remove the No 74 fuse for the fuel pump relay in the passenger compartment fusebox (see Chapter 12), then start the engine and allow it to idle until it stops. The system pressure is now relieved. Refit the fuel pump fuse.

Remember that relieving the system pressure does not remove the risk of fuel spillage – fuel will still be present in the lines, and it is wise to place absorbent rags around any connection which is to be disturbed.

Precautions

⚠️ **Warning: Petrol is extremely flammable – great care must be taken when working on any part of the fuel system. Do not smoke or allow any naked flames or uncovered light bulbs near the work area. Note that gas-powered domestic appliances with pilot flames, such as heaters, boilers and tumble dryers, also present a fire hazard – bear this in mind if you are working in an area where such appliances are present. Always keep a suitable fire extinguisher close to the work area and familiarise yourself with its operation before starting work. Wear eye protection when working on fuel systems and wash off any fuel spilt on bare skin immediately with soap and water. Note that fuel vapour is just as dangerous as liquid fuel; a vessel that has just been emptied of liquid fuel will still contain vapour and can be potentially explosive. Petrol is a highly dangerous and volatile liquid, and the precautions necessary when handling it cannot be overstressed.**

• Many of the operations described in this Chapter involve the disconnection of fuel lines, which may cause an amount of fuel spillage. Before commencing work, refer to the above Warning and the information in Safety first! at the beginning of this manual; also see the information on depressurising the fuel system, given previously in this Section.

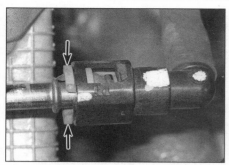

2.10a Two-tab type fitting; depress both tabs with your fingers, then pull the fuel pipe and the fitting apart

2.10b On this type of fitting, depress the two buttons on opposite sides of the fitting, then pull it off the fuel pipe

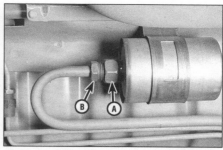

2.10c Threaded fuel pipe fitting; hold the stationary portion of the pipe or component (A) while loosening the union nut (B) with a flare-nut spanner

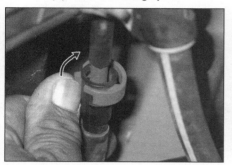

2.10d Plastic collar-type fitting; rotate the outer part of the fitting

2.10e Metal collar quick-connect fitting; pull the end of the retainer off the fuel pipe and disengage the other end from the female side of the fitting...

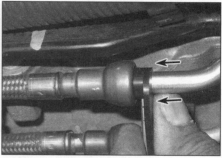

2.10f...insert a fuel pipe separator tool into the female side of the fitting, push it into the fitting and pull the fuel pipe off the pipe

• *It is strongly advised that, wherever possible, the battery negative lead is disconnected whenever there is a danger of fuel spillage. This reduces the risk of a spark causing a fire, and also prevents the fuel pump running, which could be dangerous if the fuel lines have been disconnected.*
• *When working with fuel system components, pay particular attention to cleanliness – dirt entering the fuel system may cause blockages which will lead to poor running.*

2 Fuel pipes and connections

1 Disconnect the battery as described in Chapter 5A, Section 3.
2 The fuel supply pipe connects the fuel pump in the fuel tank to the high pressure fuel pump on the engine.
3 Whenever you're working under the vehicle, be sure to inspect all fuel and evaporative emission pipes for leaks, kinks, dents and other damage. Always replace a damaged fuel pipe immediately.
4 If you find signs of dirt in the pipes during disassembly, disconnect all pipes and blow them out with compressed air. Inspect the fuel strainer on the fuel pump pick-up unit for damage and deterioration.

Steel tubing

5 It is critical that the fuel pipes be

replaced with pipes of equivalent type and specification.
6 Some steel fuel pipes have threaded fittings. When loosening these fittings, hold the stationary fitting with a spanner while turning the union nut.

Plastic tubing

⚠️ *Warning: When removing or installing plastic fuel tubing, be careful not to bend or twist it too much, which can damage it. Also, plastic fuel tubing is NOT heat resistant, so keep it away from excessive heat.*

7 When replacing fuel system plastic tubing, use only original equipment replacement plastic tubing.

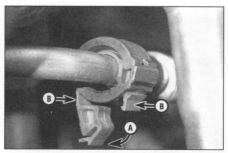

2.10g Some fittings are secured by lock tabs. Release the lock tab (A) and rotate it to the fully-opened position, squeeze the two smaller lock tabs (B)...

Flexible hoses

8 When replacing fuel system flexible hoses, use original equipment replacements, or hose to the same specification.
9 Don't route fuel hoses (or metal pipes) within 100 mm of the exhaust system or within 280 mm of the catalytic converter. Make sure that no rubber hoses are installed directly against the vehicle, particularly in places where there is any vibration. If allowed to touch some vibrating part of the vehicle, a hose can easily become chafed and it might start leaking. A good rule of thumb is to maintain a minimum of 8.0 mm clearance around a hose (or metal pipe) to prevent contact with the vehicle underbody.

Disconnecting Fuel pipe Fittings

10 Typical fuel pipe fittings:

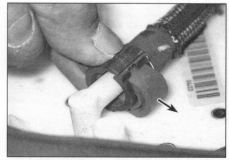

2.10h...then push the retainer out and pull the fuel pipe off the pipe

2.10i Spring-lock coupling; remove the safety cover, install a coupling release tool and close the tool around the coupling...

2.10j...push the tool into the fitting, then pull the two pipes apart

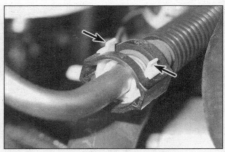

2.10k Hairpin clip type fitting: push the legs of the retainer clip together, then push the clip down all the way until it stops and pull the fuel pipe off the pipe

3.1a Release the clamp . . .

3.1b . . . and disconnect the hose from the throttle body

3 Air cleaner assembly – removal and refitting

Removal

1.8 and 2.0 litre models

1 Release the clamp and disconnect the air outlet hose from the throttle body **(see illustrations)**.
2 Release the rubber strap at the front of the air cleaner housing **(see illustration)**.
3 Pull the air cleaner assembly straight up from its rubber mountings, then disconnect the breather from the base of the housing as it's withdrawn **(see illustrations)**.

2.4 litre models

4 Undo the 2 retaining screws and detach the intake from the bonnet slam panel **(see illustration)**.
5 Gently pull the vacuum hose from the air cleaner assembly **(see illustration)**.
6 Slacken the air outlet hose clamp and disconnect the hose **(see illustration)**.
7 Slide the ECU cover upwards from place, and disconnect the wiring plugs **(see illustrations)**.
8 Disconnect the wiring plug from the mass airflow sensor.
9 Make alignment marks between the bracket

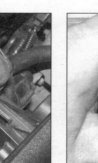

3.2 Release the rubber strap

3.3a Squeeze together the side of the collar and disconnect the breather hose . . .

3.3b . . . and remove the air cleaner assembly

3.4 Remove the air intake from the slam panel

3.5 Pull the vacuum hose (arrowed) from the front of the air cleaner assembly

and the chassis, then remove the 2 bolts securing the right-hand engine mounting to the chassis member, and push the right-hand end of the engine rearwards 20 to 30 mm.

10 Pull the air filter assembly upwards to release it from the rubber mountings, then undo the wiring guide screw, slide the assembly to the left-hand side and manoeuvre it from position **(see illustration)**.

Refitting

11 In all cases, refit by reversing the removal operations.

---

4 Accelerator pedal – removal and refitting

Removal

1 Carefully prise the panel in front of the centre console from place, releasing the 4 retaining clips **(see illustration)**.

2 Prise away the rear edge of the trim panel at the driver's side end of the facia and release the lower facia panel outer clip **(see illustration)**.

3 Undo the 3 retaining screws and remove the lower facia panel **(see illustration)**. Disconnect any wiring plugs as the panel is withdrawn.

4 Undo the three nuts securing the assembly to the bulkhead **(see illustration)**.

5 Release the cable tie, and disconnect the position sensor wiring plug as the pedal assembly is removed. No further dismantling of the assembly is recommended.

Refitting

6 Refit by reversing the removal operations.

---

5 Fuel gauge sender/ pump unit – removal and refitting

Note: *Observe the precautions in Section 1 before working on any component in the fuel system.*

Removal

1 Remove the fuel tank as described in Section 6.

4.3 Undo the 3 screws (arrowed) and remove the facia lower panel

3.6 Release the clamp (arrowed) and disconnect the outlet hose

3.7b . . . then lever over the catches and disconnect the wiring plugs

2 Unscrew the pump/sender unit plastic retaining collar using a pair of large, crossed-screwdrivers, or improvise a tool **(see illustration)**.

3 Lift the pump/sender unit from the tank

4.1 Pull the panel in front of the centre console rearwards to release the clips

4.4 Accelerator pedal assembly retaining nuts (arrowed)

3.7a Slide up the ECU cover . . .

3.10 Manoeuvre the air cleaner assembly from position

(see illustration). Discard the O-ring seal, a new one must be fitted.

4 Although a filter is fitted to the base of the fuel pump/sender unit, no separate parts are available.

4.2 Prise the facia end panel away, and remove the clip (arrowed)

5.2 Use a home-made tool to slacken the sender unit retaining collar

5.3 Carefully lift the sender/pump unit from the tank, taking care not to bend the float arm

5.5 Connect a multimeter to the sender unit terminals, and measure the resistance at full, and zero deflection – see text

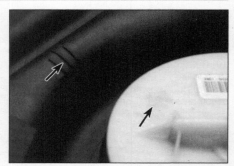

5.6 Align the mark on the tank with the arrow on the sender unit (arrowed)

5 If required, attach the leads from a multimeter to the sender unit wires (orange and green), and measure the resistance at full float deflection and zero deflection. The resistance of the unit we tested was 200 ohms at zero deflection, and 10 ohms at full deflection **(see illustration)**.

Refitting

6 Refitting is a reversal of removal, bearing in mind the following points:

a) Use a new O-ring seal smeared with petroleum jelly.

b) Position the sender/pump units, so the arrow on the cover aligns with the mark on the fuel tank **(see illustration)**.

c) Tighten the sender/pump unit retaining collar to the specified torque, where tools permit.

---

6 Fuel tank –
removal and refitting

Note: *Observe the precautions in Section 1 before working on any component in the fuel system.*

Removal

1 Before the tank can be removed, it must be drained of as much fuel as possible. To avoid the dangers and complications of fuel handling and storage, it is advisable to carry out this operation with the tank almost empty.

2 Disconnect the battery negative lead (see Chapter 5A).

3 Slacken the left-rear roadwheel bolts, then

chock the front wheels and jack up the rear of the vehicle and support it on axle stands (see *Jacking and vehicle support*). Remove the roadwheel.

4 Remove the rear section of the exhaust system as described in Section 13. Support the front section of the system to avoid placing any strain on the flexible section.

5 Undo the plastic nuts and remove the heat shield beneath the tank.

6 Release the clamps and disconnect the fuel filler and breather hoses where they join the metal pipes **(see illustration)**. Be prepared for fuel spillage. If the clamps are at all damaged, renew them.

7 On some models, it may be necessary to remove the carbon canister first as described in Chapter 4C, Section 4.

8 Press in the release buttons (prise up the white locking element on the supply pipe first) and disconnect the fuel delivery and carbon canister pipes located in front of the tank **(see illustration)**.

9 Working at the rear of the tank, press in the release button and disconnect the pipe to the carbon canister **(see illustration)**.

10 Position a trolley jack under the centre of the tank. Insert a protective wooden pad between the jack head and tank base, then raise the jack to just take the weight of the tank.

11 Undo the tank retaining straps, and carefully lower the jack and tank slightly.

12 Disconnect the fuel sender/pump unit wiring connector from the top of the tank **(see illustration)**.

13 Lower the front of the tank and slide it forward, feeding the hoses over the top of the rear subframe, and remove the tank from under the car.

14 If the tank is contaminated with sediment or water, remove the gauge sender unit and the fuel pump as described previously. Swill the tank out with clean fuel.

15 The tank is moulded from a synthetic material and if damaged it should be renewed. However, in certain cases it may be possible to have small leaks or minor damage repaired. Seek the advice of a dealer or suitable specialist concerning tank repair.

16 If a new tank is to be fitted, transfer all

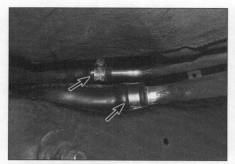

6.6 Release the clamps (arrowed) and disconnect the fuel filler and breather pipes

6.8 Prise up the white locking catch (arrowed), then press in the button and disconnect the fuel supply pipe

6.9 Press in the release button, then disconnect the carbon canister pipe from the rear of the tank (arrowed)

6.12 Depress the release clip (arrowed) and disconnect the sender unit wiring plug

the components from the old tank to the new. Always renew the seal between the fuel pump/gauge sender unit and the tank.

Refitting

17 Refitting is a reversal of removal, bearing in mind the following points:

a) *Before raising the tank to its final position, reconnect the sender/pump unit wiring plug, and clip the carbon canister hose into the top of the tank.*

b) *On completion, refill the tank with fuel and check exhaustively for signs of leakage before driving the car on the road.*

7 Fuel injection system – general information

General information

This is a microprocessor-controlled engine management system, designed to meet stringent emission control legislation whilst still providing excellent engine performance and fuel economy. This is achieved by continuously monitoring the engine using various sensors, whose data is input to the system's Electronic Control Unit (ECU). Note that the ECU may also be referred to as the ECM (Electronic Control Module). Based on this information, the ECU program and memory then determine the exact amount of fuel necessary, which is injected directly sequentially into the intake manifold, for all actual and anticipated driving conditions. The ECU also controls the engine ignition functions (see Chapter 5B), and the engine emission control systems (see Chapter 4C).

The main components of the fuel side of the system are as follows.

Electronic control unit

The ECU is a microprocessor which controls the entire operation of the fuel, ignition, engine cooling fan, camshaft position (where applicable) and emission systems. Contained in the module memory are programmes which control the fuel supply to the injectors, and their opening duration. The programme enters sub-routines to alter these parameters, according to inputs from the other components of the system. In addition to this, the engine idle speed is controlled by the ECU, which uses a motorised throttle unit. The ECU also incorporates a self-diagnostic facility, in which the entire fuel/ignition system is continuously monitored for correct operation. Any detected faults are logged as fault codes which can be downloaded using a piece of equipment called a fault code reader. In the event of a fault in the system due to loss of a signal from one of the sensors, the ECU may to an emergency (limp-home) program. This will allow the car to be driven, although engine operation and performance will be limited.

The ECU has several adaptive (self-learning) functions, enabling it to continually adapt to changing circumstances through the life of the vehicle (wear, fuel differences, etc).

The engine management ECU also receives information from the vehicle's other control modules (Central electronic module, Brake control module, Climate control module, Transmission control module (auto only), Steering wheel module, Driver information module, and the Electrical power steering module), via a databus network known as a CAN databus (Controller Area Network). On some models, a LIN (Local Interconnect Network) is used for some inter-ECU communication (Alternator control module 2005-on).

Fuel injectors

Each fuel injector consists of a solenoid-operated needle valve, which opens under commands from the ECU. Fuel from the fuel rail is then delivered sequentially through the injector nozzle into the intake manifold.

Coolant temperature sensor

This resistive device is screwed into the thermostat housing, where its element is in direct contact with the engine coolant. Changes in coolant temperature are detected by the ECU as a change in sensor resistance. The sensor is a negative temperature coefficient type, where the resistance decreases as the temperature increases. Signals from the coolant temperature sensor are also used by the temperature gauge in the instrument panel.

Manifold absolute pressure/ Intake air temperature sensor

This combined sensor measures both the pressure/vacuum and temperature of the air entering the intake manifold. The MAP sensor is a semi-conductor where a silicone membrane is actuated by the pressure acting upon it. The voltage signal from the MAP sensor changes in proportion to the pressure – as the pressure increases, so does the voltage. The temperature sensor is a negative temperature coefficient, where the resistance of the sensor decreases as the temperature increases. Note that the intake air temperature sensor is not fitted to 2.4 litre models – only the MAP sensor.

Mass airflow/ Intake air temperature sensor

2.4 litre models

The MAF sensor measures the mass of air drawn into the engine. The sensor is of the hot-wire type, containing a resistive element which has a ceramic coating. The unit is located in the air cleaner intake, and uses the intake air to alter the resistance of the element. The combined sensor also incorporates an intake air temperature sensor. This is a negative coefficient temperature sensor, where the resistance decreases as the temperature increases.

Accelerator pedal position sensor

The accelerator pedal position sensor contains two potentiometers and an analogue-to-digital converter. The pedal shaft is connected to the potentiometers, whose resistance changes relative to pedal position. The sensor transmits both an analogue and digital signal to the ECU, informing it of the pedal position and rate of change. This information is used be the ECU to control the motorised throttle control unit. No throttle cable is fitted.

Electronic throttle module

The throttle control unit regulates the amount of air entering the intake manifold. It consists of a throttle valve (disc), a DC motor and gears, and two potentiometers which report the position of the throttle valve to the ECU. There is no throttle cable fitted – the position of the throttle valve is controlled by the ECU via the electric motor.

Fuel pump

The electric fuel pump is located in the fuel tank, and totally submerged in the fuel. The unit is a two-stage device consisting of an electric motor which drives an impeller pump to draw in fuel, and a gear pump to discharge it under pressure. The fuel is then supplied to the fuel rail on the intake manifold via an in-line fuel filter.

Fuel pressure regulator

The function of the fuel pressure regulator is incorporated into the fuel tank-mounted pump module.

Stop-lamp switch

Informs the ECU of the brake pedal position, for cruise control functions.

Clutch pedal switch

Manual transmission

Informs the ECU of the clutch pedal position for cruise control functions.

Fuel pressure/ temperature sensor

2.4 litre models

This Piezo resistor in fitted to the fuel rail. As pressure acts upon the sensor, the output voltage varies proportionally. The temperature detection element of the sensor is a negative temperature coefficient sensor, where the resistance decreases as the temperature increases.

Air conditioning pressure sensor

Located in the high-pressure side of the air conditioning system, this sensor informs the ECM of the system pressure to enable control of the engine cooling fan (to cool the condenser) and the compressor, and adjusts the idle speed relative to compressor load.

8.2 The diagnostic connector is located under the driver's side of the facia

Crankshaft position/ speed sensor

1.8 and 2.0 litre models

As the engine crankshaft rotates, a toothed wheel behind the crankshaft pulley also rotates. Mounted next to this pulley is an inductive sensor. As the toothed wheel rotates, an alternating current is induced in the sensor. The rotational speed of the crankshaft is calculated by the engine management ECU from the current induced. In order that the ECU can determine the position of the crankshaft, one of the teeth on the wheel is missing. This is known as the reference position. As this gap passes the sensor, the induced current drops to zero, allowing the ECU to recognise the crankshaft position. Although the rotational position of the crankshaft can be monitored, the sensor cannot determine which 'stroke' (compression, exhaust, etc) the engine is on. For this information, the ECU must rely on the camshaft position sensor.

2.4 litre models

As the engine flywheel rotates, a series of drilled/punch holes (6° apart) on its circumference pass the tip of the sensor, fitted at the rear of the engine above the flywheel. As the sensor is inductive with a permanent magnet, the passing flywheel/holes generate an AC voltage in the sensor. The frequency of this voltage, is directly proportional to the speed of the engine. In order to monitor the position of the crankshaft, two holes are missing. These missing holes create an anomaly in the signal, from which the ECU can determine the exact

9.2 Mass airflow sensor screws (arrowed)

position of the crankshaft. The first tooth after the mission holes is located at 84° before TDC on cylinder number 1.

Camshaft position sensor

In order to determine the position of the camshaft, this sensor is located adjacent the camshaft flanges. On each flange are 'flanks' which have one tooth each. These teeth are not equally spaced (the flanks are not symmetrical), so as they pass by then sensor tip, the permanent magnetic in the sensor generates an AC voltage – the pattern of which informs the ECU of the position, and the frequency represents the speed.

Camshaft reset valve

2.4 litre models

This valve, fitted to the cylinder head, controls the flow of oil to the continuously variable valve timing (CVVT) unit on the camshaft. The flow of oil to these units determines the camshaft's radial position. The voltage to the solenoid is controlled by the engine management ECU.

8 Fuel injection system – testing and adjustment

1 If a fault appears in the fuel injection system, first ensure that all the system wiring connectors are securely connected and free of corrosion. Then ensure that the fault is not due to poor maintenance; ie, check that the air cleaner filter element is clean, the spark plugs are in good condition and correctly gapped, the cylinder compression pressures are correct, the ignition timing is correct and the engine breather hoses are clear and undamaged, referring to Chapters 1A, 2A, 2B and 5B.
2 If these checks fail to reveal the cause of the problem, a diagnostic connector is under the driver's side facia above the pedals, into which a fault code reader can be plugged **(see illustration)**. The test equipment is capable of interrogating the engine management system electronically and accessing its internal fault log.
3 Fault codes can only be extracted from the ECU using a dedicated fault code reader.

9.4 Manifold absolute pressure/Intake air temperature sensor – 2.4 litre models

A Volvo dealer will obviously have such a reader, but they are also available from other suppliers. It is unlikely to be cost-effective for the private owner to purchase a fault code reader, but a well-equipped local garage or auto electrical specialist will have one.
4 Using this equipment, faults can be pinpointed quickly and simply, even if their occurrence is intermittent. Testing all the system components individually in an attempt to locate the fault by elimination is a time-consuming operation that is unlikely to be fruitful (particularly if the fault occurs dynamically), and carries high risk of damage to the ECU's internal components.
5 Experienced home mechanics equipped with an accurate tachometer and a carefully-calibrated exhaust gas analyser may be able to check the exhaust gas CO content and the engine idle speed; if these are found to be out of specification, then the vehicle must be taken to a suitably-equipped Volvo dealer or specialist for assessment. Neither the air/ fuel mixture (exhaust gas CO content) nor the engine idle speed are manually adjustable; incorrect test results indicate the need for maintenance (possibly, injector cleaning) or a fault within the fuel injection system.

9 Fuel injection system components – removal and refitting

Note: *Refer to the precautions in Section 1 before working on any component in the fuel system. The following procedures are applicable to all fuel injection systems unless otherwise stated.*

Mass airflow/ Intake air temperature sensor

2.4 litre models

1 Remove the air cleaner assembly as described in Section 3.
2 Undo the two screws and remove the sensor from the air cleaner cover **(see illustration)**.
3 Refit by reversing the removal operations.

Manifold absolute pressure/ Intake air temperature sensor

2.4 litre models

4 The sensor is fitted to the left-hand upper end of the intake manifold **(see illustration)**.
5 Disconnect the wiring plug, then pull the sensor from the manifold.
6 Refit by reversing the removal operations.

1.8 and 2.0 litre models

7 Jack up the front of the vehicle, and support it securely on axle stands (see *Jacking and vehicle support*). Where fitted, undo the 7 Torx screws, and remove the engine undershield.
8 Disconnect the sensor wiring plug, then undo the retaining screws and remove the sensor from the lower, left-hand edge of the intake manifold **(see illustration)**.
9 Refitting is the reversal of removal.

9.8 On 1.8 and 2.0 litre models, the MAP sensor is located at the lower, left-hand edge of the manifold (arrowed)

9.12 Depress the clip and pull the wiring plug from each injector

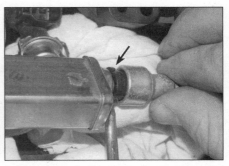

9.13 Press-in the sleeve (arrowed) and disconnect the fuel supply hose from the rail

Fuel rail and injectors

Note: *If an injector problem is suspected, it might be worth trying the effect of a proprietary injector cleaner petrol treatment before removing the injectors.*

10 Depressurise the fuel system as described in Section 1.

Removal – 1.8 and 2.0 litre models

11 Pull the plastic cover on the top of the engine straight up from its mountings.

12 Depress the clips and disconnect the wiring plug from each of the injectors (**see illustration**). Release the clips and free the wiring harness from the fuel rail.

13 Disconnect the quick-release fuel line coupling from the fuel rail by pushing back the coupling sleeves (**see illustration**). Be prepared for fuel spillage as the coupling is released. Plug the coupling after disconnection to prevent further loss of fuel.

14 Clean the area around the injectors, then remove the fuel rail mounting bolts (**see illustration**).

15 Gently work the injectors loose, and pull the rail upwards to release the injectors from the cylinder head, and remove the rail complete with injectors.

16 Prise out each retaining clip and pull the injectors from the fuel rail (**see illustration**). Discard the clip and the O-ring seal; new ones must be fitted.

Removal – 2.4 litre models

17 Remove the air cleaner assembly as described in Section 3.

18 Slacken the clamp and disconnect the air intake hose from the manifold (**see illustration 3.6**).

19 Undo the 6 bolts at the front of the intake manifold, and the 2 at the rear (**see illustrations**). Lift off the manifold upper section and place it to one side.

20 Release the clips and disconnect the wiring plug from each injector (**see illustration**).

21 Clean the area around the injectors, then undo the fuel rail mounting bolts (**see illustration**).

22 Disconnect the fuel supply hose from the fuel rail.

23 Spray some penetrating oil around the injector locations in the intake manifold,

9.14 Fuel rail mounting bolts (arrowed)

then pull the fuel rail, complete with injectors upwards from the manifold.

24 Undo the retaining screws, remove the injector retaining plate, and unclip the injectors.

9.19a The upper section of the manifold is retained by 6 screws at the front . . .

9.20 Depress the clip (arrowed) and pull the wiring plug from each injector

9.16 Prise out the clip and disconnect the injector from the rail

Refitting

25 Refit by reversing the removal operations, and noting the following points:

a) *Check that the injector O-rings and*

9.19b . . . and 2 at the rear (arrowed)

9.21 Fuel rail mounting bolts (arrowed)

9.29 Electronic throttle module screws (arrowed) – 1.8 and 2.0 litre models

9.32 Disconnect the throttle body wiring plug – 2.4 litre models

9.33 Electronic throttle module bolts (arrowed) – 2.4 litre models

manifold/cylinder head seals are in good condition, and renew them if necessary.

b) *Smear the O-rings with petroleum jelly or silicone grease as an assembly lubricant.*

c) *Ensure that all wiring and fuel line connections are correctly and securely made.*

d) *Tighten the fuel rail retaining bolts to the specified torque setting.*

Electronic throttle module

1.8 and 2.0 litre models

26 Disconnect the battery negative lead as described in Chapter 5A.

27 Pull the plastic cover on the top of the engine straight up from its mountings.

28 Slacken the clamp and disconnect the air intake hose between the electronic throttle module and the air cleaner assembly.

29 Disconnect the wiring plug, undo the four screws and remove the electronic throttle module **(see illustration)**. Discard the gasket, a new one must be fitted.

30 Refit by reversing the removal operations, using a new gasket. Fit new hose clips if necessary, and tighten the electronic throttle module retaining screws to the specified torque.

2.4 litre models

31 Remove the air cleaner assembly as described in Section 3.

32 Disconnect the electronic throttle module wiring plug **(see illustration)**.

33 Undo the 4 retaining bolts and remove the electronic throttle module **(see illustration)**. Discard the gasket and the retaining bolts – new ones must be fitted.

34 Refit by reversing the removal operations,

using a new gasket and new retaining bolts. Tighten the electronic throttle module retaining bolts to the specified torque.

Coolant temperature sensor

35 Refer to Chapter 3.

Electronic control unit

Note: *If a new control unit is fitted, it must be programmed using dedicated Volvo test equipment. Entrust this task to a Volvo dealer or suitably-equipped specialist.*

36 Disconnect the battery negative lead as described in Chapter 5A.

Caution: Wait at least two minutes after the ignition has been switched off for any residual energy to drain from the main system relay.

Removal – 1.8 and 2.0 litre models

37 Clean off the top of the ECU box lid, to make sure no debris falls inside when it is removed. Release the catch on the top of the ECU module box cover. Lift off the cover and place it to one side **(see illustration)**.

38 Undo the 3 ECU retaining screws, then release the locking levers and disconnect the wiring plugs **(see illustration)**. Remove the ECU. **Note:** *Do not touch the control module terminal pins with bare hands – there is a danger of damage due to static electricity.*

Removal – 2.4 litre models

39 Slide up and remove the ECU cover **(see illustration 3.7a)**.

40 Release the locking levers and disconnect the wiring plugs from the ECU **(see illustration 3.7b)**. **Note:** *Do not touch the control module terminal pins with bare hands – there is a danger of damage due to static electricity.*

41 Undo the 5 Torx screws and remove the ECU **(see illustration)**.

Refitting

42 Refitting is a reversal of removal.

Crankshaft position/speed sensor

1.8 and 2.0 litre models

43 Jack up the front of the vehicle and support it securely on axle stands (see *Jacking and vehicle support*). Where fitted, undo the 7 Torx screws, and remove the engine undershield **(see illustration)**.

9.37 Depress the clip and lift off the ECU cover – 1.8 and 2.0 litre models

9.38 Lever out the catches (arrowed) and disconnect the ECU plugs

9.41 Undo the screws (arrowed) and detach the ECU from the air cleaner assembly

9.43 Undo the 7 Torx screws (arrowed) and remove the engine undershield (where fitted)

44 The sensor is located adjacent to the crankshaft pulley. Disconnect the sensor wiring plug (see illustration).
45 Undo the 2 retaining bolts and remove the sensor.
46 Refitting is a reversal of removal, tightening the sensor retaining bolts securely.

2.4 litre models

47 Remove the air cleaner assembly as described in Section 3.
48 Undo the 8 bolts securing the upper section of the intake manifold, then position the manifold (with intake hose still attached), to one side. Cover the openings in the lower section of the manifold to prevent contamination.
49 The sensor is located above the transmission housing at the left-hand end of the cylinder block. Hold the radiator hose to one side, disconnect the sensor wiring plug, then undo the nut and remove the sensor. Discard the nut; a new one must be fitted.
50 Refitting is a reversal of removal, tightening the new retaining nut to the specified torque, and refit the manifold using a new gasket.

Camshaft position sensor

1.8 and 2.0 litre models

51 Remove the plastic cover on the top of the engine straight up from its mountings.
52 Disconnect the sensor wiring plug, undo the screw and remove the sensor (see illustration).
53 Refitting is a reversal of removal, tightening the retaining screw to the specified torque.

2.4 litre models

54 Slacken the clamp and disconnect the air intake hose from the intake manifold.
55 Undo the 8 retaining bolts and move the upper section of the intake manifold to one side (see illustration 9.19a and 9.19b).
56 There may be 2 sensors: one over the inlet camshaft, and one over the exhaust camshaft, both located at the left-hand end of the cylinder head cover. Disconnect the sensor(s) wiring plug (see illustration).
57 Undo the retaining screw(s) and remove the sensor(s).
58 Refitting is a reversal of removal, using a new manifold upper section gasket.

Camshaft reset valve

2.4 litre models

59 Undo the clips/screws, and remove the timing belt upper cover.
60 Clean the area around the valve to prevent any dirt ingress, then disconnect the valve wiring plug.
61 Undo the retaining screw, and remove the valve (see illustration). Discard the seal.
62 Ensure the mating faces are clean, then refit the valve using a new seal, with the bevelled edge of the seal facing downwards. Tighten the retaining screw securely.
63 Refit the timing belt cover.

9.44 Crankshaft speed/position sensor (arrowed) – 1.8 and 2.0 litre models

9.56 Inlet camshaft position sensor – 2.4 litre models

Clutch pedal position switch

64 Refer to Chapter 6.

Fuel pump module

2.4 litre models

65 Disconnect the battery negative lead as described in Chapter 5A.
66 Remove the left-hand rear seat cushion as described in Chapter 11.
67 Pull up and remove the left-hand rear door sill trim panel, then fold the carpet forwards.
68 Disconnect the module wiring plug, then pull the module upwards from its mounting pad (see illustration).
69 Refitting is the reversal of removal.

Fuel pressure sensor

2.4 litre models

70 Depressurise the fuel system as described in Section 1.

9.68 Fuel pump module – 2.4 litre models

9.52 Camshaft position sensor – 1.8 and 2.0 litre models

9.61 Camshaft reset valve – 2.4 litre models

71 Undo the screws and remove the upper timing belt cover.
72 Disconnect the sensor wiring plug.
73 Cover the alternator to prevent fuel ingress, then undo the retaining screw and remove the sensor (see illustration). Be prepared for fuel spillage.
74 Refitting is the reversal of removal. Check for fuel leakage after starting the engine.

Fuel pump suppression filter

Note: *The suppression filter is only fitted to vehicles in certain markets.*

1.8 and 2.0 litre models

75 Ensure the ignition is switched off, remove the rear seat cushion as described in Chapter 11.
76 Pull the front edge upwards, then pull the rear edge forwards, and remove the left-hand rear door sill trim panel.
77 Fold forward the carpet and undo the suppression filter retaining bolt.

9.73 Fuel pressure sensor – 2.4 litre models

11.2a Disconnect the EVAP hose . . .

11.2b . . . and brake servo hose from the front of the manifold

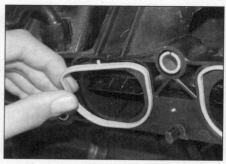

11.9 Renew the intake manifold seals

78 Note their fitted positions, then disconnect the filter wiring plugs as it is withdrawn.
79 Refitting is a reversal of removal.

Stop-light switch

80 Refer to Chapter 9, Section 17.

10 Cruise control –
general information

When fitted, the cruise control allows the vehicle to maintain a steady speed selected by the driver, regardless of gradients or prevailing winds.

The main components of the system is the control software (part of the steering wheel module), and a control switch. Brake and (when applicable) clutch pedal switches protect the engine against excessive speeds or loads should a pedal be depressed whilst the system is in use.

In operation, the driver accelerates to the desired speed, and then brings the system into use by means of the switch. The control software then monitors vehicle speed (from the wheel speed sensors) and opens or closes the throttle by means of the motorised throttle control unit. If the switch is moved to OFF, or the brake or clutch pedal is depressed, the control software immediately closes the throttle. The set speed is stored in the control module memory and the system can be reactivated by moving the switch to RESUME, provided that vehicle speed has not dropped below 25 mph.

12.3 Undo the steering column joint pinch-bolt (arrowed)

The driver can override the cruise control for overtaking simply by depressing the throttle pedal. When the pedal is released, the set speed will be resumed.

The cruise control cannot be engaged at speeds below 25 mph, and should not be used in slippery or congested conditions.

For removal and refitting procedures:
a) Steering wheel module – Chapter 10.
b) Cruise control switch – Chapter 12.
c) Electronic throttle module – Section 9 of this Chapter.

11 Inlet manifold –
removal and refitting

Note: *Observe the precautions in Section 1 before working on any component in the fuel system.*

1.8 and 2.0 litre models

Removal

1 Remove the electronic throttle module as described in Section 9.
2 Note their fitted positions and disconnect the EVAP canister and brake servo vacuum hoses from the manifold **(see illustrations)**.
3 Disconnect the wiring plug from the pressure sensor at the lower left-hand corner of the manifold.
4 Undo the fuel rail mounting bolts **(see illustration 9.14)**, and move the fuel rail and injectors to one side. Plug or cover the openings in the cylinder head to prevent contamination.
5 Undo the 2 screws securing the oil level dipstick tube, and pull it from place. Check the condition of the O-ring seal at the base of the tube and renew it if necessary.
6 The inlet manifold is secured by 7 bolts at its upper edge, and 1 bolt at its lower edge. Undo the bolts.
7 Note their fitted positions, and disconnect the vacuum hoses from the control valves on the manifold. Disconnect the crankcase breather hose and remove the manifold. Discard the seals. **Note:** *We found it preferable to disconnect the manifold geometry change-over actuator vacuum hose at the solenoid.*

Refitting

8 Refit by reversing the removal operations, using a new manifold gasket, and new seals and O-rings for the injectors if necessary.
9 Locate the manifold seals on the manifold, and place the manifold in position **(see illustration)**. Where applicable, remember to feed the crankcase ventilation hose up between the second and third ducts. Tighten the bolts securely.

2.4 litre models

Removal

10 Remove the fuel injectors as described in Section 9.
11 Slacken the lower row of manifold retaining bolts, then remove the upper and outer bolts and lift the manifold from position. Disconnect the hose between the manifold and oil separator as the manifold is withdrawn. Discard the gasket.

Refitting

12 Refitting is a reversal of removal, using new gaskets/seals where necessary, and tightening the fasteners to their specified torque where given.

12 Exhaust manifold –
removal and refitting

1.8 and 2.0 litre models

Removal

1 Disconnect the battery negative lead (see Chapter 5A).
2 Ensure the steering wheel is in the straight-ahead position, then engage the steering lock to secure the column in this position. **Note:** *If only the manifold gasket is to be renewed, ignore this Step.*
3 Working under the facia, pull up the plastic boot, make alignment marks between the steering column universal joint and the steering rack pinion. Undo the pinch-bolt and pull the joint upwards from the pinion **(see illustration)**. **Note:** *If only the manifold gasket is to be renewed, ignore this Step.*
4 Remove the plastic cover on top of the

engine by pulling it straight up from its mountings.

5 Disconnect the front and rear oxygen sensor wiring plugs **(see illustration). Note:** *If only the manifold gasket is to be renewed, ignore this Step.*

6 Undo the 4 bolts and remove the heat shield from the upper side of the manifold.

7 Undo the nuts securing the manifold to the cylinder head. Discard the nuts, new ones must be fitted.

8 Raise the front of the vehicle and support it securely on axle stands (see *Jacking and vehicle support*).

9 Undo the 2 bolts securing the mounting bracket to the catalytic converter.

10 Undo the 2 bolts and remove the SIPS crossmember from under the exhaust system **(see illustration).**

11 Undo the nuts and disconnect the exhaust pipe from the manifold/catalytic converter.

12 Detach the catalytic converter from the rubber mountings, and pull the manifold away from the cylinder head. Discard the gasket. If the manifold is only being removed to renew the gasket, no further dismantling is necessary.

13 Undo the bolts and remove the lower torque rod and mounting bracket from the between the engine/transmission casing and the subframe.

14 Make alignment marks between the front subframe and the vehicle body, then position a trolley jack under the subframe. Undo the subframe mounting bolts and lower it approximately 10 cm – just enough to manoeuvre the manifold/catalytic converter downwards, out of position, and out from under the vehicle.

Refitting

15 If a new manifold/catalytic converter is being fitted, transfer the oxygen sensors from the old manifold to the new one, using a little high-temperature copper grease on the threads.

16 Fit a new gasket between onto the mounting studs in the cylinder head, then manoeuvre the manifold/catalytic converter into place. Fit the new mounting nuts, but only finger-tighten them at this stage.

17 Reconnect the exhaust pipe to the manifold/catalytic converter, and tighten the nuts securely.

18 Refit the SIPS crossmember and tighten the bolts securely.

19 Refit and tighten the catalytic converter mounting bracket bolts.

20 Carefully raise the front subframe, aligning the previously-made marks, and the steering rack pinion with the steering column universal joint. In order to check the alignment of the subframe, Volvo use a special tool (No 999 7089) which fits through two corresponding holes in the subframe and chassis. In the absence of these tools, use two round pieces of wood – see Chapter 10, Section 15.

21 Refit and tighten the subframe mounting bolts to the specified torque.

12.5 The oxygen sensor wiring plugs are located at the left-hand end of the cylinder head

22 Refit the lower torque rod and mounting bracket, tightening the bolts to the specified torque.

23 Now tighten the nuts securing the manifold to the cylinder head.

24 The remainder of refitting is a reversal of removal, noting that a new steering column universal joint pinch-bolt should be fitted.

2.4 litre models

Removal

25 Undo the 5 bolts securing the heat shield to the exhaust manifold. Leave the shield loose on the manifold.

26 Undo the nuts securing the manifold to the cylinder head.

27 Disconnect the front oxygen sensor wiring plug, and release the wiring harness from the clips **(see illustration).**

28 Raise the front of the vehicle and support it securely on axle stands (see *Jacking and vehicle support*).

29 Undo the 2 bolts and remove the SIPS crossmember from under the exhaust pipe. Release the rear oxygen sensor wiring harness from the clip on the crossmember as it is withdrawn.

30 Disconnect the rear oxygen sensor wiring plug, then undo the nuts securing the exhaust manifold to the catalytic converter **(see illustration).**

31 Undo the nuts securing the catalytic converter to the exhaust pipe, then unhook the rubber mountings and remove the catalytic converter.

32 If it is only required to renew the gasket,

12.27 Front oxygen sensor wiring plug – 2.4 litre models

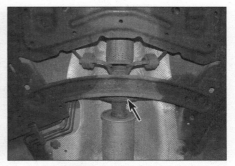

12.10 SIPS crossmember (arrowed)

pull the manifold rearwards from the cylinder head and discard the gasket.

33 If the manifold is to be renewed, undo the bolts and remove the lower torque rod and mounting bracket from between the engine/transmission casing and the subframe.

34 Lower the exhaust manifold and remove it from the vehicle.

Refitting

35 Ensure the mating faces of the cylinder head and exhaust manifold are clean, then install the new gaskets over the studs in the cylinder head. Apply anti-seize grease (Copperslip) to the manifold studs.

36 Position the heat shield on the manifold, then fit the manifold to the cylinder, tightening the new nuts to the specified torque.

37 Apply anti-seize grease (Copperslip) to their threads, then tighten the heat shield bolts securely.

38 The remainder of refitting is a reversal of removal.

13 Exhaust system –
   general information
   and component renewal

General information

1 On 2.4 litre models, the exhaust system consists of a front section which comprises a front pipe and silencer, an intermediate section which also incorporates a silencer, and a rear section comprising silencer and tailpipe. On 1.8 and 2.0 litre models, the

12.30 Catalytic converter-to-manifold nuts (arrowed)

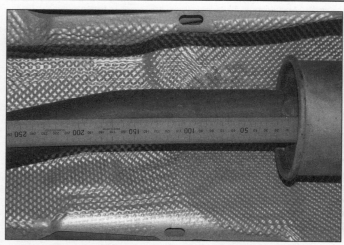

13.9 Measure back 105 mm from the rear edge of the front silencer – 1.8 and 2.0 litre models

13.11 Measure 100 mm back from the welded bracket behind the centre silencer – 2.4 litre models

system consists of a front pipe and silencer, intermediate pipe and silencer and a tail pipe. The system is suspended from the underbody on rubber mountings, and bolted to the exhaust manifold/catalytic converter at the front.

2 The exhaust system should be examined for leaks, damage and security at regular intervals (see Chapter 1A). To do this, apply the handbrake, and allow the engine to idle in a well-ventilated area. Lie down on each side of the car in turn, and check the full length of the system for leaks, while an assistant temporarily places a wad of cloth over the end of the tailpipe. If a leak is evident, stop the engine and use a proprietary repair kit to seal it. If the leak is excessive, or damage is evident, renew the section. Check the rubber mountings for deterioration, and renew them if necessary.

Front section removal

3 With the handbrake applied, jack up the front (and preferably the rear) of the car, and support it securely on axle stands (see *Jacking and vehicle support*).

4 Where fitted, undo the 7 Torx screws and remove the engine undershield.

5 Undo the nuts securing the front pipe flange to the manifold/catalytic converter.

6 Undo the nuts and bolts connecting the front and intermediate sections.

7 Separate the front pipe-to-manifold/catalytic converter joint, and remove the front section from under the car.

Rear section removal

1.8 and 2.0 litre models

8 Chock the front wheels, then jack up the rear (and preferably the front) of the car, and support it on axle stands (see *Jacking and vehicle support*).

9 If this is the original exhaust system, measure 105 mm back from the rear edge of the front silencer and cut the pipe in two using a hacksaw **(see illustration)**.

10 If this is a repair exhaust system, undo the nut securing the clamp between the two exhaust sections, unhook the rubber mountings and remove the rear section.

2.4 litre models

11 If this is the original system, measure 100 mm back from the bracket welded to the exhaust pipe behind the centre silencer **(see illustration)**. Cut the pipe using a hacksaw.

12 If this is a repair exhaust system, slacken the clamp bolt, unhook the rubber mountings and remove the rear section.

Refitting

13 Refitting is a reversal of removal, bearing in mind the following points:

a) *Use a new sealing ring or flange gasket, as applicable, on the front pipe-to-manifold joint.*

b) *When refitting the front section, loosely attach the front pipe to the manifold/catalytic converter, and the exhaust pipe to the intermediate pipe. Align the system, then tighten the front pipe-to-manifold nuts first, followed by the intermediate pipe clamp nuts.*

c) *Ensure that there is a minimum clearance of 20 mm between the exhaust system and underbody/suspension components.*

d) *Repair rear silencers are available, which slip over the end of the existing exhaust pipe, and are clamped in place. Slip the new silencer over the pipe, engage the rubber silencer mountings, then tighten the pipe clamp securely.*

Chapter 4 Part B:
Fuel and exhaust systems – diesel models

Contents

Degrees of difficulty

Easy, suitable for novice with little experience	Fairly easy, suitable for beginner with some experience 	Fairly difficult, suitable for competent DIY mechanic	Difficult, suitable for experienced DIY mechanic	Very difficult, suitable for expert DIY or professional

Specifications

General
System type: .... Direct injection common rail with Bosch or Siemens high pressure delivery pump, variable nozzle turbocharger, and intercooler

Torque wrench settings	Nm	lbf ft
Accelerator pedal securing nuts	10	7
Exhaust manifold to cylinder head:		
1.6 litre engines	24	18
2.0 litre 4-cylinder engine:		
Stage 1	15	11
Stage 2	25	18
2.0 litre 5-cylinder engine	20	15
2.4 litre engine:		
Stage 1	15	11
Stage 2	25	18
Fuel high pressure pipe union nuts*:		
1.6 litre engines:		
Stage 1	20	15
Stage 2	25	18
2.0 litre 4-cylinder engine:		
Stage 1	19	14
Stage 2	30	22
5-cylinder engines:		
Stage 1	10	7
Stage 2	Angle tighten a further 60°	
Fuel injection pump mounting screws:		
1.6 litre engines	22	16
2.0 litre 4-cylinder engine	20	15
5-cylinder engines	18	13
Fuel injector clamp screws*:		
1.6 litre engines:		
Stage 1	4	3
Stage 2	Angle-tighten a further 65°	
All other engines	13	10

Torque wrench settings (continued)

	Nm	lbf ft
Fuel pressure control valve (5-cylinder engines only):		
Fuel-rail mounted valve:		
Stage 1	60	44
Stage 2	Angle tighten a further 90°	
Stage 3	80	59
Pump-mounted valve:		
Stage 1	4	3
Stage 2	7	5
Fuel pressure sensor:	70	52
Fuel rail-to-cylinder head bolts:		
2.0 litre 4-cylinder engine	22	16
All other engines	24	18
Fuel sender locking ring	70	52
Fuel tank restraining strap bolts	24	18
Fuel temperature sensor	21	15
Intercooler securing screws	10	7
Throttle body securing bolts	10	7
Turbocharger:		
Coolant pipe to turbocharger	38	28
Oil pressure pipe to turbocharger		
1.6 litre and 2.0 litre 5-cylinder engines	18	13
2.0 litre 4-cylinder engine	38	28
2.4 litre engine	25	18
Oil feed to cylinder block	38	28
Turbocharger upper mounting bolts - 1.6 litre (80kw) engine	25	18
Turbocharger to exhaust manifold*:		
1.6 litre engines	25	18
2.0 litre 4-cylinder engine	24	18
2.0 litre 5-cylinder engine:		
Stage 1	18	13
Stage 2	24	18

Do not re-use

1 General information and precautions

General information

The operation of the fuel injection system is described in more detail in Section 6.

Fuel is drawn from a tank under the rear of the vehicle by a tank-immersed electric pump, and then forced through a filter to the injection pump. The intake camshaft driven injection pump is a tandem pump – a low pressure gear-type pump which supplies the high-pressure pump with fuel at a constant pressure, and a high-pressure piston-type pump which supplies fuel to the common fuel rail at variable pressure. Fuel is supplied from the common fuel rail to the injectors. Also inside the injection pump assembly is a pressure control valve which regulates the quantity of fuel to the high-pressure pump, and a bypass valve which returns excess fuel back to the low pressure pump. The injectors are operated by solenoids controlled by the ECU, based on information supplied by various sensors. The engine ECU also controls the preheating side of the system – refer to Chapter 5C for more details.

The EDC (electronic diesel control) system fitted, incorporates a 'drive-by-wire' system, where the traditional accelerator cable is fitted instead of an accelerator pedal position sensor. The position and rate-of-change of the accelerator pedal is reported by the position sensor to the ECU, which then adjusts the fuel injectors and fuel pressure to deliver the required amount of fuel, and optimum combustion efficiency.

The exhaust system incorporates a turbocharger, and an EGR. Further detail of the emission control systems can be found in Chapter 4D.

Precautions

• Wear gloves or use barrier cream to protect your skin from diesel fuel. Do not expose yourself to high pressure fuel spray.

• When working on diesel fuel system components, scrupulous cleanliness must be observed, and care must be taken not to introduce any foreign matter into fuel lines or components.

• After carrying out any work involving disconnection of fuel lines, it is advisable to check the connections for leaks; pressurise the system by cranking the engine several times.

• Electronic control units are very sensitive components, and certain precautions must be taken to avoid damage to these units as follows.

• When carrying out welding operations on the vehicle using electric welding equipment, the battery and alternator should be disconnected.

• Although the underbonnet-mounted modules will tolerate normal underbonnet conditions, they can be adversely affected by excess heat or moisture. If using welding equipment or pressure-washing equipment in the vicinity of an electronic module, take care not to direct heat, or jets of water or steam, at the module. If this cannot be avoided, remove the module from the vehicle, and protect its wiring plug with a plastic bag.

• Before disconnecting any wiring, or removing components, always ensure that the ignition is switched off.

• Do not attempt to improvise ECU fault diagnosis procedures using a test lamp or multimeter, as irreparable damage could be caused to the module.

• After working on fuel injection/engine management system components, ensure that all wiring is correctly reconnected before reconnecting the battery or switching on the ignition.

2 Fuel pipe and connectors

Refer to the information and photos in Chapter 4A, Section 2.

3.1a Remove the 2 expanding rivets and remove the inlet trunking

3.1b Release the clip…

3.1c …disconnect the wiring plug for the mass air flow sensor…

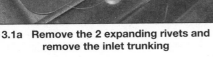

3 Air cleaner assembly –
removal and refitting

Removal

1.6 litre engines

1 Remove the 2 expanding plastic rivets and disconnect the air inlet trunking at the lock panel (see illustration). Undo the 2 bolts securing the mass air flow sensor to the side of the housing. On models fitted with the 85kw engine, unclip the wiring loom from the side of the housing, disconnect the wiring plug for the mass air flow sensor, and disconnect the small vacuum pipe. Slacken the clamp and disconnect the air outlet pipe from the side of the housing (see illustrations).
2 Release the rubber retaining strap at the front of the housing and pull the housing upwards to release it from the three mounting grommets (see illustration).

2.0 litre 4-cylinder engine

3 Disconnect the mass airflow meter wiring plug, release the harness clip, slacken the clamp, and disconnect the outlet hose from the mass airflow meter (see illustration).
4 Release the rubber retaining strap at the front of the housing and pull the housing upwards to release it from the three mounting grommets (see illustration 3.2).

5-cylinder engines

5 Undo the screws/clamp and disconnect the air outlet pipe from air cleaner housing. Undo the 2 screws and disconnect the air inlet trunking at the lock panel, and pull the air inlet pipe from the air cleaner housing.
6 Pull the housing upwards to release it from its mounting grommets.

Refitting

7 Refitting is a reversal of removal. Make sure the outlet and intake ducts are clipped securely into position (where applicable) and that any wiring plugs are refitted.

3.1d …and disconnect the vacuum pipe

4 Fuel tank –
removal and refitting

Note: Observe the precautions in Section 1 before working on any component in the fuel system.

Removal

1 Before the tank can be removed, it must be drained of as much fuel as possible. To avoid the dangers and complications of fuel handling and storage, it is advisable to carry out this operation with the tank almost empty.
2 Disconnect the battery negative lead (see Chapter 5A).
3 Slacken the left-rear roadwheel bolts, then chock the front wheels then jack up the rear of the vehicle and support it on axle stands

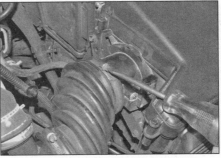

3.1e Disconnect the outlet pipe from the air cleaner housing

(see Jacking and vehicle support). Remove the roadwheel.
4 Disconnect the intermediate/rear section of the exhaust system at the connection behind the catalytic converter, and unhook the rubber mountings. Support the front section of the system to avoid placing any strain on the flexible section.
5 Undo the plastic nuts and remove the heat shield for access to the fuel pipes.
6 Slacken the clips and disconnect the fuel filler and breather pipes. Be prepared for fuel spillage.
7 Prise up the locking catches, depress the buttons and disconnect the fuel pipes from the front of the tank (see illustration).
8 Position a trolley jack under the centre of the tank. Insert a protective wooden pad between the jack head and tank base, then raise the jack to just take the weight of the tank.

3.2 Release the rubber retaining strap (arrowed)

3.3 Disconnect the mass air flow meter wiring plug

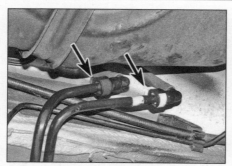

4.7 Prise up the catches (arrowed) and depress the buttons to disconnect the hoses

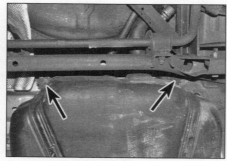

4.9a Fuel tank strap rear bolts (arrowed) . . .

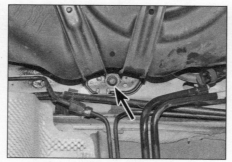

4.9b . . . and front bolt (arrowed)

4.11 Depress the locking collars to disconnect hoses from the sender unit

13 If the tank is contaminated with sediment or water, remove the gauge sender unit as described previously. Swill the tank out with clean fuel.
14 The tank is moulded from a synthetic material and if damaged, it should be renewed. However, in certain cases it may be possible to have small leaks or minor damage repaired. Seek the advice of a dealer or suitable specialist concerning tank repair.
15 If a new tank is to be fitted, transfer all the components from the old tank to the new. Always renew the seal and plastic nut securing the gauge sender unit. Once used, they may not seat and seal properly on a new tank.

Refitting

16 Refitting is a reversal of removal, bearing in mind the following points:
 a) *Before raising the tank to its final position, reconnect the sender unit wiring plug.*
 b) *On completion, bleed the fuel system as described in Section 7.*

9 Undo the tank retaining straps, and carefully lower the jack and tank slightly **(see illustrations)**.
10 Disconnect the fuel sender unit wiring connector.

11 Depress the locking collars and disconnect the fuel connections from the sender unit **(see illustration)**.
12 Lower the jack and tank, and remove the tank from under the car.

<table>
<tr><td>5</td><td>Accelerator pedal –
removal and refitting</td><td></td></tr>
</table>

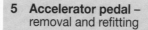

Removal

1 Carefully prise the panel in front of the centre console from place, releasing the 4 retaining clips **(see illustration)**.
2 Prise away the rear edge of the trim panel at the driver's side end of the facia and release the lower facia panel outer clip **(see illustration)**.
3 Undo the 3 retaining screws and remove the lower facia panel **(see illustration)**. Disconnect any wiring plugs as the panel is withdrawn.
4 Undo the 3 nuts securing the assembly to the bulkhead **(see illustration)**.
5 Release the cable tie, and disconnect the position sensor wiring plug as the pedal assembly is removed. No further dismantling of the assembly is recommended.

Refitting

6 Refit by reversing the removal operations.

5.1 Pull the panel in front of the centre console rearwards to release the clips

5.2 Prise the facia end panel away, and remove the clip (arrowed)

<table>
<tr><td>6</td><td>Fuel injection system –
general information</td></tr>
</table>

The system is under the overall control of the Electronic Diesel Control (EDC) system, which also controls the preheating system (see Chapter 5C).
Fuel is supplied from the rear-mounted fuel tank, via an electrically-powered lift pump (controlled by the central electronic module) and fuel filter, to the fuel injection pump. The fuel injection pump supplies fuel under high pressure to the common fuel rail. The fuel rail provides a reservoir of fuel under pressure

5.3 Undo the 3 screws (arrowed) and remove the facia lower panel

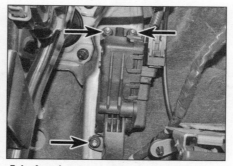

5.4 Accelerator pedal assembly retaining nuts (arrowed)

ready for the injectors to deliver direct to the combustion chamber. The individual fuel injectors incorporate solenoids which, when operated, allow the high pressure fuel to be injected. The solenoids are controlled by the EDC electric control module (ECU). The fuel injection pump purely provides high pressure fuel. The timing and duration of the injection is controlled by the ECU, based on the information received from the various sensors. In order to increase combustion efficiency and reduce combustion noise (diesel 'knock'), a small amount of fuel is injected before the main injection takes place – this is known as Pre- or Pilot-injection.

Additionally, the engine management ECU activates the preheating system (Chapter 5C), and the exhaust gas recirculation (EGR) system (see Chapter 4D).

The system uses the following sensors.
a) *Crankshaft sensor – informs the ECU of the crankshaft speed and position.*
b) *Coolant temperature sensor – informs the ECU of engine temperature.*
c) *Mass airflow/intake air temperature sensor – informs the ECU of the mass and temperature of air entering the intake tract.*
d) *Wheel speed sensor – informs the ECU of the vehicle speed.*
e) *Accelerator pedal position sensor – informs the ECU of throttle position, and the rate of throttle opening/closing.*
f) *Fuel high-pressure sensor – informs the ECU of the pressure of the fuel in the common rail.*
g) *Camshaft position sensor – informs the ECU of the camshaft position so that the engine firing sequence can be established.*
h) *Stop-light switch – informs the ECU when the brakes are being applied*
i) *Manifold absolute pressure sensor – informs the ECU of the boost pressure generated by the turbocharger.*
j) *Air conditioning pressure sensor – informs the ECU of the high-pressure side of the air conditioning circuit, in case a raised idle speed is required to compensate for compressor load.*

On all models, a 'drive-by-wire' throttle control system is used. The accelerator pedal is not physically connected to the fuel injection pump with a traditional cable, but instead is monitored by a dual potentiometer mounted on the pedal assembly, which provides the engine control unit (ECU) with a signal relating to accelerator pedal movement.

The signals from the various sensors are processed by the ECU, and the optimum fuel quantity and injection timing settings are selected for the prevailing engine operating conditions.

Catalytic converter(s), a particulate filter (depending on model and market) and an exhaust gas recirculation (EGR) system are fitted, to reduce harmful exhaust gas emissions.

Details of this and other emissions control system equipment are given in Chapter 4D.

If there is an abnormality in any of the readings obtained from any sensor, the ECU enters its back-up mode. In this event, the ECU ignores the abnormal sensor signal, and assumes a pre-programmed value which will allow the engine to continue running (albeit at reduced efficiency). If the ECU enters this back-up mode, the warning light on the instrument panel will come on, and the relevant fault code will be stored in the ECU memory.

If the warning light comes on, the vehicle should be taken to a Volvo dealer or specialist at the earliest opportunity. A complete test of the Electronic Diesel Control (EDC) system can then be carried out, using a special electronic test unit which is simply plugged into the system's diagnostic connector. The connector is located below the driver's side of the facia above the pedals.

7 Fuel system – priming and bleeding

1 After disturbing the fuel system before the high-pressure fuel injection pump, the system must be bled. To do this, Volvo technicians use a hand pump (No 951 2898) that sucks fuel from the tank, and forces it through the filter. In the absence of this tool, use a hand-held vacuum pump.
2 Remove the plastic cover on the top of the engine by pulling it straight up from its mountings at the front and right-hand edges, then pull it forwards.

Using the Volvo pump

3 Disconnect the fuel supply pipe quick-release connector from the high-pressure fuel injection pump, and place the end of the pipe in a suitable container to catch the emerging fuel.
4 Disconnect the fuel supply hose to the fuel filter, and connect the hand pump (or equivalent) between the hose and the filter. Ensure the arrow on the pump is pointing towards the fuel filter.

7.9 Depress the release tab (arrowed) and disconnect the fuel return hose

5 Operate the pump until there is a continuous flow of fuel into the container.
6 Reattach the pipe to the high-pressure pump, then operate the pump until strong resistance is felt.
7 Operate the starter motor and run the engine until it reaches normal operating temperature. *Caution: Do not operate the starter motor for more than 10 seconds, then wait 30 seconds before trying again.*
8 Stop the engine, and remove the hand pump. Wipe up any fuel spillage, and refit the engine cover.

Using a hand-held vacuum pump

9 Depress the release tab and disconnect the fuel return connection adjacent to the fuel filter **(see illustration)**.
10 Connect the vacuum pump pipe to the return hose, and continue to pull a vacuum until bubble-free fuel emerges from the hose. The progress of the fuel emerging from the filter can be observed through the transparent hose leading to the high-pressure pump **(see illustrations)**.
11 Reconnect the fuel return hose.
12 Operate the starter motor and run the engine until it reaches normal operating temperature. *Caution: Do not operate the starter motor for more than 10 seconds, then wait 30 seconds before trying again.*
13 Stop the engine. Wipe up any fuel spillage, and refit the engine cover.

7.10a Using a vacuum pump, draw the fuel through the system . . .

7.10b . . . until bubble-free fuel emerges through the transparent hose (arrowed) leading to the high-pressure pump

8.2 We used a home-made tool to unscrew the sender unit plastic collar

8.3a Lift the sender unit from the tank . . .

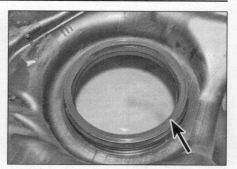

8.3b . . . discard the seal (arrowed), a new one must be fitted

8 Fuel gauge sender/ pump units – removal and refitting

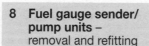

Note: *Observe the precautions in Section 1 before working on any component in the fuel system.*

Removal

1 Remove the fuel tank as described in Section 4.
2 Unscrew the sender unit plastic retaining collar using a pair of large, crossed-screwdrivers, or improvise a tool **(see illustration)**.
3 Lift the sender unit from the tank **(see illustrations)**. Discard the O-ring seal, a new one must be fitted. On models with a fuel-fired auxiliary heater, undo the plug for the suction pipe on the underside of the level sensor, and transfer the pipe to the new sensor (if renewed). No separate parts are available.
4 If required, attach the leads from a multimeter to the sender unit wires, and measure the resistance at full float deflection and zero deflection **(see illustration)**. The resistance of the unit we tested was 200 ohms at full deflection and 10 ohms at zero deflection.

Refitting

5 Refitting is a reversal of removal, bearing in mind the following points:
a) Use a new O-ring seal smeared with petroleum jelly.

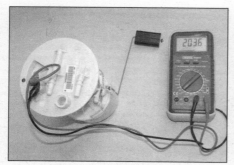

8.4 Use a multimeter to measure the sender unit resistance at full, and zero float arm deflection

b) Position the sender unit so the arrow on the cover aligns with the marks on the fuel tank **(see illustration)**.
c) Tighten the sender unit retaining collar to the specified torque, where tools permit.

9 Fuel injection system – testing and adjustment

Testing

1 If a fault appears in the fuel injection system, first ensure that all the system wiring connectors are securely connected and free from corrosion. Ensure that the fault is not due to poor maintenance; i.e. check that the air cleaner filter element is clean, that the cylinder compression pressures are correct (see Chapter 1B, 2C, 2D or 2E), and that the engine breather hoses are clear and undamaged.
2 If the engine will not start, check the condition of the glow plugs (see Chapter 5C).
3 If these checks fail to reveal the cause of the problem, the vehicle should be taken to a Volvo dealer or specialist for testing using special electronic equipment which is plugged into the diagnostic connector. The tester should locate the fault quickly and simply, avoiding the need to test all the system components individually, which is time-consuming, and also carries a risk of damaging the ECU.

Adjustment

4 The engine idle speed, maximum speed

8.5 The arrow on the sender cover must align with the marks on the fuel tank (arrowed)

and fuel injection timing are all controlled by the ECU. Whilst in theory it is possible to check the settings, if they are found to be in need of adjustment, the car will have to be taken to a suitably-equipped Volvo dealer or specialist. They will have access to the necessary diagnostic equipment required to test and (where possible) adjust the settings.

10 Fuel injection pump – removal and refitting

Caution: Be careful not to allow dirt into the injection pump or injector pipes during this procedure.
Note: *Any rigid high-pressure fuel pipes disturbed must be renewed.*

Removal

1 Disconnect the battery negative lead (see Chapter 5A). On 5 cylinder engines, remove the battery as described in Chapter 5A and the air cleaner assembly as described in Section 3.
2 Remove the plastic cover from the top of the engine, by pulling it straight up from its mountings.

1.6 litre engines

3 Remove the timing belt as described in Chapter 2C. Note that on models fitted with the 85kw engine, the inlet manifold must be removed as described in Section 17.
4 On the 80kW engine, undo the 2 bolts at the manifold, slacken the clamp at the EGR valve, unbolt the support bracket, and remove the air pipe.
5 On the 80kW engine, remove the glow plug wiring harness. Disconnect the wiring plug, disconnect the wiring at the glow plugs, and undo the 2 harness retaining bolts.
6 Depress the locking buttons and disconnect the fuel supply and return hoses from the pump. Plug the openings to prevent contamination.
7 Undo the 3 bolts and remove the bracket at the rear of the pump, and disconnect the wiring plug from the pump.
8 Unscrew the pipe unions, undo the bolt for the support bracket (where fitted), and remove the high-pressure fuel pipe between the pump

10.14 Slacken the clamp (arrowed) and disconnect the air ducting

10.15 Remove the pipe (arrowed) between the high-pressure fuel pump and the fuel rail

10.16a Slide out the clip and disconnect the fuel supply hose . . .

and the fuel rail. Discard the pipe, a new one must be fitted. Plug the openings to prevent contamination.

9 Hold the pump sprocket stationary, and loosen the centre nut securing it to the pump shaft.

10 The fuel pump sprocket is a taper fit on the pump shaft and it will be necessary to make up a tool to release it from the taper. Partially unscrew the sprocket retaining nut, fit the home made tool, and secure it to the sprocket with two 7.0mm bolts and nuts. Prevent the sprocket rotating as before and screw down the nuts, forcing the sprocket off the shaft taper.

11 Once the taper is released, remove the tool, unscrew the nut fully, and remove the sprocket from the pump shaft.

12 Undo the 3 bolts and remove the pump from the mounting bracket.

2.0 litre 4-cylinder engine

13 Remove the air cleaner housing as described in Section 3, and the vacuum pump as described in Chapter 9.

14 Slacken the clamp and disconnect the air ducting from the mass airflow sensor. Move the ducting to one side for access to the pump (see illustration).

15 Undo the unions and remove the high-pressure fuel pipe between the pump and the fuel rail (see illustration). Discard the pipe, a new one must be fitted.

16 Note their fitted positions, depress the release tabs, and disconnect the fuel supply and return pipes from the pump (see illustrations). Be prepared for fuel spillage.

10.16b . . . then depress the release tab (arrowed) and disconnect the fuel return hose

Plug the openings to prevent contamination.

17 Note their fitted positions, and disconnect the wiring plugs from the pump.

18 Undo the 3 retaining bolts and pull the pump from the cylinder head (see illustration). Discard the gasket.

5-cylinder engines

19 Slacken the unions, then remove the high-pressure fuel pipe between the pump and the common (fuel) rail. Discard the pipe, a new one must be fitted. Plug or cover the fuel rail and pump ports to prevent dirt ingress.

20 Release the clamps and disconnect the supply and return hoses from the pump. If the metal hose clamps are damaged during removal, update them with traditional worm-drive clamps. Plug or seal the pump ports to prevent dirt ingress.

21 Disconnect sensor wiring plugs from the pump.

22 Remove the three retaining screws, and

10.18 Undo the 3 bolts and remove the pump (arrowed)

remove the fuel pump. Recover the connecting piece between the end of the camshaft and the pump drive – this is easily lost as the pump is removed (see illustrations). Discard the seal, a new one must be fitted. With the exception of the control valve (see Section 12), no internal components of the pump are available. If the pump is faulty, the complete unit may have to be renewed – consult a Volvo dealer or specialist.

Caution: Do not rotate the pump once removed - it's important that it retains its original position if refitted.

Refitting

23 Ensure that the mating surfaces of the pump and engine are clean and dry, and fit a new O-ring seal or gasket where appropriate. Lubricate the seal with clean engine oil.

24 Position the fuel pump, ensuring any connecting piece is in place. On the 2.0 litre 4-cylinder engine ensure that the slot in the

10.22a Pump retaining screws on 5-cylinder engines

10.22b Recover the connecting piece between the end of the camshaft and the pump drive

10.22c The pump connecting piece must align with the slots in the end of the inlet camshaft

10.24 Ensure the pump drive dog (arrowed) is aligned with the slot in the end of the camshaft

10.26 Use a crows-foot adapter to tighten the pipe union, and a second spanner to counterhold the pump port. Do not allow the pump port to rotate

Removal

1.6 litre engines

1 On the 80kw engine slacken the clamps, unbolt any support brackets, and remove the air pipe between the manifold and the EGR valve. On the 85kw engine remove the inlet manifold as described in Section 17.

2 On the 80kw engine, undo the securing bolt, disconnect the wiring from the glow plugs, and move the wiring harness to one side. Undo the 3 bolts and lift the injector wiring guide from place. On both engines, disconnect the wiring plugs from the top of each injector **(see illustration)**. Depending on the engine fitted, release the clamp and connector or extract the retaining clip and disconnect the leak off pipe from each injector **(see illustrations)**.

3 Clean the area around the high-pressure fuel pipes between the injectors and the fuel rail, then unscrew the pipe unions. Use a second spanner to counter-hold the union screwed into the injector body. The injectors screwed-in unions must not be allowed to move. Remove the bracket above the fuel rail unions, then remove the pipes. Plug the openings in the fuel rail and injectors to prevent dirt ingress.

4 Remove any covers, unscrew the injector retaining screw/bolts, and carefully pull or lever the injector from place. If necessary, use an open-ended spanner and twist the injector to free it from position. Do not lever against or pull on the solenoid housing at the top of the injector.

5 Remove the copper washer and upper seal from each injector or from the cylinder head if they remained in place during injector removal. Cover the injector holes in the cylinder head to prevent dirt ingress.

Other engines

6 On the 2.0 litre 4-cylinder engine, remove the cylinder head cover/intake manifold as described in Chapter 2D and unclip the cover from each injector.

7 On the 2.4 litre engine, remove the air cleaner housing as described in Section 3.

8 Make sure the areas around the high-pressure fuel pipe unions from the fuel rail to the injectors is scrupulously clean and free from debris, etc. If possible, use a vacuum cleaner and a degreaser to clean the area.

9 Carefully prise out the retaining clips, then disconnect the fuel return hoses from the injectors **(see illustrations 11.2b and 11.2c)**. Take care not to drop the retaining clips as they are removed, and check the condition of the O-ring seals – renew if necessary.

10 Undo the unions, then remove the high-pressure fuel pipes from the fuel rail to the injectors **(see illustration)**. Discard the fuel pipes, new ones must be fitted. Use a second open-ended spanner on the injector port to counterhold when slackening the pipe union **(see illustration)**. Be prepared for fuel spillage and plug/cover the ports in the injectors and fuel rail to prevent dirt ingress.

end of the camshaft and the pump drive dog are aligned **(see illustration)**. Tighten the pump mounting bolts to the specified torque.

25 Reconnect the fuel supply and return hoses to the pump, and secure them with new clamps.

26 Fit the new high-pressure fuel pipe between the pump and common rail, then tighten to the specified torque, using a crow's-foot adapter if required **(see illustration)**.

27 The remainder of refitting is a reversal of removal, bearing in mind the following points:
   a) The fuel system may need to be bled so refer to Section 7.
   b) Once the engine has started, thoroughly check for fuel leaks from the disturbed

pipes/hoses. If a leak is detected, **do not** attempt to cure it by further tightening of the pipe unions.

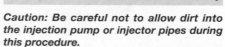

11 Fuel injectors – removal and refitting

Caution: Be careful not to allow dirt into the injection pump or injector pipes during this procedure.

Note: *If the injectors are to be refitted, plug all openings, and store them upright in their original order. They must be refitted to their original positions.*

11.2a Depress the clip and disconnect the wiring plugs from the injectors

11.2b Prise down the lower edge of the retaining clip (shown with the return hose disconnected for clarity)...

11.2c ...then pull the return hoses from the injectors

11.10a Undo the pipe union on the common rail

11.10b Use a second spanner to prevent the port on the injector from turning whilst slackening the union

11.11a Injector clamp nuts (arrowed)

11.11b Slide the copper sealing washer from the injector

11.11c The injectors should be stored upright

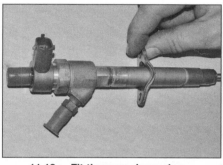

11.13a Fit the new clamp ring…

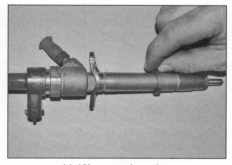

11.13b …and washer

11 Disconnect the wiring plug from each injector, unscrew the two nuts securing each injector clamp (complete with spacers where fitted), and carefully remove the injectors. Slide the copper sealing washer from the end of each injector. Discard the sealing washers – new ones must be fitted (see illustrations). Cover the injector hole in the cylinder head to prevent dirt ingress. If the injectors are to be refitted, plug all openings and store them upright in their original order. They must be refitted to their original positions (see illustration).

Refitting

12 Ensure that the injectors and seats in cylinder head are clean, dry and free from soot. It's essential the sealing surfaces are dirt-free, otherwise leakage will occur.
13 Fit new clamp rings, washers, circlips (where applicable) and sealing washers to the injectors, and refit them to the cylinder head (see illustrations).
14 Fit new rigid high pressure pipes between the common rail and the injectors. Starting at the common rail, tighten the pipe unions to

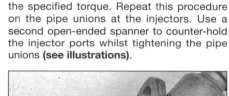

11.13c We fabricated a tool out of sheet metal to allow the circlip to slide over the end of the injector

the specified torque. Repeat this procedure on the pipe unions at the injectors. Use a second open-ended spanner to counter-hold the injector ports whilst tightening the pipe unions (see illustrations).

11.13d The circlip must locate in the groove

11.13e Refit the injectors into the cylinder head

11.14a Fit the new pipes to the injectors/ common rail…

11.14b …and use a crows-foot adapter to tighten the union nuts

12.8 Crankshaft position sensor – 1.6 litre engines

12.13 Crankshaft position sensor – 2.0 litre 4-cylinder engine

12.17 Crankshaft position sensor – 5-cylinder engines

15 The remainder of refitting is a reversal of removal, bearing in mind the following points:

a) *Check the condition of the fuel return hoses, and renew if any appear damaged or perished.*

b) *Ensure all wiring connectors and harnesses are correctly refitted and secured.*

c) *Depending on the engine fitted, different 'classes' of injector may be available as spare parts. You should refer to a Volvo dealer or parts specialist before purchasing replacements.*

d) *If new injectors are fitted, new software may need to be downloaded to the engine management ECM from Volvo. Entrust this task to a Volvo dealer or specialist.*

e) *Once the engine has started, thoroughly check for fuel leaks from the disturbed pipes/hoses.*

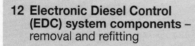

12 Electronic Diesel Control (EDC) system components – removal and refitting

Crankshaft position/ speed sensor

1.6 litre engines

1 Remove the plastic engine cover by pulling it straight up from its mountings.

2 Unclip the fuel hoses from their bracket on top of the upper pulley cover.

3 Remove the auxiliary drivebelt as described in Chapter 1B.

4 Raise the front of the vehicle and support it securely on axle stands (see *Jacking and vehicle support*). Undo the fasteners and remove the engine undershield.

5 To lock the crankshaft, working underneath the engine, insert Volvo tool No. 999 7169 into the hole in the right-hand face of the engine block casting over the lower section of the flywheel. Rotate the crankshaft until the tool engages in the corresponding hole in the flywheel.

6 Remove the crankshaft pulley as described in Chapter 2C.

7 Unclip the wiring loom from the front face of the upper cover, undo the 5 securing bolts for

each and remove the upper and lower pulley covers.

8 Disconnect the wiring plug, remove the retaining bolt, and carefully remove the sensor **(see illustration)**.

9 Refitting is the reverse of removal.

2.0 litre 4-cylinder engine

10 Slacken the right-hand front road wheel nuts, then raise the front of the vehicle and support it securely on axle stands (see *Jacking and vehicle support*). Remove the roadwheel.

11 Release the fasteners and remove the right-hand front wheel arch liner.

12 The sensor is located adjacent to the crankshaft pulley. Disconnect the sensor wiring plug.

13 Slacken and remove the retaining bolt and carefully remove the sensor **(see illustration)**.

14 Refitting is the reverse of removal, tightening the retaining bolt securely.

5-cylinder engines

15 Remove the EGR cooler and valve assembly, as described in Chapter 4D.

16 The sensor is located above the flywheel. Trace the wiring back from the sensor, and disconnect the wiring plug.

17 Slacken and remove the retaining bolt and carefully remove the sensor from its mounting **(see illustration)**.

18 Refitting is the reverse of removal, tightening the retaining bolt securely.

Mass airflow sensor

19 On 1.6 litre engines, remove the plastic

12.25 Manifold absolute pressure sensor (arrowed)

cover on top of the engine, and disconnect the air pipe between the air cleaner housing and the turbocharger.

20 On all engines, ensure the ignition is switched off then release the retaining clip and disconnect the wiring connector from the airflow sensor **(see illustration 3.1c)**.

21 Undo the screws then remove the airflow sensor from the air inlet pipe or air cleaner housing, along with its sealing ring where fitted.

22 Refitting is the reverse of removal, lubricating the new sealing ring.

Coolant temperature sensor

23 Refer to Chapter 3 for removal and refitting details.

Accelerator pedal position sensor

24 The sensor is secured to the accelerator pedal. Refer to Section 5 of this Chapter on pedal removal. Note that at the time of writing, the sensor was not available separately from the pedal assembly.

Manifold absolute pressure sensor

25 On all except the 2.4 litre engine, the MAP sensor is mounted on the inlet manifold, although the exact location differs slightly according to the engine fitted. However, the process for removal is the same in each case. **(see illustration)**.

26 Remove the plastic cover on the top of the engine.

27 Ensure the ignition is switched off then disconnect the wiring connector from the sensor.

28 Slacken and remove the retaining bolt and remove the sensor from the vehicle.

29 On the 2.4 litre engine, the sensor is mounted on the intercooler. Remove the intercooler as described in Section 16, disconnect the wiring plug, remove the retaining bolt, and remove the sensor

30 Refitting is the reverse of removal, tightening the sensor retaining bolt securely.

Stop-light switch

31 The engine control module receives a signal from the stop-light switch which

12.36a 3 wiring plugs are connected to the ECU . . .

12.36b . . . fold back the catches . . .

12.36c . . . and pull the plugs from the ECU

indicates when the brakes are being applied. Stop-light switch removal and refitting details can be found in Chapter 9.

Electronic control unit (ECU)

Note: *If a new control unit is fitted, it must be programmed using dedicated Volvo test equipment. Entrust this task to a Volvo dealer or suitably-equipped specialist.*

32 Disconnect the battery negative lead (see Chapter 5A), then wait at least 2 minutes before commencing work, to allow any stored electrical energy to dissipate.

33 Slacken the left-hand front roadwheel nuts, then raise the front of the vehicle and support it securely on axle stands (see *Jacking and vehicle support*). Remove the roadwheel.

34 Remove the securing screws, and remove the wheelarch liner.

35 Undo the 4 screws (6 screws on 5-cylinder engines) and remove the ECU cover.

36 Release the locking catches, and disconnect the wiring plugs from the ECU **(see illustrations)**.

37 Undo the screws or release the clips as applicable and remove the ECU.

38 Refitting is a reversal of removal, ensuring the cover's rubber seal (where fitted) is correctly positioned in the groove.

Fuel pressure sensor

5-cylinder engines

39 Remove the swirl control valve/motor as described in this section.

40 Disconnect the wiring plug from the sensor, located at the left-hand end of the fuel rail **(see illustration)**.

41 Unscrew the pressure sensor. Plug the openings to prevent contamination.

42 Refitting is a reversal of removal, tightening the sensor to the specified torque.

All other engines

43 Volvo advise that the sensor should not be loosened or removed. If this component fails it is possible that the fuel rail may need to be replaced so you should refer to a Volvo dealer or parts specialist.

Fuel pressure control valve

5-cylinder engines – fuel rail-mounted valve

44 Remove the fuel rail as described in this section.

45 Disconnect the wiring plug and unscrew the control valve from the right-hand end of the fuel rail **(see illustration)**.

46 Refitting is a reversal of removal.

2.0 litre 5-cylinder engine – pump-mounted valve

47 Pull the plastic cover on top of the engine upwards to remove it.

48 Clean the area around the valve on the pump, then disconnect the valve wiring plug.

49 Undo the 2 bolts and remove the valve from the pump. Be prepared for fluid spillage. Plug or cover the opening to prevent contamination.

50 Refitting is a reversal of removal, lubricating the valve O-ring before fitting.

2.4 litre engine – pump-mounted valve

51 Remove the air cleaner assembly as described in Section 3.

52 Clean the area around the valve on the pump, then disconnect the valve wiring plug.

53 Undo the 3 Torx bolts and remove the valve by slowing rotating it and pulling it from the pump. Be prepared for fluid spillage. Plug or cover the openings to prevent contamination **(see illustration)**.

54 Refitting is a reversal of removal, lubricating the valve O-ring before fitting.

All other engines

55 It would appear that the valve cannot be separated from the fuel rail or injection. Consult a Volvo dealer or specialist.

Fuel rail

56 For all engines, follow the relevant steps in Section 10 to enable the removal of the high-pressure pipes between the fuel injectors and the fuel rail. Discard the pipes, new ones must be fitted. On models fitted with the 1.6 litre (80kw) engine it is also necessary to remove the EGR valve/cooler as described in Chapter 4D.

57 Unscrew the unions and remove the high-pressure fuel pipe between the injection pump and the fuel rail. Discard the pipe, a new one must be fitted. Disconnect any wiring plugs from the fuel rail, such as one for the fuel pressure sensor shown on the 2.0 litre 4-cylinder engine **(see illustration)**.

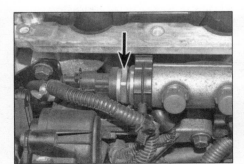

12.40 Fuel pressure sensor (arrowed)

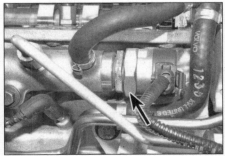

12.45 Fuel pressure control valve (arrowed)

12.53 Fuel pressure control valve (arrowed) – pump-mounted valve

12.57 The fuel pressure sensor is on the underside of the common fuel rail (arrowed)

12.59 Use a 'crow's-foot' adapter to tighten the union nuts

12.63 The intake air temperature sensor is located on the intake manifold (arrowed)

12.68 Swirl valve motor control arm

12.69 Undo the bolts (arrowed) securing the swirl valve control motor

12.72 Camshaft position sensor – 2.0 litre 4-cylinder engine

58 Undo the retaining nuts and remove the fuel rail.
59 To refit, position the fuel rail but only hand-tighten the nuts at this stage. Fit the new high-pressure fuel pipes between the injectors and the fuel rail, and the injection pump and the fuel rail, and tighten the unions to the specified torque **(see illustration)**.
60 Now tighten the fuel rail retaining nuts to the specified torque.
61 The remainder of refitting is a reversal of removal, noting the relevant points in Section 11.

Intake air temperature sensor

Note: *On models fitted with the 1.6 litre (85kw) or 5-cylinder engine, the sensor is an integral part of the mass air flow sensor. Refer to the relevant part of this section.*

1.6 litre (80kw) and 2.0 litre 4-cylinder engine

62 Remove the plastic cover from over the top of the engine by pulling it straight up from its mountings.
63 Disconnect the sensor wiring plug **(see illustration)**.
64 Undo the retaining bolt and pull the sensor from position.
65 Apply a little petroleum jelly to ease the sensor in to place, then tighten the retaining bolt securely.
66 Reconnect the sensor wiring plug and refit the engine cover.

Swirl damper actuator (5-cylinder engines only)

67 Remove the plastic cover from over the

top of the engine, by pulling it straight up from its mountings.
68 Pull the control arm from the valve/motor **(see illustration)**.
69 Undo the 2 bolts and remove the control valve/motor **(see illustration)**.
70 Refitting is a reversal of removal. Note that if a new valve/motor has been fitted, the values stored in the ECU must be reset using dedicated diagnostic equipment. Entrust this task to a Volvo dealer or suitably-equipped specialist.

Camshaft position sensor

71 Remove the plastic cover from over the top of the engine, by pulling it straight up from its mountings.
72 Depending on the engine fitted, the sensor is located at the right-hand end or at the rear

12.76 On the 2.0 litre 4-cylinder engine, the turbocharger boost pressure regulator valve is located at the left-hand end of the cylinder head

of the cylinder head cover. Ensure that the ignition is switched off, and disconnect the wiring plug from the sensor **(see illustration)**.
73 Undo the screw and remove the sensor.
74 Fit the sensor into the cover ensuring it is correctly located on any dowels. Position the sensor so that the nipple of the sensor is just in contact with the camshaft signal wheel. Tighten the sensor retaining bolt to the specified torque.

Turbocharger boost pressure regulator valve

75 Raise the front of the vehicle and support it securely on axle stands (see *Jacking and vehicle support*). Remove the engine undershield on 1.6 litre models. Remove the air-cleaner housing on the 2.0 litre 4-cylinder model as described in Section 3.
76 Disconnect the wiring plug, then undo the 2 regulator retaining nuts **(see illustration)**.
77 Note their fitted locations and disconnect the vacuum hoses as the regulator is withdrawn.
78 Refitting is a reversal of removal

Fuel temperature sensor

Note: *This is fitted only to 5-cylinder engines.*
79 Remove the plastic cover from over the top of the engine, by pulling it straight up from its mountings.
80 The sensor is located on the top/front edge of the high pressure pump at the left-hand end of the cylinder head. Disconnect the sensor wiring plug **(see illustration)**.

12.80 The fuel temperature sensor is located on the high-pressure fuel pump

12.87 Disconnect the inlet pipe from the throttle body

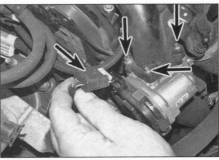

12.88a Undo the 3 bolts (arrowed) securing the throttle body to the inlet pipe...

81 Clean the area around the sensor, then unscrew it from the pump. Be prepared for fluid spillage. Plug the opening to prevent contamination.

82 Refitting is a reversal of removal, tightening the sensor to the specified torque.

Throttle body

Removal

All engines

83 Remove the plastic engine cover by pulling it straight up from its mountings.

1.6 litre (80kW) engine

84 Disconnect the 4 wiring plugs from the throttle body assembly.

85 Slacken the clamps and disconnect the 3 air pipes from the throttle body. There is a pipe at the top and bottom and one on the left-hand side.

86 Undo the mounting bolt located adjacent to the oil filler cap, and the mounting bolt each side of the assembly. The throttle body can now be removed.

1.6 litre (85kW) engine

87 Disconnect the wiring plug from the throttle body assembly, slacken the clamp, and disconnect the air inlet pipe at the bottom of the unit **(see illustration)**.

88 Undo the 3 bolts securing the throttle body to the inlet pipe, undo the lower mounting bolt, and remove the throttle body **(see illustrations)**. Note that the lower mounting bolt can be difficult to reach and access can be improved by removing the flexible section of the outlet pipe from the turbocharger.

2.0 litre 4-cylinder engine

89 Slacken the clamp and disconnect the air inlet pipe from the bottom of the throttle body assembly.

90 Undo the securing screws for the two sensors and move them to one side. Disconnect the vacuum hose.

91 Undo the 3 mounting bolts and remove the throttle body.

5-cylinder engines

92 Remove the air cleaner housing as described in Section 3.

93 Slacken the clamp and disconnect the air inlet pipe from the throttle body assembly.

12.88b ...and undo the lower mounting bolt

94 Disconnect the wiring plug, undo the 4 mounting bolts, and remove the throttle body **(see illustration)**.

Refitting

95 In all cases, refitting is a reversal of removal. If a new throttle body has been fitted, the stored values in the engine management ECU must be reset. Entrust this task to a Volvo dealer or suitably-equipped specialist.

13 Turbocharger – description and precautions

Description

A turbocharger increases engine efficiency by raising the pressure in the inlet manifold above atmospheric pressure. Instead of the air simply being sucked into the cylinders, it is forced in. Additional fuel is supplied by the injection pump in proportion to the increased air intake.

Energy for the operation of the turbocharger comes from the exhaust gas. The gas flows through a specially-shaped housing (the turbine housing) and in so doing spins the turbine wheel. The turbine wheel is attached to a shaft, at the end of which is another vaned wheel known as the compressor wheel. The compressor wheel spins in its own housing and compresses the inducted air on the way to the inlet manifold.

The compressed air passes through an intercooler. This is an air-to-air heat exchanger, mounted with the radiator at the front of the

12.94 Throttle body retaining bolts (top two bolts arrowed)

vehicle. The purpose of the intercooler is to remove from the inducted air some of the heat gained in being compressed. Because cooler air is denser, removal of this heat further increases engine efficiency.

The turbocharger has adjustable guide vanes controlling the flow of exhaust gas into the turbine, the vanes being controlled by the engine management ECU. At lower engine speeds, the vanes close together, giving a smaller exhaust gas entry port, and therefore higher gas speed, which increases boost pressure at low engine speed. At high engine speed, the vanes are turned to give a larger exhaust gas entry port, and therefore lower gas speed, effectively maintaining a reasonably constant boost pressure over the engine rev range. This is known as a Variable Nozzle Turbocharger (VNT).

The turbo shaft is pressure-lubricated by an oil feed pipe from the main oil gallery. The shaft 'floats' on a cushion of oil. A drain pipe returns the oil to the sump.

Precautions

• The turbocharger operates at extremely high speeds and temperatures. Certain precautions must be observed to avoid premature failure of the turbo or injury to the operator.

• **Do not** operate the turbo with any parts exposed. Foreign objects falling onto the rotating vanes could cause excessive damage and (if ejected) personal injury.

• **Do not** race the engine immediately after start-up, especially if it is cold. Give the oil a few seconds to circulate.

• **Always** allow the engine to return to idle

14.7a Air outlet pipe bolts (top bolt arrowed)

14.7b Undo the nut and bolt for the support bracket

14.8 Undo the 4 bolts (arrowed) for the turbocharger heat shield

14.9 Undo the bolts and remove the inlet pipe stub (left-hand bolt arrowed)

speed before switching it off – do not blip the throttle and switch off, as this will leave the turbo spinning without lubrication.
• Allow the engine to idle for several minutes before switching off after a high-speed run.
• Observe the recommended intervals for oil and filter changing, and use a reputable oil of the specified quality (see *Lubricants and fluids*). Neglect of oil changing, or use of inferior oil, can cause carbon formation on the turbo shaft and subsequent failure.

14 Turbocharger – removal and refitting

Removal

Note: *On models fitted with the 2.0 litre 4-cylinder engine, remove the exhaust*

14.10 Oil pressure pipe union

manifold as described in Section 17 and unbolt the turbocharger. On models fitted with the 2.4 litre engine, the turbocharger is integral to the exhaust manifold and cannot be removed separately.

1.6 litre (80kw) engine

1 Remove the catalytic converter as described in Chapter 4D.
2 Undo the clamp at the throttle body, undo the 2 bolts at the turbocharger, and remove the air outlet pipe.
3 Unscrew the oil pressure pipe from the turbocharger. Undo the clips and disconnect the vacuum pipes from the turbocharger.
4 Undo the 2 lower bolts connecting the turbocharger to the exhaust manifold. Undo the bolts and remove the heatshield over the turbocharger.
5 Undo the upper mounting bolt and mounting nuts and remove the turbocharger.

14.17 Turbocharger oil return pipe

1.6 litre (85kw) engine

6 Remove the particulate filter as described in Chapter 4D.
7 Undo the 2 bolts securing the air outlet pipe to the turbocharger, and the nut and bolt for the support bracket adjacent to the throttle body **(see illustrations)**.
8 Undo the securing bolt and remove the dipstick guide tube. Undo the 4 bolts and remove the heatshield bracket above the turbocharger **(see illustration)**, and the 4 bolts that secure the heatshield above the exhaust manifold.
9 Slacken the clamps and remove the air pipe between the and cleaner housing and the turbocharger. Undo the 2 bolts and remove the air inlet pipe stub from the turbocharger **(see illustration)**. Disconnect the wiring plug and the vacuum pipe from the actuator.
10 Unscrew the oil pressure pipe from the turbocharger **(see illustration)**, slacken the clamps, and disconnect the hose below the turbocharger.
11 Undo the 4 bolts at the exhaust manifold and remove the turbocharger.

2.0 litre 5-cylinder engine

12 Remove the particulate filter as described in Chapter 4D.
13 Remove the air pipe at the front of the engine. Slacken the clamp at the air cleaner housing, the clamp at the rear of the cylinder head on the right-hand side, the clamp for the breather hose, and undo the bolt for the support bracket.
14 Slacken the clamp for the air inlet pipe at the turbocharger, undo the bolt for the support bracket at the rear of the cylinder head, and remove the inlet pipe.
15 Raise the front of the vehicle and support it securely on axle stands (see *Jacking and vehicle support*). Remove the engine undershield.
16 Undo the clamps, undo the bolt for the support bracket, and remove the air pipe beneath the engine.
17 Unscrew the oil pressure pipe from the turbocharger, and undo the 2 screws and disconnect the oil return pipe **(see illustration)**.
18 Undo the lower mounting bolt and the 4 upper bolts at the exhaust manifold and remove the turbocharger.

Refitting

19 Refitting is a reversal of removal, noting the following points:
  a) Ensure all mating surfaces are clean and dry.
  b) Renew all O-rings, seals and gaskets.
  c) Tighten all fasteners to the specified torque where available.
  d) Prior to starting the engine, remove the fuel pump relay and operate the starter until the oil pressure light extinguishes. Refit the relay, start the engine, and check for leaks.

15 Turbocharger –
examination and overhaul

1 With the turbocharger removed, inspect the housing for cracks or other visible damage.
2 Spin the turbine or the compressor wheel to verify that the shaft is intact and to feel for excessive shake or roughness. Some play is normal since in use the shaft is 'floating' on a film of oil. Check that the wheel vanes are undamaged.
3 The wastegate and actuator are integral with the turbocharger, and cannot be checked or renewed separately. Consult a Volvo dealer or other specialist if it is thought that the wastegate may be faulty.
4 If the exhaust or induction passages are oil-contaminated, the turbo shaft oil seals have probably failed. (On the induction side, this will also have contaminated the intercooler which if necessary should be flushed with a suitable solvent.)
5 No DIY repair of the turbo is possible. A new unit may be available on an exchange basis.

16 Intercooler –
removal and refitting

1 Remove the front bumper as described in Chapter 11, release the clips and remove the plastic bumper bar cover from place.
2 Undo the upper screws securing the lower air baffle. Note that these are hard to reach and removing them requires a degree of patience.
3 Slacken the clamps and disconnect the air pipes from the intercooler, and undo the bolt each side at the bottom of the intercooler. Lift the intercooler upwards slightly to disengage the hooks and remove the intercooler downwards **(see illustrations)**. On 2.4 litre models, disconnect the wiring plug for the manifold absolute pressure sensor prior to removal.
4 Refitting is a reversal of removal.

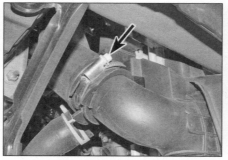
16.3a Slacken the intercooler hose clamps (arrowed) . . .

16.3b . . . on both sides (arrowed)

16.3c Undo the intercooler mounting bolts each side (arrowed) . . .

16.3d . . . then lift it up to disengage the hooks, and lower it

17 Manifolds –
removal and refitting

Intake manifold

1 On models with the 1.6 litre (80kw) or 2.0/2.4 litre engine, the intake manifold is integral with the cylinder head cover – refer to Chapter 2C, 2D or 2E.

1.6 litre (85kw) engine

2 Disconnect the battery negative lead as described in Chapter 5A.
3 Remove the manifold absolute pressure sensor as described in Section 12. Follow steps 8 to 10 for fuel filter removal as described in Chapter 1B, but instead of removing the filter itself undo the 3 bolts and remove the filter housing.

4 Release the clips for the fuel filter pipes and the cable harness from the top of the engine, and move to one side **(see illustration)**.
5 Slacken the clamp and disconnect the air inlet pipe from the bottom of the throttle body. Undo the lower mounting bolt for the throttle body - note that access is difficult and can be improved by removing the flexible section of the air pipe adjacent to the throttle body **(see illustrations)**.
6 Slacken the clamp and disconnect the inlet air pipe from the induction pipe flange at the rear of the cylinder head on the right-hand side. Undo the nut and bolt for the inlet pipe support bracket **(see illustrations)**.
7 Disconnect the wiring plug from the EGR valve, then undo the two bolts securing the EGR pipe to the inlet manifold. Undo the bolt for the EGR valve support bracket at the engine block.
8 Undo the 2 bolts for the EGR pipe at the

17.4 Unclip the fuel pipes from their brackets (arrowed)

17.5a Disconnect the inlet pipe from the throttle body...

17.5b ...and undo the lower mounting bolt

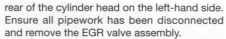

17.6a Disconnect the inlet pipe from the flange

17.6b Undo the nut and bolt for the support bracket...

17.6c ...and lift the pipe and the throttle body from place

rear of the cylinder head on the left-hand side. Ensure all pipework has been disconnected and remove the EGR valve assembly.

9 Undo the 2 bolts at the inlet pipe flange at the rear of the cylinder head and the 3 bolts securing the manifold to the cylinder head. The manifold can now be withdrawn.

10 Refitting is a reversal of removal.

Exhaust manifold

Removal

1.6 litre engines

11 Remove the turbocharger as described in Section 14. Undo the 10 nuts securing the exhaust manifold to the cylinder head and recover any spacers.

2.0 litre 4-cylinder engine

12 Remove the plastic cover from over the

top of the engine by pulling it straight up from its mountings at the front and right-hand edges, then pull it forwards.

13 Drain the cooling system as described in Chapter 1B.

14 Remove the battery as described in Chapter 5A, then undo the 3 bolts and remove the battery tray.

15 Disconnect the gearchange cables from the transmission levers, and support bracket as described in Chapter 7A.

16 Slacken the clamps, undo the nut and bolt, then remove the charge air pipe from under the engine oil sump.

17 Remove the driveshafts as described in Chapter 8. Note that there is no need to remove the left-hand driveshaft from the transmission casing. **Note:** *This is not necessary if the manifold/turbocharger is only*

being removed to renew the cylinder head and/or gasket.

18 Suspend the right-hand end of the engine with an engine hoist, then undo the bolts securing the right-hand engine mounting to the bracket on the engine block. Allow the engine come forward a little.

19 Undo the bolts and remove the lower torque rod from the rear of the engine. **Note:** *This is not necessary if the manifold/turbocharger is only being removed to renew the cylinder head and/or gasket.*

20 Undo the bolts securing the steering rack to the subframe, then support the rack using straps or similar, suspending it from a suitable location in the engine compartment. **Note:** *This is not necessary if the manifold/turbocharger is only being removed to renew the cylinder head and/or gasket.*

21 Place a trolley jack under the subframe, then undo the subframe mounting bolts and lower it. Remove the subframe from under the vehicle. **Note:** *This is not necessary if the manifold/turbocharger is only being removed to renew the cylinder head and/or gasket.*

22 Undo the bolts securing the EGR cooler to the EGR valve and the intake manifold.

23 Disconnect the wiring plug, then undo the 2 bolts at the top, slacken the Allen screw underneath and remove the EGR valve (see Chapter 4D).

24 Slacken the clips and disconnect the hoses from the EGR cooler **(see illustration)**.

25 Slacken the nut, release the clips and remove the heat shield from right-hand end of the EGR cooler.

26 Undo the nuts securing the EGR cooler to the exhaust manifold, and the nut securing the bracket to the exhaust manifold, then manoeuvre the EGR cooler out from place.

27 Undo the bolts and remove the air intake ducting and resonator from the turbocharger **(see illustrations)**.

28 Remove the catalytic converter as described in Chapter 4D.

29 Disconnect the wiring plug and the vacuum pipe from the turbocharger vane position sensor/actuator **(see illustration)**.

30 Disconnect the oil feed and return pipes from the turbocharger. Recover the sealing washers, and be prepared for oil spillage.

17.24 Slacken the clips and disconnect the hoses from the EGR cooler (right-hand clip arrowed)

17.27a One bolt secures the intake ducting and resonator to the bracket (arrowed) . . .

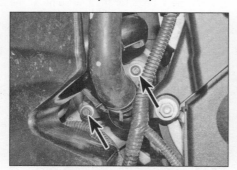

17.27b . . . and 2 secure it to the turbocharger (arrowed)

17.29 Turbocharger vane position sensor/actuator wiring plug and vacuum hose (arrowed)

17.30a   Turbocharger oil feed banjo bolt (arrowed)

17.30b   Turbocharger oil return hose retaining bolts (arrowed)

17.30c   The oil feed banjo bolt incorporates a filter

17.31   Turbocharger lower mounting bolt (arrowed)

17.32   Undo the nuts and recover the manifold spacers

17.34   Undo the nuts (arrowed) securing the turbocharger to the manifold

Note that there is a filter fitted into the oil feed banjo bolt **(see illustrations)**.

31 Slacken the turbocharger lower bracket bolt **(see illustration)**.

32 Pull the heat shield upwards to unclip it from the top surface, then undo the nuts securing the exhaust manifold to the cylinder head, and recover the spacers **(see illustration)**. Pull the manifold from the mounting studs. If the manifold is being removed to renew the gasket to the cylinder head, no further dismantling is required. Remove the gasket.

33 Lower the manifold and turbocharger downwards from the vehicle.

34 If required, undo the nuts and detach the turbocharger from the manifold **(see illustration)**.

5-cylinder engines

35 Remove the plastic cover from the top of the engine, and drain the cooling system as described in Chapter 1B.

36 Remove the catalytic converter as described in Chapter 4D.

37 Undo the 4 nuts/bolts and remove the heatshield above the exhaust manifold.

38 Raise the front of the vehicle and support it securely on axle stands (see *Jacking and vehicle support*). Remove the engine undershield. Undo the clamps and the support bracket bolt and remove the charge air pipe beneath the engine. Slacken the clamp and disconnect the inlet pipe from the turbocharger.

39 Undo the 2 screws for the pipe support bracket at the turbocharger. Unscrew the

unions and disconnect the oil feed, oil return, and coolant pipes from the turbocharger.

40 Slacken the clamp and disconnect the EGR cooler pipe from the end of the exhaust manifold. Disconnect the wiring plug from the turbocharger actuator.

41 Undo the 10 nuts securing the exhaust manifold/turbocharger to the cylinder head and recover any spacers.

Refitting

42 Examine all the manifold studs for signs of damage and corrosion; remove all traces of corrosion, and repair or renew any damaged studs.

43 Ensure the mating surfaces of the exhaust manifold and cylinder head are clean and dry. Position new gasket, and refit the exhaust manifold to the cylinder head. Tighten the nuts to the specified torque.

44 The remainder of refitting is a reversal of removal, noting the following points:

a) *Apply a little high-temperature anti-seize grease to the manifold studs.*

b) *Where necessary replenish the cooling system as described in Chapter 1B.*

c) *On 2.0 litre 4-cylinder engines, fit a new oil feed banjo bolt.*

18   Exhaust system – general information and component renewal

General information

1 The exhaust system consists of two sections: the front pipe with the catalytic

converter, and the rear section with the intermediate and rear silencers. A particulate filter is available on some vehicles depending on the engine fitted.

2 If required, the rear silencer can be replaced independently of the remainder of the system, by cutting the old silencer from the pipe, and slipping the new one over the cut end.

Removal

3 The exhaust system is joined together by a mixture of flanged, or sliding joints **(see illustration)**. Apply plenty of penetrating fluid to the fasteners prior to removal, undo the fasteners, unhook the rubber mountings, and manoeuvre the system from under the vehicle.

Rear silencer

4 If the rear silencer is the only part of the system requiring replacement, cut the old silencer from the rear section of the system using pipe cutters or a hacksaw. The exact

18.3   Exhaust pipe flange joint

point where the cut is made can differ depending on the engine fitted so you should check with a Volvo dealer before cutting the system. Free the silencer from its mountings, and remove it from the vehicle.

5 Clean up and de-burr the end of the existing exhaust pipe with a file/emery tape etc.

6 Replacement rear silencers are available, which slip over the end of the existing exhaust pipe, and are clamped in place. Slip the new silencer over the pipe, engage the rubber silencer mountings, then tighten the pipe clamp securely.

Refitting

7 Each section is refitted by reversing the removal sequence, noting the following points:

a) *Ensure that all traces of corrosion have been removed from the flanges and renew all gaskets.*

b) *Inspect the rubber mountings for signs of damage or deterioration, and renew as necessary.*

c) *Prior to tightening the exhaust system fasteners to the specified torque, ensure that all rubber mountings are correctly located, and that there is adequate clearance between the exhaust system and vehicle underbody.*

Chapter 4 Part C:
Emission control systems – petrol models

Contents

Degrees of difficulty

Easy, suitable for novice with little experience	Fairly easy, suitable for beginner with some experience	Fairly difficult, suitable for competent DIY mechanic	Difficult, suitable for experienced DIY mechanic	Very difficult, suitable for expert DIY or professional

Specifications

Torque wrench settings	Nm	lbf ft
Catalytic converter to manifold (2.4 litre models only)*	24	18
Oxygen sensor:		
1.8 and 2.0 litre models	20	15
2.4 litre models	45	33

* Do not re-use

1 General information

All models covered by this manual have various features built into the fuel and exhaust systems to help minimise harmful emissions. These features fall broadly into three categories; crankcase emission control, evaporative emission control, and exhaust emission control. The main features of these systems are as follows.

Crankcase emission control

To reduce the emissions of unburned hydrocarbons from the crankcase into the atmosphere, a Positive Crankcase Ventilation (PCV) system is used. The engine is sealed, and the blow-by gases and oil vapour are drawn from inside the crankcase, through an oil separator, into the inlet tract, to be burned by the engine during normal combustion.

Under conditions of high manifold depression (idling, deceleration) the gases will be sucked positively out of the crankcase. Under conditions of low manifold depression (acceleration, full-throttle running) the gases are forced out of the crankcase by the (relatively) higher crankcase pressure; if the engine is worn, the raised crankcase pressure (due to increased blow-by) will cause some of the flow to return under all manifold conditions.

Evaporative emission control

Petrol models

The evaporative emission control (EVAP) system is used to minimise the escape of unburned hydrocarbons into the atmosphere. To do this, the fuel tank filler cap is sealed, and a carbon canister is used to collect and store petrol vapours generated in the tank. When the engine is running, the vapours are cleared from the canister by an ECM controlled electrically-operated EVAP purge valve, into the inlet tract, to be burned by the engine during normal combustion.

To ensure that the engine runs correctly when idling, the valve only opens when the engine is running under load; the valve then opens to allow the stored vapour to pass into the inlet tract.

Exhaust emission control

Oxygen (lambda) sensors

To minimise the amount of pollutants which escape into the atmosphere, all models are fitted with a catalytic converter in the exhaust system. The system is of the closed-loop type, in which two heated oxygen sensors in the exhaust system provide the engine management ECM with constant feedback on the oxygen content of the exhaust gases. This enables the ECU to adjust the mixture by altering injector opening time, thus providing the best possible conditions for the converter

to operate. The system functions in the following way.

The oxygen sensors (also known as a lambda sensors) have built-in heating elements, activated by the ECM to quickly bring the sensor's tip to an efficient operating temperature. The sensor's tip is sensitive to oxygen, and sends the control module a varying voltage depending on the amount of oxygen in the exhaust gases; if the inlet air/fuel mixture is too rich, the exhaust gases are low in oxygen, so the sensor sends a voltage signal proportional to the oxygen detected, the voltage altering as the mixture weakens and the amount of oxygen in the exhaust gases rises. Peak conversion efficiency of all major pollutants occurs if the inlet air/fuel mixture is maintained at the chemically-correct ratio for complete combustion of petrol – 14.7 parts (by weight) of air to 1 part of fuel (the stoichiometric ratio). The sensor output voltage alters in a large step at this point, the ECM using the signal change as a reference point, and correcting the inlet air/fuel mixture accordingly, by altering the fuel injector opening time.

Exhaust gas recirculation (EGR) system

An EGR control valve is only fitted to 1.8 and 2.0 litre models.

The EGR system is designed to recirculate small quantities of exhaust gas into the inlet tract, and therefore into the combustion process. This reduces the level of oxides of

3.4 Oil separator – 1.8 and 2.0 litre models

nitrogen present in the final exhaust gas which is released into the atmosphere.

The volume of exhaust gas recirculated is controlled by an electrically-operated solenoid valve. The solenoid, valve, and cooler is an assembly mounted at the left-hand end of the cylinder head between the intake and exhaust manifold.

The EGR system is controlled by the engine management ECM, which receives information on engine operating parameters from its various sensors.

Catalytic converters

Catalytic converters are fitted to all petrol models. One catalytic converter is integral with the exhaust manifold, and another is normally fitted into the front section of the exhaust pipe.

**2   Catalytic converter –
      general information
      and precautions**

On petrol models, a three-way catalytic converter is incorporated into the exhaust manifold and the front section of the exhaust pipe, whilst on diesel models, an oxidation catalytic converter is fitted downstream from the turbocharger.

The catalytic converter is a reliable and simple device, which needs no maintenance in itself, but there are some facts of which an owner should be aware if the converter is to function properly for its full service life.

a) *DO NOT use leaded petrol or LRP – the lead will coat the precious metals, reducing their converting efficiency, and will eventually destroy the converter.*

b) *Always keep the ignition and fuel systems well-maintained in accordance with the manufacturer's schedule (see Chapter 1A).*

c) *If the engine develops a misfire, do not drive the vehicle at all (or at least as little as possible) until the fault is cured.*

d) *DO NOT push- or tow-start the vehicle – this will soak the catalytic converter in unburned fuel, causing it to overheat when the engine does start.*

e) *DO NOT switch off the ignition at high engine speeds, ie, do not blip the throttle immediately before switching off.*

3.12 The electrically-heated oil separator is located on the front face of the cylinder block – 2.4 litre models

f) *DO NOT use fuel or engine oil additives – these may contain substances harmful to the catalytic converter.*

g) *DO NOT continue to use the vehicle if the engine burns oil to the extent of leaving a visible trail of blue smoke.*

h) *Remember that the catalytic converter operates at very high temperatures. DO NOT, therefore, park the vehicle in dry undergrowth, over long grass or piles of dead leaves, after a long run.*

i) *Remember that the catalytic converter is FRAGILE. Do not strike it with tools during servicing work.*

j) *In some cases, a sulphurous smell (like that of rotten eggs) may be noticed from the exhaust. This is common to many catalytic converter-equipped vehicles. Once the vehicle has covered a few thousand miles, the problem should disappear – in the meantime, try changing the brand of petrol used.*

k) *The catalytic converter used on a well-maintained and well-driven vehicle should last for between 50 000 and 100 000 miles. If the converter is no longer effective, it must be renewed.*

**3   Crankcase emission control
      system – checking and
      component renewal**

Checking

1 The components of this system require no attention other than to check that the hoses are clear and undamaged.

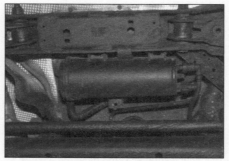

4.5 The carbon canister (arrowed) is attached to the rear subframe

Oil separator renewal

2 The oil separator is located on the front facing side of the cylinder block, below the intake manifold.

1.8 and 2.0 litre petrol models

3 Remove the intake manifold as described in Part A of this Chapter.

4 Unbolt the oil separator from the cylinder block/crankcase, and withdraw it. Remove and discard the gasket (**see illustration**).

5 Flush out or renew the oil separator as necessary.

6 On reassembly, fit a new gasket, and tighten the bolts securely.

7 The remainder of refitting is a reversal of removal.

2.4 litre models

8 Remove the air cleaner assembly as described in Chapter 4A.

9 Undo the engine oil level dipstick guide tube bolt, then pull the tube from the sump.

10 Undo the wiring connector bracket bolts, and move the bracket/harness to one side.

11 Remove the clips securing the connecting hoses to the separator. If the clips are in less than perfect condition, obtain new clips for reassembly.

12 Undo the 4 retaining bolts and remove the unit from the engine (**see illustration**).

13 Refit the oil separator using a reversal of removal. Refit the air cleaner assembly as described in Part A of this Chapter.

**4   Evaporative emission control
      system – checking and
      component renewal**

Checking

1 Poor idle, stalling and poor driveability can be caused by an inoperative canister vacuum valve, a damaged canister, split or cracked hoses, or hoses connected to the wrong fittings. Check the fuel filler cap for a damaged or deformed gasket.

2 Fuel loss or fuel odour can be caused by liquid fuel leaking from fuel lines, a cracked or damaged canister, an inoperative canister vacuum valve, and disconnected, misrouted, kinked or damaged vapour or control hoses.

3 Inspect each hose attached to the canister for kinks, leaks and cracks along its entire length. Repair or renew as necessary.

4 Inspect the canister. If it is cracked or damaged, renew it. Look for fuel leaking from the bottom of the canister. If fuel is leaking, renew the canister, and check the hoses and hose routing.

Component renewal

Carbon canister

5 The canister is located under the rear of the vehicle, attached to the rear subframe (**see illustration**).

6 Note their fitted locations, then press in the release buttons, and disconnect the hoses from the canister **(see illustration)**.
7 Undo the two retaining screws and lower the canister from place.
8 Refitting is a reversal of removal.

Canister purge valve (EVAP)

9 The canister purge valve is mounted in the engine compartment, on the left-hand end of the cylinder head. Remove the battery and battery tray as described in Chapter 5A.
10 Note their fitted positions, then disconnect the vacuum pipes and wiring plug from the valve **(see illustration)**.
11 Unclip the valve from the bracket.
12 Refitting is a reversal of removal.

---

5 Exhaust emission control systems – checking and component renewal

Checking

1 Checking of the system as a whole entails a close visual inspection of all hoses, pipes and connections for condition and security. Apart from this, any known or suspected faults should be attended to by a Volvo dealer or suitably-equipped specialist.

Oxygen (lambda) sensor renewal

Note: *The sensor is delicate, and will not work if it is dropped or knocked, if its power supply is disrupted, or if any cleaning materials are used on it.*

1.8 and 2.0 litre petrol models

2 Pull the plastic cover on the top of the engine straight up from its mountings.
3 Disconnect the heated oxygen sensor wiring connector, and release the wiring from any cable-ties.
4 Unscrew the sensor from the exhaust manifold, and collect the sealing washer (where fitted) **(see illustration)**.
5 On refitting, clean the sealing washer (where fitted) and renew it if it is damaged or worn. Apply a smear of anti-seize compound to the sensor's threads, then refit the sensor, tightening it to the specified torque. Reconnect the wiring and secure with cable-ties where applicable.

2.4 litre models

6 Raise the front of the vehicle and support it securely on axle stands (see *Jacking and vehicle support*). If removing the front sensor, undo the 7 Torx screws and remove the engine undershield.
7 Disconnect the sensor wiring plug, and release the wiring harness from any retaining clips.
8 Undo the sensor and recover the sealing washer (where fitted) **(see illustration)**.
9 On refitting, clean the sealing washer (where fitted) and renew it if it is damaged or worn. Apply a smear of anti-seize compound to the sensor's threads, then

4.6 Depress the release buttons (arrowed) and disconnect the hoses

refit the sensor, tightening it to the specified torque. Reconnect the wiring and secure with cable-ties where applicable.

Catalytic converter(s) renewal

1.8 and 2.0 litre petrol models

10 The catalytic converter(s) is part of the exhaust manifold. Refer to Part A of this Chapter for renewal procedures and additional information.

2.4 litre petrol models

11 Note its fitted position, then disconnect front oxygen sensor wiring plug **(see illustration)**. Release the sensor wiring harness from any retaining clips.
12 Remove the front right-hand driveshaft as described in Chapter 8.
13 Undo the bolts and remove the SIPS front crossmember from beneath the catalytic converter.

5.4 Unscrew the oxygen sensor from the manifold – upper sensor shown

5.11 Oxygen sensor wiring plug (arrowed)

4.10 The purge valve (arrowed) is located at the left-hand end of the cylinder head

14 Disconnect the rear oxygen sensor wiring plug, and release the wiring harness from any retaining clips.
15 Undo the nuts securing the catalytic converter to the exhaust manifold and the exhaust system.
16 Unhook the catalytic converter from the rubber mountings and lower is from the vehicle **(see illustration)**.
17 Refitting is a reversal of removal, noting the following points:
 a) Fit new gaskets.
 b) Use new nuts to secure the catalytic converter to the exhaust pipe and manifold.
 c) Tighten all fasteners to the specified torque where given.

EGR solenoid/valve renewal

1.8 and 2.0 litre petrol models

18 Remove the plastic cover on the top of

5.8 Rear oxygen sensor – 2.4 litre models

5.16 Catalytic converter mountings and SIPS crossmember (arrowed)

5.23 EGR valve (arrowed) – 1.8 and 2.0 litre models

the engine by pulling it straight up from its mountings.

19 Remove the air cleaner assembly as described in Chapter 4A.

20 Drain the coolant as described in Chapter 1A.

21 Undo the 4 retaining nuts securing the coolant outlet housing to the left-hand end of the cylinder head.

22 Undo the nut securing the oxygen sensor connector bracket, then pull the coolant outlet housing from the cylinder head. Discard the gasket.

23 Disconnect the solenoid wiring plug, then undo the screws and detach the solenoid/valve from the EGR tube **(see illustration)**. Discard the gasket.

24 Refitting is a reversal of removal, renewing the gasket where applicable.

Chapter 4 Part D:
Emission control systems – diesel models

Contents

Degrees of difficulty

Easy, suitable for novice with little experience	Fairly easy, suitable for beginner with some experience	Fairly difficult, suitable for competent DIY mechanic	Difficult, suitable for experienced DIY mechanic	Very difficult, suitable for expert DIY or professional

Specifications

Torque wrench settings	Nm	lbf ft
Catalytic converter to turbocharger*:		
1.6 litre (80kw) engine	25	18
1.6 litre (85kw) engine	24	18
2.0 litre 5-cylinder engine	7	5
2.0 litre 4-cylinder and 2.4 litre engine	24	18
EGR valve mounting bolts:		
1.6 litre (80kw) and 2.0 litre 4-cylinder engines	10	7
5-cylinder engines	50	37
EGR cooler bolts:		
2.0 litre 4-cylinder engine, to EGR valve	10	7
2.0 litre 4-cylinder engine, to exhaust manifold:		
Stage 1	15	12
Stage 2	25	18
2.0 litre 5-cylinder engine	50	37
2.4 litre engine	24	18
Exhaust flange nuts/bolts*	50	37
Exhaust gas temperature sensor:		
1.6/2.0 litre engines	30	22
2.4 litre engine	45	33
Oil separator bolts	20	15
Oxygen sensor	45	33
SIPS crossmember	50	37

* Do not re-use

3.5a Undo the 4 bolts (arrowed) securing the fuel filter bracket...

3.5b ...and the single Torx screw on the side (arrowed)...

3.5c ...then lift the filter from place

1 General information

Emission control systems

All models covered by this manual have various features built into the fuel and exhaust systems to help minimise harmful emissions. These features fall broadly into three categories; crankcase emission control, evaporative emission control, and exhaust emission control. Additionally, diesel models may be equipped with a particulate emission filter which uses porous silicon carbide substrate to trap particulates of carbon as the exhaust gases pass through.

The main features of these systems are as follows.

Crankcase emission control

Crankcase gases are taken via hoses from the cylinder head and the cylinder block, into a cyclone type oil separator. Here, the gases are forced to twist past two cones. As the gases pass the cones, oil is thrown out and condenses on the walls of the separator, where it then returns to the sump. The gases are admitted into the intake system, via a pressure limiting valve.

Exhaust gas recirculation system

This system is designed to recirculate small quantities of exhaust gas into the inlet tract, and therefore into the combustion process. This reduces the level of oxides of nitrogen present in the final exhaust gas which is released into the atmosphere.

The volume of exhaust gas recirculated is controlled by an electrically-operated solenoid valve. The solenoid, valve and cooler is an assembly mounted at the left-hand end or rear of the cylinder head between the intake and exhaust manifold.

The EGR system is controlled by the engine management ECM, which receives information on engine operating parameters from its various sensors.

Particulate filter system

The particulate filter is combined with the catalytic converter in the exhaust system, and

its purpose it to trap particulates of carbon (soot) as the exhaust gases pass through, in order to comply with latest emission regulations.

The filter can be automatically regenerated (cleaned) by the system's ECM on-board the vehicle. The engine's high pressure injection system is utilised to inject fuel into the exhaust gases during the post-injection period; this causes the filter temperature to increase sufficiently to oxidise the particulates, leaving an ash residue.

2 Catalytic converter – general information and precautions

The catalytic converter is a reliable and simple device, which needs no maintenance in itself, but there are some facts of which an owner should be aware if the converter is to function properly for its full service life.

a) Always keep the fuel system well-maintained in accordance with the manufacturer's schedule (see Chapter 1).

b) If the engine develops a misfire, do not drive the vehicle at all (or at least as little as possible) until the fault is cured.

c) DO NOT push – or tow-start the vehicle – this will soak the catalytic converter in unburned fuel, causing it to overheat when the engine does start.

d) DO NOT switch off the ignition at high engine speeds, ie, do not blip the throttle immediately before switching off.

e) DO NOT use fuel or engine oil additives – these may contain substances harmful to the catalytic converter.

3.7 Oil filter housing/separator retaining nuts (arrowed)

f) DO NOT continue to use the vehicle if the engine burns oil to the extent of leaving a visible trail of blue smoke.

g) Remember that the catalytic converter operates at very high temperatures. DO NOT, therefore, park the vehicle in dry undergrowth, over long grass or piles of dead leaves, after a long run.

h) Remember that the catalytic converter is FRAGILE. Do not strike it with tools during servicing work.

i) In some cases, a sulphurous smell (like that of rotten eggs) may be noticed from the exhaust. This is common to many catalytic converter-equipped vehicles. Once the vehicle has covered a few thousand miles, the problem should disappear – in the meantime, try changing the brand of diesel used.

j) The catalytic converter used on a well-maintained and well-driven vehicle should last for between 50 000 and 100 000 miles. If the converter is no longer effective, it must be renewed.

3 Crankcase emission control system – checking and component renewal

Checking

1 The components of this system require no attention other than to check that the hoses are clear and undamaged.

Oil separator renewal

Note: *The process described below is for the 2.0 4-cylinder engine.*

2 Drain the engine oil and coolant as described in Chapter 1B.

3 Pull the plastic cover on the top of the engine upwards from its mountings at the front and right-hand edges, then pull it forwards.

4 Release both wiring harnesses from the retaining clips on the fuel filter bracket.

5 Release the fuel pipe from the clip, then undo the 4 bolts/1 screw and lift up the fuel filter and its bracket, and place it on top of the engine **(see illustrations)**.

6 Slacken the clips and remove the air inlet pipe from the intake manifold.

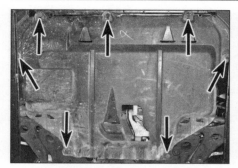

4.4 Engine undershield retaining Torx screws (arrowed)

4.5a Disconnect the flexible hose at the air cleaner housing

4.5b Intercooler hose support bracket bolt (arrowed) at the transmission housing

7 Disconnect the oil pressure switch wiring plug, then undo the nuts and detach the oil filter housing/separator from the engine block **(see illustration)**. Be prepared for oil and coolant spillage. Plug or seal the openings to prevent contamination.

8 Release the clips and disconnect the hoses as the unit is withdrawn.

9 Refitting is a reversal of removal, noting the following points:

  a) *Renew the oil filter housing/separator O-ring seal.*

  b) *Replenish the engine oil and coolant as described in Chapter 1B.*

---

4 Exhaust emission control systems – checking and component renewal

Checking

1 Checking of the system as a whole entails a close visual inspection of all hoses, pipes and connections for condition and security. Apart from this, any known or suspected faults should be attended to by a Volvo dealer or suitably equipped specialist.

Catalytic converter/ particulate filter renewal

2 There are slight variations in the removal and refitting procedure depending on the year of manufacture. Removal and refitting is essentially the same for all models.

1.6 litre engine

3 Remove the plastic cover on top of the engine by pulling it straight up from its mountings.

4 Raise the front of the vehicle and support it securely on axle stands (see *Jacking and vehicle support*). Undo the 7 Torx screws and remove the engine undershield **(see illustration)**.

5 Slacken the clamps and disconnect the flexible pipe between the air cleaner housing and the turbocharger inlet **(see illustration)**. Working from beneath, slacken the clamps and disconnect the 2 intercooler hoses and undo the bolt for the support bracket on the transmission housing **(see illustration)**.

6 Slacken the clamp and disconnect the charge air hose at the front of the engine, and

4.6a Slacken the clamp and disconnect the flexible section from the charge air hose

4.6b Undo the support bracket bolt (arrowed)

undo the bolt for the support bracket located behind the turbocharger inlet pipe **(see illustrations)**.

7 Unscrew the oxygen sensor and temperature sensor at the top of the catalyst/filter, collect the sealing washers (where fitted)

4.7a Unscrew the sensors (arrowed)...

4.7b ...and disconnect the sensor wiring plug

and disconnect the wiring plug above the alternator **(see illustrations)**.

8 Undo the 4 bolts and remove the heatshield above the turbocharger. Undo the 4 bolts and remove the heatshield surrounding the catalyst/filter **(see illustrations)**.

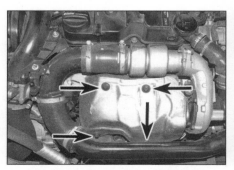

4.8a Turbocharger heat shield bolts (arrowed)

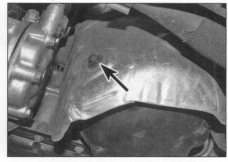

4.8b Undo the bolts for the catalyst/filter heat shield – one of the lower bolts arrowed

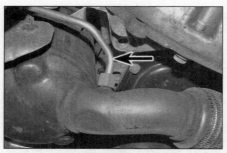

4.9 One of the catalyst/filter pressure pipes. Don't unscrew the union – trace the metal pipe back and disconnect the rubber hose

4.11 Undo the clamp connecting the catalyst/filter to the turbocharger

4.13 Undo the bolts securing the SIPS crossmember (arrowed)

9 Disconnect the hoses from the pressure pipes at the top and bottom of the catalyst/filter on the left-hand side **(see illustration)**.
10 Undo the nuts and disconnect the catalyst/filter at the exhaust pipe flange.
11 Undo the mounting nut and bolt on either side of the catalyst/filter, undo the clamp at the turbocharger **(see illustration)**, and carefully withdraw the catalyst/filter from under the vehicle.

2.0 litre 4-cylinder engine

12 Raise the front of the vehicle and support it securely on axle stands (see *Jacking and vehicle support*). Undo the 7 Torx screws and remove the engine undershield **(see illustration 4.4)**.
13 Undo the bolts and remove the SIPS crossmember from beneath the catalytic converter-to-exhaust pipe connection **(see illustration)**.
14 Undo the nuts and disconnect the catalytic converter from the exhaust pipe **(see illustration)**. Recover the gasket.
15 Unhook the rubber mountings from the catalytic converter adjacent to the front subframe.
16 Undo the 4 nuts securing the support bracket to the catalytic converter and the lower, rear engine/transmission mounting.
17 Slacken the clamp and detach the catalytic converter from the turbocharger **(see illustration)**. Withdraw the catalytic converter from under the vehicle.

2.0 litre 5-cylinder engine

18 Remove the plastic engine cover by pulling it straight up from its mountings.

4.14 Undo the nuts (arrowed) and detach the catalytic converter from the exhaust pipe

19 Unscrew the oxygen sensor and temperature sensor, collect the sealing washers (where fitted), and disconnect their wiring plugs.
20 Undo the 4 bolts and remove the exhaust manifold/turbocharger heatshield. Undo the clips and disconnect the pressure sensor pipes located at the top of the catalyst/filter.
21 Undo the bolts and remove the SIPS crossmember from beneath the catalytic converter-to-exhaust pipe connection **(see illustration 4.13)**.
22 Slacken the clamp and disconnect the pipe between the catalytic converter/particulate filter and the turbocharger. Slacken the clamp and disconnect the pipe between the catalytic converter/particulate filter and the forward section of the exhaust. Unhook the forward section of the exhaust from its rubber mountings.
23 Slacken the clamp that secures the catalytic converter/particulate filter and remove the unit.

2.4 litre 5-cylinder engine

24 To remove the catalytic converter, start by removing the plastic engine cover by pulling it straight up from its mountings.
25 Unscrew and remove the oxygen sensor and temperature sensor, collect the sealing washers (where fitted), and disconnect their wiring plugs. They are located in the exhaust pipe just below the heatshield for the exhaust manifold.
26 Remove the battery and battery tray as described in Chapter 5A.
27 Undo the 4 bolts and remove the exhaust manifold/turbocharger heat shield.

4.17 Catalytic convertor-to-turbocharger clamp bolt (arrowed)

28 Undo the 2 bolts for the catalytic converter support bracket, the bolts securing the catalytic converter to the turbocharger, and the bolts connecting the catalytic converter to the front section of the exhaust system.
29 Unhook the forward section of the exhaust from its rubber mountings, and remove the catalytic converter.
30 To remove the particulate filter, unscrew the temperature sensors (collecting the sealing washers where fitted) and disconnect the wiring plugs. Undo the bolts at the front and rear of the filter that connect it to the exhaust system, and unhook the exhaust mounting. The filter can now be removed.

Refitting

31 Refitting is a reversal of removal, noting the following points:
a) *Ensure that all traces of corrosion have been removed from the flanges and renew all gaskets.*
b) *Use new clamps to secure the catalytic converter/particulate filter to the turbocharger.*
c) *Use new nuts to secure the catalytic converter/particulate filter to the exhaust pipe.*
d) *Inspect the rubber mountings for signs of damage or deterioration, and renew as necessary.*
e) *Prior to the tightening the exhaust system fasteners to the specified torque, ensure that all rubber mountings are correctly located, and that there is adequate clearance between the exhaust system and vehicle underbody.*
f) *On refitting the oxygen or temperature sensors, clean the sealing washer (where fitted) and renew if it is damaged or worn. Apply a smear of anti-seize compound to the sensor's threads, then refit the sensor, tightening it to the specified torque. Reconnect the wiring and secure with cable ties where applicable.*

EGR valve/cooler

Note: *If the EGR valve is replaced it must be adapted to the engine using diagnostic equipment. Consult a Volvo dealer or suitably equipped specialist.*

1.6 litre (80 kw) engine

32 To remove the EGR valve, start by removing the plastic cover on top of the engine.

33 Slacken the clamp for the air pipe at the EGR valve, undo the 2 bolts securing the pipe to the inlet manifold at the right-hand end of the cylinder head, undo the bolt for the support bracket, and remove the pipe.

34 Disconnect the wiring plug, undo the 2 securing bolts, and remove the EGR valve.

35 To remove the EGR cooler, start by draining the cooling system as described in Chapter 1B.

36 Undo the retaining clamps/clips and disconnect all coolant pipes from the cooler. Slacken the clamps, disconnect the inlet pipe from the end of the cooler and between the cooler and the EGR valve **(see illustration)**, undo the securing bolt, and remove the cooler.

37 Refitting is a reversal of removal for both components, ensuring that the cooling system is replenished where necessary.

1.6 litre (85kw) engine

38 Refer to the process for the removal of the inlet manifold, as described in Chapter 4B.

2.0 litre 4-cylinder engine

39 Remove the plastic cover from the top of the engine by pulling it upwards at the right-hand and front edges, then pull it forwards.

40 Raise the front of the vehicle and support it securely on axle stands (see *Jacking and vehicle support*). Undo the 7 Torx screws and remove the engine undershield **(see illustration 4.4)**.

41 Take the weight of the engine with an engine hoist. If a hoist is not available, use a trolley jack beneath the engine, with a block of wood between the jack head and the sump to prevent damage.

42 Undo the 2 nuts and 2 bolts, then remove the right-hand engine mounting assembly.

43 Undo the 2 bolts and remove the lower torque rod from the rear of the engine/transmission.

44 Release the clamp and disconnect the air ducting from the intake manifold.

45 Lower the engine approximately 8 cm, and move it forward slightly.

46 Remove the clamp securing the EGR pipe to the exhaust manifold **(see illustration)**.

4.36 EGR valve pipe clamp (arrowed)

47 Undo the screws securing the EGR valve to the EGR cooler and the 2 screws securing the valve to the cylinder head **(see illustration)**. In order to improve access, disconnect the charge air pipe by the air cleaner, and remove the pipe bracket screw adjacent to the EGR valve, then bend the pipe out of the way.

48 Slacken the mounting screw under the EGR valve a few turns, withdrawn the valve. Discard the gasket.

49 Refitting is a reversal of removal, noting the following points:
a) *Renew the valve-to-cooler gasket.*
b) *Tighten the fasteners to the specified torque where given.*
c) *Replenish the cooling system as described in Chapter 1B.*

2.0 litre 5-cylinder engine

50 Drain the cooling system as described in Chapter 1B.

51 Remove the air filter housing as described in Chapter 4B, and the throttle body assembly as described in Chapter 4B.

52 Slacken the clamps and remove any pipework and support brackets from the EGR valve/cooler, and disconnect the wiring plugs.

53 Undo the 2 bolts that secure the EGR cooler to the exhaust manifold pipe. Undo the 3 bolts securing the EGR valve/cooler to the cylinder block, and remove the unit. The EGR valve can be separated from the EGR cooler by undoing the 4 bolts that connect the components.

54 Refitting is a reversal of removal noting the points in step 49 above. Note that the system may need to be reset using Volvo diagnostic

equipment in which case you should consult a Volvo dealer or suitably equipped specialist.

2.4 litre engine

55 Drain the cooling system as described in Chapter 1B.

56 Remove the EGR actuator valve by removing the throttle body as described in Chapter 4B, disconnecting the wiring plug, and undoing the 4 bolts that secure the actuator valve.

57 Remove the battery and battery box as described in Chapter 5A.

58 Slacken the clamp and disconnect the air pipe between the inlet manifold and the EGR valve. Undo the bolt securing the pipe bracket to the top of the EGR valve.

59 Release the clamps and disconnect the pipes from the EGR cooler, and slacken the clamp that connects the EGR cooler to the exhaust manifold.

60 Undo the bolt for the EGR cooler support bracket, the 2 bolts securing the EGR valve to the cylinder block, and remove the unit. The EGR valve can be separated from the EGR cooler by undoing the 4 bolts that connect the components.

61 Refitting is a reversal of removal.

Particulate filter differential pressure sensor

62 The location of the sensor differs depending on the engine fitted. On models fitted with the 1.6 litre engine it is located on the side of the air filter housing (80 kW) or the side of the battery box (85 kW) **(see illustration)**, while on other engines it is located at the rear of the engine bay or cylinder head **(see illustration)**.

4.46 Release the clamp (arrowed)

4.47 The EGR valve is secured by 2 screws to the cylinder head, and one Allen screw on its underside (arrowed)

4.62a On the 85kW 1.6 litre engine, the sensor is on the side of the battery box

4.62b Particulate filter differential pressure sensor located at the rear of the cylinder head

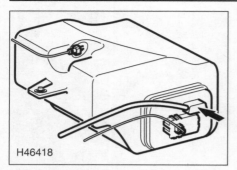

4.66 Detach the quick-release connectors and the level sensor wiring plug (arrowed)

Note that on models fitted with the 2.0 litre 5-cylinder engine, it is necessary to remove the vacuum actuator for the turbocharger in order to gain access to the sensor.

63 On all engines disconnect the sensor wiring plug, undo the clips and disconnect the hoses, and undo any retaining screws. The sensor can now be withdrawn.

Note: *After renewing the pressure differential sensor, the values for the sensor stored in the ECM must be adapted. This requires access to dedicated Volvo diagnostic equipment, and should be entrusted to a Volvo dealer or suitably-equipped specialist.*

Additive tank renewal

Caution: Do not allow the additive to come into contact with skin, eyes or vehicle paintwork.

64 The tank is mounted underneath the rear of the vehicle, attached to the subframe. Raise the rear of the vehicle and support it securely on axle stands (see *Jacking and vehicle support*).

65 Disconnect the tank level sensor wiring plug.

66 Release the quick-release connectors and disconnect the pipes from the tank **(see illustration)**. Be prepared for fluid spillage. Plug or seal the openings to prevent contamination.

67 Undo the 3 screws and remove the tank. Note that new tanks are only available as complete units – no separate parts are available. Consult a Volvo dealer or specialist.

68 Refitting is a reversal of removal. Note that after the tank has been refitted/renewed, the additive feed hose must be filled with additive, and the control module adapted. This can only be carried out using Volvo test equipment. Consult a Volvo dealer or specialist.

Additive dosage control module (ADM) renewal

69 Ensure the ignition is switched off, then remove the rear seat cushion as described in Chapter 11.

70 Lift up the carpet on the left-hand side under the seat, undo the 2 nuts and remove the ADM. Disconnect the ADM wiring plug as the unit is withdrawn.

71 Refitting is a reversal of removal. Note that if the ADM has been renewed, the new unit must be programmed using software downloaded from Volvo. Consult a Volvo dealer or specialist.

Chapter 5 Part A:
Starting and charging systems

Contents

Degrees of difficulty

Easy, suitable for novice with little experience	**Fairly easy,** suitable for beginner with some experience	**Fairly difficult,** suitable for competent DIY mechanic	**Difficult,** suitable for experienced DIY mechanic	**Very difficult,** suitable for expert DIY or professional

Specifications

System

Type . . . . 12 volt, negative earth

Battery

Type . . . . Low-maintenance or maintenance-free sealed for life
Capacity . . . . 60 to 90 Ah (depending on model)
Charge condition:
　Poor . . . . 12.5 volts
　Normal . . . . 12.6 volts
　Good . . . . 12.7 volts

Alternator

Output . . . . 120 or 150A

Starter motor

Type:
　Petrol engines:
　　1.8 and 2.0 litre engines . . . . 1.1 kW
　　2.4 litre engines. . . . . 1.4 kW
　Diesel engines:
　　1.6 litre engines. . . . . 1.7 kW
　　2.0 litre engines. . . . . 2 kW
　　2.4 litre engines. . . . . 2.2 kW

Torque wrench settings	Nm	lbf ft
Alternator mounting bolts:		
Petrol engines:		
1.8 and 2.0 litre engines	24	18
2.4 litre engines	24	18
Diesel engines:		
1.6 litre 80kw engine	24	18
1.6 litre 85kw engine	48	35
2.0 litre 4-cylinder engine:		
M6	10	7
M10	50	37
5-cylinder engines	24	18
Battery clamp bolts	10	7
Engine crossmember nuts	24	18
Starter motor mounting bolts:		
Petrol engines:		
1.8 and 2.0 litre engines	35	26
2.4 litre petrol engines	40	30
Diesel engines:		
1.6 litre engines	35	26
All other engines	50	37

1 General information and precautions

General information

The engine electrical system consists mainly of the charging and starting systems. Because of their engine-related functions, these components are covered separately from the body electrical devices such as the lights, instruments, etc (which are covered in Chapter 12). Information on the diesel preheating system is covered in Chapter 5C.

The electrical system is of the 12 volt negative earth type.

The battery is of the low-maintenance or maintenance-free (sealed for life) type, and is charged by the alternator, which is belt-driven from the crankshaft pulley.

The starter motor is of the pre-engaged type, incorporating an integral solenoid. On starting, the solenoid moves the drive pinion into engagement with the flywheel ring gear before the starter motor is energised. Once the engine has started, a one-way clutch prevents the motor armature being driven by the engine until the pinion disengages from the flywheel.

Precautions

⚠️ **Warning: It is necessary to take extra care when working on the electrical system to avoid damage to semi-conductor devices (diodes and transistors), and to avoid the risk of personal injury. In addition to the precautions given in 'Safety first!' observe the following when working on the system:**

• **Always remove rings, watches, etc before working on the electrical system. Even with the battery disconnected, capacitive discharge could occur if a component's live terminal is earthed through a metal object. This could cause a shock or nasty burn.**

• **Do not reverse the battery connections. Components such as the alternator, electronic control units, or any other components having semi-conductor circuitry could be irreparably damaged.**

• **Never disconnect the battery terminals, the alternator, any electrical wiring or any test instruments when the engine is running.**

• **Do not allow the engine to turn the alternator when the alternator is not connected.**

• **Never test for alternator output by 'flashing' the output lead to earth.**

• **Always ensure that the battery negative lead is disconnected when working on the electrical system.**

• **If the engine is being started using jump leads and a slave battery, connect the batteries positive-to-positive and negative-to-negative (see Jump starting). This also applies when connecting a battery charger.**

• **Never use an ohmmeter of the type incorporating a hand-cranked generator for circuit or continuity testing.**

• **Before using electric-arc welding equipment on the car, disconnect the battery, alternator and components such as the electronic control units (where applicable) to protect them from the risk of damage.**

2 Battery – testing and charging

Testing

Standard and low-maintenance battery

1 If the vehicle covers a small annual mileage, it is worthwhile checking the specific gravity of the electrolyte every three months to determine the state of charge of the battery. Use a hydrometer to make the check, and compare the results with the following table. Note that the specific gravity readings assume an electrolyte temperature of 15°C (60°F); for every 10°C (18°F) below 15°C (60°F) subtract 0.007. For every 10°C (18°F) above 15°C (60°F) add 0.007.

	Above 25°C	Below 25°C
Fully-charged	1.210 to 1.230	1.270 to 1.290
70% charged	1.170 to 1.190	1.230 to 1.250
Discharged	1.050 to 1.070	1.110 to 1.130

2 If the battery condition is suspect, first check the specific gravity of electrolyte in each cell. A variation of 0.040 or more between any cells indicates loss of electrolyte or deterioration of the internal plates.

3 If the specific gravity variation is 0.040 or more, the battery should be renewed. If the cell variation is satisfactory but the battery is discharged, it should be charged as described later in this Section.

Maintenance-free battery

4 In cases where a sealed for life maintenance-free battery is fitted, topping-up and testing of the electrolyte in each cell may not be possible. The condition of the battery can therefore only be tested using a battery condition indicator or a voltmeter.

5 Certain models may be fitted with a maintenance-free battery, with a built-in charge condition indicator. The indicator is located in the top of the battery casing, and indicates the condition of the battery from its colour. The charge conditions denoted by the colour of the indicator should be printed on a label attached to the battery – if not, consult a Volvo dealer or automotive electrician for advice.

6 If testing the battery using a voltmeter, connect the voltmeter across the battery and note the voltage. The test is only accurate if the battery has not been subjected to any kind of charge for the previous six hours. If this is not the case, switch on the headlights

for 30 seconds, then wait four to five minutes before testing the battery after switching off the headlights. All other electrical circuits must be switched off, so check that the doors and tailgate are fully shut when making the test.

7 If the voltage reading is less than 12.2 volts, then the battery is discharged, whilst a reading of 12.2 to 12.4 volts indicates a partially-discharged condition.

8 If the battery is to be charged, it should be removed from the vehicle and charged on the bench as described later in this section. If a modern 'intelligent' battery charger is used, the battery can be charged in situ once disconnected – as described in Section 3.

Charging

Note: *The use of a modern 'intelligent' battery charger is recommended. These chargers can safely charge all types of battery, regardless of the state of charge of the battery.*

Standard and low-maintenance battery

9 Rapid boost charges which are claimed to restore the power of the battery in 1 to 2 hours are not recommended, as they can cause serious damage to the battery plates through overheating. If the battery is completely flat, recharging should take at least 24 hours.

10 While charging the battery, note that the temperature of the electrolyte should never exceed 37.8°C (100°F).

Maintenance-free battery

11 This battery type takes considerably longer to fully recharge than the standard type, the time taken being dependent on the extent of discharge, but it can take anything up to three days.

12 If the battery is to be charged from a fully-discharged state (condition reading less than 12.2 volts) it must be recharged with a modern 'intelligent' battery charger. Where this is not available then the battery should be charged by a local garage, auto electrician or the main dealer.

3 Battery – disconnecting, reconnecting, removal and refitting

Disconnecting the battery

Caution: Wait at least 5 minutes after turning off the ignition switch before disconnect the battery. This is to allow sufficient time for the various control modules to store information.

1 Lower the drivers window and remove the key from the ignition. Note the warning above.

2 The battery is located on the left-hand side of the engine compartment. Open the cover to gain access to the battery. On models fitted with an engine compartment crossmember, pull up the plastic covers, undo the retaining nuts and move the crossmember out of the way **(see illustrations)**.

3 Loosen the clamp nut and disconnect the battery negative lead (-) **(see illustration)**.

4 Move the negative (earth) lead away from the terminal. Cover the lead (or battery terminal) with a suitable insulator (a plastic bag is ideal) or simply secure it to the side with a cable tie.

Reconnecting the battery

5 Reconnect the negative lead. Push it down until it is flush with the battery terminal post and then tighten the nut to the specified torque.
6 Refit the battery cover and close the bonnet.
7 Reach through the open drivers window and turn on the sidelights. Wait a minute or so to allow the on board computer systems to boot up and for the battery voltage to stabilise.
8 Start the vehicle (from outside where possible) and then open and close all the power windows. Adjust the clock time and re-activate the audio unit by inserting the security code (where applicable).
9 To restore the electric window automatic opening/closing function (where fitted) ensure all windows and doors are closed, and then lock the vehicle via the driver's door. Now unlock the driver's door, and then lock it again – hold the key in the locking position for at least one second.

Removal

10 Remove the battery cover and disconnect the battery as described above.
11 Slacken the clamp nut and disconnect the battery positive lead terminal (**see illustration**).
12 On models fitted with the 1.6 litre engine, undo the retaining bolts for the differential pressure sensor and move it to one side.

3.2a   Where fitted, pull up the plastic cover each end and undo the crossmember nut

3.3   Slacken the clamp nut and disconnect the battery negative lead

Unhook the pipe from the side of the battery box, release any wiring loom securing clips and using a screwdriver, release the front section of the battery box and pull it towards the front of the vehicle (**see illustrations**).

3.2b   Release the clip and remove the cover over the battery

3.11   Slacken the clamp nut and disconnect the battery positive terminal

13 Unscrew the 2 nuts and remove the battery retaining clamp (**see illustrations**).
14 Lift the battery out of the engine compartment (**see illustration**). If required, the battery tray can be removed by undoing

3.12a   Undo the bolts for the differential pressure sensor...

3.12b   ...unhook the pipe from the side of the battery box...

3.12c   ...and release the front section of the battery box and pull it forwards

3.13a   Undo the nuts for the battery clamp ...

3.13b   ...and remove the clamp

3.14a   Lift the battery from its tray

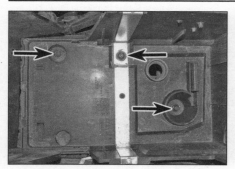

3.14b   If required, undo the 3 bolts and remove the battery tray

3.21a   Auxiliary battery wiring plug

Note: *Refer to the warnings given in 'Safety first!' and in Section 1 of this Chapter before starting work.*

1 If the ignition/no-charge warning light fails to illuminate when the ignition is switched on, first check the alternator wiring connections for security. If all is satisfactory, the alternator maybe at fault and should be renewed or taken to an auto-electrician for testing and repair.

2 If the ignition warning light illuminates when the engine is running, stop the engine and check that the drivebelt is correctly tensioned (see Chapter 1A or 1B) and that the alternator connections are secure. If all is so far satisfactory, have the alternator checked by an auto-electrician for testing and repair.

3 If the alternator output is suspect even though the warning light functions correctly, the regulated voltage may be checked as follows.

4 Connect a voltmeter across the battery terminals and start the engine.

5 Increase the engine speed until the voltmeter reading remains steady; the reading should be between 13.5 and 14.8 volts.

6 Switch on as many electrical accessories (eg, the headlights, heated rear window and heater blower) as possible, and check that the alternator maintains the regulated voltage between 13.5 and 14.8 volts.

7 If the regulated voltage is not as stated, the fault may be due to worn brushes, weak brush springs, a faulty voltage regulator, a faulty diode, a severed phase winding, or worn or damaged slip-rings. The brushes and slip-ring may be checked (see Section 6), but if the fault persists the alternator should be renewed or taken to an auto-electrician for testing and repair.

3.21b   Undo the bolt for the battery cover

3.23   The cover just fits over the auxiliary battery and clips into place at the rear of the battery box

the 3 bolts in the base, unclipping any wiring or pipes, and lifting the tray from place **(see illustration).**

Refitting

15 Position the battery in the battery box.

16 Refit the retaining clamp and tighten the retaining nuts securely. Clip the front section of the battery box in place, ensuring that any wiring loom clips have been refitted.

17 Reconnect the battery positive lead, followed by the negative lead. Smear a little petroleum jelly on the terminals. Ensure no-one is inside the vehicle whilst the battery is reconnected.

18 Refit the battery cover, followed by the engine compartment crossmember (where fitted). Tighten the retaining nuts securely.

19 After reconnecting the battery, the engine

may run erratically until it's been driven for a few minutes to allow the ECM to relearn driving characteristics. Initialise the central locking system by unlocking the vehicle with the remove control or key.

Auxiliary Battery

Note: *On models fitted with the Stop/Start system, an auxiliary battery is located in front of the left-hand side front wheel.*

20 Remove the front bumper as described in Chapter 11.

21 Disconnect the wiring plug, and undo the bolt for the battery cover **(see illustrations).**

23 Slide the cover towards the left-hand side of the vehicle, and then lift it from position. The battery can now be lifted from its tray **(see illustration).**

24 Refitting is a reversal of removal.

Removal

1 Disconnect the battery negative lead (see Section 3)

2 Remove the auxiliary drivebelt as described in Chapter 1A or 1B.

1.8 and 2.0 litre petrol engines

3 Remove the plastic cover on the top of the engine by pulling it straight upwards from its mountings.

4 Undo and remove the alternator upper mounting bolt.

5 Raise the vehicle and support it securely on axle stands (see *Jacking and vehicle support*). Where fitted, undo the 7 Torx screws and remove the engine undershield **(see illustration).**

6 Disconnect the wiring plugs and the lead from the terminal stud at the rear of the alternator **(see illustration).**

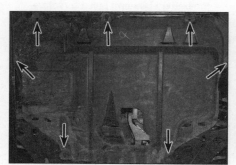

5.5 Undo the 7 Torx screws and remove the engine undershield

5.6 Disconnect the wiring plug, then pull off the rubber cap and disconnect the lead from the terminal stud

5.8 Wheel arch liner plastic nuts

5.9 Pull off the rubber cap, disconnect the terminal lead and then disconnect the wiring plug

5.14 Remove the flexible section of pipe (arrowed)

5.18 Undo the bolts (arrowed) and lift off the fuel filter cover

5.19a Undo the Torx screw on the side of the filter (arrowed)…

5.19b …then lift the filter from place

7 Undo the 2 lower mounting bolts and lift out the alternator.

2.4 litre petrol engines

8 Jack up the front of the vehicle (see *Jacking and vehicle support*), then remove the right-hand front roadwheel. Undo the Torx screws/plastic nuts and remove the wheel arch liner **(see illustration)**.
9 Disconnect the wiring plug and the lead from the terminal stud at the rear of the alternator **(see illustration)**.
10 Remove the retaining bolts and remove the alternator.

1.6 litre diesel engine (80kW)

11 Disconnect the sensor(s) wiring plug(s), then undo the retaining bolts and remove the air inlet tube/anti-shudder valve. Recover the seal and renew if necessary.
12 Slacken the clamps, disconnect the air inlet pipes, undo the retaining bolts, and remove the throttle body assembly.

1.6 litre diesel engine (85 kW)

13 Pull the plastic cover on top of the engine upwards to release it from its mountings.
14 Slacken the clamps, undo the nut and bolt securing the retaining bracket, and remove the flexible section of air pipe adjacent to the throttle body **(see illustration)**.
15 Remove the throttle body as described in Chapter 4B, Section 12.
16 Move any remaining air pipes to one side, along with any sections of the wiring harness. Unclip the wiring harness from the bracket above the alternator and disconnect the two

wiring plugs. Undo the 3 bolts and remove the tensioner for the auxiliary drivebelt, along with the bracket above the alternator.
17 Slacken and remove the air-conditioning compressor bolts. DO NOT disconnect the refrigerant lines. Manoeuvre the alternator past the compressor and remove it.

2.0 litre 4-cylinder models

18 Undo the bolts and remove the cover from over the fuel filter assembly **(see illustration)**.
19 Disconnect the wiring plug, then undo the screw and lift the fuel filter from position with the hoses still attached **(see illustrations)**.
20 Remove the lower filter bracket/protective cover and then disconnect the wiring plugs from the alternator **(see illustration 5.9)**.
21 Remove the single lower bolt, the front bolts and the upper bolt **(see illustration)**. Lift up and remove the alternator.

5.21 The 2.0 litre (4-cylinder) alternator mounting bolts

5-cylinder engines

22 Pull the plastic cover on top of the engine upwards to release it from its mountings.
23 Slacken the clamp for the outlet pipe from the air cleaner housing, the clamp at the rear of the cylinder head on the right-hand side, undo the bolt for the securing bracket, and remove the air pipe at the front of the engine. Undo the 2 bolts and remove the intake trunking from the lock panel.
24 Remove the rubber cover and disconnect the alternator B+ wire by removing the bolt and then disconnect the control wiring plug **(see illustration 5.9)**.
25 Remove the mounting bolts **(see illustrations)** and then remove the alternator.

Refitting

26 For all engines refitting is a reversal of

5.25a The upper mounting bolt…

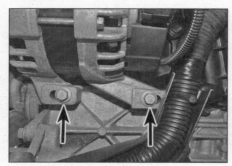

5.25b …and the lower mounting bolts

6.3 Undo the 3 nuts and remove the plastic cover

6.4 Brush holder screws (arrowed)

removal, remembering to tighten the various fasteners to their specified torque where given.

6 Alternator –
brush holder/regulator module renewal

1 Remove the alternator, as described in Section 5.
2 Place the alternator on a clean work surface, with the pulley facing down.
3 Undo the cover nuts/screws, then lift the plastic cover from the rear of the alternator **(see illustration)**.
4 Undo the screws and carefully remove the brush holder from the alternator **(see illustration)**.
5 Inspect the brushes for wear and damage. No specifications for brush length are given by Volvo, but excessive wear should be obvious **(see illustration)**.
6 Clean and inspect the surfaces of the slip-rings on the end of the alternator shaft, working through the holder location hole **(see illustration)**. If they are excessively worn, or damaged, the alternator must be renewed.
7 To refit the brush holder, push the brushes back into their holders, then insert a 1.5mm Allen key (or extended paper clip) through the hole in the brush cover to hold the brushes in their retracted positions **(see illustration)**.
8 Lower the brush holder over the slip-rings and securely tighten the retaining screws. Remove the Allen key (or paper clip).

7 Starting system –
testing

Note: *Refer to the precautions given in 'Safety first!' and in Section 1 of this Chapter before starting work.*
1 If the starter motor fails to operate when the ignition key is turned to the appropriate position, the following possible causes may be to blame:
a) *The battery is faulty.*
b) *The electrical connections between the switch, solenoid, battery and starter motor are somewhere failing to pass the necessary current from the battery through the starter to earth.*
c) *The solenoid is faulty.*
d) *The starter motor is mechanically or electrically defective.*
2 To check the battery, switch on the headlights. If they dim after a few seconds, this indicates that the battery is discharged – recharge (see Section 2) or renew the battery. If the headlights glow brightly, operate the ignition switch and observe the lights. If they dim, then this indicates that current is reaching the starter motor, therefore the fault must lie in the starter motor. If the lights continue to glow brightly (and no clicking sound can be heard from the starter motor solenoid), this indicates that there is a fault in the circuit or solenoid –

see following paragraphs. If the starter motor turns slowly when operated, but the battery is in good condition, then this indicates that either the starter motor is faulty, or there is considerable resistance somewhere in the circuit.
3 If a fault in the circuit is suspected, disconnect the battery leads (including the earth connection to the body), the starter/solenoid wiring and the engine/transmission earth strap. Thoroughly clean the connections, and reconnect the leads and wiring, then use a voltmeter or test light to check that full battery voltage is available at the battery positive lead connection to the solenoid, and that the earth is sound. Smear petroleum jelly around the battery terminals to prevent corrosion – corroded connections are amongst the most frequent causes of electrical system faults.
4 If the battery and all connections are in good condition, check the circuit by disconnecting the wire from the solenoid blade terminal. Connect a voltmeter or test light between the wire end and a good earth (such as the battery negative terminal), and check that the wire is live when the ignition switch is turned to the start position. If it is, then the circuit is sound – if not, the circuit wiring can be checked as described in Chapter 12.
5 The solenoid contacts can be checked by connecting a voltmeter or test light between the battery positive feed connection on the starter side of the solenoid, and earth. When the ignition switch is turned to the start position, there should be a reading or lighted

6.5 Inspect the brushes for wear or damage

6.6 Inspect the alternator shaft slip-rings for wear or damage

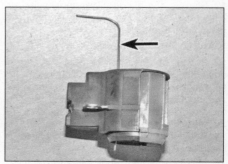

6.7 Insert a paper clip through the hole in the cover to retain the brushes prior to refitting (arrowed)

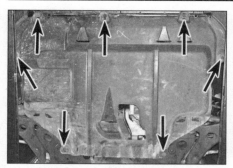

8.2 Undo the 7 Torx screws (arrowed) and remove the engine undershield

8.3 Undo the nut and slide the wiring terminal from the stud

8.4 Remove the wiring harness bracket from the starter motor retaining studs/bolts

bulb, as applicable. If there is no reading or lighted bulb, the solenoid is faulty and should be renewed.

6 If the circuit and solenoid are proved sound, the fault must lie in the starter motor. In this event, it may be possible to have the starter motor overhauled by a specialist, but check on the cost of spares before proceeding, as it may prove more economical to obtain a new or exchange motor.

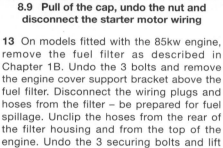

8.9 Pull of the cap, undo the nut and disconnect the starter motor wiring

8.10 Note the position of the locating dowel

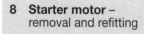

8 Starter motor – removal and refitting

Removal

1 Disconnect the battery negative lead as described in Section 3.

1.8 and 2.0 litre petrol models

2 Raise the front of the vehicle and support it securely on axle stands (see *Jacking and vehicle support*). Where fitted, undo the 7 Torx screws and remove the engine undershield **(see illustration)**.

3 Disconnect the wiring from the starter solenoid **(see illustration)**.

4 Undo the retaining nuts and move the wiring bracket to one side **(see illustration)**.

5 Unbolt the starter motor rear support bracket from the cylinder block – where fitted.

6 Undo the mounting studs and remove the starter motor. Discard the gasket.

2.4 litre petrol models

7 Remove the air cleaner assembly as described in Chapter 4A, Section 3.

8 Unclip the coolant hose, then slacken the hose bracket and bend it to one side for access to the starter motor bolts.

9 Disconnect the wiring from the starter motor **(see illustration)**.

10 Undo the mounting bolts and remove the starter motor **(see illustration)**.

1.6 litre diesel engines

11 Remove the plastic cover on top of the engine.

12 Disconnect the battery negative lead and on models fitted with the 80 kW engine, remove the battery and battery box as described in Section 3.

13 On models fitted with the 85kw engine, remove the fuel filter as described in Chapter 1B. Undo the 3 bolts and remove the engine cover support bracket above the fuel filter. Disconnect the wiring plugs and hoses from the filter – be prepared for fuel spillage. Unclip the hoses from the rear of the filter housing and from the top of the engine. Undo the 3 securing bolts and lift the filter housing from place.

14 Undo the 2 upper starter motor mounting bolts located at the bell housing.

15 Raise the front of the vehicle and support it securely on axle stands (see *Jacking and vehicle support*). Undo the 7 Torx screws and remove the engine undershield **(see illustration 8.2)**.

16 On models fitted with the 80kW engine, undo the 3 bolts securing the bracket to the rear of the subframe, undo the mounting bolt,

disconnect the 2 vacuum hoses, and remove the vacuum capsule in front of the starter motor.

17 Disconnect the wiring from the starter motor solenoid, undo the lower mounting bolt, and remove the unit. Note the position of any locating dowels and ensure they are positioned correctly when refitting.

2.0 litre 4-cylinder engine

18 Raise the front of the vehicle and support it securely on axle stands (see *Jacking and vehicle support*). Undo the 7 Torx screws and remove the engine undershield **(see illustration 8.2)**.

19 Undo the M8 and M6 nuts, then pull the plastic cover over the starter wiring connections to the right-hand side to disconnect them **(see illustration)**.

20 Undo the mounting bolts and remove the starter downwards **(see illustration)**.

8.19 Undo the nuts (arrowed) and disconnect the wiring

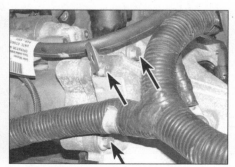

8.20 Starter motor bolts (arrowed) – 2.0 litre 4-cylinder engine

5-cylinder engines

21 Disconnect the battery negative lead as described in Section 3.

22 Remove the throttle body assembly as describe in Chapter 4B Section 12.

23 Unclip the wiring harness from around the starter motor, disconnect the wiring from the starter motor solenoid, and undo the 3 mounting bolts. The motor can now be withdrawn.

Refitting

24 Refitting is a reversal of removal. Tighten all fasteners to their specified torque where given.

9 Starter motor –
   testing and overhaul

If the starter motor is thought to be suspect, it should be removed and taken to an auto-electrician for testing. Most auto-electricians will be able to supply and fit brushes at a reasonable cost. However, check on the cost of repairs before proceeding, as it may prove more economical to obtain a new or exchange motor.

Chapter 5 Part B:
Ignition system – petrol models

Contents

Degrees of difficulty

Easy, suitable for novice with little experience 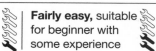 | **Fairly easy,** suitable for beginner with some experience | **Fairly difficult,** suitable for competent DIY mechanic | **Difficult,** suitable for experienced DIY mechanic | **Very difficult,** suitable for expert DIY or professional

Specifications

General

System type . . . . Distributorless engine management system
Firing order:
  4-cylinder models. . . . . 1-3-4-2 (No 1 cylinder at the timing chain end of the engine)
  5-cylinder models. . . . . 1-2-4-5-3 (No 1 cylinder at timing belt end of engine)

Spark plugs

Type . . . . See Chapter 1A Specifications

Ignition timing

Checking . . . . The ignition timing is constantly altered by the engine management ECU, and cannot be checked without specialist equipment

Ignition coil

Primary resistance . . . . Not available
Secondary resistance. . . . . Not available

Knock sensor

Resistance:
  1.8 and 2.0 litre petrol models . . . . 4.9 M ohms
  2.4 litre models. . . . . Not available

Torque wrench settings

	Nm	lbf ft
Ignition coil	10	7
Knock sensors	20	15

1 General information

The ignition system is responsible for igniting the compressed fuel/air charge in each cylinder in turn at precisely the right moment for the prevailing engine speed and load. This is achieved by using a sophisticated engine management system, which utilises computer technology and electromagnetic circuitry to achieve the required ignition characteristics.

The main components of the ignition side of the system are the ignition coils (with integral power stage and HT caps), the spark plugs and knock sensor(s). The ignition system is under the overall control of the engine management ECU, therefore many of the sensors used by the ECU have an influence on the ignition system. The operation of the system is as follows.

On 2.4 litre models, the ECU computes engine speed and crankshaft position from a series of holes drilled in the periphery of the engine flywheel, with an RPM sensor whose inductive head runs just above the drilled flywheel periphery. As the crankshaft rotates, the land (or 'teeth') between the drilled holes in the flywheel, passes the crankshaft position/speed sensor, which transmits a pulse to the ECU every time a tooth passes it. There is one missing hole in the flywheel periphery, which allows the land (or tooth) at that point to be twice as wide as the others. The ECU recognises the absence of a pulse from the position/speed sensor at this point, and uses it to establish the TDC position for No 1 piston. The time interval between pulses, and the location of the missing pulse, allow the ECU to accurately determine the position of the crankshaft and its speed. The camshaft position sensor enhances this information by detecting whether a particular piston is on an inlet or an exhaust cycle.

On 1.8 and 2.0 litre models, the crankshaft speed/position sensor is located adjacent to the crankshaft pulley at the right-hand end of the engine. The permanent magnet inductive sensor generates an alternating current as the toothed wheel behind the pulley rotates. The current and frequency generated increases as the engine speed increases. At TDC on the toothed wheel is a reference position. As this position passes the sensor, the generated voltage and frequency drop to zero, allowing the ECU to identify the position of the crankshaft. As with the 2.4 litre engine, the camshaft position sensor enhances this information by detecting whether a particular piston is on an inlet or an exhaust cycle.

Information on engine load is supplied to the ECU via the mass airflow sensor and the manifold absolute pressure sensor on certain models. The engine load is determined by computation based on the quantity of air being drawn into the engine. Further information is sent to the ECU from a knock sensor (two sensors on 2.4 litre models). This sensor is sensitive to vibration, and detects the knocking which occurs when the engine starts to pink (pre-ignite). Sensors monitoring coolant temperature, accelerator pedal position, roadspeed, and automatic transmission gear position (where applicable), provide additional input signals to the ECU on vehicle operating conditions.

From this constantly-changing data, the ECU selects, and if necessary modifies, a particular ignition advance setting from a map of ignition characteristics stored in its memory.

With the firing point established, the ECU sends a signal to the ignition power stage, which is an electronic switch controlling the current to the ignition coil primary windings. On receipt of the signal from the ECU, the power stage interrupts the primary current to the ignition coil, which induces a high-tension voltage in the coil secondary windings. This HT voltage is passed through the integral HT caps to the spark plugs. Each cylinder has its own small ignition coil, attached directly to each spark plug, and wired back to the ECU.

In the event of a fault in the system due to loss of a signal from one of the sensors, the ECU reverts to an emergency (limp-home) program. This will allow the car to be driven, although engine operation and performance will be limited. A warning light on the instrument panel will illuminate if the fault is likely to cause an increase in harmful exhaust emissions.

To facilitate fault diagnosis, the ignition system is provided with an on-board diagnostic facility, which can be interrogated using suitable diagnostic equipment (fault code reader). The diagnostic connector is located under the driver's side of the facia, above the pedals **(see illustration)**.

1.9 The diagnostic connector is located under the driver's side of the facia

2 Ignition system – testing

⚠️ *Warning: Voltages produced by an electronic ignition system are considerably higher than those produced by conventional ignition* systems. *Extreme care must be taken when working on the system if the ignition is switched on. Persons with surgically-implanted cardiac pacemaker devices should keep well clear of the ignition circuits, components and test equipment.*

General

1 The components of the ignition system are normally very reliable; most faults are far more likely to be due to loose or dirty connections, or to tracking of HT voltage due to dirt, dampness or damaged insulation, than to the failure of any of the system's components. **Always** check all wiring thoroughly before condemning an electrical component, and work methodically to eliminate all other possibilities before deciding that a particular component is faulty.

2 The old practice of checking for a spark by holding the live end of an HT cap a short distance away from the engine is **not** recommended; not only is there a high risk of a powerful electric shock, but the ECU, or HT coil may be damaged. Similarly, **never** try to diagnose misfires by pulling off one HT coil at a time.

3 The following tests should be carried out when an obvious fault such as non-starting or a clearly detectable misfire exists. Some faults, however, are more obscure and are often disguised by the fact that the ECU will adopt an emergency program (limp-home) mode to maintain as much driveability as possible. Faults of this nature usually appear in the form of excessive fuel consumption, poor idling characteristics, lack of performance, knocking or pinking noises from the engine under certain conditions, or a combination of these conditions. Where problems such as this are experienced, the best course is to refer the car to a suitably-equipped garage for diagnostic testing using dedicated test equipment.

Engine will not start

Note: *Remember that a fault with the anti-theft alarm or immobiliser will give rise to apparent starting problems. Make sure that the alarm or immobiliser has been deactivated, referring to the vehicle handbook for details.*

4 If the engine either will not turn over at all, or only turns very slowly, check the battery and starter motor. Connect a voltmeter across the battery terminals (meter positive probe to battery positive terminal) then note the voltage reading obtained while turning the engine over on the starter for (no more than) ten seconds. If the reading obtained is less than approximately 9.5 volts, first check the battery, starter motor and charging system as described in Chapter 5A.

Engine misfires

5 An irregular misfire is probably due to a loose connection to one of the ignition coils or system sensors.

6 With the ignition switched off, check carefully through the system, ensuring that all connections are clean and securely fastened.

7 Regular misfiring indicates a problem with one of the ignition coils or spark plugs. As no resistance values are available, testing the coils is best left to a Volvo dealer or suitably-equipped specialist.

8 Any further checking of the system components should be carried out after first checking the ECU for fault codes.

3 Fault finding –
general information and preliminary checks

Note: *Both the ignition and fuel systems must ideally be treated as one interrelated engine management system. Although the contents of this section is mainly concerned with the ignition side of the system, many of the components perform dual functions, and some of the following procedures of necessity relate to the fuel system.*

General information

1 The fuel and ignition systems on all engines covered by this manual incorporate an on-board diagnostic system to facilitate fault finding and system testing. Should a fault occur, the ECU stores a series of fault codes for subsequent read-out via the 16-pin diagnostic connector located under the driver's side of the facia above the pedals **(see illustration 1.9)**.

2 If driveability problems have been experienced and engine performance is suspect, the on-board diagnostic system can be used to pinpoint any problem areas, but this requires special test equipment. Once this has been done, further tests may often be necessary to determine the exact nature of the fault; ie, whether a component itself has failed, or whether it is a wiring or other interrelated problem.

3 Apart from visually checking the wiring and connections, any testing will require the use of a fault code reader at least. A Volvo dealer will obviously have such a reader, but they are also available from other suppliers. It is unlikely to be cost-effective for the private owner to purchase a fault code reader, but a well-equipped local garage or auto electrical specialist will have one.

Preliminary checks

Note: *When carrying out these checks to trace a fault, remember that if the fault has appeared only a short time after any part of the vehicle has been serviced or overhauled, the first place to check is where that work was carried out, however unrelated it may appear, to ensure that no carelessly-refitted components are causing the problem.*

Note: *If you are tracing the cause of a partial engine fault, such as lack of performance, in addition to the checks outlined below, check the compression pressures. Check also that the fuel filter and air cleaner element have been renewed at the recommended intervals.*

Refer to Chapters 1A and 2A or 2B for details of these procedures.

Note: *Remember that any fault codes which have been logged will have to be cleared from the ECU memory using a dedicated fault code reader (see paragraph 3) before you can be certain the cause of the fault has been fixed.*

4 Check the condition of the battery connections (see Chapter 5A) – remake the connections or renew the leads if a fault is found. Use the same techniques to ensure that all earth points in the engine compartment provide good electrical contact through clean, metal-to-metal joints, and that all are securely fastened.

5 Next work methodically around the engine compartment, checking all visible wiring, and the connections between sections of the wiring loom. What you are looking for at this stage is wiring that is obviously damaged by chafing against sharp edges, or against moving suspension/transmission components and/or the auxiliary drivebelt, by being trapped or crushed between carelessly-refitted components, or melted by being forced into contact with hot engine castings, coolant pipes, etc. In almost all cases, damage of this sort is caused in the first instance by incorrect routing on reassembly after previous work has been carried out (see the note at the beginning of this sub-Section).

6 Obviously wires can break or short together inside the insulation so that no visible evidence betrays the fault, but this usually only occurs where the wiring loom has been incorrectly routed so that it is stretched taut or kinked sharply; either of these conditions should be obvious on even a casual inspection. If this is thought to have happened and the fault proves elusive, the suspect section of wiring should be checked very carefully during the more detailed checks which follow.

7 Depending on the extent of the problem, damaged wiring may be repaired by rejoining the break or splicing-in a new length of wire, using solder to ensure a good connection, and remaking the insulation with adhesive insulating tape or heat-shrink tubing, as desired. If the damage is extensive, given the implications for the vehicle's future reliability, the best long-term answer may well be to renew that entire section of the loom, however expensive this may appear.

8 When the actual damage has been repaired, ensure that the wiring loom is re-routed correctly, so that it is clear of other components, is not stretched or kinked, and is secured out of harm's way using the plastic clips, guides and ties provided.

9 Check all electrical connectors, ensuring that they are clean, securely fastened, and that each is locked by its plastic tabs or wire clip, as appropriate. If any connector shows external signs of corrosion (accumulations of white or green deposits, or streaks of 'rust'), or if any is thought to be dirty, it must be unplugged and cleaned using electrical contact cleaner. If the connector pins are

severely corroded, the connector must be renewed; note that this may mean the renewal of that entire section of the loom.

10 If the cleaner completely removes the corrosion to leave the connector in a satisfactory condition, it would be wise to pack the connector with a suitable material which will exclude dirt and moisture, and prevent the corrosion from occurring again; a Volvo dealer may be able to recommend a suitable product.

11 Working methodically around the engine compartment, check carefully that all vacuum hoses and pipes are securely fastened and correctly routed, with no signs of cracks, splits or deterioration to cause air leaks, or of hoses that are trapped, kinked, or bent sharply enough to restrict airflow. Check with particular care at all connections and sharp bends, and renew any damaged or deformed lengths of hose.

12 Working from the fuel tank, via the filter, to the fuel rail (and including the feed and return), check the fuel lines, and renew any that are found to be leaking, trapped or kinked. Check particularly the ends of the hoses – these can crack and perish sufficiently to allow leakage.

13 Unclip the air cleaner cover, and check that the air filter is not clogged or soaked. A clogged air filter will obstruct the inlet airflow, causing a noticeable effect on engine performance. Renew the filter if necessary; refer to Chapter 1A Section 26 for further information, if required.

14 Start the engine and allow it to idle.

Caution: Working in the engine compartment while the engine is running requires great care if the risk of personal injury is to be avoided; among the dangers are burns from contact with hot components, or contact with moving components such as the radiator cooling fan or the auxiliary drivebelt. Refer to Safety first! at the front of this manual before starting, and ensure that your hands, and any long hair or loose clothing, are kept well clear of hot or moving components at all times.

15 Working from the air inlet, via the air cleaner assembly and the mass air flow sensor to the throttle control unit and inlet manifold (and including the various vacuum hoses and pipes connected to these), check for air leaks. Usually, these will be revealed by sucking or hissing noises, but minor leaks may be traced by spraying a solution of soapy water on to the suspect joint; if a leak exists, it will be shown by the change in engine note and the accompanying air bubbles (or sucking-in of the liquid, depending on the pressure difference at that point). If a leak is found at any point, tighten the fastening clamp and/or renew the faulty components, as applicable.

16 Similarly, work from the cylinder head, via the manifold to the tailpipe, to check that the exhaust system is free from leaks. The simplest way of doing this, if the vehicle can be raised and supported safely and with complete security while the check is made, is

4.2 Press down the clip and disconnect the coil wiring plug

4.6 Depress the clip and disconnect the wiring plug (arrowed)

to temporarily block the tailpipe while listening for the sound of escaping exhaust gases; any leak should be evident. If a leak is found at any point, tighten the fastening clamp bolts and/or nuts, renew the gasket, and/or renew the faulty section of the system, as necessary, to seal the leak.

17 It is possible to make a further check of the electrical connections by wiggling each electrical connector of the system in turn as the engine is idling; a faulty connector will be immediately evident from the engine's response as contact is broken and remade. A faulty connector should be renewed to ensure that the future reliability of the system; note that this may mean the renewal of that entire section of the loom.

18 If the preliminary checks have failed to reveal the fault, the car must be taken to a Volvo dealer or suitably-equipped garage

5.4 Knock sensor (arrowed) – 1.8 and 2.0 litre models

4.3 Undo the coil retaining bolt (arrowed)

4.7 Undo the retaining bolt and lift the coil from position

for diagnostic testing using electronic test equipment.

4 Ignition HT coils – removal and refitting

Removal

1.8 and 2.0 litre engines

1 Remove the plastic cover on the top of the engine by pulling it straight up from its mountings.

2 Disconnect the ignition coils(s) wiring plug(s) **(see illustration)**. It is safest to work on one coil at a time. However, if the coils and their wiring plugs are marked for position, all four could be removed at once.

3 Each coil is secured by one bolt. Undo the

5.6 Front knock sensor (arrowed) – 2.4 litre models

bolt(s) and carefully pull the coil(s) from the cylinder head **(see illustration)**.

2.4 litre models

4 Remove the upper section of the intake manifold/cylinder head cover as described in Chapter 4A.

5 If the ignition coils for cylinders 1 or 2 are to be removed, release the clips and remove the timing belt upper cover. Refer to Chapter 2B, Section 3.

6 Disconnect the ignition coils(s) wiring plug(s) **(see illustration)**. It is safest to work on one coil at a time. However, if the coils and their wiring plugs are marked for position, all five could be removed at once.

7 Unscrew the coil retaining bolt, then pull the coil and HT cap out of the recess in the cylinder head **(see illustration)**.

Refitting

8 Align the coil with the mounting bolt hole, then push it down firmly onto the spark plug. Tighten the retaining bolt to the specified torque.

9 Press the wiring plug until it can be heard to 'click' into place.

10 The remainder of refitting is a reversal of removal.

5 Knock sensor(s) – removal and refitting

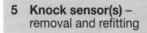

Removal

1.8 and 2.0 litre models

1 The knock sensor is located on the front facing side of the cylinder block under the intake manifold.

2 Refer to Chapter 4A and remove the intake manifold.

3 Disconnect the wiring connector from the knock sensor.

4 Note the fitted position of the sensor, it is essential that it is refitted to its original position. Undo the retaining bolt and remove the sensor **(see illustration)**.

2.4 litre models

5 Remove the air cleaner assembly as described in Chapter 4A.

6 Note their fitted positions, it is essential that they are fitted to their original positions. Undo the bolts and remove the sensors **(see illustration)**. Disconnect the wiring plugs as the sensors are withdrawn.

Refitting

7 Refitting is a reversal of removal, noting the following points:

a) The sensor(s) must be refitted in their original positions, with the wiring harness angle exactly as before.

b) Tightening the retaining bolt to the specified torque is absolutely essential. Failure to do so could impair the performance of the sensor, causing engine damage.

Chapter 5 Part C:
Preheating system – diesel models

Contents

Degrees of difficulty

Easy, suitable for novice with little experience	Fairly easy, suitable for beginner with some experience	Fairly difficult, suitable for competent DIY mechanic	Difficult, suitable for experienced DIY mechanic	Very difficult, suitable for expert DIY or professional

Specifications

Torque wrench setting	Nm	lbf ft
Glow plugs	8	6

1 General information

To assist cold starting, diesel engine models are fitted with a preheating system, which comprises a relay, and glow plugs. The system is controlled by the Electronic Diesel Control (EDC) system, using information provided by the coolant temperature sensor (see Chapter 4B).

The glow plugs are miniature electric heating elements, encapsulated in a metal case with a probe at one end, and an electrical connection at the other. Each combustion chamber has a glow plug threaded into it. When the glow plug is energised, it heats up rapidly causing the temperature of the air charge drawn into each of the combustion chambers to rise. Each glow plug probe is positioned directly in line with the incoming spray of fuel from the injector. Hence the fuel passing over the glow plug probe is also heated, allowing its optimum combustion temperature to be achieved more readily.

The duration of the preheating period is governed by the Electronic Diesel Control (EDC) system control module (ECM), using information provided by the coolant temperature sensor. The ECM alters the preheating time (the length for which the glow plugs are supplied with current) to suit the prevailing conditions.

The EDC control unit also turns on the glow plugs during the engine warm up phase (as required) and during DPF (Diesel Particulate Filter) regeneration, on models fitted with a particulate filter. The glow plugs should be considered part of the emission control systems, as much as part of the starting system.

A warning light informs the driver that preheating is taking place. The lamp extinguishes when sufficient preheating has taken place to allow the engine to be started, but power will still be supplied to the glow plugs for a further period, known as post-heating, to reduce exhaust emissions. If no attempt is made to start the engine, the power supply to the glow plugs is switched off to prevent battery drain and glow plug burn-out.

2 Preheating system – testing

1 Full testing of the system can only be carried out using specialist diagnostic equipment which is connected to the engine management system diagnostic wiring connector (see Chapter 12). If the preheating system is thought to be faulty, some preliminary checks of the glow plug operation may be made as described in the following paragraphs.
2 Connect a voltmeter or 12 volt test lamp between the glow plug supply cable, and a good earth point on the engine.
Caution: Make sure that the live connection is kept well clear of the engine and bodywork.
3 Have an assistant activate the preheating system by inserting the remote unit and turning the key (or ignition dial on models

fitted with Keyless Drive) to position II, and check that battery voltage is applied to the glow plug electrical connection. **Note:** The supply voltage will be less than battery voltage initially, but will rise and settle as the glow plug heats up. It will then drop to zero when the preheating period ends and the safety cut-out operates.
4 If no supply voltage can be detected at the glow plug, then the glow plug relay or the supply cable may be faulty.
5 To locate a faulty glow plug, disconnect the supply cables and measure the resistance between each glow plug and earth. No precise specification is available, but a resistance of one or two ohms is typical. A much higher value or a reading of infinity (open-circuit) denotes a fault.
6 Any further testing should be done by a specialist using the appropriate diagnostic equipment.

3 Glow plugs – removal, inspection and refitting

Removal

All engines

1 Remove the plastic cover from the top of the engine.

1.6 litre engines

2 The glow plugs are fitted into the rear face of the cylinder head. On models fitted with the 80kW engine, undo the 2 nuts securing the glow plug wiring bracket above the EGR cooler.

3.3a Undo the nut and bolt for the support bracket

3.3b Induction pipe flange at the rear of the cylinder head

3.7 Disconnect the coolant hoses from the EGR cooler (arrowed)

3.9 Undo the nuts (arrowed) securing the electrical connections to the glow plugs

3.10 Unscrew the glow plugs from the cylinder head

4.2 Disconnect the wiring plug, and unclip the relay from its bracket

3 On models fitted with the 85kW engine, undo the nut and bolt that support the induction pipe at the throttle body, slacken the clamp at the induction pipe flange at the rear of the cylinder head and pull the pipe forwards a little. Remove the insulation padding at the rear of the cylinder head, then undo the 5 bolts that secure the bracket below the induction pipe flange. Undo the bolt for the wiring bracket **(see illustrations)**.

4 Unplug the wiring connector from each glow plug and move the wiring loom to one side.

5 Unscrew each plug from the cylinder head using a deep socket.

2.0 litre 4-cylinder engine

6 The glow plugs are fitted into the rear face of the cylinder head. Remove the EGR solenoid/valve as described in Chapter 4D.

7 Clamp the coolant hoses connected to the EGR cooler on the rear of the cylinder head, using hose clamps, then release the clips and disconnect the hoses from the cooler **(see illustration)**.

8 Undo the bolts/nuts and remove the EGR cooler.

9 Undo the nuts (1 per plug) and disconnect the wiring harness from the glow plugs **(see illustration)**.

10 Unscrew each glow plug from the cylinder head using a deep socket **(see illustration)**.

5-cylinder engines

11 The glow plugs are fitted into the front face of the cylinder head. Unplug the wiring connector from each glow plug then unscrew each plug from the cylinder head.

Inspection

12 Inspect the glow plugs for signs of damage. Burnt or eroded glow plug tips can be caused by a bad injector spray pattern. Have the injectors checked if this sort of damage is found.

13 If the glow plugs are in good condition, check them electrically, as described in Section 2.

Refitting

All engines

14 Thoroughly clean the glow plugs, and the glow plug seating areas in the cylinder head.

15 Apply a smear of anti-seize compound to the glow plug threads, then refit the glow plug and tighten it to the specified torque.

16 Reconnect the wiring to the glow plug.

17 The remainder of refitting is a reversal of removal.

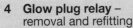

4 Glow plug relay – removal and refitting

Note: *The location of the relay differs depending on the engine fitted.*

1 On models fitted with the 1.6 litre 80kw or 2.0 4-cylinder engine it is located in the underbonnet fusebox on the left-hand side of the engine bay. With the relay identified it can simply be pulled from position.

2 On models fitted with the 1.6 litre 85kw or 2.0/2.4 litre 5-cylinder engine it is located behind the front bumper on the left-hand side **(see illustration)**. Remove the front bumper as described in Chapter 11. Disconnect the wiring plug and unclip the relay from its bracket. Refitting is a reversal of removal.

Chapter 6
Clutch

Contents

Degrees of difficulty

Easy, suitable for novice with little experience	**Fairly easy,** suitable for beginner with some experience	**Fairly difficult,** suitable for competent DIY mechanic	**Difficult,** suitable for experienced DIY mechanic	**Very difficult,** suitable for expert DIY or professional

Specifications

General
Clutch type . . . . Single dry plate, diaphragm spring, self-adjusting, hydraulic actuation

Torque wrench settings

	Nm	lbf ft
Clutch cover retaining bolts	24	18
Pedal retaining nuts	24	18
Release bearing and slave cylinder mounting bolts	10	7

1 General information

A single dry plate diaphragm spring clutch is fitted to all manual transmission models. The clutch is hydraulically-operated via a master and slave cylinder. All models have an internally-mounted slave cylinder and release bearing combined into one unit.

The main components of the clutch are the clutch cover and pressure plate, the driven plate (sometimes called the friction plate or disc) and the release bearing. The pressure plate is bolted to the flywheel, with the driven plate sandwiched between them. The centre of the driven plate carries female splines which mate with the splines on the transmission input shaft. The release bearing acts on the diaphragm spring fingers of the pressure plate.

When the engine is running and the clutch pedal is released, the diaphragm spring clamps the pressure plate, driven plate and flywheel firmly together. Drive is transmitted through the friction surfaces of the flywheel and pressure plate to the linings of the driven plate, and thus to the transmission input shaft.

The slave cylinder is incorporated into the release bearing – when the slave cylinder operates, the release bearing moves against the diaphragm spring fingers. As the spring pressure on the pressure plate is relieved, the flywheel and pressure plate spin without moving the driven plate. As the pedal is released, spring pressure is restored and the drive is gradually taken up.

The clutch hydraulic system consists of a master cylinder, a slave cylinder and the associated pipes and hoses. The fluid reservoir is shared with the brake master cylinder.

2 Clutch pedal – removal and refitting

Removal and refitting of the clutch pedal is included in the master cylinder removal and refitting procedure described below.

3 Clutch master cylinder – removal and refitting

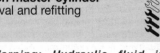 **Warning: Hydraulic fluid is poisonous; wash off immediately and thoroughly in the case of skin contact, and seek immediate medical advice if any fluid is swallowed or gets into the eyes. Certain types of hydraulic fluid are inflammable, and may ignite when allowed into contact with hot components; when servicing any hydraulic system, it is safest to assume that the fluid IS inflammable, and to take precautions against the risk of fire as though it is petrol that is being handled. Hydraulic fluid is also an effective paint stripper, and will attack plastics; if any is spilt, it should be washed off immediately, using copious quantities of clean water. Finally, it is hygroscopic (it absorbs moisture from the air) – old fluid may be contaminated and unfit for further use. When topping-up or renewing the fluid, always use the recommended type, and ensure that it comes from a freshly-opened sealed container.**

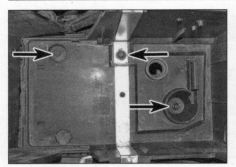

3.1 Undo the 3 bolts (arrowed) and remove the battery tray

3.2 Where fitted, remove the bulkhead soundproofing panel

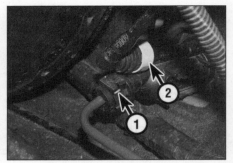

3.4 Clutch pressure pipe locking pin (1) and supply pipe locking collar (2)

3.9 Depress the clip each side and separate the pushrod from the pedal

3.10 Clutch pedal bracket nuts (arrowed – facia removed for clarity)

3.11 Rotate the master cylinder (arrowed) anti-clockwise

Removal

1 Remove the battery as described in Chapter 5A, then undo the 3 bolts and remove the battery box **(see illustration)**.

2 Release the retaining clip, undo the plastic nut and remove the soundproofing panel at the engine compartment bulkhead (where fitted) **(see illustration)**.

3 Disconnect the clutch position sensor (where fitted) at the engine compartment bulkhead, as described in Section 8.

4 Pull out the locking pin and disconnect the clutch hydraulic fluid pressure pipe in the engine compartment from the master cylinder **(see illustration)**. Be prepared for fluid spillage. Plug or seal the openings to prevent contamination.

5 Press in the locking collar and carefully pull the clutch hydraulic fluid supply pipe in the engine compartment from the master cylinder. Be prepared for fluid spillage. Plug or seal the openings to prevent contamination, and position the end of the supply pipe higher than the reservoir.

6 Remove the lower facia panel on the driver's side, as described in Chapter 11.

7 On models fitted with a clutch pedal position sensor, remove the sensor as described in Section 8.

8 On models fitted with a start inhibitor switch, disconnect the wiring plug, depress the locking tab, and remove the switch from the pedal bracket.

9 On all models, depress the lock clips each side, and separate the master cylinder pushrod from the pedal **(see illustration)**.

10 Undo the 4 nuts and pull the pedal, bracket and master cylinder approximately 50mm rearwards **(see illustration)**. Access to the upper nut is limited – dexterity and patience will be required. Be prepared for fluid spillage.

11 Rotate the master cylinder anti-clockwise (from the cabin), and separate the master cylinder from the pedal bracket. Volvo technicians use a special tool (No 999 7172) to rotate the master cylinder. If the master cylinder is tight, in the absence of this tool, use a hammer and punch **(see illustration)**.

12 Manoeuvre the pedal and bracket from under the facia. No further dismantling is recommended. If faulty, the pedal and bracket must be renewed as an assembly.

Refitting

13 Refit by reversing the removal operations. Note the following points:

a) Tighten all fasteners securely.

b) Renew the seal between the master cylinder and the bulkhead.

4.3 Slave cylinder fluid pipe clip

c) Before refitting the engine compartment bulkhead soundproofing panel, bleed the clutch hydraulic system as described in Section 5.

d) Check the operation of the clutch before refitting the lower facia panel.

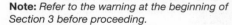

4 Clutch slave cylinder – removal and refitting

Note: *Slave cylinder internal components are not available separately, and no repair or overhaul of the cylinder is possible. In the event of a hydraulic system fault, or any sign of fluid leakage, the unit should be renewed. On all transmissions the slave cylinder and release bearing are a single assembly, commonly known as to as a Concentric Slave Cylinder (CSC).*

Note: *Refer to the warning at the beginning of Section 3 before proceeding.*

Removal

1 Remove the transmission as described in Chapter 7A. The internal slave cylinder cannot be removed with the transmission in place.

2 Release the rubber seal from the transmission, and move it inwards down the pipe.

3 On models fitted with the M66 transmission, prise out the clip and disconnect the fluid pipe junction from the pipe **(see illustration)**.

4 Remove the bolts securing the cylinder and release bearing assembly to the transmission, and remove the assembly, feeding the fluid pipe in through the transmission aperture **(see illustration)**.

Refitting

5 Refit by reversing the removal operations, noting the following points:

a) *Tighten the release bearing assembly mounting bolts to the specified torque.*

b) *Depending on the transmission fitted, Volvo recommend applying a layer of sealant to the new slave cylinder before refitting. You should check with a Volvo dealer or specialist to establish whether this is required.*

c) *Volvo recommend the use of new seals when refitting the quick-release pipe connections.*

d) *Refit the transmission as described in Chapter 7A.*

e) *Bleed the clutch hydraulic system on completion (Section 5).*

5 Clutch hydraulic system – bleeding

Note: *Refer to the warning at the beginning of Section 3 before proceeding.*

1 Top-up the hydraulic fluid reservoir on the brake master cylinder with fresh clean fluid of the specified type (see *Weekly checks*).

2 Remove the dust cap, and fit a length of clear hose over the bleed screw on the slave cylinder **(see illustration)**. Place the other end of the hose in a jar containing a small amount of hydraulic fluid.

3 Slacken the bleed screw, then have an assistant depress the clutch pedal. Tighten the bleed screw when the pedal is depressed. Have the assistant release the pedal, then slacken the bleed screw again.

4 Repeat the process until clean fluid, free of air bubbles, emerges from the bleed screw. Tighten the screw at the end of a pedal downstroke, and remove the hose and jar. Refit the dust cover.

5 Top-up the hydraulic fluid reservoir.

6 Pressure bleeding equipment may be used if preferred – refer to the information in Chapter 9, Section 2.

6 Clutch assembly – removal, inspection and refitting

⚠️ **Warning: Dust created by clutch wear and deposited on the clutch components may contain asbestos, which is a health hazard. DO NOT blow it out with compressed air or inhale any of it. DO NOT use petrol or petroleum-based solvents to clean off the dust. Brake system cleaner or methylated spirit should be used to flush the dust into a suitable receptacle. After the clutch components are wiped clean with rags, dispose of the contaminated rags and the used cleaner in a sealed, marked container.**

Note: *Volvo tools 999 7068 and 999 5662*

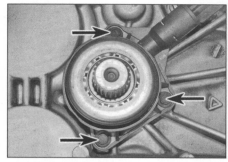

4.4 Undo the bolts and remove the slave cylinder

may be required to reset the self-adjusting mechanism and compress the diaphragm spring prior to clutch removal, although it is possible to successfully carry out the procedure using improvised home-made tools. Volvo also use a tool (999 7120), bolted to the engine mating face, to lock the flywheel in place. Again, a home-made tool or the assistance of another person will suffice.

Removal

1 Access to the clutch may be gained in one of two ways. Either the engine/transmission assembly can be removed as described in Chapter 2F, and the transmission then separated from the engine, or the engine may be left in the car and the transmission removed independently as described in Chapter 7A. If the clutch is to be refitted, use paint or marker pen to mark the position of the clutch cover relative to the flywheel.

With Volvo special tools

2 Fit Volvo 'counterhold' tool 999 7068 to the clutch cover to reset the self-adjusting mechanism. The pins of the tool must engage in the groove in front of the adjuster springs, then hold the tool against the plate. Engage the hooks at the end of the tool springs in the centre of the three holes, located at 120° intervals along the circumference of the clutch cover.

3 Fit the Volvo compression tool 999 5662 to the clutch cover, and compress the diaphragm spring so that the self-adjusting spring is not under tension. Ensure that hooks on the underside of the compressor engage correctly without clamping the adjuster mechanism

6.4 Undo the pressure plate retaining bolts

5.2 The clutch slave cylinder bleed screw is located on the top of the transmission

springs. Screw-in the compression tool spindle for a maximum of 2 turns until the diaphragm spring has pressed the pressure plate to a 'free' position. A distinct 'click' will be heard when the pressure plate is in the 'free' position.

With or without Volvo special tools

4 Undo the screws and remove the clutch cover/pressure plate, followed by the driven plate **(see illustration)**. Note the orientation of the driven plate.

5 It is important that no oil or grease is allowed to come into contact with the friction material or the pressure plate and flywheel faces during inspection and refitting. **Note:** *If the clutch cover/pressure plate is to be refitted, do not allow the diaphragm spring to remain in the compressed state for a long period of time, or the spring may be permanently weakened.*

Inspection

6 With the clutch assembly removed, clean off all traces of clutch dust using a dry cloth. This is best done outside or in a well-ventilated area.

7 Examine the linings of the driven plate for wear and loose rivets, and the rim for distortion, cracks, broken torsion springs and worn splines. The surface of the friction linings may be highly glazed, but, as long as the friction material pattern can be clearly seen, this is satisfactory.

8 If there is any sign of oil contamination, indicated by a continuous or patchy, shiny black discolouration, the plate must be renewed and the source of the contamination traced and rectified. This will be either a leaking crankshaft oil seal or transmission input shaft oil seal – or both.

9 The driven plate must also be renewed if the lining thickness has worn down to, or just above, the level of the rivet heads. Given the amount of dismantling work necessary to gain access to the driven plate, it may be wise to fit a new plate regardless of the old one's condition.

10 Check the machined faces of the flywheel and pressure plate. If either is grooved, or heavily scored, renewal is necessary. Providing the damage is not too serious, the flywheel can be removed as described in the relevant Part of Chapter 2A, 2B, 2C, 2D or 2E, and taken to an engineering works, who may be able to clean up the surface by machining. Models

6.15a The driven plate should be marked (arrowed) to indicate which side faces the flywheel

6.18a Using some threaded rod, washers, and 2 nuts, compress the spring fingers and the pressure plate together...

fitted with a dual mass flywheel should not be machined, if scored or damaged the flywheel must be replaced.

11 The pressure plate must be renewed if any cracks are apparent, if the diaphragm spring is damaged or its pressure suspect, or if there is excessive warpage of the pressure plate face.

12 With the transmission removed, check the condition of the release bearing, as described in Section 7.

Refitting

13 It is advisable to refit the clutch assembly with clean hands, and to wipe down the pressure plate and flywheel faces with a clean dry rag before assembly begins.

14 Fit an appropriate centering tool into the hole at the end of the crankshaft. The tool must be a sliding fit in the crankshaft hole and the driven plate centre.

15 Place the driven plate in position with the longer side of the centre boss towards the

8.2 Rotate the clutch pedal position sensor anti-clockwise to remove it

6.15b Position the driven plate using a clutch aligning tool

6.18b ...then move the adjusting ring (arrowed) anti-clockwise to the stop...

flywheel, or as noted on removal. Note that the new driven plate will be marked to indicate which side faces the flywheel **(see illustrations)**.

With Volvo special tools

16 Fit the counterhold tool 999 7068 to the clutch cover, ensuring the three pins engage in the grooves in front of the adjuster springs, then hold the tool against the plate. Engage the hooks at the end of the tool springs in the centre of the three holes, located at 120° intervals along the circumference of the clutch cover.

17 Fit the Volvo compression tool 999 5662 to the clutch cover, and compress the diaphragm spring so that the self-adjusting springs are not under tension. Ensure that hooks on the underside of the compressor engage correctly without clamping the adjuster mechanism springs. The compressor spindle should be turned no more 2 turns and a distinct 'click' will be heard when the pressure plate is in the 'free' position.

Without Volvo special tools

18 Using a length of threaded rod, and some circular spacers and two nuts, compress the diaphragm spring fingers and the pressure plate together as shown. Once the fingers are compressed, use a screwdriver to move and hold the adjusting ring anti-clockwise to the stop **(see illustrations)**.

19 Slowly undo the nuts to uncompress the pressure plate assembly. The self-adjusting ring should remain in the same place (see paragraph 18). Remove the threaded rod, etc.

With or without Volvo special tools

20 Position the clutch cover/pressure plate

assembly over the dowels on the flywheel, aligning the previously-made marks (where applicable).

21 Working in a diagonal pattern, fit and evenly tighten the cover retaining screws to the specified torque.

22 Slowly release the compressor, then remove the counterhold tool from the clutch – where applicable.

23 Pull the centering tool from the plate/crankshaft, and check visually that the driven plate appears centrally located.

24 Remove the flywheel locking tool if used.

25 The engine and/or transmission can now be refitted as described in Chapter 2F or Chapter 7A.

---

7   Clutch release bearing – removal, inspection and refitting

Removal

1 Access to the clutch release bearing may be gained in one of two ways. Either the engine/transmission assembly can be removed as described in Chapter 2F, and the transmission then separated from the engine, or the engine may be left in the car and the transmission removed independently as described in Chapter 7A.

2 The release bearing and slave cylinder are combined into one unit, and cannot be separated. Refer to the slave cylinder removal procedure in Section 4.

Inspection

3 Check the bearing for smoothness of operation, and renew it if there is any roughness or harshness as the bearing is spun. It is a good idea to renew the bearing as a matter of course during clutch overhaul, regardless of its apparent condition, considering the amount of dismantling work necessary to gain access to it.

Refitting

4 Refer to Section 4.

---

8   Clutch pedal position sensor – renewal

1 For models with the sensor located adjacent to the clutch master cylinder, release the retaining clip, undo the plastic nut and remove the soundproofing panel at the engine compartment bulkhead (where fitted). Disconnect the sensor wiring plug, unclip the sensor and remove.

2 For models with the sensor located at the clutch pedal bracket, remove the driver's side lower facia panel as described in Chapter 11. Disconnect the wiring plug, then rotate the sensor anti-clockwise and pull it from the pedal bracket **(see illustration)**.

3 Refitting is a reversal of removal.

Chapter 7 Part A:
Manual transmission

Contents

Degrees of difficulty

| Easy, suitable for novice with little experience | Fairly easy, suitable for beginner with some experience | Fairly difficult, suitable for competent DIY mechanic | Difficult, suitable for experienced DIY mechanic | Very difficult, suitable for expert DIY or professional |

Specifications

General

Designation	MTX75, B6, M66, M56 or MMT6
Transmission type:	
MTX75 and M56.	Five forward gears and one reverse. Synchromesh on all gears
B6, M66 or MMT6.	Six forward gears and one reverse. Synchromesh on all gears

Lubrication

Lubricant type	See *Lubricants, fluids and tyre pressures* on page 0•16
Capacity:	
MTX75	1.8 litres
B6	1.6 litres
M66.	1.9 litres
MMT6	1.65 litres
M56.	2.0 litres

Torque wrench settings

	Nm	lbf ft
Engine mounting nuts/bolts (including torque rod)	See Chapter 2C	
Gear lever housing bolts	24	18
Oil filler/drain plugs.	35	26
Reversing light switch	24	18
Roadwheel bolts.	See Chapter 10	
Starter motor mounting bolts.	See Chapter 5A	
Subframe mounting bolts.	See Chapter 10	
Transmission-to-engine bolts.	50	37

1 General information

The manual transmission and final drive are housed in an aluminium casing, bolted directly to the left-hand side of the engine. Gear selection is by a remotely-sited lever assembly, operating the transmission selector mechanism via cables. A variety of manual transmissions are fitted to the S40/V50 range of vehicles (see Specifications).

On 1.6 litre diesel models, 1.8 and 2.0 litre petrol models, the Ford-originated transmission code is MTX75. MT standing for Manual Transmission, X for transaxle (front-wheel drive), and 75 being the distance between the input and output shafts in mm **(see illustration)**. The Volvo-originated transmission code is B6.

On 2.0 litre and 2.4 litre models, the Volvo-originated transmission bears the code M66, or MMT6. The transmission internal components comprise the input shaft, the upper and lower layshafts, the final drive differential and the selector mechanism.

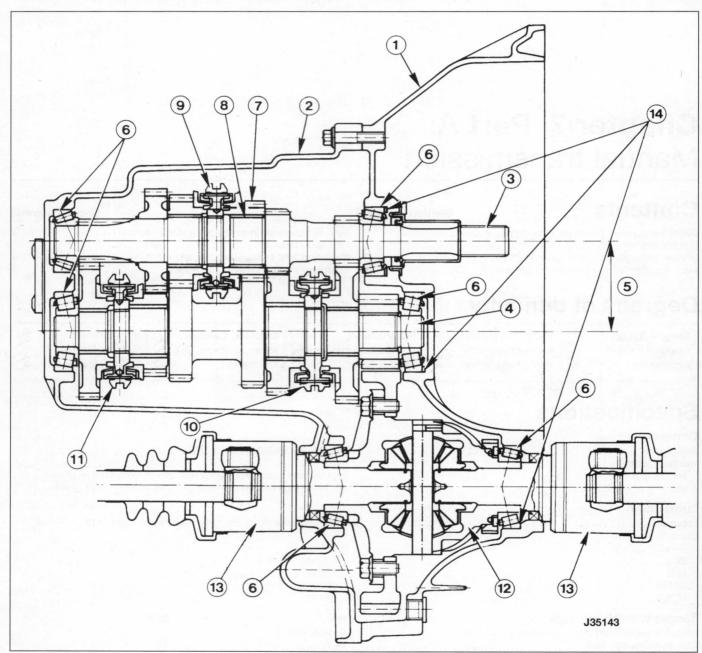

J35143

1.2 MTX 75 transmission

1 Clutch housing	5 Distance between shaft	8 Needle roller bearings	12 Differential
2 Transmission housing	centres = 75mm	9 3rd/4th gear synchro	13 Driveshafts
3 Input shaft	6 Taper roller bearings	10 1st/2nd gear synchro	14 Shims
4 Output shaft	7 4th gear	11 5th/reverse gear synchro	

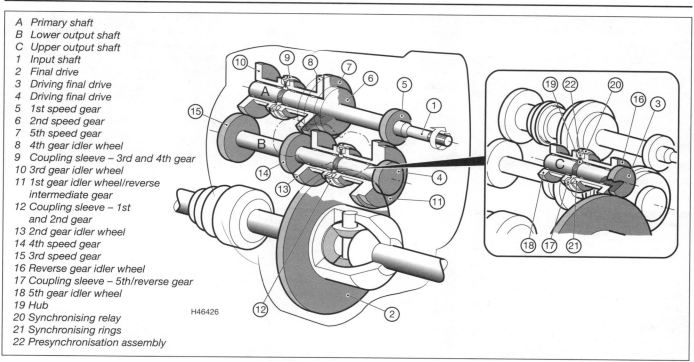

A Primary shaft
B Lower output shaft
C Upper output shaft
1 Input shaft
2 Final drive
3 Driving final drive
4 Driving final drive
5 1st speed gear
6 2nd speed gear
7 5th speed gear
8 4th gear idler wheel
9 Coupling sleeve – 3rd and 4th gear
10 3rd gear idler wheel
11 1st gear idler wheel/reverse
intermediate gear
12 Coupling sleeve – 1st
and 2nd gear
13 2nd gear idler wheel
14 4th speed gear
15 3rd speed gear
16 Reverse gear idler wheel
17 Coupling sleeve – 5th/reverse gear
18 5th gear idler wheel
19 Hub
20 Synchronising relay
21 Synchronising rings
22 Presynchronisation assembly

H46426

1.3 M56 5-speed transmission

Synchromesh is fitted to all gears **(see illustration)**.

Because of the complexity and possible unavailability of parts and special tools necessary, internal repair procedures for the manual transmission are not included for the home mechanic. For readers who wish to tackle a transmission rebuild, brief notes on overhaul are provided in Section 8. The bulk of the information in this Chapter is devoted to removal and refitting procedures.

2 Gear lever housing –
removal and refitting

Removal

1 Remove the centre console as described in Chapter 11.
2 Squeeze the gaiter at the base of the gearknob to release the clips and pull the gaiter downwards. Press down the knob and rotate it anti-clockwise as far as the stop, then pull it from the lever **(see illustration)**.

Models fitted with MTX-75, B6, M56 and M66 transmission

3 Prise off the selector inner cable socket ends from the balljoints on the levers, and disengage the outer cables from the brackets on the housing **(see illustrations)**.
4 Undo the 4 bolts securing the housing assembly to the floor **(see illustration)**.

Models fitted with MMT6 transmission

5 Disengage the left-hand outer cable from the bracket on the housing.

6 Undo the 4 bolts securing the housing assembly to the floor **(see illustration 2.4)**.
7 Lift up the housing, and prise off the selector inner cable socket joints from the base of the gear lever.
8 Release the remaining out cable from the

housing and remove the assembly from the vehicle.

Refitting

9 Refit by reversing the removal operations. Tighten the 4 bolts securely.

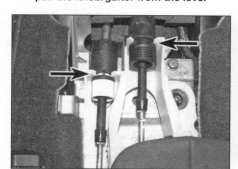

2.2 Press down, rotate anti-clockwise and pull the knob/gaiter from the lever

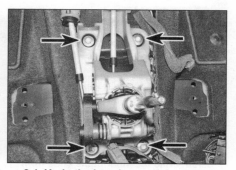

2.3a Inner cable balljoint (arrowed)

2.3b Disengage the outer cables from the brackets (arrowed)

2.4 Undo the housing retaining bolts (arrowed)

3.3a Depress the clip and remove the ECU cover

3.3b Fold out the catches and disconnect the wiring plugs

3.4 Battery support tray bolts

3.8 Undo the 4 nuts, 3 bolts and remove the mounting

3.9 Remove the mounting bracket

3 Selector cables – removal and refitting

Removal

1 Where fitted, pull up and remove the engine cover. On 2.4 litre petrol engines and 2.0 litre diesel engines remove the air cleaner assembly as described in Chapter 4A (petrol engines) or Chapter 4B (diesel engines).

2 Disconnect and then remove the battery as described in Chapter 5A Section 3.

3 On 1.8 and 2.0 litre petrol models remove the ECU cover and disconnect the ecu wiring plugs (see illustrations).

4 Undo 3 bolts and remove the battery support tray (see illustration). Note their fitted positions, and disconnect any wiring plugs as the box is withdrawn.

5 Jack up the front of the vehicle and support it securely on axle stands (see Jacking and vehicle support).

6 Remove the engine undershield.

7 On models where the selector cables are hidden by the transmission mounting bracket the transmission must be supported from below using a trolley jack (with a block of wood on the head of the jack to help spread the load). Position the jack under the bell housing and raise it to support the transmission and engine.

8 Undo the 4 nuts, 3 bolts and remove the left-hand engine/transmission mounting upper bracket (see illustration).

9 Undo the 3 bolts and remove the transmission bracket (see illustration). Lower the transmission slightly.

10 At the transmission disconnect the cables from the selector shaft, pull back the locking collars (or remove the outer cable bracket) and lift the selector cables off the transmission (see illustrations).

11 Remove the mounting for the central silencer, undo the 4 plastic nuts, and slide the heat shield rearwards for access to the grommet where the cables pass through the floor.

12 Release the cables from the retaining clips on the underside of the floor.

13 Disconnect the selector cables from the gear lever as described in Section 2.

14 Fold back the carpet each side of the centre console area, and carefully cut away the sound insulation around the cable grommet, located just in front of the heater housing. Remove the sound insulation.

15 Undo the 2 nuts securing the cable grommet to the floor, and lift the grommet from the mounting studs (see illustration).

16 Manoeuvre the cable assembly into the passenger cabin, then out of the vehicle.

Refitting

17 Manoeuvre the cable assembly into position, through the hole in the floor, up to the transmission, then fit the grommet over the mounting studs and tighten the retaining nuts securely.

3.10a Prise the inner cable ends from the levers on the transmission (MTX 75 transmission

3.10b Slide back the blue collars and pull the outer cables rearwards

3.15 Undo the cable grommet nuts (arrowed)

18 Reposition the sound insulation around the grommet, and tape over the cut.
19 The remainder is a reversal of removal. Adjust the selector cable as described in this Section.

Adjustment

20 If not already done so, remove the battery, battery support tray, ECU and air cleaner assembly as required to access to the gear selectors on the transmission.
21 Select 3rd gear using the gearchange lever (4th gear on models fitted with the 2.0 litre 5-cylinder engine).
22 Pull out the lock button on the relevant inner cable fitting cable at the selector lever on the transmission **(see illustrations)**.
23 Check that the gearchange lever is held centrally. On models fitted with the B6 transmission lock the transmission in position with a suitable rod fitted to the selector shaft **(see illustration)**.
24 Press in the lock button on inner cable fitting at the selector lever on the transmission, and check that the gear positions are readily obtainable.
25 Refit the battery box or air cleaner assembly using a reversal of the removal procedure.

4 Oil seals – renewal

Driveshaft seals

1 Remove the left- or right-hand driveshaft (as appropriate) with reference to Chapter 8, Section 2.
2 Drain the transmission oil as described in Section 6.
3 Using a large screwdriver or suitable lever, carefully prise the oil seal out of the transmission casing, taking care not to damage the casing **(see illustration)**.
4 Wipe clean the oil seal seating in the transmission casing.
5 Apply a small amount of general purpose grease to the new seal lips, then press it a little way into the casing by hand, making sure that it is square to its seating.
6 Using suitable tubing or a large socket, carefully drive the oil seal fully into position until it is flush with the casing edge **(see illustration)**.
7 Refit the driveshaft(s) as described in Chapter 8.

Input shaft oil seal

Note: *On the MTX 75 transmission the input shaft seal is integral with the clutch slave cylinder/release bearing. Renew the cylinder/bearing as described in Chapter 6, Section 4.*
8 Remove the clutch release bearing/slave cylinder as described in Chapter 6.
9 Note its fitted depth, then drill a small hole in the hard outer surface of the seal, insert a

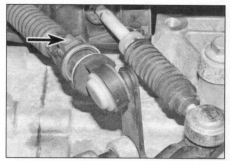

3.22a Pull out the lock button on the inner cable fitting (arrowed) – MMT6

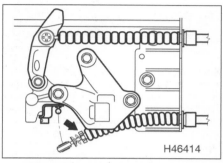

3.22c Pull out the lock button – M56

self-tapping screw, and use pliers to extract the seal **(see illustration)**.
10 Lubricate the new seal with grease and fit it to the bellhousing, lips pointing to the

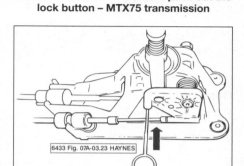

3.22b Pull back the collar and push out the lock button – MTX75 transmission

4.3 Prise the driveshaft oil seal from place

4.9 Insert a self-tapping screw and pull the seal from place

3.23 Lock the transmission selector shaft in position with a suitable drill bit or rod

gearbox side. Use a deep socket or suitable tubing to seat it **(see illustration)**.
11 Refit the release bearing/slave cylinder using a reversal of removal.

4.6 Drive the oil seal into place using a tube or socket

4.10 Drive the new seal squarely into place to its original depth

5.1a Reversing light switch (arrowed) – MTX 75

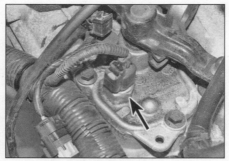

5.1b Reversing light switch (arrowed) – MMT6

2 Release the screws and remove the engine undershield, then position a suitable container beneath the transmission.

3 Unscrew and remove the drain plug and allow the oil to drain into the container **(see illustrations)**. Note that the illustrations show the MTX-75 and MMT6 transmissions but others are similar. Check the condition of the drain plug sealing washer, and renew if necessary.

4 When all the oil has drained, refit the drain plug and tighten it to the specified torque.

Refilling

Note: *For the level check to be accurate, the car must be completely level. If the front of the car has been jacked up, the rear should be jacked up also.*

5 Wipe clean the area around the filler/level plug, and unscrew the plug from the casing. It is a sensible precaution to ensure that the filler plug can be loosened before draining the oil.

6 Fill the transmission through the filler plug orifice with the correct type of oil until the oil begins to run out of the orifice **(see illustrations)**.

7 Refit the filler/level plug with a new seal, and tighten it to the specified torque.

8 Dispose of the old oil safely in accordance with environmental regulations.

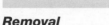

5 Reversing light switch – removal and refitting

Removal

1 Depending on the transmission fitted, the reversing light switch is located on the upper face of the transmission or on the side of the transmission casing. However the process is essentially the same for all models **(see illustrations)**.

2 Remove the air cleaner assembly as described in the relevant part of Chapter 4.

3 Disconnect the wiring plug and unscrew the switch from the transmission housing.

Refitting

4 Refit by reversing the removal operations.

6 Manual transmission oil – draining and refilling

Note: *Renewal of the transmission oil is not a service requirement and will normally only be necessary if the unit is to be removed for overhaul or renewal. However, if the car has completed a high mileage, or is used under arduous conditions (eg, extensive towing or taxi work), it would be advisable to change the oil as a precaution, especially if the gearchange quality has deteriorated.*

Draining

1 Slacken the left-hand front roadwheel bolts, then jack up the front of the vehicle and support it securely on axle stands (see *Jacking and vehicle support*). Remove the roadwheel.

7 Manual transmission – removal and refitting

Note: *Arrangements must be made to support the engine from above, to allow the engine/transmission mounting to be detached on the left-hand side. The best way to support the engine is with a bar resting in the bonnet channels with an adjustable hook appropriately placed. Trolley jacks and the help of an assistant will also be required throughout the procedure.*

Removal

1 Remove the cover from the top of the engine.

2 Remove the battery as described in Chapter 5A, Section 3.

1.8 and 2.0 litre petrol engines

3 Pull the engine management ECU cover straight up to remove it **(see illustration 3.3a)**.

4 Release the locking catches, disconnect the ECU wiring plugs and release the wiring harness from any retaining clips on the battery box **(see illustration 3.3b)**.

All engines

5 Undo the 3 bolts and remove the battery tray **(see illustration)**. Note their fitted positions, and disconnect any wiring plugs as the box is withdrawn.

6 Refer to Chapter 4A, Section 3 (petrol engines) or Chapter 4B, Section 3 (diesel engines) and remove the air cleaner assembly,

6.3a Transmission drain plug – MTX 75

6.3b Transmission drain plug (arrowed) – MMT6

6.6a Oil filler/level plug (arrowed) – MTX 75

6.6b Oil filler/level plug (arrowed) – MMT6

and all relevant inlet ducting around the left-hand side of the engine.

7 Disconnect the gearchange cables from the transmission as described in Section 3.

8 Prise out the retaining clip and disconnect the clutch hydraulic fluid pipe from the junction at the transmission bellhousing, then pull the pipe's rubber bush upwards from the bracket on the transmission. Plug or seal the openings to prevent contamination. To improve access, undo the bolts and remove the selector cables support bracket from the top of the transmission.

9 Jack up and support the front of the vehicle (see *Jacking and vehicle support*). Remove the engine undershield.

10 Refer to Section 6 and drain the transmission oil. This is not absolutely essential, but will remove the potential problem of oil spillage when the driveshafts are removed, or when the transmission is moved out of the car.

11 Remove both driveshafts as described in Chapter 8, Section 2.

12 Remove the starter motor as described in Chapter 5A, Section 8.

13 Undo the fasteners and remove the left-hand front wheel arch liner.

14 On all models fitted with 5 cylinder engines (petrol and diesel) remove the front subframe as described in Chapter 10, Section 15.

15 Note the fitted position of the earth lead on the top/front of the transmission (where fitted), then disconnect the lead, along with the reversing light switch wiring plug **(see illustration)** and the neutral position sensor wiring plug (where fitted).

16 Support the engine from above (see the note at the start of this Section), then remove the left-hand engine/transmission mounting and bracket as described in Chapter 2E Section 11.

17 Undo the bolts and remove the torque rod and the mounting bracket from the transmission. Where fitted remove the protective cover **(see illustrations)**.

18 On turbocharged engines remove the charge air pipe from under the engine/transmission **(see illustration)** and then remove the charge air pipes from the intercooler.

19 Where fitted, remove the heat shield from the catalytic converter (or DPF). On 1.6 diesel engines remove the catalytic converter (or DPF on models fitted with a particulate filter) and then remove the converter support bracket.

20 Lower the transmission enough so that when pulled from the engine the transmission will clear the chassis leg. Note that on 2.0 litre petrol engines the transmission must be pulled forward as it is lowered.

21 Withdraw the transmission squarely off the engine dowels, taking care not to allow the weight of the transmission to hang on the input shaft.

22 Lower the jack and remove the unit from under the car.

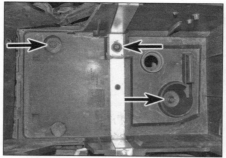

7.5 Undo the 3 bolts (arrowed) and remove the battery tray

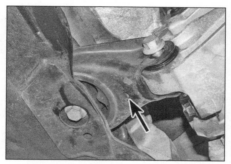

7.17a Undo the bolts and remove the lower torque rod (arrowed)

Refitting

23 Ensure the transmission input shaft is clean and free of rust or grease, then apply a little lubricant (Volvo part No 30759651) to the splines of the input shaft – wipe off any excess lubricant. Check to make sure all locating dowels are in good condition and fitted correctly.

24 Manoeuvre the transmission squarely into position, and engage it with the engine dowels. Refit the lower bolts securing the transmission to the engine, and tighten them to the specified torque.

25 Raise the engine to its approximate fitted position. Refit the engine mounting bracket and torque rod, and secure with the bolts tightened to the specified torque.

26 The remainder of refitting is a reversal of removal, noting the following points:

a) *Tighten all fasteners to their specified torque where given.*

7.18 Undo the bolt and remove the charge air pipe

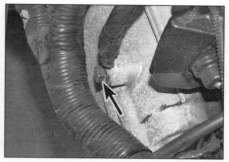

7.15 Disconnect the earth lead (arrowed) from the transmission casing

7.17b Undo the nut (arrowed) and remove the cover (2.0 litre diesel engine shown)

b) *Refit the front subframe (where applicable), aligning the previously-made marks (where applicable). The alignment of the subframe can be checked using alignment tools or a round bar or wooden dowels of 20mm diameter, through the alignment holes (see illustration).*

c) *Top-up the gearbox oil as described in Section 6 of this Chapter.*

d) *Adjust the selector lever cables as described in Section 3.*

e) *Bleed the clutch hydraulic system as described in Chapter 6.*

8 Manual transmission overhaul – general information

Overhauling a manual transmission is a difficult job for the do-it-yourselfer. It involves

7.26 Insert an alignment tool through the holes in the subframe and body (arrowed)

the dismantling and reassembly of many small parts. Numerous clearances must be precisely measured and, if necessary, changed with selected spacers and circlips. As a result, if transmission problems arise, while the unit can be removed and refitted by a competent do-it-yourselfer, overhaul should be left to a transmission specialist. Rebuilt transmissions may be available – check with your dealer parts department, motor factors, or transmission specialists. At any rate, the time and money involved in an overhaul is almost sure to exceed the cost of a rebuilt unit.

Nevertheless, it's not impossible for an experienced mechanic to rebuild a transmission, providing the special tools are available, and the job is done in a deliberate step-by-step manner, so nothing is overlooked.

The tools necessary for an overhaul include: internal and external circlip pliers, a bearing puller, a slide hammer, a set of pin punches, a dial test indicator, and possibly a hydraulic press. In addition, a large, sturdy workbench and a vice or transmission stand will be required.

During dismantling of the transmission, make careful notes of how each part comes off, where it fits in relation to other parts, and what holds it in place.

Before taking the transmission apart for repair, it will help if you have some idea what area of the transmission is malfunctioning. Certain problems can be closely tied to specific areas in the transmission, which can make component examination and renewal easier. Refer to the *Fault finding* section at the rear of this manual for information regarding possible sources of trouble.

Chapter 7 Part B:
Automatic transmission

Contents

Degrees of difficulty

Easy, suitable for novice with little experience	Fairly easy, suitable for beginner with some experience	Fairly difficult, suitable for competent DIY mechanic	Difficult, suitable for experienced DIY mechanic	Very difficult, suitable for expert DIY or professional

Specifications

General

Type .... Computer-controlled five- or six-speed, one reverse, with torque converter lock-up on three or five highest gears.

Designation .... AW55-51SN (five-speed)
TF-80SC (six speed)

Lubrication

Lubricant type .... See *Lubricants, fluids and tyre pressures* on page 0•16
Capacity:
 Drain and refill:
  AW55-51SN .... 7.65 +/- 0.15 litres
  TF-80SC .... 7.0 litres

Torque wrench settings

	Nm	lbf ft
Engine/transmission mounting bolts	See relevant part of Chapter 2 depending on engine	
Oil filler/drain plugs (AW55-51SN)	35	26
Oil filler plug (TF-80SC)	35	26
Oil drain plug (TF-80SC)	8	6
Roadwheel nuts:		
Stage 1 (All nuts)	20	15
Stage 2:		
Standard, locking and nuts with fixed conical seating	110	81
Nuts with rotating conical seating	130	96
Starter motor mounting bolts	See Chapter 5A	
Steering rack-to-subframe bolts	See Chapter 10	
Subframe bolts	See Chapter 10	
Torque converter-to-driveplate bolts*:		
AW55-51SN	35	26
TF-80SC	60	44
Transmission-to-engine bolts	50	37

* Do not re-use

2.3 Prise the end of the inner cable from the balljoint on the transmission lever (arrowed)

2.4a Prise up the blue retaining ring...

2.4b ... then pull back the collar and disengage the outer cable from the bracket

1 General information

The AW 55-51SN is a computer-controlled fully-automatic five-speed transmission, with torque converter lock-up on the highest three gears. The TF-80SC is a computer-controlled fully-automatic six-speed transmission, with torque converter lock-up on the highest five gears.

The units are controlled by a transmission control module (TCM) which receives signal inputs from various sensors relating to transmission operating conditions. Information on engine parameters are also sent to the TCM from the engine management system. From this data, the TCM can establish the optimum gear shifting speeds and lock-up engagement points according to the driving mode selected.

Drive is taken from the engine to the transmission by a torque converter. This is a type of fluid coupling, which under certain conditions has a torque multiplying effect. The torque converter is mechanically locked to the engine, under the control of the TCM, when the transmission is operating in the three highest gears. This eliminates losses due to slip, and improves fuel economy.

The engine can only be started in position P, thanks to a safety/security feature called Shiftlock. With this system, the ignition key can only be removed from the ignition/

2.10a Prise up the blue retaining ring . . .

steering lock if the selector lever is placed in position P. On restarting the car, the selector lever can only be moved from the P position once the ignition switch is turned to position II.

Most models with automatic transmission feature a Winter mode selector, with the switch located alongside the selector lever. In this mode, the transmission will allow starting from rest in a higher than normal gear to avoid wheelspin in poor road conditions.

A kickdown facility causes the transmission to shift down a gear (subject to engine speed) when the throttle is fully depressed. This is useful when extra acceleration is required. Kickdown, like the other transmission functions, is controlled by the TCM.

In addition to control of the transmission, the TCM incorporates a built-in fault diagnosis facility. If a transmission fault occurs, the transmission warning light on the instrument panel will flash; the TCM will revert to an emergency (limp-home) program which ensures that two forward gears and reverse will always be available, but gearchanging must be performed manually. If a fault of this nature does occur, the TCM stores a series of signals (or fault codes) which can be read and interpreted using suitable diagnostic equipment, for quick and accurate fault diagnosis (see Section 7). The TCM also has a facility for recording the amount of time the gearbox fluid spends above a 150°C – normally this temperature is only achieved by continuous taxi-use, or continuous use as a tow vehicle. Once a predetermined amount of time at or above this temperature is exceeded, the TCM will store a fault code, and illuminate a warning light on the instrument cluster, indicating that the fluid must be changed. However, just changing the fluid will not extinguish the warning light – this must be carried out using dedicated Volvo test equipment.

The automatic transmission is a complex unit, but if it is not abused, it is reliable and long-lasting. Repair or overhaul operations are beyond the scope of many dealers, let alone the home mechanic; specialist advice should be sought if problems arise which cannot be solved by the procedures given in this Chapter.

2 Selector cable – removal, refitting and adjustment

Removal

1 On vehicles fitted with the TF-80SC transmission, it is necessary to remove the air cleaner assembly as described in Chapter 4A (petrol) or 4B (diesel) Remove the battery and battery box as described in Chapter 5A, the left-hand engine mounting as described in Chapter 2E, and the differential pressure sensor as described in Chapter 4D. The remainder of the process is essentially the same as that described below.

2 Remove the centre console as described in Chapter 11.

3 Carefully prise the selector inner cable socket fitting from the balljoint on the transmission lever **(see illustration)**.

4 Release the selector outer cable from the bracket on the transmission **(see illustrations)**. Tie a length of string or cable to the selector cable to assist during refitting.

5 Jack up the front of the vehicle and support it securely on axle stands (see *Jacking and vehicle support*).

6 Remove the mounting for the central silencer, undo the 4 plastic nuts, and slide the heat shield rearwards for access to the grommet where the cable passes through the floor.

7 Release the cable from the retaining clip on the underside of the floor.

8 Fold back the carpet each side of the centre console area, and carefully cut away the sound insulation around the cable grommet, located just in front of the heater housing. Remove the sound insulation.

9 Undo the 2 nuts securing the cable grommet to the floor, and lift the grommet from the mounting studs.

10 Prise off the blue ring, then pull back the locking sleeve and release the outer cable from the selector lever housing bracket **(see illustrations)**.

11 Pull the cable into the passenger cabin sufficiently to enable the cable end fitting to be disengaged from the balljoint on the selector lever **(see illustration)**.

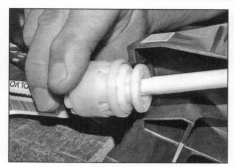

2.10b . . . then pull back the collar and disengage the outer cable from the bracket

2.11 Prise the inner cable (arrowed) from the lever balljoint

2.23 Pull the forward the spring-loaded sleeve (arrowed)

12 Manoeuvre the selector cable assembly into the passenger cabin, untie the string/cable – leaving it in place to aid refitting, then remove the selector cable out of the vehicle.

Refitting and adjustment

13 From inside the car, tie the string/cable to the selector cable carefully feed the cable through into the engine compartment, with the help of an assistant pulling the string/cable, ensuring that it is correctly routed.
14 Reconnect the cable to the selector lever and housing bracket. Ensure the cable is engaged before fitting the outer cable sleeve retaining clip.
15 Refit the cable entry grommet, and securely tighten the 2 nuts.
16 Refit the sound insulation, and tape over the splits/cuts.
17 Refit the carpet.
18 Working underneath the vehicle, clip the cable to the underside of the floor.
19 Refit the heat shield, secure the retaining nuts and refit the silencer mounting.
20 Refit the cable end fitting to the balljoint on the transmission selector lever, then refit the outer cable sleeve, and secure it with the retaining clip.
21 Lower the vehicle to the ground. Ensure the ignition is switched off.
22 Move the gear selector lever to position P (Park). Ensure that the gear lever and cable position do not move during subsequent operations.
23 Working in the engine compartment, release the selector cable adjuster by pulling forward the spring-loaded sleeve and pulling up the release lug **(see illustration)**.
24 Move the selector lever on the transmission as far forward as it will go to the P (Park) position. Ensure that P is selected by releasing the handbrake and trying to roll the car; the transmission should be locked. Re-apply the handbrake.
25 Press down the release lug on the selector cable sleeve.
26 Refit the ECM cover.
27 Refit the centre console as described in Chapter 11.

3 Selector housing and position display panel – removal and refitting

Removal

Selector housing

1 Remove the centre console as described in Chapter 11.
2 Note their fitted positions then disconnect the wiring plugs from the housing.
3 Undo the 4 bolts securing the selector housing to the vehicle floor **(see illustration)**.
4 Release the selector cable from the housing lever as described in Section 2.

Position display panel

5 Remove the centre console as describe in Chapter 11.

6 Rotate the collar at the base of the lever knob anti-clockwise and pull it downwards **(see illustration)**.
7 Grasp the lever knob with both hands, and give it a sharp jerk upwards to remove it.
8 Note their fitted positions and disconnect the connectors from the solenoid and harness switches.
9 Carefully release the 4 retaining clips and remove the display panel **(see illustrations)**.

Refitting

10 Refitting is a reversal of removal, noting the following points:
a) *If the selector housing has been renewed, the built-in position sensor must be calibrated using Volvo test equipment. Entrust this task to a Volvo dealer or suitably-equipped specialist.*
b) *Fit the knob onto the selector lever and*

3.3 Undo the 4 bolts securing the housing to the floor (left-hand bolts arrowed)

3.6 Rotate the collar anti-clockwise and pull it downwards

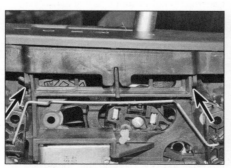

3.9a Release the clips (arrowed) on the right-hand side . . .

3.9b . . . followed by the clips (arrowed) on the left-hand side

4.5a Undo the nut and lift the lever from the TCM spindle . . .

firmly push it down into position. Pull the gaiter up around the knob, and push the lock ring upwards to secure the gaiter to the knob.

4 Transmission control module – removal and refitting

Note: *If a new control module is fitted, it must be programmed using dedicated Volvo test equipment. Entrust this task to a Volvo dealer or suitably-equipped specialist.*

Removal

1 Turn the ignition off, then wait at least 2 minutes before disconnecting the battery negative lead (see Chapter 5A). This is to ensure that any residual electrical energy has been dissipated. **Note:** *If the cooling fan runs on after the ignition has been switched off, wait until it stops then wait a further 1 minute before disconnecting the battery lead.*
2 Remove the air cleaner assembly as described in Chapter 4A (petrol) or 4B (diesel).
3 The TCM (Transmission Control Module) is located on the top of the transmission casing. Disconnect the wiring plugs from the TCM. **Note:** *Do not touch the control module terminal pins with bare hands – there is a danger of damage due to static electricity.*
4 Undo the retaining bracket screw, and

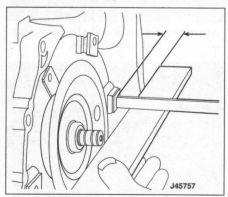

5.7 When correctly fitted, the distance between the end of the transmission casing and the mounting tabs on the converter should be 14mm

4.5b . . . then undo the 3 bolts and remove the TCM

remove the bracket to the right-hand side of the TCM. On models fitted with the TF-80SC transmission, undo the 2 bolts and remove the cable guide adjacent to the TCM.
5 Undo 3 retaining bolts, and the lever retaining nut. Pull the lever from the spindle and remove the TCM **(see illustrations)**.

Refitting

6 Ensure the gear selector is in the neutral position.
7 Locate the TCM in position, ensuring the arrows on the lever spindle and TCM casing align **(see illustration)**.
8 Refit the TCM retaining bolts, and the retaining bracket, then tighten the bolts/screws securely.
9 Refit the lever and tighten the retaining nut securely.
10 Reconnect the wiring plugs and refit the air cleaner assembly.
11 Reconnect the battery negative lead (see Chapter 5A).

5 Fluid seals – renewal

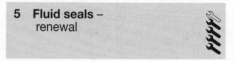

Differential side gear seals

1 The procedure is the same as that described for the manual transmission in Chapter 7A.

Input shaft/torque converter seal

2 Remove the transmission (see Section 6).
3 Pull the torque converter squarely out of the transmission. Be careful, as it is full of fluid.
4 Pull or lever out the old seal. Clean the seat and inspect the seal rubbing surface on the torque converter.
5 Lubricate the new seal with transmission fluid and fit it, lips inwards. Seat it with a piece of tube.
6 Lubricate the torque converter sleeve with transmission fluid, and slide the converter into place, pushing it in as far as it will go.
7 Check that the torque converter is fully seated by measuring the distance from the edge of the transmission housing face to the retaining bolt tabs on the converter. The dimension should be approximately 14mm **(see illustration)**.

4.7 Ensure the arrows on the TCM cover and spindle align (arrowed)

8 Refit the transmission (see Section 6).

Gear selector rod seal

9 Remove the TCM as described in Section 4.
10 Carefully prise the old oil seal from position using a small screwdriver. Take care not to damage the linkage rod.
11 Smear the lips of the new oil seal with clean automatic transmission fluid, then guide the seal over the rod (lips towards the transmission), and seat it in place using a suitable tubular spacer.
12 Refit the TCM as described in Section 4.

All seals

13 Check the transmission fluid level as described in Chapter 1A or 1B on completion.

6 Automatic transmission – removal and refitting

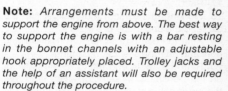

Note: *Arrangements must be made to support the engine from above. The best way to support the engine is with a bar resting in the bonnet channels with an adjustable hook appropriately placed. Trolley jacks and the help of an assistant will also be required throughout the procedure.*
Note: *The process described below is for the removal and refitting of the AW55-51SN transmission. The process for removal and refitting of the TF-80SC transmission is essentially similar, noting the following points:*
a) The left-hand engine mounting should be removed at the beginning of the process, with reference to the note above on supporting the engine.
b) To separate the transmission from the engine, the transmission must be lowered by 60mm. The upper and lower 4 bolts can then be removed. With the transmission supported using a trolley jack, the remaining bolt on each side can be removed.

Removal

1 Slacken both driveshaft hub nuts as described in Chapter 8, Section 2 and then slacken the wheel nuts Raise and support the front of the car (see *Jacking and vehicle support*). Remove the both front wheels and the engine undershield.

2 Set the steering wheel and roadwheels in the straight-ahead position. Release the steering column adjuster, and push the steering wheel in and upwards as far as it will go. Lock it in this position.

3 Disconnect the battery negative lead as described in Chapter 5A, and remove the battery box as described in Chapter 5A.

4 Undo the bolts securing the steering rack to the front subframe. Use cable ties/straps to suspend the steering rack from the vehicle body.

5 Remove both the front driveshafts as described in Chapter 8.

6 Position a trolley jack under the front subframe, make alignment marks between the subframe and vehicle body, then slacken the subframe front mounting bolts a little.

7 Detach the front exhaust pipe rubber mounting from the bracket.

8 Undo the subframe rear mounting bolts, and the rear torque rod bolts **(see illustration)**.

9 Lower the front subframe a little, and remove the front anti-roll bar clamp mounting bolts. Detach the bar from the subframe.

10 Release the wiring harness from the clips on the subframe, then remove the front mounting bolts and lower the subframe. Manoeuvre it from under the vehicle.

11 On models fitted with the TF-80SC transmission, slacken the clamps, undo the support bracket bolt, and remove the charge air-pipe beneath the engine.

12 Place a container under the transmission, then undo the retaining bolt and disconnect the fluid pipe from the front lower edge of the transmission casing **(see illustration)**. Plug or seal the openings to prevent contamination.

13 Disconnect the earth connection from the transmission casing **(see illustration)**.

14 Rotate the crankshaft, using a socket on the pulley nut, until one of the torque converter-to-driveplate retaining bolts becomes accessible through the opening on the rear facing side of the engine. Working through the opening, undo the bolt using a TX50 socket. Rotate the crankshaft as necessary and remove the remaining bolts in the same way.

15 Remove the air cleaner assembly as described in Chapter 4A or 4B.

16 Carefully prise the selector inner cable fitting from the balljoint on the transmission lever, then pull back the sleeve and detach the outer cable from the bracket **(see illustrations 2.4a and 2.4b)**.

17 Press in the collars and disconnect the fluid pipe between the oil cooler and transmission cover at the quick release couplings **(see illustration)**. Be prepared for fluid spillage.

18 Working at the front of the transmission, remove the engine coolant hose bracket, and the holder for the bracket.

19 Release transmission bleed hose from the bracket above the starter motor mounting.

20 Remove the starter motor as described in Chapter 5A.

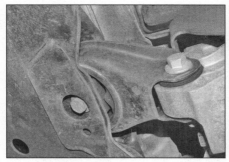

6.8 Undo the bolts and remove the rear torque rod

21 Remove the bolts at the upper edge, securing the transmission to the engine.

22 With reference to the note at the beginning of this Section, suitably support the engine from above, and adjust the support so that the load is just taken off the engine mountings.

23 Undo the left-hand engine/transmission mounting through-bolt, and lower the transmission a sufficiently to access the bolts and remove the left-hand engine/transmission mounting assembly. Check that no hoses or wiring harnesses are trapped or stretched whilst lowering the engine/transmission.

24 Lower the engine/transmission by means of the overhead support, until sufficient clearance exists to enable the transmission to be withdrawn. Take care not to lower the unit too far, or the exhaust downpipe will foul the steering rack. Also, make sure that the engine oil dipstick tube clears the radiator fan, and that no hoses or leads are trapped or stretched.

25 Securely and safely support the transmission from below on a trolley jack.

26 Remove the remaining bolts securing the transmission to the engine.

27 With the aid of an assistant, draw the transmission squarely off the engine dowels making sure that the torque converter remains in position on the transmission. Use the access hole in the transmission housing to hold the converter in place.

28 Lower the jack and remove the unit from under the car.

Refitting

29 Clean the contact surfaces on the torque converter and driveplate, and the transmission

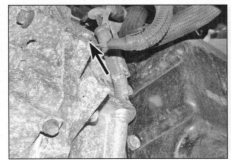

6.13 Transmission earth lead (arrowed)

6.12 Undo the bolt (arrowed) and disconnect the fluid hose

and engine mating faces. Lightly lubricate the torque converter guide projection and the engine/transmission locating dowels with grease.

30 Volvo insist that the oil cooler must be flushed using new transmission oil prior to refitting. Absolute cleanliness is essential.

31 Check that the torque converter is fully-seated by measuring the distance from the edge of the transmission housing face to the retaining bolt tabs on the converter. The dimension should be approximately 14mm **(see illustration 5.7)**.

32 Manoeuvre the transmission squarely into position, and engage it with the engine dowels. Refit the bolts securing the transmission to the engine and tighten lightly first in a diagonal sequence, then again to the specified torque.

33 Attach the torque converter to the driveplate using new bolts. Rotate the crankshaft for access to the bolts as was done for removal, then rotate the torque converter by means of the access hole in the transmission housing. Fit and tighten all the bolts hand-tight first, then tighten again to the specified torque.

34 Refit the left-hand engine/transmission mounting assembly and tighten the bolts to the specified torque.

35 Raise the engine to its approximate fitted position. Refit the left-hand engine/transmission through-bolt and tighten it to the specified torque.

36 The remainder of refitting is a reversal of removal, noting the following points:

a) Tighten all fasteners to their specified torque where given.

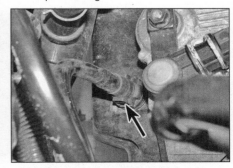

6.17 Transmission oil pipe quick-release coupling (arrowed)

6.36 Check the subframe alignment using round tools that fit through the holes in the subframe and vehicle body (arrowed)

b) *Refit the front subframe, aligning the previously-made marks (where applicable). The alignment of the subframe can be checked using alignment tools or a round bar or wooden dowel of 20mm diameter, through the alignment holes (see illustration).*
c) *Top-up the transmission fluid as described in Chapter 1A or 1B.*
d) *Adjust the selector lever cable as described in Section 2.*
e) *Reconnect the battery negative lead as described in Chapter 5A.*

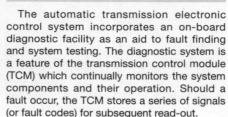

7 Automatic transmission – fault diagnosis

The automatic transmission electronic control system incorporates an on-board diagnostic facility as an aid to fault finding and system testing. The diagnostic system is a feature of the transmission control module (TCM) which continually monitors the system components and their operation. Should a fault occur, the TCM stores a series of signals (or fault codes) for subsequent read-out.

If a fault occurs, indicated by the flashing of the warning light on the instrument panel, the on-board diagnostics can be accessed using a fault code reader, for quick and accurate diagnosis. A Volvo dealer will obviously have such a reader, but they are also available from other suppliers. It is unlikely to be cost-effective for the private owner to purchase a fault code reader, but a well-equipped local garage or auto electrical specialist will have one.

In many instances, the fault may be nothing more serious than a corroded, trapped or loose wiring connection, or a loose, dirty, or badly-fitted component. Remember that if the fault has appeared only a short time after any part of the vehicle has been serviced or overhauled, the first place to check is where

that work was carried out, however unrelated it may appear, to ensure that no carelessly-refitted components are causing the problem.

Even if the source of the problem is found and fixed, diagnostic equipment may still be required, to erase the fault code from the TCM memory, and stop the warning light flashing.

If the fault cannot be easily cured, the only alternatives possible at this time are the substitution of a suspect component with a known good unit (where possible), or entrusting further work to a Volvo dealer or suitably-equipped specialist.

8 Emergency release of the selector lever

1 If the vehicle's battery is disconnected or discharged, it is possible to release the selector lever from its locked position. First, ensure the handbrake is fully applied or chock the rear wheels if it is not possible to apply the handbrake.
2 Withdraw the plastic key blade from the remote control unit, and open the small cover at the rear of the selector panel.
3 Insert the key blade into the hole revealed by opening the cover, and holding the blade down, move the selector lever to the neutral position.

Chapter 8
Driveshafts

Contents

Degrees of difficulty

Easy, suitable for novice with little experience	Fairly easy, suitable for beginner with some experience	Fairly difficult, suitable for competent DIY mechanic	Difficult, suitable for experienced DIY mechanic	Very difficult, suitable for expert DIY or professional

Specifications

General

Driveshaft type . . . . Equal-length solid-steel shafts, splined to inner and outer constant velocity joints. Intermediate shaft incorporated in right-hand driveshaft assembly
Outer constant velocity joint type. . . . . Ball-and-cage
Inner constant velocity joint type . . . . Tripod

Lubrication

Lubricant type . . . . Special grease supplied in repair kit, or suitable molybdenum disulphide grease – consult a Volvo dealer or parts specialist

CV joint grease capacity:

	Outboard joint	Inboard joint
1.8 and 2.0 litre petrol models	95 g	140 g
2.4 litre petrol models	125 g	153 g
1.6 litre diesel models	125 g	153 g
2.0 litre diesel models	120 g	174 g
2.4 litre diesel models	Not available	

Torque wrench settings

	Nm	lbf ft
Driveshaft bolt:*		
Stage 1	35	26
Stage 2	Angle-tighten a further 90°	
Lower arm balljoint to hub carrier*	70	52
Right-hand driveshaft support bearing cap bolts	24	18
Roadwheel nuts:		
Stage 1 (All nuts)	20	15
Stage 2:		
Standard, locking and nuts with fixed conical seating	110	81
Nuts with rotating conical seating	130	96

* Do not re-use

1 General information

Drive is transmitted from the differential to the front wheels by means of two solid-steel, equal-length driveshafts equipped with constant velocity (CV) joints at their inner and outer ends. Due to the position of the transmission, an intermediate shaft and support bearing are incorporated into the right-hand driveshaft assembly.

A ball-and-cage type CV joint is fitted to the outer end of each driveshaft. The joint has an outer member, which is splined to accept the wheel hub, and is threaded so that it can be fastened to the hub by a large bolt. The joint contains six balls within a cage, which engage with the inner member. The complete assembly is protected by a flexible gaiter secured to the driveshaft and joint outer member.

At the inner end, the driveshaft is splined to engage a tripod type CV joint, containing needle roller bearings and cups. On the left-hand side, the driveshaft inner CV joint engages directly with the differential sun wheel. On the right-hand side, the inner joint is integral with the intermediate shaft, the inner end of which engages with the differential sun wheel. As on the outer joints, a flexible gaiter secured to the driveshaft and CV joint outer member protects the complete assembly.

2.3 Slacken the driveshaft retaining bolt through the hole in the centre of the wheel

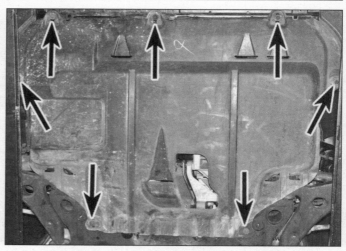

2.4 Undo the Torx screws (arrowed) and remove the engine undershield

2 Driveshafts – removal and refitting

Removal

1 Firmly apply the handbrake and chock the rear wheels. When the driveshaft bolt is to be loosened (or tightened), it is preferable to do so with the car resting on its wheels. If the car is jacked up, this places a high load on the jack, and the car could slip off.

2.7 Counterhold the anti-roll bar balljoint shank with an Allen key

2.10 Use a balljoint separator tool to detach the balljoint from the hub carrier

2 Remove the wheel trim or centre cap to gain access to the driveshaft bolt. If the wheel design does not permit this access, the safest option is to remove the wheel and fit the spare – see *Wheel changing* at the front of the manual.

3 With an assistant firmly depressing the brake pedal, slacken the driveshaft retaining bolt using a socket and a long extension bar **(see illustration)**. Note that this bolt is extremely tight – ensure that the tools used to loosen it are of good quality, and a good fit.

4 Loosen the front wheel nuts, then jack up

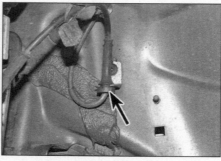

2.8 Release the ABS harness from the bracket (arrowed)

2.12 Push the lower control arm downwards, pull the hub carrier outwards, and withdraw the driveshaft

the front of the car and support it on axle stands (see *Jacking and vehicle support*). Remove the appropriate front roadwheel, then undo the 7 Torx screws and remove the engine undershield (where fitted) **(see illustration)**. If required, the wheelarch liner can be removed to improve access.

5 Remove the previously-slackened driveshaft retaining bolt. Discard the bolt – a new one must be fitted.

6 Tap the end of the driveshaft approximately 15 to 20mm into the wheel hub.

7 Undo the nut and detach the anti-roll bar link rod from the suspension struts, using an Allen key to counterhold the link balljoint **(see illustration)**.

8 Detach the brake hose from the bracket on the strut, and release the ABS wiring harness from the bracket on the wheel arch **(see illustration)**.

9 Slacken the lower control arm balljoint nut until the end of the balljoint shank is level with the top of the nut.

10 Detach the lower control arm balljoint from the hub carrier using a balljoint separator tool **(see illustration)**.

11 Push down on the suspension arm using a stout bar to release the balljoint shank from the hub carrier. Take care not to damage the balljoint dust cover during and after disconnection.

12 Swivel the suspension strut and hub carrier assembly outwards, and withdraw the driveshaft CV joint from the hub flange **(see illustration)**.

13 If removing the left-hand driveshaft, free the inner CV joint from the transmission by levering between the edge of the joint and the transmission casing with a large screwdriver or similar tool. Take care not to damage the transmission oil seal or the inner CV joint gaiter. Withdraw the driveshaft from under the wheel arch.

14 If removing the right-hand driveshaft, undo the two bolts and remove the cap from

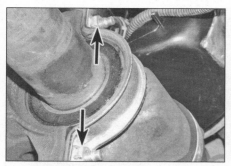

2.14 Undo the 2 nuts and remove the intermediate bearing cap (arrowed)

the intermediate shaft support bearing **(see illustration)**. Pull the intermediate shaft out of the transmission, and remove the driveshaft assembly from under the wheel arch. Note: *Do not pull the outer shaft from the intermediate shaft – the coupling will separate.*

Refitting

15 Refitting is a reversal of removal, but observe the following points.

a) *Prior to refitting, remove all traces of rust, oil and dirt from the splines of the outer CV joint, and lubricate the splines of the inner joint with wheel bearing grease.*

b) *If working on the left-hand driveshaft, ensure that the inner CV joint is pushed fully into the transmission, so that the retaining circlip locks into place in the differential gear.*

c) *Always use a new driveshaft-to-hub retaining bolt (see illustration).*

d) *Fit the same wheel as was used for loosening the driveshaft bolt, and lower the car to the ground.*

e) *Tighten all nuts and bolts to the specified torque (see Chapters 9 and 10 for brake and suspension component torque settings). When tightening the driveshaft bolt, tighten first using a torque wrench, then further, through the specified angle, using an angle-tightening gauge.*

f) *Where applicable, refit the alloy wheel on completion. Tighten the roadwheel nuts to the specified torque.*

2.15 Always renew the driveshaft retaining bolt

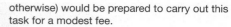

3 Outer constant velocity joint gaiter – renewal

1 Remove the driveshaft as described in Section 2.

Automatic models with a vibration damper

2 On these vehicles, after removing the inner CV joint, measure and note the distance from the end of the shaft to the edge of the damper. The damper must then be pressed from the shaft, the outer joint boot renewed, then the damper pressed back into its original position using the dimensions previously noted. If access to a hydraulic press in not available, most engineering workshops (automotive or

otherwise) would be prepared to carry out this task for a modest fee.

All models

3 Cut off the gaiter retaining clips, then slide the gaiter down the shaft to expose the outer constant velocity joint **(see illustration)**.
Caution: Do not disassemble the outer CV joint.
4 Scoop out as much grease as possible from the joint.
5 Inspect the ball tracks on the inner and outer members. If the tracks have widened, the balls will no longer be a tight fit. At the same time, check the ball cage windows for wear or cracking between the windows. If the joints appear worn, complete renewal may be the only option – check with a Volvo dealer or specialist.
6 If the joint is in satisfactory condition, obtain a repair kit from your Volvo dealer, consisting of a new gaiter, retaining clips, driveshaft screw, circlip and grease.
7 Pack the joint with the half of the grease supplied, working it well into the ball tracks, and into the driveshaft opening in the inner member **(see illustration)**.
8 Slide the rubber gaiter onto the shaft.
9 Apply the remaining grease to the joint and the inside of the gaiter.
10 Locate the outer lip of the gaiter in the groove on the joint outer member, then fit the retaining clip. Remove any slack in the clips by carefully compressing the raised section using a special pair of pincers **(see illustrations)**.
Note: *Ensure no grease is on the surfaces between the gaiter and the joint housing.*

3.3 Cut the gaiter retaining clips

3.7 Pack the outer CV joint with about half the grease supplied

3.10a Locate the outer clip on the gaiter . . .

3.10b . . . then using a special pair of pliers . . .

3.10c . . . remove any slack in the clip

3.11 Lift the inner edge of the gaiter to equalise the air pressure

3.12 The circlip on the end of the shaft must be renewed

11 Use a small screwdriver to lift the inner lip of the gaiter, allowing the air pressure inside the gaiter to equalise, then fit the inner clip to the gaiter **(see illustration)**.
12 Fit the new circlip to the end of the shaft **(see illustration)**.
13 Where applicable, press the damper into its original position. Brushing the shaft and the hole in the vibration damper with soapy water will allow the damper to slide more easily.
14 Check that the constant velocity joint moves freely in all directions, then refit the driveshaft as described in Section 2.
15 Volvo recommend lubricating the gaiter once the driveshaft is refitted by applying a small amount of spray wax (Volvo 30787812) to the outside of the gaiter.

4 Inner constant velocity joint gaiter – renewal

1 Remove the driveshaft as described in Section 2.

2 Cut through the metal clips, and slide the gaiter from the inner CV joint.
3 Clean out some of the grease from the joint, then make alignment marks between the housing and the shaft, to aid reassembly **(see illustration)**.
4 Carefully pull the housing from the tripod, twisting the housing so the tripod rollers come out one at a time. If necessary, use a soft-faced hammer or mallet to tap the housing off.

4.3 Make alignment marks between the shaft and housing

5 Clean the grease from the tripod and housing.
6 Remove the circlip, and carefully drive the tripod from the end of the shaft **(see illustrations)**. Discard the circlip, a new one (supplied in the repair kit) must be fitted. Remove the gaiter if still on the shaft.
7 Slide the new gaiter onto the shaft along with the smaller clip **(see illustration)**.
8 Refit the tripod with the bevelled edge towards the driveshaft, and drive it fully into

4.6a Remove the circlip from the end of the shaft . . .

4.6b . . . then carefully drive the tripod from the shaft

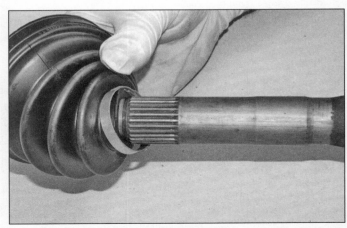

4.7 Slide the new gaiter and smaller diameter clip onto the shaft

4.8a Fit the tripod with the bevelled edge (arrowed) towards the shaft . . .

4.8b . . . then fit the new circlip

4.11 The smaller diameter of the gaiter must locate over the groove in the shaft (arrowed)

4.12 Equalise the air pressure before tightening the gaiter clip

place, until the new circlip can be installed (see illustrations).

9 Lubricate the tripod rollers with some of the grease supplied in the gaiter kit, then fill the housing and gaiter with the remainder.

10 Refit the housing to the tripod, tapping it gently into place using a soft-hammer or mallet if necessary.

11 Slide the new gaiter into place ensuring the smaller diameter of the gaiter locates over the grooves in the shaft (see illustration).

12 Fit the new retaining clips and refit the driveshaft as described in Section 2 (see illustration).

13 Volvo recommend lubricating the gaiter once the driveshaft is refitted by applying a small amount of spray wax (Volvo 30787812) to the outside of the gaiter.

5 Right-hand driveshaft support bearing – removal and refitting

Note: *At the time of writing, it would appear the support bearing was not available as a separate part. If the bearing is worn of damaged, the complete driveshaft must be renewed. Exchange driveshafts are available – check with a Volvo dealer or specialist.*

6 Driveshaft overhaul – general information

Road test the car, and listen for a metallic clicking from the front as the car is driven slowly in a circle with the steering on full-lock. Repeat the check on full-left and full-right lock. This noise may also be apparent when pulling away from a standstill with lock applied. If a clicking noise is heard, this indicates wear in the outer constant velocity joints.

If vibration, consistent with roadspeed, is felt through the car when accelerating, there is a possibility of wear in the inner constant velocity joints.

If the joints are worn or damaged, it would appear at the time of writing that no parts are available, other than boot kits, and the complete driveshaft must be renewed. Exchange driveshafts are available - check with a Volvo dealer or specialist.

Chapter 9
Braking system

Contents

Degrees of difficulty

Easy, suitable for novice with little experience 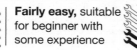	**Fairly easy,** suitable for beginner with some experience	**Fairly difficult,** suitable for competent DIY mechanic	**Difficult,** suitable for experienced DIY mechanic	**Very difficult,** suitable for expert DIY or professional

Specifications

General

System type:

Footbrake . . . . Dual-circuit hydraulic with servo assistance. Disc brakes front and rear. Anti-lock braking (ABS) on all models

Handbrake . . . . Mechanical to rear calipers

Front brakes

Type	Ventilated disc, with single-piston sliding calipers
Brake pad friction material minimum thickness	2.0 mm
Disc diameter	278, 300 or 320 mm
Disc thickness:	
New	26.0 mm
Wear limit	23.0 mm
Maximum disc run-out	0.075 mm
Maximum disc thickness variation	0.008 mm

Rear brakes

Type	Solid disc, with single-piston sliding calipers
Brake pad friction material minimum thickness	2.0 mm
Disc diameter	295 mm
Disc thickness wear limit:	9.0mm
Maximum disc run-out	0.04 mm
Maximum disc thickness variation	0.008 mm

Torque wrench settings

	Nm	lbf ft
ABS wheel sensor mounting bolts.	6	4
Brake pedal bolts.	24	18
Flexible hose unions.	23	18
Front brake disc retaining screw	10	7
Front caliper bracket bolts*	120	89
Front caliper guide pins	28	21
Master cylinder mounting nuts.	24	18
Rear caliper bracket bolts*.	70	52
Rear caliper slide rail bolts	35	26
Rigid pipe unions	18	13
Roadwheel nuts:		
Stage 1 (All nuts).	20	15
Stage 2:		
Standard, locking and nuts with fixed conical seating	110	81
Nuts with rotating conical seating	130	96
Steering column joint pinch-bolt	See Chapter 10	
Subframe mounting bolts:*.	See Chapter 10	
Vacuum pump bolts	See Chapter 2 specifications	
Vacuum servo unit mounting nuts	24	18

Do not re-use

1 General information

The brake pedal operates disc brakes on all four wheels by means of a dual circuit hydraulic system with servo assistance. The handbrake operates actuators integral with the rear brake calipers, utilising the same brake pads. An anti-lock braking system (ABS) is fitted to all models, and is described in further detail in Section 18.

The hydraulic system is split into two circuits, so that in the event of failure of one circuit, the other will still provide adequate braking power (although pedal travel and effort may increase). An axle-split system is employed, in which one circuit serves the front brakes and the other circuit the rear brakes.

The brake servo is of the direct-acting type, being interposed between the brake pedal and the master cylinder. The servo magnifies the effort applied by the driver. It is vacuum-operated with a camshaft-driven vacuum pump.

Instrument panel warning lights alert the driver to low fluid level by means of a level sensor in the master cylinder reservoir. Other warning lights remind when the handbrake is applied, and indicate the presence of a fault in the ABS system.

Note: *When servicing any part of the system, work carefully and methodically; also observe scrupulous cleanliness when overhauling any part of the hydraulic system. Always renew components (in axle sets, where applicable) if in doubt about their condition, and use only genuine Volvo parts, or at least those of known good quality. Note the warnings given in 'Safety first!' and at relevant points in this Chapter concerning the dangers of asbestos dust and hydraulic fluid.*

2 Hydraulic system – bleeding

⚠️ *Warning: Hydraulic fluid is poisonous; wash off immediately and thoroughly in the case of skin contact, and seek immediate medical advice if any fluid is swallowed or gets into the eyes. Certain types of hydraulic fluid are inflammable, and may ignite when allowed into contact with hot components; when servicing any hydraulic system, it is safest to assume that the fluid IS inflammable, and to take precautions against the risk of fire as though it is petrol that is being handled. Hydraulic fluid is also an effective paint stripper, and will attack plastics; if any is spilt, it should be washed off immediately, using copious quantities of clean water. Finally, it is hygroscopic (it absorbs moisture from the air). The more moisture is absorbed by the fluid, the lower its boiling point becomes, leading to a dangerous loss of braking under hard use. Old fluid may be contaminated and unfit for further use. When topping-up or renewing the fluid, always use the recommended type, and ensure that it comes from a freshly-opened sealed container.*

General

1 The correct functioning of the brake hydraulic system is only possible after removing all air from the components and circuit; this is achieved by bleeding the system.

2 During the bleeding procedure, add only clean, fresh hydraulic fluid of the specified type; never re-use fluid that has already been bled from the system. Ensure that sufficient fluid is available before starting work.

3 If there is any possibility of incorrect fluid being used in the system, the brake lines and components must be completely flushed with uncontaminated fluid and new seals fitted to the components.

4 If brake fluid has been lost from the master cylinder due to a leak in the system, ensure that the cause is traced and rectified before proceeding further.

5 Park the car on level ground, apply the handbrake, and switch off the ignition.

6 Check that all pipes and hoses are secure, unions tight, and bleed screws closed. Remove the dust caps and clean any dirt from around the bleed screws.

7 Unscrew the master cylinder reservoir cap, and top-up the reservoir to the MAX level line. Refit the cap loosely, and remember to maintain the fluid level at least above the MIN level line throughout the procedure, otherwise there is a risk of further air entering the system.

8 There is a number of one-man, do-it-yourself, brake bleeding kits currently available from motor accessory shops. It is recommended that one of these kits is used wherever possible, as they greatly simplify the bleeding operation, and also reduce the risk of expelled air and fluid being drawn back into the system. If such a kit is not available, the basic (two-man) method must be used, which is described in detail below.

9 If a kit is to be used, prepare the car as described previously, and follow the kit manufacturer's instructions, as the procedure may vary slightly according to the type being used; generally, they are as outlined below in the relevant sub-section.

10 Whichever method is used, the same sequence must be followed (paragraphs 11 and 12) to ensure the removal of all air from the system.

Bleeding sequence

11 If the hydraulic system has only been partially disconnected and suitable precautions were taken to minimise fluid loss, it should only be necessary to bleed that part of the system (ie, the primary or secondary circuit).

12 If the complete system is to be bled, then it should be done in the following sequence:
  a) Front left-hand brake
  b) Front right-hand brake.
  c) Rear brakes (in any order).

Bleeding

Basic (two-man) method

13 Collect a clean glass jar of reasonable size and a suitable length of plastic or rubber tubing, which is a tight fit over the bleed screw, and a ring spanner to fit the screws. The help of an assistant will also be required.

14 If not already done, remove the dust cap from the bleed screw of the first wheel to be bled **(see illustration)**, and fit the spanner and bleed tube to the screw. Place the other end of the tube in the jar, and pour in sufficient fluid to cover the end of the tube.

15 Ensure that the master cylinder reservoir fluid level is maintained at least above the MIN level line throughout the procedure.

16 Have the assistant fully depress the brake pedal several times to build-up pressure, then maintain it on the final downstroke.

17 While pedal pressure is maintained, unscrew the bleed screw (approximately one turn) and allow the compressed fluid and air to flow into the jar. The assistant should maintain pedal pressure, following it down to the floor if necessary, and should not release it until instructed to do so. When the flow stops, tighten the bleed screw again have the assistant release the pedal slowly, and recheck the reservoir fluid level.

18 Repeat the steps given in paragraphs 16 and 17 until the fluid emerging from the bleed screw is free from air bubbles. If the master cylinder has been drained and refilled, and air is being bled from the first screw in the sequence, allow approximately five seconds between cycles for the master cylinder passages to refill.

19 When no more air bubbles appear, tighten the bleed screw securely, remove the tube and spanner, and refit the dust cap. Do not overtighten the bleed screw.

20 Repeat these procedures on the remaining calipers in sequence until all air is removed from the system and the brake pedal feels firm again.

Using a one-way valve kit

21 As their name implies, these kits consist of a length of tubing with a one-way valve fitted, to prevent expelled air and fluid being drawn back into the system; some kits include a translucent container, which can be positioned so that the air bubbles can be more easily seen flowing from the end of the tube.

22 The kit is connected to the bleed screw, which is then opened **(see illustration)**. The

user returns to the driver's seat, depresses the brake pedal with a smooth steady stroke, and slowly releases it; this is repeated until the expelled fluid is clear of air bubbles.

23 Note that these kits simplify work so much that it is easy to forget the master cylinder fluid level; ensure that this is maintained at least above the MIN level line at all times.

Using a pressure-bleeding kit

Note: *This is the method recommended by Volvo if the hydraulic system has been drained either wholly or partially.*

24 These kits are usually operated by the reserve of pressurised air contained in the spare tyre. However, note that it will probably be necessary to reduce the pressure to a lower level than normal; refer to the instructions supplied with the kit.

25 By connecting a pressurised, fluid-filled container to the master cylinder reservoir, bleeding is then carried out by simply opening each bleed screw in turn (in the specified sequence) and allowing the fluid to run out, until no more air bubbles can be seen in the expelled fluid.

26 This method has the advantage that the large reservoir of fluid provides an additional safeguard against air being drawn into the system during bleeding.

27 Pressure-bleeding is particularly effective when bleeding difficult systems, or when bleeding the complete system at the time of routine fluid renewal.

All methods

28 When bleeding is complete, and firm pedal feel is restored, wash off any spilt fluid, tighten the bleed screws securely, and refit their dust caps.

29 Check the hydraulic fluid level in the master cylinder reservoir, and top-up if necessary.

30 Discard any hydraulic fluid that has been bled from the system; it will not be fit for re-use.

31 Check the feel of the brake pedal. If it feels at all spongy, air must still be present in the system, and further bleeding is required. Failure to bleed satisfactorily after a reasonable repetition of the bleeding operations may be due to worn master cylinder seals.

32 Check the operation of the clutch. Any problems noted would indicate a need to bleed the clutch system also – see Chapter 6.

2.14 Prise off the dust cap from the bleed screw (arrowed)

3 Hydraulic pipes and hoses – renewal

Note: *Before starting work, refer to the warning at the beginning of Section 2 concerning the dangers of hydraulic fluid.*

1 If any pipe or hose is to be renewed, minimise hydraulic fluid loss by removing the master cylinder reservoir cap, placing a piece of plastic film over the reservoir and sealing it with an elastic band. Alternatively, flexible hoses can be sealed, if required, using a proprietary brake hose clamp; metal brake pipe unions can be plugged (if care is taken not to allow dirt into the system) or capped immediately they are disconnected. Place a wad of rag under any union that is to be disconnected, to catch any spilt fluid.

2 If a flexible hose is to be disconnected, unscrew the brake pipe union nut before removing the spring clip which secures the hose to its mounting, where applicable. Some of the flexible hose unions are protected by a rubber cover – in this case, the pipe will have to be removed from its mounting bracket first, and the cover slid down the pipe, before the nut can be unscrewed.

3 To unscrew the union nuts, it is preferable to obtain a brake pipe spanner of the correct size; these are available from most large motor accessory shops. Failing this, a close-fitting open-ended spanner will be required, though if the nuts are tight or corroded, their flats may be rounded-off if the spanner slips. In such a case, a self-locking wrench is often the only way to unscrew a stubborn union, but it follows that the pipe and the damaged nuts must be renewed on reassembly.

4 Always clean a union and surrounding area before disconnecting it. If disconnecting a component with more than one union, make a careful note of the connections before disturbing any of them.

5 If a brake pipe is to be renewed, it can be obtained, cut to length and with the union nuts and end flares in place, from Volvo dealers. All that is then necessary is to bend it to shape, following the line of the original, before fitting it to the car. Alternatively, most motor accessory shops can make up brake pipes from kits, but

2.22 Connect the kit and open the bleed screw

this requires very careful measurement of the original, to ensure that the new one is of the correct length. The safest answer is usually to take the original to the shop as a pattern.

6 Before refitting, blow through the new pipe or hose with dry compressed air. Do not overtighten the union nuts. It is not necessary to exercise brute force to obtain a sound joint.

7 If flexible rubber hoses are renewed, ensure that the pipes and hoses are correctly routed, with no kinks or twists, and that they are secured in the clips or brackets provided. Original equipment flexible hoses have white lines along their length which clearly show if the hose is twisted.

8 After fitting, bleed the hydraulic system as described in Section 2, wash off any spilt fluid, and check carefully for fluid leaks.

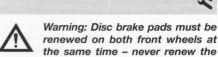

4 Front brake pads – renewal

⚠️ *Warning: Disc brake pads must be renewed on both front wheels at the same time – never renew the pads on only one wheel, as uneven braking may result. Dust created by wear of the pads may contain asbestos, which is a health hazard. Never blow it out with compressed air and do not inhale any of it. DO NOT use petroleum-based solvents to clean brake parts. Use brake cleaner or methylated spirit only. DO NOT allow any brake fluid, oil or grease to contact the brake pads or disc. Also refer to the warning at the start of Section 2 concerning the dangers of hydraulic fluid.*

1 Apply the handbrake, then slacken the front roadwheel nuts. Jack up the front of the vehicle and support it on axle stands (see *Jacking and vehicle support*). Remove both front roadwheels.

2 Follow the accompanying photos (**illustrations 4.2a to 4.2p**) for the actual pad renewal procedure. Be sure to stay in order and read the caption under each illustration, and note the following points:

a) *New pads may have an adhesive foil on the backplates. Remove this foil prior to installation.*

b) *Thoroughly clean the caliper guide surfaces, and apply a little brake assembly (silicone) grease (Volvo 116 1688) .*

c) *When pushing the caliper piston back to accommodate new pads, keep a close eye on the fluid lever in the reservoir.*

3 Depress the brake pedal repeatedly, until the pads are pressed into firm contact with the brake disc, and normal (non-assisted) pedal pressure is restored.

4 Repeat the above procedure on the remaining front brake caliper.

5 Refit the roadwheels, then lower the vehicle to the ground and tighten the roadwheel nuts to the specified torque.

6 Check the hydraulic fluid level as described in *Weekly checks*.

Caution: New pads will not give full braking efficiency until they have bedded-in. Be prepared for this, and avoid hard braking as far as possible for the first hundred miles or so after pad renewal

4.2a Use a flat-bladed screwdriver to carefully prise off the caliper retaining spring

4.2b Prise out the rubber caps . . .

4.2c . . . and use an Allen key to undo the caliper guide pin bolts (arrowed)

4.2d Slide the caliper and pads from the disc

4.2e Pull the inner brake pad from the caliper piston

4.2f If you're fitting new pads, push the piston back into the caliper using a G-clamp . . .

4.2g . . . or piston retraction tool – don't forget to keep an eye on the fluid level in the master cylinder reservoir

4.2h Clean the pad mounting surfaces using a wire brush

4.2i Measure the thickness of the pad's friction material. If it's 2.0mm or less, renew all the front pads

4.2j Fit the outer pad to the caliper mounting bracket . . .

4.2k . . . then fit the inner pad to the caliper piston

4.2l Slide the caliper with the inner pad fitted over the disc and outer pad

4.2m Hold the caliper in place, screw in the guide pin bolts, and tighten them to the specified torque

4.2n Press the rubber caps into place over the guide pin bolts (arrowed)

5 Rear brake pads – renewal

Warning: Disc brake pads must be renewed on both rear wheels at the same time – never renew the pads on only one wheel as uneven braking may result. Dust created by wear of the pads may contain asbestos, which is a health hazard. Never blow it out with compressed air and do not inhale any of it. DO NOT use petroleum-based solvents to clean brake parts. Use brake cleaner or methylated spirit only. DO NOT allow any brake fluid, oil or grease to contact the brake pads or disc. Also refer to the warning at the start of Section 2 concerning the dangers of hydraulic fluid.

1 Chock the front wheels, slacken the rear roadwheel nuts, then jack up the rear of the vehicle and support it on axle stands (see *Jacking and vehicle support*). Remove the rear wheels.
2 With the handbrake lever fully released, follow the accompanying photos **(see illustrations 5.2a to 5.2p)** for the actual pad renewal procedure. Be sure to stay in order and read the caption under each illustration, and note the following points:
a) *If re-installing the original pads, ensure they are fitted to their original positions.*
b) *Thoroughly clean the caliper guide surfaces and guide pins, and apply a little brake assembly grease (Volvo 116 1688).*

4.2o Use a pair of pliers . . .

c) *If new pads are to be fitted, use a piston retraction tool to push the piston back and twist it clockwise at the same time – keep an eye on the fluid level in the reservoir whilst retracting the piston.*
3 Depress the brake pedal repeatedly, until the pads are pressed into firm contact with the brake disc, and normal (non-assisted) pedal pressure is restored.
4 Repeat the above procedure on the remaining brake caliper.
5 If necessary, adjust the handbrake as described in Section 13.
6 Refit the roadwheels, then lower the vehicle to the ground and tighten the roadwheel nuts to the specified torque.
7 Check the hydraulic fluid level as described in *Weekly checks*.
Caution: New pads will not give full braking

4.2p . . . to refit the caliper retaining spring

efficiency until they have bedded-in. Be prepared for this, and avoid hard braking as far as possible for the first hundred miles or so after pad renewal.

5.2a Carefully remove the caliper retaining spring with a screwdriver

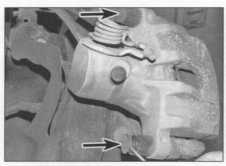

5.2b Prise out the guide pin bolts rubber caps (arrowed) . . .

5.2c . . . and unscrew the guide pin bolts using an Allen key or hexagon drive bit

5.2d Release the hydraulic hose from the bracket

5.2e Lift the caliper from the disc

5.2f Remove the outer pad . . .

5.2g . . . followed by the inner pad

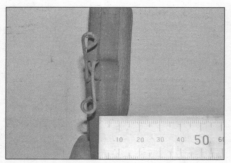

5.2h Measure the thickness of the pad's friction material, if it's 2.0mm or less, renew all the rear pads

5.2i If new pads are to be fitted, use a piston retraction tool to press the piston back into the caliper, at the same time as rotating it clockwise – keep an eye on the fluid level in the brake master cylinder

5.2j Use a wire brush to clean the pad mounting surfaces on the caliper mounting bracket

5.2k Fit the inner pad . . .

5.2l . . . followed by the outer pad

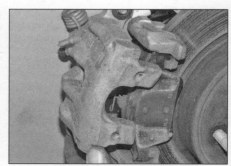

5.2m Slide the caliper over the pads

5.2n Hold the caliper in position, screw in the guide pin bolts and tighten them to the specified torque

5.2o Refit the guide pin rubber caps

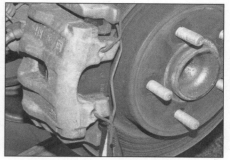

5.2p Use a pair of pliers to refit the caliper retaining spring

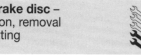

6 Front brake disc –
inspection, removal and refitting

Note: *Before starting work, refer to the warning at the beginning of Section 4 concerning the dangers of asbestos dust.*
Note: *If either disc requires renewal, BOTH should be renewed at the same time, to ensure even and consistent braking. New brake pads should also be fitted.*

Inspection

1 Remove the front brake pads as described in Section 4.
2 Inspect the disc friction surfaces for cracks or deep scoring (light grooving is normal and may be ignored). A cracked disc must be renewed; a scored disc can be reclaimed by machining, provided that the thickness is not reduced below the specified minimum.
3 Check the disc run-out using a dial test indicator with its probe positioned near the outer edge of the disc. If the run-out exceeds the figures given in the Specifications, machining may be possible, otherwise disc renewal will be necessary.
4 Excessive disc thickness variation can also cause judder. Check this using a micrometer **(see illustration)**.

Removal

5 With the brake pads and caliper removed (Section 8), undo the two mounting bolts and remove the brake caliper bracket **(see illustration 7.3)**.
6 Check whether the position of the disc in relation to the hub is marked, and if not, make your own mark as an aid to refitting. Lift off the disc **(see illustration)**.

Refitting

7 Ensure that the hub and disc mating faces are spotlessly clean. Clean any rustproofing compound off a new disc with degreaser and a rag.
8 Locate the disc on the hub with the orientation marks (where applicable) aligned.

6.4 Measure the thickness of the brake disc using a micrometer

9 Refit the brake caliper bracket and tighten the bolts to the specified torque.
10 Refit the brake pads as described in Section 4.

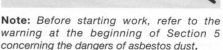

7 Rear brake disc –
inspection, removal and refitting

Note: *Before starting work, refer to the warning at the beginning of Section 5 concerning the dangers of asbestos dust.*
Note: *If either disc requires renewal, BOTH should be renewed at the same time, to ensure even and consistent braking. New brake pads should also be fitted.*

Inspection

1 With the rear brake pads removed (Section 5), the inspection procedures are the same as for the front brake disc, and reference should be made to Section 6, paragraphs 2 to 4 inclusive.

Removal

2 If not already done, remove the rear brake pads as described in Section 5. Suitably support the caliper, or suspend it using string or wire tied to a convenient suspension component.
3 Undo the two caliper mounting bracket bolts, and withdraw the bracket **(see illustration)**.
4 Remove the disc retaining clip and discard

6.6 Lift the brake disc from the studs

it (where fitted – only used during the production process).
5 Mark the position of the disc in relation to the hub, then pull off the disc. Tap it with a soft-faced mallet if necessary to free it.

Refitting

6 Ensure that the hub and disc mating faces are spotlessly clean. Clean any rustproofing compound off a new disc with degreaser and a rag.
7 Locate the disc on the hub with the orientation marks aligned.
8 Refit the brake caliper mounting bracket and tighten the bolts to the specified torque.
9 Refit the brake pads as described in Section 5.
10 Adjust the handbrake as described in Section 13.

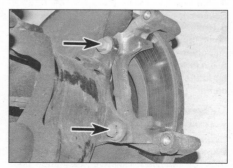

7.3 Undo the caliper mounting bracket bolts (arrowed)

8.2a Using a pedal jack to keep the brake pedal depressed

8 Front brake caliper – removal, overhaul and refitting

Note: *Before starting work, refer to the warning at the beginning of Section 2 concerning the dangers of hydraulic fluid, and to the warning at the beginning of Section 4 concerning the dangers of asbestos dust.*

Removal

1 Apply the handbrake and chock the rear wheels. Slacken the front wheel nuts, then jack up the front of the car and support it on axle stands (see *Jacking and vehicle support*). Remove the roadwheel.

2 To minimise fluid loss, have an assistant depress and hold down the brake pedal, then attach a length of plastic hose to the bleed screw on the caliper, with the other end of the hose in a clean container. Unscrew the bleed screw a turn or so and allow the fluid to flow into the container. As soon as the flow of fluid slows, close the screw, and secure the pedal in the depressed position. This can be achieved with a proprietary pedal jack, or improvised using a length of wood (broom handle, etc) cut to the right length. Alternatively, use a brake hose clamp, a G-clamp, or a similar tool with protected jaws, to gently clamp the front flexible hydraulic hose **(see illustrations)**.

3 Clean the area around the hydraulic hose-to-caliper union, then slacken the hose union half a turn. Be prepared for fluid spillage.

4 Remove the brake pads as described in Section 4.

5 Unscrew the caliper from the hydraulic hose, and wipe up any spilled brake fluid immediately. Plug or cap the open unions.

6 If it is wished to remove the caliper bracket, undo the two bolts which secure it to the hub carrier.

Overhaul

7 At the time of writing, no parts were available to overhaul the calipers. Consequently, if the calipers are faulty, they must be renewed. However, exchange units are available. Consult a Volvo dealer or parts specialist.

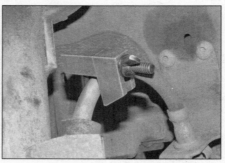

8.2b Use a hose clamp on the flexible hoses

Refitting

8 If removed, refit the caliper bracket, and tighten the bolts to the specified torque.

9 Refit the brake pads as described in Section 4, but screw the caliper onto the flexible hose before refitting it to the caliper bracket.

10 Tighten the flexible hose union ensuring that the hose is not kinked.

11 Remove the brake hose clamp and/or pedal jack, and bleed the hydraulic system as described in Section 2.

12 Apply the footbrake two or three times to settle the pads, then refit the roadwheel and lower the car. Tighten the wheel nuts in a diagonal sequence to the specified torque.

9 Rear brake caliper – removal, overhaul and refitting

Note: *Before starting work, refer to the warning at the beginning of Section 2 concerning the dangers of hydraulic fluid, and to the warning at the beginning of Section 5 concerning the dangers of asbestos dust.*

Removal

1 Apply the handbrake and chock the front wheels. Slacken the rear wheel nuts, then jack up the rear of the car and support it on axle stands (see *Jacking and vehicle support*). Remove the roadwheel.

2 To minimise fluid loss, have an assistant depress and hold down the brake pedal, then attach a length of plastic hose to the bleed screw on the caliper, with the other end of the hose in a clean container. Unscrew the bleed screw a turn or so and allow the fluid to flow into the container. As soon as the flow of fluid slows, close the screw, and secure the pedal in the depressed position. This can be achieved with a proprietary pedal jack, or improvised using a length of wood (broom handle, etc) cut to the right length. Alternatively, use a brake hose clamp, a G-clamp, or a similar tool with protected jaws, to gently clamp the rear flexible hydraulic hose **(see illustrations 8.2a and 8.2b)**.

3 Clean around the hydraulic union on the caliper, then slacken the hose union half a turn.

4 Remove the rear brake pads as described in Section 5.

5 Unclip the handbrake inner cable fitting from the lever on the caliper, then detach the outer cable from the bracket **(see illustration 14.9)**.

6 Undo the caliper from the flexible hose union. Be prepared for fluid spillage, and plug or cap the open unions.

Overhaul

7 At the time of writing, no parts were available to overhaul the calipers. Consequently, if the calipers are faulty, they must be renewed. However, exchange units are available. Consult a Volvo dealer or parts specialist.

Refitting

8 Refit the brake hose to the caliper, only finger tighten the union at this stage.

9 Re-attach the handbrake cable to the caliper lever and bracket.

10 Refit the brake pads as described in Section 5.

11 Tighten the hose union securely, ensuring the hose isn't twisted or kinked.

12 Remove the brake hose clamp and/or pedal jack, where fitted, and bleed the hydraulic system as described in Section 2.

13 Apply the footbrake two or three times to settle the pads, then refit the roadwheel and lower the car. Tighten the wheel bolts in a diagonal sequence to the specified torque.

10 Brake master cylinder – removal and refitting

Note: *Before starting work, refer to the warning at the beginning of Section 2 concerning the dangers of hydraulic fluid.*
Note: *Overhaul of the master cylinder is not possible, and internal components are not available separately. In the event of a fault in the master cylinder, the unit must be renewed.*

Removal

1 Disconnect the battery negative lead as described in Chapter 5A.

2 Depress the brake pedal repeatedly to collapse any residual vacuum in the servo, then syphon as much fluid as possible from the master cylinder reservoir, using a syringe or old poultry baster.
Caution: Do not syphon the fluid by mouth – it is poisonous.

3 Disconnect any wiring connectors from the reservoir/master cylinder.

4 On manual transmission models, depress the retaining tab and disconnect the clutch master cylinder fluid hose from the side of the reservoir **(see illustration)**. Be prepared for fluid spillage. Plug the open end of the hose and the reservoir orifice.

5 Disconnect the hydraulic pipe unions from the master cylinder **(see illustration)**.

10.4 Disconnect the level sensor wiring plug, then depress the release button (hidden on the rear of the coupling) and disconnect the clutch master cylinder fluid supply hose (arrowed)

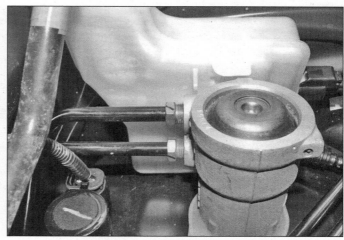

10.5 Undo the unions and disconnect the hydraulic pressure pipes from the cylinder

Be prepared for further fluid spillage. Plug or cap the openings to prevent contamination.

6 Remove the nuts which secure the master cylinder to the servo **(see illustration)**. Pull the master cylinder off the servo studs and remove it. Be careful not to spill hydraulic fluid on the paintwork.

7 If required, undo the screw and lift the reservoir from the master cylinder body **(see illustration)**. Check the condition of the two seals, and renew if necessary.

Refitting

8 If removed, lubricate the seals with clean brake fluid, refit the reservoir to the master cylinder, then tighten the retaining screw securely.

9 Place the master cylinder in position on the servo unit, and secure with the nuts tightened to the specified torque.

10 Refit the brake pipes, but do not tighten the union nuts fully at this stage.

11 Refit the fluid hose to the reservoir. Lubricate the hose end with brake hydraulic fluid to ease fitting.

12 Reconnect the reservoir/master cylinder electrical connectors.

13 Place absorbent rags under the brake pipe unions on the master cylinder, then fill the reservoir with clean hydraulic fluid of the specified type.

14 Tighten the brake pipe unions securely when hydraulic fluid can be seen seeping out.

15 Bleed the hydraulic system as described in Section 2 on completion. On manual transmission models, bleed the clutch hydraulic system as described in Chapter 6.

16 After the system has been bled, pressure test the master cylinder by depressing the brake pedal hard and holding it down for 30 seconds. Release the pedal and check for leaks around the master cylinder pipe unions.

10.6 The master cylinder is secured to the servo by two nuts (arrowed)

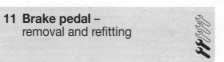

11 Brake pedal –
removal and refitting

Removal

1 Remove the steering column as described in Chapter 10, Section 14.

2 Remove the accelerator pedal as described in Chapter 4A (petrol) or 4B (diesel).

3 Remove the pin securing the servo pushrod

11.3 Prise out the metal centre and remove the pin securing the servo pushrod to the pedal

10.7 Undo the screw and pull the reservoir from the master cylinder (end of screw arrowed)

to the pedal. Discard as a new pin must be fitted **(see illustration)**.

4 Remove the stop-light switch as described in Section 17.

5 Undo the 6 nuts securing the pedal bracket to the brake servo and bulkhead **(see illustration)**.

Refitting

6 Manoeuvre the pedal into position. Renew all retaining bolts and tighten to the specified torque.

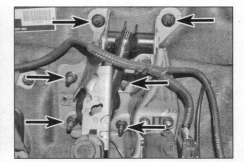

11.5 Undo the 6 nuts (arrowed) securing the pedal bracket

11.7 Push the new servo pushrod pin in until it clicks into place

7 Reconnect the servo pushrod to the pedal, and fit the new pin **(see illustration)**.
8 Refit the steering column as described in the Chapter 10.
9 Check the operation of the brake lights.

12 Vacuum servo unit – removal and refitting

Removal

1 As the air conditioning circuit must be disturbed, have the system evacuated by a refrigerant engineer.
2 Depress the brake pedal several times to dissipate any vacuum in the servo unit.
3 Remove the brake master cylinder as described in Section 10.
4 Remove the windscreen wiper motor as described in Chapter 12.

12.5a Undo the scrivets (arrowed) . . .

12.9 Spread the circlip (arrowed) and pull the pedal sensor from the servo

5 Release the wiring harnesses from their clips, then undo the 2 scrivets and remove the protective cover over the brake servo **(see illustrations)**.
6 Undo the fasteners and remove the air conditioning low pressure pipe. Plug/seal the openings to prevent contamination. Discard the O-ring seals, new ones must be fitted.
7 Unclip the high-pressure air conditioning pipe from the retaining clip and move it to one side.
8 Prise the pressure sensor from the servo (where fitted).
9 Disconnect the wiring plug, then carefully spread the circlip, and pull the pedal sensor from the servo **(see illustration)**. Discard the O-ring seal, a new one must be fitted.
10 Undo the unions and remove the two fluid pipes between the master cylinder and the ABS unit. Plug/seal the openings to prevent contamination.
11 Remove the lower facia panel on the driver's side as described in Chapter 11.
12 Undo the 2 bolts and remove the upper timing belt cover **(see illustration)**.
13 Raise the front of the vehicle, and support it securely on axle stands (see *Jacking and vehicle support*). Undo the 7 Torx screws and remove the engine undershield (where fitted).
14 Support the engine with a trolley jack. Place a block of wood between the jack head and the sump to prevent damage.
15 Undo the bolts and remove the right-hand engine mounting assembly, then lower the engine approximately 6 cm.

12.5b . . . and remove the cover over the servo

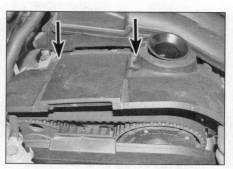

12.12 Undo the 2 bolts (arrowed) and remove the timing belt upper cover

16 Remove the pin securing the servo pushrod to the brake pedal **(see illustration 11.7)**. Note that the pin cannot be entirely separated, and a new one must be fitted upon reassembly.
17 Undo the 4 nuts securing the servo to the pedal bracket/bulkhead **(see illustration)**. Manoeuvre the servo from the engine compartment.

Refitting

18 Refitting is a reversal of removal bearing in mind the following points:
a) *Tighten all nuts and bolts to the specified torque.*
b) *Refit the master cylinder as described in Section 10.*
c) *Refit the windscreen wiper as described in Chapter 12.*
d) *Check and if necessary, bleed the hydraulic system as described in Section 2 on completion.*
e) *Have the air-conditioning system re-charged by a suitably equipped specialist.*

13 Handbrake – adjustment

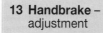

Note: *The handbrake should only be adjusted when the brake discs/pads are cool.*
1 Before carrying out the adjustment, apply the handbrake firmly 5 times. Chock the front wheels and release the handbrake.
2 Remove the cup holder from the centre console by pulling it straight up and then prise out the plastic trim piece located in the base of the cupholder recess. Slacken the adjusting nut until the end of the adjusting rod is level with the top surface of the nut **(see illustrations)**.
3 Raise the rear of the vehicle and support it securely on axle stands (see *Jacking and vehicle support*).
4 Depress the foot brake pedal 5 times to ensure the rear caliper adjustment is correct.
5 One at a time, rotate the rear wheels to check there is no abnormal friction.
6 Working inside the vehicle, with the lever in the rest position, tighten the adjusting nut

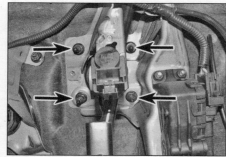

12.17 Undo the 4 nuts (arrowed) securing the servo to the pedal bracket

until 7.0mm of the rod's thread protrudes from the nut, then tighten the nut further until light friction can be felt at the wheels.

7 Pull the handbrake lever up to at least 5 notches, 5 times, then release the lever and check that there is still light friction at the wheels. If necessary, tighten the adjustment nut.

8 Undo the adjustment nut one complete revolution, apply the handbrake (at least 5 notches, 5 times).

9 Release the lever and check that there is no friction from the handbrake mechanism at the wheels. If there is undo the adjustment nut, apply the handbrake (at least 5 notches, 5 times) and check again.

10 When the adjustment is satisfactory, refit the trim piece in the base of the cupholder recess and the cupholder itself, and lower the vehicle to the ground.

14 Handbrake cable – removal and refitting

Removal

1 Loosen the rear wheel nuts and chock the front wheels. Jack up the rear of the car and support it on axle stands (see *Jacking and vehicle support*). Remove the rear roadwheels.

2 Slacken the handbrake cable adjustment nut completely with reference to Section 13.

3 Undo the 2 nuts securing the exhaust

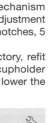

13.2a Prise out the piece of trim covering the adjusting nut…

catalytic converter to the centre silencer, and undo the centre silencer mounting bracket nut. Use wire or string to suspend the catalytic converter from the vehicle body.

4 Detach the exhaust intermediate section rubber mounting, then position the exhaust system to one side. Suspend the exhaust system using wire or string to prevent damage.

5 Undo the 4 plastic nuts and remove the heat shield from below the handbrake lever **(see illustration)**.

6 Undo the 2 plastic nuts and 1 screw securing the air baffle on the appropriate side **(see illustration)**.

7 Undo the 7 plastic nuts and remove the heat shield above the rear/intermediate silencer **(see illustration)**.

8 Depress the retaining clips and pull the outer cable fittings from the mounting bracket,

13.2b …and undo the adjusting nut until it's level with the adjusting rod

then detach the handbrake front inner cable from the equaliser bracket **(see illustrations)**.

9 Disconnect the inner cables from the calipers at the rear **(see illustration)**.

10 Unclip the cable and withdraw it from under the vehicle. Note the rear cable is only available as a complete assembly.

Front cable

11 Remove the centre console as described in Chapter 11.

12 Slacken and remove the handbrake adjusting nut at the lever **(see illustrations 13.2a and 13.2b)**.

13 Undo the exhaust centre silencer mounting bracket bolt, then undo the 6 plastic nuts and slide the heat shield above the silencer forwards to access the cables.

14 Detach the cable from the equaliser bracket at the rear **(see illustration 14.8b)**,

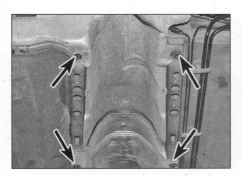

14.5 Undo the 4 nuts (arrowed) and remove the heat shield

14.6 Remove the air baffle (arrowed) on the appropriate side

14.7 Remove the heat shield above the silencer

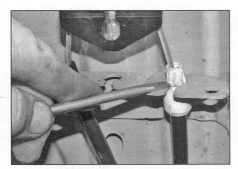

14.8a Depress the clips and detach the outer cables from the bracket . . .

14.8b . . . then disconnect the front inner cable from the equaliser bracket

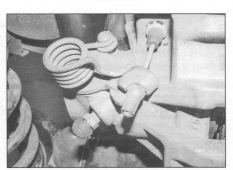

14.9 Detach the cable from the caliper lever

14.14 With the adjusting nut (arrowed) removed, pull the inner cable from the lever

and the lever at the front **(see illustration)**. Remove the cable.

Refitting

15 Refitting is a reversal of removal, remembering to adjust the handbrake as described in Section 13.

15 Handbrake lever –
removal and refitting

Removal

1 Remove the centre console as described in Chapter 11.
2 Undo the cable adjuster nut from the handbrake cable **(see illustrations 13.2a and 13.2b)**.
3 Disconnect the wiring connector from the handbrake warning light switch.

15.4 Handbrake lever assembly retaining bolts (arrowed)

17.3 Depress the tab and disconnect the switch wiring plug (arrowed)

4 Undo the 3 bolts securing the lever assembly to the floor **(see illustration)**.
5 Refitting is a reversal of removal. Adjust the handbrake as described in Section 13 on completion.

16 Handbrake warning switch –
removal and refitting

1 Remove the centre console as described in Chapter 11.
2 Undo the retaining screw and remove the switch **(see illustration)**.
3 Disconnect the wiring plug as the switch is withdrawn.
4 Refitting is a reversal of removal.

17 Stop-light switch –
removal and refitting

Removal

1 Ensure the ignition is switched off.
2 Remove the lower facia panel on the driver's side as described in Chapter 11.
3 Disconnect the switch wiring plug **(see illustration)**.
4 Rotate the switch clockwise until it releases from the bracket.
5 Compress the switch side retaining catches and withdraw the switch from the pedal bracket. Disconnect the wiring connector(s) and remove the switch **(see illustration)**.

16.2 Handbrake warning switch retaining screw (arrowed)

17.5 Rotate the stop-light switch clockwise to remove it

Refitting

6 Make sure the brake pedal is in the 'at rest' position, then refit the switch, rotating it anti-clockwise until it locks in place. Note that the switch 'self-adjusts' on installation.
7 Reconnect the wiring plug.
8 Refit the lower facia panel.

18 Anti-lock braking system (ABS) –
general information

The anti-lock braking system, fitted as standard equipment on all models, monitors the rotational speed of the wheels under braking. Sudden deceleration of one wheel, indicating that lock-up is occurring, causes the hydraulic pressure to that wheel's brake to be reduced or interrupted momentarily.

The main components of the system are the wheel sensors, the electronic control module (ECM) and the hydraulic modulator assembly.

One sensor is fitted to each wheel, together with a pulse wheel carried on the wheel/ driveshaft hub. The sensors monitor the rotational speeds of the wheels, and are able to detect when there is a risk of wheel locking (low rotational speed). The wheel sensors also provide vehicle speed information to the speedometer.

Information from the sensors is fed to the ECM, which operates solenoid valves in the hydraulic modulator. The solenoid valves restrict the hydraulic fluid supply to any caliper detected to be on the verge of locking.

Should a fault develop in the system, the ECM illuminates a warning light on the instrument panel and disables the system. Normal braking will still be available, but without the anti-lock function. In the event of a fault, the ECM stores a series of signals (or fault codes) for subsequent read-out using diagnostic equipment (see Section 20).

Electronic brake force distribution (EBD) is incorporated into the ABS system, and regulates the proportion of braking force applied to the front and rear wheels.

On cars equipped with a traction control system, the ABS system performs a dual role. In addition to detecting when a wheel is locking under braking, the system also detects a wheel that is spinning under acceleration. When this condition is detected, the brake on that wheel is momentarily applied to reduce, or eliminate, the wheel spin. When the rotational speed of the spinning wheel is detected to be equal to the other wheels, the brake is released. On vehicles equipped with stability control the same sensors, solenoids and pipes are used. However, vehicles are also equipped with a combined yaw rate and lateral acceleration sensor, and a steering wheel angle sensor.

19 Anti-lock braking system (ABS) components – removal and refitting

Removal

Front wheel sensor

1 Loosen the appropriate front wheel bolts and chock the rear wheels. Jack up the front of the car and support it on axle stands (see *Jacking and vehicle support*). Remove the roadwheel.
2 Undo the screw which secures the sensor to the hub carrier **(see illustrations)** and disconnect the wiring plug. Withdraw the sensor, and unclip the wiring from any brackets.

Rear wheel sensor

3 Loosen the appropriate rear wheel bolts and chock the front wheels. Jack up the rear of the car and support it on axle stands (see *Jacking and vehicle support*). Remove the roadwheel.
4 Undo the screw which secures the sensor to the hub **(see illustration)** and disconnect the wiring plug. Withdraw the sensor, and unclip the wiring from any brackets.

Brake control module (BCM)

5 Remove the hydraulic modulator as described in this Section.
6 Disconnect the wiring plug, undo the screw at each corner, and remove the module.
7 No further dismantling is recommended. Ensure that no dirt, etc, is allowed to enter the modulator or BCM/pump assembly.
8 If the BCM has been renewed, the software for the unit must be downloaded from Volvo.

Hydraulic modulator

Note: *Before starting work, refer to the warning at the beginning of Section 2 concerning the dangers of hydraulic fluid.*
Caution: Absolute cleanliness is essential. Even the smallest ingress of dirt can cause the system to fail.
9 To minimise fluid loss, have an assistant depress and hold down the brake pedal, then attach a length of plastic hose to the bleed screw on a caliper, with the other end of the hose in a clean container. Unscrew the bleed screw a turn or so and allow the fluid to flow into the container. As soon as the flow of fluid slows, close the screw, and secure the pedal in the depressed position. This can be achieved with a proprietary pedal jack, or improvised using a length of wood (broom handle, etc) cut to the right length **(see illustration 8.2a)**.
10 Remove the battery as described in Chapter 5A, then undo the 3 bolts and remove the battery box. Disconnect any relevant wiring plugs as the box is withdrawn.
11 Clean the area around the brake pipe unions on the modulator, and note their fitted positions, then detach the pipes from the modulator **(see illustration)**. Plug or seal the openings to prevent contamination. Be prepared for fluid spillage.
12 Disconnect the Brake Control Module

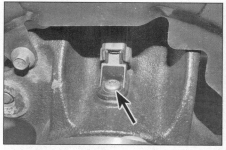

19.2a Undo the sensor retaining Torx bolt (arrowed – shown with the disc removed for clarity) . . .

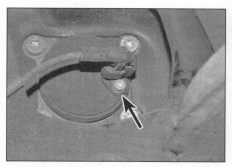

19.4 Undo the rear wheel speed sensor Torx bolt (arrowed)

19.2b . . . then carefully prise the sensor up from the hub carrier

19.11 Undo the pipe unions on the modulator

wiring plug, undo the fasteners and remove the modulator assembly.
13 No further dismantling is recommended. Note, that when the system is bled on completion, pressure-bleeding equipment will be necessary.

Brake pedal position sensor

14 Depress the brake pedal two or three times to dissipate any vacuum remaining in the servo unit.
15 Disconnect the wiring connector from the pedal sensor located on the front face of the vacuum servo unit (similar to that shown in illustration 12.9).
16 Open the circlip and withdraw the sensor from the servo. Recover the O-ring and spacer sleeve from the sensor if fitted.

Refitting

17 In all cases, refitting is a reversal of the removal operations but note the following points:
a) Clean off all dirt from the wheel sensors and mounting locations before refitting with a stiff brush.
b) Bleed the hydraulic system as described in Section 2 after refitting the hydraulic modulator.
c) Where fitted use a new O-ring on the brake pedal position sensor, and ensure that the colour-coded spacer sleeve matches the colour code of the servo unit.
d) If the BCM or BSC have been removed and refitted, then the dynamic stability control system may need to be recalibrated. This can be achieved using

Volvo test equipment. Alternatively, this can be carried out by driving the car for a distance of approximately 20 miles under the following conditions:
Low lateral acceleration (no sharp cornering).
Smooth road surface (no potholes, grooves, etc)
Good surface traction (not slippery).

20 Anti-lock braking system (ABS) – fault diagnosis

1 The anti-lock braking system incorporates a sophisticated on-board diagnostic system to facilitate fault finding and system testing. Should a fault occur, the BCM stores a series of signals (or fault codes) for subsequent read-out via the diagnostic socket located under the facia, above the driver's pedals **(see illustration)**.

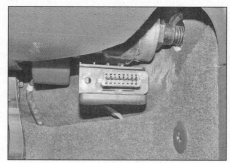

20.1 The diagnostic socket is located under the driver's side of the facia

21.3 The EGR pipe clamp is secured by a nut (arrowed)

21.4 Depress the button (arrowed) and disconnect the pipe from the vacuum pump

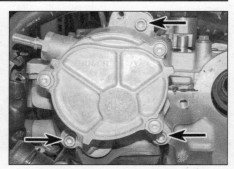

21.5 Vacuum pump retaining bolts (arrowed)

21.10a Renew the pump O-ring seals (arrowed)

21.10b Ensure the drive lugs engage with the slot in the end of the camshaft (arrowed)

2 If problems have been experienced, the on-board diagnostic system can be used to pinpoint any problem areas, but this requires special test equipment. Once this has been done, further tests may often be necessary to determine the exact nature of the fault; ie, whether a component itself has failed, or whether it is a wiring or other interrelated problem. Apart from visually checking the wiring and connections, any testing will require the use of a fault code reader at least. A Volvo dealer will obviously have such a reader, but they are also available from other suppliers. It is unlikely to be cost-effective for the private owner to purchase a fault code reader, but a well-equipped local garage or auto electrical specialist will have one.

3 Note that the BCM is in constant communication with the vehicle's other control modules via a databus communication network. Traditional fault finding, using the method of backprobing the connectors, etc, should not be attempted at the network connectors.

21 Vacuum pump – removal and refitting

Note: *Only fitted to diesel engines.*

Removal

1 Pull the plastic cover from over the engine straight up from its mountings. Note that on 1.6 litre engines, the cover may be held in position by 2 bolts.

1.6 litre engines

2 Depress the release button and remove the main vacuum hose from the pump, then pull the smaller hose from the pump. Undo the 2 retaining bolts and carefully withdraw the pump.

2.0 litre 4-cylinder engine

3 Remove the clamp for the EGR pipe on the vacuum pump, and release the fuel pipe from the clips (see illustration).

4 Depress the release button, and disconnect the vacuum hose from the pump (see illustration).

5 Undo the 3 bolts and remove the pump from the cylinder head (see illustration). Be prepared for fluid spillage. Discard the O-ring seals, new ones must be fitted. No dismantling of the pump is recommended.

5-cylinder engines

6 Remove the battery and battery tray as described in Chapter 5A.

7 Undo the bolt for the pipe support bracket, located at the left-hand end of the cylinder head above the vacuum pump.

8 Undo the quick-release connector and disconnect the vacuum hose from the pump.

9 Undo the 3 retaining bolts and remove the pump from the cylinder head. Be prepared for fluid spillage. Discard the O-ring seals, new ones must be fitted. No dismantling of the pump is recommended.

Refitting

10 Fit new O-ring seals to the pump mating face, then align the pump drive lugs with the slots in the end of the exhaust camshaft, and fit the pump to the cylinder head – tighten the bolts to the specified torque (see illustrations).

11 The remainder of refitting is a reversal of removal.

Chapter 10
Suspension and steering

Contents

Degrees of difficulty

Easy, suitable for novice with little experience	**Fairly easy,** suitable for beginner with some experience	**Fairly difficult,** suitable for competent DIY mechanic	**Difficult,** suitable for experienced DIY mechanic	**Very difficult,** suitable for expert DIY or professional

Specifications

Front suspension
Type . . . .   Independent, with MacPherson struts incorporating coil springs and telescopic shock absorbers. Anti-roll bar fitted to all models

Rear suspension
Type . . . .   Fully-independent, multi-link with coil springs and hydraulic telescopic shock absorbers. Anti-roll bar fitted to all models

Steering
Type . . . .   Power-assisted rack-and-pinion
Steering fluid type . . . .   See *Lubricants, fluids and tyre pressures* on page 0•16

Wheel alignment and steering angles
Front wheel:
  Camber angle. . . . .   -0.6° ± 0.7°
  Castor angle. . . . .   3.6° ± 1.5°
  Toe setting . . . .   0.2° ± 0.1° toe-in
Rear wheel:
  Camber angle. . . . .   -1.5° ± 1.0°
  Toe setting . . . .   0.3° ± 0.1° toe-in

Tyres
Tyre pressures . . . .   See sticker on the driver's-side B-pillar

Torque wrench settings

	Nm	lbf ft
Front suspension		
ABS sensor	5	4
Anti-roll bar clamp bolts*	50	37
Anti-roll bar connecting link nuts*	50	37
Anti-roll bar connecting link-to-front strut bolt*	60	44
Balljoint to hub carrier bolts*	50	37
Control arm to subframe*:		
Front bolt	175	129
Rear bolts:		
Stage 1	60	44
Stage 2	Angle-tighten a further 90°	
Driveshaft bolt*:		
Stage 1	35	26
Stage 2	Angle-tighten a further 90°	
Engine compartment cross stay bolts (if fitted)	24	18
Hub carrier balljoint-to-control arm nut*	70	52
Subframe mounting bolts:*		
Front	120	89
Rear	280	207
Subframe rear mounting brackets to body	24	18
Suspension strut to hub carrier	90	66
Suspension strut piston nut*	50	37
Suspension strut upper mounting to body*	30	22
Rear suspension		
Anti-roll bar-to-subframe bolts	50	37
Anti-roll bar-to-lower control arms	50	37
Lateral link/hub carrier to body	120	89
Lower control arm to hub carrier	110	81
Lower control arm to subframe	110	81
Rear hub bearing assembly	65	48
Shock absorber lower mounting bolt:		
Normal suspension	115	85
Self-levelling suspension (Nivomat)	225	166
Shock absorber upper mounting bolts	25	18
Shock absorber upper mounting nut:*		
Normal suspension	25	18
Self-levelling suspension (Nivomat)	60	44
Tie-rod bolts	110	81
Upper control arm to hub carrier/lateral link and subframe	110	81
Steering		
EPS/pump mounting bolts	25	18
Steering column mounting bolts*	25	18
Steering rack mounting bolts	80	59
Steering shaft universal joint pinch-bolt*	25	18
Steering wheel bolt*	65	48
Track rod end balljoint nuts*	50	37
Track rod locknuts	63	45
Roadwheels		
Roadwheel nuts:		
Stage 1 (All nuts)	20	15
Stage 2:		
Standard, locking and nuts with fixed conical seating	110	81
Nuts with rotating conical seating	130	96

* Do not re-use

1 General information

The independent front suspension is of the MacPherson strut type, incorporating coil springs and integral telescopic shock absorbers. The struts are located by transverse control arms, which are attached to the front subframe via rubber bushes at their inner ends, and incorporate a balljoint at their outer ends. The hub carriers, which carry the hub bearings, brake calipers and the hub/disc assemblies, are bolted to the MacPherson struts, and connected to the control arms through the balljoints. A front anti-roll bar is fitted to all models, and is attached to the subframe and to the MacPherson struts via link arms.

The rear suspension is of the fully independent, multi-link type, consisting of an upper and lower control arm mounted via rubber bushes to the lateral link/hub carrier and rear subframe. The lateral link is attached to the vehicle body at the front end and incorporates the hub carrier at the rear. The assembly is located by a tie-rod each side. Coil springs are fitted between the lower control arm and the subframe. Separate hydraulic telescopic shock absorbers are fitted between the hub carrier and the vehicle body.

2.2 Remove the driveshaft bolt (arrowed)

2.7 Use a balljoint separator tool to detach the lower arm balljoint from the hub carrier

2.9 Lever the control arm downwards, pull the hub carrier outwards, and withdraw the end of the driveshaft from the hub flange

Power-assisted rack-and-pinion steering is fitted as standard equipment. Power assistance is derived from a hydraulic pump, driven by an electric motor, controlled by the Electronic Power Steering module (EPS).

Note: *Many of the components described in this Chapter are secured by nuts and bolts tightened by the angle-tightening method. These particular nuts and bolts are indicated in the torque wrench settings section of the specifications. When these fastenings are disturbed, it is often required that **new** nuts and/or bolts are always used when refitting, as indicated in the Specifications. Self-locking nuts are also used in many areas, and these should also be renewed, particularly if resistance cannot be felt when the locking portion passes over the bolt or stud thread.*

2 Front hub carrier and bearing – removal and refitting

Note: *The hub bearing is a sealed, pre-adjusted and prelubricated, double-row ball type, and*

is intended to last the car's entire service life without maintenance or attention. The hub flange and bearing are serviced as a complete assembly, and these components cannot be dismantled or renewed individually.

Removal

1 Slacken the driveshaft retaining bolt as described in Chapter 8, Section 2, then slacken the wheel nuts, raise and support the front of the car and remove the roadwheel.

2 Remove the driveshaft retaining bolt **(see illustration)**. Discard the bolt: a new one must be used on reassembly.

3 Remove the front brake disc as described in Chapter 9.

4 Undo the 4 bolts and remove the brake backplate.

5 Undo the retaining nut, then disconnect the steering track rod end balljoint from the hub carrier. If necessary, use a balljoint separator tool **(see illustration 19.3a and 19.3b)**.

6 Disconnect the wiring plug, undo the Torx screw and remove the ABS wheel sensor from the hub carrier – refer to Chapter 9 if necessary.

7 Slacken the nut until it is level with the end

of the balljoint shank, then using a balljoint separator tool, detach the suspension control arm balljoint from the hub carrier. Use an Allen key in the end of the balljoint shank to prevent it from rotating as the nut is slackened **(see illustration)**.

8 Use a stout bar to lever the control arm downwards and move the hub carrier over the end of the balljoint shank. Take care not to damage the balljoint dust cover during and after disconnection.

9 Swivel the hub carrier assembly outwards, and withdraw the driveshaft CV joint from the hub flange **(see illustration)**.

10 Remove the bolt securing the hub carrier to the shock absorber. Insert a flat-bladed tool into the gap and very slightly spread the hub carrier where it clamps onto the lower end of the shock absorber. Tap the hub carrier downwards from the shock absorber at the same time. Note which way the bolt is inserted – from the front **(see illustrations)**.

11 The hub and bearing must now be removed from the hub carrier as an assembly. Due to the design of the assembly, we found it impossible to press the new hub/bearing into the carrier without using Volvo special tools

2.10a With the bolt removed, spread the hub carrier slightly using a large screwdriver . . .

2.10b . . . then gently tap the hub carrier downwards from the shock absorber

2.11a Using the Volvo special tool to support the hub carrier, press the hub flange and bearing out . .

No 999 7090 (see illustrations). The bearing will be rendered unserviceable by removal and cannot be re-used.

Refitting

12 Prior to refitting, remove all traces of metal adhesive, rust, oil and dirt from the splines and threads of the driveshaft outer CV joint and the bearing housing mating surface on the hub carrier.

13 The remainder of refitting is a reversal of removal, but observe the following points:
a) *Ensure that the hub and brake disc mating faces are spotlessly clean, and refit the disc with the orientation marks aligned.*
b) *A new driveshaft retaining screw should be used.*
c) *Ensure that the ABS sensor, and the sensor location in the hub carrier, are perfectly clean before refitting.*
d) *Tighten all nuts and bolts to the specified torque (see Chapter 9 for brake component torque settings).*

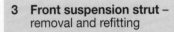

3 Front suspension strut – removal and refitting

Removal

1 Slacken the driveshaft retaining bolt as described in Chapter 8, Section 2, then slacken the wheel nuts, raise and support the front of the car and remove the roadwheel.

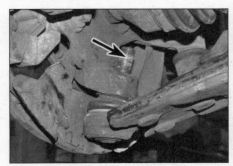

3.4 Pull the control arm downwards until the end of the balljoint shank (arrowed) is through the bottom of the hub carrier

2.11b . . . then assemble the special tool around the new bearing/flange assembly . . .

2.11d . . . then press the hub carrier . . .

2 Remove the driveshaft retaining bolt. Discard the bolt: a new one must be used on reassembly.

3 Slacken the nut until it is level with the end of the balljoint shank, then using a balljoint separator tool, detach the suspension control arm balljoint from the hub carrier. Use an Allen key in the end of the balljoint shank to prevent it from rotating as the nut is slackened (see illustration 2.7).

4 Use a stout bar to lever the control arm downwards and push the end of the balljoint shank down through the hub carrier (see illustration). Take care not to damage the balljoint dust cover during and after disconnection.

5 Undo the 2 bolts securing the brake caliper mounting bracket to the hub carrier and pull the caliper from the disc. Use string or wire to suspend the caliper from the vehicle bodywork, etc. Do not place any strain on the brake hose.

3.7 Undo the nut securing the anti-roll bar balljoint to the suspension strut – use an Allen key to counterhold the balljoint shank

2.11c . . position the hub carrier over the new bearing and the special tool in place on the hub carrier . .

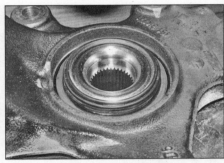

2.11e . . . fully onto the bearing

6 Swivel the hub carrier assembly outwards, and withdraw the driveshaft CV joint from the hub flange.

7 Undo the nut securing the anti-roll bar link balljoint to the suspension strut. Use an Allen key to counterhold the balljoint shank (see illustration).

8 Remove the bolt securing the hub carrier to the shock absorber. Insert a flat-bladed tool into the gap and very slightly spread the hub carrier where it clamps onto the lower end of the shock absorber. Tap the hub carrier downwards from the shock absorber at the same time. Note which way the bolt is inserted – from the front (see illustrations 2.10a and 2.10b).

9 From within the engine compartment, pull up the plastic covers, undo the retaining nuts and remove the engine compartment cross-stay (where fitted) (see illustration).

3.9 Pull up the covers, then undo the nuts and remove the engine compartment cross-stay (where fitted)

10 Undo the 3 bolts securing the strut upper mounting to the body – **do not** attempt to loosen the centre nut **(see illustration)**. Note that new nuts will be required for refitting.

11 Manoeuvre the strut out from underneath the wheel arch.

Refitting

12 Refitting is a reversal of removal, but observe the following points:

a) *Tighten all nuts and bolts to the specified torque, using new nuts/bolts where necessary.*

b) *Have the headlamp aim checked and if necessary, adjusted.*

---

4 Front suspension strut – dismantling, inspection and reassembly

⚠️ *Warning: Before attempting to dismantle the suspension strut, a suitable tool to hold the coil spring in compression must be obtained. Adjustable coil spring compressors which can be positively secured to the spring coils are readily available, and are recommended for this operation. Any attempt to dismantle the strut without such a tool is likely to result in damage or personal injury.*

Dismantling

1 Remove the strut from the car as described in Section 3.

2 Slacken the piston nut 1/2 a turn, while holding the protruding portion of the piston

3.10 Support the suspension strut, then undo the 3 bolts/studs and lower it from the wheel arch

rod with an Allen key **(see illustration)**. Do not remove the nut at this stage.

3 Fit the spring compressors to the coil springs, and tighten the compressors until the load is taken off the spring seats **(see illustration)**.

4 Remove the piston nut, then make alignment marks where the ends of the spring contact the upper and lower seats **(see illustration)**. Discard the nut – a new one must be fitted.

5 Remove the upper mounting/spring seat, bump stop and gaiter followed by the spring **(see illustration)**. Do not attempt to separate the spring seat from the mounting or the bearing balls will fall out.

Inspection

6 With the strut assembly now completely dismantled, examine all the components for wear, damage or deformation. Renew any of the components as necessary.

7 Examine the shock absorber for signs of fluid leakage, and check the strut piston for signs of pitting along its entire length. Test the operation of the shock absorber, while holding it in an upright position, by moving the piston through a full stroke and then through short strokes of 50 to 100mm. In both cases, the resistance felt should be smooth and continuous. If the resistance is jerky, or uneven, or if there is any visible sign of wear or damage, renewal is necessary.

8 If any doubt exists about the condition of the coil spring, gradually release the spring compressor, and check the spring for distortion and signs of cracking. Since no minimum free length is specified by Volvo, the only way to check the tension of the spring is to compare it to a new component. Renew the spring if it is damaged or distorted, or if there is any doubt as to its condition.

9 Inspect all other components for signs of damage or deterioration, and renew any that are suspect.

10 If a new shock absorber is being fitted, hold it vertically and pump the piston a few times to prime it.

Reassembly

11 Reassembly is a reversal of dismantling, but ensure that the spring is fully compressed before fitting. Make sure that the spring ends are correctly located in the upper and lower seats, aligning the marks made on removal, then tighten the new shock absorber piston retaining nut and strut mounting bolts to the specified torque **(see illustrations)**.

4.2 Hold the strut piston rod with an Allen key, and slacken the retaining nut

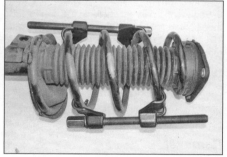

4.3 Fit the compressors to the springs

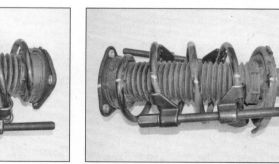

4.4 Make alignment marks between the spring and seats

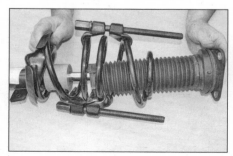

4.5 With the springs fully compressed, remove the mounting/seat/bump stop and gaiter, followed by the spring

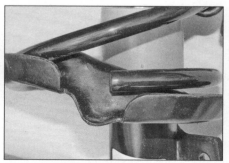

4.11a Ensure the spring ends are correctly located in their seats

4.11b Tighten the new piston rod nut to the specified torque

5.5a Control arm front mounting bolt (arrowed) . . .

5.5b . . . and rear mounting bolts (arrowed)

5 Front suspension control arm and balljoint – removal, overhaul and refitting

Note: *The balljoint is not available separately from the control arm. If defective the control arm/balljoint assembly must be renewed.*

Removal

1 Slacken the driveshaft retaining bolt as described in Chapter 8, Section 2, then slacken the wheel nuts, raise and support the front of the car and remove the roadwheel. Also remove the engine undershield **(see illustration 6.1)**.

2 Remove the driveshaft retaining bolt. Discard the bolt: a new one must be used on reassembly.

3 Slacken the nut until it is level with the end of the balljoint shank, then using a balljoint separator tool, detach the suspension control arm balljoint from the hub carrier. Use an Allen key in the end of the balljoint shank to prevent it from rotating as the nut is slackened **(see illustration 2.7)**.

4 Use a stout bar to lever the control arm downwards and over the end of the balljoint shank **(see illustration 3.4)**. Take care not to damage the balljoint dust cover during and after disconnection.

5 Undo the two bolts securing the control arm rear mounting and the single bolt securing the front mounting and manoeuvre the control arm from under the vehicle **(see illustrations)**. Discard the bolts, new one must be fitted.

Overhaul

6 Thoroughly clean the control arm and the area around the control arm mountings. Inspect the arm for any signs of cracks, damage or distortion, and carefully check the inner pivot bushes for signs of swelling, cracks or deterioration of the rubber.

7 If either bush requires renewal, the work should be entrusted to a Volvo dealer or specialist. A hydraulic press and suitable spacers are required to remove and refit the bushes and a setting gauge is needed for accurate positioning of the bushes in the arm.

Refitting

8 Locate the arm in its mountings, and fit the new mounting bolts. Tighten the bolts to their specified torque.

9 Engage the balljoint shank in the control arm, then tighten the new nut to the specified torque.

10 The remainder of refitting is a reversal of removal.

6 Front anti-roll bar – removal and refitting

Removal

1 Slacken the driveshaft retaining bolt as described in Chapter 8, Section 2, then slacken the wheel nuts, raise and support the front of the car and remove the roadwheel. Also remove the engine undershield **(see illustration)**.

2 Remove the driveshaft retaining bolt. Discard the bolt: a new one must be used on reassembly. Push the driveshaft through the hub by approximately 10 to 15 mm.

3 Slacken the nut until it is level with the end of the balljoint shank, then using a balljoint separator tool, detach the suspension control arm balljoint from the hub carrier. Use an Allen key in the end of the balljoint shank to prevent it from rotating as the nut is slackened **(see illustration 2.7)**.

4 Use a stout bar to lever the control arm downwards and over the end of the balljoint shank **(see illustration 3.4)**. Take care not to damage the balljoint dust cover during and after disconnection.

5 Undo the bolt each side securing the steering rack to the subframe, then suspend the rack from the vehicle body work using string/wire or cable ties **(see illustration 15.11)**.

6 Undo the nut each side securing the lower end of the anti-roll bar links to the bar. Use a Torx bit to counterhold the nut.

7 Position a sturdy trolley jack beneath, and in contact with, the rear of the subframe.

8 Undo the bolt each side securing the front of the subframe to the body approximately 6 turns **(see illustration)**. Note that new subframe front mounting bolts will be required for refitting.

9 Undo the bolt at the lower rear of the engine securing the lower torque rod to the bracket on the transmission/engine.

10 Unhook the exhaust system rubber mountings from the brackets on the rear of the subframe, disconnect the oxygen sensor wiring plug (where fitted), then undo the bolts each side securing the rear mounting brackets to the subframe and vehicle body, and recover the washers **(see illustration)**. Note that new subframe mounting bolts will be required for refitting.

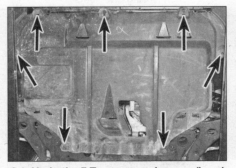

6.1 Undo the 7 Torx screws (arrowed) and remove the engine undershield

6.8 Undo the subframe front mounting bolt each side approximately 6 turns

6.10 Undo the bolt (arrowed) each side securing the mounting brackets to the subframe and body

6.12 Undo the anti-roll bar clamp bolts each side (arrowed)

6.13 The anti-roll bar bushes are split to facilitate renewal, and are shaped to fit the bar profile

6.16 Align the front subframe by inserting aligning tools (arrowed) through the holes in the subframe into the corresponding holes in the vehicle body

11 Carefully lower the jack and allow the subframe to drop slightly at the rear, so that the anti-roll bar clamp bolts are accessible.
12 Undo the bolts securing the anti-roll bar clamps on each side of the subframe, and manipulate the anti-roll bar out from under the car **(see illustration)**. Discard the bolts, new ones must be fitted.
13 Examine the anti-roll bar for signs of damage or distortion, and the connecting links and mounting bushes for signs of deterioration of the rubber. The bushes are split along their length and must be fitted in their original positions **(see illustration)**.

Refitting

14 Manipulate the anti-roll bar into position on the subframe. Fit the new clamp bolts and tighten to the specified torque.
15 Raise the subframe at the rear, fit the rear mounting brackets to the body, and tighten the bolts (new where applicable) hand-tight only at this stage.
16 The alignment of the subframe must be checked by inserting round tools through the holes in the sidemembers. Volvo tools (part No 999 7089) may be available. Alternatively, using two lengths of wooden dowel, 20mm in diameter, and approximately 150mm in length **(see illustration)**.
17 With the subframe correctly aligned, fit new front subframe mounting bolts, and tighten all subframe bolts to the specified torque.
18 The remainder of refitting is a reversal of removal.

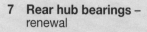

7 Rear hub bearings –
renewal

1 The rear hub bearings cannot be renewed separately, and are supplied with the rear hub as a complete assembly.
2 Remove the brake disc as described in Chapter 9.
3 Undo the bolt and remove the ABS wheel speed sensor from the hub carrier **(see illustration)**.
4 Undo the four Torx bolts and withdrawn the bearing assembly from the hub carrier.

5 Fit the new assembly to the hub carrier then insert and tighten the bolts to the specified torque.
6 Refit the ABS wheel speed sensor and brake disc as described in Chapter 9.

8 Rear hub carrier/lateral link –
removal and refitting

Removal

1 Remove the relevant rear coil spring as described in Section 10.
2 Undo the fasteners and remove the air baffle plate from the relevant side **(see illustration)**.
3 Remove the lower mounting bolt and pull the shock absorber from the lateral link.

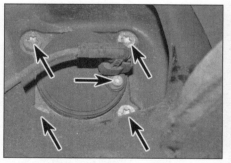

7.3 Rear ABS sensor bolt (arrowed) and rear hub bearing bolts (arrowed)

8.7 Detach the handbrake cable clip from the lateral link

4 Undo the retaining bolt and withdraw the ABS wheel sensor from hub carrier/lateral link. Do not disconnect the wheel sensor wiring plug.
5 Undo the bolts securing the upper control arm and tie-rod to the lateral link/hub carrier **(see illustrations 11.4, 11.7a and 11.7b)**.
6 Undo the bolt and detach the lower control arm from the lateral link/hub carrier **(see illustrations 11.10a and 11.10b)**.
7 Undo the screw and detach the handbrake cable retaining clip from the lateral link **(see illustration)**.
8 Release the ABS wheel speed sensor wiring harness from the clips on the lateral link.
9 Undo the 2 bolts securing the front mounting to the vehicle body, and withdraw the lateral link from under the vehicle **(see illustration)**.

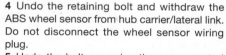

8.2 Undo the nuts (arrowed) and remove the air baffle

8.9 Lateral link/hub carrier front mounting bolts

8.15 The distance from the hub centre to the wheel arch must be 350 mm

10 Renewal of the bush at the front of the lateral link requires the use of Volvo special tools and a hydraulic press. Therefore it is recommended that this task should be entrusted to a Volvo dealer or suitably-equipped specialist.

Refitting

11 Manoeuvre the lateral link into position and tighten the 2 front mounting bolts to the specified torque.
12 Refit the ABS wheel speed sensor wiring harness clips to the link.
13 Position the handbrake cable and refit the cable retaining clip.
14 Refit the upper control arm, lower control arm and tie-rod, but don't tighten the bolt yet. The lateral link must be in the 'normal' position before the bolts are tightened.
15 Position a trolley jack under the shock absorber mounting of the lower control arm and raise the hub carrier assembly to the 'normal' position. Measure the distance from

the lower edge of the top of the wheel arch to the centre of the wheel hub **(see illustration)**. On all models the distance must be 350mm.
16 Tighten the upper control arm, lower control arm and tie-rod bolts to their specified torque.
17 The remainder of refitting is a reversal of removal.

9 Rear shock absorber – removal and refitting

Removal

1 Slacken the rear roadwheel nuts, then chock the front wheels then jack up the rear of the vehicle and support it on axle stands (see *Jacking and vehicle support*). Remove the rear wheels.
2 Place a trolley jack under the hub carrier and raise the suspension a little to take the load off the shock absorber.
3 Undo the 2 bolts securing the upper end of the shock absorber to the vehicle body **(see illustration)**.
4 Undo the lower mounting bolt, and pull the shock absorber from the hub carrier **(see illustration)**.
5 If required, undo the nut and pull the upper mounting from the shock absorber **(see illustration)**.
6 Check the condition of the shock absorber and renew as necessary.

Refitting

7 Refitting is a reversal of removal, tightening all nuts and bolts to the specified torques.

10 Rear coil spring – removal and refitting

Removal

1 Slacken the roadwheel nuts, then chock the front wheels and raise the rear of the vehicle. Support it securely on axle stands (see *Jacking and vehicle support*). Remove the roadwheels.

Left-hand side spring

2 Attach spring compressors to the spring and compress the spring. Volvo specify tools No 951 2911 and 951 2897. Alternative spring compressors may be available **(see illustration)**.

Right-hand side spring

3 Remove the shock absorber as described in Section 9, then lower the trolley jack a little.
4 Attach spring compressors to the spring and compress the spring. Volvo specify tools No 951 2911 and 951 2897. Alternative spring compressors may be available **(see illustration 10.2)**.

Both sides

5 Lift out the spring from its location.
6 Examine all the components for wear or damage, and renew as necessary.

Refitting

7 Refit the rubber seats to the control arm and spring, ensuring the ends of the spring locate correctly **(see illustrations)**.

9.3 Shock absorber upper mounting bolts (arrowed)

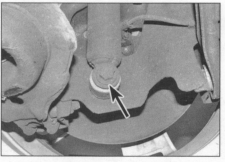

9.4 Shock absorber lower mounting bolt (arrowed)

9.5 Undo the shock absorber upper mounting nut (arrowed)

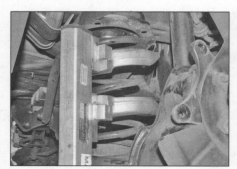

10.2 Remove the rear springs using spring compressors

10.7a The lug (arrowed) on the underside of the seat must locate in the hole in the arm

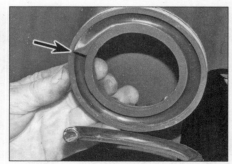

10.7b The end of the spring must fit against the stop in the rubber seat (arrowed)

11.4 Tie-rod mounting bolts (arrowed)

11.7a Upper control arm inner bolt (arrowed) . . .

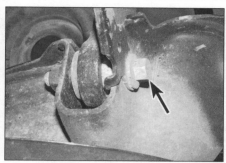

11.7b . . . and outer bolt (arrowed)

8 Refit the compressed spring onto the seat in the lower control arm. Rotate the spring until the spring engages correctly in the control arm grooves.
9 Raise the control arm by means of the jack, and engage the upper end of the spring in its recess in the body.
10 Refit the shock absorber (where applicable), securing it in place before removing the jack. Tighten all nuts and bolts to the specified torque.
11 Release and remove the spring compressor.
12 The remainder of refitting is a reversal of removal.

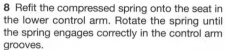
11 Rear suspension link arms – removal and refitting

Removal

1 Loosen the rear wheel nuts. Chock the front wheels, then jack up the rear of the vehicle and support it on axle stands (see *Jacking and vehicle support*). Remove the appropriate rear roadwheel(s).

Tie-rod

2 Remove the rear spring as described in Section 10.
3 If not already done so, position a trolley jack under the hub carrier/lateral link, and raise the hub carrier a little to take the tension from the tie-rod bolts.
4 Undo the outer and inner bolts, then remove the tie-rod **(see illustration)**.

Upper control arm

5 Remove the rear spring as described in Section 10.
6 If not already done so, position a trolley jack under the hub carrier/lateral link, and raise the hub carrier a little to take the tension from the control arm bolts.
7 Undo the outer and inner bolts, then remove the control arm **(see illustrations)**.

Lower control arm

8 Remove the coil spring as described in Section 10.
9 Undo the nuts and detach the anti-roll bar links from the control arm and anti-roll bar **(see illustration 12.2)**.

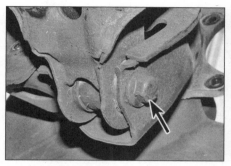

11.10a Undo the lower control arm outer bolt (arrowed) . . .

10 Mark the position of the inner bolt eccentric washer in relation to the arm, then undo the inner and outer control arm bolts, rotate the anti-roll bar approximately 30° and remove the control arm **(see illustrations)**.
11 Examine the condition of the metal-elastic bushes in the control arm. If renewal is necessary, the bushes must be pressed from the arm and new ones pressed into place. This necessitates the use of a hydraulic press. Entrust this task to a Volvo dealer or suitably-equipped garage.

Refitting

12 Refitting any of the control arms/tie rods is essentially a reversal of removal, noting the following points:
a) Tighten all fasteners to their specified torque where given, using a little thread-locking compound.

12.2 Rear anti-roll bar-to-control arm bolt (arrowed)

11.10b . . . then mark the position of the eccentric washer (arrowed) and remove the bolt

b) Before tightening any control arm/tie-rod mounting bolts, ensure the suspension is in the 'normal' position as described Section 8 of this Chapter.

12 Rear anti-roll bar – removal and refitting

Removal

1 Chock the front wheels, then jack up the rear of the vehicle and support it on axle stands (see *Jacking and vehicle support*).
2 Undo the nuts securing the outer ends of the anti-roll bar **(see illustration)**. Take care not to damage the rubber boots.
3 Undo the nuts securing the anti-roll bar clamps to the subframe, manoeuvre the anti-roll bar from under the vehicle **(see illustration)**.

12.3 Undo the screws (arrowed) securing the anti-roll bar clamps

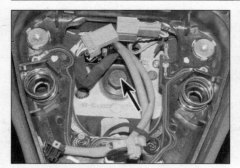

13.4 Slacken the steering wheel centre bolt (arrowed)

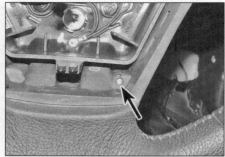

13.5a Remove the locking screw from the storage position (arrowed) . . .

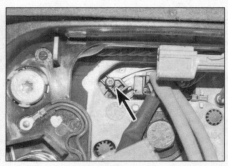

13.5b . . . and insert it to lock the contact unit in place (arrowed)

4 Examine the anti-roll bar for signs of damage or distortion, and the connecting links and mounting bushes for signs of deterioration of the rubber. The bushes are split along their length and must be fitted in their original positions.

Refitting

5 Position the anti-roll bar, then fit and tighten the bolts securing the anti-roll bar clamps to the subframe.
6 Refit the anti-roll bar links and tighten the nuts to the specified torque, using a Torx bit to counterhold the nuts.
7 The remainder of refitting is a reversal of removal.

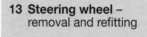

13 Steering wheel –
removal and refitting

⚠️ **Warning: Handle the airbag unit with extreme care as a precaution against personal injury, and always hold it with the cover facing away from the body. If in doubt concerning any proposed work involving the airbag unit or its control circuitry, consult a Volvo dealer.**

Removal

1 Drive the car forwards, and park it with the front wheels in the straight-ahead position.
2 Remove the driver's airbag as described in Chapter 12.
3 Disconnect the green wiring plug at the top of the steering wheel aperture.

4 Undo the steering wheel centre retaining bolt **(see illustration)**.
5 Ensure the steering wheel is in the 'straight-ahead' position, then remove the lower screw from its storage position and insert it into the hole to lock the rotary contact reel **(see illustrations)**.
6 Lift the steering wheel off the column shaft, and feed the wiring and plastic strip through the hole in the wheel.

Refitting

7 Ensure that the front wheels are still in the straight-ahead position.
8 Feed the wiring through the hole in the steering wheel, then engage the wheel with the steering column shaft. Ensure that the marks made on removal are aligned, and that the pegs on the contact reel engage with the recesses on the steering wheel hub. Note that the upper shroud is attached to the instrument panel surround. Do not attempt to turn the steering wheel with the contact reel locked, otherwise the reel will be damaged.
9 Refit the steering wheel retaining bolt, and tighten it finger-tight only.
10 Referring to the information in Chapter 12, remove the airbag contact reel locking screw, and refit the screw and plastic strip to the location provided in the steering wheel.
11 Tighten the new steering wheel retaining bolt to the specified torque.
12 Refit the airbag unit to the steering wheel as described in Chapter 12.

14 Steering column –
removal and refitting

Removal

1 Disconnect the battery negative lead – see Chapter 5A.
2 Fully extend the steering column, then remove the steering wheel (see Section 13).
3 Undo the fasteners and remove the lower facia panel on the driver's side – see Chapter 11.
4 Undo the 4 screws and remove the knee bolster and air duct from under the steering column (where fitted).
5 Undo the three Torx screws from under the steering column lower shroud, and prise the upper and lower shrouds apart to release the retaining pegs. Remove the lower shroud, and lift the upper shroud out of the way. If required, unclip the gaiter between the upper shroud and the facia **(see illustrations)**.
6 The wiper/washer switch and turn indicator switch are retained by 2 screws each. Undo the screws and pull the switches out to the sides **(see illustration)**.
7 Undo the 2 screws, release the clip, and pull the contact reel/steering wheel module rearwards. Disconnect the wiring plugs as the assembly is withdrawn **(see illustrations)**.
8 Disconnect any remaining wiring plugs, then release clips securing the wiring harness to the guide on the underside of the column.

14.5a Undo the 3 Torx screws (arrowed) . . .

14.5b . . . then prise apart the shrouds and unclip the gaiter (arrowed)

14.6 Undo the screws (arrowed) and pull the switches from the module

9 Carefully pull the steering column lower gaiter from place, releasing the clips **(see illustration)**.

10 Undo the steering column lower pinch-bolt and pull the joint upwards from the pinion **(see illustration)**. Ensure the column adjustment lever is released before detaching the joint from the pinion. Discard the pinch-bolt, a new one must be fitted.

11 Undo the 4 retaining bolts and manoeuvre the column from the vehicle **(see illustration)**. Discard the bolts, new ones must be fitted.

12 If required, drill out the security screws, press in the retaining pin, and remove the steering lock from the column **(see illustration)**. No further dismantling of the assembly is recommended.

Refitting

13 Refitting is a reversal of removal, bearing in mind the following points:
a) Lubricate universal joint splines with grease before engaging the steering column.
b) When fitting the new column retaining bolts, the shortest bolts are nearest the bulkhead.
c) Use a new universal joint pinch-bolt.
d) If refitting the steering lock, tighten the new security screws until their heads snap off.

15 Steering rack – removal and refitting

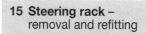

Removal

1 Drive the car forwards and park it with the steering wheels in the straight-ahead position. Remove the ignition key to lock the steering in this position.

2 Remove the lower facia panel on the driver's side as described in Chapter 11.

3 Remove the steering column lower gaiter, then undo the pinch-bolt and pull the joint upwards from the pinion **(see illustrations 14.9 and 14.10)**. Ensure the column adjustment lever is released before detaching the joint from the pinion. Discard the pinch-bolt, a new one must be fitted.

4 Loosen the front wheel nuts. Chock the rear wheels then jack up the front of the vehicle and support it on axle stands (see *Jacking and vehicle support*). Remove both front roadwheels.

5 Slacken and remove the bolt securing the driveshaft to the hub on each side, and push the driveshaft through the hub approximately 10 to 15mm. Have an assistant depress the brake pedal to prevent the hub from rotating. Discard the bolt, a new one must be used.

6 Undo the 7 Torx screws and remove the engine undershield **(see illustration 6.1)**.

7 Measure the length of the track rod on one side, relative to the steering rack housing, and make a note of the dimension measured.

8 Undo the retaining nut, then disconnect the

14.7a Undo the 2 screws (arrowed) . . .

14.7b . . . depress the clip (arrowed) and pull the module from the column

14.9 Pull the column lower gaiter upwards

14.10 Undo the steering column lower pinch-bolt (arrowed)

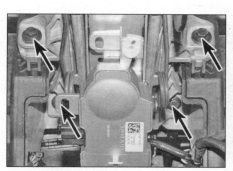

14.11 Steering column retaining bolts (arrowed)

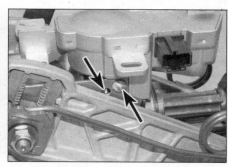

14.12 Drill out the securing bolt each side (arrowed) then depress the clip (arrowed)

steering track rod end balljoint from the hub carrier. If necessary, use a balljoint separator tool **(see illustrations 19.3a and 19.3b)**.

9 Slacken the nut until it is level with the end of the balljoint shank, then using a balljoint separator tool, detach the suspension control arm balljoint from the hub carrier. Use an Allen key in the end of the ball joint shank to prevent it from rotating as the nut is slackened.

10 Use a stout bar to lever the control arm downwards and over the end of the balljoint shank. Take care not to damage the balljoint dust cover during and after disconnection **(see illustration 3.4)**.

11 Undo the bolt each side securing the steering rack to the subframe, then suspend the rack from the vehicle body work using string/wire or cable ties **(see illustration)**.

12 Undo the nut each side securing the lower end of the anti-roll bar links to the bar. Use a Torx bit to counterhold the nut.

13 Position a sturdy trolley jack beneath the subframe.

14 Undo the bolt at the lower rear of the engine securing the lower torque rod to the bracket on the transmission/engine.

15.11 Undo the bolt each side securing the steering rack to the subframe

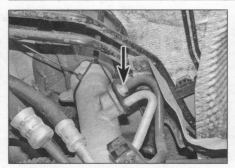

15.18 Fluid unions retaining bolt (arrowed)

15 Undo the bolt each side securing the front of the subframe to the body **(see illustration 6.8)**. Note that new subframe front mounting bolts will be required for refitting.

16 Unhook the exhaust system rubber mountings from the brackets on the rear of the subframe, disconnect the oxygen sensor wiring plug, then undo the bolts each side securing the rear mounting brackets to the subframe and body, and recover the washers **(see illustration 6.10)**. Note that new bolts will be required for refitting.

17 Carefully lower the subframe.

18 Undo the retaining bolt and pull the fluid pipe unions from the steering rack **(see illustration)**. Be prepared for fluid spillage. Plug or seal the openings to prevent contamination. Discard the O-ring seals, new ones must be fitted.

19 Release the string/cable ties/wire, and manoeuvre the steering rack sideways from the engine compartment.

Refitting

20 Set the length of the track rod to the previously-recorded dimension by turning the pinion shaft as necessary.

21 Manipulate the steering rack into position, and support it as during removal.

22 Engage the steering shaft universal joint with the pinion shaft, and push it fully home.

23 Refit the fluid pipes to the steering rack using new O-ring seals, and tighten the retaining bolts securely.

24 Raise the subframe into position, and engage the steering rack bolts.

25 Fit the subframe rear mounting brackets

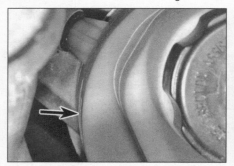

17.4 The power steering fluid level is just visible through the reservoir body (arrowed)

16.2 Release the clips (arrowed) and remove the gaiter

to the body, then insert the new front and rear subframe mounting bolts. Only hand-tighten them at this stage.

26 The alignment of the subframe must be checked by inserting round tools through the holes in the sidemembers. Volvo tools (part No 999 7089) may be available. Alternatively, using two lengths of wooden dowel, 20mm in diameter, and approximately 150mm in length **(see illustration 6.16)**.

27 With the subframe correctly aligned, tighten all subframe bolts to the specified torque.

28 Fit the new universal joint pinch-bolt and tighten it to the specified torque.

29 The remainder of refitting is a reversal of removal, noting the following points:
a) *Tighten all fasteners to their specified torque where given.*
b) *Bleed the power steering system as described in Section 17.*
c) *Have the front wheel alignment checked at the earliest opportunity.*

16 Steering rack gaiters – renewal

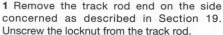

1 Remove the track rod end on the side concerned as described in Section 19. Unscrew the locknut from the track rod.

2 Release the two clips and peel off the gaiter **(see illustration)**.

3 Clean out any dirt and grit from the inner end of the track rod and (when accessible) the rack.

4 Wrap insulating tape around the track

18.4 Undo the pressure pipe bracket bolt (arrowed)

rod threads to protect the new gaiter whilst installing.

5 Refit the track rod end locknut.

6 Refit the track rod end as described in Section 19.

17 Steering rack – bleeding

1 Ensure the handbrake is applied.

2 The power steering fluid reservoir is located on the right-hand side of the engine compartment, just behind the headlight. Remove the right-hand side headlight as described in Chapter 12.

3 Wipe clean the area around the reservoir filler neck, and unscrew the filler cap/dipstick from the reservoir.

4 The fluid level in the reservoir is visible through the reservoir body. If necessary use a torch to enhance visibility **(see illustration)**.

5 If topping-up is necessary, use clean fluid of the specified type (see *Weekly checks*). Check for leaks if frequent topping-up is required. Do not run the engine without fluid in the reservoir.

6 After component renewal, or if the fluid level has been allowed to fall so low that air has entered the hydraulic system, bleeding must be carried out as follows.

7 Fill the reservoir to the correct level as described above.

8 Start the engine and turn the steering wheel from full lock one way, to full lock the other way. Repeat this 5 times then top-up the fluid level as necessary.

9 Turn the steering wheel slowly to the full left lock position, then turn the steering wheel slowly to the full right lock position, and hold it there for 2-3 seconds.

10 Turn the steering wheel slowly to the full left lock position 5 times, then turn the steering wheel slowly to the full right lock position, and hold it there for 2-3 seconds.

11 Top-up the fluid level again if necessary.

12 Repeat paragraphs 8 to 10 until the steering operation is satisfactory.

13 On completion, stop the engine, recheck the fluid level then refit the headlight.

18 Electronic power steering module/pump – removal and refitting

Removal

1 Remove the right-hand side headlight as described in Chapter 12.

2 Remove the front bumper as described in Chapter 11, then remove the right-hand wheel arch liner.

3 Use a syringe to extract as much fluid as possible from the pump reservoir.

4 Undo the pressure pipe union lock bracket bolt a few turns and remove the bracket **(see illustration)**.

18.5 Disconnect the wiring plugs from the EPS module

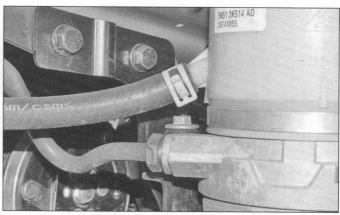

18.6 Disconnect the fluid return and pressure pipes

18.7 EPS module retaining bolts (arrowed)

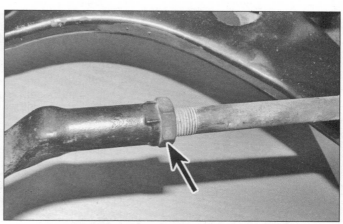

19.2 Slacken the track rod end locknut (arrowed)

5 Disconnect the wiring plugs from the EPS module (Electronic Power Steering) **(see illustration)**.

6 Release the clip and disconnect the fluid return pipe from the reservoir, then undo the union and disconnect the pressure pipe **(see illustration)**. Plug or seal the openings to prevent contamination. Be prepared for fluid spillage.

7 Undo the 3 bolts and remove the assembly **(see illustration)**.

8 No individual parts are available for the EPS/pump. If faulty, exchange units are available from Volvo.

Refitting

9 Refitting is a reversal of removal, bearing in mind the following points:
a) Use a new O-ring on pressure pipe union.
b) Tighten the mounting bolts to the specified torque.
c) If a new EPS has been fitted, suitable software will need to be downloaded from Volvo. Consult your local dealer or specialist.
d) Refill/top-up the fluid reservoir, and bleed the system as described in Section 17.

19 Track rod end – removal and refitting

Removal

1 Loosen the appropriate front wheel nuts. Chock the rear wheels, then jack up the front of the vehicle and support it on axle stands (see *Jacking and vehicle support*). Remove the appropriate front roadwheel.

19.3a Use an Allen key to counterhold the track rod end balljoint shank

2 Counterhold the track rod, and slacken the track rod end locknut by half a turn **(see illustration)**. If the locknut is now left in this position, it will act as a further guide for refitting.

3 Unscrew the track rod end balljoint nut, using and Allen key to counterhold the balljoint shank. Separate the balljoint from the steering arm with a proprietary balljoint separator, then remove the nut and disengage the balljoint from the arm **(see illustrations)**.

19.3b Use a separator tool to detach the track rod end from the hub carrier

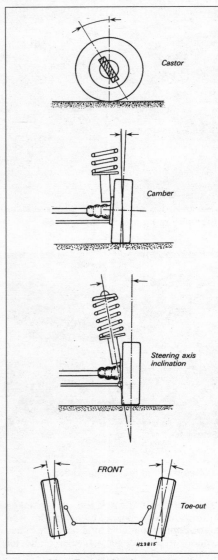

20.1 Front wheel geometry

4 Unscrew the track rod end from the track rod, counting the number of turns needed to remove it. Make a note of the number of turns, so that the tracking can be reset (or at least approximated) on refitting.

Refitting

5 Screw the track rod end onto the track rod by the same number of turns noted during removal.
6 Engage the balljoint in the steering arm. Fit a new nut and tighten it to the specified torque.
7 Counterhold the track rod and tighten the locknut.
8 Refit the front wheel, lower the car and tighten the wheel nuts in a diagonal sequence to the specified torque.
9 Have the front wheel toe-in (tracking) checked and adjusted by a Volvo dealer or suitably-equipped repairer.

20 Wheel alignment and steering angles – general information

1 A car's steering and suspension geometry is defined in four basic settings – all angles are expressed in degrees; the relevant settings are camber, castor, steering axis inclination, and toe setting **(see illustration)**. On the models covered by this manual, only the front camber and the front and rear wheel toe settings are adjustable.
2 Camber is the angle at which the front wheels are set from the vertical when viewed from the front or rear of the car. Negative camber is the amount (in degrees) that the wheels are tilted inward at the top from the vertical.
3 The front camber angle is adjusted by slackening the steering knuckle-to-suspension strut mounting bolts and repositioning the hub carrier assemblies as necessary.
4 Castor is the angle between the steering axis and a vertical line when viewed from each side of the car. Positive castor is when the steering axis is inclined rearward at the top.
5 Steering axis inclination is the angle (when viewed from the front of the vehicle) between the vertical and an imaginary line drawn through the front suspension strut upper mounting and the control arm balljoint.
6 Toe setting is the amount by which the distance between the front inside edges of the roadwheels (measured at hub height) differs from the diametrically opposite distance measured between the rear inside edges of the roadwheels. Toe-in is when the roadwheels point inwards, towards each other at the front, while toe-out is when they splay outwards from each other at the front.
7 The front wheel toe setting is adjusted by altering the length of the steering track rods on both sides. This adjustment is normally referred to as the tracking.
8 The rear wheel toe setting is adjusted by altering the position of the rear suspension transverse arm-to-trailing arm mountings.
9 With the exception of the front and rear toe settings, and the front camber angles, all other suspension and steering angles are set during manufacture, and no adjustment is possible. It can be assumed, therefore, that unless the vehicle has suffered accident damage, all the preset angles will be correct.
10 Special optical measuring equipment is necessary to accurately check and adjust the front and rear toe settings and front camber angles, and this work should be carried out by a Volvo dealer or similar expert. Most tyre-fitting centres have the expertise and equipment to carry out at least a front wheel toe setting (tracking) check for a nominal charge.

Chapter 11
Bodywork and fittings

Contents

Degrees of difficulty

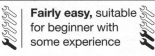

Easy, suitable for novice with little experience	**Fairly easy,** suitable for beginner with some experience	**Fairly difficult,** suitable for competent DIY mechanic	**Difficult,** suitable for experienced DIY mechanic	**Very difficult,** suitable for expert DIY or professional

Specifications

Torque wrench settings	Nm	lbf ft
Bonnet hinge bolts	24	18
Bonnet lock bolts	24	18
Boot lid bolts	24	18
Boot lid lock bolts	20	15
Door carrier bolts	10	7
Door hinge bolts	24	18
Facia		
To A-pillar (inner 2 bolts)	24	18
To A-pillar (outer bolt in door shut)	50	37
To bukhead	24	18
Front seat retaining bolts	40	30
Front seat belt anchorage to seat	45	33
Front seat belt tensioner/inertia reels	40	30
Rear seat backrest bolts	50	37
Rear seat cushion retaining bolts	25	18
Rear seat belt inertia reel nut	40	30
Rear seat belt lower anchorages	50	37
Tailgate hinge bolts	24	18
Tailgate lock bolts	20	15

1 General information

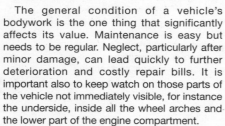

The bodyshell is made of pressed-steel sections. Most components are welded together, but some use is made of structural adhesives. The doors and door pillars are reinforced against side impacts as part of the side impact protection system (SIPS).

A number of structural components and body panels are made of galvanised steel to provide a high level of protection against corrosion. Extensive use is also made of plastic materials, mainly in the interior, but also in exterior components. The front and rear bumpers are moulded from a synthetic material that is very strong and yet light. Plastic components such as wheel arch liners are fitted to the underside of the vehicle to further improve corrosion resistance.

2 Maintenance – bodywork and underframe

The general condition of a vehicle's bodywork is the one thing that significantly affects its value. Maintenance is easy but needs to be regular. Neglect, particularly after minor damage, can lead quickly to further deterioration and costly repair bills. It is important also to keep watch on those parts of the vehicle not immediately visible, for instance the underside, inside all the wheel arches and the lower part of the engine compartment.

The basic maintenance routine for the bodywork is washing preferably with a lot of water, from a hose. This will remove all the loose solids which may have stuck to the vehicle. It is important to flush these off in such a way as to prevent grit from scratching the finish. The wheel arches and underframe need washing in the same way to remove any accumulated mud which will retain moisture and tend to encourage rust. Oddly enough, the best time to clean the underframe and wheel arches is in wet weather when the mud is thoroughly wet and soft. In very wet weather the underframe is usually cleaned of large accumulations automatically and this is a good time for inspection.

Periodically, except on vehicles with a wax-based underbody protective coating, it is a good idea to have the whole of the underframe of the vehicle steam-cleaned so that a thorough inspection can be carried out to see what minor repairs and renovations are necessary. Steam-cleaning is available at many garages, and is necessary for removal of the accumulation of oily grime which sometimes is allowed to become thick in certain areas. If steam-cleaning facilities are not available, there are one or two excellent grease solvents available which can be brush applied; the dirt can then be simply hosed off. Note that these methods should not be used on vehicles with wax-based underbody protective coating, or the coating will be removed. Such vehicles should be inspected annually, preferably just prior to winter, when the underbody should be washed down and any damage to the wax coating repaired using underseal. Ideally, a completely fresh coat should be applied. It would also be worth considering the use of such wax-based protection for injection into door panels, sills, box sections, etc, as an additional safeguard against rust damage where such protection is not provided by the vehicle manufacturer.

After washing paintwork, wipe off with a chamois leather to give an unspotted clear finish. A coat of clear protective wax polish will give added protection against chemical pollutants in the air. If the paintwork sheen has dulled or oxidised, use a cleaner/polisher combination to restore the brilliance of the shine. This requires a little effort, but such dulling is usually caused because regular washing has been neglected. Care needs to be taken with metallic paintwork, as special non-abrasive cleaner/polisher is required to avoid damage to the finish.

Always check that the door and ventilator opening drain holes and pipes are completely clear, so that water can be drained out. Brightwork should be treated in the same way as paintwork. Windscreens and windows can be kept clear of the smeary film which often appears by the use of a proprietary glass cleaner. Never use any form of wax or other body or chromium polish on glass, especially not on the windscreen or tailgate.

3 Maintenance – upholstery and carpets

Mats and carpets should be brushed or vacuum cleaned regularly to keep them free of grit. If they are badly stained, remove them from the vehicle for scrubbing or sponging, and make quite sure they are dry before refitting. Seats and interior trim panels can be kept clean by wiping with a damp cloth and a proprietary upholstery cleaner. If they do become stained (which can be more apparent on light-coloured upholstery) use a little liquid detergent and a soft nail brush to scour the grime out of the grain of the material. Do not forget to keep the headlining clean in the same way as the upholstery. When using liquid cleaners inside the vehicle, do not over-wet the surfaces being cleaned. Excessive damp could get into the seams and padded interior causing stains, offensive odours or even rot.

4 Minor body damage – repair

Minor scratches

If the scratch is very superficial, and does not penetrate to the metal of the bodywork, repair is very simple. Lightly rub the area of the scratch with a paintwork renovator, or a very fine cutting paste, to remove loose paint from the scratch, and to clear the surrounding bodywork of wax polish. Rinse the area with clean water.

In the case of metallic paint, the most commonly-found 'scratches' are not in the paint, but in the lacquer top coat, and appear white. If care is taken , these can sometimes be rendered less obvious by very careful use of paintwork renovator (which would otherwise not be used on metallic paintwork); otherwise, repair of these scratches can be achieved by applying lacquer with a fine brush.

Apply touch-up paint to the scratch using a fine paint brush; continue to apply fine layers of paint until the surface of the paint in the scratch is level with the surrounding paintwork. Allow the new paint at least two weeks to harden: then blend it into the surrounding paintwork by rubbing the scratch area with a paintwork renovator or a very fine cutting paste. Finally, apply wax polish.

Where the scratch has penetrated right through to the metal of the bodywork, causing the metal to rust, a different repair technique is required. Remove any loose rust from the bottom of the scratch with a penknife, then apply rust-inhibiting paint, to prevent the formation of rust in the future. Using a rubber or nylon applicator fill the scratch with bodystopper paste. If required, this paste can be mixed with cellulose thinners, to provide a very thin paste which is ideal for filling narrow scratches. Before the stopper-paste in the scratch hardens, wrap a piece of smooth cotton rag around the top of a finger. Dip the finger in cellulose thinners, and then quickly sweep it across the surface of the stopper-paste in the scratch; this will ensure that the surface of the stopper-paste is slightly hollowed. The scratch can now be painted over as described earlier in this Section.

Dents

When deep denting of the vehicle's bodywork has taken place, the first task is to pull the dent out, until the affected bodywork almost attains its original shape. There is little point in trying to restore the original shape completely, as the metal in the damaged area will have stretched on impact, and cannot be reshaped fully to its original contour. It is better to bring the level of the dent up to a point which is about 3mm below the level of the surrounding bodywork. In cases where the dent is very shallow anyway, it is not worth trying to pull it out at all. If the underside of the dent is accessible, it can be hammered out gently from behind, using a mallet with a wooden or plastic head. Whilst doing this, hold a suitable block of wood firmly against the outside of the panel to absorb the impact from the hammer blows and thus prevent a large area of the bodywork from being 'belled-out'.

Should the dent be in a section of the bodywork which has a double skin or some other factor making it inaccessible from behind, a different technique is called for. Drill several small holes through the metal inside the area – particularly in the deeper section. Then screw long self-tapping screws into the holes just sufficiently for them to gain a good purchase in the metal. Now the dent can be pulled out by pulling on the protruding heads of the screws with a pair of pliers.

The next stage of the repair is the removal of the paint from the damaged area, and from an inch or so of the surrounding 'sound' bodywork. This is accomplished most easily by using a wire brush or abrasive pad on a power drill, although it can be done just as effectively by hand using sheets of abrasive paper. To complete the preparation for filling, score the surface of the bare metal with a screwdriver or the tang of a file, or alternatively, drill small holes in the affected area. This will provide a really good 'key' for the filler paste.

To complete the repair, see the Section on filling and re-spraying.

Rust holes or gashes

Remove all paint from the affected area, and from an inch or so of the surrounding 'sound' bodywork, using an abrasive pad or a wire brush on a power drill. If these are not available, a few sheets of abrasive paper will do the job just as effectively. With the paint removed, you will be able to gauge the severity of the corrosion, and therefore decide whether to renew the whole panel (if this is possible) or to repair the affected area. New body panels are not as expensive as most people think, and it is often quicker and more satisfactory to fit a new panel than to attempt to repair large areas of corrosion.

Remove all fittings from the affected area, except those which will act as a guide to the original shape of the damaged bodywork. Then, using tin snips or a hacksaw blade, remove all loose metal and any other metal badly affected by corrosion. Hammer the edges of the hole inwards in order to create a slight depression for the filler paste.

Wire-brush the affected area to remove the powdery rust from the surface of the remaining metal. Paint the affected area with rust-inhibiting paint; if the back of the rusted area is accessible treat this also.

Before filling can take place, it will be necessary to block the hole in some way. This can be achieved by the use of aluminium or plastic mesh, or aluminium tape.

Aluminium or plastic mesh or glass fibre matting is probably the best material to use for a large hole. Cut a piece to the approximate size and shape of the hole to be filled, then position it in the hole so that its edges are below the level of the surrounding bodywork. It can be retained in position by several blobs of filler paste around its periphery.

Aluminium tape should be used for small or very narrow holes. Pull a piece off the roll and trim it to the approximate size and shape required, then pull off the backing paper (if used) and stick the tape over the hole; it can be overlapped if the thickness of one piece is insufficient. Burnish down the edges of the tape with the handle of a screwdriver or similar, to ensure that the tape is securely attached to the metal underneath.

Filling and re-spraying

Before using this Section, see the Sections on dent, deep scratch, rust holes and gash repairs.

Many types of bodyfiller are available, but generally speaking those proprietary kits which contain a tin of filler paste and a tube of resin hardener are best for this type of repair; some can be used directly from the tube. A wide, flexible plastic or nylon applicator will be found invaluable for imparting a smooth and well contoured finish to the surface of the filler.

Mix up a little filler on a clean piece of card or board – measure the hardener carefully (follow the maker's instructions on the pack) otherwise the filler will set too rapidly or too slowly. Using the applicator, apply the filler paste to the prepared area; draw the applicator across the surface of the filler to achieve the correct contour and to level the filler surface. As soon as a contour that approximates to the correct one is achieved, stop working the paste – if you carry on too long the paste will become sticky and begin to 'pick up' on the applicator. Continue to add thin layers of filler paste at twenty-minute intervals until the level of the filler is just proud of the surrounding bodywork.

Once the filler has hardened, excess can be removed using a metal plane or file. From then on, progressively finer grades of abrasive paper should be used, starting with a 40-grade production paper and finishing with 400-grade wet-and-dry paper. Always wrap the abrasive paper around a flat rubber, cork, or wooden block – otherwise the surface of the filler will not be completely flat. During the smoothing of the filler surface the wet-and-dry paper should be periodically rinsed in water. This will ensure that a very smooth finish is imparted to the filler at the final stage.

At this stage the 'dent' should be surrounded by a ring of bare metal, which in turn should be encircled by the finely 'feathered' edge of the good paintwork. Rinse the repair area with clean water, until all of the dust produced by the rubbing-down operation has gone.

Spray the whole repair area with a light coat of primer – this will show up any imperfections in the surface of the filler. Repair these imperfections with fresh filler paste or bodystopper, and once more smooth the surface with abrasive paper. If bodystopper is used, it can be mixed with cellulose thinners to form a really thin paste which is ideal for filling small holes. Repeat this spray and repair procedure until you are satisfied that the surface of the filler, and the feathered edge of the paintwork are perfect. Clean the repair area with clean water and allow to dry fully.

The repair area is now ready for final spraying. Paint spraying must be carried out in a warm, dry, windless and dust free atmosphere. This condition can be created artificially if you have access to a large indoor working area, but if you are forced to work in the open, you will have to pick your day very carefully. If you are working indoors, dousing the floor in the work area with water will help to settle the dust which would otherwise be in the atmosphere. If the repair area is confined to one body panel, mask off the surrounding panels; this will help to minimise the effects of a slight mis-match in paint colours. Bodywork fittings (eg chrome strips, door handles etc) will also need to be masked off. Use genuine masking tape and several thicknesses of newspaper for the masking operations.

Before commencing to spray, agitate the aerosol can thoroughly, then spray a test area (an old tin, or similar) until the technique is mastered. Cover the repair area with a thick coat of primer; the thickness should be built up using several thin layers of paint rather than one thick one. Using 400 grade wet-and-dry paper, rub down the surface of the primer until it is really smooth. While doing this, the work area should be thoroughly doused with water, and the wet-and-dry paper periodically rinsed in water. Allow to dry before spraying on more paint.

Spray on the top coat, again building up the thickness by using several thin layers of paint. Start spraying in the centre of the repair area and then, with a single side-to-side motion, work outwards until the whole repair area and about 50mm of the surrounding original paintwork is covered. Remove all masking material 10 to 15 minutes after spraying on the final coat of paint.

Allow the new paint at least two weeks to harden, then, using a paintwork renovator or a very fine cutting paste, blend the edges of the paint into the existing paintwork. Finally, apply wax polish.

Plastic components

With the use of more and more plastic body components by the vehicle manufacturers (eg bumpers, spoilers, and in some cases major body panels), rectification of more serious damage to such items has become a matter of either entrusting repair work to a specialist in this field, or renewing complete components. Repair of such damage by the DIY owner is not really feasible owing to the cost of the equipment and materials required for effecting such repairs. The basic technique involves making a groove along the line of the crack in the plastic using a rotary burr in a power drill. The damaged part is then welded back together by using a hot-air gun to heat up and fuse a plastic filler rod into the groove. Any excess plastic is then removed and the area rubbed down to a smooth finish. It is important that a filler rod of the correct plastic is used, as body components can be made of a variety of different types (eg polycarbonate, ABS, polypropylene).

6.3 Prise off the clips and pull the support struts from the mounting studs

6.4 Undo the bonnet hinge nuts

Damage of a less serious nature (abrasions, minor cracks etc) can be repaired by the DIY owner using a two-part epoxy filler repair material. Once mixed in equal proportions, this is used in similar fashion to the bodywork filler used on metal panels. The filler is usually cured in twenty to thirty minutes, ready for sanding and painting.

If the owner is renewing a complete component himself, or if he has repaired it with epoxy filler, he will be left with the problem of finding a suitable paint for finishing which is compatible with the type of plastic used. At one time the use of a universal paint was not possible owing to the complex range of plastics encountered in body component applications. Standard paints, generally speaking, will not bond to plastic or rubber satisfactorily. However, it is now possible to obtain a plastic body parts finishing kit which consists of a pre-primer treatment, a primer

and coloured top coat. Full instructions are normally supplied with a kit, but basically the method of use is to first apply the pre-primer to the component concerned and allow it to dry for up to 30 minutes. Then the primer is applied and left to dry for about an hour before finally applying the special coloured top coat. The result is a correctly-coloured component where the paint will flex with the plastic or rubber, a property that standard paint does not normally possess.

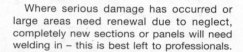

5 Major body damage – repair

Where serious damage has occurred or large areas need renewal due to neglect, completely new sections or panels will need welding in – this is best left to professionals.

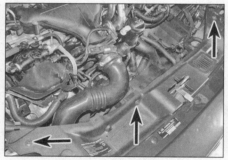

7.1 Undo the 3 bolts (arrowed) and remove the plastic panel

7.2 Release the coolant expansion tank from its fixings and move it to one side

7.4a Disconnect the cable from the lock levers . . .

7.4b . . . and the release lever

If the damage is due to impact, it will also be necessary to check completely the alignment of the body shell structure. Due to the principle of construction, the strength and shape of the whole can be affected by damage to a part. In such instances, the services of a Volvo agent with specialist checking jigs are essential. If a body is left misaligned, it is first of all dangerous as the car will not handle properly and secondly uneven stresses will be imposed on the steering, engine and transmission, causing abnormal wear or complete failure. Tyre wear may also be excessive.

6 Bonnet – removal, refitting and adjustment

Removal

1 Open the bonnet, and disconnect the hoses from the washer jets, as described in Chapter 12.
2 Where applicable, disconnect the washer jet's wiring plugs and pull the loom from the bonnet.
3 Mark around the hinge bracket on the underside of the bonnet with a felt tip pen for reference when refitting. Prise out the clip and pull the support from place **(see illustration)**.
4 With the aid of an assistant, support the bonnet and remove the hinge bolts **(see illustration)**. Lift off the bonnet and store it in a safe place.

Refitting and adjustment

5 Before refitting, place pads of rags under the corners of the bonnet near the hinges to protect the paintwork from damage.
6 Fit the bonnet and insert the hinge bolts. Just nip the bolts up in their previously marked positions.
7 Reconnect the washer tube and wiring plugs.
8 Shut the bonnet and check its fit. If necessary slacken the bolts and reposition the bonnet.
9 Tighten the hinge bolts securely when adjustment is correct and refit the support.

7 Bonnet release cable – removal, refitting and adjustment

Removal

1 Undo the 3 bolts and remove the plastic trim attached to the bonnet slam panel **(see illustration)**.
2 Lift out the coolant expansion tank and move it to one side **(see illustration)**.
3 Remove the trim panel above the driver's pedals – refer to Section 25 if necessary.
4 Disconnect the cable ends from the lock levers and release catch, note the cable routing, release it from the retaining clips and remove it **(see illustrations)**.

Refitting and adjustment

5 Refit by reversing the removal operations.

8 Bonnet lock – removal and refitting

Removal

1 Remove the front bumper as described in Section 21. Undo the 3 bolts and remove the plastic trim attached to the bonnet slam panel **(see illustration 7.1)**.
2 Remove the fixings and fold down the upper air baffle.
3 Detach the release cable and wiring plug from the lock **(see illustration)**.
4 Undo the two lock retaining bolts and remove the lock.

Refitting

5 Refitting is a reversal of removal. Only finger-tighten the lock retaining bolts, then shut the bonnet to centralise the catch. Tighten the retaining bolts securely.

9 Doors – removal, refitting and adjustment

Removal

1 Disconnect the battery negative lead (see Chapter 5A).
2 Open the door and support it with a jack or axle stand, using rags to protect the paintwork.
3 Disconnect the front door electrical wiring. Pull back the rubber boot, then use a small screwdriver to release the clip and unplug the connector. If removing a rear door, release the convoluted sleeve from the door pillar, pull the connector from the pillar, depress the clip and separate the two halves of the connector **(see illustrations)**.
4 Release the door check strap by undoing the bolt securing it to the pillar bracket.
5 Undo the upper and lower hinge bolts at the pillar **(see illustrations)**.
6 With the help of an assistant, lift the door upwards to disengage the hinge pins, then remove the door.

Refitting and adjustment

7 Refit the door by reversing the removal operations.
8 On some models Volvo technicians use a special tool to adjust the position of the door hinges. If adjustment is required the task should be entrusted to a Volvo dealer or suitably-equipped specialist.

10 Door interior trim panel – removal and refitting

Removal

1 Ensure the ignition is switched off. Wait

8.3 Bonnet lock cable and wiring plug (arrowed)

9.3b Pull back the sleeve, release the clip and disconnect the rear door connector

at least one minute for any stored electrical energy to dissipate before commencing work.
2 Prise off the trim on the inside of the door grab handle, then prise up the handle and switch assembly **(see illustrations)**.

10.2a Prise away the inner trim from the door grab handle (arrowed) . . .

10.3a In the handle aperture, undo the 2 screws – front door (arrowed) . . .

9.3a Prise up the clip and disconnect the front door harness

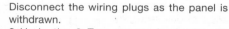

9.5 Undo the door hinge bolts (arrowed)

Disconnect the wiring plugs as the panel is withdrawn.
3 Undo the 2 Torx screws in the handle aperture **(see illustrations)**.
4 The door trim panel is further secured

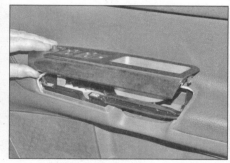

10.2b . . . then prise up the switch panel/ handle

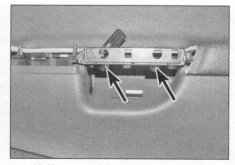

10.3b . . . and 2 screws – rear door (arrowed)

10.4a Metal clip (arrowed) securing the top of the door trim panel

10.4b Plastic clips (arrowed) secure the sides and bottom of the door trim panel

10.4c Pull the panel from the door to release the clips

10.6 Disconnect the interior handle cable as the panel is withdrawn

by metal and plastic clips around the base and front/rear/top edges of the panel. Use a flat-bladed tool to carefully prise the panel from the door frame **(see illustrations)**.

5 Lift the panel over the door lock knob, then

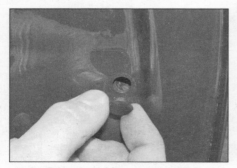

11.2a Prise the rubber grommet from the end of the door

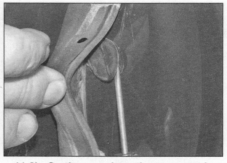

11.2b On the rear door, the grommet is behind the rubber weatherstrip

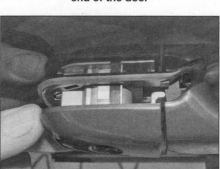

11.3a Pull out the lock cylinder/blanking plug . . .

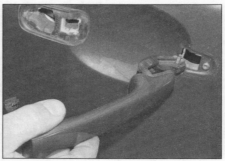

11.3b . . . outer handle . . .

pull the panel away from the door sufficiently to gain access to the various wiring plugs/cables behind it. Noting their locations, disconnect the wiring from the window, door mirror and door locking switches (where applicable).

6 Release the clips and disconnect the cable end from the interior handle (where applicable) **(see illustration)**.

Refitting

7 Refitting is a reversal of removal. Obtain and fit new fasteners for the base/edges of the panel if any were broken during removal. Check the operation of all switches before finally fitting the trim panel into place.

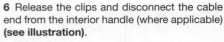

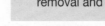

11 Door handle and lock components – removal and refitting

Outer handle

Removal

1 On models with the keyless entry system, disconnect the battery negative lead as described in Chapter 5A.

2 Prise out the rubber grommet from the end of the door **(see illustrations)**.

3 Undo the Torx screw in the grommet aperture a maximum of 5 complete turns, and pull the lock cylinder/blanking plug, outer handle and rubber seal from the door **(see illustrations)**.

4 On models with the keyless entry system, pull the outer handle wiring plug forwards and secure it in the 'parking position' before disconnecting it. Otherwise there is a risk the connector will fall into the door and be difficult to retrieve without removing the door trim panel.

Refitting

5 Refitting is a reversal of removal.

Front door lock cylinder

6 Remove of the lock cylinder is described within the outer door handle removal procedure described previously in this Section.

Front door lock assembly

Removal

7 Lower the front window by approximately 290mm.

8 Disconnect the battery negative lead as described in Chapter 5A.

9 Remove the door window as described

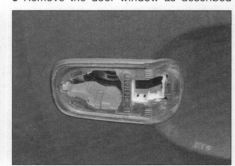

11.3c . . . and rubber seal

in Section 12, but instead of removing the window slide it fully upwards and tape it in position.

10 Remove the outer door handle as described in this Section.

11 Disconnect the door mirror wiring plug from the door cassette assembly.

12 Remove the 3 Torx bolts at the rear end of the door securing the lock mechanism, and the single Torx screw at the base of the glass guide **(see illustration)**.

13 Undo the Torx screw securing the outer door handle frame **(see illustration)**.

14 Undo the 9 screws securing the door cassette assembly **(see illustration)**.

15 Prise up the locking catch and disconnect the wiring plug from the door **(see illustration 9.3a)**.

16 Reach inside the door frame, slide up the plastic catch, then squeeze together the clips on the outside and push the connector/harness into the door **(see illustration)**.

17 Manoeuvre the cassette assembly from the door **(see illustration)**.

18 Remove the lock button, disconnect the lock wiring plug, and the interior handle release cable from the lock mechanism **(see illustrations)**.

19 Drill out the rivet at the base of the mechanism **(see illustration)**.

20 Unclip the outer handle mechanism from the cassette, and disconnect the 2 release cables **(see illustrations)**.

21 Unhook the lock mechanism, and manoeuvre it from the cassette assembly.

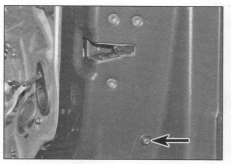

11.12 Undo the 3 Torx bolts securing the lock, and the single screw at the base of the glass guide (arrowed)

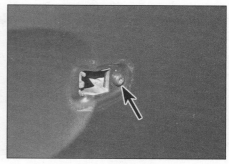

11.13 Outer door handle frame retaining screw (arrowed)

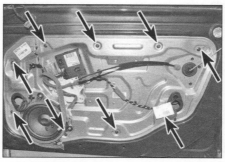

11.14 The door cassette is secured by 9 screws (arrowed)

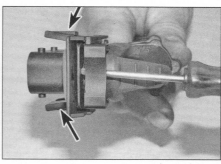

11.16 Prise up the catch, squeeze together the clips (arrowed) and pull the connector into the door – shown removed from door for clarity

11.17 Manoeuvre the cassette from the door

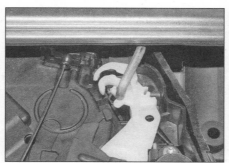

11.18a Disconnect the lock button rod . . .

11.18b . . . then prise out the clip (arrowed) and disconnect the lock wiring plug

11.19 Remove the rivet at the base of the lock (arrowed)

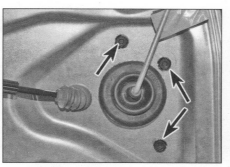

11.20a Release the 3 clips (arrowed) . . .

11.20b . . . then disconnect the 2 cables from the lock

11.28 Rear door lock Torx bolts

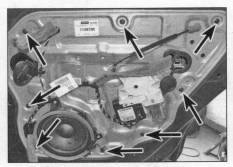

11.29 The rear door cassette is secured by 8 screws (arrowed)

11.30 Peel back the gaiter and disconnect the lock button rod

Refitting

22 Refitting is a reversal of the removal procedure. Check for correct operation before refitting the door trim.

Rear door lock assembly

Removal

23 Lower the rear window by approximately 150mm.
24 Disconnect the battery negative lead as described in Chapter 5A.
25 Remove the door window as described in Section 12, but instead of removing the window slide it fully upwards and tape it in position.
26 Remove the outer door handle as described in this Section.
27 Undo the Torx screw securing the outer handle frame to the door (see illustration 11.13).
28 Remove the 3 Torx bolts at the rear end

of the door securing the lock mechanism (see illustration).
29 Undo the 8 screws securing the door cassette assembly (see illustration).
30 Peel back the rubber gaiter and detach the lock button (see illustration).
31 Pull back the gaiter and disconnect the door wiring plug from the pillar, then press the harness and sleeve into the door (see illustration 9.3b).
32 Manoeuvre the cassette assembly from the door (see illustration).
33 Disconnect the lock wiring plug, and the interior handle release cable from the lock mechanism (see illustration).
34 Drill out the rivet at the base of the mechanism (see illustration).
35 Disconnect the outer handle release cable (see illustration).
36 Unhook the lock mechanism, and manoeuvre it from the cassette assembly.

Refitting

37 Refitting is a reversal of the removal procedure. Check for correct operation before refitting the door trim.

Interior handles

38 Both the front and rear interior handles are integral with the door trim panels, and not available separately.

12 Door window glass, motor, and regulator - removal and refitting

Front door window regulator

Removal

1 Lower the front window by approximately 290mm.
2 Disconnect the battery negative lead as described in Chapter 5A.
3 Remove the door window as described in this Section. However, instead of removing the window slide it fully upwards and tape it in position.
4 Remove the outer door handle as described in the previous Section.
5 Disconnect the door mirror wiring plug from the door cassette assembly.
6 Remove the 3 bolts at the rear end of the door securing the lock mechanism, and the single screw at the base of the glass guide (see illustration 11.12).
7 Undo the Torx screw securing the outer handle frame to the door (see illustration 11.13).
8 Undo the 9 screws securing the door cassette assembly (see illustration 11.14).
9 Prise up the locking catch and disconnect the wiring plug from the door (see illustration 9.3a).
10 Reach inside the door frame, slide up the plastic catch, then squeeze together the clips on the outside and push the connector/harness into the door (see illustration 11.16).
11 Manoeuvre the cassette assembly from the door (see illustration 11.17).
12 Drill out the four rivets, and manoeuvre the regulator assembly from the cassette (see illustration).

11.32 Manoeuvre the cassette assembly from the door

11.33 Disconnect the cable from the lock

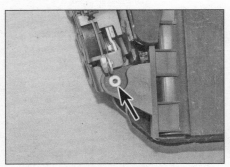

11.34 Drill out the rivet (arrowed)

11.35 Disconnect the outer handle release cable

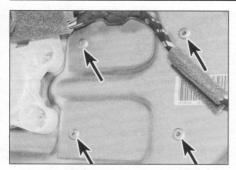

12.12 Drill out the rivets (arrowed) and remove the window regulator

12.23 Rear window regulator retaining rivets (arrowed)

12.27 Prise open the covers and slacken the clamp screws (arrowed) 2 turns

12.28 Manoeuvre the glass upwards from the door

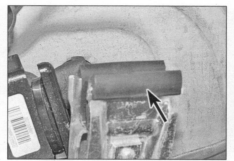

12.29a The clamp rubber should be renewed (arrowed) . . .

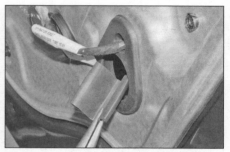

12.29b . . . this can be done working through the cassette aperture using thin-nosed pliers

Refitting

13 Refitting is a reversal of the removal procedure. If a new regulator has been fitted, before use, the window position may need to be initialised. This can only be carried out using Volvo test equipment. Entrust this task to a Volvo dealer or suitably-equipped specialist.

Rear door window regulator

Removal

14 Lower the rear window by approximately 150mm.
15 Disconnect the battery negative lead as described in Chapter 5A.
16 Remove the door window as described in this Section, but instead of removing the window slide it fully upwards and tape it in position.
17 Remove the outer door handle as described in the previous Section.
18 Remove the 3 bolts at the rear end of the door securing the lock mechanism **(see illustration 11.28)**.
19 Undo the 8 screws securing the door cassette assembly **(see illustration 11.29)**.
20 Peel back the rubber gaiter and detach the lock button **(see illustration 11.30)**.
21 Pull back the gaiter and disconnect the door wiring plug from the pillar, then press the harness and sleeve into the door.
22 Manoeuvre the cassette assembly from the door **(see illustration 11.32)**.
23 Drill out the 4 rivets, and manoeuvre the regulator from the cassette **(see illustration)**.

Refitting

24 Refitting is a reversal of the removal

procedure. If a new regulator has been fitted, before use, the window position may need to be initialised. This can only be carried out using Volvo test equipment. Entrust this task to a Volvo dealer or suitably-equipped specialist.

Front door window glass

Removal

25 Lower the window by approximately 290mm.
26 Remove the door inner trim panel as described in Section 10.
27 Prise open the plastic covers, and slacken the window clamp screws 2 turns only **(see illustration)**.
28 Pull the window upwards and manoeuvre it from the door **(see illustration)**.
29 The rear window clamp rubber should be renewed if the window is removed. Use a pair of thin-nosed pliers, and pull the rubber through the access hole in the cassette assembly **(see illustrations)**.

12.36a Prise up the outer rubber strip . . .

Refitting

30 If removed, fit a new rubber into the rear window clamp using thin-nosed pliers, then use a long, flat tool to push the rubber into place in the clamp.
31 Manoeuvre the glass into position, ensuring it's central in the clamping rubbers.
32 Tighten the clamping screws securely, and refit the plastic covers.
33 The remainder of refitting is a reversal of removal.

Rear door window glass

Removal

34 Lower the window approximately 150mm.
35 Remove the door inner trim panel as described in Section 10.
36 Use a flat-bladed tool to prise out and remove the inner and outer rubber strips either side of the window **(see illustrations)**.
37 Carefully pull the inner and outer triangular

12.36b . . . and the inner rubber strip

12.37a Pull the outer triangular trim away to release the push-on clips . . .

12.37b . . . followed by the inner trim

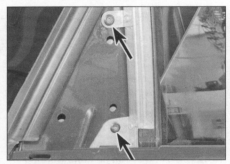

12.38 Drill out the 2 rivets (arrowed)

12.39 Prise out the plastic covers and slacken the clamp screws 3 turns (arrowed)

trims from the rear corner of the window frame **(see illustrations)**.
38 Drill out the 2 rivets securing the rear window guide **(see illustration)**.
39 Slacken the window clamping screws 3 complete revolutions **(see illustration)**.

40 Release the inner rubber seal at the rear of the door, then pull up and remove the window trim and glass channel **(see illustrations)**.
41 Lift up the glass and manoeuvre it from the door.

12.40a Prise out the rubber seal . . .

12.40b . . . then lift out the glass channel

12.45 Front window electric motor retaining bolts (arrowed)

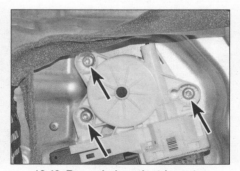

12.49 Rear window electric motor retaining bolts (arrowed)

Refitting

42 Refitting is a reversal of removal, noting the following points:
a) *Tighten the window glass clamping screws securely.*
b) *Check the position of the window before completely refitting the door trim panel. If necessary the position can be adjusted by slackening the clamp screws and repositioning the glass.*

Front window electric motor

Removal

43 Remove the door inner trim panel as described in Section 10.
44 Note their fitted positions, then disconnect the 3 wiring plugs from the motor.
45 Undo the 3 retaining bolts and pull the motor assembly from the regulator **(see illustration)**.

Refitting

46 Refitting is a reversal of removal. Note that if a new motor assembly has been fitted, software must be downloaded to the control unit. Consult a Volvo dealer or specialist.

Rear window electric motor

Removal

47 Remove the door inner trim panel as described in Section 10.
48 Disconnect the wiring plug from the motor.
49 Undo the 3 retaining bolts and pull the motor assembly from the regulator **(see illustration)**.

Refitting

50 Refitting is a reversal of removal. Note that if a new motor assembly has been fitted, software must be downloaded to the control unit. Consult a Volvo dealer or specialist.

13 Boot lid – removal and refitting

Removal

1 Remove the warning triangle from the trim panel (where fitted).
2 Carefully pull the grab handle recess trim from the boot panel **(see illustration)**.

13.2 Pull the grab handle recess from the trim panel

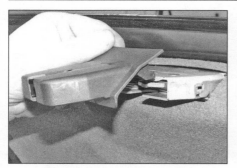

13.3 Pull the boot lock cover from place

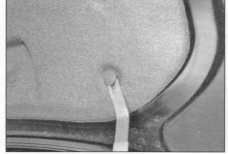

13.4 Prise out the 10 clips

13.7 Mark around the hinges, and undo the screws (arrowed)

3 Pull the boot lock plastic cover from place **(see illustration)**.
4 Release the 10 clips and remove the boot inner trim panel **(see illustration)**.
5 Note their fitted positions, then disconnect the boot wiring plugs, and release the loom grommet from the boot lid.
6 Remove the boot lid support struts as described in Section 18.
7 Mark around the hinges to aid alignment on refitting, then undo the two screws each side securing the hinges to the boot lid **(see illustration)**. Have an assistant support the boot lid, pull the wiring loom out from the boot lid as it's withdrawn.

Refitting

8 Refitting is a reversal of removal. Check the fit and closure of the boot lid, and adjust if necessary.

---

14 Boot lid lock components – removal and refitting

Removal

1 Remove the boot lid interior trim panel as described in Section 13, and pull off the plastic cover over the boot lock if fitted.
2 Disconnect the lock wiring plug, undo the 3 screws, and withdraw the lock from the tailgate **(see illustration)**.
3 To remove the exterior handle, open the boot lid, undo the 4 screws, and pull the

handle assembly from position. Disconnect the wiring plug as the handle is withdrawn.

Refitting

4 Refitting is a reversal of removal.

---

15 Tailgate interior trim panel – removal and refitting

Removal

1 Open the tailgate and use a flat-bladed tool to remove the grab handle **(see illustration)**.
2 To remove the lower trim panel, release the 6 clips - there are 4 at the upper edge of the panel nearest the window, and 2 at the lower edge **(see illustration)**.
3 To remove the upper trim panel, remove

the lower panel as described above. Release the clip at each side and the 4 clips at the top edge of the tailgate **(see illustrations)**.

Refitting

4 Refitting is a reversal of removal.

---

16 Tailgate – removal and refitting

Removal

1 Open the tailgate, and remove the interior trim panels as described in Section 15.
2 Disconnect the wiring plugs for the lock mechanism, wiper motor, and high-level brake light, and unclip the wiring harness from the tailgate. Disconnect the washer jet hose **(see illustration)**.

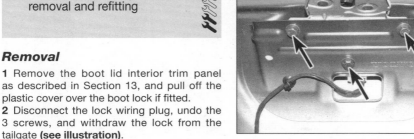

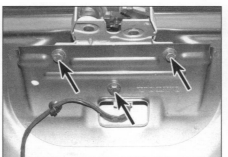

14.2 Undo the boot lock bolts (arrowed)

15.1 Pull the grab handle trim downwards

15.2 Pull the trim panel away from the tailgate to release the clips

15.3a Pull the sides of the upper trim towards each other . . .

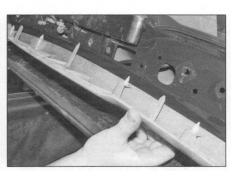

15.3b . . . then pull the trim away from the hinges

16.2 Disconnect the wiring plugs and the earth connections

3 Have an assistant support the tailgate, then disconnect the tailgate struts as described in Section 18.

4 Make alignment marks between the tailgate hinges and the bodywork to aid refitting, then undo the hinge bolts and remove the tailgate **(see illustration)**. Feed the harness through the tailgate as it's withdrawn.

Refitting

5 Refitting is a reversal of removal.

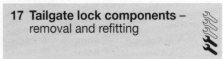

17 Tailgate lock components – removal and refitting

Removal

1 Remove the tailgate lower trim panel as described in Section 15.

2 Disconnect the lock wiring plug, undo the

17.2 Tailgate lock retaining bolts (arrowed)

18.1 Prise off the clips and detach the ends of the support struts from the ball-stud mountings

16.4 Make alignment marks then undo the tailgate hinge bolts (arrowed)

3 screws securing the lock mechanism to the tailgate and withdraw the lock **(see illustration)**.

3 To remove the exterior handle, open the tailgate, undo the 4 screws, and pull the handle assembly from position. Disconnect the wiring plug as the handle is withdrawn **(see illustrations)**.

Refitting

4 Refitting is a reversal of removal.

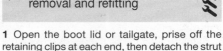

18 Boot lid/tailgate support struts – removal and refitting

1 Open the boot lid or tailgate, prise off the retaining clips at each end, then detach the strut from the mounting balljoints **(see illustration)**.

2 Refitting is a reversal of removal. Note that the struts contain gas under pressure - if new ones have been fitted, the old ones should be

17.3a Undo the handle assembly Torx screws (arrowed)

20.2 Carefully release the mirror glass from the clips

disposed of safely, and should on no account be incinerated.

19 Windscreen and other fixed glass – removal and refitting

Special equipment and techniques are needed for successful removal and refitting of the windscreen, rear window and side windows. Have the work carried out by a Volvo dealer or a windscreen specialist.

20 Mirrors and associated components – removal and refitting

⚠ *Warning: If the mirror glass is broken, wear gloves to protect your hands. This is good advice, in fact, even if the glass is not broken, due to the risk of glass breakage.*

Door mirror glass

1 Pivot the mirror glass into the mirror housing as far as possible on the lower edge.

2 Insert a blunt, flat-bladed tool behind the upper edge of the glass and prise the glass from the mounting. Take care – excessive force will cause the glass to break. Disconnect the wiring plugs as the glass is withdrawn **(see illustration)**.

3 Refitting is a reversal of removal.

Door mirror motor

4 Remove the mirror glass as described above.

5 Undo the central nut. Disconnect the wiring,

17.3b Disconnect the wiring plug as the assembly is removed

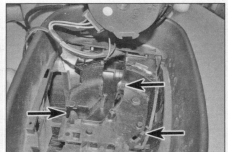

20.5 Mirror motor retaining clips (arrowed)

and using a small screwdriver release the 3 clips that secure the motor to the mirror housing **(see illustration)**.

6 Refitting is a reversal of removal.

Door mirror cover

7 Remove the mirror glass as described previously.

8 Insert a small screwdriver into the access hole in the mirror housing and release the clip **(see illustration)**.

9 Carefully prise the cover from the mirror.

10 Refitting is a reversal of removal ensuring the lip of the cover fits correctly around the edge of the mirror housing.

Door mirror (complete unit)

11 Remove the door interior trim panel as described in Section 10 and disconnect the mirror wiring plug inside the door.

12 Support the mirror, undo the retaining bolt, and withdraw the mirror from the door **(see illustration)**. Release the rubber grommet from the door as the mirror is withdrawn.

13 Refitting is a reversal of removal.

Interior mirror

14 Prise apart the 2 halves of the cover over the mirror base/sensor **(see illustration)**.

15 Disconnect the mirror wiring plug (where applicable).

16 Twist the mirror base 90° and remove it from the windscreen mounting **(see illustration)**.

Note: *Some models may be fitted with an Electronic Compass. Recalibration of the unit may be required on refitting and you should refer to a Volvo dealer.*

17 Refitting is a reversal of removal.

Blind Spot Information System

18 An optional Blind Spot Information System (BLIS) may be fitted to warn the driver of a vehicle in the 'blind spot' area not visible in the door mirror on both sides of the car. The system uses digital camera technology to detect a vehicle in the 'blind spot' area on each side of the car and illuminate a warning light on the inside door panel next to the mirror. A switch on the facia panel allows the driver to enable the system when required. It should be noted that the system does not

20.8 Release the clip and pull the cover forwards

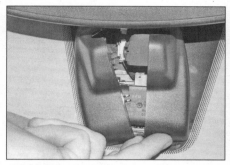
20.14 Prise apart the mirror base covers

react to bicycles or mopeds, and at night-time will only react to vehicles with headlamps switched on.

19 The camera is located in the door mirror lower cowl and may be removed by first removing the door mirror cover as described earlier in this Section.

20 The warning light is located on the triangular trim panel over the door mirror mounting nut, and may be removed with reference to the door interior trim panel removal procedure described in Section 10 of this Chapter.

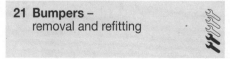

21 Bumpers – removal and refitting

Note: *The bumpers consist of several sections, and once the bumper assembly has*

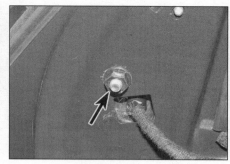
20.12 Exterior mirror retaining nut (arrowed)

20.16 Twist the mirror base 90° to detach it from the windscreen

been removed as described below, further dismantling can take place. Refer to a Volvo dealer for advice on which sections are available separately.

Front bumper removal

1 Open the bonnet and disconnect the battery negative terminal as described in Chapter 5A.

2 Working underneath the vehicle, release the tabs or screws that secure the lower baffle to the radiator support bracket **(see illustration)**.

3 Press in the centre pins and remove the 5 plastic expansion rivets at the top edge of the bumper **(see illustrations)**.

4 Undo the Torx bolt at each end of the bumper at the top edge **(see illustration)**.

5 Undo the 5 screws/bolts securing the bumper to the wheel arch liner each side **(see illustration)**.

6 Where fitted, carefully prise the headlamp

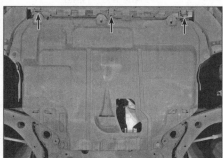
21.2 A number of tabs secure the lower baffle to the radiator support bracket (3 are arrowed)

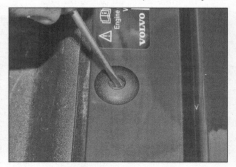
21.3a Push in the centre pins . . .

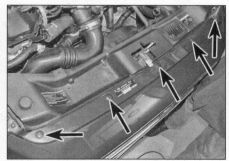
21.3b . . . and prise out the 5 plastic rivets (arrowed)

21.4 Undo the Torx screw in each upper corner (arrowed)

21.5 The bumper is secured to the wheel arch liner with 5 bolts (arrowed)

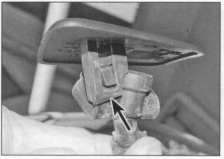

21.6 Release the clip (arrowed) on the underside securing the headlight washer jet cover

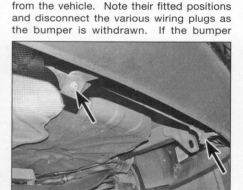

21.7 Remove the headlight, and release the bumper catch (arrowed) with a screwdriver

washer jet covers from the bumper, then gently pull them forwards. Press up the clip in the underside and remove the covers **(see illustration)**.

7 With the help of an assistant, pull the

bumper sides outwards slightly to release the clips, then pull it forward and remove it from the vehicle. Note their fitted positions and disconnect the various wiring plugs as the bumper is withdrawn. If the bumper

is reluctant to release from the clips under the headlights, remove the headlights as described in Chapter 12, and release the catches with a screwdriver **(see illustration)**.

Front bumper refitting

8 Refitting is a reversal of removal taking care to ensure that the bumper aligns correctly with surrounding body panels.

Rear bumper removal

S40 models

9 Open the boot lid, and undo the screw at each side of the boot lid aperture **(see illustration)**.

10 Undo the 2 screws on the underside of the bumper **(see illustration)**.

11 Undo the 5 screws each side securing the bumper to the wheel arch liner **(see illustration)**.

12 With the help of an assistant, pull the bumper sides outwards slightly to release the clips at the top edge each side, then pull it rearwards and remove it from the vehicle. Note their fitted positions and disconnect any wiring plugs as the bumper is withdrawn.

V50 models

13 Open the tailgate, and undo the screw at each side of the tailgate aperture **(see illustration)**.

14 Undo the 2 screws on the underside of the bumper **(see illustration)**.

15 Undo the 5 screws each side securing the bumper to the wheel arch liner **(see illustration)**.

16 With the help of an assistant, pull the

21.9 Undo the 2 Torx screws (arrowed) each side of the boot aperture

21.10 Remove the 2 Torx screws (arrowed) on the underside of the bumper

21.11 5 Torx screws secure the bumper to the wheel arch liner

21.13 Remove the Torx screw each side in the tailgate aperture (arrowed)

21.14 Undo the 2 Torx screws on the underside (arrowed)

21.15 5 Torx screws secure the wheel arch liner to the bumper

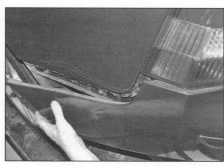

21.16 Pull out the top edges to release the clips

bumper sides outwards slightly to release the clips at the top edge each side, then pull it rearwards and remove it from the vehicle **(see illustration)**. Note their fitted positions and disconnect any wiring plugs as the bumper is withdrawn.

Rear bumper refitting - all models

17 Refitting is a reversal of removal taking care to ensure that the bumper aligns correctly with surrounding body panels.

22 Front grille panel – removal and refitting

Removal

1 Volvo say the grille can be removed with the bumper in place. In practice this proved

difficult and there is a risk of damage to the grille and surrounding paintwork, so we recommend removing the bumper first. Using a flat-bladed tool, release the retaining clips around the edge of the grille - there are 4 at the top, 4 at the bottom, and 1 each side towards the top. Remove the grille **(see illustration)**.

Refitting

2 Refit by reversing the removal operations, ensuring the clips are securely engaged.

23 Front seat and motors – removal and refitting

Note: *All models are equipped with a SIPS airbag, fitted into the side of the front seat backrest, as part of the Side Impact Protection System; refer to Chapter 12 for further information on the SRS and SIPS systems.*

Front Seat

Removal

1 Raise the seat base to its maximum height. Ensure that the ignition is switched off, then disconnect the battery negative lead as described in Chapter 5A. Wait at least 5 minutes for any residual electrical energy to dissipate before proceeding.
2 It's advisable to 'earth' the seat frame before removal to protect against static electricity discharge. Strip the insulation from both ends of a long length of electrical cable, and secure one end to the metal parts of the seat frame

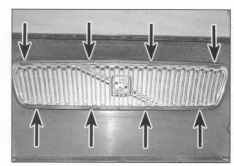

22.1 Front grille retaining clips (arrowed)

and the other end to a bare metal part of the vehicle body or similar.
3 Undo the bolt under the front of the seat and disconnect the wiring plug **(see illustration)**. Take great care not to damage the connectors.
4 On the passenger's seat, undo the screw at the front edge of the seat side panel **(see illustration)** and pivot the front of the panel upwards to access the seat belt clip **(see illustration)**. The seat belt clip on the driver's side can be accessed without removing the side panel.
5 Use a small screwdriver to depress the quick-release catch through the hole in the cover, and pull the seat belt lower anchorage from the outside of the seat **(see illustrations)**.
6 Remove the plastic covers and undo the 4 seat mounting bolts **(see illustrations)**.
7 Lift the seat and manoeuvre it from the

23.3 The connector is secured by a single bolt (arrowed)

23.4a Undo the screw (arrowed) securing the seat side panel

23.4b Pivot the side panel upwards

23.5a Depress the clip and release the outer seat belt mounting – driver's side . . .

23.5b . . . and passenger's side

23.6a Slide the plastic covers from the rails . . .

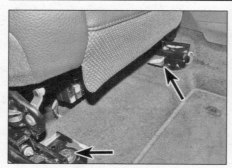

23.6b . . . then undo the seat retaining bolts (arrowed)

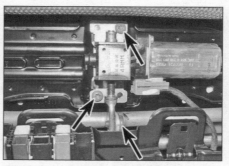

23.12 Front seat height adjustment motor bolts (arrowed)

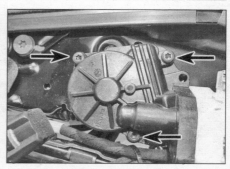

23.16 Rear height adjustment motor outer bolts (arrowed)

23.19 Front-to-rear motor retaining screws (arrowed)

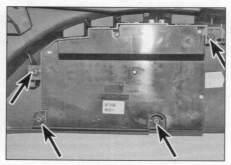

23.23 Power seat module retaining screws (arrowed)

vehicle. As the seats are very heavy, the help of an assistant would be a good idea. Note their fitted positions, and disconnect any wiring plugs as the seat is withdrawn. Take great care not to damage the connectors.

Refitting

8 Locate the seat over the guide pins, reconnect the wiring, and insert the retaining bolts. Tighten the bolts securely and refit the bolt covers.

9 Reconnect the seat belt lower anchorage, ensuring that the catch is fully engaged. Refit the seat side panel where removed.

10 Make sure that no-one is inside the car, then reconnect the battery negative lead.

Seat motors

Front height adjustment motor

11 Remove the seat as previously described in this Section.

12 Undo the 3 bolts and remove the motor **(see illustration)**. Disconnect the wiring plug as the motor is withdrawn.

13 Refitting is a reversal of removal.

Rear height adjustment motor

14 Raise the seat to its highest position (if possible).

15 Undo the screw at the front edge of the seat side panel, then pull the panel upwards from place.

16 Release the cable tie securing the wiring harness to the motor, then undo the 4 bolts (1 on the inside edge) and remove the motor **(see illustration)**. Disconnect the wiring plug as the motor is withdrawn.

17 Refitting is a reversal of removal

Front-to-rear adjustment motor

18 Remove the front seat as described previously in this section.

19 Undo the 2 screws and remove the motor and cables **(see illustration)**. Disconnect the wiring plug as the motor is withdrawn.

20 Refitting is a reversal of removal.

Power seat module

21 Raise the seat to its highest position (if possible).

22 Undo the screw at the front edge of the seat side panel, then pull the panel upwards from place.

23 Undo the 4 retaining screws and detach the module from the side panel **(see illustration)**, disconnecting the wiring plugs as the module is withdrawn.

24 Refitting is a reversal of removal. if a new module has been fitted, suitable software must be downloaded. Consult a Volvo dealer or specialist.

24 Rear seat – removal and refitting

Removal

1 Pivot the seat cushion forwards, then undo the retaining bolts and remove the cushion **(see illustration)**.

2 Grip the upper edge of the side cushion, and pull it forwards, then upwards from position **(see illustration)**.

3 Undo the backrest hinge clip bolt (located at the base of the backrest, closest to the door), and prise up the clip **(see illustration)**.

24.1 Prise off the covers and undo the seat retaining bolts

24.2 Pull the top edge forwards, then lift the side cushion from place

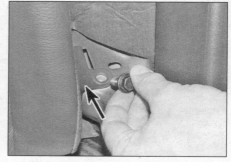

24.3 Undo the bolt and lift the clip (arrowed)

4 Lift the backrest from place noting how the hinge pins interlock **(see illustration)**. To remove the '60%' backrest, undo the bolt securing the seat belt and stalk to the vehicle floor.

Refitting

5 Refit by reversing the removal operations.

25 Interior trim –
removal and refitting

Note: *Refer to earlier Sections of this Chapter for specific procedures covering door and tailgate interior trim panels.*

General

1 The interior trim panels are secured using either screws or various types of trim fasteners, usually studs or clips.
2 Check that there are no other panels overlapping the one to be removed, or other components hindering removal; usually there is a sequence that has to be followed, and this will only become obvious on close inspection.
3 Some of the interior panels will additionally be retained by the screws which are used to secure other items, such as the grab handles.
4 Remove all visible retainers, such as screws, noting that these may be hidden under small plastic caps. If the panel will not come free, it is held by internal clips or fasteners. These are usually situated around the edges of the panel, and can be prised up to release them; note, however, that they can break quite easily, so new ones should be available. The best way of releasing such clips is to use a large flat-bladed screwdriver or other wide-bladed tool. Note that in many cases, the adjacent sealing strip must be prised back to release a panel.
5 When removing a panel, **never** use excessive force or the panel may be damaged; always check carefully that all fasteners or other relevant components have been removed or released before attempting to withdraw a panel.
6 Refitting is a reversal of removal; secure the fasteners by pressing them firmly into place and ensure that all disturbed components are correctly secured to prevent rattles.

Carpets

7 The passenger compartment floor carpet is in three sections; front left, front right and rear, and is secured at the sides by the front and rear sill trim panels.
8 Carpet removal and refitting is reasonably straightforward, but is very time-consuming because all adjoining trim panels must be removed first, as must components such as the seats and seat belt lower anchorages.

Headlining

9 The headlining is clipped to the roof, and can be withdrawn only once all fittings such

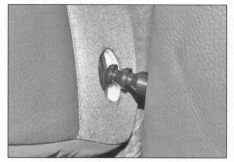
24.4 The seat hinge pins interlock

as grab handles, sun visors, sunroof (if fitted), fixed window glass, and related trim panels have been removed and the relevant sealing strips have been prised clear.
10 Note that headlining removal and refitting requires considerable skill and experience if it is to be carried out without damage, and is therefore best entrusted to a dealer or automotive upholstery specialist.

Rear parcel shelf

S40 models only

11 Release the catches and fold down the rear seat backrests.
12 Carefully prise out and remove the luggage compartment light unit on the underside of the parcel shelf **(see illustration)**.
13 Undo the bolts securing the lower ends of the outer rear seat belts.
14 Reach underneath and release the clips

25.12 Prise out the luggage compartment light

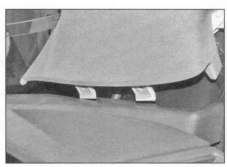
25.18 Note how the lower edge of the A-pillar trim hooks into place

each side by pressing the shelf upwards adjacent to the suspension turrets **(see illustration)**.
15 Pull the shelf forwards a little, then prise out the seat belt guide trims and thread the belts through the shelf as it's withdrawn.
16 Refitting is a reversal of removal.

A-pillar trims

17 Pull the rubber weatherstrip from the door aperture adjacent to the A-pillar.
18 Pull the top of the A-pillar trim inwards towards the centre of the passenger cabin, then unhook the clip at the top of the trim **(see illustration)**.
19 Refitting is a reversal of removal. If any clips are damaged, new ones should be used when refitting, so as not to impair the inflatable safety curtain performance.

B-pillar trims

20 Pull the front door sill trim panel straight up to release it from the retaining clips. Repeat the procedure on the rear door sill trim panel **(see illustration)**.
21 Move the front seat as far forward as possible, then pull the rubber weatherstrips from the door apertures adjacent to the B-pillar.
22 Depress the quick-release catch at the side and remove the seat belt lower anchorage from the outside of the seat **(see illustrations 23.5a and 23.5b)**.
23 Carefully prise out the cover, then undo the retaining screw at the top of the upper B-pillar trim **(see illustration)**.

25.14 Press the parcel shelf upwards to release the clips by the suspension turrets

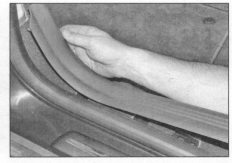
25.20 Pull the sill trim upwards to release the clips

25.23 Prise out the cover and undo the screw at the top of the pillar trim (arrowed)

25.24a Pull the lower edge of the pillar trim inwards . . .

25.24b . . . and the upper trim downwards/ inwards

25.25a Depress the clip (arrowed) to separate the two halves of the pillar trim

25.25b Release the clips and detach the seat belt aperture trim

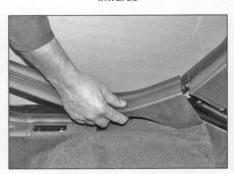

25.28 Pull the sill trim panel upwards to release the clips

24 Pull the lower edge of the lower B-pillar trim in towards the centre of the cabin to release the clips, then pull the upper trim inwards/downwards to release the clips **(see illustrations)**.

25 Press in the clip to separate the upper trim from the lower. Prise out the aperture trim and feed the seat belt through the panel as it's withdrawn **(see illustrations)**.
26 Refitting is a reversal of removal.

C-pillar trims

S40 models

27 Fold down the rear seat backrest, grip the upper edge of the side cushion, and pull it forwards, then upwards from position **(see illustration 24.2)**.
28 Pull the rubber weatherstrip from the door aperture adjacent to the pillar trim panel, then pull the rear door sill trim upwards to release the clips **(see illustration)**.
29 Pull the lower section of the pillar trim in towards the centre of the vehicle to release the push-in clips **(see illustration)**.
30 Pull the top of the rear section of the pillar trim in towards the centre of the vehicle to release the push-in clips, then lift it from place. Slide the 'holder' clip from the panel as it's withdrawn. Note that if at all damaged, the 'holder' clip should be renewed **(see illustrations)**.
31 Pull the front section of the pillar trim inwards to release the push-in clips **(see illustration)**.
32 Refitting is a reversal of removal.

V50 models

33 Fold down the rear seat backrest, grip the upper edge of the side cushion, and pull it forwards, then upwards from position **(see illustration 24.2)**.
34 Pull the rubber weatherstrip from the door aperture adjacent to the pillar trim panel.
35 Pull the lower C-pillar trim panel inwards and release the 4 push-in clips **(see illustration)**.

25.29 The lower section of the pillar trim is secured by 4 push-in clips

25.30a Note the hook at the base of the pillar trim (arrowed)

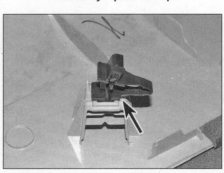

25.30b If the 'holder' clip is damaged during removal, renew it (arrowed)

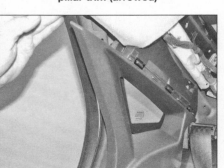

25.31 Pull the trim inwards to release the clips

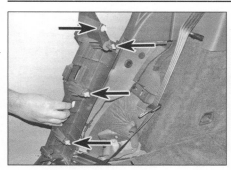

25.35 The panel is retained by 4 push-in clips (arrowed)

25.36 Prise out the cover and undo the screw (arrowed)

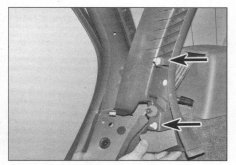

25.37 2 push-in clips secure the C-pillar trim panel (arrowed)

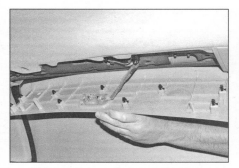

25.39 Pull down the central tailgate aperture trim panel

25.42 The D-pillar trim is secured by 4 push-in clips. Note how the top of the trim hooks behind the headlining (arrowed)

25.45 Undo the 2 plastic screws (arrowed)

36 Prise out the cover, and undo the retaining screw at the top of the panel **(see illustration)**.

37 Pull the upper C-pillar trim panel inwards and release the 2 push-in clips **(see illustration)**.

38 Refitting is a reversal of removal.

D-pillar trims

V50 models only

39 Remove the cant rail trim panel located at the rear of the headlining. Carefully release the retaining clips and remove the panel, disconnecting the wiring plug for the light unit as the panel is withdrawn **(see illustration)**.

40 Pull the rubber weatherstrip from the tailgate aperture adjacent to the pillar trim.

41 Starting from the rear edge, pull the top, side trim panel away from position a little - there is no need to remove it completely **(see illustration 25.56)**.

42 Pull the top pillar trim panel in towards the centre of the vehicle, disengaging it from the guide by the headlining as it's withdrawn and lower it from position **(see illustration)**.

43 Refitting is a reversal of removal.

Luggage compartment side panel

S40 models

44 Lift out the luggage compartment floor panel.

45 Undo the 2 plastic screws, then prise the boot sill trim panel upwards to release the clips **(see illustration)**.

46 Release the 4 panel-retaining clips in the luggage compartment **(see illustration)**.

47 Fold down the rear seat backrest, then release the retaining clips for the parcel shelf at the suspension turrets **(see illustration**

25.14). Release the clip in the centre of the side panel trim.

48 Lift the panel over the hook at the top and luggage stowage eye at the base, then remove the panel, disconnecting any wiring plugs as it's withdrawn.

49 Refitting is a reversal of removal.

V50 models

50 Lift out the luggage compartment floor panel.

51 Prise open the covers and undo the screw in each, then remove the luggage securing eyes **(see illustration)**.

52 Undo the single bolt securing the panel over the seat belt inertia reel, and remove the panel by pulling it upwards **(see illustration)**.

53 Undo the retaining bolt at the front, upper edge of the side panel **(see illustration)**.

54 Pull away the rubber weatherstrip from the tailgate aperture adjacent to the panel.

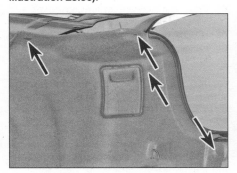

25.46 Release the 4 clips (arrowed)

25.51 Prise open the cover, then undo the screw behind

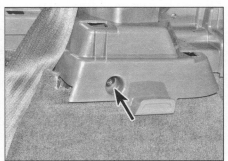

25.52 Remove the Torx bolt (arrowed) at the edge of the panel

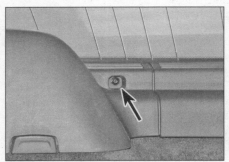

25.53 Undo the Torx bolt (arrowed) and pull the panel upwards to release the clips

25.56 Pull the side panel inwards to release the push-in clips

25.58 Prise the end panel from the passenger's side of the facia, then remove the clip (arrowed)

25.60 Pull the panel in front of the centre console rearwards to release the clips

55 Fold down the rear seat backrest and remove the side cushion as described in Section 24

56 Starting at the rear edge, pull the panel inwards to release the 2 retaining clips, then repeat this at the front edge, and remove

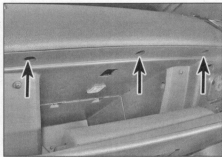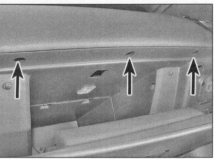

25.62a Undo the 3 screws at the top of the glovebox (arrowed) . . .

it from the luggage compartment **(see illustration)**.

57 Refitting is a reversal of removal, noting that to aid refitment, pull the tailgate sill trim panel upwards on the relevant side before refitting the side panel.

25.62b . . . and the 2 lower screws (arrowed)

Glovebox

58 Carefully prise the passenger side facia end panel from position **(see illustration)**.
59 Prise out the clip at the end of the facia.
60 Using a flat-bladed tool, prise the panel in front of the centre console rearwards to release the push-in clips **(see illustration)**.
61 Apply masking tape to the edge of the centre console to prevent accidental damage whilst the glovebox is withdrawn.
62 Open the glovebox, pull out the rubber mat, then undo the 5 retaining screws and pull the glovebox rearwards to release the 2 clips at the top edge. Disconnect any wiring plugs as the glovebox is withdrawn **(see illustrations)**.
63 If required, undo the 4 screws and remove the inner glovebox.
64 Refitting is a reversal of removal.

Sun visor

65 Prise out the out mounting cover and undo the 2 screws **(see illustration)**.
66 Unclip the sun visor from the inboard mounting and remove it. Disconnect the wiring plug as the sun visor is withdrawn **(see illustration)**.
67 To remove the inboard mounting, prise down the retaining tab and remove the mounting from the headlining **(see illustration)**.
68 Refitting is a reversal of removal.

Grab Handle

69 Hold down the grab handle, prise open the plastic covers and undo the 2 retaining screws **(see illustration)**.
70 Refitting is a reversal of removal.

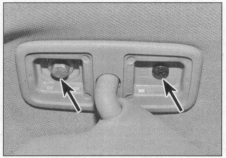

25.65 Sunvisor outer mounting screws (arrowed)

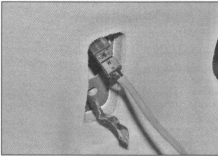

25.66 Pull out the sunvisor wiring, and disconnect the plug

25.67 Prise out the plug, and pull down the inner mounting

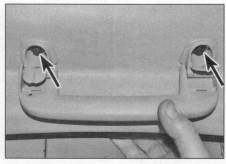

25.69 Prise down the covers, and undo the grab handle retaining screws (arrowed)

Driver's side lower facia panel

71 Carefully prise the driver's side facia end panel from position **(see illustration)**.

72 Remove the panel clip at the end of the facia.

73 Using a flat-bladed tool, prise the panel in front of the centre console rearwards to release the push-in clips.

74 Undo the 3 lower facia panel retaining screws, and release the 2 clips at the top of the panel either side of the steering column surround **(see illustration)**.

75 Pull the lower facia panel downwards and manoeuvre it from the cabin. Disconnect the light unit wiring plug as the panel is withdrawn.

76 Refitting is a reversal of removal.

---

26 Seat belts –
general information, removal and refitting

1 All models are equipped with pyrotechnic front seat belt tensioners as part of the Supplemental Restraint System (SRS). The system is designed to instantaneously take up any slack in the seat belt in the case of a sudden frontal impact, therefore reducing the possibility of injury to the front seat occupants. Each front seat is fitted with the system, the tensioner being situated behind the upper B-pillar trim panel.

2 The seat belt tensioner is triggered, with the driver's and passenger's airbag, by a frontal impact above a predetermined force. Lesser impacts, including impacts from behind, will not trigger the system.

3 When the system is triggered, the explosive gas in the tensioner mechanism retracts and locks the seat belt through a cable which acts on the inertia reel. This prevents the seat belt moving, and keeps the occupant firmly in position in the seat. Once the tensioner has been triggered, the seat belt will be permanently locked and the assembly must be renewed. If any abnormal rattling noises are heard when pulling out or retracting the belt, this also indicates that the tensioner has been triggered.

4 There is a risk of injury if the system is triggered inadvertently when working on

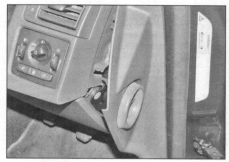

25.71 Remove the facia end panel

the vehicle, and it is therefore strongly recommended that any work involving the seat belt tensioner system is entrusted to a Volvo dealer. Note the following warnings before contemplating any work on the front seat belts.

⚠️ **Warning: Switch off the ignition, disconnect the battery negative lead, and wait for at least 5 minutes for any residual electrical energy to dissipate before starting work involving the front seat belts.**

• **Do not expose the tensioner mechanism to temperatures in excess of 100°C (212°F).**

• **If the tensioner mechanism is dropped, it must be renewed, even it has suffered no apparent damage.**

• **Do not allow any solvents to come into contact with the tensioner mechanism.**

• **Do not attempt to open the tensioner mechanism, as it contains explosive gas.**

• **Tensioners from other vehicles, even from the same model and year, must not be fitted.**

• **Tensioners must be discharged before they are disposed of, but this task should be entrusted to a Volvo dealer or specialist.**

Removal

Front seat belts

5 Switch off the ignition, then disconnect the battery negative lead as described in Chapter 5A. Wait for at least 5 minutes before proceeding.

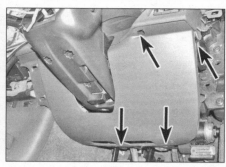

25.74 Lower facia panel screws and clip (arrowed)

6 Remove the appropriate front seat as described in Section 23.

7 Remove the B-pillar trim as described in Section 25.

8 Disconnect the wiring plug, slacken the pyrotechnic tube clamp bolt, then undo the 2 bolts and remove the seat belt inertia reel **(see illustrations)**. This wiring plug should never be disconnected (or reconnected) while the battery negative lead is connected.

Rear seat belts

9 Switch off the ignition then disconnect the battery negative lead as described in Chapter 5A. Wait for at least 5 minutes before proceeding.

Outer seat belts - S40 models

10 Remove the parcel shelf as described in Section 25.

11 Disconnect the pretensioner wiring plug, then undo the retaining nut and lift the inertia reel from place **(see illustration)**. Access to the buckles and floor anchorages is gained by tipping the seat cushion forwards.

Outer seat belts - V50 models

12 Fold down the rear seat backrest, then remove the retaining screw and remove the panel over the inertia reel **(see illustration 25.52)**.

13 Undo the inertia reel retaining nut, and disconnect the wiring plug **(see illustration)**.

14 Undo the seat belt lower anchorage bolt and remove the belt from the cabin.

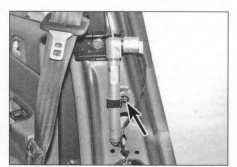

26.8a Pyrotechnic tube clamp bolt (arrowed)

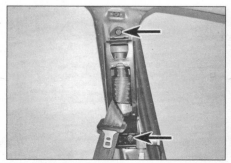

26.8b Seat belt inertia reel mounting bolts (arrowed)

26.11 Undo the inertia reel nut – S40 models

26.13 Rear seat outer belt inertia reel nut (arrowed)

26.15 The centre seat belt buckle is bolted to the floor

26.18a Undo the Torx screw (arrowed) . . .

26.18b . . . then remove the plastic end cap

26.19 Prise out the seat belt guide trim

26.21 The cargo net cover brackets are secured by Allen screws

Centre seat belt

Note: *Removing the centre rear seat belt inertia reels involves removal of the seat cover. Patience and dexterity are required to successfully remove and refit the cover.*

15 Access to the buckles and floor anchorages is gained by tipping the seat cushion forwards **(see illustration)**.

16 To access to the inertia reels, remove the rear seat back, as described in Section 24.

17 Press in the headrest release button, and pull the headrests from the backrest.

18 Undo the Torx screw and remove the plastic end cap from the top of the backrest **(see illustrations)**.

19 Carefully prise up and remove the seat belt guide trim from the top of the backrest **(see illustration)**.

20 Working at the rear of the backrest, slide the cargo net cover to the outside, and remove it.

21 Undo the Allen screws and remove the 2 brackets from the rear of the backrest **(see illustration)**.

22 Prise out the 2 plastic clips and pull the cover from the rear of the backrest **(see illustrations)**.

23 Using a blunt, flat-bladed tool, carefully release the edge of the upholstery from the frame **(see illustration)**.

24 Fold the centre armrest down (where applicable), undo the two retaining Torx screws, and disengage the armrest from the locating lugs **(see illustration)**.

25 Release the armrest aperture fabric from the frame and lift the upholstery and foam upwards **(see illustration)**.

26 Lift out the polystyrene covers, depress the clips and slide out the headrest mounting tubes **(see illustrations)**.

27 Lift up and fold back the seat cover/foam to expose the inertia reel.

28 Squeeze together the sides of the plastic cover over the inertia reel, and remove it.

26.22a Prise out the plastic clips . . .

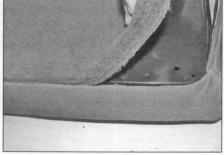

26.22b . . . and pull the backrest cover away

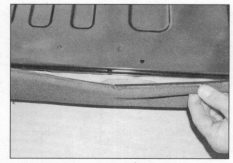

26.23 Carefully prise the upholstery from the frame

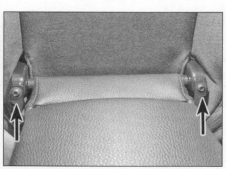

26.24 Undo the Torx screws (arrowed) securing the centre armrest

26.25 Release the armrest fabric from the frame

26.26a Lift away the polystyrene cover . . .

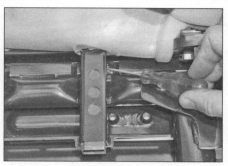
26.26b . . . then depress the clip and pull out the headrest mounting tubes

29 Undo the 2 Torx screws securing the seat belt guide to the seat backrest (see illustration).
30 Undo the retaining nut and manoeuvre the inertia reel from place (see illustration)

Refitting

31 In all cases, refit by reversing the removal operations. Tighten the seat belt mountings to the specified torque. When refitting the seat belts, note the following points:
a) *Reconnect the front seat belt lower anchorage, ensuring that the catch is fully engaged.*
b) *Make sure that no-one is inside the car. Switch on the ignition, then reconnect the battery negative lead. Switch the ignition off, then on again, and check that the airbag warning light comes on, then goes out within 15 seconds.*

27 Centre console – removal and refitting

Removal

1 Fully apply the handbrake, then move the gear or selector lever to neutral – note that it may be necessary to move the gear or selector lever as the console is removed.
2 Ensure the front seats are in the fully lowered, rearmost position.
3 Disconnect the battery negative terminal as described in Chapter 5A.

Early models (up to July 2007)

4 Using a flat-bladed plastic or wooden tool, carefully prise up the handbrake lever gaiter from the console, and pull it over the lever (see illustrations).
5 Carefully pull the panel in front of the centre console rearwards to release the push-in clips.
6 Using a small screwdriver, depress the catch at one of the upper corners of the audio panel, and carefully prise the panel rearwards on that side. Repeat the operation on the other side of the audio panel (see illustrations 27.17a and 27.17b).
7 Push the Infotainment Control Module (ICM) rearwards from the console (see illustration). Disconnect the wiring plugs as the module is withdrawn.

26.29 The seat belt guide is secured by 2 Torx screws (arrowed)

26.30 Seat belt inertia reel retaining nut (arrowed)

8 Carefully prise up the cigarette lighter/power outlet panel (see illustration). Disconnect the wiring plugs as the panel is withdrawn.

9 Undo the 4 screws securing the console centre panel (see illustrations).
10 Lift the centre panel slightly, then unclip the gear lever gaiter (manual transmission only) (see

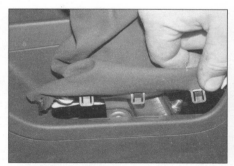
27.4a Unclip the handbrake lever gaiter...

27.4b ...and pull it from the lever

27.7 Reach behind and push the Infotainment Control Module from place

27.8 The cigarette lighter/power outlet panel simply pulls upwards from place

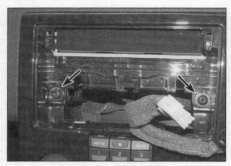

27.9a Undo the 2 Torx screws at the top of the panel . . .

27.9b . . . and the 2 at the lower edge

27.10 The gaiter unclips from the panel

27.11 Unclip the panel and undo the 2 Torx screws

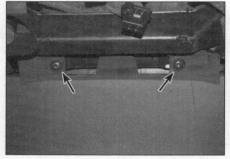

27.12 Undo the 2 Torx screws at the front of the console

27.16 Unclip the gear lever gaiter

illustration). Remove the panel, disconnecting the wiring plugs as the panel is withdrawn.
11 Unclip the panel under the central armrest, and undo the 2 console retaining Torx screws exposed **(see illustration)**.

12 Undo the 2 Torx screws at the front of the console **(see illustration)**.
13 Lift up the rear of the console, and disconnect the wiring plug for the rear ashtray/accessory power socket.

14 Lifting the rear edge first, manoeuvre the centre console over the handbrake and gearchange/selector levers, and out from the vehicle. On automatic models, feed the selector lever panel through the aperture as the console is removed.
15 The various sections of the console are held together by various nuts and screws, visible from beneath.

Later models (from July 2007)

16 Remove the lower facia panel in front of the centre console as described in Section 25. Unclip the gaiter for the handbrake lever from the console **(see illustration)**.
17 Remove the audio panel. Using a small screwdriver, depress the catch at one of the upper corners of the audio panel, and carefully prise the panel rearwards on that side. Repeat the operation on the other side of the audio panel **(see illustrations)**.
18 Push the Infotainment Control Module (ICM) rearwards from the console **(see illustration 27.7)**. Disconnect the wiring plugs as the module is withdrawn. On early models release the power outlet panel, disconnect the wiring plug and remove the panel.
19 Open the centre armrest and undo the 2 screws located in the base of the armrest unit **(see illustration)**.
20 Undo the 2 Torx screws at the front of the console and the 2 screws in the audio module aperture **(see illustrations 27.9a and 27.12)**.
21 Using a flat-bladed tool, prise up the storage tray at the front of the console and the trim panel around the handbrake lever **(see illustrations)**.

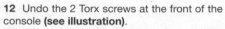

27.17a Insert a screwdriver to press the clip outwards and prise out the panel – note the tape to prevent damage

27.17b View from inside the panel to show how the clip is released

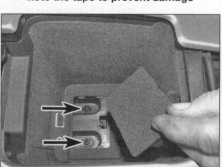

27.19 Remove the trim panel and undo the 2 screws

27.21a Unclip the storage tray from the front of the console

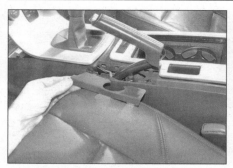

27.21b Unclip the trim panel from around the handbrake lever

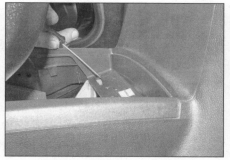

27.22 Use a screwdriver to gently lift the retaining clip

27.23 Undo the 2 screws

22 Using a screwdriver, lift the clip on the left-hand side exposed by removal of the storage tray at the front of the console (see illustration). Slide the lower console towards the rear of the cabin.

23 Undo the 2 screws located just behind the gear or selector lever (see illustration).

24 Disconnect the wiring plug at the rear of the climate control panel and the 2 wiring plugs located between the air vent trunking at the front of the console (see illustration). The console can now be removed from the cabin, manoeuvring it over the gear/selector lever as it's withdrawn (see illustration).

Refitting

25 Refitting is a reversal of removal.

---

28 Facia –
removal and refitting

27.24a Disconnect the 2 plugs (arrowed) between the ventilation trunking

27.24b Withdraw the console

and disengage the front edge from the facia (see illustration 25.20).

9 Pull back the carpets on both sides, disconnect the wiring plugs in the boxes each

side, then undo the bolts and disconnect the 2 earth connections each side (see illustrations).

10 Rotate the fasteners anti-clockwise and

Removal

1 Ensure the front seats are in the rearmost positions, set the temperature control to the maximum cooling position, then disconnect the battery negative lead (see Chapter 5A). Wait at least 5 minutes before proceeding to allow any residual electrical energy to dissipate.

2 Remove the driver's side lower facia panel and the glovebox as described in Section 25.

3 Remove the centre console as described in Section 27.

4 Release the 2 clips and remove the sound insulation panel on the passenger's side (see illustration).

5 The air ducts on the driver's and passenger's side are secured to the crossmember by 1 screw each. Undo the screws and remove the air ducts (see illustration).

6 Remove the A-pillar trim panels as described in Section 25.

7 Undo the 2 Torx screws, remove the instrument panel frame trim, and release the moulding from the upper steering column (see illustration).

8 On both driver and passenger side, pull up the rear edge of the front door sill trim panel,

28.4 Undo the fasteners and remove the sound insulation panel

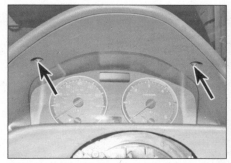

28.7 Undo the instrument panel frame trim screws (arrowed)

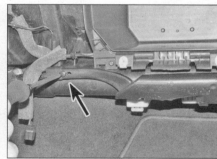

28.5 Undo the screw (arrowed) each side securing the air ducts

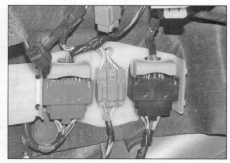

28.9a Open the plastic boxes on each side and disconnect the wiring plugs

28.9b Undo the earth connections on the passenger's side . . .

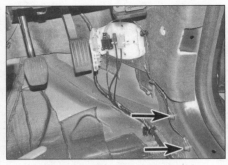

28.9c . . . and on the driver's side (arrowed)

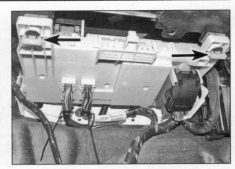

28.10 Undo the fusebox/CEM fasteners (arrowed)

28.12 Lever over the catch and disconnect the supplementary restraint system module wiring plug (arrowed)

28.13 Pull the centre air duct downwards and remove it

28.14 Remove the brackets each side (arrowed)

lower the central electrical module (CEM) from the facia. Note their fitted positions, then disconnect the CEM wiring plugs, release the wiring harness clips, and remove the CEM **(see illustration)**.
11 Disconnect the reversing light wiring plug from the selector mechanism (automatic transmission models only), and release the wiring harness clips.
12 Located in the centre console area, disconnect the air bag module wiring plug **(see illustration)**.
13 Remove the centre air duct - start by pulling down the top edge **(see illustration)**.
14 Undo the retaining bolts securing the facia floor brackets on the passenger's and driver's side. Release the wiring harness clips and remove the brackets **(see illustration)**.
15 Undo the screws securing the heater matrix assembly cover, and manoeuvre the cover from place **(see illustration)**.
16 Remove the steering column as described in Chapter 10.
17 Remove the windscreen wiper motor as described in Chapter 12.
18 Remove the 2 facia retaining bolts in the engine compartment **(see illustration)**.
19 Undo the 2 retaining bolts and remove the audio unit, disconnecting the wiring plugs as the unit is withdrawn **(see illustration)**.
20 Undo the 2 retaining bolts in the centre of the facia **(see illustration)**.
21 Prise out the plastic locking catch and disconnect the wiring plugs from each door.
22 Undo the bolt each end of the facia in the door aperture as far as possible **(see illustration)**.
23 Screw in the facia crossmember spacer each side **(see illustration)**.
24 Remove the upper retaining bolts each

28.15 The heater matrix cover is secured by various screws (arrowed) around its edge

28.18 Undo the 2 bolts in the engine compartment behind the wiper motor position

28.19 Media player retaining Torx bolts (arrowed)

28.20 Undo the 2 bolts in the centre of the facia (arrowed)

end of the facia, and screw in some 8mm threaded rod **(see illustration)**.

25 Remove the passenger's side lower retaining bolt, and slacken the driver's side bolt 5mm. Pull the passenger's side of the facia rearwards approximately 140mm **(see illustration)**.

26 Disconnect the heater distribution box damper motor wiring plug (passenger's side) and the blower motor plug (driver's side).

27 Remove the lower retaining bolt on the driver's side of the facia. With the help of an assistant, undo the threaded rods and manoeuvre the facia through the passenger door opening.

Refitting

28 Manoeuvre the facia into position, and insert the threaded rods into the facia upper mounting bolt holes. Ensure the top edge of the facia engages correctly with guides by the windscreen, and central locating pins in the opening for the centre console engage correctly with the heater housing. Ensure that no wires become trapped as the facia is lowered into position.

29 Reconnect the heater distribution and blower motor wiring plugs.

30 Insert the facia lower retaining bolts finger-tight at this stage.

31 Screw in the facia end retaining bolts (located in the door apertures), then screw in the spacers until they contact the crossmember. Check the position of the facia by aligning the mounting holes in the engine compartment. If necessary, adjust the facia position by rotating the end spacers. With the facia aligned, hold the spacers, and tighten all the retaining bolts.

32 The remainder of refitting is a reversal of removal.

33 On cars equipped with a passenger's airbag, make sure that no-one is inside the car. Switch on the ignition, then reconnect the battery negative lead. Switch the ignition off, then on again, and check that the SRS warning light comes on, then goes out after approximately 7 seconds.

28.22 Undo the bolt at each end of the facia in the door pillar area . . .

28.24 Remove the upper facia bolt each end and screw in some 8 mm threaded rod

28.23 . . . then screw the spacer away from the crossmember (arrowed)

28.25 Pull the facia rearwards approximately 140 mm

29 Sunroof – general information

An electrically-operated sunroof is available as standard or optional equipment, according to model.

The sunroof is maintenance-free, but any adjustment or removal and refitting of the component parts should be entrusted to a dealer or specialist, due to the complexity of the unit and the need to remove much of the interior trim and headlining to gain access. The latter operation is involved, and requires care and specialist knowledge to avoid damage.

If the sunroof action becomes sluggish, the slides and/or cables may need lubricating – consult a Volvo dealer or specialist for advice on a suitable product to use. Further checks in the event of non-operation are limited to checking the fuse and wiring, with reference to the wiring diagrams at the end of Chapter 12.

Drain tubes

It is advisable to check the sunroof water drain tubes on a periodic basis. If they become blocked, they may be cleared by probing them with a length of suitable cable (an old speedometer drive cable is ideal). The front drain tubes terminate at the front bulkhead at the rear of the engine bay. The rear drain tubes terminate ahead of the rear wheels inside the wheelarches.

Chapter 12
Body electrical system

Contents

Degrees of difficulty

Easy, suitable for novice with little experience | **Fairly easy,** suitable for beginner with some experience | **Fairly difficult,** suitable for competent DIY mechanic | **Difficult,** suitable for experienced DIY mechanic | **Very difficult,** suitable for expert DIY or professional

Specifications

General
System type . . . . 12 volt, negative earth
Fuses . . . . See wiring diagrams at end of Chapter and sticker on control box lid for specific vehicle details

Bulbs — Wattage
Direction indicators 21
Direction indicator side repeaters . . . . 5 capless
Foglight:
  Front. 55 H11
  Rear 21
Headlight:
  Dipped 55 H7
  Main 55 HB3
Gas discharge headlights:
  Dipped 35 DS2
  Main 55 HB3
Glovebox light . . . . 3 capless
High-level stop-light. . . . . LEDs
Interior light 5
Number plate light 5
Luggage compartment light. . . . . 5 capless
Reversing light 21
Sidelights 5
Stop-light 21
Tail light. 5
Vanity mirror 1.2

Torque wrench settings

	Nm	lbf ft
Airbag (passenger side):		
Retaining bolts	10	7
Airbag control module	10	7
Airbag side crash sensors	6	4
Anti-theft alarm siren	10	7
Audio module/amplifier	10	7
Door panel switch module	10	7
Handbrake switch mounting	10	7
Horn	10	7
Light units (rear)	10	7
Rear wiper motor bolts	10	7
Tailgate wiper arm nut	24	18
Windscreen wiper linkage bolts/nuts	10	7
Windscreen wiper motor	10	7
Windscreen wiper arm nuts	21	15

1 General information and precautions

General information

The electrical system is of 12 volt negative earth type. Power for the lights and all electrical accessories is supplied by a lead-acid type battery, which is charged by the belt-driven alternator.

This Chapter covers repair and service procedures for the various electrical components not associated with the engine. Information on the battery, alternator and starter motor can be found in Chapter 5A.

Precautions

⚠ *Warning: Before carrying out any work on the electrical system, read through the precautions given in 'Safety first!' at the beginning of this manual.*

2 Electrical fault finding – general information

Note: *Refer to the precautions given in this Chapter before starting work. The following tests relate to testing of the main electrical circuits, and should not be used to test delicate electronic circuits, particularly where an electronic control unit is used.*

General

1 A typical electrical circuit consists of an electrical component, any switches, relays, motors, fuses, fusible links or circuit breakers related to that component, and the wiring and connectors which link the component to both the battery and the chassis. To help to pinpoint a problem in an electrical circuit, wiring diagrams are included at the end of this Chapter.

2 Before attempting to diagnose an electrical fault, first study the appropriate wiring diagram, to obtain a complete understanding of the components included in the particular circuit concerned. The possible sources of a fault can be narrowed down by noting if other components related to the circuit are operating properly. If several components or circuits fail at one time, the problem is likely to be related to a shared fuse or earth connection.

3 Electrical problems usually stem from simple causes, such as loose or corroded connections, a faulty earth connection, a blown fuse, a melted fusible link, or a faulty relay. Visually inspect the condition of all fuses, wires and connections in a problem circuit before testing the components. Use the wiring diagrams to determine which terminal connections will need to be checked in order to pinpoint the trouble-spot.

4 The basic tools required for electrical fault finding include a circuit tester or voltmeter (a 12 volt bulb with a set of test leads can also be used for certain tests); an ohmmeter (to measure resistance and check for continuity); a battery and set of test leads; and a jumper wire, preferably with a circuit breaker or fuse incorporated, which can be used to bypass suspect wires or electrical components. Before attempting to locate a problem with test instruments, use the wiring diagram to determine where to make the connections.

⚠ *Warning: Under no circumstances may live measuring instruments such as ohmmeters, voltmeters or a bulb and test leads be used to test any of the SRS airbag, SIPS bag, or pyrotechnical seat belt circuitry. Any testing of these components must be left to a Volvo dealer, as there is a danger of activating the system if the correct procedures are not followed.*
Caution: The Volvo S40/V50 electrical system is complex. Many of the ECMs are connected via a 'Databus' system, where they are able to share information from the various sensors, and communicate with each other. For instance, as the automatic gearbox approaches a gear ratio shift point, it signals the engine management ECM via the Databus. As the gearchange is made by the transmission ECM, the engine management ECM retards the ignition timing, momentarily reducing engine output to ensure a smoother transition from one gear ratio to the next. Due to the design of the Databus system, it is not advisable to backprobe the ECMs with a multimeter in the traditional manner. Instead, the electrical systems are equipped with a sophisticated self-diagnosis system, which can interrogate the various ECMs to reveal the stored fault codes, and help pinpoint faults. In order to access the self-diagnosis system, specialist test equipment (fault code reader/scanner) is required. Refer to your Volvo dealer or suitably-equipped specialist.

5 To find the source of an intermittent wiring fault (usually due to a poor or dirty connection, or damaged wiring insulation), a wiggle test can be performed on the wiring. This involves wiggling the wiring by hand to see if the fault occurs as the wiring is moved. It should be possible to narrow down the source of the fault to a particular section of wiring. This method of testing can be used in conjunction with any of the tests described in the following sub-Sections.

6 Apart from problems due to poor connections, two basic types of fault can occur in an electrical circuit – open-circuit, or short-circuit.

7 Open-circuit faults are caused by a break somewhere in the circuit, which prevents current from flowing. An open-circuit fault will prevent a component from working.

8 Short-circuit faults are caused by a short somewhere in the circuit, which allows the current flowing in the circuit to escape along an alternative route, usually to earth. Short-circuit faults are normally caused by a breakdown in wiring insulation, which allows a feed wire to touch either another wire, or an earthed component such as the bodyshell. A short-circuit fault will normally cause the relevant circuit fuse to blow.

Finding an open-circuit

9 To check for an open-circuit, connect one lead of a circuit tester or the negative lead of a voltmeter either to the battery negative terminal or to a known good earth.

10 Connect the other lead to a connector in the circuit being tested, preferably nearest to the battery or fuse. At this point, battery

2.20a The main earth connections are on both front suspension turrets (right-hand turret arrowed)...

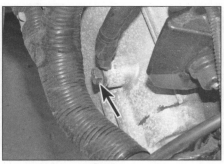

2.20b . . . the front of the transmission casing (arrowed) . . .

2.20c . . . and in the passenger compartment (both sides)

voltage should be present, unless the lead from the battery or the fuse itself is faulty (bearing in mind that some circuits are live only when the ignition switch is moved to a particular position).

11 Switch on the circuit, then connect the tester lead to the connector nearest the circuit switch on the component side.

12 If voltage is present (indicated either by the tester bulb lighting or a voltmeter reading, as applicable), this means that the section of the circuit between the relevant connector and the switch is problem-free.

13 Continue to check the remainder of the circuit in the same fashion.

14 When a point is reached at which no voltage is present, the problem must lie between that point and the previous test point with voltage. Most problems can be traced to a broken, corroded or loose connection.

Finding a short-circuit

15 To check for a short-circuit, first disconnect the load(s) from the circuit (loads are the components which draw current from a circuit, such as bulbs, motors, heating elements, etc).

16 Remove the relevant fuse from the circuit, and connect a circuit tester or voltmeter to the fuse connections.

17 Switch on the circuit, bearing in mind that some circuits are live only when the ignition switch is in a particular position.

18 If voltage is present (indicated either by the tester bulb lighting or a voltmeter reading, as applicable), this means that there is a short-circuit.

19 If no voltage is present during this test, but the fuse still blows with the load(s) reconnected, this indicates an internal fault in the load(s).

Finding an earth fault

20 The battery negative terminal is connected to earth – the metal of the engine/transmission and the vehicle body – and many systems are wired so that they only receive a positive feed, the current returning via the metal of the car body **(see illustrations)**. This means that the component mounting and the body form part of that circuit. Loose or corroded mountings can therefore cause a range of electrical faults, ranging from total failure of a circuit, to a puzzling partial failure. In particular, lights may shine dimly (especially when another

circuit sharing the same earth point is in operation), motors (eg, wiper motors or the radiator cooling fan motor) may run slowly, and the operation of one circuit may have an apparently-unrelated effect on another.

21 Note that on many vehicles, earth straps are used between certain components, such as the engine/transmission and the body, usually where there is no metal-to-metal contact between components, due to flexible rubber mountings, etc.

22 To check whether a component is properly earthed, disconnect the battery and connect one lead of an ohmmeter to a known good earth point. Connect the other lead to the wire or earth connection being tested. The resistance reading should be zero; if not, check the connection as follows.

23 If an earth connection is thought to be faulty, dismantle the connection, and clean both the bodyshell and the wire terminal (or the component earth connection mating surface) back to bare metal. Be careful to remove all traces of dirt and corrosion, then use a knife to trim away any paint, so that a clean metal-to-metal joint is made. On reassembly, tighten the joint fasteners securely; if a wire terminal is being refitted, use serrated washers between the terminal and the bodyshell, to ensure a clean and secure connection.

24 When the connection is remade, prevent the onset of corrosion in the future by applying a coat of petroleum jelly or silicone-based grease, or by spraying on (at regular intervals) a proprietary ignition sealer, or a water-dispersant lubricant.

3 Fuses and relays – general information

Fuses

1 The fuses are located in the central fusebox situated on the left-hand side of the engine compartment and in the Central Electrical Module (CEM) located beneath the glovebox **(see illustrations)**.

2 If a fuse blows, the electrical circuit(s) protected by that fuse will cease to operate. The fuse positions and the circuits protected depends on vehicle specification, model year and country. Refer to the wiring diagrams at the rear of this manual, and the sticker on the fusebox lid which gives details for the particular vehicle.

3 To remove a fuse, first switch off the ignition, then lift up the cover on the fusebox or lower the CEM as described in Section 8. Using the plastic removal tool provided, pull the fuse out of its terminals. The wire within the fuse should be visible; if the fuse is blown, the wire will be broken or melted.

4 Always renew a fuse with one of an identical rating; never use a fuse with a different rating from the original, or substitute anything else, as it may lead to a fire. Never renew a fuse more than once without tracing the source of the trouble. The fuse rating is stamped on top of the fuse; note that fuses are also colour-coded for easy recognition. Spare fuses are provided in the fusebox.

3.1a Release the clip (arrowed) and remove the engine compartment fusebox cover

3.1b Central Electrical Module located beneath the glovebox

4.5a Most electrical connectors have a single release tab that you depress to release the connector

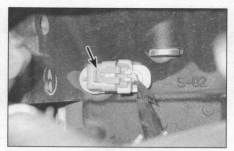

4.5b Some electrical connectors have a retaining tab which must be pried up to free the connector

4.5c Some connectors have two release tabs that you must squeeze to release the connector

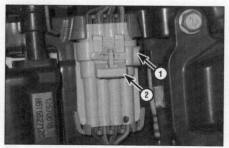

4.5d Some connectors use wire retainers that you squeeze to release the connector

4.5e Critical connectors often employ a sliding lock (1) that you must pull out before you can depress the release tab (2)

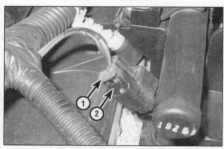

4.5f Here's another sliding-lock style connector, with the lock (1) and the release tab (2) on the side of the connector

5 Persistent blowing of a particular fuse indicates a fault in the circuit(s) protected. Where more than one circuit is involved, switch on one item at a time until the fuse blows, so showing in which circuit the fault lies.

6 Besides a fault in the electrical component concerned, a blown fuse can also be caused by a short-circuit in the wiring to the component. Look for trapped or frayed wires allowing a live wire to touch vehicle metal, and for loose or damaged connectors.

7 Note that only the blade-type fuses should ever be renewed by the DIY mechanic. If one of the large fusible links in the main fusebox blows, this indicates a serious electrical fault, which should be diagnosed by a Volvo dealer or automotive electrical specialist.

Relays – general

8 A relay is an electrically-operated switch, which is used for the following reasons:
a) *A relay can switch a heavy current remotely from the circuit in which the*

current is flowing, allowing the use of lighter-gauge wiring and switch contacts.
b) *A relay can receive more than one control input, unlike a mechanical switch.*
c) *A relay can have a timer function – for example an intermittent wiper delay.*

9 If a circuit which includes a relay develops a fault, remember that the relay itself could be faulty. A basic test of relay operation is to have an assistant switch on the item concerned, while you listen for a click from the relay. This would at least determine whether the relay is switching or not, but is not conclusive proof that a relay is working.

10 Most relays have four or five terminals – two terminals supplying current to its solenoid winding to provide the switching, a main current input and either one or two outputs to either supply or isolate the component concerned (depending on its configuration). Using the wiring diagrams at the end of this Chapter, test to ensure that all connections deliver the expected voltage or good earth.

11 Ultimately, testing is by substitution of a known good relay, but be careful – relays which look similar are not necessarily identical for purposes of substitution.

12 The relays are found in the fusebox, on the passenger's side of the engine compartment, and in the Central Electrical Module.

13 To remove a relay, make sure that the ignition is switched off, then pull the relay from its socket. Push the new relay firmly in to refit.

4 Electrical connectors

1 Most electrical connections on these vehicles are made with multiwire plastic connectors. The mating halves of many connectors are secured with locking clips molded into the plastic connector shells. The mating halves of some large connectors, such as some of those under the instrument panel, are held together by a bolt through the center of the connector.

2 To separate a connector with locking clips, use a small screwdriver to pry the clips apart carefully, then separate the connector halves. Pull only on the shell, never pull on the wiring harness, as you may damage the individual wires and terminals inside the connectors. Look at the connector closely before trying to separate the halves. Often the locking clips are engaged in a way that is not immediately clear. Additionally, many connectors have more than one set of clips.

3 Each pair of connector terminals has a male half and a female half. When you look at

4.5g On some connectors the lock (1) must be pulled out to the side and removed before you can lift the release tab (2)

4.5h Some critical connectors, like the multi-pin connectors at the ECM employ pivoting locks that must be flipped open

5.3 The steering module switches are retained by 2 screws each (arrowed)

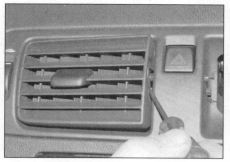

5.5a Prise out the vent grille . . .

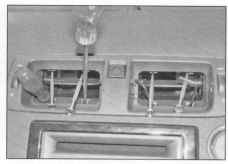

5.5b . . . then release the 8 clips and prise out the vent surround

the end view of a connector in a diagram, be sure to understand whether the view shows the harness side or the component side of the connector. Connector halves are mirror images of each other, and a terminal shown on the right side end-view of one half will be on the left side end-view of the other half.

4 It is often necessary to take circuit voltage measurements with a connector connected. Whenever possible, carefully insert a small straight pin (not your meter probe) into the rear of the connector shell to contact the terminal inside, then clip your meter lead to the pin. This kind of connection is called "backprobing." When inserting a test probe into a terminal, be careful not to distort the terminal opening. Doing so can lead to a poor connection and corrosion at that terminal later. Using the small straight pin instead of a meter probe results in less chance of deforming the terminal connector. "T" pins are a good choice as temporary meter connections. They allow for a larger surface area to attach the meter leads too.

5 Typical electrical connectors are shown in the accompanying photos (4.5a to 4.5h).

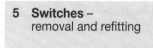

5 Switches –
   removal and refitting

Steering column multi-function switches

1 Disconnect the battery negative lead as described in Chapter 5A.

5.9a Undo the instrument surround screws (arrowed) . . .

5.7 Disconnect the optic cable from the media player (shown with the unit removed for clarity)

2 Remove the steering column shrouds as described in Chapter 10.

3 Remove the switch in question. Each switch is secured by two screws **(see illustration)**. Remove the screws and pull the switch out to the side carefully.

4 Refit the relevant switch using a reversal of removal.

Ignition/starter switch

Removal

5 Release the retaining clips, then carefully prise the centre air vents from the facia **(see illustrations)**.

6 Remove the driver's side lower facia panel and centre console as described in Chapter 11.

7 Release the optic cable retaining clips from the underside of the media player module (where fitted), by pressing the clips outwards

5.9b . . . and pull it from place

5.8 Media player retaining Torx bolts (arrowed)

and downwards **(see illustration)**. Take care not to kink or stretch the optic cables.

8 Undo the 2 retaining bolts and pull the media player module (where fitted) from the facia. Disconnect the wiring plugs as the unit is withdrawn **(see illustration)**.

9 Undo the 2 screws and pull the instrument cluster surround trim from place **(see illustrations)**.

10 The ignition switch is retained by 2 screws. Reach through the apertures, undo the screws, disconnect the wiring plugs and manoeuvre the switch from the facia **(see illustration)**.

Refitting

11 Refitting is a reversal of removal.

Headlight switch

12 Ensure the switch is in the '0' position.

5.10 The ignition switch is secured by 2 Torx screws (arrowed – viewed from the rear of the facia)

5.13 Prise the end panel from the facia

5.14a Push the switch module from place

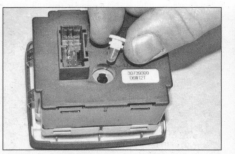

5.14b Twist the bulbholder anti-clockwise and pull it from the switch (the bulb is integral with the holder)

13 Remove the facia end-panel as described in Chapter 11 (see illustration).
14 Working from behind the facia, release the clips at the top and bottom of the switch and push it outwards from the facia, disconnecting

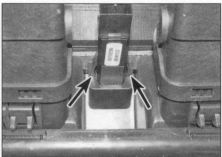

5.17 Release the clips (arrowed) and push the hazard switch from the panel

the wiring plug as the switch is withdrawn (see illustration). If required, twist the bulbholder on the rear of the unit anti-clockwise, pull it from position and renew the illumination bulb (see illustration).

5.20a Prise the trim from the inside of the grab handle . . .

5.20b . . . then prise the panel upwards to release the clips

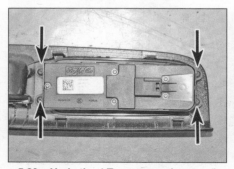

5.20c Undo the 4 Torx screws (arrowed) and pull the switch from the panel surround

5.26 Undo the screw (arrowed) for the handbrake warning light switch

15 Refitting is a reversal of removal.

Hazard warning light switch

16 Remove the centre air vent as described in Chapter 3 (see illustrations 5.5a and 5.5b).
17 Disconnect the wiring plug from the switch and use a thin-bladed screwdriver to release the clips on each side of the switch (see illustration). Push the switch from the panel.
18 Refitting is a reversal of removal.

Centre console switches

19 The switches are integral to the centre console panel. Refer to Chapter 11 for removal of the centre console.

Door panel switches

Front and rear doors

20 For the driver's door, use a flat-bladed tool to carefully release the grab handle recess trim. Using the same tool, release the 6 remaining clips by carefully levering the switch panel from the door, disconnect the wiring plug, and withdraw the panel from the door (see illustrations). Undo the 4 screws on the underside of the panel and remove the switches (see illustration).
21 While the procedure for the front passenger door and rear doors is the same, note that the switch panel is attached by 5 clips and only 2 screws are used to retain the switch.
22 Refitting is a reversal of removal, but test the operation of the switch before refitting the switch panel.

Door/tailgate courtesy light microswitches

23 The courtesy light microswitches are incorporated in the door/tailgate/boot lock assembly, together with the central locking motor.

Brake light switch

24 Refer to Chapter 9, Section 17.

Handbrake warning light switch

25 Remove the centre console as described in Chapter 11.
26 Undo the screw at the rear of the handbrake mounting bracket, release the clip, and withdraw the switch (see illustration).
27 Refitting is a reversal of removal

Steering wheel switches

28 Remove the driver's airbag as described in Section 25.
29 Using a flat-bladed tool, carefully prise the switch panel from the wheel and disconnect the wiring plug as the switch is withdrawn (see illustration).
30 Refitting is a reversal of removal.

Sunroof switch

31 Remove the overhead interior light unit as described in Section 10.
32 Release the retaining clips, disconnect the wiring plug, and remove the switch.
33 Refitting is a reversal of removal.

Central locking switch

34 Remove the driver's door trim panel as described in Chapter 11.

35 Release the retaining clips at the top and bottom of the switch, disconnect the wiring plug, and remove the switch **(see illustration)**.

36 Refitting is a reversal of removal.

---

6 Instrument panel – removal and refitting

Note 1: *The instrument panel includes the immobiliser control unit and its function is included in the vehicle's self-diagnosis program. If the instrument panel has a fault, it would be prudent to have the vehicle's fault code memory interrogated by a Volvo dealer or specialist, prior to removing the panel.*

Note 2: *If the instrument panel is being substituted with a new or exchange unit, the assistance of a Volvo dealer or specialist is required to download necessary software, and initialise/adapt the various instrument panel functions.*

Removal

1 In order to preserve the mileage record, the vehicle must be put in 'standby' mode as follows. Remove the ignition key, close all the doors and boot lid/tailgate, lock the vehicle and wait 2 minutes. The vehicle is now in standby mode.

2 Unlock the vehicle, fully extend the steering column, and move it to its lowest position.

3 Undo the 2 Torx screws securing the instrument panel surround at its upper edge, and pull it from position **(see illustration)**.

4 Undo the 2 retaining screws (one at each end), lift the panel and manoeuvre it from position **(see illustration)**.

5 Disconnect the wiring plug(s) as the panel is withdrawn.

Refitting

6 Refitting is a reversal of removal, but see the note at the beginning of this section.

---

7 Electrical system sensors – removal and refitting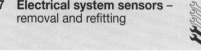

Note: *Not all sensors are fitted to all models.*

Vehicle speed sensor

1 Vehicle speed information for the speedometer is provided by the anti-lock braking system (ABS) wheel sensors, and this is in place of the vehicle speed sensor which is often found on modern cars. If the speedometer does not work, therefore, this indicates a possible problem with the signal from the ABS wheel sensors. Check the wiring connections to the wheel sensors, and to the ABS control unit – if no fault is revealed, refer to a Volvo dealer or suitably-equipped garage for diagnostic testing.

5.29 Carefully prise the switch pad from the steering wheel

6.3 Undo the instrument surround screws

Brake fluid level sensor

2 The brake fluid level sensor is a float incorporated in the master cylinder reservoir. The sensor and reservoir are an assembly; renew the reservoir if the unit is faulty – see Chapter 9.

Oil level sensor

3 Fitted to 5-cylinder engines, the oil level sensor is located on the sump.

4 Wait until the engine is cold. Chock the rear wheels, then jack up the front of the car and support it on axle stands (see *Jacking and vehicle support*).

5 Release the screws and remove the engine undershield.

6 Drain the engine oil as described in Chapter 1A (petrol) or 1B (diesel).

7 Undo the 3 bolts and remove the sensor from the sump **(see illustration)**. Expect some oil spillage as the sensor is withdrawn.

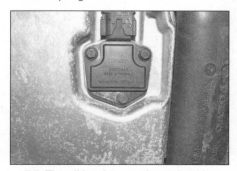

7.7 The oil level sensor is retained by 3 bolts

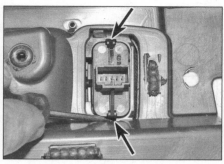

5.35 Release the clips (arrowed) and press the central locking switch from the panel

6.4 Instrument panel retaining Torx screws (arrowed)

8 Refitting is a reversal of removal, refilling the engine with the specified quantity of oil.

9 Refitting is a reversal of removal, tightening the sensor to the specified torque.

Fuel level sender unit

10 Refer to Chapter 4A (petrol) or 4B (diesel).

Coolant temperature sensor

11 Refer to Chapter 3.

Outside temperature sensor

12 Remove the passenger side door mirror glass and cover as described in Chapter 11.

13 Using a small screwdriver, release the clip and pull the sensor from the mirror housing. Disconnect the wiring plug as the sensor is withdrawn.

14 Refitting is a reversal of removal.

Air conditioning evaporator temperature sensor

15 Refer to Chapter 3.

Clutch pedal position sensor

16 Refer to Chapter 6.

Yaw rate/lateral acceleration sensor (Body Sensor Cluster)

17 The BSC (body sensor cluster stability sensor) is located under the right-hand front seat. Disconnect the battery negative lead as described in Chapter 5A.

18 Remove the right-hand front seat as described in Chapter 11.

19 Fold the carpet to one side then undo the 2 screws/bolts securing the sensor bracket to the

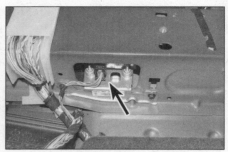

7.19 The body stability sensor cluster is located under the carpet on the driver's side (arrowed)

floor **(see illustration)**. Note the sensor fitted position, and disconnect the wiring plug as the sensor bracket is withdrawn. Take care when handling the sensor as it is easily damaged - if it is dropped, a new one must be fitted.

20 Refitting is a reversal of removal. **Note:** *If a new sensor has been fitted, it must be calibrated using Volvo dedicated test equipment. Entrust this task to a Volvo dealer or suitably-equipped specialist.*

8 Central electronic module (CEM) – general information, removal and refitting

General information

The central electronic module (CEM) manages the functions of a number of items including the headlights, foglights, windscreen washers, tailgate washer

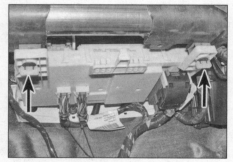

8.3 Rotate the fasteners anti-clockwise (arrowed)

9.4a Rotate the bulbholder (arrowed) anti-clockwise (left-hand headlight) or clockwise (right-hand headlight)

8.2 Push in the centre pins, pull the out the plastic rivets, and remove the panel under the passenger's side of the facia

(where applicable), brake lights, headlamp washers (where applicable), central locking, immobiliser, headlamp range adjustment, indicators, blindspot information system, courtesy lighting, rear electric windows, fuel pump, starter motor, speed-sensitive power steering, heated seats, and the horn, but also acts as a bridge between the high-speed and low-speed communication networks (Databuses). Consequently, it monitors the signals between most of the vehicles sensors, actuators and control modules. As the CEM communicates with all other modules, it contains the vehicle's self-diagnosis system and stores any fault codes generated. The CEM also contains information specific to the vehicle: VIN, build details, and vehicle equipment options. Consequently, if the CEM needs renewing, the stored information must be retrieved prior to removal, and then programmed into the new unit once fitted.

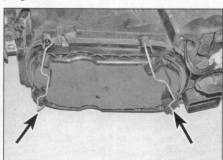

9.3 Push the clips outwards and remove the cover from the headlight (arrowed)

9.4b The main beam bulb is integral with the holder

Central electronic module removal

Note: *If the CEM is to be renewed, stored information must be retrieved and then programmed into the new CEM. As this task requires the use of dedicated Volvo test equipment, entrust it to a Volvo dealer or suitably-equipped specialist.*

1 Disconnect the battery negative lead as described in Chapter 5A.

2 Push in the centre pins of the 2 plastic expanding rivets securing the trim panel beneath the glovebox, pull the rivets from place and remove the panel **(see illustration)**.

3 Unscrew the 2 fasteners at the forward edge of the CEM, gently pivot the front of the unit downwards, and lift the mountings at the rear from the securing bracket **(see illustration)**. Disconnect the wiring plugs and withdraw the CEM completely.

4 Refitting is a reversal of removal. **Note:** *If a new unit has been fitted, suitable software will need to be downloaded and installed from Volvo. Entrust this task to a Volvo dealer or suitably-equipped specialist.*

9 Bulbs (exterior lights) – renewal

1 Whenever a bulb is renewed, note the following points:

a) *Remember that if the light has just been in use, the bulb may be extremely hot.*
b) ***Do not*** *touch the bulb glass with the fingers, as the small deposits can cause the bulb to cloud over.*
c) *Always check the bulb contacts and holder, ensuring that there is clean metal-to-metal contact. Clean off any corrosion or dirt before fitting a new bulb.*
d) *Wherever bayonet-type bulbs are fitted, ensure that the live contacts bear firmly against the bulb contact.*
e) *Always ensure that the new bulb is of the correct rating and that it is completely clean before fitting it.*

Headlight

Note: *This section does not cover bulb renewal on models fitted with gas discharge headlights; refer to Section 11 for renewal details.*

Main beam

2 Remove the headlight unit as described in Section 11.

3 Push the retaining clips outwards and remove the plastic cover from the rear of the headlight **(see illustration)**.

4 Rotate the bulbholder anti-clockwise (left-hand headlight) or clockwise (right-hand headlight) and pull the bulbholder from the headlight **(see illustrations)**. Note that the bulb is integral with the holder. If the bulb is to be refitted, do not touch the glass with the fingers. If the glass is accidentally touched, clean it with methylated spirit.

5 Fit the new bulb using a reversal of the removal procedure.

9.8a Release the retaining clip . . .

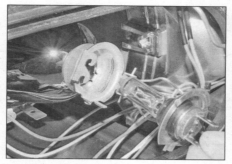

9.8b . . . and pull the dipped beam bulb
from the headlight reflector

9.11 Pull the sidelight bulbholder
(arrowed) from the headlight

Dipped beam

6 Remove the headlight as described in Section 11.
7 Push the retaining clips outwards and remove the plastic cover from the rear of the headlight **(see illustration 9.3)**.
8 Disconnect the wiring plug from the rear of the bulb, then release the retaining clip and remove the bulb from the headlight, noting which way around it's fitted **(see illustrations)**. If the bulb is to be refitted, do not touch the glass with the fingers. If the glass is accidentally touched, clean it with methylated spirit.
9 Fit the new bulb using a reversal of the removal procedure.

Sidelight

10 Remove the headlight unit as described in Section 11, then remove the cover from the rear of the headlight **(see illustration 9.3)**.
11 Pull the bulbholder from the headlight unit **(see illustration)**. Pull only on the bulbholder – not the cable.
12 Pull the wedge-type bulb directly from the bulbholder.
13 Fit the new bulb using a reversal of the removal procedure.

Front foglight

14 Remove the foglight as described in Section 11.
15 Disconnect the wiring from the bulbholder.
16 Rotate the bulbholder anti-clockwise and pull it from the foglight **(see illustration)**. Note that the bulb is integral with the bulbholder.
17 Fit the new bulb using a reversal of the removal procedure.

Front direction indicator

18 Remove the headlight as described in Section 11.
19 Rotate the bulbholder anti-clockwise and pull it from the headlight **(see illustration)**.
20 Depress and twist the bulb to remove it from the bulbholder **(see illustration)**.
21 Fit the new bulb using a reversal of the removal procedure.

Direction indicator side repeater

22 Remove the door mirror cover as described in Chapter 11.
23 Release the clip and manoeuvre the

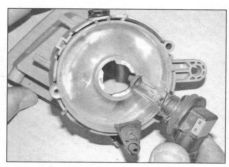

9.16 Rotate the front foglight bulbholder
anti-clockwise and remove it

side repeater from the mirror housing **(see illustrations)**.
24 Pull the wedge-type bulb from the bulbholder.
25 Fit the new bulb using a reversal of the removal procedure.

9.20 . . . then depress and twist the bulb

9.23b . . . and remove the side repeater

9.19 Rotate the directional indicator
bulbholder anti-clockwise to remove it . . .

Headlight-mounted side marker

26 Remove the headlight as described in Section 11.
27 Rotate the bulbholder/wiring plug anti-clockwise and pull them from the headlight **(see illustration)**.

9.23a Release the clip . . .

9.27 Rotate the side marker bulbholder/
wiring plug anti-clockwise and pull them
from the headlight

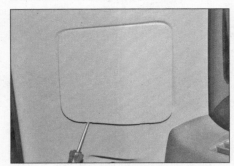

9.30a Carefully prise the relevant bulb access panel from place – V50 models

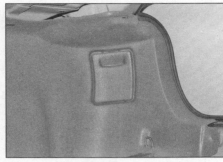

9.30b Rear light access panel – S40 models

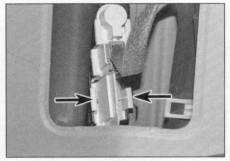

9.32a Squeeze together the clips (arrowed) and remove the bulbholder assembly – V50 upper lights shown . . .

28 Pull the capless, wedge-type bulb from the holder.
29 Fit a new bulb using a reversal of the removal procedure.

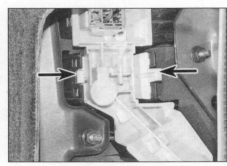

9.32b . . . and lower lights bulbholder clips (arrowed) – V50 models

Rear combination light

30 Working in the luggage compartment, unclip and remove the appropriate access panel on the relevant side (see illustrations).

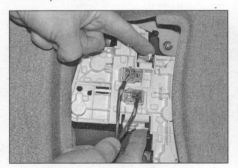

9.32c Bulbholder retaining clips – S40 models

9.33 Press and twist the relevant bulb to remove it

9.39 Undo the Torx screws and pull the down the number plate light – V50 models

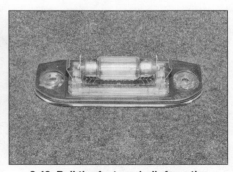

9.40 Pull the festoon bulb from the contacts

31 Disconnect the wiring plug from the bulbholder assembly.
32 Squeeze the plastic tabs and withdraw the bulbholder from the rear light unit (see illustrations).
33 Press and twist the relevant bulb anti-clockwise, and withdraw it from the bulbholder (see illustration).
34 Fit the new bulb using a reversal of the removal procedure.

Number plate light

S40 models

35 The number plate lights are located in the boot lid or tailgate, just above the number plate. For better access to the retaining screws, open the boot lid/tailgate. Undo the retaining screw and prise down the lens (see illustration 9.39).
36 Rotate the bulbholder anti-clockwise and pull it from the lens.
37 Pull the festoon-type bulb from its holder.
38 Fit the new bulb using a reversal of the removal procedure.

V50 models

39 Undo the retaining Torx screws, and pull the lens from the tailgate (see illustration).
40 Pull the festoon-type bulb from the contacts (see illustration).
41 Fit the new bulb using a reversal of the removal procedure.

High-level stop-light

42 The high-level stop-light is illuminated by non-renewable LEDs (Light Emitting Diodes). If faulty, the complete stop-light assembly must be renewed as described in Section 11.

---

10 Bulbs (interior lights) – renewal

---

1 Whenever a bulb is renewed, note the following points:
a) *Remember that if the light has just been in use, the bulb may be extremely hot.*
b) *Always check the bulb contacts and holder, ensuring that there is clean metal-to-metal contact between the bulb and its live and earth. Clean off any corrosion or dirt before fitting a new bulb.*
c) *Wherever bayonet-type bulbs are fitted, ensure that the live contact(s) bear firmly against the bulb contact.*
d) *Always ensure that the new bulb is of the correct rating and that it is completely clean before fitting it.*

Interior/reading lights
Front

2 Carefully pull the light unit down squarely from the headlining (see illustration).
3 Twist the bulbholder and remove it (see illustrations). Note that the bulb is integral with the holder.

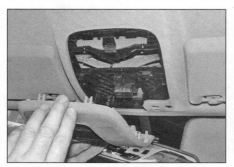

10.2 Pull the interior light downwards squarely to release the clips

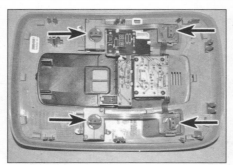

10.3a Twist the relevant bulbholder (arrowed) . . .

10.3b . . . and pull it from place

10.4a Prise the rear light lens/cover from place . . .

10.4b . . . and pull the capless bulb from the holder

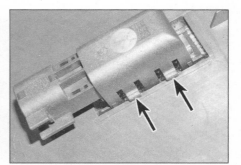

10.7 Depress the clips (arrowed) and free the light from the glovebox

Rear

4 Prise free the light unit lens, then pull the capless bulb from the holder **(see illustrations)**.
5 Fit the new bulb using a reversal of the removal procedure.

Glovebox/footwell light

6 Remove the glovebox as described in Chapter 11.
7 Release the clips and prise the light unit from the glovebox **(see illustration)**.
8 Insert a flat-bladed screwdriver behind the end of the lens, depress the retaining clip and prise free the light lens **(see illustration)**.
9 Pull the capless bulb from its holder.
10 Fit the new bulb using a reversal of the removal procedure. Note that the lens will only fit one way round.

Sunvisor/vanity mirror light

11 Ensure the mirror lid is closed, then carefully prise out the mirror/cover from the sunvisor, using a small screwdriver **(see illustration)**.
12 Pull the festoon-type bulb from the contacts **(see illustration)**.
13 Fit the new bulb using a reversal of the removal procedure.

Instrument panel bulbs

14 On all models covered by this Manual, it is not possible to renew the instrument panel bulbs individually as they are of LED design and soldered to a printed circuit board. It is not possible to renew a single LED. Where an LED is not functioning, the complete instrument panel must be renewed.

Luggage compartment light

15 Insert a flat-bladed screwdriver behind the end of the lens, depress the retaining clip and prise free the light lens/unit **(see illustration)**.
16 Pull the festoon bulb from its holder.

10.8 Release the clip and remove the lens

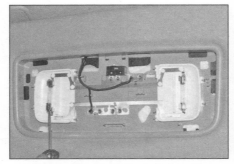

10.12 . . . then pull the bulb from the contacts

17 Fit the new bulb using a reversal of the removal procedure.

Switch illumination

18 Most switch illumination bulbs are built

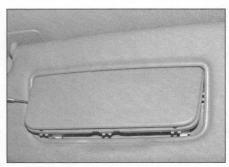

10.11 Carefully prise the mirror/cover away . . .

10.15 Depress the clip and prise down the luggage compartment light

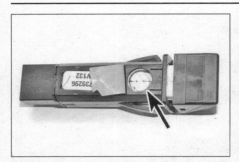

10.19 Twist the bulbholder anti-clockwise and remove it – hazard warning switch shown (arrowed)

11.2 Pull the headlight outwards to release the lug from the locating hole (arrowed)

into the switch itself, and cannot be renewed separately. Refer to Section 5 and remove the switch. However, the illumination bulbs for the light switch module and hazard warning switches can

11.5 Unclip the foglight surround from the bumper

11.6b Foglight retaining screw (arrowed) – later models

11.1 Pull up the headlight locking pin (arrowed)

11.3 Depress the clip and disconnect the headlight wiring plug (arrowed)

be renewed – remove the relevant switch as described in Section 5.

19 Twist the bulbholder anti-clockwise and remove it. The bulb is integral with the holder (**see illustration**).

11.6a Foglight retaining screw – early models

11.7 Ensure the dowels (arrowed) are correctly located

20 Refitting is a reversal of removal.

Heater/air conditioning control panel illumination

21 The control panel is illuminated by non-renewable LEDs. If defective, the control panel may need to be renewed.

11 Exterior light units – removal and refitting

Headlight unit

Caution: On models equipped with gas discharge headlights, disconnect the battery negative lead as described in Chapter 5A, prior to working on the headlights.

Removal

1 Open the bonnet, and pull up the headlight locking pin (**see illustration**).

2 Pull the headlight to the outside, then forwards (**see illustration**). Take care not to damage the vehicle paintwork as the headlight is removed.

3 Depress the retaining clip, and disconnect the wiring plug from the rear of the headlight (**see illustration**).

Refitting

4 Refitting is a reversal of the removal procedure. On completion check for satisfactory operation, and have the headlight beam adjustment checked as soon as possible.

Front foglight

Removal

5 Using a screwdriver, release the 4 retaining clips and pull the foglight surround trim from the bumper (**see illustration**).

6 Undo the mounting screw, withdraw the foglight from the front bumper, and disconnect the wiring (**see illustrations**).

Refitting

7 Refitting is a reversal of removal, ensuring that the locating dowels are positioned correctly (**see illustration**). Have the foglight beam setting checked at the earliest opportunity. An approximate adjustment can be made by positioning the car 10 metres in front of a wall marked with the centre point of the foglight lens. Turn the adjustment screw as required. Note that only height adjustment is possible – there is no lateral adjustment.

Direction indicator side repeater

Removal and refitting

8 The procedure is as described for bulb renewal in Section 9.

Rear combination light

S40 models

9 With the boot lid open, fold forward the access flap, squeeze together the retaining clips and remove the bulbholder assembly (**see illustration 9.32c**).

10 Undo the 4 retaining nuts and pull the light unit from position **(see illustration)**.
11 Refitting is a reversal of removal. Ensure that the seal is correctly positioned.

V50 models

12 Remove the access covers from the D-pillar trim panel, then squeeze together the retaining clips and remove the bulbholder assemblies **(see illustration 9.32a and 9.32b)**.
13 Undo the 4 retaining nuts, and remove the light unit **(see illustration)**.
14 Refitting is a reversal of removal. Ensure that the seal is correctly positioned.

Number plate light

15 The procedure is as described for bulb renewal in Section 9.

High-level stop-light

V50 models

16 Remove the tailgate trim panel as described in Section 16 of Chapter 11.
17 Press in the centre pins and prise out the 2 plastic expanding rivets, then disconnect the wiring plug, and slide the light unit from position **(see illustrations)**.
18 Refitting is a reversal of removal.

S40 models

19 On these models, the high-level stop-light is bonded to the headlining. In order to renew the light unit, the headlining must be lowered, and the light detached from the lining. This is an involved procedure, requiring experience and great care. Consequently, it is recommended that the task be entrusted to a Volvo dealer or specialist.

Beam adjustment

20 Accurate adjustment of the headlight beam is only possible using optical beam setting equipment, and this work should therefore be carried out by a Volvo dealer or suitably-equipped workshop.
21 For reference, the headlights can be adjusted using the adjuster screws, accessible via the top of each light unit **(see illustration)**.
22 Some models are equipped with an electrically-operated headlight beam adjustment system which is controlled through the switch in the facia. On these models, ensure that the switch is set to the basic O position before adjusting the headlight aim.

Setting up for left- or right-hand driving

23 It is possible to adjust the headlight beams for driving on the right-hand, or left-hand side of the road. Remove the headlight as described in this Section.
24 Release the clips and remove the cover from the rear of the headlight **(see illustration 9.3)**.
25 Move the lever at the lower edge of the reflector to the left for driving on the left-hand side of the road (RHD), or to the right for driving on the right-hand side of the road (LHD).

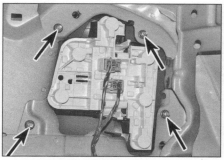

11.10 Rear light retaining nuts (arrowed) – S40 models

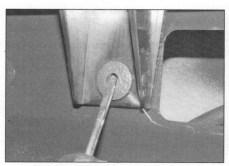

11.17a Press in the centre pins, and remove the plastic expanding rivets . . .

12 Bi-Xenon gas discharge headlight system – component removal, refitting, and adjustment

General information

1 Bi-Xenon gas discharge headlights were available as an optional extra on all models covered in this manual. The headlights are fitted with bulbs that produce light by means of an electric arc, rather than by heating a metal filament as in conventional halogen bulbs. The arc is generated by a control circuit which operates at high voltages. The intensity of the emitted light means that the headlight beam has to be controlled dynamically to avoid dazzling other road users. An electronic control unit monitors the vehicle's pitch and overall ride height by sensors

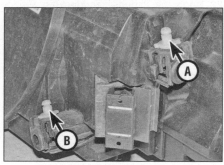

11.21 Headlight beam adjustment screws (shown with the headlight removed)

A Horizontal adjustment
B Vertical adjustment

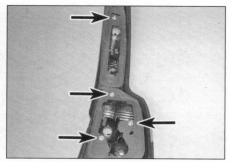

11.13 Rear light unit retaining nut studs – shown with the unit removed for clarity

11.17b . . . then slide the high-level stop-light from place

mounted on the front and rear suspension and adjusts the beam range accordingly, using the range control motors built into the headlight units.

⚠ **Warning: The discharge bulb starter circuitry operates at extremely high voltages. To avoid the risk of electric shock, ensure that the battery negative cable is disconnected before working on the headlight units (see Chapter 5A), then additionally switch the dipped beam on and off to discharge any residual voltage.**

Bulb renewal

Headlight main beam

2 Remove the headlight as described in Section 11.
3 Push the retaining clips outwards, and remove the plastic cover from the rear of the headlight **(see illustration 9.3)**.
4 Disconnect the wiring plug from the rear of the bulb, then release the retaining clip and pull the bulb from the reflector **(see illustration 9.4a)**. Note how the lugs on the bulb engage with the slots in the reflector. If the bulb is to be refitted, do not touch the glass with the fingers. If the glass is accidentally touched, clean it with methylated spirit.
5 Fit the new bulb using a reversal of the removal procedure.

Headlight dipped beam

Caution: The dipped beam bulb is under gas pressure of at least 10 bars, therefore it is recommended that protective glasses are worn during this procedure.

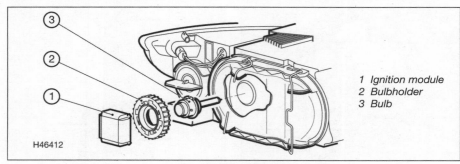

1 Ignition module
2 Bulbholder
3 Bulb

H46412

12.8 Xenon bulb details

6 Remove the headlight unit as described in Section 11.

7 Release the retaining clips and detach the plastic cover from the rear of the light unit **(see illustration 9.3)**.

8 Disconnect the wiring plug, then remove the ignition module, followed by the bulbholder and bulb **(see illustration)**. If the glass is accidentally touched, clean it with methylated spirit.

9 Fit the new bulb using a reversal of the removal procedure, ensuring the lug at the top of the lamp engages correctly with the corresponding slot in the reflector.

Sidelight

10 Remove the headlight unit as described in Section 11.

11 Pull the bulbholder from the headlight unit **(see illustration 9.11)**. Pull only on the bulbholder – not the cable.

12 Pull the wedge-type bulb directly from the bulbholder.

13 Fit the new bulb using a reversal of the removal procedure.

Gas discharge lamp control module/ballast

Removal

14 Two control modules are fitted – one for each headlight. The unit on the driver's side serves as a 'master' and communicates with the central electronic module (integral with the passenger's cabin fusebox) via a LIN (Local Interconnect Network), whilst the other control unit is the 'slave' and communicates only with the 'master'. The control units are responsible

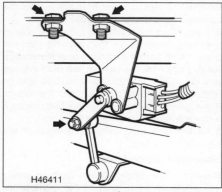

H46411

12.21 Ride height sensor mounting bolts and control arm bolt (arrowed)

for moving the Bi-Xenon bulb from the dipped position to the main beam position, and for controlling the headlight automatic levelling motors, based on signals received from the suspension height sensors. Integral with the control units are the ballast units. These units are responsible for converting the current from DC to AC, and regulating the voltage to the bulb. The voltage required to start the bulb is approximately 1000 V, and about 100 V to maintain the arc between the bulb's electrodes.

15 Release the fasteners and pull back the front edge of the wheel arch liner on the relevant side.

16 Undo the ballast support bracket retaining bolt, and disconnect the wiring plug.

17 Manoeuvre the ballast/control module from position.

Refitting

18 Refitting is a reversal of removal. Note that if a new unit has been fitted, new software will need to be downloaded from Volvo. Consult a Volvo dealer or specialist.

Front ride height sensor

Removal

19 The sensor is mounted on the lower control arm of the left-hand wheel. Apply the handbrake, then jack up the front of the vehicle and support it on axle stands (see *Jacking and vehicle support*).

20 Undo the plastic nut and fold out the wheel arch liner.

21 Undo the bolt securing the sensor arm bracket to the control arm **(see illustration)**.

22 Undo the 2 bolts securing the sensor body to the mounting bracket.

23 Disconnect the wiring plus as the sensor is withdrawn.

Refitting

24 Refitting is a reversal of removal. Note that if a new sensor has been fitted, then a calibration procedure must be carrier out. This requires access to Volvo diagnostic equipment – entrust this task to a Volvo dealer or suitably-equipped specialist.

Rear ride height sensor

Removal

25 The sensor is secured to the left-hand lower control arm and the rear subframe. Chock the front wheels, then jack up the rear

of the vehicle and support it on axle stands (*see Jacking and vehicle support*). Remove the left-hand rear road wheel.

26 Undo the nut securing the link to the sensor arm **(see illustration 12.21)**.

27 Undo the 2 bolts securing the sensor to the subframe. Disconnect the wiring plug as the sensor is withdrawn.

Refitting

28 Refitting is a reversal of removal. Note that if a new sensor has been fitted, then a calibration procedure must be carried out. This requires access to Volvo diagnostic equipment – entrust this task to a Volvo dealer or suitably-equipped specialist.

Setting-up for left- or right-hand driving

29 On models equipped with gas discharge headlights, the 'dipping' characteristics of the unit can be set-up for countries who drive on the left or right. Remove the headlight as described in Section 11.

30 Release the clips and remove the plastic cover from the rear of the headlight behind the dipped beam location.

31 Press the lever on the side of the reflector upwards for driving on the right, and down for driving on the left.

Beam adjustment

32 The basic alignment procedure of the headlights is the same as normal Halogen headlights (see Section 11). However, before the procedure is attempted, the ride height sensors must be calibrated using dedicated Volvo test equipment. Therefore this task should be entrusted to a Volvo dealer or suitably-equipped specialist.

Range control positioning motor

33 The range control motors are integral with the headlights, and cannot be renewed separately. If faulty, the complete headlight must be renewed.

---

13 Headlight control module - removal and refitting

1 The headlamp control module is located beneath the wheelarch liner of the left-hand front wheel.

2 Loosen the left-hand side front wheel nuts and chock the rear wheels. Jack up the front of the car and support it on axle stands (see *Jacking and vehicle support*). Remove the front roadwheel and undo the 6 screws securing the front section of the wheelarch liner.

3 Undo the securing screws, release the locking catch, and disconnect the wiring plug. The module can now be removed.

4 Refitting is a reversal of removal. **Note:** *If a new module has been fitted, suitable software will need to be downloaded and installed. Entrust this task to a Volvo dealer or suitably equipped specialist.*

14.2a Unclip the cover from the bumper mounting bar

14.2b Horn retaining bolt (arrowed)

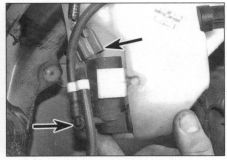

16.2 Disconnect the pump hoses and wiring plug (arrowed)

14 Horn – removal and refitting

1 Volvo advise that the horn units can be reached by removing the grille. However, given the difficulty in removing the grille with the bumper in place, we recommend removing the front bumper (Chapter 11) to prevent the risk of damage.
2 With the front bumper removed, unclip the plastic cover from the bumper mounting bar (see illustration), unbolt the horn from its bracket and remove it (see illustration). Disconnect the wiring plug as the horn is removed.
3 Refitting is a reversal of removal.

15 Sunroof motor – removal and refitting

Removal

1 Pull the front interior light console downwards from position, and disconnect the wiring plugs.
2 Slacken the 3 bolts securing the interior light console frame.
3 Disconnect the wiring plug, then undo the 3 bolts and manoeuvre the sunroof motor/control module from position.

Refitting

4 Refitting is a reversal of removal. However, the motor/control module must be calibrated as below.

Calibration

Installing a previously-used motor

5 With the sunroof closed, and the ignition switch in position I, press the sunroof control switch rear edge upwards until the sunroof is in its tilt position. Release the control switch.
6 Move the control switch forwards for approximately 30 seconds, until the sunroof moves approximately 2mm and the motor stops. Release the control switch.
7 Move the control switch forwards within 0.5 seconds of releasing it, and hold it there while the sunroof completes one movement cycle (moves to its fully open position and then to its fully closed position). When the motor stops, calibration is complete.

Installing a new motor

8 With the sunroof closed, and the ignition switch in position I, press the sunroof control switch rear edge upwards until the sunroof is in its tilt position. Release the control switch.
9 Move the control switch forwards within 0.5 seconds of releasing it, and hold it there while the sunroof completes one movement cycle (moves to its fully open position and then to its fully closed position). When the motor stops, calibration is complete.

16 Washer system components – removal and refitting

Windscreen and tailgate washer pump

Removal

1 Remove the lower section of the washer reservoir as described below.
2 Note the fitted location, then pull the hose(s) from the pump, and disconnect the pump wiring plug (see illustration).
3 Place a container under the reservoir, and be prepared for spillage.
4 Grip the washer pump and pull it out of the reservoir.

Refitting

5 Refitting is a reversal of removal.

Headlamp washer pump

6 Refer to the section above for the windscreen and tailgate washer pump.

Washer reservoir

Removal

7 Remove the plenum cover. Start by removing the wiper arms as described in Section 17 and remove the 4 fasteners along the front edge of the plenum cover. Remove the 2 centre fastenings below the base of the windscreen by depressing the centre pin and turning the catches anti-clockwise by a quarter of a turn (see illustrations).

16.7a Prise-in the centre pins and prise out the 4 plastic rivets – 2 in the centre (arrowed) . . .

16.7b . . .and 1 at each end (arrowed) . . .

16.7c . . . then rotate the central clips (arrowed) 90° anti-clockwise and remove the scuttle panel

16.8 Undo the screw (arrowed) at the filler neck

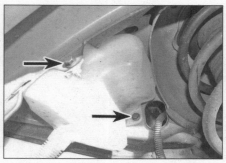

16.10a Upper reservoir mounting bolts (arrowed)

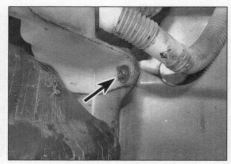

16.10b Undo the lower reservoir lower mounting screw (arrowed)…

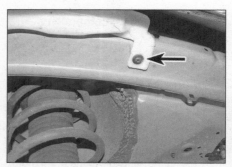

16.10c …and the upper mounting screw (arrowed)

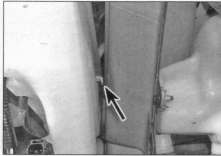

16.10d The hook on the side of the reservoir…

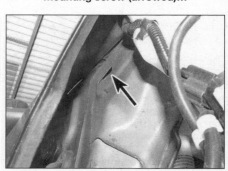

16.10e …locates in the hole in the inner wing

8 Undo the securing screw located at the filler neck **(see illustration)**.

9 Loosen the right-hand side front wheel nuts and chock the rear wheels. Jack up the front of the car and support it on axle stands (see *Jacking and vehicle support*). Remove the right-hand side front roadwheel, undo the screws and remove the wheelarch liner. There are 5 screws securing the liner to the front bumper, one screw either side of the suspension strut, and 3 screws at the lower rear edge of the liner.

10 Undo the 2 bolts securing the upper section of the reservoir **(see illustration)**, and the 2 screws securing the lower section **(see illustrations)**. The lower section is also located by a hook approximately half way up the side of the reservoir that locates in a slot in the inner wing - a long screwdriver can be used to release the hook **(see illustrations)**. Note that for washer pump removal, only

the lower section of the reservoir need be removed. The two sections are joined by a short pipe that can be pulled from the lower section, although you should be prepared for spillage.

Refitting

11 Refitting is a reversal of removal, ensuring that the plenum cover seals are correctly located against the front wings and windscreen.

Windscreen washer jets

12 The windscreen washer jets can be adjusted by inserting a pin into the jet and altering the aim as required. To remove a washer jet, open the bonnet, and disconnect the hose from the jet.

13 Where applicable, disconnect the wiring plug, then squeeze together the clips and remove the jet **(see illustration)**.

Washer fluid level sensor

14 The level sensor is located on the front of the lower section of the washer reservoir **(see illustration)**. To remove the sensor, remove the wheelarch liner as described above in order to gain access to the lower section of the reservoir. Disconnect the sensor wiring plug and pull the sensor from place.

17 Wiper arms –
removal and refitting

1 If the wipers are not in their parked position, switch on the ignition, and allow the motor to automatically park.

2 Before removing an arm, mark its parked position on the glass with a strip of adhesive tape. Prise off the cover and unscrew the spindle nut **(see illustration)**. Ease the arm

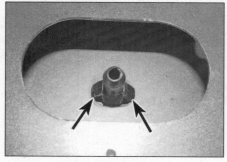

16.13 Squeeze together the clips (arrowed) and remove the jet

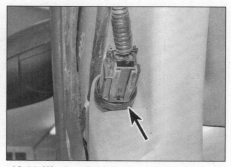

16.14 Washer fluid level sensor (arrowed)

17.2 Prise up the cover and undo the wiper spindle nut

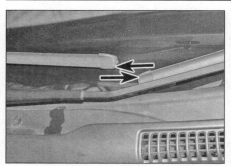

17.3 The end of the upper wiper blade should rest 10mm above the end of the lower one (arrowed)

from the spindle by rocking it slowly from side-to-side. If necessary use a puller to remove the arms.

3 Refitting is a reversal of removal, but before tightening the spindle nuts, position the wiper blades as marked before removal. If the position of the blades has been lost, or the windscreen renewed, position the blades so that the end of the uppermost blade is 10mm above the lower blade **(see illustration)**.

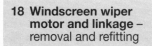

18 Windscreen wiper motor and linkage – removal and refitting

Removal

1 Switch the wipers on, then off again to ensure that the motor and linkage are parked.
2 Remove the windscreen wiper arms as described in Section 17.
3 Remove the plenum cover as described in Section 16 and remove the cover over the wiper motor (where fitted) **(see illustration)**.
4 Disconnect the wiper motor wiring plug.
5 Undo the 4 bolts and manoeuvre the wiper motor linkage from position **(see illustrations)**.
6 Using a screwdriver, carefully prise the linkage arm from the balljoint stud.
7 To aid refitting, measure the distance between the arm and the end stop as shown **(see illustration)**.
8 Undo the nut and remove the arm from the motor spindle.
9 Undo the three Torx bolts and remove the motor.

Refitting

10 When refitting, with the motor/linkage back in place, reconnect the wiring plug then operate the touch-wipe button to set the motor in the rest position. Refit the crank in the same position as on removal using the measurement made, and tighten the retaining nut securely. The remainder of refitting is a reversal of removal.

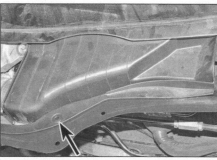

18.3 Press in the centre pin, prise out the rivet and remove the cover over the wiper motor (arrowed)

18.5b ... and 1 at the outside end (arrowed)

19 Tailgate wiper motor – removal and refitting

Removal

1 Switch the wiper on then off again to ensure that the motor and linkage are parked.
2 Remove the tailgate wiper arm as described in Section 17.
3 Remove the tailgate upper and lower interior trim panels as described in Chapter 11.
4 Disconnect the wiring plug, undo the three motor retaining bolts and withdraw it from the tailgate **(see illustration)**.

Refitting

5 Refit the motor to the tailgate and secure with the three mounting bolts.

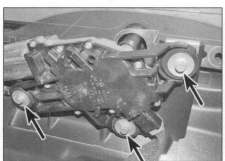

19.4 Tailgate wiper motor mounting bolts (arrowed)

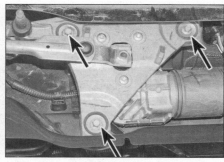

18.5a The wiper linkage is secured by 3 bolts around the motor area (arrowed) . . .

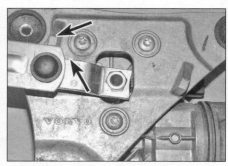

18.7 Measure the distance between the end-stop and the arm (arrowed)

6 If a new motor is being fitted, temporarily reconnect the wiring connector at the car, switch on the motor then switch it off again to ensure that it is parked.
7 Refitting is a reversal of removal.

20 Audio units – removal and refitting

Facia mounted audio units

Removal

1 Remove the centre console as described in Chapter 11 and ensure no discs are in the unit.
2 Undo the 2 retaining screws and pull the unit forward from the facia until the wiring plugs are accessible **(see illustration)**.

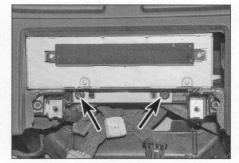

20.2 Undo the 2 Torx screws (arrowed) and withdraw the player module

20.6 Audio module retaining nuts (arrowed)

3 Disconnect the wiring plugs and remove the unit. Be aware that the wiring may be of the fibre optic variety and should not be bent excessively as this can cause damage. **Note:** *If a new Volvo audio unit has been fitted, suitable software will need to be downloaded and installed from Volvo. Entrust this task to a Volvo dealer or suitably-equipped specialist.*

Refitting

4 Refitting is a reversal of removal.

Audio module/amplifier

5 Remove the left-hand side trim panel in the luggage compartment as described in Chapter 11.
6 Undo the retaining nuts, disconnect the wiring plugs, and remove the unit **(see illustration)**. Be aware that the wiring may

20.12a Use a screwdriver to depress the catch in the upper corner of the audio display panel – note the use of tape to protect the panel

20.12b View from inside the panel to show how the catch is released

20.11 Pull the panel in front of the centre console rearwards to release the clips

be of the fibre optic variety and should not be bent excessively as this can cause damage.
7 Refitting is the reversal of removal. **Note:** *If a new Volvo audio unit has been fitted, suitable software will need to be downloaded and installed from Volvo. Entrust this task to a Volvo dealer or suitably-equipped specialist.*

Antenna Amplifier

8 Remove the C-pillar trim as described in Chapter 11.
9 Disconnect the 3 wiring plugs, undo the securing screw, and use a small screwdriver to release the securing clips.
10 Refitting is a reversal of removal.
Note: *On estate models this operation requires the release of the rear section of the headlining. We recommend this task is entrusted to a Volvo dealer.*

Information and Entertainment Display

11 Carefully pull the panel behind the centre console rearwards to release the clips **(see illustration)**.
12 Using a small screwdriver, depress the catch at one of the upper corners of the display panel, and carefully prise the panel rearwards on that side. Repeat the operation on the other side of the panel **(see illustrations)**.
13 Reach behind and push the display module forwards from the console, disconnecting the wiring plugs as the module is withdrawn **(see illustration)**.

Radio Control Module

14 On S40 models, remove the parcel shelf as described in Chapter 11.

20.13 Push the module display from place

15 On V50 models, remove the right-hand side luggage compartment trim panel as described in Chapter 11.
16 On all models, undo the retaining nut and bolt, disconnect the wiring plug, and remove the module.
Note: *If a new Volvo audio unit has been fitted, suitable software will need to be downloaded and installed from Volvo. Entrust this task to a Volvo dealer or suitably-equipped specialist.*

21 Speakers – removal and refitting

Facia speaker (where fitted)

1 Carefully prise up the speaker/display unit grille on the top of the facia.
2 Undo the screws and lift the speaker/display unit up. Disconnect the wiring and remove the speaker.
3 Refitting is a reversal of removal, making sure the speaker is correctly located.

Front door speakers

4 A tweeter is located in the forward edge of the door (adjacent to the door mirror). Remove the door trim panel as described in Chapter 11. Unclip the speaker grille, use a small screwdriver to release the securing clip, rotate the speaker anti-clockwise a little and withdraw it from the door panel, withdrawing the wiring and plug through the speaker aperture.
5 To remove the main speakers, remove the door trim panel as described in Chapter 11.
6 Drill out the 4 rivets securing the speaker to the door carrier. Remove the speaker and disconnect the wiring plug **(see illustration 21.9)**.
7 Refitting is a reversal of removal.

Rear door speakers

8 Remove the door trim panel as described in Chapter 11.
9 Drill out the 3 rivets securing the speaker to the door carrier. Remove the speaker and disconnect the wiring plug **(see illustration)**.
10 Refitting is a reversal of removal.

21.9 Drill out the rivets and remove the speaker (arrowed)

22 Anti-theft alarm and immobiliser system – general information

Note: *This information is applicable only to the systems fitted by Volvo as original equipment. All models are equipped with an anti-theft alarm, and most are also equipped with an ignition immobiliser.*

Immobiliser

The electronic immobiliser is automatically activated when the remote unit is removed from the starter panel on the facia. When activated, it cuts the ignition circuit, preventing the engine from being started.

The system is disarmed when the remote unit is inserted into the starter panel on the facia, as follows. The remote unit contains a transponder micro-chip, and the starter panel contains a reader. When the remote unit enters the starter panel, the reader recognises the signal from the micro-chip, and de-activates the immobiliser. It is essential that the tag showing the remote number is not lost (this will be supplied with the car when new). Any duplicate remotes will have to be obtained from a Volvo dealer, who will need the remote number to supply a duplicate.

Any problems or work involving the immobiliser system should be entrusted to a Volvo dealer or specialist, as dedicated electronic equipment is required to diagnose faults, or to 'match' the various components.

Alarm

An anti-theft alarm system is fitted as standard equipment. The alarm has switches on all the doors (including the tailgate), and the bonnet. If the tailgate, bonnet or any of the doors are opened or the ignition switch is switched on whilst the alarm is set, the alarm siren will sound and the hazard warning lights will flash. The alarm also has an immobiliser function which makes the ignition inoperable whilst the alarm is triggered.

Signals from the alarm system switches and contacts which are integral with the door, bonnet and tailgate locks are sent to a central control unit inside the car once the system is set. The control unit monitors the signals and activates the alarm if any of the signal loops are broken, or if an attempt is made to start the car (or to hot-wire the ignition).

The status of the system is displayed by means of a flashing LED.

Should the alarm system become faulty, bear in mind the following points:
a) *As with other electrical equipment, many faults are caused by poor connections or bad earths.*
b) *Check the operation of all the door, bonnet and boot lid/tailgate switches, and the operation of all interior lights.*
c) *The alarm system may behave oddly if the vehicle battery is in poor condition, or if its terminals are loose.*

23.2 Undo the 2 bolts for the bracket, and the 2 bolts securing the siren to the bracket (arrowed)

d) *If the system is operating correctly, but gives too many false alarms, a Volvo dealer or specialist may be able to reduce the sensitivity of some of the system sensors.*
e) *Ultimately, the vehicle may have to be taken to a Volvo dealer or a suitably-equipped garage for examination. They will have access to a special diagnostic tester which will quickly trace any fault present in the system.*

23 Anti-theft alarm system components – removal and refitting

Siren

1 Remove the plenum cover as described in Section 16. The siren is located on the left-hand side.
2 Undo the 2 bolts for the siren bracket and the 2 bolts securing the siren to the bracket, disconnect the wiring plug, and remove the unit **(see illustration)**.
3 Refitting is a reversal of removal.

Intrusion sensor

4 The sensors are located in the centre of the headlining. Using a flat-bladed tool, release the clips and remove the cover **(see illustration)**.
5 Release the 3 securing clips, disconnect the wiring plug, and remove the unit.
6 Refitting is a reversal of removal.

24 Airbag System – general information and precautions

General information

A supplemental restraint system is fitted in various forms as standard or optional equipment depending on model and territory.

The main system component is a driver's airbag, which is designed to prevent serious chest and head injuries to the driver during an accident. Similar airbags for the front seat passenger, side airbags (built into the side

23.4 Intrusion sensor cover

of the front seats), and side curtain airbags are also standard fitment. Side impact crash sensors are located on the B and C-pillars of the vehicle, with frontal sensors located each side of the radiator fan assembly on the lock carrier/crossmember. The module incorporates a deceleration sensor, and a microprocessor ECU, to monitor the severity of the impact and trigger the airbag where necessary. The airbag is inflated by a gas generator, which forces the bag out of the module cover in the centre of the steering wheel, or out of a cover on the passenger's side of the facia/seat cover/ headlining. A contact reel behind the steering wheel at the top of the steering column ensures that a good electrical connection is maintained with the airbag at all times as the steering wheel is turned in each direction.

In addition to the airbag units, the supplemental restraint system also incorporates pyrotechnic seat belt tensioners operated by gas cartridges in the belt inertia reel assembly. The pyrotechnic units are also triggered by the crash sensor, in conjunction with the airbags, to tighten the seat belts and provide additional collision protection.

All models also incorporate a side impact protection system (SIPS) as standard equipment. In its basic form, the SIPS system is essentially an integral part of the vehicle structure in which strengthening agents are used to distribute side impacts through the bodywork. This is done by reinforcing the lower areas of the doors and door pillars, and providing strengthening bars in the seats and centre console. In this way, side impacts are absorbed by the body structure as a whole, giving exceptional impact strength.

Precautions

⚠️ *Warning: The safe handling of the SRS components requires the use of Volvo special equipment. Any attempt to dismantle the airbag module, SIPS bag, crash sensors, contact reel, seat belt tensioners or any associated wiring or components without this equipment, and the specialist knowledge needed to use it correctly, could result in severe personal injury and/or malfunction of the system.*

• *Before carrying out any work on the SRS components, disconnect the battery and wait for at least 10 minutes for any residual electrical energy to dissipate before proceeding.*
• *Handle the airbag unit with extreme care as a precaution against personal injury, and always hold it with the cover facing away from the body. If in doubt concerning any proposed work involving the airbag unit or its control circuitry, consult a Volvo dealer.*
• *Note that the airbag(s) must not be subjected to temperatures in excess of 90°C (194°F). When the airbag is removed, ensure that it is stored with the pad up to prevent possible inflation.*
• *Do not allow any solvents or cleaning agents to contact the airbag assemblies. They must be cleaned using only a damp cloth.*

• *The airbag(s) and control unit are both sensitive to impact. If either is dropped or damaged they should be renewed.*
• *Disconnect the airbag control unit wiring plug prior to using arc-welding equipment on the vehicle.*

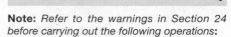

25 Airbag system components - removal and refitting

Note: *Refer to the warnings in Section 24 before carrying out the following operations:*
1 Disconnect the battery negative terminal (see Chapter 5A). Wait at least 5 minutes for any residual electrical energy to dissipate before commencing work. **Note:** *If removing the driver's airbag, turn the steering wheel 90° from straight-ahead before disconnecting the battery, otherwise the steering lock will engage.*

Driver's airbag

2 Set the steering wheel to straight-ahead, then turn it 90° to the left or right. Release the steering column adjustment lever, and pull the wheel out and down as far as possible.
3 Locate the access hole in the reverse side of the steering wheel, and insert a flat-bladed screwdriver into the hole, then pull the handle upwards to release the retaining clip **(see illustration)**. Turn the airbag 180° and release the clip on the other side.
4 Temporarily touch the striker plate of the front door to discharge any electrostatic electricity. Return the steering wheel to the straight-ahead position, then carefully lift the airbag assembly away from the steering wheel and disconnect the wiring connectors from the rear of the unit **(see illustration)**. Note that the airbag must not be knocked or dropped, and should be stored the correct way up with its padded surface uppermost.
5 On refitting, reconnect the wiring connectors and locate the airbag unit in the steering wheel, making sure the wire does not become trapped, and push the airbag into place to engage the retaining clips. Switch on the ignition, **then** reconnect the battery negative lead (see Chapter 5A). Ensure no-one is in the vehicle when the battery is reconnected.

Airbag wiring contact unit

6 The contact unit is integral with the steering wheel module (SWM). Removal and refitting of the unit is described in Section 28 of this Chapter.

Passenger airbag

7 Remove the passenger's glovebox, centre console, and driver's side lower facia panel as described in Chapter 11.
8 Remove the facia loudspeaker as described in Section 21 (where fitted).
9 Undo the 2 screws and remove the instrument cluster surround trim **(see illustration 6.3)**.
10 Carefully prise the covers from each end of the facia **(see illustration)**.
11 Working underneath the facia, undo the 2 airbag lower mounting bolts **(see illustration)**.
12 Disconnect the airbag wiring plug **(see illustration)**.
13 Undo the 2 cover bolts on the underside of the facia panel **(see illustrations)**.

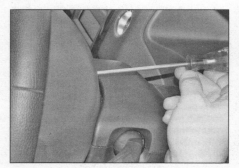

25.3 Insert a flat-bladed screwdriver, and lift the handle to release the airbag clip

25.4 Disconnect the wiring plugs from the rear of the airbag

25.10 Prise the end panels from the facia

25.11 Undo the 2 airbag lower mounting bolts (arrowed)

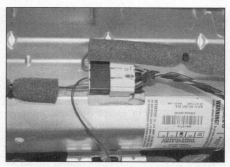

25.12 Disconnect the airbag wiring plug

25.13a Undo the bolts on the underside of the facia – to the right . . .

25.13b . . . and left of the airbag (arrowed)

14 Undo the 3 screws at the centre, lower section of the facia panel **(see illustrations)**.
15 Undo the bolt in the facia speaker aperture (where applicable), and disconnect the hazard warning switch wiring plug.
16 Undo the screw at each end of the facia panel **(see illustration)**.
17 Lift the facia panel slightly, disconnect the light switch and ignition switch wiring plugs, then lift the panel away.
18 Undo the 8 nuts and remove the airbag **(see illustration)**.
19 Refitting is a reversal of removal. Ensure that the wiring connector is securely reconnected. Ensure that no-one is inside the vehicle. Switch on the ignition, then reconnect the battery negative lead.

Airbag control unit

Removal

20 Disconnect the battery negative lead as described in Chapter 5A. Wait at least 10 minutes before proceeding, to allow and residual electrical energy to dissipate.
21 Remove the centre console as described in Chapter 11.
22 Release the locking catches and disconnect the 2 wiring plugs.
23 Note its fitted location, undo the 4 screws and remove the module **(see illustration)**.

Refitting

24 Refitting is a reversal of removal, ensuring the module is fitted with the arrow on its top surface facing forwards.
25 On completion, make sure that no-one is inside the car. Switch on the ignition, then reconnect the battery negative lead. Switch the ignition off, then on again, and check that the SRS warning light comes on, then goes out within 7 seconds. **Note:** *If a new control unit has been fitted, suitable software will need to be downloaded and installed from Volvo. Entrust this task to a Volvo dealer or suitably-equipped specialist.*

Side airbags

26 The side airbag units are built into the front seats, and their removal requires that the seat fabric be removed. This is not considered to be a DIY operation, and should be referred to a Volvo dealer or upholstery specialist.

Side crash sensors

Removal

27 The side crash sensors are fitted to the B-pillar (between the driver's and passenger's doors), and at the base of the C-pillar. The battery should be disconnected, as described in Chapter 5A, before any work is undertaken on the sensors.
28 To remove the sensor on the B-pillar, remove the pillar trim (as applicable) as described in Chapter 11. Release the clips and disconnect the wiring plug from the sensor **(see illustration)**. Undo the retaining screws and remove the sensor.
29 To remove the sensor at the base of the C-pillar, remove the rear seat side pad and the C-pillar trim as described in Chapter 11. Undo the retaining screws and remove the sensor **(see illustration 25.28)**.

Refitting

30 Refit the sensor(s) to the pillar(s) and tighten the retaining screws to the specified torque. Reconnect the wiring plug.
31 The remainder of refitting is a reversal of removal.

Front crash sensors

Removal

32 The front crash sensors are located each side of the radiator fan assembly on the lock carrier/crossmember. Disconnect the battery, as described in Chapter 5A, before removing the sensors.
33 Disconnect the wiring plug from the sensor, undo the retaining screws and remove the sensor **(see illustration)**.

Refitting

34 Refitting is a reversal of removal.

25.14a Remove the screws in the centre (arrowed) . . .

25.14b . . . and the one to the right of the ignition switch (arrowed)

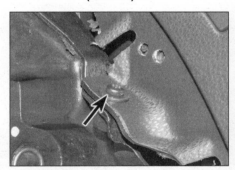

25.16 Undo the screw (arrowed) at each end of the facia

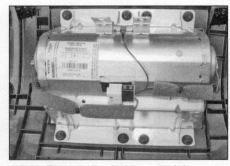

25.18 Remove the 8 airbag retaining nuts

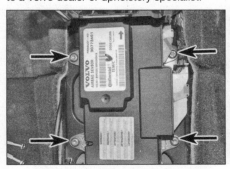

25.23 SRS module retaining screws (arrowed)

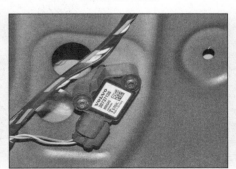

25.28 Crash sensors are located in the B-pillar and C-pillar

25.33 The front crash sensors are located either side of the radiator

Side curtain airbag

35 In order to remove the side curtain airbag(s), the headlining must be removed. This is not considered a DIY operation, and should be entrusted to a Volvo dealer or upholstery specialist.

Passenger airbag deactivation switch

36 Where fitted, the switch to deactivate the front passenger airbag is located in the trim panel at the end of the facia on the passenger side.
37 To remove the switch, first disconnect the battery negative terminal as described in Chapter 5A.
38 Carefully prise off the trim panel, pull forward slightly, and disconnect the wiring plug.
39 On the rear of the panel, release the securing clips and remove the switch.
40 Refitting is a reversal of removal.

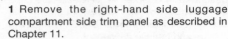

26 Parking assistance system – removal and refitting

Control module

1 The parking assistance module (PAM) is located behind the luggage compartment right-hand side trim panel. Remove the panel as described in Chapter 11.
2 Undo the 2 bolts, remove the module and disconnect the wiring plugs.
3 Refitting is a reversal of removal. A new unit may require recalibration and this should be entrusted to a Volvo dealer or suitably-equipped specialist.

Sensors

4 The sensors are set into the rear bumper. Remove the rear bumper as described in Chapter 11.

5 Disconnect the wiring plug from each sensor.
6 Spread the retaining clips and pull the sensor from the inside of the bumper.
7 Refitting is a reversal of removal.

27 Fuel filler flap locking motor – removal and refitting

1 Remove the right-hand side luggage compartment side trim panel as described in Chapter 11.
2 Open the fuel filler flap and undo the 2 screws adjacent to the catch. Disconnect the wiring plug and slide the motor from the bracket. The motor can now be withdrawn **(see illustration)**.
3 Refitting is a reversal of removal.

28 Electronic Control Modules – removal and refitting

Steering Wheel Module

General information

1 The steering wheel module is fitted to the top of the steering column, and manages the signals for the following functions (where applicable):
a) Steering wheel angle information.
b) Steering wheel angle rate of change.
c) Audio systems volume control.
d) Phone module menu selection and volume.
e) Traffic information menu.
f) Windscreen washer and wipers.
g) Tailgate washers and wipers.
h) Headlamp washers.
i) Cruise control.

27.2 Undo the filler flap motor Torx screws (arrowed)

j) Turn signal lamps.
k) Indicator lamps.
l) Dipped and main beam.
m) Trip computer/driver's information module test display.
n) Rain sensor module.
o) Parking heater.

2 The steering wheel module is in constant communication with the vehicle's other control modules via an information network, known as a 'Databus'.
3 Should a fault occur, the module is equipped with a sophisticated self-diagnosis facility, which can be interrogated via the vehicle's diagnostic connector located under the driver's side of the facia, using a fault code reader.

Removal

4 Refer to Chapter 10 and remove the steering wheel.
5 Undo the three T25 Torx screws from under the steering column lower shroud, unclip the gaiter and prise the upper and lower shrouds apart to release the retaining pegs. Remove the lower shroud, and lift the upper shroud out of the way **(see illustrations)**.
6 The wiper/washer switch and turn indicator switch are retained by 2 screws each. Undo

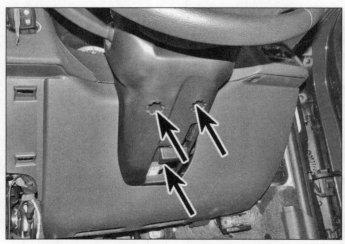

28.5a Undo the lower shroud screws (arrowed)

28.5b Unclip the rubber gaiter and separate the column shrouds

28.6 The steering module switches are retained by 2 screws each (arrowed)

28.7a Undo the 2 screws (arrowed) . . .

28.7b . . . then press in the clip (arrowed) and slide the module from the column

the screws and pull the switches out to the sides **(see illustration)**.

7 Undo the 2 screws, release the clip, and pull the contact reel/steering wheel module rearwards. Disconnect the wiring plugs as the assembly is withdrawn **(see illustrations)**.

Refitting

8 Refitting is a reversal of removal. If a new steering wheel module/contact reel has been fitted, software for the new unit must be downloaded from Volvo. Consult a Volvo dealer or specialist.

Keyless Vehicle Module

9 Remove the left-hand side front seat as described in Chapter 11.

10 Release the catches and disconnect the 5 wiring plugs from the unit, undo the 2 screws, and remove the module.

11 Refitting is a reversal of removal.

Rain Sensor Module

12 Carefully prise-off the interior mirror mounting cover **(see illustration)**.

13 Disconnect the sensor wiring plug, release the 2 catches, and remove the module **(see illustration)**.

14 Refitting is a reversal of removal.

Seat Heating Module

15 The seat heating module is fitted to the underside of the front seats. It is possible to access the module once the seat has been placed in its highest position. Alternatively, remove the front seat as described in Chapter 11.

16 Prise up the centre pin, then lever-out the plastic expanding rivet securing the module to the seat frame. Disconnect the wiring plug and remove the module.

17 Refitting is a reversal of removal.

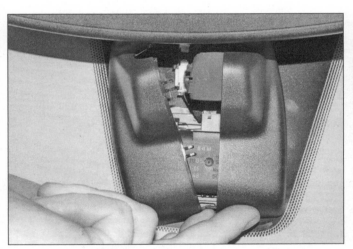

28.12 Prise apart the mirror mounting covers

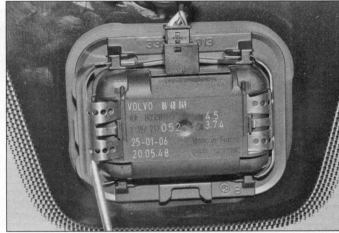

28.13 Release the catches and disconnect the sensor wiring plug

VOLVO S40/V50 wiring diagrams from March '04 to June '07

Diagram 1

Key to symbols

Solenoid actuator	Bulb	Wire splice, soldered joint, or unspecified connector
Heating element	Switch	Connecting wires
Earth point & location (E7)	Fuse/fusible link **F26**	Diode
Wire colour (red with yellow tracer) Rd/Ye	Resistor	Light-emitting diode
Dashed outline denotes part of a larger item, containing in this case an electronic or solid state device	Variable resistor	Item number **12**
	Variable resistor	Motor/pump **M**

Earth locations

E1   On engine
E2   LH strut tower
E3   LH strut tower
E4   Base of LH 'A' pillar
E5   Base of LH 'A' pillar
E6   RH strut tower
E7   Base of RH 'A' pillar
E8   LH rear of luggage compartment
E9   RH rear of luggage compartment
E10 Base of LH 'B' pillar
E11 LH strut tower
E12 Base of RH 'A' pillar
E13 Base of LH 'A' pillar
E14 Base of RH 'A' pillar
E15 Base of RH 'B' pillar

Engine fusebox ④

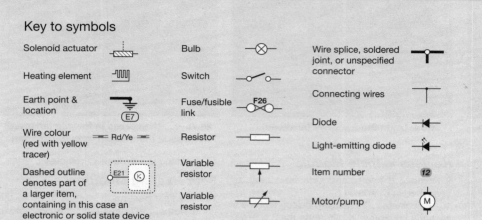

Fuse	Rating	Circuit protected	Fuse	Rating	Circuit protected
F1	50A	Engine cooling fan	F20	15A	Horn
F2	80A	Power steering	F21	20A	Additional heater
F3	60A	Passenger fusebox supply	F22	-	Spare
F4	60A	Passenger fusebox supply	F23	10A	Engine management/transmission control
F5	80A	Climate control, additional heater	F24	20A	Heated fuel filter
F6	60/70A	Glow plugs (4/5 cylinders)	F25	-	Spare
F7	30A	ABS pump	F26	15A	Ignition switch
F8	20A	ABS valves	F27	10A	A/C compressor
F9	30A	Engine functions	F28	-	Spare
F10	40A	Ventilation fan	F29	15A	Front foglight
F11	20A	Headlight washers	F30	3A	Engine management
F12	30A	Heated rear window	F31	10A	Voltage regulator
F13	30A	Starter motor relay	F32	10A	Engine management
F14	40A	Trailer wiring	F33	20A	Engine management
F15	-	Spare	F34	10A	Engine management
F16	30A	Infotainment system	F35	15A	Engine management
F17	30A	Windscreen wipers	F36	10A	Engine management
F18	40A	Passenger fusebox supply			
F19	-	Spare			

Passenger fusebox ⑥

Fuse	Rating	Circuit protected	Fuse	Rating	Circuit protected	Fuse	Rating	Circuit protected
F37	-	Spare	F62	20A	Sunroof	F75	-	Spare
F38	-	Spare	F63	20A	Supply to rear RH door	F76	-	Spare
F39	-	Spare	F64	5A	Audio system	F77	-	Luggage compartment accessory connector
F40	-	Spare	F65	5A	Infotainment system			
F41	-	Spare	F66	10A	Infotainment system, climate control	F78	-	Spare
F42	-	Spare	F67	-	Spare	F79	5A	Reversing light
F43	15A	Phone, audio system	F68	5A	Cruise control, steering wheel control unit	F80	-	Spare
F44	10A	SRS system	F69	5A	Climate control, rain sensor	F81	20A	Supply to rear LH door
F45	15A	Accessory connectors	F70	-	Spare	F82	25A	Supply to front RH door
F46	5A	Interior lighting, glovebox light	F71	-	Spare	F83	25A	Supply to front LH door
F47	5A	Interior lighting	F72	-	Spare	F84	25A	Passenger's electric seat
F48	15A	Washer	F73	5A	Sunroof, over head console, rear seatbelt reminder, autodim mirror	F85	25A	Driver's electric seat
F49	10A	SRS system	F74	15A	Fuel pump relay	F86	5A	Interior lighting, electric seats fuel level display
F50	-	Spare						
F51	10A	Parking assistance, headlight levelling, additional heater						
F52	5A	Transmission control, ABS						
F53	10A	Power steering						
F54	10A	Engine management						
F55	20A	Remote control, keyless control						
F56	10A	Alarm						
F57	15A	Diagnostic connector, stop light						
F58	7.5A	RH main beam, auxiliary lights						
F59	7.5A	LH main beam						
F60	15A	Driver's seat heater						
F61	15A	Passenger's seat heater						

H33663

Wire colours

Bk	Black	**Pk**	Pink
Ye	Yellow	**Vt**	Violet
Bu	Blue	**Og**	Orange
Bn	Brown	**Wh**	White
Gn	Green	**Rd**	Red
Gy	Grey	**Lgn**	Lt. Green

*   Models with automatic
    transmission

Key to items

1 Battery
2 Alternator
3 Starter motor
4 Engine fusebox
   R2 = horn relay
   R13 = starter relay
5 Ignition switch
6 Passenger fusebox
7 Transmission control unit
8 Engine control unit
9 Clutch pedal switch
   (manual transmission)
10 Steering wheel control unit
11 Clock springs
12 Horn switch
13 Horn
14 Cooling fan control unit
15 Climate control pressure switch
16 Coolant temperature sensor
17 Cooling fan motor
18 Power steering control unit
19 ABS control unit

Diagram 2

H33664

Starting & charging

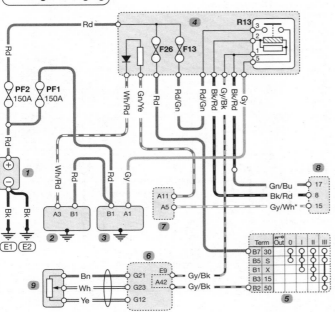

Horn

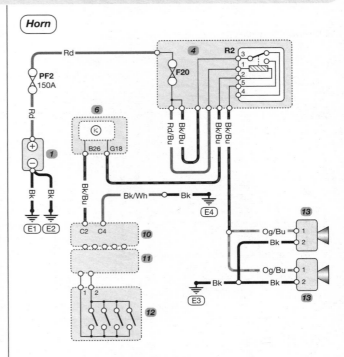

Engine cooling fan

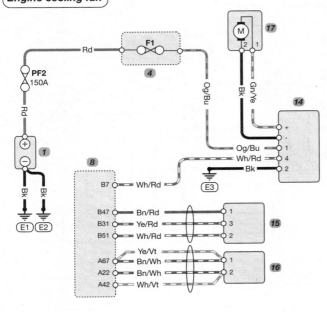

Electronic power steering

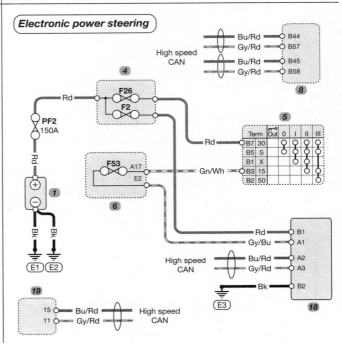

Wire colours

Bk	Black	**Pk**	Pink
Ye	Yellow	**Vt**	Violet
Bu	Blue	**Og**	Orange
Bn	Brown	**Wh**	White
Gn	Green	**Rd**	Red
Gy	Grey	**Lgn**	Lt. Green

* Models with Bi-Xenon headlights

Key to items

1 Battery
4 Engine fusebox
5 Ignition switch
  a = inhibitor
  b = reader
6 Passenger fusebox
  a = control unit
  R8 = main beam relay
10 Steering wheel control unit
22 Steering column lock unit

23 Light switch
  a = off/side/headlight
  b = 'lights on' indicator
24 LH headlight unit
  a = dip beam
  b = main beam
  c = sidelight
25 RH headlight unit
  (as above)
26 LH headlight discharge control unit

27 RH headlight discharge control unit
28 Number plate light assembly
29 LH rear light unit
  a = stop/tail light
  b = tail light
30 RH rear light unit
  a = stop/tail light
  b = tail light

Diagram 3

H33665

Start control system

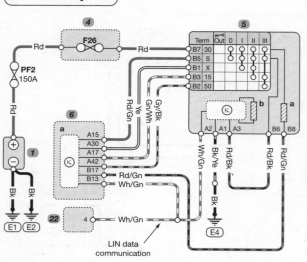

Headlights (without Bi-Xenon)

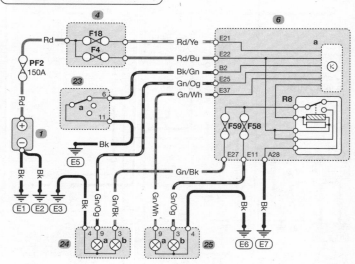

Side & tail lights

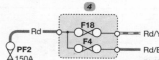
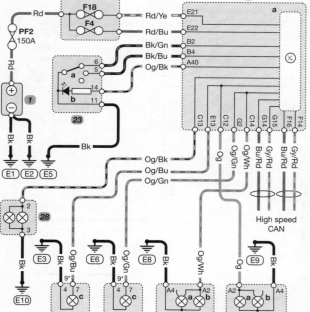

Headlights (with Bi-Xenon)

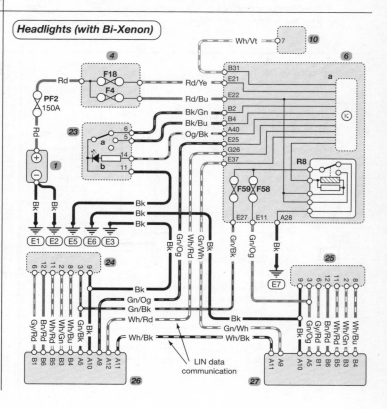

Wire colours

Bk	Black	Pk	Pink
Ye	Yellow	Vt	Violet
Bu	Blue	Og	Orange
Bn	Brown	Wh	White
Gn	Green	Rd	Red
Gy	Grey	Lgn	Lt. Green

* Models with Bi-Xenon headlights

Key to items

1 Battery
4 Engine fusebox
  R4 = front foglight relay
6 Passenger fusebox
  a = control unit
  R2 = reversing light relay
  R8 = main beam relay
7 Transmission control unit
23 Light switch
  c = rear foglight
  d = front foglight

24 LH headlight unit
  d = direction indicator
25 RH headlight unit
  d = direction indicator
29 LH rear light unit
  a = stop/tail light
  c = reversing light
  d = rear foglight
  e = direction indicator
30 RH rear light unit
  (as above)

33 Fuse in holder
34 Auxiliary light switch
35 Auxiliary light relay
36 LH auxiliary light
37 RH auxiliary light
38 High level stop light
39 RH rear window suppressor
40 Driver information control unit
41 Stop light switch
42 Reversing light switch
  (manual transmission)

43 LH front foglight
44 RH front foglight
45 LH mirror assembly
46 RH mirror assembly
47 LH front door control unit
48 RH front door control unit
49 Hazard warning switch

Diagram 4

H33666

Auxiliary lighting

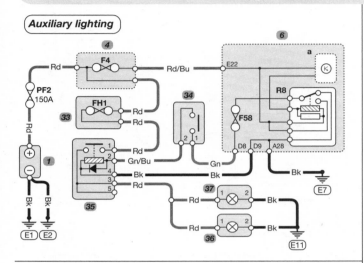

Stop & reversing lights

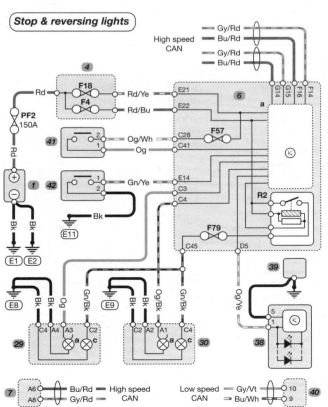

Front & rear foglights

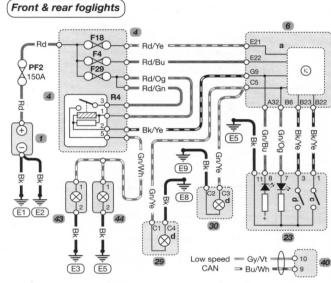

Direction indicators & hazard warning lights

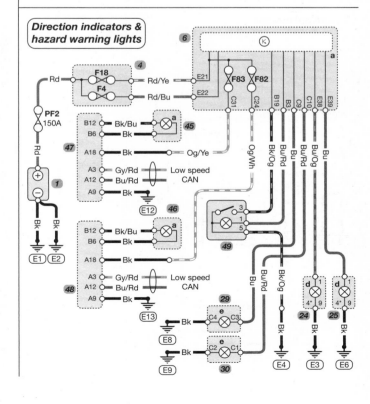

Wire colours				Key to items		

Wire colours

Bk	Black	Pk	Pink
Ye	Yellow	Vt	Violet
Bu	Blue	Og	Orange
Bn	Brown	Wh	White
Gn	Green	Rd	Red
Gy	Grey	Lgn	Lt. Green

Key to items

1 Battery
4 Engine fusebox
  R9 = Headlight washer relay
5 Ignition switch
6 Passenger fusebox
  a = control unit
  R7A = windscreen washer relay
  R7B = rear window washer relay
  R18 = comfort functions relay

10 Steering wheel control unit
23 Light switch
  a = off/side/headlight
  b = 'lights on' indicator
30 RH rear light unit
  a = stop/tail light
41 Stop light switch
53 Trailer control unit
54 7 pin trailer socket

55 13 pin trailer socket
56 Headlight washer pump
57 Wiper motor control unit
58 Rain sensor
59 Windscreen washer pump

Diagram 5

H33667

7 pin trailer socket

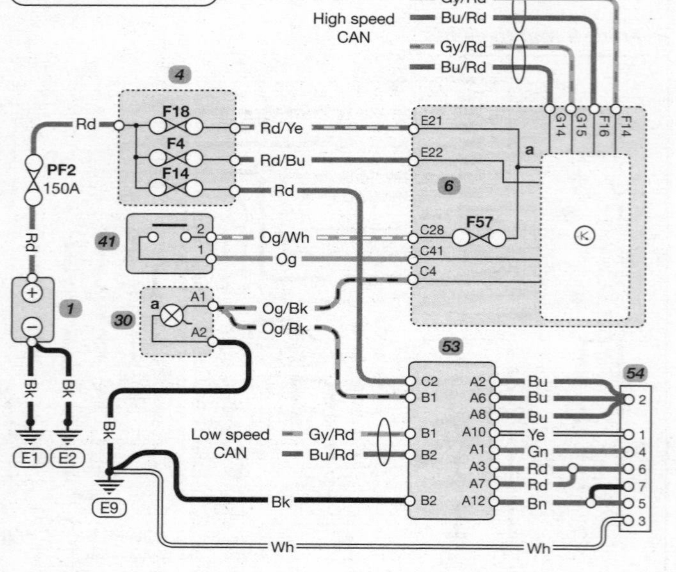

13 pin trailer socket

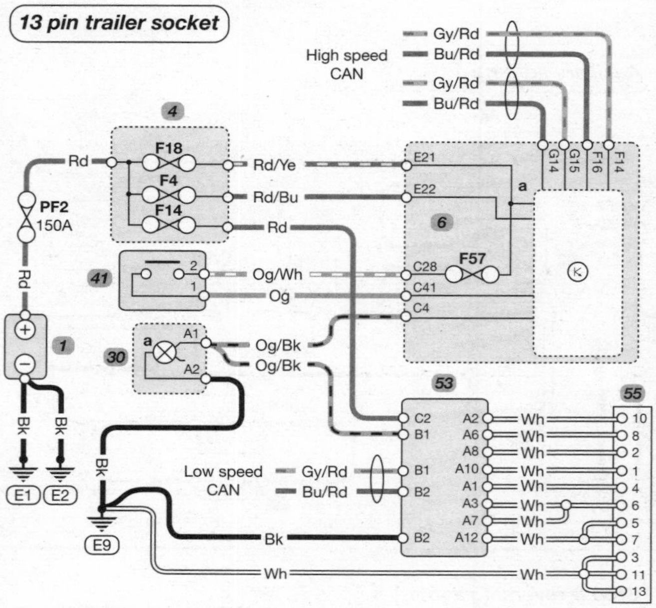

Headlight washer

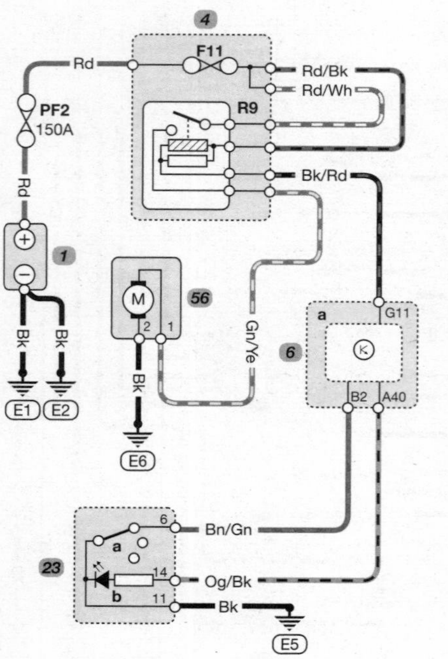

Wash/wipe

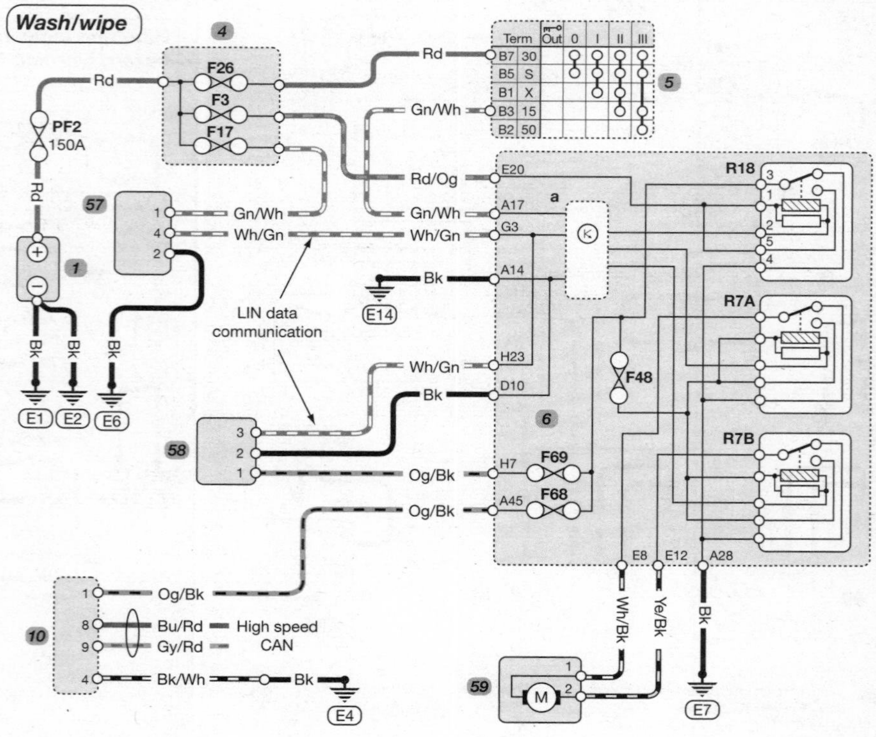

Term	Out	0	I	II	III
B7	30				
B5	S				
B1	X				
B3	15				
B2	50				

LIN data communication

High speed CAN

Low speed CAN

Wire colours

Bk	Black	**Pk**	Pink
Ye	Yellow	**Vt**	Violet
Bu	Blue	**Og**	Orange
Bn	Brown	**Wh**	White
Gn	Green	**Rd**	Red
Gy	Grey	**Lgn**	Lt. Green

Key to items

1 Battery
4 Engine fusebox
6 Passenger fusebox
  a = control unit
10 Steering wheel control unit
23 Light switch
  e = tailgate release
28 Number plate light assembly

47 LH front door control unit
48 RH front door control unit
60 LH rear door control unit
61 RH rear door control unit
62 Remote receiver
63 Fuel filler flap motor
64 Tailgate lock motor
65 SRS control unit

66 Tailgate lock switch
67 Door lock assembly
68 Central locking switch

Diagram 6

H33668

Central locking

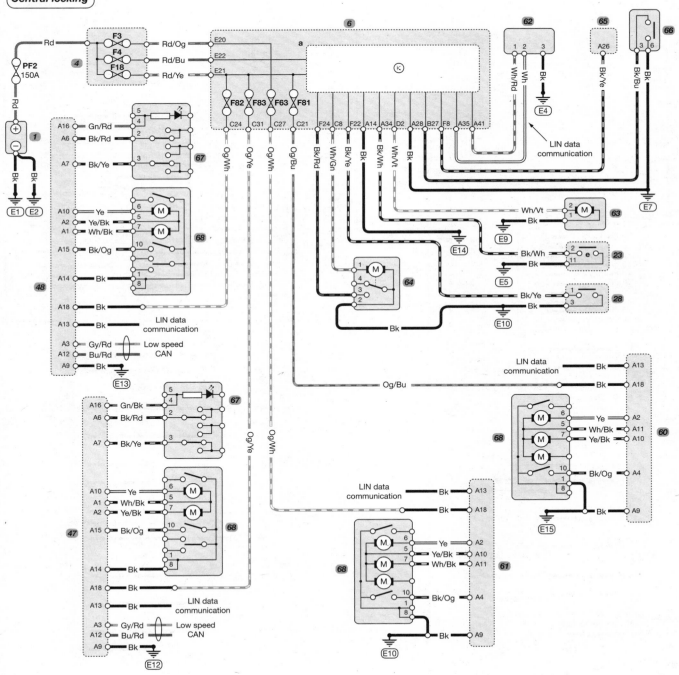

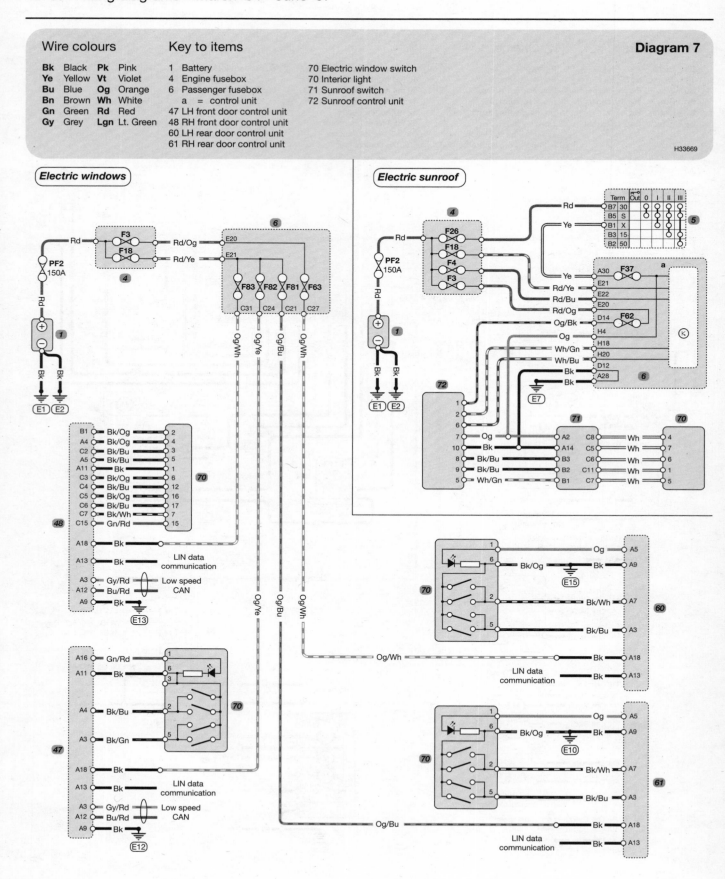

Diagram 7

Wire colours

Bk	Black	Pk	Pink
Ye	Yellow	Vt	Violet
Bu	Blue	Og	Orange
Bn	Brown	Wh	White
Gn	Green	Rd	Red
Gy	Grey	Lgn	Lt. Green

Key to items

1 Battery
4 Engine fusebox
6 Passenger fusebox
   a = control unit
47 LH front door control unit
48 RH front door control unit
60 LH rear door control unit
61 RH rear door control unit

70 Electric window switch
70 Interior light
71 Sunroof switch
72 Sunroof control unit

H33669

Electric windows

Electric sunroof

Wire colours

Bk	Black	Pk	Pink
Ye	Yellow	Vt	Violet
Bu	Blue	Og	Orange
Bn	Brown	Wh	White
Gn	Green	Rd	Red
Gy	Grey	Lgn	Lt. Green

Key to items

1 Battery
4 Engine fusebox
 R10 = heated rear window
5 Ignition switch
6 Passenger fusebox
 a = control unit
 R11B = infotainment system
10 Steering wheel control unit
39 RH rear window suppressor
45 LH mirror assembly
46 RH mirror assembly
47 LH front door control unit
48 RH front door control unit
75 Traffic message control unit
76 AM/FM tuner control unit
77 Heated rear window control unit
78 Heated rear window
79 Infotainment control unit
80 Media player
81 Audio unit
82 Centre speaker (dashboard)
83 RH rear door
84 RH rear door tweeter
85 Passenger's door speaker
86 Passenger's door tweeter
87 LH rear door speaker
88 LH rear door tweeter
89 Driver's door speaker
90 Driver's door tweeter
91 Microphone
92 LH rear window suppressor
93 Climate control system control unit
94 Heated mirror/rear window switch
95 Door mirror control switch

Diagram 8

H33670

Audio system

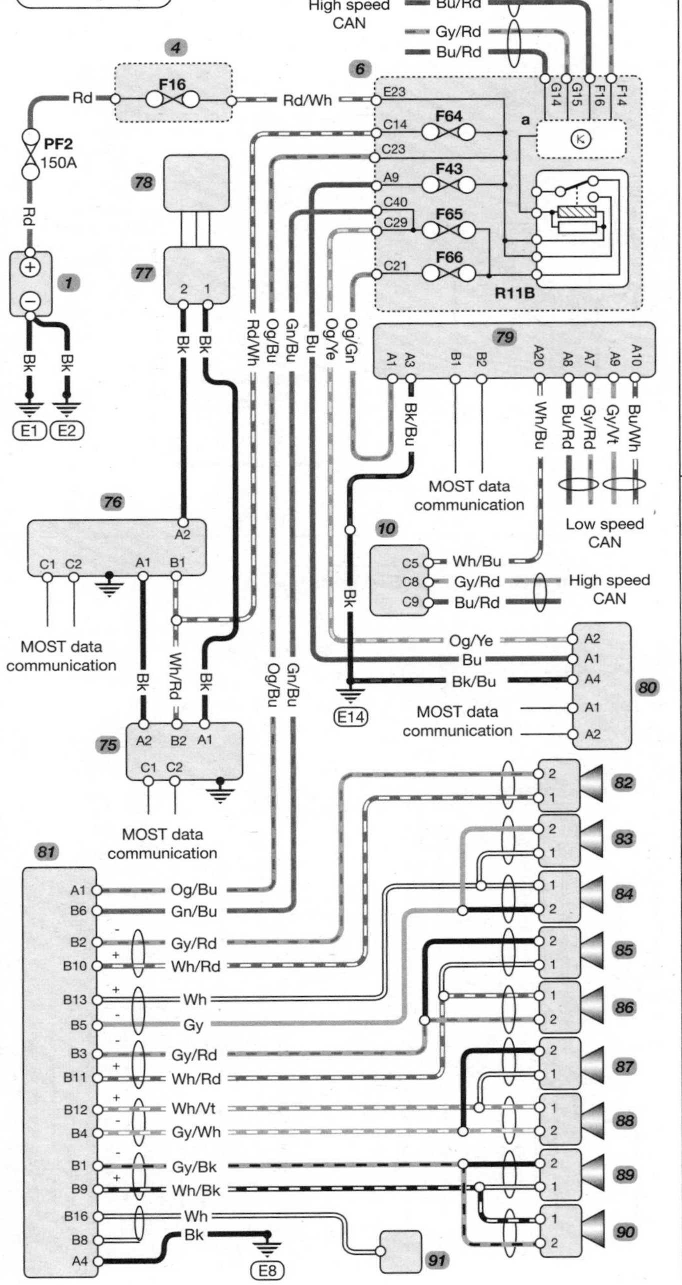

Heated rear window

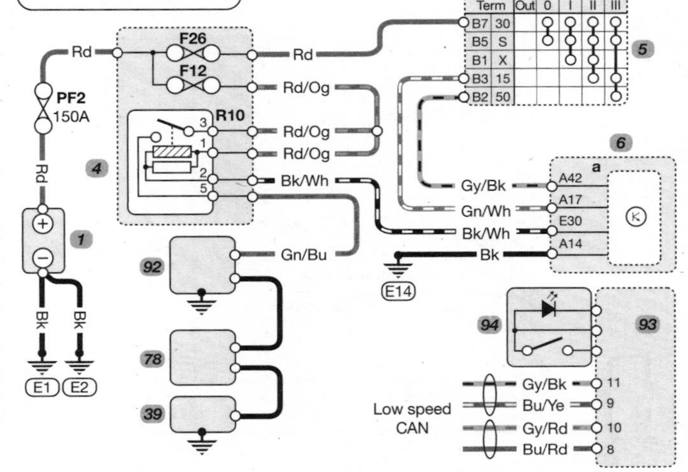

Heated & electric mirrors

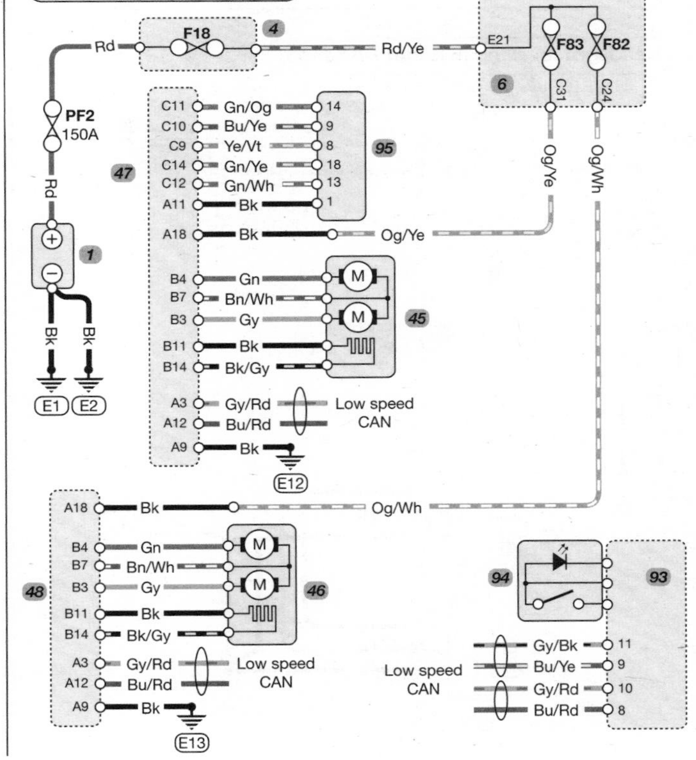

Wire colours

Bk	Black	**Pk**	Pink
Ye	Yellow	**Vt**	Violet
Bu	Blue	**Og**	Orange
Bn	Brown	**Wh**	White
Gn	Green	**Rd**	Red
Gy	Grey	**Lgn**	Lt. Green

Key to items

1 Battery
4 Engine fusebox
5 Ignition switch
6 Passenger fusebox
  a = control unit
  R3 = comfort relay
  R8 = main beam relay
23 Light switch
  f = headlight levelling
24 LH headlight unit
  e = headlight levelling

25 RH headlight unit
  e = headlight levelling
26 LH headlight discharge control unit
27 RH headlight discharge control unit
100 Diagnostic connector
101 Front 12v connector
102 Rear 12v connector
103 Luggage compartment 12v connector
104 Front level sensor
105 Rear level sensor

Diagram 9

H33671

Diagnostic connector

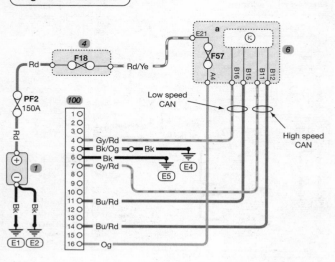

12v accessory connectors

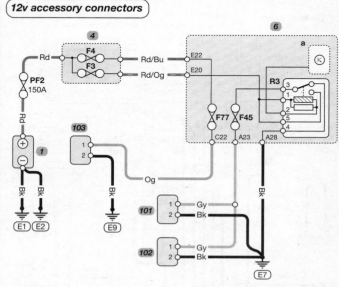

Headlight levelling (without Bi-Xenon)

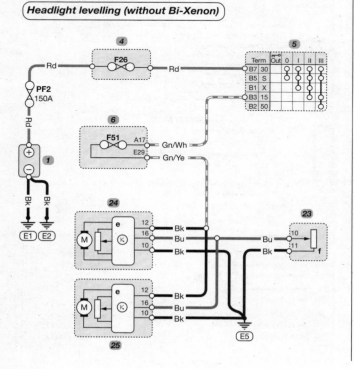

Headlight levelling (with Bi-Xenon)

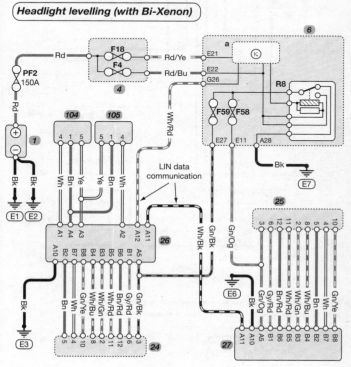

VOLVO S40/V50 wiring diagrams from July '07 to 2013   Diagram 1

Key to symbols

Symbol name		Symbol name		Symbol name	
Solenoid actuator		Bulb		Wire splice, soldered joint, or unspecified connector	
Heating element		Switch		Connecting wires	
Earth point & location	E7	Fuse/fusible link	F26	Diode	
Wire colour (red with yellow tracer)	Rd/Ye	Resistor		Light-emitting diode	
Dashed outline denotes part of a larger item, containing in this case an electronic or solid state device	E21 (K)	Variable resistor		Item number	12
		Variable resistor		Motor/pump	M

Earth locations

E1	On engine
E2	LH strut tower
E3	LH strut tower
E4	Base of LH 'A' pillar
E5	Base of LH 'A' pillar
E6	RH strut tower
E7	Base of RH 'A' pillar
E8	LH rear of luggage compartment
E9	RH rear of luggage compartment
E10	Base of LH 'B' pillar
E11	LH strut tower
E12	Base of RH 'A' pillar
E13	Base of LH 'A' pillar
E14	Base of RH 'A' pillar
E15	Base of RH 'B' pillar

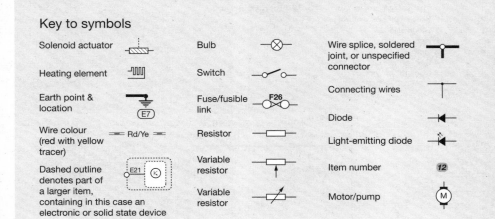

Engine fusebox ④

Fuse	Rating	Circuit protected	Fuse	Rating	Circuit protected
F1	50A	Engine cooling fan	F20	15A	Horn
F2	80A	Power steering	F21	20A	Additional heater
F3	60A	Passenger fusebox supply	F22	-	Spare
F4	60A	Passenger fusebox supply	F23	10A	Engine management/transmission control
F5	80A	Climate control, additional heater	F24	20A	Heated fuel filter
F6	60/70A	Glow plugs (4/5 cylinders)	F25	-	Spare
F7	30A	ABS pump	F26	15A	Ignition switch
F8	20A	ABS valves	F27	10A	A/C compressor
F9	30A	Engine functions	F28	-	Spare
F10	40A	Ventilation fan	F29	15A	Front foglight
F11	20A	Headlight washers	F30	3A	Engine management
F12	30A	Heated rear window	F31	10A	Voltage regulator
F13	30A	Starter motor relay	F32	10A	Engine management
F14	40A	Trailer wiring	F33	20A	Engine management
F15	-	Spare	F34	10A	Engine management
F16	30A	Infotainment system	F35	15A	Engine management
F17	30A	Windscreen wipers	F36	10A	Engine management
F18	40A	Passenger fusebox supply			
F19	-	Spare			

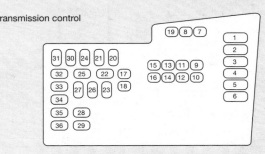

Passenger fusebox ⑥

Fuse	Rating	Circuit protected	Fuse	Rating	Circuit protected	Fuse	Rating	Circuit protected
F37	-	Spare	F62	20A	Sunroof	F75	-	Spare
F38	-	Spare	F63	20A	Supply to rear RH door	F76	-	Spare
F39	-	Spare	F64	5A	Audio system	F77	-	Luggage compartment accessory connector
F40	-	Spare	F65	5A	Infotainment system			
F41	-	Spare	F66	10A	Infotainment system, climate control	F78	-	Spare
F42	-	Spare	F67	-	Spare	F79	5A	Reversing light
F43	15A	Phone, audio system	F68	5A	Cruise control, steering wheel control unit	F80	-	Spare
F44	10A	SRS system	F69	5A	Climate control, rain sensor	F81	20A	Supply to rear LH door
F45	15A	Accessory connectors	F70	-	Spare	F82	25A	Supply to front RH door
F46	5A	Interior lighting, glovebox light	F71	-	Spare	F83	25A	Supply to front LH door
F47	5A	Interior lighting	F72	-	Spare	F84	25A	Passenger's electric seat
F48	15A	Washer	F73	5A	Sunroof, over head console, rear seatbelt reminder, autodim mirror	F85	25A	Driver's electric seat
F49	10A	SRS system				F86	5A	Interior lighting, electric seats fuel level display
F50	-	Spare	F74	15A	Fuel pump relay			
F51	10A	Parking assistance, headlight levelling, additional heater						
F52	5A	Transmission control, ABS						
F53	10A	Power steering						
F54	10A	Engine management						
F55	20A	Remote control, keyless control						
F56	10A	Alarm						
F57	15A	Diagnostic connector, stop light						
F58	7.5A	RH main beam, auxiliary lights						
F59	7.5A	LH main beam						
F60	15A	Driver's seat heater						
F61	15A	Passenger's seat heater						

H47633

Wire colours

Bk Black   **Pk** Pink
Ye Yellow   **Vt** Violet
Bu Blue   **Og** Orange
Bn Brown   **Wh** White
Gn Green   **Rd** Red
Gy Grey   **Lgn** Lt. Green

Key to items

1 Battery
2 Alternator
3 Starter motor
4 Engine fusebox
   R2 = horn relay
   R13 = starter relay
5 Ignition switch
6 Passenger fusebox
9 Clutch pedal switch
   (manual transmission)
10 Steering wheel control unit
11 Clock springs
12 Horn switch
13 Horn
14 Cooling fan control unit
17 Cooling fan motor
18 Power steering control unit
19 ABS control unit

Diagram 2

H47634

Starting & charging

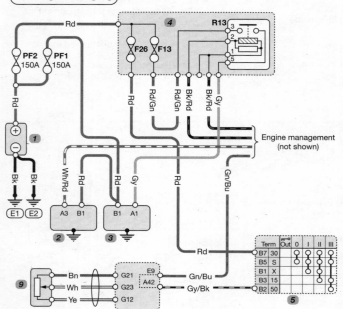

Horn

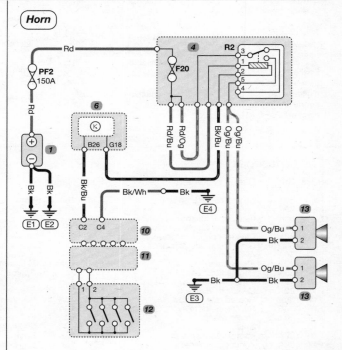

Engine cooling fan

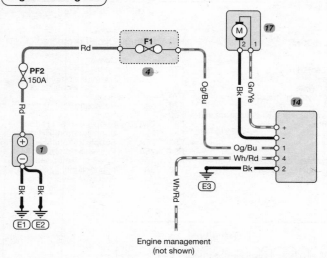

Electronic power steering

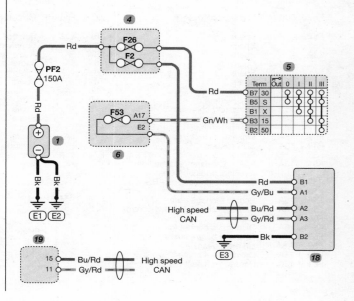

Wire colours

Bk	Black	**Pk**	Pink
Ye	Yellow	**Vt**	Violet
Bu	Blue	**Og**	Orange
Bn	Brown	**Wh**	White
Gn	Green	**Rd**	Red
Gy	Grey	**Lgn**	Lt. Green

Key to items

1 Battery
4 Engine fusebox
5 Ignition switch
  a = inhibitor
  b = reader
6 Passenger fusebox
  a = control unit
  R8 = main beam relay
10 Steering wheel control unit
22 Steering column lock unit
23 Light switch
  a = off/side/headlight
  b = 'lights on' indicator

24 LH headlight unit
  a = dip beam/xenon
  b = main beam
  c = sidelight
25 RH headlight unit
  (as above)
28 Number plate light assembly
29 LH rear light unit 1
  a = stop light
  b = tail light
30 RH rear light unit 1
  (as above)

31 LH rear light unit 2
  a = tail light
32 RH rear light unit 2
  (as above)

Diagram 3

H47635

Start control system

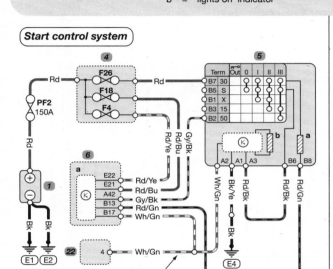

Headlights (without Bi-Xenon)

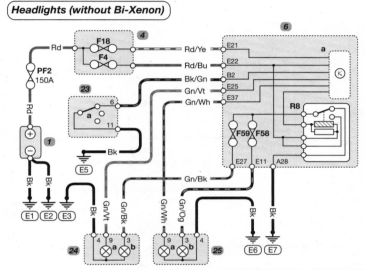

Side & tail lights

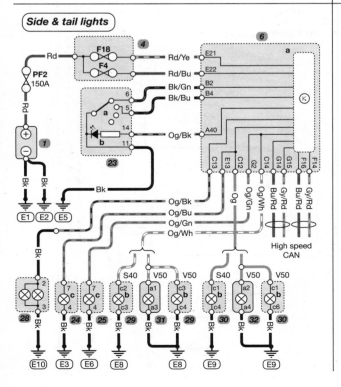

Headlights (with Bi-Xenon)

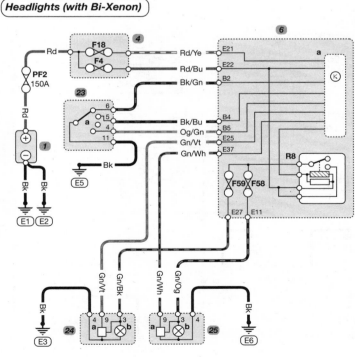

Wire colours

Bk	Black	**Pk**	Pink
Ye	Yellow	**Vt**	Violet
Bu	Blue	**Og**	Orange
Bn	Brown	**Wh**	White
Gn	Green	**Rd**	Red
Gy	Grey	**Lgn**	Lt. Green

* V50 models

Key to items

1 Battery
4 Engine fusebox
  R4 = front foglight relay
6 Passenger fusebox
  a = control unit
  R2 = reversing light relay
  R8 = main beam relay
7 Transmission control unit
23 Light switch
  c = rear foglight
  d = front foglight

24 LH headlight unit
  d = direction indicator
25 RH headlight unit
  d = direction indicator
29 LH rear light unit
  a = stop light
  c = reversing light
  d = rear foglight
  e = direction indicator
30 RH rear light unit
  (as above)

33 Fuse in holder
34 Auxiliary light switch
35 Auxiliary light relay
36 LH auxiliary light
37 RH auxiliary light
38 High level stop light
39 RH rear window suppressor
40 Driver information control unit
41 Stop light switch
42 Reversing light switch
  (manual transmission)

43 LH front foglight
44 RH front foglight
45 LH mirror assembly
46 RH mirror assembly
47 LH front door control unit
48 RH front door control unit
49 Hazard warning switch

Diagram 4

H47636

Auxiliary lighting

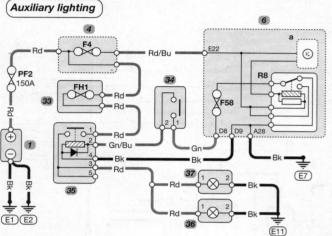

Front & rear foglights

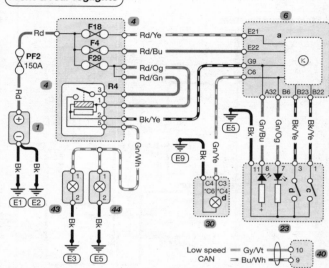

Stop & reversing lights

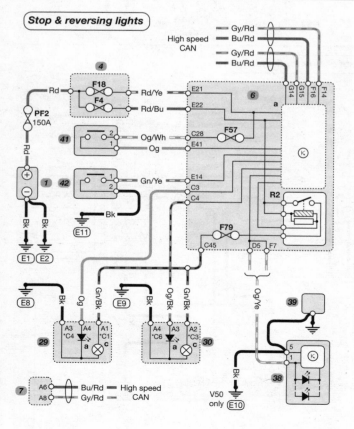

Direction indicators & hazard warning lights

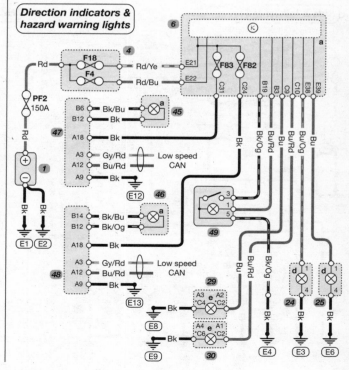

Wire colours

Bk	Black	**Pk**	Pink
Ye	Yellow	**Vt**	Violet
Bu	Blue	**Og**	Orange
Bn	Brown	**Wh**	White
Gn	Green	**Rd**	Red
Gy	Grey	**Lgn**	Lt. Green

Key to items

1 Battery
4 Engine fusebox
  R9   = headlight washer relay
5 Ignition switch
6 Passenger fusebox
  a   = control unit
  R7A = windscreen washer relay
  R7B = rear window washer relay
  R11A = rear wiper relay (V50)
  R18 = comfort functions relay

10 Steering wheel control unit
23 Light switch
  a   = off/side/headlight
  b   = 'lights on' indicator
30 RH rear light unit
  a   = stop light
32 Rear wiper motor (V50)
41 Stop light switch
53 Trailer control unit
54 7 pin trailer socket

55 13 pin trailer socket
56 Headlight washer pump
57 Wiper motor control unit
58 Rain sensor
59 Windscreen washer pump

Diagram 5

H47637

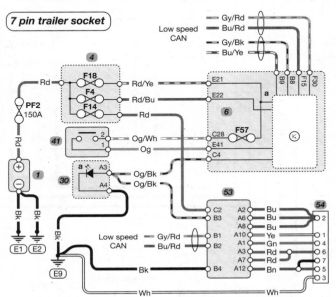

7 pin trailer socket

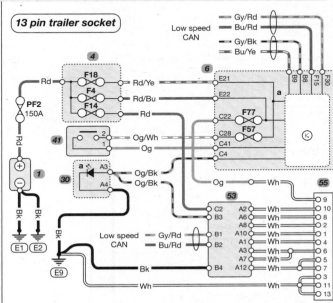

13 pin trailer socket

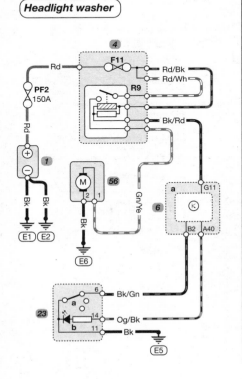

Headlight washer

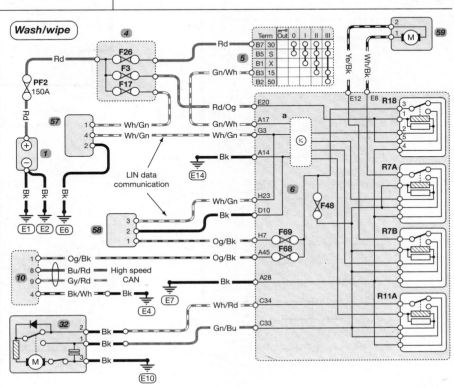

Wash/wipe

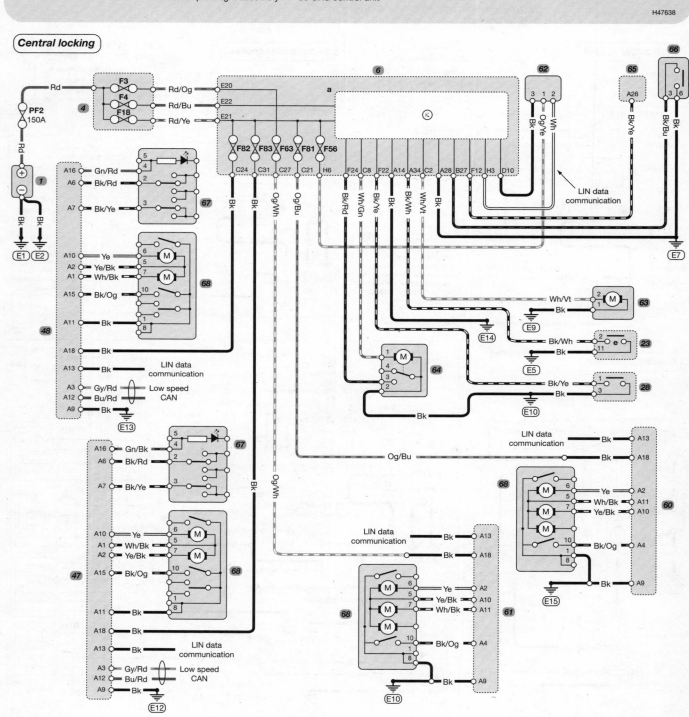

Wire colours

Bk	Black	**Pk**	Pink
Ye	Yellow	**Vt**	Violet
Bu	Blue	**Og**	Orange
Bn	Brown	**Wh**	White
Gn	Green	**Rd**	Red
Gy	Grey	**Lgn**	Lt. Green

Key to items

1 Battery
4 Engine fusebox
6 Passenger fusebox
    a = control unit
10 Steering wheel control unit
23 Light switch
    e = tailgate release
28 Number plate light assembly

47 LH front door control unit
48 RH front door control unit
60 LH rear door control unit
61 RH rear door control unit
62 Remote receiver
63 Fuel filler flap motor
64 Tailgate lock motor
65 SRS control unit

66 Tailgate lock switch
67 Door lock assembly
68 Central locking switch

Diagram 6

H47638

Central locking

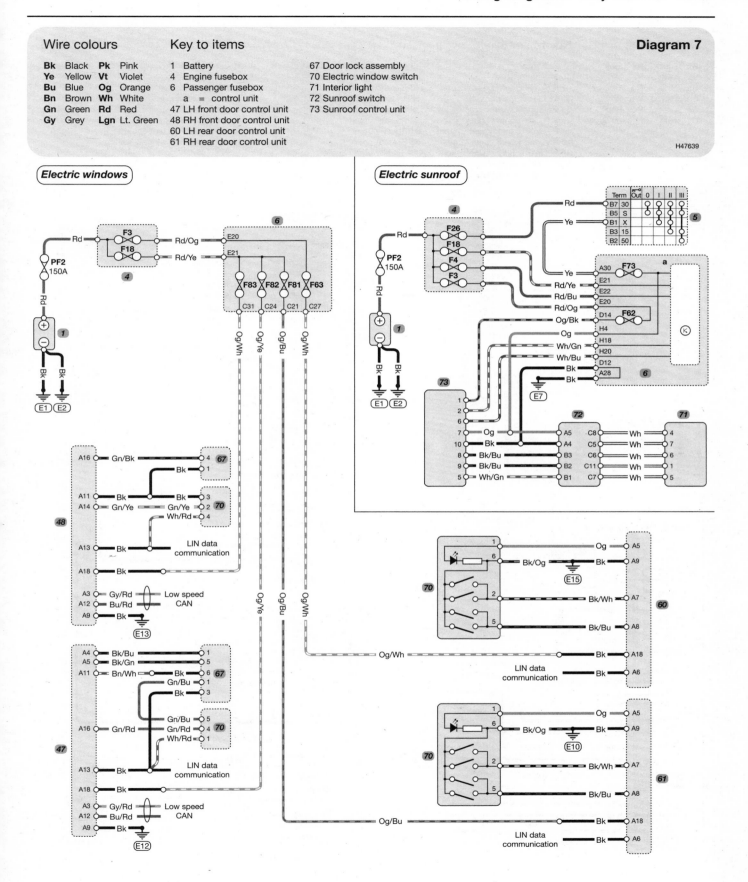

Wire colours

Bk	Black	**Pk**	Pink
Ye	Yellow	**Vt**	Violet
Bu	Blue	**Og**	Orange
Bn	Brown	**Wh**	White
Gn	Green	**Rd**	Red
Gy	Grey	**Lgn**	Lt. Green

Key to items

1 Battery
4 Engine fusebox
6 Passenger fusebox
   a = control unit
47 LH front door control unit
48 RH front door control unit
60 LH rear door control unit
61 RH rear door control unit
67 Door lock assembly
70 Electric window switch
71 Interior light
72 Sunroof switch
73 Sunroof control unit

Diagram 7

H47639

Electric windows

Electric sunroof

Wire colours

Bk	Black	Pk	Pink
Ye	Yellow	Vt	Violet
Bu	Blue	Og	Orange
Bn	Brown	Wh	White
Gn	Green	Rd	Red
Gy	Grey	Lgn	Lt. Green

Key to items

1 Battery
4 Engine fusebox
R10 = heated rear window
5 Ignition switch
6 Passenger fusebox
   a = control unit
   R11B = infotainment system
10 Steering wheel control unit
39 RH rear window suppressor
45 LH mirror assembly
46 RH mirror assembly

47 LH front door control unit
48 RH front door control unit
70 Electric window switch
78 Heated rear window
79 Infotainment control unit
80 Auxiliary input
81 Audio unit
83 RH rear door
84 RH rear door tweeter
85 Passenger's door speaker
86 Passenger's door tweeter

87 LH rear door speaker
88 LH rear door tweeter
89 Driver's door speaker
90 Driver's door tweeter
91 Microphone
92 LH rear window suppressor
93 Climate control system control unit
94 Heated mirror/rear window switch

Diagram 8

H47640

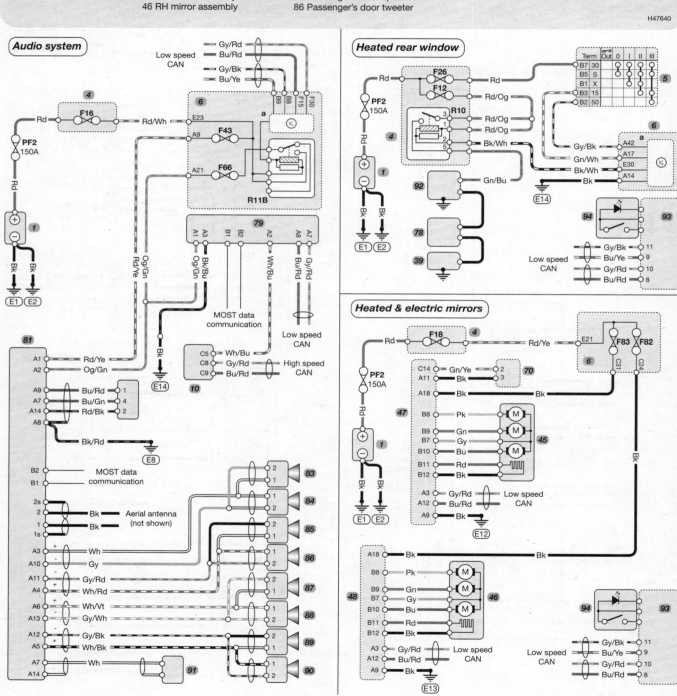

Wire colours			Key to items		Diagram 9

Wire colours

Bk	Black	Pk	Pink
Ye	Yellow	Vt	Violet
Bu	Blue	Og	Orange
Bn	Brown	Wh	White
Gn	Green	Rd	Red
Gy	Grey	Lgn	Lt. Green

Key to items

1 Battery
4 Engine fusebox
5 Ignition switch
6 Passenger fusebox
   a = control unit
   R1 = interior lighting relay
   R3 = comfort relay
10 Steering wheel control unit
23 Light switch
   f = headlight levelling
24 LH headlight unit
   e = headlight levelling
25 RH headlight unit
   e = headlight levelling
26 LH headlight discharge control unit
27 RH headlight discharge control unit
100 Diagnostic connector
101 Front 12v connector
102 Rear 12v connector
103 Luggage compartment 12v connector
104 Front level sensor
105 Rear level sensor
106 Headlight levelling control unit

H47649

Diagnostic connector

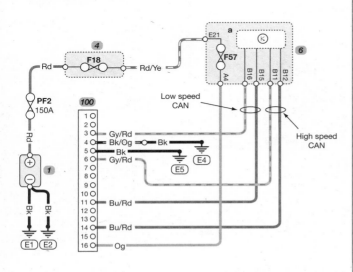

12v accessory connectors

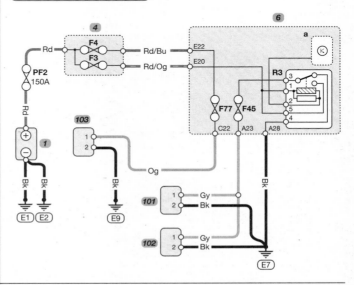

Headlight levelling (without Bi-Xenon)

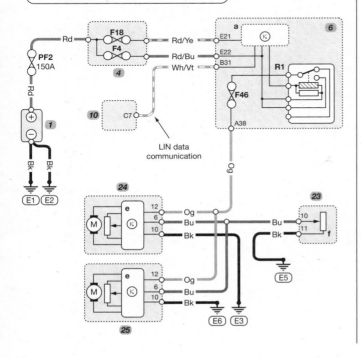

Headlight levelling (with Bi-Xenon)

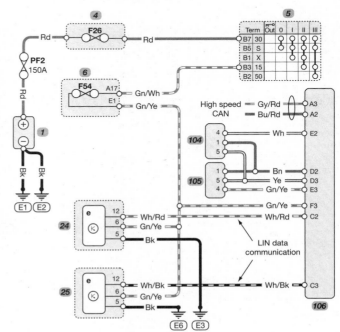

Dimensions and weights

Note: *All figures are approximate, and may vary according to model. Refer to manufacturer's data for exact figures.*

Dimensions

Overall length	
S40	4468 to 4470 mm
V50	4510 to 4514 mm
Overall width.	1770 mm
Overall height	1452 mm
Wheelbase	2640 mm

Weights

Kerb weight	Refer to decal on driver's door pillar
Maximum roof rack load	75 kg
Maximum towing weight	
Trailer without brakes.	650 to 700kg
Trailer with brakes.	1200 to 1500kg

Fuel economy

Although depreciation is still the biggest part of the cost of motoring for most car owners, the cost of fuel is more immediately noticeable. These pages give some tips on how to get the best fuel economy.

Working it out

Manufacturer's figures

Car manufacturers are required by law to provide fuel consumption information on all new vehicles sold. These 'official' figures are obtained by simulating various driving conditions on a rolling road or a test track. Real life conditions are different, so the fuel consumption actually achieved may not bear much resemblance to the quoted figures.

How to calculate it

Many cars now have trip computers which will

display fuel consumption, both instantaneous and average. Refer to the owner's handbook for details of how to use these.

To calculate consumption yourself (and maybe to check that the trip computer is accurate), proceed as follows.

1. Fill up with fuel and note the mileage, or zero the trip recorder.
2. Drive as usual until you need to fill up again.
3. Note the amount of fuel required to refill the tank, and the mileage covered since the previous fill-up.
4. Divide the mileage by the amount of fuel used to obtain the consumption figure.

For example:

Mileage at first fill-up (a) = 27,903
Mileage at second fill-up (b) = 28,346
Mileage covered (b – a) = 443
Fuel required at second fill-up = 48.6 litres

The half-completed changeover to metric units in the UK means that we buy our fuel

in litres, measure distances in miles and talk about fuel consumption in miles per gallon. There are two ways round this: the first is to convert the litres to gallons before doing the calculation (by dividing by 4.546, or see Table 1). So in the example:

48.6 litres ÷ 4.546 = 10.69 gallons
443 miles ÷ 10.69 gallons = 41.4 mpg

The second way is to calculate the consumption in miles per litre, then multiply that figure by 4.546 (or see Table 2).

So in the example, fuel consumption is:

443 miles ÷ 48.6 litres = 9.1 mpl
9.1 mpl x 4.546 = 41.4 mpg

The rest of Europe expresses fuel consumption in litres of fuel required to travel 100 km (l/100 km). For interest, the conversions are given in Table 3. In practice it doesn't matter what units you use, provided you know what your normal consumption is and can spot if it's getting better or worse.

Table 1: conversion of litres to Imperial gallons

litres	1	2	3	4	5	10	20	30	40	50	60	70
gallons	0.22	0.44	0.66	0.88	1.10	2.24	4.49	6.73	8.98	11.22	13.47	15.71

Table 2: conversion of miles per litre to miles per gallon

miles per litre	5	6	7	8	9	10	11	12	13	14
miles per gallon	23	27	32	36	41	46	50	55	59	64

Table 3: conversion of litres per 100 km to miles per gallon

litres per 100 km	4	4.5	5	5.5	6	6.5	7	8	9	10
miles per gallon	71	63	56	51	47	43	40	35	31	28

Maintenance

A well-maintained car uses less fuel and creates less pollution. In particular:

Filters

Change air and fuel filters at the specified intervals.

Oil

Use a good quality oil of the lowest viscosity specified by the vehicle manufacturer (see *Lubricants and fluids*). Check the level often and be careful not to overfill.

Spark plugs

When applicable, renew at the specified intervals.

Tyres

Check tyre pressures regularly. Under-inflated tyres have an increased rolling resistance. It is generally safe to use the higher pressures specified for full load conditions even when not fully laden, but keep an eye on the centre band of tread for signs of wear due to over-inflation.

When buying new tyres, consider the 'fuel saving' models which most manufacturers include in their ranges.

Driving style

Acceleration

Acceleration uses more fuel than driving at a steady speed. The best technique with modern cars is to accelerate reasonably briskly to the desired speed, changing up through the gears as soon as possible without making the engine labour.

Air conditioning

Air conditioning absorbs quite a bit of energy from the engine – typically 3 kW (4 hp) or so. The effect on fuel consumption is at its worst in slow traffic. Switch it off when not required.

Anticipation

Drive smoothly and try to read the traffic flow so as to avoid unnecessary acceleration and braking.

Automatic transmission

When accelerating in an automatic, avoid depressing the throttle so far as to make the transmission hold onto lower gears at higher speeds. Don't use the 'Sport' setting, if applicable.

When stationary with the engine running, select 'N' or 'P'. When moving, keep your left foot away from the brake.

Braking

Braking converts the car's energy of motion into heat – essentially, it is wasted. Obviously some braking is always going to be necessary, but with good anticipation it is surprising how much can be avoided, especially on routes that you know well.

Carshare

Consider sharing lifts to work or to the shops. Even once a week will make a difference.

Electrical loads

Electricity is 'fuel' too; the alternator which charges the battery does so by converting some of the engine's energy of motion into electrical energy. The more electrical accessories are in use, the greater the load on the alternator. Switch off big consumers like the heated rear window when not required.

Freewheeling

Freewheeling (coasting) in neutral with the engine switched off is dangerous. The effort required to operate power-assisted brakes and steering increases when the engine is not running, with a potential lack of control in emergency situations.

In any case, modern fuel injection systems automatically cut off the engine's fuel supply on the overrun (moving and in gear, but with the accelerator pedal released).

Gadgets

Bolt-on devices claiming to save fuel have been around for nearly as long as the motor car itself. Those which worked were rapidly adopted as standard equipment by the vehicle manufacturers. Others worked only in certain situations, or saved fuel only at the expense of unacceptable effects on performance, driveability or the life of engine components.

The most effective fuel saving gadget is the driver's right foot.

Journey planning

Combine (eg) a trip to the supermarket with a visit to the recycling centre and the DIY store, rather than making separate journeys.

When possible choose a travelling time outside rush hours.

Load

The more heavily a car is laden, the greater the energy required to accelerate it to a given speed. Remove heavy items which you don't need to carry.

One load which is often overlooked is the contents of the fuel tank. A tankful of fuel (55 litres / 12 gallons) weighs 45 kg (100 lb) or so. Just half filling it may be worthwhile.

Lost?

At the risk of stating the obvious, if you're going somewhere new, have details of the route to hand. There's not much point in achieving record mpg if you also go miles out of your way.

Parking

If possible, carry out any reversing or turning manoeuvres when you arrive at a parking space so that you can drive straight out when you leave. Manoeuvering when the engine is cold uses a lot more fuel.

Driving around looking for free on-street parking may cost more in fuel than buying a car park ticket.

Premium fuel

Most major oil companies (and some supermarkets) have premium grades of fuel which are several pence a litre dearer than the standard grades. Reports vary, but the consensus seems to be that if these fuels improve economy at all, they do not do so by enough to justify their extra cost.

Roof rack

When loading a roof rack, try to produce a wedge shape with the narrow end at the front. Any cover should be securely fastened – if it flaps it's creating turbulence and absorbing energy.

Remove roof racks and boxes when not in use – they increase air resistance and can create a surprising amount of noise.

Short journeys

The engine is at its least efficient, and wear is highest, during the first few miles after a cold start. Consider walking, cycling or using public transport.

Speed

The engine is at its most efficient when running at a steady speed and load at the rpm where it develops maximum torque. (You can find this figure in the car's handbook.) For most cars this corresponds to between 55 and 65 mph in top gear.

Above the optimum cruising speed, fuel consumption starts to rise quite sharply. A car travelling at 80 mph will typically be using 30% more fuel than at 60 mph.

Supermarket fuel

It may be cheap but is it any good? In the UK all supermarket fuel must meet the relevant British Standard. The major oil companies will say that their branded fuels have better additive packages which may stop carbon and other deposits building up. A reasonable compromise might be to use one tank of branded fuel to three or four from the supermarket.

Switch off when stationary

Switch off the engine if you look like being stationary for more than 30 seconds or so. This is good for the environment as well as for your pocket. Be aware though that frequent restarts are hard on the battery and the starter motor.

Windows

Driving with the windows open increases air turbulence around the vehicle. Closing the windows promotes smooth airflow and

reduced resistance. The faster you go, the more significant this is.

And finally . . .

Driving techniques associated with good fuel economy tend to involve moderate acceleration and low top speeds. Be considerate to the needs of other road users who may need to make brisker progress; even if you do not agree with them this is not an excuse to be obstructive.

Safety must always take precedence over economy, whether it is a question of accelerating hard to complete an overtaking manoeuvre, killing your speed when confronted with a potential hazard or switching the lights on when it starts to get dark.

Conversion factors

Length (distance)

Inches (in)	x 25.4	= Millimetres (mm)	x 0.0394	= Inches (in)
Feet (ft)	x 0.305	= Metres (m)	x 3.281	= Feet (ft)
Miles	x 1.609	= Kilometres (km)	x 0.621	= Miles

Volume (capacity)

Cubic inches (cu in; in³)	x 16.387	= Cubic centimetres (cc; cm³)	x 0.061	= Cubic inches (cu in; in³)
Imperial pints (Imp pt)	x 0.568	= Litres (l)	x 1.76	= Imperial pints (Imp pt)
Imperial quarts (Imp qt)	x 1.137	= Litres (l)	x 0.88	= Imperial quarts (Imp qt)
Imperial quarts (Imp qt)	x 1.201	= US quarts (US qt)	x 0.833	= Imperial quarts (Imp qt)
US quarts (US qt)	x 0.946	= Litres (l)	x 1.057	= US quarts (US qt)
Imperial gallons (Imp gal)	x 4.546	= Litres (l)	x 0.22	= Imperial gallons (Imp gal)
Imperial gallons (Imp gal)	x 1.201	= US gallons (US gal)	x 0.833	= Imperial gallons (Imp gal)
US gallons (US gal)	x 3.785	= Litres (l)	x 0.264	= US gallons (US gal)

Mass (weight)

Ounces (oz)	x 28.35	= Grams (g)	x 0.035	= Ounces (oz)
Pounds (lb)	x 0.454	= Kilograms (kg)	x 2.205	= Pounds (lb)

Force

Ounces-force (ozf; oz)	x 0.278	= Newtons (N)	x 3.6	= Ounces-force (ozf; oz)
Pounds-force (lbf; lb)	x 4.448	= Newtons (N)	x 0.225	= Pounds-force (lbf; lb)
Newtons (N)	x 0.1	= Kilograms-force (kgf; kg)	x 9.81	= Newtons (N)

Pressure

Pounds-force per square inch (psi; lbf/in²; lb/in²)	x 0.070	= Kilograms-force per square centimetre (kgf/cm²; kg/cm²)	x 14.223	= Pounds-force per square inch (psi; lbf/in²; lb/in²)
Pounds-force per square inch (psi; lbf/in²; lb/in²)	x 0.068	= Atmospheres (atm)	x 14.696	= Pounds-force per square inch (psi; lbf/in²; lb/in²)
Pounds-force per square inch (psi; lbf/in²; lb/in²)	x 0.069	= Bars	x 14.5	= Pounds-force per square inch (psi; lbf/in²; lb/in²)
Pounds-force per square inch (psi; lbf/in²; lb/in²)	x 6.895	= Kilopascals (kPa)	x 0.145	= Pounds-force per square inch (psi; lbf/in²; lb/in²)
Kilopascals (kPa)	x 0.01	= Kilograms-force per square centimetre (kgf/cm²; kg/cm²)	x 98.1	= Kilopascals (kPa)
Millibar (mbar)	x 100	= Pascals (Pa)	x 0.01	= Millibar (mbar)
Millibar (mbar)	x 0.0145	= Pounds-force per square inch (psi; lbf/in²; lb/in²)	x 68.947	= Millibar (mbar)
Millibar (mbar)	x 0.75	= Millimetres of mercury (mmHg)	x 1.333	= Millibar (mbar)
Millibar (mbar)	x 0.401	= Inches of water (inH₂O)	x 2.491	= Millibar (mbar)
Millimetres of mercury (mmHg)	x 0.535	= Inches of water (inH₂O)	x 1.868	= Millimetres of mercury (mmHg)
Inches of water (inH₂O)	x 0.036	= Pounds-force per square inch (psi; lbf/in²; lb/in²)	x 27.68	= Inches of water (inH₂O)

Torque (moment of force)

Pounds-force inches (lbf in; lb in)	x 1.152	= Kilograms-force centimetre (kgf cm; kg cm)	x 0.868	= Pounds-force inches (lbf in; lb in)
Pounds-force inches (lbf in; lb in)	x 0.113	= Newton metres (Nm)	x 8.85	= Pounds-force inches (lbf in; lb in)
Pounds-force inches (lbf in; lb in)	x 0.083	= Pounds-force feet (lbf ft; lb ft)	x 12	= Pounds-force inches (lbf in; lb in)
Pounds-force feet (lbf ft; lb ft)	x 0.138	= Kilograms-force metres (kgf m; kg m)	x 7.233	= Pounds-force feet (lbf ft; lb ft)
Pounds-force feet (lbf ft; lb ft)	x 1.356	= Newton metres (Nm)	x 0.738	= Pounds-force feet (lbf ft; lb ft)
Newton metres (Nm)	x 0.102	= Kilograms-force metres (kgf m; kg m)	x 9.804	= Newton metres (Nm)

Power

Horsepower (hp)	x 745.7	= Watts (W)	x 0.0013	= Horsepower (hp)

Velocity (speed)

Miles per hour (miles/hr; mph)	x 1.609	= Kilometres per hour (km/hr; kph)	x 0.621	= Miles per hour (miles/hr; mph)

Fuel consumption*

Miles per gallon, Imperial (mpg)	x 0.354	= Kilometres per litre (km/l)	x 2.825	= Miles per gallon, Imperial (mpg)
Miles per gallon, US (mpg)	x 0.425	= Kilometres per litre (km/l)	x 2.352	= Miles per gallon, US (mpg)

Temperature

Degrees Fahrenheit = (°C x 1.8) + 32   Degrees Celsius (Degrees Centigrade; °C) = (°F – 32) x 0.56

It is common practice to convert from miles per gallon (mpg) to litres/100 kilometres (l/100km), where mpg x l/100 km = 282

Spare parts are available from many sources, including maker's appointed garages, accessory shops, and motor factors. To be sure of obtaining the correct parts, it may sometimes be necessary to quote the vehicle identification number. If possible, it can also be useful to take the old parts along for positive identification. Items such as starter motors and alternators may be available under a service exchange scheme – any parts returned should always be clean.

Our advice regarding spare part sources is as follows:

Officially-appointed garages

This is the best source of parts which are peculiar to your car, and are not otherwise generally available (eg, badges, interior trim, certain body panels, etc). It is also the only place at which you should buy parts if the vehicle is still under warranty.

Accessory shops

These are very good places to buy materials and components needed for the maintenance of your car (oil, air and fuel filters, spark plugs, light bulbs, drivebelts, oils and greases, brake pads, touch-up paint, etc). Parts like this sold by a reputable shop are of the same standard as those used by the car manufacturer.

Motor factors

Good factors will stock all the more important components which wear out comparatively quickly and can sometimes supply individual components needed for the overhaul of a larger assembly. They may also handle work such as cylinder block reboring, crankshaft regrinding and balancing, etc.

Tyre and exhaust specialists

These outlets may be independent or members of a local or national chain. They frequently offer competitive prices when compared with a main dealer or local garage, but it will pay to obtain several quotes before making a decision. Also ask what 'extras' may be added to the quote – for instance, fitting a new valve and balancing the wheel are both often charged on top of the price of a new tyre.

Other sources

Beware of parts or materials obtained from market stalls, car boot sales or similar outlets. Such items are not always sub-standard, but there is little chance of compensation if they do prove unsatisfactory. In the case of safety-critical components such as brake pads there is the risk not only of financial loss but also of an accident causing injury or death.

Second-hand components or assemblies obtained from a car breaker can be a good buy in some circumstances, but this sort of purchase is best made by the experienced DIY mechanic.

Vehicle identification numbers

Modifications are a continuing and unpublicised process in vehicle manufacture, quite apart from major model changes. Spare parts manuals and lists are compiled upon a numerical basis, the individual vehicle identification numbers being essential to correct identification of the component concerned.

When ordering spare parts always give as much information as possible. Quote the vehicle type and year, vehicle identification number (VIN), and engine number, as appropriate.

The vehicle identification number (VIN) appears in a number of locations, including on a plastic tag attached to the passenger side of the facia panel, visible through the windscreen, and stamped onto the bulkhead panel (see illustrations)

The engine number is stamped on the right-hand end of the cylinder block.

The transmission identification numbers are located on a plate attached to the top of the transmission casing, or cast into the casing itself.

The VIN plate mounted on the right-hand rear door pillar...

...on a plate on the fascia (visible through the windscreen)...

...and on the top of the engine compartment bulkhead

Whenever servicing, repair or overhaul work is carried out on the car or its components, observe the following procedures and instructions. This will assist in carrying out the operation efficiently and to a professional standard of workmanship.

Joint mating faces and gaskets

When separating components at their mating faces, never insert screwdrivers or similar implements into the joint between the faces in order to prise them apart. This can cause severe damage which results in oil leaks, coolant leaks, etc upon reassembly. Separation is usually achieved by tapping along the joint with a soft-faced hammer in order to break the seal. However, note that this method may not be suitable where dowels are used for component location.

Where a gasket is used between the mating faces of two components, a new one must be fitted on reassembly; fit it dry unless otherwise stated in the repair procedure. Make sure that the mating faces are clean and dry, with all traces of old gasket removed. When cleaning a joint face, use a tool which is unlikely to score or damage the face, and remove any burrs or nicks with an oilstone or fine file.

Make sure that tapped holes are cleaned with a pipe cleaner, and keep them free of jointing compound, if this is being used, unless specifically instructed otherwise.

Ensure that all orifices, channels or pipes are clear, and blow through them, preferably using compressed air.

Oil seals

Oil seals can be removed by levering them out with a wide flat-bladed screwdriver or similar implement. Alternatively, a number of self-tapping screws may be screwed into the seal, and these used as a purchase for pliers or some similar device in order to pull the seal free.

Whenever an oil seal is removed from its working location, either individually or as part of an assembly, it should be renewed.

The very fine sealing lip of the seal is easily damaged, and will not seal if the surface it contacts is not completely clean and free from scratches, nicks or grooves. If the original sealing surface of the component cannot be restored, and the manufacturer has not made provision for slight relocation of the seal relative to the sealing surface, the component should be renewed.

Protect the lips of the seal from any surface which may damage them in the course of fitting. Use tape or a conical sleeve where possible. Where indicated, lubricate the seal lips with oil before fitting and, on dual-lipped seals, fill the space between the lips with grease.

Unless otherwise stated, oil seals must be fitted with their sealing lips toward the lubricant to be sealed.

Use a tubular drift or block of wood of the appropriate size to install the seal and, if the seal housing is shouldered, drive the seal down to the shoulder. If the seal housing is unshouldered, the seal should be fitted with its face flush with the housing top face (unless otherwise instructed).

Screw threads and fastenings

Seized nuts, bolts and screws are quite a common occurrence where corrosion has set in, and the use of penetrating oil or releasing fluid will often overcome this problem if the offending item is soaked for a while before attempting to release it. The use of an impact driver may also provide a means of releasing such stubborn fastening devices, when used in conjunction with the appropriate screwdriver bit or socket. If none of these methods works, it may be necessary to resort to the careful application of heat, or the use of a hacksaw or nut splitter device. Before resorting to extreme methods, check that you are not dealing with a left-hand thread!

Studs are usually removed by locking two nuts together on the threaded part, and then using a spanner on the lower nut to unscrew the stud. Studs or bolts which have broken off below the surface of the component in which they are mounted can sometimes be removed using a stud extractor.

Always ensure that a blind tapped hole is completely free from oil, grease, water or other fluid before installing the bolt or stud. Failure to do this could cause the housing to crack due to the hydraulic action of the bolt or stud as it is screwed in.

For some screw fastenings, notably cylinder head bolts or nuts, torque wrench settings are no longer specified for the latter stages of tightening, "angle-tightening" being called up instead. Typically, a fairly low torque wrench setting will be applied to the bolts/nuts in the correct sequence, followed by one or more stages of tightening through specified angles.

When checking or retightening a nut or bolt to a specified torque setting, slacken the nut or bolt by a quarter of a turn, and then retighten to the specified setting. However, this should not be attempted where angular tightening has been used.

Locknuts, locktabs and washers

Any fastening which will rotate against a component or housing during tightening should always have a washer between it and the relevant component or housing.

Spring or split washers should always be renewed when they are used to lock a critical component such as a big-end bearing retaining bolt or nut. Locktabs which are folded over to retain a nut or bolt should always be renewed.

Self-locking nuts can be re-used in non-critical areas, providing resistance can be felt when the locking portion passes over the bolt or stud thread. However, it should be noted that self-locking stiffnuts tend to lose their effectiveness after long periods of use, and should then be renewed as a matter of course.

Split pins must always be replaced with new ones of the correct size for the hole.

When thread-locking compound is found on the threads of a fastener which is to be re-used, it should be cleaned off with a wire brush and solvent, and fresh compound applied on reassembly.

Special tools

Some repair procedures in this manual entail the use of special tools such as a press, two or three-legged pullers, spring compressors, etc. Wherever possible, suitable readily-available alternatives to the manufacturer's special tools are described, and are shown in use. In some instances, where no alternative is possible, it has been necessary to resort to the use of a manufacturer's tool, and this has been done for reasons of safety as well as the efficient completion of the repair operation. Unless you are highly-skilled and have a thorough understanding of the procedures described, never attempt to bypass the use of any special tool when the procedure described specifies its use. Not only is there a very great risk of personal injury, but expensive damage could be caused to the components involved.

Environmental considerations

When disposing of used engine oil, brake fluid, antifreeze, etc, give due consideration to any detrimental environmental effects. Do not, for instance, pour any of the above liquids down drains into the general sewage system, or onto the ground to soak away. Many local council refuse tips provide a facility for waste oil disposal, as do some garages. You can find your nearest disposal point by calling the Environment Agency on 08708 506 506 or by visiting www.oilbankline.org.uk.

Note: It is illegal and anti-social to dump oil down the drain. To find the location of your local oil recycling bank, call 08708 506 506 or visit www.oilbankline.org.uk.

The jack supplied with the vehicle tool kit should **only** be used for changing the roadwheels in an emergency – see *Wheel changing* at the front of this book. When carrying out any other kind of work, raise the vehicle using a heavy-duty hydraulic (or 'trolley') jack, and always supplement the jack with axle stands positioned under the vehicle jacking points. If the roadwheels do not have to be removed, consider using wheel ramps – if wished, these can be placed under the wheels once the vehicle has been raised using a hydraulic jack, and the vehicle lowered onto the ramps so that it is resting on its wheels.

Only ever jack the vehicle up on a solid, level surface. If there is even a slight slope, take great care that the vehicle cannot move as the wheels are lifted off the ground. Jacking up on an uneven or gravelled surface is not recommended, as the weight of the vehicle will not be evenly distributed, and the jack may slip as the vehicle is raised.

As far as possible, do not leave the vehicle unattended once it has been raised, particularly if children are playing nearby.

Before jacking up the front of the car, ensure that the handbrake is firmly applied. When jacking up the rear of the car, place wooden chocks in front of the front wheels, and engage first gear (or P).

The jack supplied with the vehicle locates in the sill flanges, at the points marked on each side of the car **(see illustration)**. Ensure that the jack head is correctly engaged before attempting to raise the vehicle.

When using a hydraulic jack or axle stands, the jack head or axle stand head may be placed under one of the four jacking points inboard of the door sills. When jacking or supporting the vehicle at these points, always use a block of wood between the jack head or axle stand, and the vehicle body. It is also considered good practice to use a large block of wood when supporting under other areas, to spread the load over a wider area, and reduce the risk of damage to the underside of the car (it also helps to prevent the underbody coating from being damaged by the jack or axle stand). **Do not** jack the vehicle under any other part of the sill, engine sump, floor pan, subframe, or directly under any of the steering or suspension components.

Never work under, around, or near a raised vehicle, unless it is adequately supported on stands. Do not rely on a jack alone, as even a hydraulic jack could fail under load. Makeshift methods should not be used to lift and support the car during servicing work.

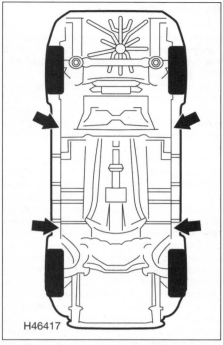

H46417

The jack supplied with the vehicle locates inboard of the sill flanges (arrowed)

Introduction

A selection of good tools is a fundamental requirement for anyone contemplating the maintenance and repair of a motor vehicle. For the owner who does not possess any, their purchase will prove a considerable expense, offsetting some of the savings made by doing-it-yourself. However, provided that the tools purchased meet the relevant national safety standards and are of good quality, they will last for many years and prove an extremely worthwhile investment.

To help the average owner to decide which tools are needed to carry out the various tasks detailed in this manual, we have compiled three lists of tools under the following headings: *Maintenance and minor repair, Repair and overhaul*, and *Special*. Newcomers to practical mechanics should start off with the *Maintenance and minor repair* tool kit, and confine themselves to the simpler jobs around the vehicle. Then, as confidence and experience grow, more difficult tasks can be undertaken, with extra tools being purchased as, and when, they are needed. In this way, a *Maintenance and minor repair* tool kit can be built up into a *Repair and overhaul* tool kit over a considerable period of time, without any major cash outlays. The experienced do-it-yourselfer will have a tool kit good enough for most repair and overhaul procedures, and will add tools from the *Special* category when it is felt that the expense is justified by the amount of use to which these tools will be put.

Maintenance and minor repair tool kit

The tools given in this list should be considered as a minimum requirement if routine maintenance, servicing and minor repair operations are to be undertaken. We recommend the purchase of combination spanners (ring one end, open-ended the other); although more expensive than open-ended ones, they do give the advantages of both types of spanner.

☐ *Combination spanners:*
 Metric – 8 to 19 mm inclusive
☐ *Adjustable spanner – 35 mm jaw (approx.)*
☐ *Spark plug spanner (with rubber insert) – petrol models*
☐ *Spark plug gap adjustment tool – petrol models*
☐ *Set of feeler gauges*
☐ *Brake bleed nipple spanner*
☐ *Screwdrivers:*
 Flat blade – 100 mm long x 6 mm dia
 Cross blade – 100 mm long x 6 mm dia
 Torx – various sizes (not all vehicles)
☐ *Combination pliers*
☐ *Hacksaw (junior)*
☐ *Tyre pump*
☐ *Tyre pressure gauge*
☐ *Oil can*
☐ *Oil filter removal tool (if applicable)*
☐ *Fine emery cloth*
☐ *Wire brush (small)*
☐ *Funnel (medium size)*
☐ *Sump drain plug key (not all vehicles)*

Repair and overhaul tool kit

These tools are virtually essential for anyone undertaking any major repairs to a motor vehicle, and are additional to those given in the *Maintenance and minor repair* list. Included in this list is a comprehensive set of sockets. Although these are expensive, they will be found invaluable as they are so versatile – particularly if various drives are included in the set. We recommend the half-inch square-drive type, as this can be used with most proprietary torque wrenches.

The tools in this list will sometimes need to be supplemented by tools from the *Special* list:

☐ *Sockets to cover range in previous list (including Torx sockets)*
☐ *Reversible ratchet drive (for use with sockets)*
☐ *Extension piece, 250 mm (for use with sockets)*
☐ *Universal joint (for use with sockets)*
☐ *Flexible handle or sliding T "breaker bar" (for use with sockets)*
☐ *Torque wrench (for use with sockets)*
☐ *Self-locking grips*
☐ *Ball pein hammer*
☐ *Soft-faced mallet (plastic or rubber)*
☐ *Screwdrivers:*
 Flat blade – long & sturdy, short (chubby), and narrow (electrician's) types
 Cross blade – long & sturdy, and short (chubby) types
☐ *Pliers:*
 Long-nosed
 Side cutters (electrician's)
 Circlip (internal and external)
☐ *Cold chisel – 25 mm*
☐ *Scriber*
☐ *Scraper*
☐ *Centre-punch*
☐ *Pin punch*
☐ *Hacksaw*
☐ *Brake hose clamp*
☐ *Brake/clutch bleeding kit*
☐ *Selection of twist drills*
☐ *Steel rule/straight-edge*
☐ *Allen keys (inc. splined/Torx type)*
☐ *Selection of files*
☐ *Wire brush*
☐ *Axle stands*
☐ *Jack (strong trolley or hydraulic type)*
☐ *Light with extension lead*
☐ *Universal electrical multi-meter*

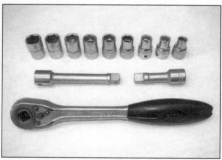

Sockets and reversible ratchet drive

Brake bleeding kit

Torx key, socket and bit

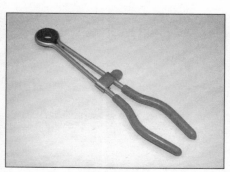

Hose clamp

Angular-tightening gauge

Special tools

The tools in this list are those which are not used regularly, are expensive to buy, or which need to be used in accordance with their manufacturers' instructions. Unless relatively difficult mechanical jobs are undertaken frequently, it will not be economic to buy many of these tools. Where this is the case, you could consider clubbing together with friends (or joining a motorists' club) to make a joint purchase, or borrowing the tools against a deposit from a local garage or tool hire specialist.

The following list contains only those tools and instruments freely available to the public, and not those special tools produced by the vehicle manufacturer specifically for its dealer network. You will find occasional references to these manufacturers' special tools in the text of this manual. Generally, an alternative method of doing the job without the vehicle manufacturers' special tool is given. However, sometimes there is no alternative to using them. Where this is the case and the relevant tool cannot be bought or borrowed, you will have to entrust the work to a dealer.

- ☐ Angular-tightening gauge
- ☐ Valve spring compressor
- ☐ Valve grinding tool
- ☐ Piston ring compressor
- ☐ Piston ring removal/installation tool
- ☐ Cylinder bore hone
- ☐ Balljoint separator
- ☐ Coil spring compressors (where applicable)
- ☐ Two/three-legged hub and bearing puller
- ☐ Impact screwdriver
- ☐ Micrometer and/or vernier calipers
- ☐ Dial gauge
- ☐ Tachometer
- ☐ Fault code reader
- ☐ Cylinder compression gauge
- ☐ Hand-operated vacuum pump and gauge
- ☐ Clutch plate alignment set
- ☐ Brake shoe steady spring cup removal tool
- ☐ Bush and bearing removal/installation set
- ☐ Stud extractors
- ☐ Tap and die set
- ☐ Lifting tackle

Buying tools

Reputable motor accessory shops and superstores often offer excellent quality tools at discount prices, so it pays to shop around.

Remember, you don't have to buy the most expensive items on the shelf, but it is always advisable to steer clear of the very cheap tools. Beware of 'bargains' offered on market stalls, on-line or at car boot sales. There are plenty of good tools around at reasonable prices, but always aim to purchase items which meet the relevant national safety standards. If in doubt, ask the proprietor or manager of the shop for advice before making a purchase.

Care and maintenance of tools

Having purchased a reasonable tool kit, it is necessary to keep the tools in a clean and serviceable condition. After use, always wipe off any dirt, grease and metal particles using a clean, dry cloth, before putting the tools away. Never leave them lying around after they have been used. A simple tool rack on the garage or workshop wall for items such as screwdrivers and pliers is a good idea. Store all normal spanners and sockets in a metal box. Any measuring instruments, gauges, meters, etc, must be carefully stored where they cannot be damaged or become rusty.

Take a little care when tools are used. Hammer heads inevitably become marked, and screwdrivers lose the keen edge on their blades from time to time. A little timely attention with emery cloth or a file will soon restore items like this to a good finish.

Working facilities

Not to be forgotten when discussing tools is the workshop itself. If anything more than routine maintenance is to be carried out, a suitable working area becomes essential.

It is appreciated that many an owner-mechanic is forced by circumstances to remove an engine or similar item without the benefit of a garage or workshop. Having done this, any repairs should always be done under the cover of a roof.

Wherever possible, any dismantling should be done on a clean, flat workbench or table at a suitable working height.

Any workbench needs a vice; one with a jaw opening of 100 mm is suitable for most jobs. As mentioned previously, some clean dry storage space is also required for tools, as well as for any lubricants, cleaning fluids, touch-up paints etc, which become necessary.

Another item which may be required, and which has a much more general usage, is an electric drill with a chuck capacity of at least 8 mm. This, together with a good range of twist drills, is virtually essential for fitting accessories.

Last, but not least, always keep a supply of old newspapers and clean, lint-free rags available, and try to keep any working area as clean as possible.

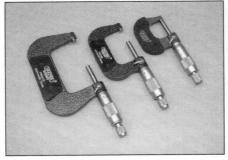

Micrometers

Dial test indicator ("dial gauge")

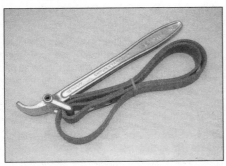

Oil filter removal tool (strap wrench type)

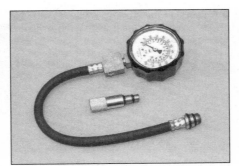

Compression tester

Bearing puller

This is a guide to getting your vehicle through the MOT test. Obviously it will not be possible to examine the vehicle to the same standard as the professional MOT tester. However, working through the following checks will enable you to identify any problem areas before submitting the vehicle for the test.

It has only been possible to summarise the test requirements here, based on the regulations in force at the time of printing. Test standards are becoming increasingly stringent, although there are some exemptions for older vehicles.

An assistant will be needed to help carry out some of these checks.

The checks have been sub-divided into four categories, as follows:

1 Checks carried out **FROM THE VEHICLE INTERIOR**

2 Checks carried out **WITH THE VEHICLE ON THE GROUND**

3 Checks carried out **WITH THE VEHICLE RAISED AND THE WHEELS FREE TO TURN**

4 Checks carried out on **YOUR VEHICLE'S EXHAUST EMISSION SYSTEM**

1 Checks carried out **FROM THE VEHICLE INTERIOR**

Handbrake (parking brake)

☐ Test the operation of the handbrake. Excessive travel (too many clicks) indicates incorrect brake or cable adjustment.
☐ Check that the handbrake cannot be released by tapping the lever sideways. Check the security of the lever mountings.

☐ If the parking brake is foot-operated, check that the pedal is secure and without excessive travel, and that the release mechanism operates correctly.
☐ Where applicable, test the operation of the electronic handbrake. The brake should engage and disengage without excessive delay. If the warning light does not extinguish, or a warning message is displayed when the brake is disengaged, this could indicate a fault which will need further investigation.

Footbrake

☐ Depress the brake pedal and check that it does not creep down to the floor, indicating a master cylinder fault. Release the pedal, wait a few seconds, then depress it again. If the pedal travels nearly to the floor before firm resistance is felt, brake adjustment or repair is necessary. If the pedal feels spongy, there is air in the hydraulic system which must be removed by bleeding.

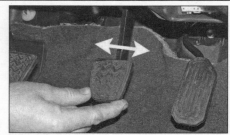

☐ Check that the brake pedal is secure and in good condition. Check also for signs of fluid leaks on the pedal, floor or carpets, which would indicate failed seals in the brake master cylinder.
☐ Check the servo unit (when applicable) by operating the brake pedal several times, then keeping the pedal depressed and starting the engine. As the engine starts, the pedal will move down. If not, the vacuum hose or the servo itself may be faulty.

Steering wheel and column

☐ Examine the steering wheel for fractures or looseness of the hub, spokes or rim.
☐ Move the steering wheel from side to side and then up and down. Check that the steering wheel is not loose on the column, indicating wear or a loose retaining nut. Continue moving the steering wheel as before, but also turn it slightly from left to right.
☐ Check that the steering wheel is not loose on the column, and that there is no abnormal movement of the steering wheel, indicating wear in the column support bearings or couplings.

☐ Check that the ignition lock (where fitted) engages and disengages correctly.
☐ Steering column adjustment mechanisms (where fitted) must be able to lock the column securely in place with no play evident.

Windscreen, mirrors and sunvisor

☐ The windscreen must be free of cracks or other significant damage within the 'swept area' of the windscreen. This is the area swept by the windscreen wipers. A second test area, known as 'Zone A', is the part of the swept area 290 mm wide, centred on the steering wheel centre line. Any damage in Zone A that cannot be contained in a 10 mm diameter circle, or any damage in the remainder of the swept area that cannot be contained in a 40 mm diameter circle, may cause the vehicle to fail the test.

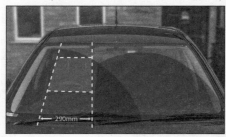

☐ Any items that may obscure the drivers view, such as stickers, sat-navs, anything hanging from the interior mirror, should be removed prior to the test.
☐ Vehicles registered after 1st August 1978 must have a drivers side mirror, and either an interior mirror, or a passenger's side mirror. Cameras (or indirect vision devices) may replace the mirrors, but they must function correctly.
☐ The driver's sunvisor must be capable of being stored in the "up" position.

Seat belts, seats and supplementary restraint systems (SRS)

Note: *The following checks are applicable to all seat belts, front and rear.*

☐ Examine the webbing of all the belts (including rear belts if fitted) for cuts, serious fraying or deterioration. Fasten and unfasten each belt to check the buckles. If applicable, check the retracting mechanism. Check the security of all seat belt mountings accessible from inside the vehicle, ensuring any height adjustable mountings lock securely in place.

☐ Where the seat belt is attached to a seat, the frame and mountings of the seat form part of the belt mountings, and are to be inspected as such.

☐ Any airbag, or SRS warning light must extinguish a few seconds after the ignition is switched on. Failure to do so indicates a fault which must be investigated.

☐ Seat belts with pre-tensioners, once activated, have a "flag" or similar showing on the seat belt stalk. This, in itself, is a reason for test failure.

☐ Check that the original airbag(s) is/are present, and not obviously defective.

☐ The seats themselves must be securely attached and the backrests must lock in the upright position. The driver's seat must also be able to slide forwards/rearwards, and lock in several positions.

Doors

☐ Both front doors must be able to be opened and closed from outside and inside, and must latch securely when closed.

☐ The rear doors must open from the outside.

☐ Examine all door hinges, catches and striker plates for missing, deteriorated, or insecure parts that could effect the opening and closing of the doors.

Speedometer

☐ The vehicle speedometer must be present, and appear operative. The figures on the speedometer must be legible, and illuminated when the lights are switched on.

2 Checks carried out WITH THE VEHICLE ON THE GROUND

Vehicle identification

☐ Number plates must be in good condition, secure and legible, with letters and numbers correctly spaced – spacing at (A) should be 33 mm and at (B) 11 mm. At the front, digits must be black on a white background and at the rear

black on a yellow background. Other background designs (such as honeycomb) are not permitted.

☐ The VIN plate and/or homologation plate must be permanently displayed and legible.

Electrical equipment

☐ Switch on the ignition and check the operation of the horn.

☐ Check the windscreen washers and wipers, examining the wiper blades; renew damaged or perished blades. The wiper blades must clear a large enough area of the windscreen to provide an 'adequate' view of the road, and be able to be parked in a position where they will not affect the drivers' view.

☐ On vehicles first used from 1st September 2009, the headlight washers (where fitted) must operate correctly.

☐ Check the operation of the stop-lights. This includes any lights that appear to be connected – Eg. high-level lights.

☐ Check the operation of the sidelights and number plate lights. The lenses and reflectors must be secure, clean and undamaged.

☐ Check the operation and alignment of the headlights. The headlight reflectors must not be tarnished and the lenses must be undamaged. Where plastic lenses are fitted, check they haven't deteriorated to the extent where they affect the light ouput or beam image. It's often possible to restore the plastic lens using a suitable polish or aftermarket treatment.

☐ Where HID or LED headlights are fitted, check the operation of the cleaning and self-levelling functions.

☐ The headlight main beam warning lamp must be functional.

☐ On vehicles first used from 1st March 2018, the daytime running lights (where fitted) must operate correctly.

☐ Switch on the ignition and check the operation of the direction indicators (including the instrument panel tell-tale) and the hazard warning lights. Operation of the sidelights and stop-lights must not affect the indicators – if it does, the cause is usually a bad earth at the rear light cluster. Indicators should flash at a rate of between 60 and 120 times per minute – faster or slower than this could indicate a fault with the flasher unit or a bad earth at one of the light units.

☐ The hazard warning lights must operate with the ignition on and off.

☐ Check the operation of the rear foglight(s), including the warning light on the instrument panel or in the switch. Note that the foglight

must be positioned in the centre or driver's side of the vehicle. If only the passenger's side illuminates, the test will fail.

☐ The warning lights must illuminate in accordance with the manufacturers' design (this includes any warning messages). For most vehicles, the ABS and other warning lights should illuminate when the ignition is switched on, and (if the system is operating properly) extinguish after a few seconds. Refer to the owner's handbook.

☐ On vehicles first used from 1st September 2009, the reversing lights must operate correctly when reverse gear is selected.

☐ Check the vehicle battery for security and leakage.

☐ Check the visible/accessible vehicle wiring is adequately supported, with no evidence of damage or deterioration that could result in a short-circuit.

Footbrake

☐ Examine the master cylinder, brake pipes and servo unit for leaks, loose mountings, corrosion or other damage. If ABS is fitted, this unit should also be examined for signs of leaks or corrosion.

☐ The fluid reservoir must be secure and the fluid level must be between the upper (A) and lower (B) markings.

☐ Check the fluid in the reservoir for signs of contamination.

☐ Inspect both front brake flexible hoses for cracks or deterioration of the rubber. Turn the steering from lock to lock, and ensure that the hoses do not contact the wheel, tyre, or any part of the steering or suspension mechanism. With the brake pedal firmly depressed, check the hoses for bulges or leaks under pressure.

Steering and suspension

☐ Have your assistant turn the steering wheel from side to side slightly, up to the point where the steering gear just begins to transmit this movement to the roadwheels. Check for excessive free play between the steering wheel and the steering gear, indicating wear or insecurity of the steering column joints, the column-to-steering gear coupling, or the steering gear itself. With a standard (380 mm diameter) steering wheel, there should be no more than 13 mm of free play for rack-and-pinion systems, and no more than 75 mm for non-rack-and-pinion designs.

☐ Have your assistant turn the steering

wheel more vigorously in each direction, so that the roadwheels just begin to turn. As this is done, examine all the steering joints, linkages, fittings and attachments. Renew any component that shows signs of wear or damage. On vehicles with hydraulic power steering, check the security and condition of the steering pump, drivebelt and hoses.

☐ Note that all movement checks on power steering systems are carried out with the engine running.

☐ Check that the vehicle is standing level, and at approximately the correct ride height.

Exhaust system

☐ Start the engine. With your assistant holding a rag over the tailpipe, check the entire system for leaks. Repair or renew leaking sections.

3 Checks carried out **WITH THE VEHICLE RAISED AND THE WHEELS FREE TO TURN**

Jack up the front and rear of the vehicle, and securely support it on axle stands. Position the stands clear of the suspension assemblies. Ensure that the wheels are clear of the ground and that the steering can be turned from lock to lock.

Steering mechanism

☐ Have your assistant turn the steering from lock to lock. Check that the steering turns smoothly, and that no part of the steering mechanism, including a wheel or tyre, fouls any brake hose or pipe or any part of the body structure.

☐ Examine the steering rack rubber gaiters for damage or insecurity of the retaining clips. If power steering is fitted, check for signs of damage or leakage of the fluid hoses, pipes or connections. Also check for excessive stiffness or binding of the steering, a missing split pin or locking device, or severe corrosion of the body structure within 30 cm of any steering component attachment point.

☐ Check the track rod end ball joint dust covers. Any covers that are missing, seriously damaged, deteriorated or insecure, may fail inspection.

Front and rear suspension and wheel bearings

☐ Starting at the front right-hand side, grasp the roadwheel at the 3 o'clock and 9 o'clock positions and rock gently but firmly. Check for free play or insecurity at the wheel bearings, suspension balljoints, or suspension mountings, pivots and attachments.

☐ Now grasp the wheel at the 12 o'clock and 6 o'clock positions and repeat the previous inspection. Spin the wheel, and check for roughness or tightness of the front wheel bearing.

☐ If excess free play is suspected at a component pivot point, this can be confirmed by using a large screwdriver or similar tool and levering between the mounting and the component attachment. This will confirm whether the wear is in the pivot bush, its retaining bolt, or in the mounting itself (the bolt holes can often become elongated).

☐ Carry out all the above checks at the other front wheel, and then at both rear wheels.

Springs and shock absorbers

☐ Examine the suspension struts (when applicable) for serious fluid leakage, corrosion, or damage to the casing. Also check the security of the mounting points.

☐ If coil springs are fitted, check that the spring ends locate in their seats, and that the spring is not corroded, cracked or broken.

☐ If leaf springs are fitted, check that all leaves are intact, that the axle is securely attached to each spring, and that there is no deterioration of the spring eye mountings, bushes, and shackles.

☐ The same general checks apply to vehicles fitted with other suspension types, such as torsion bars, hydraulic displacer units, etc. Ensure that all mountings and attachments are secure, that there are no signs of excessive wear, corrosion or damage, and (on hydraulic types) that there are no fluid leaks or damaged pipes.

☐ Check any suspension and anti-roll bar link ball joint dust covers. Any covers that are missing, seriously damaged, deteriorated or insecure, may fail inspection.

☐ Examine each shock absorber for signs of leakage, corrosion of the casing, missing, detached or worn pivots and/or rubber bushes.

Driveshafts (fwd vehicles only)

☐ Rotate each front wheel in turn and inspect the inner and outer joint gaiters for splits or damage. Also check that each driveshaft is straight and undamaged.

Braking system

☐ If possible without dismantling, check brake pad wear and disc condition. Ensure that the friction lining material has not worn excessively, (A) and that the discs are not fractured, pitted, scored or badly worn (B). As a general rule, if the friction material is less than 1.5 mm thick, the inspection will fail.

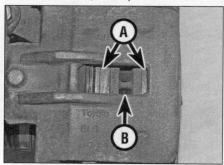

☐ Examine all the rigid brake pipes underneath the vehicle, and the flexible hose(s) at the rear. Look for corrosion, chafing or insecurity of the pipes, and for signs of bulging under pressure, chafing, splits or deterioration of the flexible hoses.

☐ Look for signs of fluid leaks at the brake calipers or on the brake backplates. Repair or renew leaking components.

☐ Slowly spin each wheel, while your assistant depresses and releases the footbrake. Ensure that each brake is operating and does not bind when the pedal is released.

☐ Examine the handbrake mechanism, checking for frayed or broken cables, excessive corrosion, or wear or insecurity of the linkage. Check that the mechanism works on each relevant wheel, and releases fully, without binding.

☐ Check the ABS sensors' wiring for signs of damage, deterioration or insecurity.

☐ It is not possible to test brake efficiency without special equipment, but a road test can be carried out later to check that the vehicle pulls up in a straight line.

Fuel and exhaust systems

☐ Inspect the fuel tank (including the filler cap), fuel pipes, hoses and unions. All components must be secure and free from leaks. Locking fuel caps must lock securely and the key must be provided for the MOT test.

☐ Examine the exhaust system over its entire length, checking for any damaged, broken or missing mountings, security of the retaining clamps and rust or corrosion.

☐ If the vehicle was originally equipped with a catalytic converter or particulate filter, one must be fitted.

Wheels and tyres

☐ Examine the sidewalls and tread area of each tyre in turn. Check for cuts, tears, lumps, bulges, separation of the tread, and exposure of the ply or cord due to wear or damage. Check that the tyre bead is correctly seated on the wheel rim, that the valve is sound and properly seated, and that the wheel is not distorted or damaged.

☐ Check that the tyres are of the correct size for the vehicle, that they are of the same size and type on each axle, and that the pressures are correct. The vehicle will fail the test if the tyres are obviously under-inflated.

☐ Check the tyre tread depth. The legal minimum at the time of writing is 1.6 mm over the central three-quarters of the tread width. Abnormal tread wear may indicate incorrect front wheel alignment or wear in steering or suspension components.

☐ Check that all wheel bolts/nuts are present.

☐ If the spare wheel is fitted externally or in a separate carrier beneath the vehicle, check that mountings are secure and free of excessive corrosion.

Body corrosion

☐ Check the condition of the entire vehicle structure for signs of corrosion in load-bearing areas. (These include chassis box sections, side sills, cross-members, pillars, and all suspension, steering, braking system and seat belt mountings and anchorages.) Any corrosion which has seriously reduced the thickness of a load-bearing area (or is within 30 cm of safety-related components such as steering or suspension) is likely to cause the vehicle to fail. In this case professional repairs are likely to be needed.

☐ Damage or corrosion which causes sharp or otherwise dangerous edges to be exposed will also cause the vehicle to fail.

Towbars

☐ Check the condition of mounting points (both beneath the vehicle and within boot/hatchback areas) for signs of corrosion, ensuring that all fixings are secure and not worn or damaged. There must be no excessive play in detachable tow ball arms or quick-release mechanisms.

☐ Examine the security and condition of the towbar electrics socket. If the later 13-pin socket is fitted, the MOT tester will check its' wiring functions/connections are correct.

General leaks

☐ The vehicle will fail the test if there is a fluid leak of any kind that poses an environmental risk.

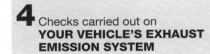

4 Checks carried out on **YOUR VEHICLE'S EXHAUST EMISSION SYSTEM**

Petrol models

☐ The engine should be warmed up, and running well (ignition system in good order, air filter element clean, etc).

☐ Before testing, run the engine at around 2500 rpm for 20 seconds. Let the engine drop to idle, and watch for smoke from the exhaust. If the idle speed is too high, or if dense blue or black smoke emerges for more than 5 seconds, the vehicle will fail. Typically, blue smoke signifies oil burning (engine wear); black smoke means unburnt fuel (dirty air cleaner element, or other fuel system fault).

☐ An exhaust gas analyser for measuring carbon monoxide (CO) and hydrocarbons (HC) is now needed. If one cannot be hired or borrowed, have a local garage perform the check.

CO emissions (mixture)

☐ The MOT tester has access to the CO limits for all vehicles from 1st August 1992. The CO level is measured at idle speed, and at 'fast idle' (2500 to 3000 rpm). The following limits are given as a general guide:
At idle speed – Less than 0.3% CO
At 'fast idle' – Less than 0.2% CO
Lambda reading – 0.97 to 1.03

☐ If the CO level is too high, this may point to poor maintenance, a fuel injection system problem, faulty lambda (oxygen) sensor or catalytic converter. Try an injector cleaning treatment, and check the vehicle's ECU for fault codes.

HC emissions

☐ The MOT tester has access to HC limits for all vehicles. The HC level is measured at 'fast idle' (2500 to 3000 rpm). The following limits are given as a general guide:
At 'fast idle' – Less than 200 ppm

☐ Excessive HC emissions are typically caused by oil being burnt (worn engine), or by a blocked crankcase ventilation system ('breather'). If the engine oil is old and thin, an oil change may help. If the engine is running badly, check the vehicle's ECU for fault codes.

Diesel models

☐ If the vehicle was fitted with a DPF (Diesel Particulate Filter) when it left the factory, it will fail the test if the MOT tester can see smoke of any colour emitting from the exhaust, or finds evidence that the filter has been tampered with.

☐ The only emission test for diesel engines is measuring exhaust smoke density, using a calibrated smoke meter.

☐ This test involves accelerating the engine to its maximum unloaded speed a minimum of once, and a maximum of 6 times. With the smoke meter connected, the engine is accelerated quickly to its maximum speed. If the smoke level is at or below the limit specified, the vehicle will pass. If the level is more than the specified limit then two further accelerations are carried out, and an average of the readings calculated. If the vehicle is still over the limit, a further three accelerations are carried out, with the average of the last three calculated after each check.
Note: *On engines with a timing belt, it is VITAL that the belt is in good condition before the test is carried out.*

Vehicles registered after 1st July 2008
Smoke level must not exceed 1.5m-1 – Turbo-charged and non-Turbocharged engines

Vehicles registered before 1st July 2008
Smoke level must not exceed 2.5m-1 – Non-turbo vehicles
Smoke level must not exceed 3.0m-1 – Turbocharged vehicles:

☐ If excess smoke is produced, try fitting a new air cleaner element, or using an injector cleaning treatment. If the engine is running badly, where applicable, check the vehicle's ECU for fault codes. Also check the vehicle's EGR system, where applicable. At high mileages, the injectors may require professional attention.

Engine

☐ Engine fails to rotate when attempting to start
☐ Engine rotates, but will not start
☐ Engine difficult to start when cold
☐ Engine difficult to start when hot
☐ Starter motor noisy or excessively-rough in engagement
☐ Engine starts, but stops immediately
☐ Engine idles erratically
☐ Engine misfires at idle speed
☐ Engine misfires throughout the driving speed range
☐ Engine hesitates on acceleration
☐ Engine stalls
☐ Engine lacks power
☐ Engine backfires
☐ Oil pressure warning light illuminated with engine running
☐ Engine runs-on after switching off
☐ Engine noises

Cooling system

☐ Overheating
☐ Overcooling
☐ External coolant leakage
☐ Internal coolant leakage
☐ Corrosion

Fuel and exhaust systems

☐ Excessive fuel consumption
☐ Fuel leakage and/or fuel odour
☐ Excessive noise or fumes from exhaust system

Clutch

☐ Pedal travels to floor – no pressure or very little resistance
☐ Clutch fails to disengage (unable to select gears)
☐ Clutch slips (engine speed increases, with no increase in vehicle speed)
☐ Judder as clutch is engaged
☐ Noise when depressing or releasing clutch pedal

Manual transmission

☐ Noisy in neutral with engine running
☐ Noisy in one particular gear
☐ Difficulty engaging gears
☐ Jumps out of gear
☐ Vibration
☐ Lubricant leaks

Automatic transmission

☐ Fluid leakage
☐ Transmission fluid brown, or has burned smell
☐ General gear selection problems
☐ Transmission will not downshift (kickdown) with accelerator fully depressed
☐ Engine will not start in any gear, or starts in gears other than Park or Neutral
☐ Transmission slips, shifts roughly, is noisy, or has no drive in forward or reverse gears

Driveshafts

☐ Clicking or knocking noise on turns (at slow speed on full-lock)
☐ Vibration when accelerating or decelerating

Braking system

☐ Vehicle pulls to one side under braking
☐ Noise (grinding or high-pitched squeal) when brakes applied
☐ Excessive brake pedal travel
☐ Brake pedal feels spongy when depressed
☐ Excessive brake pedal effort required to stop vehicle
☐ Judder felt through brake pedal or steering wheel when braking
☐ Brakes binding
☐ Rear wheels locking under normal braking

Suspension and steering systems

☐ Vehicle pulls to one side
☐ Wheel wobble and vibration
☐ Excessive pitching and/or rolling around corners, or during braking
☐ Wandering or general instability
☐ Excessively-stiff steering
☐ Excessive play in steering
☐ Lack of power assistance
☐ Tyre wear excessive

Electrical system

☐ Battery will not hold a charge for more than a few days
☐ Ignition/no-charge warning light remains illuminated with engine running
☐ Ignition/no-charge warning light fails to come on
☐ Lights inoperative
☐ Instrument readings inaccurate or erratic
☐ Horn inoperative, or unsatisfactory in operation
☐ Windscreen wipers inoperative, or unsatisfactory in operation
☐ Windscreen washers inoperative, or unsatisfactory in operation
☐ Electric windows inoperative, or unsatisfactory in operation
☐ Central locking system inoperative, or unsatisfactory in operation

Introduction

The vehicle owner who does his or her own maintenance according to the recommended service schedules should not have to use this section of the manual very often. Modern component reliability is such that, provided those items subject to wear or deterioration are inspected or renewed at the specified intervals, sudden failure is comparatively rare. Faults do not usually just happen as a result of sudden failure, but develop over a period of time. Major mechanical failures in particular are usually preceded by characteristic symptoms over hundreds or even thousands of miles. Those components which do occasionally fail without warning are often small and easily carried in the vehicle.

With any fault finding, the first step is to decide where to begin investigations. Sometimes this is obvious, but on other occasions, a little detective work will be necessary. The owner who makes half a dozen haphazard adjustments or replacements may be successful in curing a fault (or its symptoms), but will be none the wiser if the fault recurs, and ultimately may have spent more time and money than was necessary. A calm and logical approach will be found to be more satisfactory in the long run. Always take into account any warning signs or abnormalities that may have been noticed in the period preceding the fault – power loss, high or low gauge readings, unusual

smells, etc – and remember that failure of components such as fuses or spark plugs may only be pointers to some underlying fault.

The pages which follow provide an easy-reference guide to the more common problems which may occur during the operation of the vehicle. These problems and their possible causes are grouped under headings denoting various components or systems, such as Engine, Cooling system, etc. The general Chapter which deals with the problem is also shown in brackets; refer to the relevant part of that Chapter for system-specific information. Whatever the fault, certain basic principles apply. These are as follows:

Verify the fault. This is simply a matter of

being sure that you know what the symptoms are before starting work. This is particularly important if you are investigating a fault for someone else, who may not have described it very accurately.

Don't overlook the obvious. For example, if the vehicle won't start, is there fuel in the tank? (Don't take anyone else's word on this particular point, and don't trust the fuel gauge either). If an electrical fault is indicated, look for loose or broken wires before digging out the test gear.

Cure the disease, not the symptom. Substituting a flat battery with a fully-charged one will get you off the hard shoulder, but if the underlying cause is not attended to, the new battery will go the same way. Similarly, changing oil-fouled spark plugs for a new set will get you moving again, but remember that the reason for the fouling (if it wasn't simply an incorrect grade of plug) will have to be established and corrected.

Don't take anything for granted. Particularly, don't forget that a 'new' component may itself be defective (especially if it's been rattling around in the boot for months), and don't leave components out of a fault diagnosis sequence just because they are new or recently-fitted. When you do finally diagnose a difficult fault, you'll probably realise that all the evidence was there from the start.

Consider what work, if any, has recently been carried out. Many faults arise through careless or hurried work. For instance, if any work has been performed under the bonnet, could some of the wiring have been dislodged or incorrectly routed, or a hose trapped? Have all the fasteners been properly tightened? Were new, genuine parts and new gaskets used? There is often a certain amount of detective work to be done in this case, as an apparently-unrelated task can have far-reaching consequences.

Engine

Engine fails to rotate when attempting to start

- ☐ Battery terminal connections loose or corroded (see *Weekly checks*)
- ☐ Battery discharged or faulty (Chapter 5A)
- ☐ Broken, loose or disconnected wiring in the starting circuit (Chapter 5A)
- ☐ Defective starter solenoid or ignition switch (Chapter 5A or 12)
- ☐ Defective starter motor (Chapter 5A)
- ☐ Starter pinion or flywheel ring gear teeth loose or broken (Chapter 2A, 2B, 2C, 2D, 2E or 5A)
- ☐ Engine earth strap broken or disconnected (Chapter 12)
- ☐ Engine suffering 'hydraulic lock' (eg, from water ingested after traversing flooded roads, or from a serious internal coolant leak) – consult a Volvo dealer or specialist for advice
- ☐ Automatic transmission not in position P or N (Chapter 7B)

Engine rotates, but will not start

- ☐ Fuel tank empty
- ☐ Battery discharged (engine rotates slowly) (Chapter 5A)
- ☐ Battery terminal connections loose or corroded (see *Weekly checks*)
- ☐ Ignition components damp or damaged – petrol models (Chapter 1A or 5B)
- ☐ Worn, faulty or incorrectly-gapped spark plugs – petrol models (Chapter 1A)
- ☐ Broken, loose or disconnected wiring in the ignition circuit – petrol models (Chapter 1A or Chapter 5B)
- ☐ Immobiliser fault, or 'uncoded' remote unit being used (Chapter 12)
- ☐ Crankshaft sensor fault (Chapter 4A or 4B)
- ☐ Preheating system faulty – diesel engines (Chapter 5C)
- ☐ Fuel injection system fault – petrol models (Chapter 4A)
- ☐ Air in fuel system – diesel engines (Chapter 4B)
- ☐ Major mechanical failure (eg, timing belt snapped) (Chapter 2A, 2B, 2C, 2D or 2E)

Engine difficult to start when cold

- ☐ Battery discharged (Chapter 5A)
- ☐ Battery terminal connections loose or corroded (see *Weekly checks*)
- ☐ Preheating system faulty – diesel engines (Chapter 5C)
- ☐ Fuel injection system fault – petrol models (Chapter 4A)
- ☐ Wrong grade of engine oil used (*Weekly checks*, Chapter 1)
- ☐ Low cylinder compression (Chapter 2A, 2B, 2C, 2D or 2E)

Engine difficult to start when hot

- ☐ Air filter element dirty or clogged (Chapter 1A or 1B)
- ☐ Fuel injection system fault – petrol models (Chapter 4A)
- ☐ Low cylinder compression (Chapter 2A, 2B, 2C, 2D or 2E)

Starter motor noisy or excessively-rough in engagement

- ☐ Starter pinion or flywheel ring gear teeth loose or broken (Chapter 2A, 2B, 2C, 2D, 2E or 5A)
- ☐ Starter motor mounting bolts loose or missing (Chapter 5A)
- ☐ Starter motor internal components worn or damaged (Chapter 5A)

Engine starts, but stops immediately

- ☐ Loose or faulty electrical connections in the ignition circuit – petrol models (Chapter 1A and Chapter 5B)
- ☐ Vacuum leak at the throttle body or inlet manifold – petrol models (Chapter 4A)
- ☐ Blocked injectors/fuel injection system fault – petrol models (Chapter 4A)
- ☐ Air in fuel, possibly due to loose fuel line connection – diesel models (Chapter 4B)

Engine idles erratically

- ☐ Air filter element clogged (Chapter 1A or 1B)
- ☐ Vacuum leak at the throttle body, inlet manifold or associated hoses – petrol models (Chapter 4A)
- ☐ Uneven or low cylinder compression (Chapter 2A, 2B, 2C, 2D or 2E)
- ☐ Camshaft lobes worn (Chapter 2A, 2B, 2C, 2D or 2E)
- ☐ Timing belt (or chain) incorrectly fitted (Chapter 2A, 2B, 2C, 2D or 2E)
- ☐ Blocked injectors/fuel injection system fault – petrol models (Chapter 4A)
- ☐ Faulty injectors – diesel models (Chapter 4B)

Engine misfires at idle speed

- ☐ Worn, faulty or incorrectly-gapped spark plugs – petrol models (Chapter 1A)
- ☐ Vacuum leak at the throttle body, inlet manifold or associated hoses – petrol models (Chapter 4A)
- ☐ Blocked injectors/fuel injection system fault – petrol models (Chapter 4A)
- ☐ Faulty injector(s) – diesel models (Chapter 4B)
- ☐ Uneven or low cylinder compression (Chapter 2A, 2B, 2C, 2D or 2E)
- ☐ Disconnected, leaking, or perished crankcase ventilation hoses (Chapter 4C or 4D)

Engine misfires throughout the driving speed range

- ☐ Fuel filter choked – diesel models (Chapter 1B)
- ☐ Fuel pump faulty, or delivery pressure low – petrol models (Chapter 4A)
- ☐ Fuel tank vent blocked, or fuel pipes restricted – petrol models (Chapter 4A)
- ☐ Vacuum leak at the throttle body, inlet manifold or associated hoses – petrol models (Chapter 4A)
- ☐ Worn, faulty or incorrectly-gapped spark plugs – petrol models (Chapter 1A)
- ☐ Faulty injector(s) – diesel models (Chapter 4B)
- ☐ Faulty ignition coil – petrol models (Chapter 4A)
- ☐ Uneven or low cylinder compression (Chapter 2A, 2B, 2C, 2D or 2E)
- ☐ Blocked injector/fuel injection system fault – petrol models (Chapter 4A)
- ☐ Blocked catalytic converter (Chapter 4D)
- ☐ Engine overheating (Chapter 3)

Engine (continued)

Engine hesitates on acceleration

- ☐ Worn, faulty or incorrectly-gapped spark plugs – petrol models (Chapter 1A)
- ☐ Vacuum leak at the throttle body, inlet manifold or associated hoses – petrol models (Chapter 4A)
- ☐ Blocked injectors/fuel injection system fault – petrol models (Chapter 4A)
- ☐ Faulty injector(s) – diesel models (Chapter 4B)
- ☐ Faulty clutch pedal switch (Chapter 6)

Engine stalls

- ☐ Vacuum leak at the throttle body, inlet manifold or associated hoses – petrol models (Chapter 4A)
- ☐ Fuel filter choked – diesel models (Chapter 1B)
- ☐ Fuel pump faulty, or delivery pressure low – petrol models (Chapter 4A)
- ☐ Fuel tank vent blocked, or fuel pipes restricted – petrol models (Chapter 4A)
- ☐ Blocked injectors/fuel injection system fault – petrol models (Chapter 4A)
- ☐ Faulty injector(s) – diesel models (Chapter 4B)

Engine lacks power

- ☐ Air filter element blocked (Chapter 1A or 1B)
- ☐ Fuel filter choked (Chapter 1A or 1B)
- ☐ Engine overheating (Chapter 3)
- ☐ Accelerator position sensor faulty – petrol models (Chapter 4A)
- ☐ Vacuum leak at the throttle body, inlet manifold or associated hoses – petrol models (Chapter 4A)
- ☐ Blocked injectors/fuel injection system fault – petrol models (Chapter 4A)
- ☐ Faulty injector(s) – diesel models (Chapter 4B)
- ☐ Fuel pump faulty, or delivery pressure low – petrol models (Chapter 4A)
- ☐ Uneven or low cylinder compression (Chapter 2A, 2B, 2C, 2D or 2E)
- ☐ Blocked catalytic converter – petrol models (Chapter 4C)
- ☐ Brakes binding (Chapter 9)
- ☐ Clutch slipping (Chapter 6)

Engine backfires

- ☐ Timing belt (or chain) incorrectly fitted (Chapter 2A, 2B, 2C, 2D or 2E)
- ☐ Vacuum leak at the throttle body, inlet manifold or associated hoses – petrol models (Chapter 4A)
- ☐ Blocked injectors/fuel injection system fault – petrol models (Chapter 4A)
- ☐ Blocked catalytic converter – petrol models (Chapter 4C)

Oil pressure warning light illuminated with engine running

- ☐ Low oil level, or incorrect oil grade (see Weekly checks)
- ☐ Faulty oil pressure sensor, or wiring damaged (Chapter 12)
- ☐ Worn engine bearings and/or oil pump (Chapter 2A, 2B, 2C, 2D or 2E)
- ☐ High engine operating temperature (Chapter 3)
- ☐ Oil pump pressure relief valve defective (Chapter 2A, 2B, 2C, 2D or 2E)
- ☐ Oil pump pick-up strainer clogged (Chapter 2A, 2B, 2C, 2D or 2E)

Engine runs-on after switching off

- ☐ Excessive carbon build-up in engine (Chapter 2A, 2B, 2C, 2D or 2E)
- ☐ High engine operating temperature (Chapter 3)
- ☐ Fuel injection system fault – petrol models (Chapter 4A)

Engine noises

Pre-ignition (pinking) or knocking during acceleration or under load

- ☐ Ignition system fault – petrol models (Chapter 1A or 5B)
- ☐ Incorrect grade of spark plug – petrol models (Chapter 1A)
- ☐ Vacuum leak at the throttle body, inlet manifold or associated hoses – petrol models (Chapter 4A)
- ☐ Excessive carbon build-up in engine (Chapter 2A, 2B, 2C, 2D or 2E)
- ☐ Blocked injector/fuel injection system fault – petrol models (Chapter 4A)
- ☐ Faulty injector(s) – diesel models (Chapter 4B)

Whistling or wheezing noises

- ☐ Leaking inlet manifold or throttle body gasket – petrol models (Chapter 4A)
- ☐ Leaking exhaust manifold gasket or pipe-to-manifold joint (Chapter 4A or 4B)
- ☐ Leaking vacuum hose – petrol models (Chapter 9)
- ☐ Blowing cylinder head gasket (Chapter 2A, 2B, 2C, 2D or 2E)

Tapping or rattling noises

- ☐ Worn valve gear or camshaft (Chapter 2A, 2B, 2C, 2D or 2E)
- ☐ Ancillary component fault (coolant pump, alternator, etc) (Chapter 3, 5A, etc)

Knocking or thumping noises

- ☐ Worn big-end bearings (regular heavy knocking, perhaps less under load) (Chapter 2F)
- ☐ Worn main bearings (rumbling and knocking, perhaps worsening under load) (Chapter 2F)
- ☐ Piston slap – most noticeable when cold, caused by piston/bore wear (Chapter 2F)
- ☐ Ancillary component fault (coolant pump, alternator, etc) (Chapter 3, 5A, etc)
- ☐ Engine mountings worn or defective (Chapter 2E)
- ☐ Front suspension or steering components worn (Chapter 10)

Cooling system

Overheating

- ☐ Insufficient coolant in system (see *Weekly checks*)
- ☐ Thermostat faulty (Chapter 3)
- ☐ Radiator core blocked, or grille restricted (Chapter 3)
- ☐ Cooling fan faulty, or control module fault (Chapter 3)
- ☐ Inaccurate coolant temperature sender (Chapter 3)
- ☐ Airlock in cooling system (Chapter 1A or 1B)
- ☐ Expansion tank pressure cap faulty (Chapter 3)

Overcooling

- ☐ Thermostat faulty (Chapter 3)
- ☐ Inaccurate coolant temperature sender (Chapter 3)
- ☐ Cooling fan faulty (Chapter 3)

External coolant leakage

- ☐ Deteriorated or damaged hoses or hose clips (Chapter 3)
- ☐ Radiator core or heater matrix leaking (Chapter 3)
- ☐ Expansion tank pressure cap faulty (Chapter 1)
- ☐ Coolant pump internal seal leaking (Chapter 3)
- ☐ Coolant pump gasket leaking (Chapter 3)
- ☐ Boiling due to overheating (Chapter 3)
- ☐ Cylinder block core plug leaking (Chapter 2F)

Internal coolant leakage

- ☐ Leaking cylinder head gasket (Chapter 2A, 2B, 2C, 2D or 2E)
- ☐ Cracked cylinder head or cylinder block (Chapter 2F)

Corrosion

- ☐ Infrequent draining and flushing (Chapter 1A or 1B)
- ☐ Incorrect coolant mixture or inappropriate coolant type (see *Weekly checks*)

Fuel and exhaust systems

Excessive fuel consumption

- ☐ Air filter element dirty or clogged (Chapter 1A or 1B)
- ☐ Fuel injection system fault – petrol models (Chapter 4A)
- ☐ Engine management system fault (Chapter 4A or 4B)
- ☐ Tyres under-inflated (see *Weekly checks*)
- ☐ Brakes binding (Chapter 9)
- ☐ Fuel leak, causing apparent high consumption (Chapter 1A or 1B)

Fuel leakage and/or fuel odour

- ☐ Damaged or corroded fuel tank, pipes or connections (Chapter 1A or 1B)

Excessive noise or fumes from exhaust system

- ☐ Leaking exhaust system or manifold joints (Chapter 4A or 4B)
- ☐ Leaking, corroded or damaged silencers or pipe (Chapter 4A or 4B)
- ☐ Broken mountings causing body or suspension contact (Chapter 2E)

Clutch

Pedal travels to floor – no pressure or very little resistance

- ☐ Air in hydraulic system/faulty master or slave cylinder (Chapter 6)
- ☐ Faulty hydraulic release system (Chapter 6)
- ☐ Clutch pedal return spring detached or broken (Chapter 6)
- ☐ Broken clutch release bearing or fork (Chapter 6)
- ☐ Broken diaphragm spring in clutch pressure plate (Chapter 6)

Clutch fails to disengage (unable to select gears)

- ☐ Air in hydraulic system/faulty master or slave cylinder (Chapter 6)
- ☐ Faulty hydraulic release system (Chapter 6)
- ☐ Clutch disc sticking on transmission input shaft splines (Chapter 6)
- ☐ Clutch disc sticking to flywheel or pressure plate (Chapter 6)
- ☐ Faulty pressure plate assembly (Chapter 6)
- ☐ Clutch release mechanism worn or incorrectly assembled (Chapter 6)

Clutch slips (engine speed increases, with no increase in vehicle speed)

- ☐ Faulty hydraulic release system (Chapter 6)
- ☐ Clutch disc linings excessively worn (Chapter 6)
- ☐ Clutch disc linings contaminated with oil or grease (Chapter 6)
- ☐ Faulty pressure plate or weak diaphragm spring (Chapter 6)

Judder as clutch is engaged

- ☐ Clutch disc linings contaminated with oil or grease (Chapter 6)
- ☐ Clutch disc linings excessively worn (Chapter 6)
- ☐ Faulty or distorted pressure plate or diaphragm spring (Chapter 6).
- ☐ Worn or loose engine or transmission mountings (Chapter 2E)
- ☐ Clutch disc hub or transmission input shaft splines worn (Chapter 6)

Noise when depressing or releasing clutch pedal

- ☐ Worn clutch release bearing (Chapter 6)
- ☐ Worn or dry clutch pedal bushes (Chapter 6)
- ☐ Worn or dry clutch master cylinder piston (Chapter 6)
- ☐ Faulty pressure plate assembly (Chapter 6)
- ☐ Pressure plate diaphragm spring broken (Chapter 6)
- ☐ Broken clutch disc cushioning springs (Chapter 6)

Manual transmission

Noisy in neutral with engine running

☐ Lack of oil (Chapter 7A)
☐ Input shaft bearings worn (noise apparent with clutch pedal released, but not when depressed) (Chapter 7A)*
☐ Clutch release bearing worn (noise apparent with clutch pedal depressed, possibly less when released) (Chapter 6)

Noisy in one particular gear

☐ Worn, damaged or chipped gear teeth (Chapter 7A)*

Difficulty engaging gears

☐ Clutch fault (Chapter 6)
☐ Worn or damaged gearchange cables (Chapter 7A)
☐ Lack of oil (Chapter 7A)
☐ Worn synchroniser units (Chapter 7A)*

Jumps out of gear

☐ Worn or damaged gearchange cables (Chapter 7A)
☐ Worn synchroniser units (Chapter 7A)*
☐ Worn selector forks (Chapter 7A)*

Vibration

☐ Lack of oil (Chapter 7A)
☐ Worn bearings (Chapter 7A)*

Lubricant leaks

☐ Leaking driveshaft or selector shaft oil seal (Chapter 7A)
☐ Leaking housing joint (Chapter 7A)*
☐ Leaking input shaft oil seal (Chapter 7A)*

Although the corrective action necessary to remedy the symptoms described is beyond the scope of the home mechanic, the above information should be helpful in isolating the cause of the condition, so that the owner can communicate clearly with a professional mechanic.

Automatic transmission

Note: *Due to the complexity of the automatic transmission, it is difficult for the home mechanic to properly diagnose and service this unit. For problems other than the following, the vehicle should be taken to a dealer service department or automatic transmission specialist. Do not be too hasty in removing the transmission if a fault is suspected, as most of the testing is carried out with the unit still fitted. Remember that, besides the sensors specific to the transmission, many of the engine management system sensors described in Chapter 4 are essential to the correct operation of the transmission.*

Fluid leakage

☐ Automatic transmission fluid is usually dark red in colour. Fluid leaks should not be confused with engine oil, which can easily be blown onto the transmission by airflow.
☐ To determine the source of a leak, first remove all built-up dirt and grime from the transmission housing and surrounding areas using a degreasing agent, or by steam-cleaning. Drive the vehicle at low speed, so airflow will not blow the leak far from its source. Raise and support the vehicle, and determine where the leak is coming from. The following are common areas of leakage:
   a) *Fluid pan*
   b) *Dipstick tube*
   c) *Transmission-to-fluid cooler unions (Chapter 7B)*

Transmission fluid brown, or has burned smell

☐ Transmission fluid level low (Chapter 1A or 1B)

General gear selection problems

☐ Chapter 7B deals with checking the selector cable on automatic transmissions. The following are common problems which may be caused by a faulty cable or sensor:
   a) *Engine starting in gears other than Park or Neutral.*
   b) *Indicator panel indicating a gear other than the one actually being used.*
   c) *Vehicle moves when in Park or Neutral.*
   d) *Poor gear shift quality or erratic gear changes.*

Transmission will not downshift (kickdown) with accelerator pedal fully depressed

☐ Low transmission fluid level (Chapter 1A or 1B)
☐ Faulty transmission sensor or wiring (Chapter 7B)
☐ Faulty selector cable (Chapter 7B)

Engine will not start in any gear, or starts in gears other than Park or Neutral

☐ Faulty transmission sensor or wiring (Chapter 7B)
☐ Faulty selector cable (Chapter 7B)

Transmission slips, shifts roughly, is noisy, or has no drive in forward or reverse gears

☐ Transmission fluid level low (Chapter 1A or 1B)
☐ Faulty transmission sensor or wiring (Chapter 7B)

Note: *There are many probable causes for the above problems, but diagnosing and correcting them is considered beyond the scope of this manual. Having checked the fluid level and all the wiring as far as possible, a dealer or transmission specialist should be consulted if the problem persists.*

Driveshafts

Vibration when accelerating or decelerating
- [ ] Worn inner constant velocity joint (Chapter 8)
- [ ] Bent or distorted driveshaft (Chapter 8)
- [ ] Worn intermediate bearing (Chapter 8)

Clicking or knocking noise on turns (at slow speed on full-lock)
- [ ] Worn outer constant velocity joint (Chapter 8)
- [ ] Lack of constant velocity joint lubricant, possibly due to damaged gaiter (Chapter 8)
- [ ] Worn intermediate bearing (Chapter 8)

Braking system

Note: *Before assuming that a brake problem exists, make sure that the tyres are in good condition and correctly inflated, that the front wheel alignment is correct, and that the vehicle is not loaded with weight in an unequal manner. Apart from checking the condition of all pipe and hose connections, any faults occurring on the anti-lock braking system should be referred to a Volvo dealer or specialist for diagnosis.*

Vehicle pulls to one side under braking
- [ ] Worn, defective, damaged or contaminated brake pads on one side (Chapter 9)
- [ ] Seized or partially-seized brake caliper piston (Chapter 9)
- [ ] A mixture of brake pad lining materials fitted between sides (Chapter 9)
- [ ] Brake caliper mounting bolts loose (Chapter 9)
- [ ] Worn or damaged steering or suspension components (Chapter 10)

Noise (grinding or high-pitched squeal) when brakes applied
- [ ] Brake pad friction lining material worn down to metal backing (Chapter 9)
- [ ] Excessive corrosion of brake disc (may be apparent after the vehicle has been standing for some time (Chapter 9)
- [ ] Foreign object (stone chipping, etc) trapped between brake disc and shield (Chapter 9)

Excessive brake pedal travel
- [ ] Faulty master cylinder (Chapter 9)
- [ ] Air in hydraulic system (Chapter 9)
- [ ] Faulty vacuum servo unit (Chapter 9)

Brake pedal feels spongy when depressed
- [ ] Air in hydraulic system (Chapter 9)
- [ ] Deteriorated flexible rubber brake hoses (Chapter 1A or 1B)
- [ ] Master cylinder mounting nuts loose (Chapter 9)
- [ ] Faulty master cylinder (Chapter 9)

Excessive brake pedal effort required to stop vehicle
- [ ] Faulty vacuum servo unit (Chapter 9)
- [ ] Faulty vacuum pump – diesel models (Chapter 9)
- [ ] Disconnected, damaged or insecure brake servo vacuum hose (Chapter 9)
- [ ] Primary or secondary hydraulic circuit failure (Chapter 9)
- [ ] Seized brake caliper piston (Chapter 9)
- [ ] Brake pads incorrectly fitted (Chapter 9)
- [ ] Incorrect grade of brake pads fitted (Chapter 9)
- [ ] Brake pad linings contaminated (Chapter 9)

Judder felt through brake pedal or steering wheel when braking

Note: *Under heavy braking on models equipped with ABS, vibration may be felt through the brake pedal. This is a normal feature of ABS operation, and does not constitute a fault*
- [ ] Excessive run-out or distortion of discs (Chapter 9)
- [ ] Brake pad linings worn (Chapter 1A or 1B)
- [ ] Brake caliper mounting bolts loose (Chapter 9)
- [ ] Wear in suspension or steering components or mountings (Chapter 1A or 1B)
- [ ] Front wheels out of balance (see *Weekly checks*)

Brakes binding
- [ ] Seized brake caliper piston (Chapter 9)
- [ ] Faulty handbrake mechanism (Chapter 9)
- [ ] Faulty master cylinder (Chapter 9)

Rear wheels locking under normal braking
- [ ] Rear brake pad linings contaminated or damaged (Chapter 9)
- [ ] Rear brake discs warped (Chapter 9)

Suspension and steering

Note: *Before diagnosing suspension or steering faults, be sure that the trouble is not due to incorrect tyre pressures, mixtures of tyre types, or binding brakes.*

Vehicle pulls to one side

- [ ] Defective tyre (see *Weekly checks*)
- [ ] Excessive wear in suspension or steering components (Chapter 1A, 1B or 10)
- [ ] Incorrect front wheel alignment (Chapter 10)
- [ ] Accident damage to steering or suspension components

Wheel wobble and vibration

- [ ] Front wheels out of balance (vibration felt mainly through the steering wheel) (see *Weekly checks*)
- [ ] Rear wheels out of balance (vibration felt throughout the vehicle) (see *Weekly checks*)
- [ ] Roadwheels damaged or distorted (see Weekly checks)
- [ ] Faulty or damaged tyre (see Weekly checks)
- [ ] Worn steering or suspension joints, bushes or components (Chapter 1A, 1B or 10)
- [ ] Wheel nuts loose (Chapter 1A or 1B)

Excessive pitching and/or rolling around corners, or during braking

- [ ] Defective shock absorbers (Chapter 10)
- [ ] Broken or weak spring and/or suspension component (Chapter 10)
- [ ] Worn or damaged anti-roll bar or mountings (Chapter 10)

Wandering or general instability

- [ ] Incorrect front wheel alignment (Chapter 10)
- [ ] Worn steering or suspension joints, bushes or components (Chapter 1A, 1B or 10)
- [ ] Roadwheels out of balance (see *Weekly checks*)
- [ ] Faulty or damaged tyre (see Weekly checks)
- [ ] Wheel nuts loose (Chapter 1A or 1B)
- [ ] Defective shock absorbers (Chapter 10)

Excessively-stiff steering

- [ ] Seized steering linkage balljoint or suspension balljoint (Chapter 1A ,1B or 10)

- [ ] Broken or incorrectly-adjusted auxiliary drivebelt (Chapter 1A or 1B)
- [ ] Incorrect front wheel alignment (Chapter 10)
- [ ] Steering rack damaged (Chapter 10)

Excessive play in steering

- [ ] Worn steering column/intermediate shaft joints (Chapter 10)
- [ ] Worn track rod balljoints (Chapter 10)
- [ ] Worn steering rack (Chapter 10)
- [ ] Worn steering or suspension joints, bushes or components (Chapter 1A, 1B or 10)

Lack of power assistance

- [ ] Broken or incorrectly-adjusted auxiliary drivebelt (Chapter 1A or 1B)
- [ ] Incorrect power steering fluid level (see *Weekly checks*)
- [ ] Restriction in power steering fluid hoses (Chapter 1A or 1B)
- [ ] Faulty power steering pump (Chapter 10)
- [ ] Faulty steering rack (Chapter 10)

Tyre wear excessive

Tyres worn on inside or outside edges

- [ ] Tyres under-inflated (wear on both edges) (see *Weekly checks*)
- [ ] Incorrect camber or castor angles (wear on one edge only) (Chapter 10)
- [ ] Worn steering or suspension joints, bushes or components (Chapter 1A, 1B or 10)
- [ ] Excessively-hard cornering or braking
- [ ] Accident damage

Tyre treads exhibit feathered edges

- [ ] Incorrect toe-setting (Chapter 10)

Tyres worn in centre of tread

- [ ] Tyres over-inflated (see *Weekly checks*)

Tyres worn on inside and outside edges

- [ ] Tyres under-inflated (see *Weekly checks*)

Tyres worn unevenly

- [ ] Tyres/wheels out of balance (see *Weekly checks*)
- [ ] Excessive wheel or tyre run-out
- [ ] Worn shock absorbers (Chapter 10)
- [ ] Faulty tyre (see Weekly checks)

Electrical system

Note: *For problems associated with the starting system, refer to the faults listed under 'Engine' earlier in this Section.*

Battery will not hold a charge for more than a few days

- [ ] Battery defective internally (Chapter 5A)
- [ ] Battery terminal connections loose or corroded (see *Weekly checks*)
- [ ] Auxiliary drivebelt worn or incorrectly adjusted (Chapter 1A or 1B)
- [ ] Alternator not charging at correct output (Chapter 5A)
- [ ] Alternator or voltage regulator faulty (Chapter 5A)
- [ ] Short-circuit causing continual battery drain (Chapter 12)

Ignition/no-charge warning light remains illuminated with engine running

- [ ] Auxiliary drivebelt broken, worn, or incorrectly adjusted (Chapter 1A or 1B)
- [ ] Internal fault in alternator or voltage regulator (Chapter 5A)
- [ ] Broken, disconnected, or loose wiring in charging circuit (Chapter 12)

Ignition/no-charge warning light fails to come on

- [ ] Warning light bulb blown (Chapter 12)
- [ ] Broken, disconnected, or loose wiring in warning light circuit (Chapter 12)
- [ ] Alternator faulty (Chapter 5A)

Electrical system (continued)

Lights inoperative

- ☐ Bulb blown (Chapter 12)
- ☐ Corrosion of bulb or bulbholder contacts (Chapter 12)
- ☐ Blown fuse (Chapter 12)
- ☐ Faulty relay (Chapter 12)
- ☐ Broken, loose, or disconnected wiring (Chapter 12)
- ☐ Faulty switch (Chapter 12)

Instrument readings inaccurate or erratic

Fuel or temperature gauges give no reading

- ☐ Faulty gauge sender unit (Chapter 4A or 4B)
- ☐ Wiring open-circuit (Chapter 12)
- ☐ Faulty instrument cluster (Chapter 12)

Fuel or temperature gauges give continuous maximum reading

- ☐ Faulty gauge sender unit (Chapter 4A or 4B)
- ☐ Wiring short-circuit (Chapter 12)
- ☐ Faulty instrument cluster (Chapter 12)

Horn inoperative, or unsatisfactory in operation

Horn operates all the time

- ☐ Horn push either earthed or stuck down (Chapter 12)
- ☐ Horn cable-to-horn push earthed (Chapter 12)

Horn fails to operate

- ☐ Blown fuse (Chapter 12)
- ☐ Cable or connections loose, broken or disconnected (Chapter 12)
- ☐ Faulty horn (Chapter 12)

Horn emits intermittent or unsatisfactory sound

- ☐ Cable connections loose (Chapter 12)
- ☐ Horn mountings loose (Chapter 12)
- ☐ Faulty horn (Chapter 12)

Windscreen wipers inoperative, or unsatisfactory in operation

Wipers fail to operate, or operate very slowly

- ☐ Wiper blades stuck to screen, or linkage seized or binding (Chapter 12)
- ☐ Blown fuse (Chapter 12)
- ☐ Battery discharged (Chapter 5A)
- ☐ Cable or connections loose, broken or disconnected (Chapter 12)
- ☐ Faulty wiper motor (Chapter 12)

Wiper blades sweep over too large or too small an area of the glass

- ☐ Wiper blades incorrectly fitted, or wrong size used (see *Weekly checks)*
- ☐ Wiper arms incorrectly positioned on spindles (Chapter 12)
- ☐ Excessive wear of wiper linkage (Chapter 12)
- ☐ Wiper motor or linkage mountings loose or insecure (Chapter 12)

Wiper blades fail to clean the glass effectively

- ☐ Wiper blade rubbers dirty, worn or perished (see *Weekly checks)*
- ☐ Wiper blades incorrectly fitted, or wrong size used (see Weekly checks)
- ☐ Wiper arm tension springs broken, or arm pivots seized (Chapter 12)
- ☐ Insufficient windscreen washer additive to adequately remove road film (see *Weekly checks)*

Windscreen washers inoperative, or unsatisfactory in operation

One or more washer jets inoperative

- ☐ Blocked washer jet
- ☐ Disconnected, kinked or restricted fluid hose (Chapter 12)
- ☐ Insufficient fluid in washer reservoir (see *Weekly checks)*

Washer pump fails to operate

- ☐ Broken or disconnected wiring or connections (Chapter 12)
- ☐ Blown fuse (Chapter 12)
- ☐ Faulty washer switch (Chapter 12)
- ☐ Faulty washer pump (Chapter 12)

Washer pump runs for some time before fluid is emitted from jets

- ☐ Faulty one-way valve in fluid supply hose (Chapter 12)

Electric windows inoperative, or unsatisfactory in operation

Window glass will only move in one direction

- ☐ Faulty switch (Chapter 12)

Window glass slow to move

- ☐ Battery discharged (Chapter 5A)
- ☐ Regulator seized or damaged, or in need of lubrication (Chapter 11)
- ☐ Door internal components or trim fouling regulator (Chapter 11)
- ☐ Faulty motor (Chapter 11)

Window glass fails to move

- ☐ Blown fuse (Chapter 12)
- ☐ Faulty relay (Chapter 12)
- ☐ Broken or disconnected wiring or connections (Chapter 12)
- ☐ Faulty motor (Chapter 11)
- ☐ Faulty control module (Chapter 11)

Central locking system inoperative, or unsatisfactory in operation

Complete system failure

- ☐ Remote handset battery discharged, where applicable
- ☐ Blown fuse (Chapter 12)
- ☐ Defective control module (Chapter 12)
- ☐ Broken or disconnected wiring or connections (Chapter 12)
- ☐ Faulty motor (Chapter 11)

Latch locks but will not unlock, or unlocks but will not lock

- ☐ Remote handset battery discharged, where applicable
- ☐ Faulty master switch (Chapter 12)
- ☐ Broken or disconnected latch operating rods or levers (Chapter 11)
- ☐ Faulty control module (Chapter 12)
- ☐ Faulty motor (Chapter 11)

One solenoid/motor fails to operate

- ☐ Broken or disconnected wiring or connections (Chapter 12)
- ☐ Faulty operating assembly (Chapter 11)
- ☐ Broken, binding or disconnected latch operating rods or levers (Chapter 11)
- ☐ Fault in door latch (Chapter 11)

A

ABS (Anti-lock brake system) A system, usually electronically controlled, that senses incipient wheel lockup during braking and relieves hydraulic pressure at wheels that are about to skid.

Air bag An inflatable bag hidden in the steering wheel (driver's side) or the dash or glovebox (passenger side). In a head-on collision, the bags inflate, preventing the driver and front passenger from being thrown forward into the steering wheel or windscreen.

Air cleaner A metal or plastic housing, containing a filter element, which removes dust and dirt from the air being drawn into the engine.

Air filter element The actual filter in an air cleaner system, usually manufactured from pleated paper and requiring renewal at regular intervals.

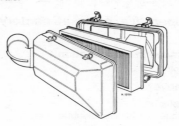

Air filter

Allen key A hexagonal wrench which fits into a recessed hexagonal hole.

Alligator clip A long-nosed spring-loaded metal clip with meshing teeth. Used to make temporary electrical connections.

Alternator A component in the electrical system which converts mechanical energy from a drivebelt into electrical energy to charge the battery and to operate the starting system, ignition system and electrical accessories.

Alternator (exploded view)

Ampere (amp) A unit of measurement for the flow of electric current. One amp is the amount of current produced by one volt acting through a resistance of one ohm.

Anaerobic sealer A substance used to prevent bolts and screws from loosening. Anaerobic means that it does not require oxygen for activation. The Loctite brand is widely used.

Antifreeze A substance (usually ethylene glycol) mixed with water, and added to a vehicle's cooling system, to prevent freezing of the coolant in winter. Antifreeze also contains chemicals to inhibit corrosion and the formation of rust and other deposits that would tend to clog the radiator and coolant passages and reduce cooling efficiency.

Anti-seize compound A coating that reduces the risk of seizing on fasteners that are subjected to high temperatures, such as exhaust manifold bolts and nuts.

Anti-seize compound

Asbestos A natural fibrous mineral with great heat resistance, commonly used in the composition of brake friction materials. Asbestos is a health hazard and the dust created by brake systems should never be inhaled or ingested.

Axle A shaft on which a wheel revolves, or which revolves with a wheel. Also, a solid beam that connects the two wheels at one end of the vehicle. An axle which also transmits power to the wheels is known as a live axle.

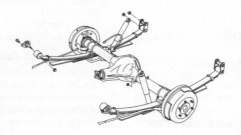

Axle assembly

Axleshaft A single rotating shaft, on either side of the differential, which delivers power from the final drive assembly to the drive wheels. Also called a driveshaft or a halfshaft.

B

Ball bearing An anti-friction bearing consisting of a hardened inner and outer race with hardened steel balls between two races.

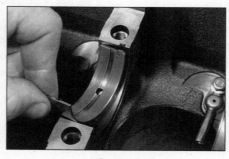

Bearing

Bearing The curved surface on a shaft or in a bore, or the part assembled into either, that permits relative motion between them with minimum wear and friction.

Big-end bearing The bearing in the end of the connecting rod that's attached to the crankshaft.

Bleed nipple A valve on a brake wheel cylinder, caliper or other hydraulic component that is opened to purge the hydraulic system of air. Also called a bleed screw.

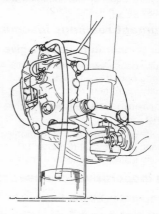

Brake bleeding

Brake bleeding Procedure for removing air from lines of a hydraulic brake system.

Brake disc The component of a disc brake that rotates with the wheels.

Brake drum The component of a drum brake that rotates with the wheels.

Brake linings The friction material which contacts the brake disc or drum to retard the vehicle's speed. The linings are bonded or riveted to the brake pads or shoes.

Brake pads The replaceable friction pads that pinch the brake disc when the brakes are applied. Brake pads consist of a friction material bonded or riveted to a rigid backing plate.

Brake shoe The crescent-shaped carrier to which the brake linings are mounted and which forces the lining against the rotating drum during braking.

Braking systems For more information on braking systems, consult the *Haynes Automotive Brake Manual*.

Breaker bar A long socket wrench handle providing greater leverage.

Bulkhead The insulated partition between the engine and the passenger compartment.

C

Caliper The non-rotating part of a disc-brake assembly that straddles the disc and carries the brake pads. The caliper also contains the hydraulic components that cause the pads to pinch the disc when the brakes are applied. A caliper is also a measuring tool that can be set to measure inside or outside dimensions of an object.

Camshaft A rotating shaft on which a series of cam lobes operate the valve mechanisms. The camshaft may be driven by gears, by sprockets and chain or by sprockets and a belt.

Canister A container in an evaporative emission control system; contains activated charcoal granules to trap vapours from the fuel system.

Canister

Carburettor A device which mixes fuel with air in the proper proportions to provide a desired power output from a spark ignition internal combustion engine.

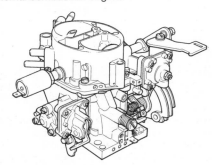

Carburettor

Castellated Resembling the parapets along the top of a castle wall. For example, a castellated balljoint stud nut.

Castellated nut

Castor In wheel alignment, the backward or forward tilt of the steering axis. Castor is positive when the steering axis is inclined rearward at the top.

Catalytic converter A silencer-like device in the exhaust system which converts certain pollutants in the exhaust gases into less harmful substances.

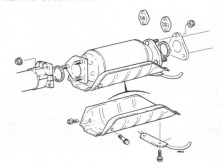

Catalytic converter

Circlip A ring-shaped clip used to prevent endwise movement of cylindrical parts and shafts. An internal circlip is installed in a groove in a housing; an external circlip fits into a groove on the outside of a cylindrical piece such as a shaft.

Clearance The amount of space between two parts. For example, between a piston and a cylinder, between a bearing and a journal, etc.

Coil spring A spiral of elastic steel found in various sizes throughout a vehicle, for example as a springing medium in the suspension and in the valve train.

Compression Reduction in volume, and increase in pressure and temperature, of a gas, caused by squeezing it into a smaller space.

Compression ratio The relationship between cylinder volume when the piston is at top dead centre and cylinder volume when the piston is at bottom dead centre.

Constant velocity (CV) joint A type of universal joint that cancels out vibrations caused by driving power being transmitted through an angle.

Core plug A disc or cup-shaped metal device inserted in a hole in a casting through which core was removed when the casting was formed. Also known as a freeze plug or expansion plug.

Crankcase The lower part of the engine block in which the crankshaft rotates.

Crankshaft The main rotating member, or shaft, running the length of the crankcase, with offset "throws" to which the connecting rods are attached.

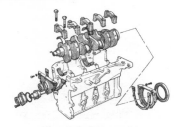

Crankshaft assembly

Crocodile clip See Alligator clip

D

Diagnostic code Code numbers obtained by accessing the diagnostic mode of an engine management computer. This code can be used to determine the area in the system where a malfunction may be located.

Disc brake A brake design incorporating a rotating disc onto which brake pads are squeezed. The resulting friction converts the energy of a moving vehicle into heat.

Double-overhead cam (DOHC) An engine that uses two overhead camshafts, usually one for the intake valves and one for the exhaust valves.

Drivebelt(s) The belt(s) used to drive accessories such as the alternator, water pump, power steering pump, air conditioning compressor, etc. off the crankshaft pulley.

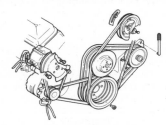

Accessory drivebelts

Driveshaft Any shaft used to transmit motion. Commonly used when referring to the axleshafts on a front wheel drive vehicle.

Driveshaft

Drum brake A type of brake using a drum-shaped metal cylinder attached to the inner surface of the wheel. When the brake pedal is pressed, curved brake shoes with friction linings press against the inside of the drum to slow or stop the vehicle.

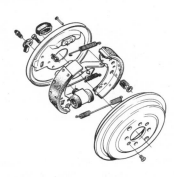

Drum brake assembly

E

EGR valve A valve used to introduce exhaust gases into the intake air stream.

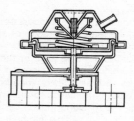
EGR valve

Electronic control unit (ECU) A computer which controls (for instance) ignition and fuel injection systems, or an anti-lock braking system. For more information refer to the *Haynes Automotive Electrical and Electronic Systems Manual*.

Electronic Fuel Injection (EFI) A computer controlled fuel system that distributes fuel through an injector located in each intake port of the engine.

Emergency brake A braking system, independent of the main hydraulic system, that can be used to slow or stop the vehicle if the primary brakes fail, or to hold the vehicle stationary even though the brake pedal isn't depressed. It usually consists of a hand lever that actuates either front or rear brakes mechanically through a series of cables and linkages. Also known as a handbrake or parking brake.

Endfloat The amount of lengthwise movement between two parts. As applied to a crankshaft, the distance that the crankshaft can move forward and back in the cylinder block.

Engine management system (EMS) A computer controlled system which manages the fuel injection and the ignition systems in an integrated fashion.

Exhaust manifold A part with several passages through which exhaust gases leave the engine combustion chambers and enter the exhaust pipe.

Exhaust manifold

F

Fan clutch A viscous (fluid) drive coupling device which permits variable engine fan speeds in relation to engine speeds.

Feeler blade A thin strip or blade of hardened steel, ground to an exact thickness, used to check or measure clearances between parts.

Feeler blade

Firing order The order in which the engine cylinders fire, or deliver their power strokes, beginning with the number one cylinder.

Flywheel A heavy spinning wheel in which energy is absorbed and stored by means of momentum. On cars, the flywheel is attached to the crankshaft to smooth out firing impulses.

Free play The amount of travel before any action takes place. The "looseness" in a linkage, or an assembly of parts, between the initial application of force and actual movement. For example, the distance the brake pedal moves before the pistons in the master cylinder are actuated.

Fuse An electrical device which protects a circuit against accidental overload. The typical fuse contains a soft piece of metal which is calibrated to melt at a predetermined current flow (expressed as amps) and break the circuit.

Fusible link A circuit protection device consisting of a conductor surrounded by heat-resistant insulation. The conductor is smaller than the wire it protects, so it acts as the weakest link in the circuit. Unlike a blown fuse, a failed fusible link must frequently be cut from the wire for replacement.

G

Gap The distance the spark must travel in jumping from the centre electrode to the side

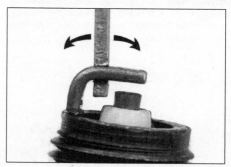
Adjusting spark plug gap

electrode in a spark plug. Also refers to the spacing between the points in a contact breaker assembly in a conventional points-type ignition, or to the distance between the reluctor or rotor and the pickup coil in an electronic ignition.

Gasket Any thin, soft material - usually cork, cardboard, asbestos or soft metal - installed between two metal surfaces to ensure a good seal. For instance, the cylinder head gasket seals the joint between the block and the cylinder head.

Gasket

Gauge An instrument panel display used to monitor engine conditions. A gauge with a movable pointer on a dial or a fixed scale is an analogue gauge. A gauge with a numerical readout is called a digital gauge.

H

Halfshaft A rotating shaft that transmits power from the final drive unit to a drive wheel, usually when referring to a live rear axle.

Harmonic balancer A device designed to reduce torsion or twisting vibration in the crankshaft. May be incorporated in the crankshaft pulley. Also known as a vibration damper.

Hone An abrasive tool for correcting small irregularities or differences in diameter in an engine cylinder, brake cylinder, etc.

Hydraulic tappet A tappet that utilises hydraulic pressure from the engine's lubrication system to maintain zero clearance (constant contact with both camshaft and valve stem). Automatically adjusts to variation in valve stem length. Hydraulic tappets also reduce valve noise.

I

Ignition timing The moment at which the spark plug fires, usually expressed in the number of crankshaft degrees before the piston reaches the top of its stroke.

Inlet manifold A tube or housing with passages through which flows the air-fuel mixture (carburettor vehicles and vehicles with throttle body injection) or air only (port fuel-injected vehicles) to the port openings in the cylinder head.

J

Jump start Starting the engine of a vehicle with a discharged or weak battery by attaching jump leads from the weak battery to a charged or helper battery.

L

Load Sensing Proportioning Valve (LSPV) A brake hydraulic system control valve that works like a proportioning valve, but also takes into consideration the amount of weight carried by the rear axle.

Locknut A nut used to lock an adjustment nut, or other threaded component, in place. For example, a locknut is employed to keep the adjusting nut on the rocker arm in position.

Lockwasher A form of washer designed to prevent an attaching nut from working loose.

M

MacPherson strut A type of front suspension system devised by Earle MacPherson at Ford of England. In its original form, a simple lateral link with the anti-roll bar creates the lower control arm. A long strut - an integral coil spring and shock absorber - is mounted between the body and the steering knuckle. Many modern so-called MacPherson strut systems use a conventional lower A-arm and don't rely on the anti-roll bar for location.

Multimeter An electrical test instrument with the capability to measure voltage, current and resistance.

N

NOx Oxides of Nitrogen. A common toxic pollutant emitted by petrol and diesel engines at higher temperatures.

O

Ohm The unit of electrical resistance. One volt applied to a resistance of one ohm will produce a current of one amp.

Ohmmeter An instrument for measuring electrical resistance.

O-ring A type of sealing ring made of a special rubber-like material; in use, the O-ring is compressed into a groove to provide the sealing action.

O-ring

Overhead cam (ohc) engine An engine with the camshaft(s) located on top of the cylinder head(s).

Overhead valve (ohv) engine An engine with the valves located in the cylinder head, but with the camshaft located in the engine block.

Oxygen sensor A device installed in the engine exhaust manifold, which senses the oxygen content in the exhaust and converts this information into an electric current. Also called a Lambda sensor.

P

Phillips screw A type of screw head having a cross instead of a slot for a corresponding type of screwdriver.

Plastigage A thin strip of plastic thread, available in different sizes, used for measuring clearances. For example, a strip of Plastigage is laid across a bearing journal. The parts are assembled and dismantled; the width of the crushed strip indicates the clearance between journal and bearing.

Plastigage

Propeller shaft The long hollow tube with universal joints at both ends that carries power from the transmission to the differential on front-engined rear wheel drive vehicles.

Proportioning valve A hydraulic control valve which limits the amount of pressure to the rear brakes during panic stops to prevent wheel lock-up.

R

Rack-and-pinion steering A steering system with a pinion gear on the end of the steering shaft that mates with a rack (think of a geared wheel opened up and laid flat). When the steering wheel is turned, the pinion turns, moving the rack to the left or right. This movement is transmitted through the track rods to the steering arms at the wheels.

Radiator A liquid-to-air heat transfer device designed to reduce the temperature of the coolant in an internal combustion engine cooling system.

Refrigerant Any substance used as a heat transfer agent in an air-conditioning system. R-12 has been the principle refrigerant for many years; recently, however, manufacturers have begun using R-134a, a non-CFC substance that is considered less harmful to the ozone in the upper atmosphere.

Rocker arm A lever arm that rocks on a shaft or pivots on a stud. In an overhead valve engine, the rocker arm converts the upward movement of the pushrod into a downward movement to open a valve.

Rotor In a distributor, the rotating device inside the cap that connects the centre electrode and the outer terminals as it turns, distributing the high voltage from the coil secondary winding to the proper spark plug. Also, that part of an alternator which rotates inside the stator. Also, the rotating assembly of a turbocharger, including the compressor wheel, shaft and turbine wheel.

Runout The amount of wobble (in-and-out movement) of a gear or wheel as it's rotated. The amount a shaft rotates "out-of-true." The out-of-round condition of a rotating part.

S

Sealant A liquid or paste used to prevent leakage at a joint. Sometimes used in conjunction with a gasket.

Sealed beam lamp An older headlight design which integrates the reflector, lens and filaments into a hermetically-sealed one-piece unit. When a filament burns out or the lens cracks, the entire unit is simply replaced.

Serpentine drivebelt A single, long, wide accessory drivebelt that's used on some newer vehicles to drive all the accessories, instead of a series of smaller, shorter belts. Serpentine drivebelts are usually tensioned by an automatic tensioner.

Serpentine drivebelt

Shim Thin spacer, commonly used to adjust the clearance or relative positions between two parts. For example, shims inserted into or under bucket tappets control valve clearances. Clearance is adjusted by changing the thickness of the shim.

Slide hammer A special puller that screws into or hooks onto a component such as a shaft or bearing; a heavy sliding handle on the shaft bottoms against the end of the shaft to knock the component free.

Sprocket A tooth or projection on the periphery of a wheel, shaped to engage with a chain or drivebelt. Commonly used to refer to the sprocket wheel itself.

Starter inhibitor switch On vehicles with an automatic transmission, a switch that prevents starting if the vehicle is not in Neutral or Park.

Strut See MacPherson strut.

T

Tappet A cylindrical component which transmits motion from the cam to the valve stem, either directly or via a pushrod and rocker arm. Also called a cam follower.

Thermostat A heat-controlled valve that regulates the flow of coolant between the cylinder block and the radiator, so maintaining optimum engine operating temperature. A thermostat is also used in some air cleaners in which the temperature is regulated.

Thrust bearing The bearing in the clutch assembly that is moved in to the release levers by clutch pedal action to disengage the clutch. Also referred to as a release bearing.

Timing belt A toothed belt which drives the camshaft. Serious engine damage may result if it breaks in service.

Timing chain A chain which drives the camshaft.

Toe-in The amount the front wheels are closer together at the front than at the rear. On rear wheel drive vehicles, a slight amount of toe-in is usually specified to keep the front wheels running parallel on the road by offsetting other forces that tend to spread the wheels apart.

Toe-out The amount the front wheels are closer together at the rear than at the front. On front wheel drive vehicles, a slight amount of toe-out is usually specified.

Tools For full information on choosing and using tools, refer to the *Haynes Automotive Tools Manual*.

Tracer A stripe of a second colour applied to a wire insulator to distinguish that wire from another one with the same colour insulator.

Tune-up A process of accurate and careful adjustments and parts replacement to obtain the best possible engine performance.

Turbocharger A centrifugal device, driven by exhaust gases, that pressurises the intake air. Normally used to increase the power output from a given engine displacement, but can also be used primarily to reduce exhaust emissions (as on VW's "Umwelt" Diesel engine).

U

Universal joint or U-joint A double-pivoted connection for transmitting power from a driving to a driven shaft through an angle. A U-joint consists of two Y-shaped yokes and a cross-shaped member called the spider.

V

Valve A device through which the flow of liquid, gas, vacuum, or loose material in bulk may be started, stopped, or regulated by a movable part that opens, shuts, or partially obstructs one or more ports or passageways. A valve is also the movable part of such a device.

Valve clearance The clearance between the valve tip (the end of the valve stem) and the rocker arm or tappet. The valve clearance is measured when the valve is closed.

Vernier caliper A precision measuring instrument that measures inside and outside dimensions. Not quite as accurate as a micrometer, but more convenient.

Viscosity The thickness of a liquid or its resistance to flow.

Volt A unit for expressing electrical "pressure" in a circuit. One volt that will produce a current of one ampere through a resistance of one ohm.

W

Welding Various processes used to join metal items by heating the areas to be joined to a molten state and fusing them together. For more information refer to the *Haynes Automotive Welding Manual*.

Wiring diagram A drawing portraying the components and wires in a vehicle's electrical system, using standardised symbols. For more information refer to the *Haynes Automotive Electrical and Electronic Systems Manual*.

Note: *References throughout this index are in the form* "Chapter number" • "Page number". *So, for example, 2C•15 refers to page 15 of Chapter 2C.*

Note: *References throughout this index are in the form* "**Chapter number**" • "**Page number**". *So, for example, 2C•15 refers to page 15 of Chapter 2C.*

Note: *References throughout this index are in the form* "**Chapter number**" • "**Page number**". *So, for example, 2C•15 refers to page 15 of Chapter 2C.*

Note: *References throughout this index are in the form* **"Chapter number"** • **"Page number"**. *So, for example, 2C•15 refers to page 15 of Chapter 2C.*

Note: *References throughout this index are in the form* "Chapter number" • "Page number". *So, for example, 2C•15 refers to page 15 of Chapter 2C.*

Preserving Our Motoring Heritage

< *The Model J Duesenberg Derham Tourster. Only eight of these magnificent cars were ever built – this is the only example to be found outside the United States of America*

Almost every car you've ever loved, loathed or desired is gathered under one roof at the Haynes Motor Museum. Over 300 immaculately presented cars and motorbikes represent every aspect of our motoring heritage, from elegant reminders of bygone days, such as the superb Model J Duesenberg to curiosities like the bug-eyed BMW Isetta. There are also many old friends and flames. Perhaps you remember the 1959 Ford Popular that you did your courting in? The magnificent 'Red Collection' is a spectacle of classic sports cars including AC, Alfa Romeo, Austin Healey, Ferrari, Lamborghini, Maserati, MG, Riley, Porsche and Triumph.

A Perfect Day Out

Each and every vehicle at the Haynes Motor Museum has played its part in the history and culture of Motoring. Today, they make a wonderful spectacle and a great day out for all the family. Bring the kids, bring Mum and Dad, but above all bring your camera to capture those golden memories for ever. You will also find an impressive array of motoring memorabilia, a comfortable 70 seat video cinema and one of the most extensive transport book shops in Britain. The Pit Stop Cafe serves everything from a cup of tea to wholesome, home-made meals or, if you prefer, you can enjoy the large picnic area nestled in the beautiful rural surroundings of Somerset.

John Haynes O.B.E., Founder and Chairman of the museum at the wheel of a Haynes Light 12. >

< *Graham Hill's Lola Cosworth Formula 1 car next to a 1934 Riley Sports.*

The Museum is situated on the A359 Yeovil to Frome road at Sparkford, just off the A303 in Somerset. It is about 40 miles south of Bristol, and 25 minutes drive from the M5 intersection at Taunton.

Open 9.30am - 5.30pm (10.00am - 4.00pm Winter) 7 days a week, *except Christmas Day, Boxing Day and New Years Day*

Special rates available for schools, coach parties and outings Charitable Trust No. 292048